Intellectual Property for Paralegals

Paralegals

The Law of Trademarks, Copyrights, Patents, and Trade Secrets

Third Edition

Intellectual Property for Paralegals

The Law of Trademarks, Copyrights, Patents, and Trade Secrets

Third Edition

Deborah E. Bouchoux, Esq.

Georgetown University

DELMAR
CENGAGE Learning

Australia • Brazil • Japan • Korea • Mexico • Singapore • Spain • United Kingdom • United States

DELMAR
CENGAGE Learning™

Intellectual Property: The Law of Trademarks, Copyrights, Patents, and Trade Secrets, Third Edition
Deborah E. Bouchoux

Vice President, Career and Professional Editorial: Dave Garza

Director of Learning Solutions: Sandy Clark

Senior Acquisitions Editor: Shelley Esposito

Managing Editor: Larry Main

Product Manager: Patricia Osborn

Editorial Assistant: Melissa Zaza

Vice President, Career and Professional Marketing: Jennifer McAvey

Marketing Director: Wendy Mapstone

Marketing Manager: Gerard McAvey

Marketing Coordinator: Jonathan Sheehan

Production Director: Wendy Troeger

Production Manager: Mark Bernard

Content Project Manager: Steven Couse

Art Director: Joy Kocsis

Technology Project Manager: Sandy Charette

Production Technology Analyst: Thomas Stover

For product information and technology assistance, contact us at
Professional & Career Group Customer Support, 1-800-648-7450
For permission to use material from this text or product,
submit all requests online at **cengage.com/permissions**.
Further permissions questions can be e-mailed to
permissionrequest@cengage.com.

Library of Congress Control Number: 2008922256
ISBN-13: 978-1428318366
ISBN-10: 1428318364

Delmar

5 Maxwell Drive
Clifton Park, NY 12065-2919
USA

Cengage Learning products are represented in Canada by Nelson Education, Ltd.

For your lifelong learning solutions, visit **delmar.cengage.com**
Visit our corporate website at **cengage.com**.

Notice to the Reader

Publisher does not warrant or guarantee any of the products described herein or perform any independent analysis in connection with any of the product information contained herein. Publisher does not assume, and expressly disclaims, any obligation to obtain and include information other than that provided to it by the manufacturer. The reader is expressly warned to consider and adopt all safety precautions that might be indicated by the activities described herein and to avoid all potential hazards. By following the instructions contained herein, the reader willingly assumes all risks in connection with such instructions. The publisher makes no representations or warranties of any kind, including but not limited to, the warranties of fitness for particular purpose or merchantability, nor are any such representations implied with respect to the material set forth herein, and the publisher takes no responsibility with respect to such material. The publisher shall not be liable for any special, consequential, or exemplary damages resulting, in whole or part, from the readers' use of, or reliance upon, this material.

Printed in the United States of America
1 2 3 4 5 XX 10 09 08

TABLE OF CONTENTS

To access the appendices, go to http://www.paralegal.delmar.cengage.com.

PREFACE

The Congress shall have power to promote the progress of science and useful arts, by securing for limited times to authors and inventors the exclusive right to their respective writings and discoveries.

U.S. Const. art. 1, § 8, cl. 8

The field of intellectual property (typically referred to as IP) is one that continues its rapid growth. Just a few years ago, individuals who identified themselves as practitioners in the field of intellectual property were met with blank stares. Now IP professionals are in constant demand, and it is a rare issue of any legal newspaper that does not include advertisements for IP practitioners. Many experts believe this rapid growth can be attributed to the spread of computer and communications technologies throughout the world. Reflecting this, technology-related legislation is continually introduced in Congress. Trademark and patent applications filed at the U.S. Patent and Trademark Office continue to grow. Similarly, there is increased emphasis on the need to enhance protection of written materials, including computer software, through copyright registration.

Today's competitive businesses recognize that nearly 80 percent of their value can lie in their intellectual property. With increased technology and global communication come greater challenges to protect intellectual property. Misappropriation or infringement of valuable proprietary information is a keystroke away. Thus, companies and law firms value the expertise of IP professionals who can assist in adopting strategies to ensure IP assets are fully protected.

IP practice groups make extensive use of paralegals. Paralegals are involved in nearly every stage of trademark and patent prosecution and maintenance practice and in the area of copyright registrations and IP audits. The field offers significant opportunities for client contact, challenging issues, and personal and intellectual growth. The specialized nature of IP practice produces highly capable and efficient paralegals whose contributions are valued by both other legal professionals and clients. Expertise in the field is recognized by salaries that are typically higher than those for other paralegals. In addition to law firm IP practice, many paralegals are employed in-house at companies with significant IP assets. These paralegals work closely with in-house counsel to meet the company's needs. In brief, the field provides significant and rewarding opportunities for career satisfaction.

The recent increased interest in intellectual property coupled with nearly daily changes in IP law has caused a relative scarcity in texts that provide both sound foundational concepts together with the practical advice needed to ensure success for IP paralegals.

This text provides a comprehensive guide to each field within the umbrella of intellectual property, namely, trademarks, copyrights, patents, trade secrets, and unfair competition. The methods by which each is created, procedures to register or protect each, duration of rights, protection from infringement, and new and international developments will be addressed for each of these fields of intellectual property.

Each chapter begins with an introduction to the topics covered therein and concludes with a brief overview of the material presented. Information is arranged in a building-block approach so the reader is presented with comprehensive coverage of each topic. Discussions of each field of intellectual property conclude with a section on the new and emerging issues in that field and then an overview of international implications, such as the methods by which intellectual property can be protected in other countries.

The substantive overview of each topic is complemented by the use of forms, sample agreements, checklists, and other practical guides. References to useful resources and Web sites are provided in each chapter and online in Appendix C so readers can gather additional information. The specific tasks in which IP professionals are involved are fully addressed. Discussion questions are provided to ensure thorough understanding of each topic. Finally, each chapter presents questions requiring readers to access Internet Web sites that are of particular interest to IP professionals. A glossary at the end of the text highlights critical terms, and selected trademark, copyright, and patent statutes are provided in Appendix E at http://www.paralegal.delmar.cengage.com.

The field of intellectual property is one of the most dynamic and challenging of all legal specialties. Many of the issues are cutting edge: How can a domain name be protected? How can a company ensure its trade secrets are not misappropriated by an employee? What is the best way to protect a computer program that may be obsolete in three years? How can a business be sure its Web site does not infringe that of a third party? How can intellectual property be protected in a global economy? How can movies and songs be protected against piracy?

Providing assistance to IP owners thus provides unique opportunities for learning and growth. Moreover, the field of intellectual property is inherently interesting. All of us see and recognize trademarks each day. All of us read books, watch movies, and use inventions. Thus, readers bring a wealth of practical and firsthand knowledge to the study of IP law. This text allows readers to link their experience as consumers with the substantive information presented to ensure IP owners are provided a full range of strategies and methods to protect their valuable assets.

ADDITIONS AND ENHANCEMENTS TO THE THIRD EDITION

Each chapter includes the following enhanced and new features:

- Trivia (a "fun" section pointing out interesting IP facts, statistics, and trivia; for example, one of the chapters on patents notes that the youngest patentee in the United States is a 4-year-old)
- Case Illustration (a short "brief" of a case that illustrates some of the principles discussed in that chapter)
- Case Study and Activities (a factual scenario involving a fictional company, Vision Corp., requiring students to identify various IP problems Vision is encountering and suggest strategies to solve those problems; as a large hotelier, Vision has a host of trademarks, copyrighted materials, and patented inventions for its luxury hotels)
- Internet Resources (a short section is given at the end of each chapter with Web sites specific to the information previously discussed in that chapter)
- Ethics Edge (a short ethics tip or pointer relevant to one of the topics discussed in that chapter)
- Using Internet Resources (a section requiring readers to access numerous Web sites and answer questions that are typical of those that occur in real-life IP practice)

This edition also includes a discussion of domain names as trademarks, an enhanced discussion in chapter 18 on patent searching, and new charts, lists, and timelines, including the following:

- timeline in chapter 4 for intent-to-use marks
- checklist in chapter 4 for trademark applications
- chart showing due dates for documents required to maintain a trademark in force
- list of do's and don'ts for trademark use
- chart analyzing a trademark infringement case
- chart showing infringement remedies in trademark cybersquatting cases
- chart showing copyright notice requirements
- list of copyright infringement myths
- chart comparing and contrasting utility, design, and plant patents
- chart outlining the novelty and statutory bars to patentability
- timeline showing the process for applications under the Patent Cooperation Treaty

Readers will also find new information on electronic systems at the U.S. Patent and Trademark Offices for filing trademark and patent applications, and discussion of new legislation, including the following:

- Trademark Dilution Revision Act of 2006
- Family Entertainment and Copyright Act of 2005
- Patent Reform Act of 2007 (pending)

Finally, this third edition contains discussions of cutting-edge IP issues such as the 2005 U.S. Supreme Court decision holding the Grokster peer-to-peer file-sharing network liable for copyright infringement, infringement of trademarks by phishing, the 2007 U.S. Supreme Court decision tightening the standards for determining obviousness for patentability, the new copyright preregistration procedures, an expanded discussion of the Digital Millennium Copyright Act's takedown provisions, the rise of patent trolls, proposals for patent reform, and a discussion of the use of the International Trade Commission as an alternative to IP infringement litigation in federal court.

Note to readers. Throughout this text, helpful Web sites, fees, and addresses are given. Due to the transitory nature of some Web sites and frequent changes in fees and other similar information, it is possible that such information may not be current at the time you read this text. The Web site of the U.S. Patent and Trademark Office, http://www.uspto.gov, provides current fee and address information. Similarly, the Web site of the Copyright Office, http://www.copyright.gov, provides up-to-date information for frequently changing topics and fees.

SUPPLEMENTAL TEACHING MATERIALS

- **The Instructor's Manual with Test Bank** is available online at http://www.paralegal.delmar.cengage.com in the Instructor's Lounge under Resource. Written by the author of the text, the *Instructor's Manual* contains suggested syllabi, lecture notes, answers to the text questions, useful Web sites, and a test bank.
- **Online Companion™**—The Online Companion™ Web site can be found at http://www.paralegal.delmar.cengage.com in the Resource section of the Web site. The Online Companion™ contains the following:
  - Chapter Summaries
  - Trivia
  - Internet Resources
  - Appendices
- **Web Page**—Come visit our Web site at www.paralegal.delmar.cengage.com, where you will find valuable information specific to this book such as hot links and sample materials to download.

Please note the Internet resources are of a time-sensitive nature and
URL addresses may often change or be deleted.

Contact us at www.paralegal.delmar.cengage.com

ACKNOWLEDGMENTS

No text is the product solely of its author. Many individuals contributed significantly to the development of this text. As always, my first thoughts go to Susan M. Sullivan, Program Director of the Paralegal Program at the University of San Diego. Sue gave me my first opportunity to teach and has always provided support and encouragement. She is a respected colleague and valued friend.

My former Program Director, Gloria Silvers of the Paralegal Studies Program at Georgetown University in Washington, DC, displayed enthusiasm and passion for education. She was of invaluable assistance and a tremendous source of encouragement.

Special thanks to the reviewers who evaluated the manuscript on behalf of the publisher and provided clear and concise analysis. Their comments and suggestions were of great assistance.

Vicki Brown
Carl Sandburg College

David Moser
Belmont University

Adam Epstein
Central Michigan University

Kent Thomas
Southeastern Career College

Konnie Kustrom
Eastern Michigan University

Bernard Behrend
Duquesne University

Giselle Franco
Keiser College

Anita Whitby
Kaplan University

Finally, my most sincere appreciation to the following individuals at Delmar Cengage Learning, who provided guidance and support throughout the development of this text: Shelley Esposito, Melissa Riveglia, Patricia Osborn, and Steven Couse. I also wish to express my appreciation to Arunesh Shukla for his assistance in the composition process.

Last, but of course, not least, deepest thanks and love to my husband, Don, and our children, Meaghan, Elizabeth, Patrick, and Robert, for their amazing patience and understanding while I worked on this text.

Much of the basic information in this text relating to trademarks, copyrights, and patents is from the Web sites of the U.S. Patent and Trademark Office and the U.S. Copyright Office, and the author wishes to acknowledge these agencies. No copyright is claimed in any of the materials or forms of these agencies, including but not limited to Exhibits 4–1, 4–3, 4–4, 4–6, 4–8, 4–9, 4-11, 5–4, 6–1, 12–1, 13–2, 18–1, 18–2, 18-3, 18–4, 18–6, 19–2, Appendix D, Form 7, and Exhibit E.

LIST OF EXHIBITS

Introduction to Intellectual Property

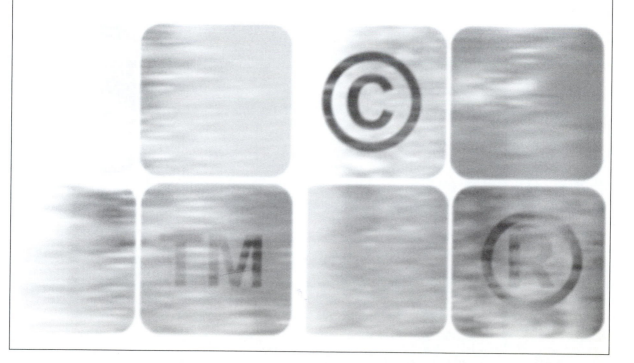

Chapter 1

Introduction to Intellectual Property Law

CHAPTER OVERVIEW

Intellectual property law protects the results of human creative endeavor. Intellectual property is generally thought to comprise four separate fields of law: trademarks, copyrights, patents, and trade secrets. A *trademark* is a word, name, symbol, or device used to identify and distinguish one's goods or services and to indicate their source. Rights in trademarks are created by use of a mark; registration with the U.S. Patent and Trademark Office (USPTO) is not required, although it offers certain advantages. *Copyright* protects original works of authorship, including literary, musical, dramatic, artistic, and other works. Just as trademarks are protected from the moment of their first public use, copyright exists from the moment of creation of a work in fixed form; registration of a copyright with the U.S. Copyright Office, while affording certain benefits, is not required. A *patent* is a grant from the U.S. government that permits its owner to exclude others from making, selling, using, or importing an invention. Patents exist only upon issuance by the USPTO. A *trade secret* consists of any valuable commercial information that, if known by a competitor, would provide some benefit or advantage to the competitor. No registration or other formalities are required to create a trade secret, and trade secrets endure as long as reasonable efforts are made to protect their secrecy.

INTELLECTUAL PROPERTY LAW BASICS

Intellectual Property Defined

There are three distinct types of property that individuals and companies can own: *real property* refers to land or real estate; *personal property* refers to specific items and things that can be identified, such as jewelry, cars, and artwork; and *intellectual property* refers to the fruits or product of human creativity, including literature, advertising slogans, songs, or new inventions. Thus, property that is the result of thought, namely, intellectual activity, is called **intellectual property.** In some foreign countries, intellectual property is referred to as **industrial property.**

Many of the rights of ownership common to real and personal property are also common to intellectual property. Intellectual property can be bought, sold, and licensed. Similarly, it can be protected against theft or infringement by others. Nevertheless, there are some restrictions on use. For example, if you were to purchase the latest bestseller by John Grisham, you would be entitled to read the book, sell it to another, or give it away. You would not, however, be entitled to make photocopies of the book and then distribute and sell those copies to others. Those rights are retained by the author of the work and are protected by copyright law.

The Rationale for Protection of Intellectual Property

Intellectual property is a field of law that aims at protecting the knowledge created through human effort in order to stimulate and promote further creativity. Authors who write books and musicians who compose songs would be unlikely to engage in further creative effort unless they could realize profit from their endeavors. If their work could be misappropriated and sold by others, they would have no incentive to create further works. Pharmaceutical companies would not invest millions of dollars into research and development of new drugs unless they could be assured that their inventions would enable them to recover these costs and develop additional drugs. Thus, not only the creators of intellectual property but the public as well benefit from protecting intellectual property.

On the other hand, if the owner of intellectual property is given complete and perpetual rights to his or her invention or work, the owner would have a monopoly and be able to charge excessive prices for the invention or work, which would harm the public. Intellectual property law attempts to resolve these conflicting goals so that owners' rights to reap the rewards of their efforts are balanced against the public need for a competitive marketplace. Thus, for example, under federal law, a patent for a useful invention will last for only 20 years from the date an application for the patent is filed with the USPTO. After that period of time, the patent expires, and anyone is free to produce and sell the product.

TYPES OF INTELLECTUAL PROPERTY

The term *intellectual property* is usually thought of as comprising four separate, but often overlapping, legal fields: trademarks, copyrights, patents, and trade secrets. Although each of these areas will be discussed in detail in the chapters that follow, a brief introduction to each discipline is helpful. (See chart on inside front and back covers of text comparing and contrasting the various types of intellectual property.)

Trademarks and Service Marks

What Is Protectable.   A trademark or service mark is a word, name, symbol, or device used to indicate the source, quality, and ownership of a product or service. A **trademark** is used in the marketing of a product (such as REEBOK® for shoes), while a **service mark** typically identifies a service (such as STARBUCKS® for restaurant services). A trademark or service mark identifies and distinguishes the products or services of one person from those of another.

In addition to words, trademarks can also consist of slogans (such as THE KING OF BEERS® for Budweiser beer), designs (such as the familiar "swoosh" that identifies Nike products), or sounds (such as the distinctive giggle of the Pillsbury Doughboy).

T r a d e m a r k s provide guarantees of quality and consistency of the product or service they identify. Thus, upon encountering the golden arches that identify a McDonald's restaurant, consumers understand the Big Mac they purchase in Chicago will be the same quality as one purchased in Seattle.

Companies expend a great deal of time, effort, and money in establishing consumer recognition of and confidence in their marks. Yet not all words, phrases, or symbols are entitled to protection as trademarks. A chain of stores that sells electronic goods could not obtain a registered trademark for "Electronic Goods" inasmuch as the name is generic, yet CIRCUIT CITY® is a nationally recognized mark for the retail sale of electronic goods and equipment. Marks may not be protectable if they are generic in nature or merely descriptive of the type of products or services they identify. Generally, marks that are protectable are those that are coined (such as KODAK®), arbitrary (such as SHELL® for gasoline), or suggestive (such as STAPLES® for office supplies).

Federal Registration of Trademarks. Interstate use of trademarks is governed by federal law, namely, the United States Trademark Act (also called the Lanham Act), found at 15 U.S.C. §§ 1051 *et seq.* See Appendix E. Additionally, trademarks are provided for in all 50 states so that marks that cannot be federally registered with the USPTO because they are not used in interstate commerce can be registered in the state in which they are used.

In the United States, trademarks are generally protected from their date of first public use. Registration of a mark is not required to secure protection for a mark, although it offers numerous advantages, such as allowing the registrant to bring an action in federal court for infringement of the mark. Applications for federal registration of trademarks are made with the USPTO. Registration is a fairly lengthy process, generally taking anywhere from 12 to 24 months or even longer. The filing fee is $375 per mark per class of

goods or services covered by the mark, although applicants are entitled to a fee reduction if they file applications electronically.

A trademark registration is valid for 10 years and may be renewed for additional 10-year periods thereafter as long as the mark is in use in interstate commerce. Additionally, registrants are required to file an affidavit with the USPTO between the fifth and sixth years after registration and every 10 years to verify the mark is in continued use. Marks not in use are then available to others.

Trademarks are among the most visible items of intellectual property, and it has been estimated that the average resident of the United States encounters approximately 1,500 different trademarks each day and 30,000 if one visits a supermarket. A properly selected, registered, and protected mark can be of great value to a company or individual desiring to establish and expand market share. There  is perhaps no better way to maintain a strong position in the marketplace than to build goodwill and consumer recognition in the identity selected for products and services and then to protect that identity under federal trademark law.

Copyrights

What Is Protectable.   **Copyright** is a form of protection governed exclusively by federal law (17 U.S.C. §§ 101 *et seq.*) granted to the authors of original works of authorship, including literary, dramatic, musical, artistic, and certain other works. See Appendix E. Thus, books, songs, plays, jewelry, movies, sculptures, paintings, and choreographic works are all protectable. Computer software is also protectable by copyright.

Copyright protection is available for more than merely serious works of fiction or art. Marketing materials, advertising copy, and cartoons are also protectable. Copyright is available for original works; no judgment is made about their literary or artistic quality. Nevertheless, certain works are not protectable by copyright, such as titles, names, short phrases, or lists of ingredients. Similarly, ideas, methods, and processes are not protectable by copyright, although the expression of those ideas is.

Copyright protection exists automatically from the time a work is created in fixed form. Thus, similar to trademark law, securing a registration for a work (with the U.S. Copyright Office) is not required for a work to be protected, although registration does provide significant advantages, such as establishing a public record of the copyright claim and providing a basis upon which an infringement suit may be brought in federal court and in which statutory damages and attorneys' fees may be recovered.

The owner of a copyright has the right to reproduce the work, prepare derivative works based on the original work (such as a sequel to the original), distribute copies of the work, and to perform and display the work. Generally, violations of such rights are protectable by infringement actions. Nevertheless, some uses of copyrighted works are considered "fair use" and do not constitute infringement, such as use of an insignificant portion of a work for noncommercial purposes or parody of a copyrighted work.

Federal Registration of Copyrights.   Neither publication nor registration of a work is required for copyright protection, in as much as works are protected under federal copyright law from the time of their creation in a fixed form. Registration, however, is inexpensive, requiring only a $45 filing fee (for applications filed in paper form), and the process is expeditious. In most cases, the Copyright Office processes applications within four to five months.

Generally, copyrighted works are automatically protected from the moment of their creation for a term generally enduring for the author's life plus an additional 70 years after the author's death. After that time, the work will fall

into the public domain and may be reproduced, distributed, or performed by anyone. The policy underlying the long period of copyright protection is that it may take several years for a painting, book, or opera to achieve its true value, and, thus, authors should receive a length of protection that will enable the work to appreciate to its greatest extent.

Patents

What Is Protectable.   A **patent** is a grant from the U.S. government that permits its owner to prevent others from making, using, importing, or selling an invention. There are three types of patents: utility patents, which are the most common patents and which cover useful inventions and discoveries (such as the typewriter, the automobile, and genetically altered mice); design patents, which cover new, original, and ornamental designs for articles (such as furniture); and plant patents, which cover new and distinct asexually reproduced plant varieties (such as hybrid flowers or trees).

Patent protection is available only for useful, novel, and nonobvious inventions. Generally, patent law prohibits the patenting of an invention that is merely an insignificant addition to or minor alteration of something already known. Moreover, some items cannot be protected by patent, such as pure scientific principles.

Federal Registration of Patents.   Patents are governed exclusively by federal law (35 U.S.C. §§ 100 *et seq.*). See Appendix E. To obtain a patent, an inventor must file an application with the USPTO (the same agency that issues trademark registrations) that fully describes the invention. Patent prosecution is expensive, time-consuming, and complex. Costs can run into the thousands of dollars, and it generally takes over two years for the USPTO to issue a patent.

Patent protection exists for 20 years from the date of filing of an application for utility patents (assuming that certain fees are paid to maintain the patent in force) and plant patents and 14 years from the date of grant for design patents. After this period of time, the invention falls into the public domain and may be used by any person without permission.

Patents promote the public good in that patent protection incentivizes inventors. In return for fully describing the invention in the patent application, the inventor is granted an exclusive but limited period of time within which to exploit the invention. After the patent expires, any member of the public is free to use, manufacture, or sell the invention. Thus, patent law strikes a balance between the need to protect inventors and the need to allow public access to important discoveries.

Trade Secrets

What Is Protectable. A **trade secret** consists of any valuable business information that, if known by a competitor, would afford the competitor some benefit or advantage. There is no limit to the type of information that can be protected as trade secrets; recipes, marketing plans, financial projections, and methods of conducting business can all constitute trade secrets. There is no requirement that a trade secret be unique or complex; thus, even something as simple and nontechnical as a list of customers can qualify as a trade secret as long as it affords its owner a competitive advantage and is not common knowledge.

If trade secrets were not protectable, companies would have no incentive to invest time, money, and effort in research and development that ultimately benefits the public. Trade secret law thus promotes the development of new methods and processes of doing business in the marketplace.

Protection of Trade Secrets. Although trademarks, copyrights, and patents are all subject to extensive statutory schemes for their protection, application, and registration, there is no federal law relating to trade secrets and no formalities are required to obtain rights to trade secrets.

Trade secrets are generally protectable under various state statutes and cases and by contractual agreements between parties. For example, employers often require employees to sign confidentiality agreements in which employees agree not to disclose proprietary information owned by the employer.

If properly protected, trade secrets may last forever. On the other hand, if companies fail to take reasonable measures to maintain the secrecy of the information, trade secret protection may be lost. Thus, disclosure of the information should be limited to those with a "need to know" it so as to perform their duties, confidential information should be kept in secure or restricted areas, and employees with access to proprietary information should sign **nondisclosure agreements.** If such measures are taken, a trade secret can be protected in perpetuity.

Another method by which companies protect valuable information is by requiring employees to sign agreements promising not to compete with the employer after leaving the job. Such covenants are strictly scrutinized by courts, but generally, if they are reasonable in regard to time, scope, and subject matter, they are enforceable.

Other Intellectual Property Rights

Although the most common types of intellectual property are trademarks, copyrights, patents, and trade secrets, other intellectual property rights exist and will be discussed in the chapters that follow. Some of these rights include semiconductor chip protection, plant variety protection, the right of publicity, and rights relating to unfair competition, including passing off, misappropriation, and false advertising.

Additionally, intellectual property rights often intersect and overlap. Thus, the formula for Coca-Cola is a trade secret, while the distinctive script in which the words COCA-COLA® are displayed is a trademark. Generally, computer programs may be protectable under copyright law, patent law, and as trade secrets, while the name for a computer program, such as WINDOWS®, qualifies for trademark protection. Jewelry may be protected both under copyright and design patent law. Legal practitioners in the field of intellectual property law must fully understand how the various types of intellectual property intersect so that clients can achieve the widest possible scope of protection. For example, although an item of jewelry can be protected as a design patent, securing a patent is complex and expensive. Moreover, a design patent lasts only 14 years from the date of grant of the patent. In contrast, securing copyright protection for the same article of jewelry is easy and inexpensive. More importantly, copyright protection endures during the life of the work's creator and for 70 years thereafter. Trade secrets that are properly protected can endure perpetually. Thus, intellectual property owners need to consider the complementary relationships among trademark, copyright, patent, and trade secrets law so as to obtain the broadest possible protection for their assets.

AGENCIES RESPONSIBLE FOR INTELLECTUAL PROPERTY REGISTRATION

United States Patent and Trademark Office

The agency charged with granting patents and registering trademarks is the **United States Patent and Trademark Office (USPTO),** one of several bureaus within the U.S. Department of Commerce. The USPTO, founded more than 200 years ago, employs more than 8,000 employees and is presently located in five buildings in Alexandria, Virginia. Mailing addresses vary depending on whether the matter relates to patents or trademarks. The USPTO is physically located at 600 Dulany Street, Alexandria, Virginia 22314. Its Web site is http://www.uspto.gov. The USPTO Web site offers a wealth of information, including basic information about trademarks and patents,

fee schedules, forms, and the ability to search and apply for trademarks and patents. Since 1991, under the Omnibus Budget Reconciliation Act, the USPTO has operated in much the same way as a private business, providing valued products and services to customers in exchange for fees that are used to fully fund USPTO operations. It uses no taxpayer funds.

The USPTO is one of the busiest of all government agencies, and as individuals and companies begin to understand the value of intellectual property, greater demands are being made on the USPTO. For example, from 2001 to 2006, the number of trademark applications received by the USPTO increased by 18 percent, and the number of patent applications received increased 28 percent. In 2006, the USPTO issued 183,187 patents and registered 147,118 trademarks.

Legislation passed in 1997 established the USPTO as a performance-based organization that is managed by professionals, resulting in the creation of a new political position, Under Secretary of Commerce for Intellectual Property. Changing the USPTO from a mere governmental agency to a governmental corporation made the USPTO equivalent to other similar organizations, such as the Tennessee Valley Authority and the Federal Deposit Insurance Corporation. Performance-based organizations have considerable flexibility in personnel matters and set specific goals and objectives to achieve. In brief, the USPTO operates more like a business with greater autonomy over its budget, hiring, and procurement. Additionally, the USPTO Web site's searchable database includes information about all U.S. patents from the first patent issued in 1790 to the most recent, with full information for all patents since 1976 and the text and images of more than four million pending and registered federal trademarks. Users can view, download, and print the images of these patents and trademarks. The USPTO is continuing its transition from paper to electronic filing for both trademarks and patents. Ninety-four percent of trademark applications and about 14 percent of patent applications were filed electronically in 2006.

The USPTO is led by the Under Secretary of Commerce for Intellectual Property and Director of the United States Patent and Trademark Office (the "Director"), who is appointed by the President. The Secretary of Commerce appoints a Commissioner for patents and a Commissioner for trademarks.

Cases relating to IP law are published in a variety of sources. One excellent topical reporter is *United States Patent Quarterly* (U.S.P.Q.), covering IP cases (relating to patents, trademarks, copyrights, and trade secrets) from 1929 to 1986, and U.S.P.Q.2d, covering IP cases from 1987 to date. In addition to publishing various federal cases relating to patents and trademarks, this set, published by BNA, Inc., also publishes administrative decisions of the Commissioner of Patents and Trademarks. Subscribers to the set receive weekly advance sheets with the most current cases; bound volumes are issued quarterly. Most law firms that specialize in IP work subscribe to this set. The set is also available through Lexis-Nexis and Westlaw, the computer-assisted legal research systems.

Additionally, a number of cases are available through the USPTO Web site.

Library of Congress

The **Library of Congress,** sometimes referred to as "Jefferson's Legacy," was established in 1800 as a legislative library. It is America's oldest national cultural institution and is the largest library in the world. Thomas Jefferson is considered the founder of the Library of Congress, and his personal library is at the heart of the library in as much as in 1814 the library's 3,000 volumes were burned by the British, and the next year Jefferson sold his personal library collection of 6,487 volumes to the Library of Congress for $23,950 the next year.

The U.S. Copyright Office has been a part of the Library of Congress since 1870 and is in charge of examining the approximately 600,000 copyright applications filed each year, issuing registrations, and maintaining copyright deposits in its vast collection.

The Library of Congress is located at 101 Independence Avenue SE, Washington, DC 20559-6000, and its Web site is http://www.copyright.gov. Basic information about copyrights, forms, and other valuable information can be obtained for free and downloaded from the Copyright Office's Web site.

ETHICS EDGE: Duty of Competence

The duty of competent legal representation is so important that it is the first substantive statement promulgated by the Model Rules of the American Bar Association. Rule 1.1 provides that competent representation requires the legal knowledge, skills, thoroughness, and preparation necessary for the representation of a client. Thus, while only an attorney may give legal advice and counsel a client as to the best strategy to protect his or her intellectual property, paralegals are expected to provide competent assistance. Paralegals thus have a duty to keep current with IP developments and cases in order to fulfill this duty of competence.

INTERNATIONAL ORGANIZATIONS, AGENCIES, AND TREATIES

There are a number of international organizations and agencies that promote the use and protection of intellectual property. Although these organizations are discussed in more detail in the chapters to follow, a brief introduction may be helpful.

- **International Trademark Association (INTA)** is a not-for-profit international association composed chiefly of trademark owners and practitioners. More than 5,000 trademark owners and professionals in more than 190 countries belong to INTA, together with others interested in promoting trademarks. INTA offers a wide variety of educational seminars and publications, including many worthwhile materials available at no cost on the Internet (see INTA's home page at http://www.inta.org). INTA is located at 655 Third Avenue, 10th Floor, New York, NY 10017-5617 (212/642-1700).
- **World Intellectual Property Organization (WIPO)** was founded in 1883 and is a specialized agency of the United Nations whose purposes are to promote intellectual property throughout the world and to administer 24 treaties dealing with intellectual property, including the Paris Convention, Madrid Protocol, the Trademark Law Treaty, and the Berne Convention. More than 180 nations are members of WIPO. WIPO is headquartered in Geneva, Switzerland, and its home page is http://www.wipo.int.

There are also a number of international agreements and treaties that affect intellectual property. Among them are the following.

- **Berne Convention for the Protection of Literary and Artistic Works (the Berne Convention).** The Berne Convention was created in 1886 under the leadership of Victor Hugo to protect literary and artistic works. It has more than 160 member nations. The United States became a party to the Berne Convention in 1989. The Berne Convention is administered by WIPO and is based on the precept that each member nation must treat nationals of other member countries like its own nationals for purposes of copyright (the principle of "national treatment").
- **Madrid Protocol.** The Madrid Protocol came into existence in 1996 and allows trademark protection for more than 70 countries, including all 27 countries of the European Union, by means of a centralized trademark filing procedure. The United States implemented the terms of the Protocol in late 2003. This treaty facilitates a one-stop, low-cost, efficient system for the international registration of trademarks by permitting a U.S. trademark owner to file for international registration in any number of member countries by filing a single standardized application form with the USPTO, in English, with a single set of fees.
- **Paris Convention.** One of the first treaties or "conventions" designed to address trademark protection in foreign countries was the Paris Convention of 1883, adopted to facilitate international patent and trademark protection. The Paris Convention is based on the principle of reciprocity so that foreign trademark and patent owners may obtain in a member country the same legal protection for their marks and patents as can citizens of those member countries. Perhaps the most significant benefit provided by the Paris Convention is that of priority. An applicant for a trademark has six months after filing an application

in any of the more than 170 member nations to file a corresponding application in any of the other member countries of the Paris Convention and obtain the benefits of the first filing date. Similar priority is afforded for utility patent applications, although the priority period is one year rather than six months. The Paris Convention is administered by WIPO.

- **North American Free Trade Agreement (NAFTA).** The NAFTA came into effect on January 1, 1994, and is adhered to by the United States, Canada, and Mexico. The NAFTA resulted in some changes to U.S. trademark law, primarily with regard to marks that include geographical terms.
- **General Agreement on Tariffs and Trade (GATT).** GATT was concluded in 1994 and is adhered to by most of the major industrialized nations in the world. The most significant changes to U.S. intellectual property law from GATT are that nonuse of a trademark for three years creates a presumption the mark has been abandoned and that the duration of a utility patent is now 20 years from the filing date of the application (rather than 17 years from the date the patent issued, as was previously the case).

(See Appendix A, Table of Treaties.)

THE INCREASING IMPORTANCE OF INTELLECTUAL PROPERTY RIGHTS

While people have always realized the importance of protecting intellectual property rights, the rapidly developing pace of technology has led to increased awareness of the importance of intellectual property assets. Some individuals and companies offer only knowledge. Thus, computer consultants, advertising agencies, Internet companies, and software implementers sell only brainpower. Similarly, some forms of intellectual property, such as domain names and moving images shown on a company's Web page, did not even exist until relatively recently. Internet domain names such as www.ibm.com are valuable assets that must be protected against infringement.

The International Intellectual Property Alliance estimates that total copyright industries accounted for 11 percent of the U.S. gross domestic product in 2005 and that more than 11 million workers are employed by these industries. Additionally, more than $110 billion of U.S. exports now depend on some form of intellectual property protection, including pharmaceuticals, motor vehicles, and aircraft and associated equipment.

Moreover, the rapidity with which information can be communicated through the Internet has led to increasing challenges in the field of intellectual property. Within hours after the world premiere of the movie *Episode III—Revenge of the Sith*, counterfeit copies were available on the streets of New York City for just a few dollars, and the movie was also available on the Web site BitTorrent for free downloading. Books, movies, and songs can now be copied, infringed, and sold illegally with the touch of a keystroke.

The Office of the United States Trade Representative has estimated that U.S. industries lose between $200 billion and $250 billion annually from piracy, counterfeiting of goods, and other intellectual property infringements.

In many cases, the most valuable assets a company owns are its intellectual property assets. For example, the value of the trademarks and service marks owned by the Coca-Cola Company has been estimated at more than $70 billion, making it the world's most valuable brand. Thus, companies must act aggressively to protect these valuable assets from infringement or misuse by others. The field of intellectual property law aims to protect the value of such investments.

Trivia

- The value of Microsoft Corporation's trademarks is estimated to be $65.1 billion.
- For businesses in the food or luxury goods sector, the value of their brands and related intellectual property is estimated at between 70 percent and 90 percent of the total value of their businesses.
- The Department of Commerce has stated that the combined copyright and trademark industries represent the second-fastest growing sector of the U.S. economy.
- The USPTO receives more than five million pieces of mail each year; it is the world's largest recipient of overnight mail.
- The USPTO estimates that piracy, counterfeiting, and the theft of IP cost about $250 billion and 750,000 jobs each year.
- Some of our U.S. presidents have been prolific inventors:
  - Thomas Jefferson invented the swivel chair, a macaroni machine, and a cipher wheel (used to code and decode messages). Jefferson did not apply for any patents, believing all people should have access to new technology.
  - George Washington registered a trademark for his brand of flour in 1772.
  - Abraham Lincoln, the only president to hold a patent, patented an invention in 1849 for a method of steering a boat through shallow waters. The model, made by Lincoln himself, is in the Smithsonian Institution. You may view the patent at the USPTO'S Web site by searching for Patent. No. 6,469.

CHAPTER SUMMARY

The term *intellectual property* is generally thought of as comprising four overlapping fields of law: trademarks (protecting names, logos, symbols, and other devices indicating the quality and source of products and services); copyrights (protecting original works of authorship); patents (grants by the federal government allowing their owners to exclude others from making, using, or selling the owner's invention); and trade secrets (any commercial information that, if known by a competitor, would afford the competitor an advantage in the marketplace). Patents must be issued by the federal government, while rights in trademarks are created by use of marks, and rights in copyright exist from the time a work is created in fixed form. Nevertheless, registration of trademarks and copyrights offers certain advantages and benefits. Trade secrets are governed by various state laws, and registration is not required for existence and ownership of a trade secret. Trademarks and trade secrets can endure perpetually as long as they are protected, while copyrights and patents will fall into the public domain and be available for use by anyone after their terms expire.

As our world becomes increasingly reliant on technological advances, greater demands and challenges are made on IP practitioners. The field is an exciting and challenging one and offers significant opportunities for hands-on involvement by IP professionals.

CASE ILLUSTRATION—POLICIES UNDERLYING INTELLECTUAL PROPERTY LAW

Case: *Sony Corporation of America v. Universal City Studios, Inc.*, 464 U.S. 417 (1984)

Facts: Owners of television programs sued the makers of home videotape recorders, alleging that the sale of the videotape recorders facilitated copyright infringement.

Holding: There was no copyright infringement. Taping television programs is acceptable "time-shifting." Moreover, the videotape recorders were capable of substantial noninfringing uses. The limited grant given by copyright is a means by which an important public purpose may be achieved. It is intended to motivate the creative activity of authors and inventors by the provision of a special reward, and to allow the public access to the products of their genius after the limited period of exclusive control has expired. The primary object of granting a patent or copyright monopoly lies in the general benefit derived by the public from the labors of authors. The reward given to the author or artist is the impetus for release to the public of the products of creative genius.

CASE STUDY AND ACTIVITIES

Case Study.   Your firm's client, Vision Corp. ("Vision"), owns numerous luxury hotels in the western region of the United States. These hotels have lushly landscaped gardens, gift and retail shops, golf courses, restaurants that feature upscale cuisine, swimming pools, tot lots with games and rides for children, and other features common to upscale hotels. The most luxurious hotels are named "V" and hotels that are slightly less luxurious operate under the name "Vision Court." Television commercials that advertise the hotels feature a cartoon-type spokesman, called "Vee," who routinely repeats the company's signature slogan, "Make your vacation your own Vision Quest." The hotels sell a variety of souvenirs in their gift shops, including cookbooks featuring recipes from the hotel restaurants, originally designed jewelry, key chains, and coffee mugs, all of which display the company's logo, a large "V" with eagles' wings inside a circle. Due to the success of the hotels, Vision is considering building hotels along the eastern seaboard and is conducting confidential market and customer surveys to determine the level of interest in such hotels.

CASE STUDY AND ACTIVITIES (CONT'D)

Activities.   Identify the trademarks, copyrights, patentable matter, and trade secrets Vision might own.

ROLE OF PARALEGAL

Because of the increasing array of intellectual property (IP) that can be created in our high-tech society and the increasing ease with which it can be infringed, intellectual property law is a growing practice area. Ten years ago, few law firms had intellectual property law departments, and intellectual property matters were handled by small firms that specialized in the field. Today, nearly every large law firm has a department devoted exclusively to intellectual property, and IP professionals are courted and valued. The *National Law Journal* has reported that attorneys in the field of intellectual property law were the highest paid of all legal specialties. Every legal newspaper and journal contains advertisements for IP paralegals, and in many cases specialists in the field of intellectual property law are paid more than their counterparts in other fields. For example, the *National Law Journal* reported that compensation for intermediate attorneys in intellectual property was the highest of all practice fields, outstripping some areas by nearly $30,000 annually. Similarly, the National Association of Legal Assistants has reported that paralegals who devote more than 40 percent of their time to IP matters make nearly 30 percent more than the average paralegal.

Among the tasks commonly performed by IP paralegals are the following:

- assisting in trademark searching to clear marks for use and preparing, filing, and monitoring trademark registration applications, maintenance, and renewal documents;
- preparing, filing, and monitoring copyright registration applications;
- assisting in patent searching and preparing, filing, and monitoring patent applications;
- docketing dates to maintain trademark and patent registrations in force;
- serving as a liaison with clients and keeping them informed of all matters relating to their IP portfolios;
- drafting license agreements for licensing of trademarks, copyrights, and patents;
- preparing employment agreements and noncompetition agreements;
- assisting in intellectual property audits to determine the extent and value of a client's intellectual property; and
- assisting in protection of trade secrets by developing and implementing policies for protection of trade secrets.

Many of the issues presented in intellectual property law are cutting-edge issues: protection of Internet domain names; copyright piracy on the Internet; downloading of music from Internet file-sharing sites; importation of counterfeited or "knockoff" goods; and development and patenting of wonder drugs. Thus, the field is exciting and presents unique opportunities for learning and growth. Additionally, there is a great deal of client contact, and playing a part in a client's selection of a new name or mark for a product, bringing a new product to market, and protecting that property from infringement or misappropriation by others is interesting and exciting.

In sum, intellectual property is a growing, exciting, and dynamic area, offering unique opportunities and challenging work. The field changes on nearly a daily basis, the issues are interesting, and IP paralegals are valued members of a legal team devoted to ensuring that clients receive the broadest possible scope of protection for their creative assets.

INTERNET RESOURCES

Federal statutes governing intellectual property:	http://www.gpoaccess.gov http://www.law.cornell.edu http://www.findlaw.com
Trademark and patent information, forms, and fees:	http://www.uspto.gov
Copyright information, forms, and fees:	http://www.copyright.gov
International treaties and agreements:	http://www.wipo.int
General information on intellectual property topics:	http://www.findlaw.com http://www.megalaw.com

DISCUSSION QUESTIONS

1. Indicate whether the following items would be protectable as trademarks, copyright, patents, or trade secrets:
   • A new composition by singer John Mayer
   • A book by former Secretary of State George Shultz
   • The ad slogan "Got Milk?"
   • A new type of computer keyboard
   • A company's plans to acquire another company in a hostile takeover
2. Author Toni Morrison wrote the novel *Beloved* in 1987. How long does copyright protection for this work last?
3. Merck & Co., Inc., applied for a patent on September 14, 1989, for a drug to treat manic depression, and the patent was granted on January 1, 1991. How long does patent protection for this drug last?
4. Assume that Merck has filed a trademark application for the name of its new drug. How long will trademark protection for this mark last?
5. Merck has maintained a number of its files, tests, and surveys related to a drug that was not productive in a secure facility. How long will protection for these materials last?
6. Samantha applied for a design patent for a bracelet on April 15, 2005, and the patent was granted on July 25, 2006. How long does patent protection for this drug last?

DISCUSSION QUESTIONS (CONT'D)

7. The novel *Red Badge of Courage* was written in 1895 by author Stephen Crane (1871–1900). Can a play based on the novel be written by a playwright? Why or why not?
8. In what way do "knock-off" handbags designed to look like legitimate handbags pose a threat to designers and makers of handbags?

USING INTERNET RESOURCES

1. Access the Web site of the USPTO.
   a. Who is the current Under Secretary of Commerce for Intellectual Property and Director of the USPTO?
   b. Review the glossary. What is the definition of "patent"?
   c. Review the fee schedule for trademarks. What is the fee to file an application to renew a trademark?
   d. Review the fee schedule for patents. What is the basic filing for a utility patent application, a design patent application, and a plant patent application?
2. Access the Web site of the Copyright Office.
   a. What is the telephone number of the Copyright Office?
   b. Review the FAQs. How is copyright different from patents or trademarks?
   c. Review the fee schedule. What is the fee for obtaining an additional certificate of registration of a copyright?
3. Locate the U.S. Code. What is the general subject matter of 15 U.S.C. § 1058?

For additional resources, go to www.paralegal.delmar.cengage.com.

PART
II

The Law of Trademarks

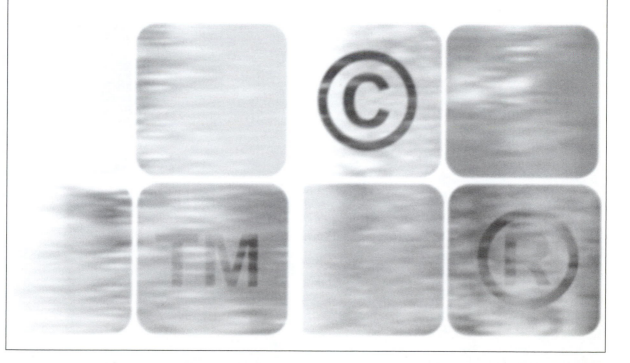

Chapter 2

Foundations of Trademark Law

CHAPTER OVERVIEW

Trademarks surround us every day and help us make valuable and informed decisions about the products and services we purchase. There are four types of marks: *trademarks* are used for goods; *service marks* are used for services; *certification marks* are used to certify some quality of a product or service: and *collective marks* indicate membership in an organization. Some marks, namely those that are coined or "made up," like EXXON®, are stronger than others, namely those that describe or suggest something about a good or service. Not all matter is protectable; marks that disparage a person or that are scandalous cannot be protected. On the other hand, even some unusual devices can be protected, such as sounds and fragrances. Trademarks come into existence through use; they need not be registered with the U.S. Patent and Trademark Office (USPTO) to be protected, although federal registration affords several advantages to a trademark owner.

INTRODUCTION

Although there was some use of trademarks or symbols in the Middle East and Far East several centuries ago, contemporary trademark law can be traced back to use of trademarks during the medieval period in Europe by merchants who sought to distinguish the goods they sold from those sold by others by applying a mark or symbol to their goods. By viewing the mark, purchasers would immediately be able to identify the craftsperson who made the goods and make an informed decision about the quality of the materials. The use of symbols by medieval craftspeople to distinguish

19

and identify their goods is the direct antecedent for the modern use of trademarks such as COCA-COLA®, MICROSOFT®, and CREST®. (See Exhibit 2–1 for History of Trademarks.)

PURPOSE AND FUNCTION OF TRADEMARKS

Trademarks perform two critical functions in the marketplace: They provide assurance that goods are of a certain quality and consistency and they assist consumers in making decisions about the purchase of goods. If a trademark such as NIKE® could be counterfeited and used by an-

other on inferior merchandise, there would be no incentive for the owners of the NIKE mark to produce high-quality shoes and to expend money establishing consumer recognition of the products offered under the NIKE marks. Thus, protection of trademarks results in increased competition in the marketplace, with both the producer of goods and services and the consumer as the ultimate beneficiaries. Businesses benefit because they can reap the rewards of their investment in developing and marketing a product without fearing another business will deceive consumers by using the same or a confusingly similar mark for like goods, and consumers benefit because they are able to identify and purchase desired goods.

EXHIBIT 2–1
History of Trademarks
(From USPTO Web
site at http://www.
uspto.gov)

The U.S. Patent and Trademark Office believes that the importance of trademarks dates back 7,000 years to about 5000 B.C., when drawings showing bison with distinctive symbols on their flanks appeared in the caves of prehistoric man. These were likely some kind of ownership mark, that is, a trademark that identified those particular bison as being the property of a unique owner and distinguished those bison from the bison of others.

By 500 B.C., a real economic use of trademarks can be documented in ancient Rome, where evidence has been found of bricks stamped with the mark of the brick manufacturer.

There is little to be found about the use and growth of trademarks between the fall of the Roman Empire and the Renaissance. The Renaissance, however, brought with it a celebration of the arts, and trademarks reemerged in a significant way. In about the 12th century, trade guilds began using marks to identify goods made by their members. In 1266, the earliest English law on trademarks, the Bakers Marking Law, came into being. This law allowed bakers to identify their breads by stamping a mark on the loaf or pricking the loaf in a particular and recognizable pattern.

The first reference to trademark infringement litigation occurred in 1618 when a clothier who produced inferior cloth used the mark of a superior cloth producer and was brought to court in the English case of *Southern v. How*, 79 Eng. Rep. 1243 (K.B. 1618).

The origin of American trademark protection came in the sailcloth manufacturing industry. In 1791, as a result of concerns of sailcloth makers, Thomas Jefferson recommended the creation of trademark legislation based on the Commerce Clause of the Constitution. In 1879, the United States finally enacted its first trademark legislation and the first registered trademark was registered under that law. The mark, used to identify liquid paints by Averill Paints was dominated by the depiction of an eagle.

The value inherent in achieving consumer loyalty to a particular product or service through the maintenance of consistent quality of the products or services offered under a mark is called **goodwill.** The goodwill associated with a trademark continues to increase over time as additional sales are made of the product offered under a mark and consumers associate the mark with its owner. There is no doubt that the name recognition or goodwill inherent in a trademark can be among a company's most valuable assets. As discussed in chapter 1, the COCA-COLA marks have been valued at $70 billion, and the COCA-COLA mark is the most recognized mark in the world.

Trademarks thus provide the following functions:

- they identify one maker's goods or services and distinguish them from those offered by others;
- they indicate that all goods or services offered under the mark come from a single producer, manufacturer, or "source";
- they indicate that all goods or services offered under the mark are of consistent quality; and
- they serve as an advertising device so that consumers link a product or service being offered with a mark (e.g., when many consumers see or hear the phrase JUST DO IT®, they immediately think of Nike products).

Thus, a consumer who purchases GAP® khaki pants in Dallas is assured that the fit and style is the same as a pair that would be purchased in Philadelphia, and that the item is the product of a single source, namely, Gap Inc.

Trademark law is a part of the broader law of unfair competition or unfair trade practices. Infringement of another's trademark is a species of unfair competition. Other acts of unfair competition include false advertising and infringement of copyrights, patents, or trade names. The law of unfair competition is meant to protect con-sumers and eliminate unfair business practices. Trademark law is a vital part of the broad protection afforded by the law of unfair competition. The law of unfair competition is fully discussed in chapter 23.

TYPES OF MARKS: TRADEMARKS, SERVICE MARKS, CERTIFICATION MARKS, AND COLLECTIVE MARKS

There are four different types of marks: trademarks, service marks, certification marks, and collective marks.

The modern definition of *trademark* is that it is a word, name, symbol, or device, or a combination thereof, used by a person (including a business entity), or which a person has a bona fide intention to use in commerce, to identify and distinguish his or her goods from those manufactured or sold by others and to indicate the source of those goods (15 U.S.C. § 1127). A *service mark* is a word, name, symbol, or device, or a combination thereof, used by a person, or which a person has a bona fide intention to use in commerce to identify and distinguish the services of one person from those of others and to indicate the source of those services. Thus, a trademark

Cheerios

is used to identify goods, such as CHEERIOS® for cereal, LEXUS® for cars, or JIM BEAM® for whiskey. A service mark is used to identify *services*, such as H&R BLOCK® for accounting services, T.G.I. FRIDAYS® for restaurant services, and FED-EX® for package delivery services.

While the term *trademark* thus refers to some physical and tangible good and *service mark* refers to an intangible service, in common usage the terzm *trademark* is often used to refer to marks for both goods and services. Throughout this text, discussions related to "trademarks" will also apply to service marks unless otherwise noted. Similarly, the term **mark** will be used as a synonym for both trademarks and service marks. The federal statute governing trademark law, the U.S. Trademark Act (the Lanham Act, found at 15 U.S.C. § 1051 *et seq.*) itself, states that the term *mark* includes any trademark, service mark, collective mark, or certification mark. See Appendix E (15 U.S.C. § 1127).

A **certification mark** is a word, name, symbol, device, or combination thereof, used by a person other than its owner to certify that goods or services have certain features in regard to quality, material, mode of manufacture, or some other characteristic (or that the work done on the goods or services was performed by members of a union or other organization). Examples of certification marks are the GOOD HOUSEKEEPING® and Underwriters Laboratory seals of approval. Certification marks are, by their very nature, unlike any other types of marks. They do not indicate the origin or source of the goods or services and they are not used by the actual owner of the goods or services. Rather, the mark is placed on the goods or used in connection with the services of another to certify something about the goods or services. Thus, a toaster that carries the GOOD HOUSEKEEPING® seal of approval signifies to consumers that the toaster has been reviewed, tested, and found to meet certain standards in regard to quality, safety, price, or some other characteristic. The toaster is not made by the Good Housekeeping people. They merely certify that the goods on which their mark is placed meet certain objective and preestablished standards.

Similarly, the mark ILGWU INTERNATIONAL GARMENT WORKERS' UNION MADE AFL-CIO (& DESIGN)® certifies that the work or labor done on garments was performed by members of the registrant's union. Another type of certification mark is used to indicate regional origin, such as STILTON®, which certifies that cheese originates in certain counties in England. The owner of a certified mark may lose rights to the mark if it arbitrarily refuses to allow use of a mark by one whose products or services meet its stated certification standards.

A **collective mark** is one used by a collective membership organization, such as a labor union, fraternity, or professional society, to identify that the person displaying the mark is a member of the organization. Thus, the FUTURE FARMERS OF AMERICA® and AMERICAN BAR ASSOCIATION® marks indicate membership in certain organizations.

(See Exhibit 2–2 for further examples of the four types of marks.)

A company may use several marks. An examination of a can of Coca-Cola reveals multiple marks: the words COCA-COLA®, the stylized WAVE DESIGN®, and the slogan THINGS GO BETTER WITH COKE®. All of these marks are used on one product and all are protected by the Coca-Cola Company.

On some occasions, companies use **house marks** to establish recognition in a wide range of products or services. For example, General Mills has registered one mark, GENERAL MILLS® (with a cursive G), for numerous food products, including cereal, biscuit mixes, and mashed potatoes.

EXHIBIT 2–2 Types of Marks	Type of Mark	Example
	Trademark	COMET® (for cleanser)
	Service Mark	HYATT® (for lodging services)
	Certification Mark	UNION MADE® (for clothing)
	Collective Mark	AMERICAN BAR ASSOCIATION 1878® (for membership in an organization)

ACQUISITION OF TRADEMARK RIGHTS

In most foreign countries, trademark rights arise from registering the mark with a governmental entity. The law in the United States is quite different: Trademark rights arise from adoption and *use* of a mark, not from registration. Thus, a person using a mark may have valid and enforceable rights in a mark even though the mark is not registered with the USPTO. Such an owner will have priority (at least within a certain geographic area) even over a subsequent user who has secured a federal registration for a mark with the USPTO.

The "use" required to establish trademark rights is more than token use; it must be public use. Although significant sales are not required, there must be a bona fide business transaction, not merely some sham use. For example, sales within a company or to personal friends are insufficient to show use, while soliciting and accepting orders is usually sufficient to show commercial use.

Establishing a date of first use is critical for a trademark owner because priority of trademark rights is measured from this date. If one party first used a mark on September 15, 2007, and another first used a similar mark on October 15, 2007, the prior, or **senior, user** will be able to preclude the **junior user** from using a confusingly similar mark.

For a mark to be registrable, it must be based on use in commerce, meaning the type of commerce that can be regulated by Congress. Generally, the use is based on **interstate commerce,** or commerce between states, although it could be based on commerce between the United States and a foreign country. A purely intrastate use does not provide a basis for federal registration of a mark. The requirement of interstate commerce is satisfied if the goods or services are advertised in more than one state, offered to citizens of more than one state, or offered on the Internet, which is considered "use" in commerce because it is available to a national audience through the use of telephone or cable lines or wireless transmission.

Although the general rule is that acquisition of trademark rights stem from use, there is one exception to this rule: the **intent-to-use application.** Until 1989, the United States was one of only two countries in the world that required that a mark be in actual use before an owner could file an application to register it.

After an applicant had begun using the mark and then filed an application, the USPTO might then refuse registration of the mark on the basis it was confusingly similar to a prior mark or was subject to some other defect. The applicant would then have invested substantial money and time in developing the mark, in using it in commerce, marketing, and advertising, and in applying for registration, only to be told the mark was unregistrable. To remedy this situation, the Trademark Law Revision Act of 1988 allowed persons to file applications for marks based on a bona fide intent to use the mark in commerce in the future. If the USPTO determines the mark is unregistrable, the applicant will not have expended any sums other than the USPTO filing fee and can readily file another application for a new mark. If the USPTO determines the mark is registrable, the applicant must then commence use of the mark in commerce and provide a statement verifying such use to the USPTO before the mark can proceed to registration. Interestingly enough, however, once the mark proceeds to registration, priority is measured from the date the intent-to-use application was *filed,* even though that filing date may precede actual use in commerce by more than three years. (See Exhibit 2–3.)

Minimal or token use cannot serve as the basis for securing or maintaining a registration, ensuring that an owner does not reserve or "warehouse" a mark by making only sporadic use of it with the intent to block others from using it rather than having a true commercial intent to exploit the mark for sales. Moreover, the USPTO desires to clear its records of unused marks, or "deadwood," so that such unused marks may be available to others.

The use required is "bona fide use of a mark in the ordinary course of trade, and not made

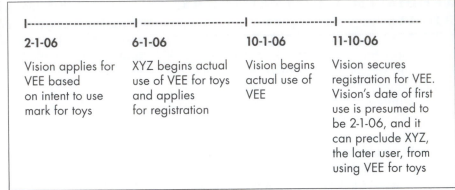

EXHIBIT 2–3
Timeline for Intent-to-Use
Applications

merely to reserve a right in a mark" (15 U.S.C. § 1127). Thus, an owner must make use of a mark as would be typical in the industry or trade. If a product is extremely expensive, such that only a few units are sold each year, this may be sufficient use if such meager sales are the norm in the relevant industry.

Just as use is required to acquire rights in a mark, continued use is required to maintain rights in a mark. Failure to use a mark for three years creates a presumption the mark has been abandoned. Abandonment is further discussed in chapter 5.

COMMON LAW RIGHTS, FEDERAL REGISTRATION UNDER THE LANHAM ACT, LAWS AND TREATIES GOVERNING TRADEMARKS, AND STATE TRADEMARK RIGHTS

Common Law Rights

As discussed, in the United States, trademark rights arise from use of a mark. It is not necessary to secure permission or registration from any governmental entity to acquire trademark rights. A party who is using a mark without any such governmental registration is said to have a **common law trademark.** This common law trademark can be enforced in any geographical area in which the mark is used. Thus, if an owner uses the mark CAKERY CRAVINGS in connection with a pastry shop in Portland, Oregon, the owner will be able to preclude later users from using a confusingly similar mark in connection with similar goods or services in its market area and in a reasonable area of expansion beyond.

Federal Registration

Although there is no requirement that a trademark owner apply for or secure federal registration of a mark with the USPTO, registration on the USPTO's Principal Register does offer several advantages:

- nationwide constructive use effective from the filing date of the application (meaning that the public is assumed to have noticed that the registrant has nationwide priority in the use of its mark as of this date);
- nationwide notice to the public of an owner's claim to a mark, thereby precluding a later user from claiming it used a mark in good faith in a remote territory and should be able to continue use;
- the ability to bar importation of goods bearing infringing trademarks (assuming

the registration is deposited with the U.S. Customs and Border Protection);

- the right under the Paris Convention to obtain a registration in various foreign countries based upon the U.S. registration;
- the right to bring an action in federal court for trademark infringement and recover lost profits, damages, costs, and possibly triple damages and attorneys' fees;
- incontestable status of the registration after five years of continuous use subsequent to the registration (meaning that the mark is immune to certain challenges), assuming appropriate documents are filed;
- the right to use the registration symbol (®) with the mark;
- a possible basis to claim priority to an Internet domain name; and
- *prima facie* (literally, "on its face") evidence of the validity of the mark and of the registration, the registrant's ownership of the mark, and the registrant's exclusive right to use the mark in connection with the identified goods and services.

Additionally, because individuals routinely search the USPTO records before adopting a new mark, a mark that is registered or applied for with the USPTO may deter a party from seeking a registration for a similar mark, thus avoiding expensive litigation.

In sum, while federal registration is not required to secure trademark rights, registration provides several advantages and enhances the level of protection an owner has for a mark.

Laws and Treaties Governing Trademarks

There are several laws and treaties governing trademarks, including the Lanham Act (many others will be further discussed in the chapters to come).

The federal statute governing trademark rights is the **Lanham Act** (also called the United States Trademark Act and found at 15 U.S.C. §§ 1051 *et seq.*), enacted in 1946 and named for Congressman Fritz Garland Lanham (D. Tex.), the then chair of the House Patent Committee (which also proposed legislation relating to trademarks) who introduced the legislation.

In addition to providing for federal trademark protection, the Lanham Act also includes statutes prohibiting unfair competition. The Lanham Act has been amended numerous times. Perhaps the most significant amendment occurred with the Trademark Law Revision Act of 1988, which provided the following two critical changes: allowing for a trademark application based on the applicant's intent to use a mark in the future (previously, applications were all based on actual use of the mark) and reducing the period of protection for federally registered marks from 20 years to 10 years (at which time the registration must be renewed). In addition to the Lanham Act, regulations relating to trademarks are found in Title 37 of the Code of Federal Regulations, entitled "Rules of Practice in Trademark Cases." These rules and regulations explain how the trademark laws are to be carried out and implemented, provide procedures to be followed at the USPTO, and generally govern the day-to-day situations that may arise at the USPTO. For example, 37 C.F.R. § 2.52 describes the format and presentation of trademark drawings.

In addition to our trademark statutes and Title 37 of the Code of Federal Regulations, rules and regulations governing trademark applications and practice can be found in the **Trademark Manual of Examining Procedure** (5th ed. 2007), (usually referred to as the "TMEP"), which is published by the USPTO and provides trademark examining attorneys, trademark applicants, and trademark attorneys with a reference work on the practices and procedures relating to the prosecution of trademark applications. In many instances, detailed information is given, and trademark practitioners keep the TMEP handy to serve as a reference tool for trademark issues and questions. For example, section 302.01 informs applicants that original documents are generally not required; photocopies are acceptable. The entire text of the TMEP is available for viewing and downloading at the USPTO Web site.

Following are key amendments to the Lanham Act:

• **North American Free Trade Agreement (NAFTA).** NAFTA was enacted in 1994 as an agreement among Canada, Mexico, and the United States. NAFTA precludes registration of marks that are primarily geographically deceptively misdescriptive.

• **Trade-Related Aspects of Intellectual Property Rights (TRIPs).** TRIPs, a treaty signed by the United States in 1994, bars registration of a mark for wine or liquor if the mark identifies a place other than the origin of the goods and was first used after 1996. Thus, a new wine cannot use the mark "Napa" unless the product originates in that region of California. TRIPs also increased the period of time of nonuse of a mark that would result in abandonment from two years to three years.

• **Trademark Law Treaty Implementation Act (TLTIA).** TLTIA, effective in late 1999, simplified several requirements relating to trademark registration and maintenance. For example, at present, the applicant need only submit one specimen showing how a mark is used rather than three, as was previously required. Additionally, a trademark applicant need no longer state the manner in which the mark is used. Finally, TLTIA established a six-month grace period for filing a renewal for a trademark registration.

• **Madrid Protocol.** The Madrid Protocol became effective in November 2003 and allows trademark applicants or registrants to file a single international trademark application and obtain protection in any of the more than 70 countries that are party to the Protocol. The Protocol thus facilitates efficient and cost-effective protection for marks on an international basis.

• **Federal Trademark Dilution Act.** The **Federal Trademark Dilution Act** protects against dilution of famous marks by preventing use of a confusingly similar mark even on unrelated goods. Thus, the owner of NIKE may prevent another individual or entity from using the NIKE mark in connection with doughnuts.

• **Anticybersquatting Consumer Protection Act.** The **Anticybersquatting Consumer Protection Act** was signed into law in late 1999 and is intended to protect the public from acts of Internet *cybersquatting,* a term used to describe the bad faith, abusive registration of Internet domain names, such as the registration of www.juliaroberts.com by one with no affiliation with Julia Roberts.

State Registration

It is possible that a mark may not qualify for federal registration, generally because it is not used in interstate commerce but is used only within the confines of one state, namely, in **intrastate commerce.** Thus, the owner of the CAKERY CRAVINGS mark used solely in Portland might seek to register the mark in Oregon. Each one of the 50 states (but not the District of Columbia) has its own trademark act. Generally, obtaining a state registration is a fairly expeditious and inexpensive process. Forms are available from each state's secretary of state, located in the state capital, and are available for downloading on the Web site of the secretary of state. The state registration (usually valid for 5 or 10 years) confers benefits only within the boundaries of the state. Thus, the owner of CAKERY CRAVINGS could not preclude another from using the same or a similar mark in Seattle, Washington. Armed with a *federal* registration, however, the owner could preclude the later Seattle user. There is no procedural or substantive advantage of securing state registrations in addition to a federal registration. The federal registration is nationwide in scope and should be sought whenever a mark qualifies for federal registration. (See Appendix B for a summary of state trademark registration provisions.)

CATEGORIES OF MARKS

Although marks can consist of words, symbols, designs, slogans, or a combination thereof, not every term is protectable. Even among marks that are protectable, some marks are stronger than others. In determining strength of marks, courts recognize several categories of marks. In ascending order of strength and protectability, the five categories are generic, descriptive, suggestive, arbitrary, and fanciful or coined marks.

- A **generic term** is not truly a mark at all but is merely a common name of a product, such as *car, soap,* or *beverage*. Such generic terms are not protectable and cannot be exclusively appropriated by one party inasmuch as they are needed by competitors to describe their goods. Thus, TOP RAMEN® serves as a trademark but "noodles" does not because it is a generic name. In some cases, marks that were once valid have become generic through misuse. Examples of words that were once trademarks but are now generic terms are *aspirin, cellophane, escalator,* and *thermos*. Thus, owners of many well-known marks take great pains to ensure their marks do not become generic. The familiar refrains "SCOTCH® brand adhesive tape" and "Q-TIP® brand cotton swabs" encountered in advertising are meant to protect marks and to ensure that consumers do not use the term *Scotch tape* to describe all adhesive tape or the term

Q-tip to refer to any cotton swab, thereby "genericizing" a once-valued trademark. Xerox's ad campaign "when you use 'Xerox' the way you use 'aspirin,' we get a headache" is similarly aimed to preserve the distinctiveness of the XEROX® mark. Generally, marks should be used as adjectives, as in "I need a KLEENEX tissue." Use of a trademark as a noun, as in "I need a Kleenex," will eventually lead to genericide of the mark and a loss of trademark rights. (See chapter 5.)

- A **descriptive mark** tells something about the product or service offered under a mark by describing some characteristic, quality, ingredient, function, feature, purpose, or use of the product or service. For example, in *In re Bed & Breakfast Registry*, 791 F.2d 157 (Fed. Cir. 1986), BED & BREAKFAST REGISTRY was held merely descriptive of lodging registration services, and in *Hunter Publishing Co. v. Caulfield Publishing Ltd.*, 1 U.S.P.Q.2d 1996 (T.T.A.B. 1986), SYSTEMS USER was held merely descriptive of a trade journal directed at users of data processing systems. Other marks that have been held descriptive include OATNUT for bread made with oats and nuts, LITTLE TAVERN for restaurant and bar services, and COASTAL WINERY for wine made on the Pacific coast. Because descriptive terms merely describe the goods or services, rather than identify the source of a product, they are not registrable with the USPTO until the consumer links the mark with a single source. That learned association is called **secondary meaning** or *acquired distinctiveness*. Descriptive marks cannot be registered until secondary meaning is shown. The USPTO assumes that secondary meaning has been acquired after five years of continuous and exclusive use of a mark. Alternatively, secondary meaning can be shown by demonstrating a significant level of advertising, sales, and consumer survey evidence to prove that when consumers encounter a mark such as SYSTEMS USER, they immediately identify it with its offeror. Such evidence allows a trademark owner to establish secondary meaning without having to wait five years. Laudatory terms such as *best, extra,* and *super* are also considered merely descriptive and are not registrable without proof of secondary meaning.

- A **suggestive mark** suggests something about the goods or services offered under the mark but does not immediately describe them. A suggestive mark requires some imagination or thought to reach a conclusion about the goods or services offered under the mark. For example, ORANGE CRUSH® was held suggestive of an orange-flavored beverage, *see Orange Crush Co. v. California Crushed Fruit Co.,* 297 F. 892 (D.C. Cir. 1924), and GREYHOUND BUS® was held suggestive of transportation services. A suggestive mark is registrable without proof of secondary meaning or distinctiveness. Other examples of suggestive marks include COPPERTONE® for suntan lotion and PLAYBOY® for magazines.
- An **arbitrary mark** is a commonly known word that is applied to an unfamiliar product. Some of the best-known arbitrary marks are CAMEL® for cigarettes, APPLE® for computers, and BLACKBERRY® for electronic handheld units. While the terms are found in a dictionary, they have no relevance when applied to the goods in question and are thus arbitrary. Arbitrary marks are registrable without proof of secondary meaning.
- **Fanciful,** or *coined,* **marks** are those that are invented and have no dictionary meaning. Marks such as KODAK®, PEPSI®, ACURA®, HONDA®, HAAGEN-DAZS®, and XEROX® are examples of fanciful

or coined marks. Such marks are the strongest marks of all and are entitled to the greatest level of protection because it will be difficult for others to claim they innocently created a highly similar mark for similar goods or services.

You can readily see that companies creating marks face a commercial dilemma. The company likely wants the name to identify something about the product or service itself so that consumers encountering the new name or mark can determine what product or service is being offered. However, if the mark communicates directly about the product, it is merely descriptive and cannot be registered without proof of secondary meaning. If a coined mark, such as XEROX, is selected, it is a strong mark, yet it tells the consumer nothing about the product or service offered and the company will need to expend substantial sums in advertising to teach consumers to link the mark with the goods.

TRADE NAMES AND BUSINESS NAMES

A **trade name** or *commercial name* is one used to identify a business or company and its goodwill, while trademarks and service marks identify goods and services. A symbol or name used only as a business name cannot be registered as a trademark or service mark. If the business name, however, also serves to identify and distinguish goods and services, it may be registrable under the Lanham Act. For example, when Hallmark places its business name on its letterhead and business cards, such use is as an unregistrable trade name or business name. When the HALLMARK (& CROWN)® mark appears on greeting cards, however, it is being used as a trademark and may be registered as such.

Some business owners falsely believe that when they incorporate in a state or file partnership or other organizational documents with a state agency, such filing serves to protect their names because the state agency will check to ensure that no similar name is already being used within the state. Thus, for example, if the secretary of state of California allows Diamond Engineers, Inc. to incorporate in California, the corporation may later have to cease using the name if it is found to infringe on a trademark. Merely allowing a company to incorporate under a name does not result in trademark rights. Approval by a state to use a name in connection with a business is merely that—the company is entitled to use the name in connection with the business itself within that state. Using the name on goods themselves or in connection with services, namely, as a trademark or service mark, is far different. Once the mark is so used in commerce, the company acquires trademark or service mark rights. (See Exhibit 2–4.)

PROTECTABLE MATTER

Introduction

The definition of a trademark or service mark is that it is a word, name, symbol, device, or any combination thereof used to identify products or services. Clearly, words such as BARNES & NOBLE® and designs or symbols such as Mercedes Benz's segmented circle or the Mr. Peanut design can function as trademarks. There are, however, a host of other items that can be protected as marks, generally because of the flexibility in the language of the Lanham Act allowing for registration of a "symbol" or "device." A symbol or device might include anything capable of conveying meaning to a person, such as sounds, smells, and shapes.

Slogans, Letters, and Numbers

A slogan can constitute a trademark if it is distinctive. Thus, the slogan HAVE IT YOUR WAY® is protectable. Alphanumeric symbols (letters and numbers) may be protectable as long as they are not merely descriptive. Thus, broadcast station call letters such as NBC® or CNN® are registrable. Similarly, numbers can function as marks. For example, Ford Motor Company has registered ZX5® for trucks and vans. If the numbers or letters describe something about the product or service offered under the mark, however, they will not be registrable unless proof of secondary meaning is shown. Thus, the mark "VT220" for computer hardware peripherals was held merely descriptive and unregistrable because "VT" stood for "video terminal" and "220" was a mere model number. Similarly, an application for registration

Type of Mark	Example	Registrability
Generic	PEANUTS (for peanuts)	Not registrable
Descriptive	BUG MIST (for insecticide)	Not registrable without proof of secondary meaning
Suggestive	SUGAR & SPICE (for cookies)	Registrable
Arbitrary	POPCORN (for feathers)	Registrable
Fanciful or coined	TRALEE (for cellular phones)	Registrable

EXHIBIT 2–4
Categories of Marks

of "888 Patents" (a telephone number) was refused because it was merely descriptive of patent-related legal services. However, once such a telephone number achieves secondary meaning, it may be registered. Thus, the mark 1-800-CALL-ATT® has been registered.

Logos and Symbols

Some of the most famous trademarks in existence consist solely of logos or symbols. Thus, registrations exist for Nike's famous "swoosh" mark, McDonald's golden arches, and Ralph Lauren's figure of a polo player on a horse. Some symbols, however, such as a peace symbol or smiley face, do not serve a trademark function and would not be registrable. Similarly, as discussed later in this chapter, logos that are purely ornamental or are mere background material may not be protectable.

Names of Performing Artists

A mark that merely serves to identify an artist or entertainer is not registrable. However, if the owner of the mark has controlled the quality of the goods or services, and the name of the artist or group has been used numerous times on different records (thereby representing an assurance of quality to the public), the name may be registered as a trademark. Thus, THE GOO GOO DOLLS® and BOB DYLAN® have been registered for musical sound recordings.

Domain Names

Domain names, for example, www.ibm.com, are registrable as trademarks or service marks only if they function as an identification of the source of goods and services. Thus, www.oakwood.com has been registered for real estate leasing services. In many cases, however, applications for domain names are refused because the domain name merely describes the goods or services offered under the mark or merely serves as an address where the applicant can be located.

Thus, www.eilberg.com was refused registration because the mark merely indicated the location on the Internet where the applicant's Web site appeared and it did not separately identify the applicant's legal services.

Another complication with domain name registration is that the USPTO has held that businesses that create a Web site for the sole purpose of advertising their own products or services cannot register a domain name used to identify that activity. Thus, www.amazon.com is registered for providing online chat rooms and bulletin boards. It is *not* registered in connection with offering books or other goods for sale. Similarly, the law firm Holland & Knight has registered www.hklaw.com in connection with its legal newsletter and *not* in connection with the offering of legal services. In many instances, the marks are found merely descriptive. Thus, LAW.COM (for providing information regarding legal services) is presently registered on the Supplemental rather than the Principal Register.

The USPTO itself has recognized that Internet domain names raise unique issues, and, thus, cases relating to registration of domain names continue to evolve.

Foreign Terms

Foreign terms are registrable as long as they comply with the requirements of the Lanham Act. Foreign wording will be translated into English and then examined by the USPTO for descriptiveness. Thus, the word *vino* would not be allowed for wine inasmuch as its immediate translation is "wine," the very product offered under the mark. Similarly, the word *optique*, a French word meaning "optic," was refused registration for eyeglasses because it was merely descriptive. *In re Optica Int'l,* 196 U.S.P.Q. 775 (T.T.A.B. 1977).

Shapes and Containers

Shapes or configurations can function as trademarks if they are distinctive rather than functional. Thus, the famous Coca-Cola bottle shape is registered with the USPTO, and a competitor who adopts a confusingly similar shape container for its product will likely be enjoined from use. The shape is not functional because it is not essential to the use or purpose of the product. If the shape aided or promoted better functioning of a bottle, such as a more efficient lip or handle, it would not be registrable. Thus, a container configuration having the appearance of an ice cream cone was found registrable as a trademark for baby pants because the shape of the container did not promote better functioning of the product.

Trade Dress

The total image of a product, such as size, shape, color, texture, packaging, and graphics, may be protected through a trademark registration. This total image is called **trade dress.** In the famous case *Two Pesos, Inc. v. Taco Cabana, Inc.,* 505 U.S. 763 (1992), the U.S. Supreme Court protected the overall image or trade dress of a Mexican restaurant chain from infringement by a competitor who used similar colors, seating configurations, and décor. When an applicant applies to register a product's design, product packaging, color, or other trade dress for goods or services, the USPTO will consider whether the trade dress is functional or distinctive. Only nonfunctional and inherently distinctive trade dress can be protected. For example, R.J. Reynolds has registered the trade dress for cigarette packaging. In other cases, trade dress that is found to lack distinctiveness is registered on the Supplemental Register (until it acquires secondary meaning). Because trade dress is often protected through the law of unfair competition, it is discussed more fully in chapter 23.

Color

Until relatively recently, a single color was not protectable as a trademark. This general rule was based on the color depletion theory: There are only a limited number of colors in the world; if businesses could appropriate a color and exclude others from using it, competition would be impaired. The present rule is that a trademark may consist of color as long as the color is not functional and the color is shown to have acquired distinctiveness either through long use or a high level of consumer recognition. Thus, Owens-Corning was allowed a registration to protect the pink color of its insulation. *In re Owens-Corning Fiberglas Corp.,* 774 F.2d 1116 (Fed. Cir. 1985). Pink has no functional or utilitarian purpose when applied to the goods and does not deprive competitors from using other colors. Similarly, in 1995, Qualitex Company was allowed to protect its green-gold ironing board pads on the basis that there was no competitive need in the industry for the green-gold color, inasmuch as numerous other colors are equally usable for similar goods. *Qualitex Co. v. Jacobson Products Co.,* 514 U.S. 159 (1995). Similarly, the colors yellow and green used by John Deere & Co. on its machines were held registrable because the colors had become distinctive of John Deere's machines and equipment. However, the color pink for surgical wound dressings was held not registrable because the color of the goods closely resembled Caucasian human skin and was thus functional. Likewise, the makers of the pink PEPTO-BISMOL® stomach medicine were unable to protect its pink color. The court held that the color pink was functional when used in connection with the medicine because the pink color had a pleasing appearance to one with an upset stomach. *Norwich Pharmacal Co. v. Sterling Drug, Inc.,* 271 F.2d 569 (2d Cir. 1959). One of the newer color registrations is for the color yellow, registered to the Lance Armstrong Foundation, Inc. for wristbands to be used in connection with charitable fundraising. The applicant claimed (and the USPTO acknowledged) that the mark had become distinctive due to its extensive renown. In sum, protecting color is still a complex and evolving legal field.

Fragrances, Sounds, and Moving Images

A fragrance can function as a trademark if it has acquired distinctiveness and is not functional. For example, in *In re Clarke*, 17 U.S.P.Q.2d 1238 (T.T.A.B. 1990), a floral fragrance was allowed as a trademark for sewing thread and embroidery yarn and was not functional when used in connection with those goods. A fragrance used in connection with products known for such features, such as perfumes or air fresheners, however, would likely be held functional and not registrable. Similarly, sounds can function as trademarks. The famous three-note chime used by NBC was the first registered sound trademark. The roar of the MGM lion, the quack of the AFLAC duck, and Woody Woodpecker's distinctive laugh are also registered. Finally, moving images may be registered. For example, Columbia Pictures has registered the moving images of the light rays surrounding its "lady Columbia" image that appears at the beginning of its movies. (U.S. Reg. No. 1,975,999).

Designs and Ornamentation

A design can function as a trademark as long as it is distinctive rather than merely functional or ornamental. Some designs are protected on their own, such as Nike's famous "swoosh" design, the alligator that appears on shirts, and Betty Crocker's spoon. If the design is merely background material, however, and does not create a separate commercial impression, or if it consists solely of some simple geometric shape, such as an oval or square, it cannot be protected without proof of secondary meaning. For example, the USPTO refused registration of two parallel colored bands placed at the top of socks as pure ornamentation. Merely decorative subject matter and pure ornamentation cannot be registered because they do not identify and distinguish goods or services and thus cannot function as trademarks.

Serialized Literary and Movie Titles

The title of a single book or movie title is generally not protectable. The title of a serialized work, such as DESPERATE HOUSEWIVES® or NEWSWEEK®, however, can be protected as a trademark or service mark.

(See Exhibit 2–5 for further examples of protectable matter.)

EXHIBIT 2–5
Protectable Matter

Protectable Matter	Example
Words	REAL TIME (for wearing apparel)
Letters	WROC (for radio broadcasting services)
Numbers	1054 (for cleaning products)
Foreign terms	CHAT ROUGE (for computer programs)
Shapes	Distinctive shape for coffee filters (as long as not functional)
Trade dress	Overall commercial impression of packaging, label, text, and graphics (for a can of chili)
Color	Blue (for container for wine, so long as not functional)
Fragrance	Floral fragrance for bookmarks
Design	CHECKERBOARD DESIGN (for food products)
Literary title	IN STYLE (for serialized magazine)

ETHICS EDGE: **Maintaining Confidentiality**

The launching of a new product or service is often a critical business decision for a client, and one whose inadvertent release would significantly harm the client's economic interests and future business plans. Thus, as clients consider, reject, and adopt marks, exercise care to ensure their materials and plans are kept in confidence.

- Keep files and drawings of proposed trademarks in secure locations.
- Be careful when communicating by e-mail, facsimile, or cell phone, to be sure that all communications are secure and confidential.
- Do not inadvertently share confidential client information with friends at social settings or in places where you may be overheard, such as at restaurants or in elevators.

EXCLUSIONS FROM TRADEMARK PROTECTION

Not every word, design, or slogan can function as a trademark. It has already been noted that generic matter cannot be registered and that merely descriptive marks cannot be registered unless secondary meaning is shown. There are several additional bars to registration found in the Lanham Act (15 U.S.C. § 1052).

Disparaging or Falsely Suggestive Marks

The Lanham Act (15 U.S.C. § 1052(a)) forbids registration of a mark that disparages, brings into contempt or disrepute, or falsely suggests an association with persons, institutions, beliefs, or national symbols. Thus, WESTPOINT for guns was held to falsely suggest a connection with the U.S. Military Academy and was refused registration. *In re Cotter & Co.*, 228 U.S.P.Q. 202 (T.T.A.B. 1985). Similarly, a registration for BAMA for shoes and stockings was canceled because the Trademark Trial and Appeal Board (TTAB) found that BAMA pointed uniquely to the University of Alabama and thus falsely suggested a connection with

the university. In April 1999, the TTAB canceled six trademark registrations owned by the NFL football team the Washington Redskins, including the mark REDSKINS, on the basis the marks disparage Native Americans. *Harjo v. Pro Football Inc.*, 50 U.S.P.Q.2d 1705 (T.T.A.B. 1999). The ruling does not prevent the team from using the marks, but it could jeopardize the revenue generated by licensing the marks because the team can no longer sue for infringement of the marks under the Lanham Act, thus severely limiting its ability to preclude knockoff or counterfeited items bearing the team's logos. In late 2003, the district court for the District of Columbia overturned the TTAB decision on procedural grounds. As of the writing of this text, there is no definitive court ruling on the question of whether the REDSKINS mark is disparaging. This complex case has been pending since 1992, when the petition to cancel the various REDSKINS registrations was filed with the Trademark Trial and Appeal Board.

Insignia

Flags, coats of arms, and other insignia of the United States or any state or any foreign nation cannot be registered.

Immoral or Scandalous Matter

Immoral or scandalous matter cannot be registered. For example, a graphic depiction of a dog defecating that was used on clothing was refused registration as scandalous. The mark was also found to disparage Greyhound Corporation because the dog was reminiscent of the Greyhound dog used by the company in connection with its transportation services. *Greyhound Corp. v. Both Worlds, Inc.*, 6 U.S.P.Q.2d 1635 (T.T.A.B. 1988). Similarly, in 2005, the TTAB upheld a refusal to register the mark WIFE BEATER for t-shirts on the basis that it was disparaging.

Names and Portraits of Living Persons

A mark comprising a name, portrait, or signature of a particular living person cannot be used without his or her written consent, and a name, signature, or portrait of a deceased U.S. president cannot be used without his widow's written consent. Thus, the portrait of the actor Paul Newman that appears on various food products must be with his written consent.

Deceptive Matter

Marks comprising deceptive matter cannot be registered. Thus, SILKEASE was held deceptive when applied to clothing not made of silk in *In re Shapely, Inc.*, 231 U.S.P.Q. 72 (T.T.A.B. 1986), and CEDAR RIDGE was held deceptive for hardboard siding not made of cedar. *Evans Products Co. v. Boise Cascade Corp.*, 218 U.S.P.Q. 160 (T.T.A.B. 1983). In most cases, marks are found to be deceptive because they falsely describe the material or content of a product or are geographically deceptively misdescriptive. Thus, SHEFFIELD used on cutlery not made in Sheffield, England, was held deceptive because of the renowned status of Sheffield for cutlery products.

Mere Surnames

A mark that is primarily merely a surname cannot be registered without proof of secondary meaning. Thus, names such as "Smith" or "Higgins" cannot be registered, while names such as "King" or "Bird" would be registrable inasmuch as they have a significance or meaning other than as surnames. A review of USPTO records discloses that McDonald's Corporation's numerous registrations for its MCDONALD'S® marks routinely claim that the mark has acquired distinctiveness through its continuous and exclusive use. The USPTO will examine telephone books to determine if a mark is primarily merely a surname. If the surname is combined with additional matter, such as other words or a design, it may be registrable. Thus, HUTCHINSON TECHNOLOGY® was registrable for computer components. *In re Hutchinson Technology, Inc.*, 852 F.2d 552 (Fed. Cir. 1988).

Geographical Terms

Marks that include geographic terms, such as references to countries, states, towns, streets, and rivers present special problems. When a geographic term is used to describe the place goods or services come from, it is considered descriptive and unregistrable if purchasers would think that the goods or services originate in the geographic place identified in the mark. Thus, THE NASHVILLE NETWORK was held primarily geographically descriptive of various entertainment services where the applicant was located in Nashville and many of the programs it distributed were produced in Nashville. *In re Opryland USA, Inc.*, 1 U.S.P.Q.2d 1409 (T.T.A.B. 1986). Similarly, CALIFORNIA PIZZA KITCHEN was primarily geographically descriptive because the restaurant services were rendered in California and elsewhere. *In re California Pizza Kitchen*, 10 U.S.P.Q. 1704 (T.T.A.B. 1998). Such marks cannot be registered without proof of secondary meaning. On the other hand, NANTUCKET® for shirts was allowed because the shirts offered under the mark did not come from Nantucket and consumers would not immediately associate Nantucket with shirts. *In re Nantucket, Inc.,* 677 F.2d 95 (C.C.P.A. 1982). Similarly, use of DUTCHBOY® for paint was held acceptable because of its arbitrariness; there is no known connection between paint and Holland. *National Lead Co. v. Wolfe,* 223 F.2d 195 (9th Cir. 1955).

As a result of NAFTA, the Lanham Act now prohibits registration of a geographically deceptively misdescriptive mark even if the mark has secondary meaning. Thus, PERRY NEW YORK for clothing not originating in New York was not registrable because consumers, upon encountering the mark, would be deceived into reacting favorably to it due to the renown of New York in the clothing and fashion industry.

Additionally, under TRIPS, and effective January 1, 1996, the Lanham Act absolutely bars registration of any geographic mark for wines and spirits not originating from the place identified in the mark. Thus, the word *Bordeaux* can only be used in connection with goods from the Bordeaux region of France. Finally, some geographic terms have become generic and can never be registered, for example, *French fries, Swiss cheese,* and *Bermuda shorts.*

Descriptive and Confusingly Similar Marks

Marks that are merely descriptive (such as CHEESE BITS for cheese-flavored snacks) or marks that are confusingly similar to those used by a senior user are not registrable. Refusals by the USPTO to register descriptive or confusingly similar marks will be discussed in detail in chapter 4.

Functional Devices

A mark or device or trade dress that is as a whole functional cannot be registered as a trademark because it would deprive others of the right to share a needed device. Thus, trademark protection might be refused for the shape of a matchbook cover when the shape functions to make the product useful. Because competitors would need to use the same shape of cover for their products to be effective, one party cannot exclusively appropriate it in perpetuity. The functionality doctrine ensures that protection for utilitarian product features be sought through patent registration, which is of limited duration. A determination by the USPTO that a proposed mark is functional is an absolute bar to registration, regardless of how distinctive a mark might be.

In one novel case, in 2006 the TTAB upheld a refusal to register a mark consisting of the flavor orange (to be used with antidepressant pills) on the dual bases that the mark was functional (because the pleasant taste performed a utilitarian function in increasing patient compliance) and that consumers would not view a flavor as a trademark but rather as an inherent feature of the product itself.

Statutorily Protected Marks

Finally, certain marks are protected by federal statute from use or confus-  ingly similar use by another (such as the wording "Smokey Bear"), marks used by various veterans' organizations, the Red Cross logo, and the Olympic rings and associated wording. There are about 70 of these special statutes.

(See Exhibit 2–6 for a table of matter that is excluded from trademark protection.)

U.S. PATENT AND TRADEMARK OFFICE

The government agency responsible for reviewing trademark applications and issuing registrations is the U.S. Patent and Trademark Office (USPTO). The official address varies depending

Nonprotectable Matter	Basis for USPTO Refusal
SQUAW (for sale of sporting goods)	Mark would disparage or bring a person or institution into contempt or disrepute
Flag of Italy (for pasta)	Insignia of a foreign nation
Graphic pictures of nude figures (for wearing apparel)	Immoral or scandalous matter
Photograph of Brad Pitt (for salad dressing) (unconsented)	Unconsented use of living person's portrait
PETERSON (for hiking boots)	Primarily merely a surname
LEATHERETTE (for gloves made of vinyl)	Deceptive
PARISIAN EROS (for perfume not from Paris)	Geographically deceptively misdescriptive
BREADSPREAD (for margarine) (without proof of secondary meaning)	Merely descriptive
NIKEE (for athletic gear)	Confusingly similar to a registered mark
SPIROS' OLYMPIC RESTAURANT (& DESIGN OF FIVE RINGS)	Statutorily protected matter
Shape of piano (needed for acoustical reasons)	Functional

Assignments	(571) 272-3350
General Assistance	(571) 272-1000; or (800) 786-9199
Intent-to-Use Unit	(571) 272-9550
Madrid Processing Unit	(571) 272-8910
Office of the Administrator for Examination	(571) 272-9100
Office of the Commissioner for Trademarks	(571) 272-8900
Office of Trademark Services	(571) 272-9401
Petitions Office	(571) 272-8950
Post-Registration	(571) 272-9500
Pre-Examination	(571) 272-9401
Publication and Issue	(571) 272-9401
Trademarks Assistance Center	(571) 272-9250; or (800) 786-9199
Trademark Status (for pending applications and registrations)	(571) 272-5400
Trademark Trial and Appeal Board	(571) 272-8500

on the particular issue involved. The USPTO is physically located in five buildings at 600 Dulany Street, Alexandria, Virginia 22314. The USPTO maintains an excellent Web site at http://www.uspto.gov, offering general information, updates on new issues, forms for downloading, a database of more than four million registered, pending, and dead trademarks, statistics, lists of USPTO fees, and a wide variety of other valuable information. (See Exhibit 2–7 for a list of frequently called USPTO telephone numbers.)

The trademark section of the USPTO is divided into a variety of different departments, such as one handling assignments, one dealing with postregistration matters, and one dealing with intent-to-use applications. Due to the spread of computer and communications technology throughout the world, the workload of the USPTO has increased significantly. New trademark applications increased by 9 percent in 2006 over 2005, with the USPTO receiving 275,790 applications.

Trivia

- The oldest U.S. trademark registration still in existence is SAMSON (with a design of a man and a lion) registered in 1884 for use on cords, line, and rope.
- The first registration of a shape and design of a container was in 1958 for Haig & Haig's pinch scotch whiskey bottle.
- Some of the famous sound marks registered include Tarzan's yell, the "Ho, Ho, Ho" of the Jolly Green Giant, and the Yahoo! yodel. (An application is pending for the sound of Homer Simpson's "D'oh.")
- The Trademark Act continues to grow in length, from just over 10,000 words in 1946 when it was first passed to nearly 25,000 words in 2000.

CHAPTER SUMMARY

Trademarks play a valuable role in our economy. They serve to distinguish one merchant's goods or services from those of another and provide assurances of quality and consistency to consumers. There are four different types of marks: trademarks (used for goods); service marks (used for services); certification marks (used to certify a quality of a good or service); and collective marks (used to show membership in an association). Rights to marks are acquired through use. There is no need to file an application for federal registration of a mark with the USPTO to acquire or maintain rights to a mark, although registration does offer significant advantages to a trademark owner.

Not all words, letters, and symbols are protectable. Generic words cannot be trademarked and descriptive marks can be trademarked only upon proof of secondary meaning. Suggestive, arbitrary, and coined marks are all registrable without proof of secondary meaning. Certain types of marks are excluded from federal protection, such as scandalous marks, deceptive marks, and geographically deceptively misdescriptive marks.

CASE ILLUSTRATION—REFUSAL TO REGISTER DECEPTIVE MARK

Case: *In re Budge Manufacturing, Co., Inc.,* 857 F.2d 773 (Fed. Cir. 1988)

Facts: The Trademark Trial and Appeal Board refused Budge's application for LOVEE LAMB for automobile seat covers made of synthetic material on the basis that the mark was deceptive.

Holding: The decision was affirmed. There is a three-part test used to determine whether a mark is deceptive: whether the term is misdescriptive of the goods; if so, whether anyone would be likely to believe the misrepresentation; and whether the misrepresentation would materially affect a purchaser's decision to buy the goods. In this case, the seat covers were made of synthetic materials and not of lamb or sheep products. Thus, the wording LAMB is misdescriptive. Purchasers are likely to believe that seat covers denominated by the term "lamb" or "sheep" are actually made from natural lamb or sheep products. Finally, natural sheepskin or lambskin products are more expensive than simulated skins and thus a misrepresentation about them is likely to affect a buyer's decision to purchase. Thus, the use of the term LAMB in the mark when used in connection with goods not made of lambskin is deceptive, and the mark cannot be registered.

CASE STUDY AND ACTIVITIES

Case Study.   Vision is considering offering a variety of new products in its hotel gift shops and would like to seek trademark registration for the marks under which the goods and services will be offered. Some of the proposed marks include the following:

- The slogan "Vacation with Vision";
- Coffee mugs with the flags of various nations on them;
- The design of a lid to be placed over the coffee mugs, which helps retain heat better than other mug covers and lids;
- The mark "El major hotel del mundo" (Spanish for "The best hotel in the world") to be displayed on T-shirts;
- The distinctive giggle of Vision's mascot, Vee; and
- The slogan "Jennifer Aniston's Favorite Hotel" to be displayed on caps and visors.

Activities.   Identify the type of mark each product or service represents (e.g., trademark, sound mark, color mark) and then indicate any possible objections the USPTO might have to each mark, if any.

ROLE OF PARALEGAL

The role of IP paralegals prior to searching and application for registration is generally limited to research, particularly research regarding whether the mark satisfies the requirements of the Lanham Act for registrability. Each element of the mark should be examined to determine whether it is descriptive, disparaging, comprises merely a surname, includes a living person's name without written consent, and so forth. Design elements of marks should also be considered to ensure the design feature is a separate and distinct portion of the mark, rather than mere background. Additionally, some preliminary discussions should take place with the mark's owner to determine whether federal registration is permissible or whether the owner will be limited to state trademark registration because the mark is not (and will not be) used in interstate commerce.

INTERNET RESOURCES

Federal statutes governing trademarks
(15 U.S.C. § 1051 *et seq.*)

http://www.gpoaccess.gov
http://www.law.cornell.edu
http://www.findlaw.com

USPTO trademark information:

http://www.uspto.gov (general information, trademark searching, and access to *Trademark Manual of Examining Procedure* for excellent information on types of marks and what may be protected)

General information on trademark topics:

http://www.findlaw.com
http://www.megalaw.com

DISCUSSION QUESTIONS

1. Classify the following marks as trademarks, service marks, collective marks, or certification marks:
   - AMERICAN BAR ASSOCIATION (to indicate membership in registrant's organization)
   - 409 (for cleaning products)
   - BRITISH AIRWAYS: THE WAY TO FLY (for transportation services)
   - PARMIGIANO-REGGIANO (used to certify that products originate in the Parma-Reggio region of Italy)
   - DR. PHIL (for television show)
   - CHIPS AHOY! (for cookies)
2. Could a bright yellow color be trademarked for road safety signs?

DISCUSSION QUESTIONS (CONT'D)

3. Could the shape of a guitar be trademarked when the shape enhances the sound produced by the guitar? Discuss.

4. Ron Nelson is opening a clothing store in Denver. He recently sold and shipped one men's shirt to his brother in New York. Is this use sufficient to support an application for federal trademark registration? What if Ron establishes a Web site that allows customers from around the United States to order his goods? Discuss.

5. What is the danger of consumers saying, "We should Google that to find out more information"?

6. Discuss whether a person could likely obtain a federal trademark registration for the following marks for the goods or services indicated, and discuss the objections, if any, that the USPTO might raise.

Mark	Goods or Services
SIMPSON	Cosmetics
PEYTON MANNING'S CHOICE	Athletic gear
MYSTIQUE	Clothing
CAFFE	Coffee beans
BEST SAUCE	Pasta sauce
OATMEAL COOKIE	Body lotion
OATMEAL KOOKIE	Oatmeal cookie
OLYMPIC RINGS	Coaching services
FANTASY	Perfume
CHOCO-BITS	Snacks with no chocolate
AVERELLA	Earphones
PENGUIN	Beverage coolers

USING INTERNET RESOURCES

1. Access the USPTO Web site and select "Trademarks" and then "Check Status." Check the status of the various federal trademark registrations and answer the questions.
   a. Check Reg. No. 2328375. What is the mark? When was it registered? For what goods was the mark registered? Whose consent is of record?
   b. Check Reg. No. 2442140. Who is the registrant? When was the mark registered? Give the description of the mark.

2. Access the USPTO Web site and select "Trademarks" and then "Search Trademarks." Use the "New User Form (Basic)" and locate the most recent mark registered to the Chicago Rabbinical Council (Reg. No. 3192909). What type of mark is this? Who is the mark used by and for what purpose?

3. Access the USPTO Web site and select "Trademarks" and then "Manual of Examining Procedure." Use the alphabetical index to answer the following questions.

a. Review the section relating to laudatory terms as marks. What mark was held to be highly laudatory and descriptive as applied to beer and ale?

b. May a columnist trademark his or her syndicated column? What section governs your answer?

4. Use an online database for federal statutes such as Cornell's Legal Information Institute. What federal statute imposes a penalty for use of SMOKEY BEAR? What is the penalty?

For additional resources, go to www.paralegal.delmar.cengage.com.

Chapter 3

Trademark Selection and Searching

CHAPTER OVERVIEW

As discussed in chapter 2, not every word, slogan, or design can be protected as a trademark or service mark. Therefore, great care must be given to selecting a mark to identify one's goods or services. Once a mark is selected, a trademark availability search should be conducted to determine if the mark is available for registration. Searches are conducted of the USPTO records, state trademark records, business directories, journals, telephone books, domain names, and Internet uses to determine whether a proposed mark may conflict with a mark already in use. Although no search can guarantee that a mark will be accepted by the USPTO for registration, a search allows a trademark owner to anticipate problems that may arise in the registration process, provides a snapshot of other marks in the marketplace, and may help avoid liability for infringement.

SELECTING AND EVALUATING A MARK

Selecting a Mark

Selection of a mark occurs in a variety of ways. Some companies hold contests and encourage employees to create a mark for a new product line or service. Other companies engage sophisticated research and branding firms that will conduct surveys and create a mark and a logo or design for the company. There are name creation software programs that help individuals and companies create marks. Once the mark is selected, it must be screened and evaluated for use and registrability. Failure to exercise this due diligence might result in the expenditure of time and money in advertising, using, and applying for a mark that is rejected for registration by the USPTO or, in the worst-case scenario, might subject the owner to damages for trademark infringement and unfair competition.

Reviewing a Proposed Mark

Once a mark is selected, it should be carefully scrutinized to ensure that it will not be excluded from protection under the Lanham Act. Considerations include whether the mark contains scandalous material, whether consent from a living person will be required, whether the mark is generic, whether it is statutorily protected, and whether the mark is descriptive of some feature of the goods and services offered under the mark. If the mark includes foreign terms, these should be translated to ensure they are not scandalous, deceptive, or merely descriptive. Many law firms specializing in trademark work use a questionnaire form or data sheet to gather basic information from clients about their marks and to aid in determining registrability (see Exhibit 3–1 for an example).

THE TRADEMARK SEARCH

Once a proposed mark has been selected, a trademark search should be conducted to ensure that the proposed mark is not confusingly similar to a mark that is the subject of a registration or pending application at the USPTO or that is in use on a common law basis.

In addition to disclosing potential conflicting marks, a search will provide some indication of the relative weakness or strength of the mark. If there are numerous marks including words similar to the proposed mark for the same or related goods, the field is said to be "crowded," and the mark, while it may achieve registration, may be weak and entitled to a narrower scope of protection than a strong, unique, and distinctive mark. For example, a review of the USPTO database shows the following registrations issued to different owners:

PARAMOUNT®   (for hardwood flooring)
PARAMOUNT®   (for paper napkins)
PARAMOUNT®   (for bowling balls)
PARAMOUNT®   (for chocolates)
PARAMOUNT®   (for entertainment motion picture services)

These numerous registrations for PARAMOUNT® show that the mark is weak, and an application to register PARAMOUNT for some distinguishable goods (e.g., cigarettes) would likely be allowed. The owner of PARAMOUNT (for cigarettes) would be able to stop later users from using PARAMOUNT for cigarettes and related products, but would have to share the field with the existing PARAMOUNT registrations and later PARAMOUNT marks used for nonsimilar goods.

A review of other marks also enables the IP team to anticipate some of the problems that may arise during the registration process and possible objections the USPTO may have to the application.

Duty to Search

A party who adopts a mark and begins using it without previously searching its availability runs the risk that a senior user will allege infringement. If the later user has begun using the infringing mark, it may need to stop using the mark and any of its marketing materials and brochures that display the offending mark. Such an error is costly and time-consuming because the party will then need to adopt another mark and begin the process of establishing consumer recognition all over again.

There is, however, another reason to conduct a trademark search prior to use or application of a trademark, namely to avoid litigation alleging trademark infringement. Liability for trademark infringement rests on a finding that two marks are likely to be confused. One factor courts consider in determining whether two marks are likely to be confused is the intent and good faith use by the second user. Recent cases have begun examining whether failure to conduct a proper search is evidence of bad faith. While a number of courts have criticized parties for failure

EXHIBIT 3–1
Trademark
Data Sheet
(U.S. Applicant)

Please provide the following information to enable us to prepare and file an application for registration of your mark with the United States Patent and Trademark Office (USPTO).

1. Describe the mark.
   a. Words: _____
   b. Logo: _____ [describe and attach sample logo] _____
   c. Are the words "stylized" (for example, should they be displayed in any particular manner, script, or typeface or is standard printing acceptable)?
   _____

2. Describe the Applicant.
   a. Full name: _____
   b. Full address: _____
   c. Type of legal entity (corporation, partnership, etc.) _____
   d. Organized under the laws of the state of _____
   e. Name of authorized person who will sign the application and other documents and his/her title: _____

3. Describe with particularity all of the goods and/or services that are or will be offered under the mark or for which protection is being sought.
   _____

4. Consult your records and state, with respect to use of the mark by you (or any predecessor) on or in connection with any of the above-described goods or services:
   a. Has the mark been used in intrastate sales or advertising? If so, give date of first use anywhere.
   _____

   b. Has the mark been used in interstate commerce within the United States? For example, has there been a transaction with an out-of-state customer or has media advertising the goods or services offered under the mark been conducted across state lines? If so, give the date the mark was first used in interstate commerce in the United States (or in foreign commerce between a foreign country and the United States). Note that use of the mark in advertising preparatory to opening a business is not sufficient.
   _____

   c. Is there a bona fide intent to use the mark in the United States if it has not yet been used in the United States? _____

5. Provide information as to how the mark is actually used (if it is in use).
   a. Newspaper or other media advertising: _____ Yes _____ No
   b. Signs or store displays: _____ Yes _____ No
   c. Direct mail, such as brochures: _____ Yes _____ No
   d. Labels, tags, packaging: _____ Yes _____ No
   e. Other (describe): _____

6. If the mark is in use, please provide at least three original specimens showing the mark as it is actually used in connection with the sale or advertising of the goods or services. If the mark is used in connection with goods, labels, tags, boxes, or other packaging are acceptable as long as they show the mark. If the mark is used in connection with services, brochures and other advertising materials are likely acceptable as long as they show the mark. If the specimens are bulky, you may provide photographs of the specimens as long as the mark is clear and legible in the photos.

to conduct a trademark search before using and applying for a mark, calling such conduct "carelessness," *SecuraComm Consulting, Inc. v. SecuraCom Inc.*, 166 F.3d 182, 188-89 (3d Cir. 1999), or stating that a search is a "very obvious and simple precaution," *First Jewellery Co. of Canada, Inc. v. Internet Shopping Network LL*, 53 U.S.P.Q.2d 1838 (S.D.N.Y. 2000), most courts have concluded that failure to perform a search, standing alone, does not prove bad faith or willful infringement. *Savin Corp. v. Savin Group*, 391 F.3d 439, 460 (2d Cir. 2004). Nevertheless, when a large company failed to conduct a trademark search until just days before the airing of a commercial when it knew of a prior use by another major marketer, the court noted the defendant was a highly sophisticated national marketer with access to every imaginable resource to avoid the slightest possibility of confusion and that failure to conduct a search was "inexcusable" and showed a "complete indifference" to the plaintiff's federal trademark rights and was a factor favoring relief to the plaintiff. *Sands, Taylor & Wood v. Quaker Oats Co.*, 18 U.S.P.Q.2d 1457 (N.D. Ill. 1990), *aff'd in part and rev'd in part*, 978 F.2d 947 (7th Cir. 1992). Finally, in *Frehling Enterprises, Inc. v. International Select Group, Inc.*, 192 F.3d 1330 (11th Cir. 1999), *cert. denied*, 531 U.S. 944 (2000), an infringement case, the court agreed that a failure to conduct a trademark search before attempting to register a trademark was "intentional blindness" and was evidence of improper intent. Thus, although there is no legal duty to perform a trademark search before using or applying for a mark, failure to do so (along with other behavior) may well be a factor suggesting improper intent. Moreover, with the numerous free sources available for those conducting trademark searches, a failure to conduct a basic search would seem careless, at best.

Because liability for trademark infringement rests on a finding that two marks are likely to be confused, a client may be able to avoid liability by showing it acted in good faith by conducting a thorough trademark search prior to using

a mark. In sum, a comprehensive trademark search can save time and money, avoid litigation, ensure a mark is available, and assist in developing a strategy to avoid possible USPTO objections.

Scope of Search

There are a variety of sources that can be reviewed to locate potentially conflicting marks. Because there are literally millions of marks registered or applied for at the USPTO, and thousands of journals, trade magazines, directories, telephone books, Internet sources, state records, and state trademark registrations that might contain other marks or business names, a computer-assisted or online search is the most effective method of searching. Moreover, an online search can be constructed to search only for similar marks used in connection with similar goods and services. Thus, if the client in our case study wishes to use VISION COURT for hotel services, there is little to be gained from looking for similar marks used in connection with candy inasmuch as consumers would not likely be confused by the coexistence of two similar marks for such dissimilar goods.

Both LEXIS® and WESTLAW®, the computer-assisted legal research systems, offer access to vast databases that may point out conflicts. One of the best-known databases is TRADEMARK-SCAN®, available through WESTLAW. TRADEMARKSCAN (federal) contains information on active registered trademarks and service marks as well as applications filed at the USPTO, while TRADEMARKSCAN (state) provides similar information on marks registered with the secretaries of state of all 50 states. Other online databases include journals, magazines, and periodicals. Most of the databases are also offered on CD-ROM, allowing IP practitioners to purchase discs and conduct their own searches. The discs are then periodically replaced and updated. The more common approach is to conduct trademark searches online.

Conducting the Trademark Search: A Two-Step Process

In nearly all instances, trademark searching is a two-step process: a preliminary search is conducted of the records of the USPTO (and possibly other databases) to make a quick determination as to whether the mark may be available or whether there is a direct conflict that would preclude use of the mark. The preliminary search is often called a **knockout search** because its primary purpose is to eliminate identical or nearly identical marks. If the results of the preliminary or knockout search indicate a mark may be available, a comprehensive search of other sources (including state trademark records, telephone directories, Internet records, and trade journals) is then conducted.

Step One: The Preliminary Search

There are a variety of sources that can be used to conduct an initial trademark search, including online subscription services, CD-ROMs, the Patent and Trademark Depository Libraries, and the USPTO Web site search services. Following are some resources commonly used for conducting a preliminary search.

Electronic Databases and CD-ROMs

- TRADEMARKSCAN online databases are owned by Thomson CompuMark, a renowned trademark search firm (discussed later), which provides information on all active registered trademarks and service marks and applications for registration filed at the USPTO. The TRADEMARKSCAN databases are primarily used as a quick screening tool to determine the availability of a new mark.
- DIALOG® is another database offered by the publisher Thomson & Thomson. Its database includes trademarks from the United States plus numerous foreign countries as well as patent and copyright information. DIALOG offers free online

training and practice (its ONTAP® service) and free practice searching at the following Web site: http://training.dialog.com/onlinecourses/trademarks/.
- SAEGIS™ is an entire suite of services provided by Thomson CompuMark that allows online worldwide trademark searching as well as searching of domain name registries and Web sites to locate common law uses of proposed marks.
- TRADEMARK.COM™ is an online search service offered by MicroPatent (discussed later), a Thomson business, offering a variety of searchable databases, including federal marks, state marks, and common law uses of potentially conflicting marks.
- LEXIS and WESTLAW, the computer-assisted research systems, offer access to vast trademark databases that may disclose potentially conflicting marks.

Many law firms subscribe to one or more of these services so they can perform an initial screening search in-house. Some of the databases can be purchased in CD-ROM format, allowing IP practitioners to purchase discs and conduct their own searches. The discs are then periodically replaced and updated. Alternatively, most IP practitioners access the various databases online, on a "pay-as-you-go" basis.

In conjunction with a preliminary or knockout search, most practitioners conduct a simple Internet search using a standard search engine. For example, entering the word mark VISION COURT into a search engine such as Google (http://www.google.com) may disclose some common law uses of the mark. Often paralegals conduct the knockout search and provide an initial review of the marks revealed. The results are communicated to the client along with recommendations for the next step to take. If a mark is intended to be used only for a short time, perhaps during a limited promotional campaign, a knockout search may be sufficient by itself.

Patent and Trademark Depository Libraries. For those located near Washington, DC, the

USPTO maintains a Public Search Facility in Alexandria, Virginia, that allows online searching of pending, registered, and dead trademarks using the trademark examining attorney automated system called X-Search. A complete trademark collection since 1870 is available online and in bound paper volumes or on microfilm. The Search Facility is open to the public every weekday. For information, call (571) 272–3275. Additionally, more than 80 libraries throughout the United States (mostly in major cities) are designated as **Patent and Trademark Depository Libraries.** These libraries receive a wealth of information from the USPTO, and trademark searching can be done at these libraries. See the USPTO Web site at http://www.uspto.gov for a list of the Patent and Trademark Depository Libraries.

USPTO Web Site. Perhaps the easiest and least expensive way to conduct a very preliminary search is to review the records of the USPTO (http://www.uspto.gov). The USPTO offers free public searching of its trademark database through its service called **Trademark Electronic Search System (TESS),** which allows searching of more than four million pending, registered, abandoned, canceled, or expired trademark records. TESS offers four search strategies.

1. **New User Form Search (Basic).** This basic search strategy is useful for finding marks made up solely of words or by searching by a trademark owner's name. Searching may also be done by trademark serial or registration number. Simply type in the name of the mark in which you are interested (e.g., VISION QUEST), and you can then review records containing those terms. Thus, results would include both VISIONQUEST and VISIONQUEST ALLIANCE. A search for VISION alone would disclose more than 8,000 entries that include the term "vision."
2. **Structured Form Search (Boolean).** The Structured Form search allows a searcher to narrow the search by locating marks relating to certain goods and services (e.g.,

VISION QUEST used for hotel services) or to locate assignments or renewals of marks. The use of Boolean connectors also helps to narrow results. Thus, a search for "VISION and QUEST" would retrieve documents with both those terms.
3. **Free Form Search (Advanced Search).** The Free Form search strategy is for more complicated searches and is generally most successful when Boolean connectors are used.
4. **Browse Dictionary (View Indexes).** The Browse Dictionary strategy allows one to review about 10 items in the USPTO's database around the search term. Thus, a search for VISION QUEST would disclose VISIOMOUSE and VISIONABLE.

The USPTO database does not easily allow phonetic searching. Thus, a search for BEAR would not disclose any marks with the term *Bare.* Additionally, searching for designs is fairly difficult. However, the site offers help and numerous strategies and tips for searching.

Once a mark is displayed on your computer screen, you will be given four separate options to obtain additional information.

• **TARR Status:** The Trademark Application and Registration Retrieval System (TARR) provides additional information about an application or registration, including a list of various actions taken by the USPTO and information on the mark's current status, such as whether it has expired because it was not renewed.
• **Assignment Status:** If the mark has been assigned, you will be given the names of the assignor and assignee and the date the assignment was recorded with the USPTO.
• **Trademark Document Retrieval (TDR):** TDR allows views of actual images of documents in the USPTO's files, such as the drawing of the mark, images of specimens of the mark, notice of publication, and certificate of registration.

This "electronic file wrapper" provides invaluable information. TDR is not yet available for older records. You may access TDR after conducting a search, or you may access it independently if you have a serial or registration number.

- **TTAB Status:** If the mark is involved in proceedings at the Trademark Trial and Appeal Board, you will be linked to documents pertaining to these proceedings.

If you already know a trademark application number or serial number, once you access the USPTO Web site, select "Trademarks" and then "Check Status." Enter the pertinent number in the search box, and you will be linked to the TARR database and information.

The USPTO site itself acknowledges its limitations and counsels users as follow: "After searching the USPTO database, even if *you* think the results are 'O.K.,' do **not** assume that your mark can be registered at the USPTO. After you file an application, the USPTO must do its own search and other review, and might refuse to register your mark." Nevertheless, despite their limitations, the USPTO search systems TESS and TARR are excellent sources for obtaining initial information, and with practice, one can become fairly proficient in conducting a knockout search or obtaining basic information about the marks owned by any one party. Although a search of these databases can provide a quick answer to very basic questions about availability of marks (much the same way a knockout search does), it is no substitute for a thorough search of other possible uses of marks, such as those used as Internet domain names, unregistered marks, and those registered with individual states. Moreover, trademark applications are not immediately entered into the database, resulting in incomplete data.

In addition to the records of the USPTO, a preliminary search should review records of well-known publicly accessible Internet databases. Thus, a simple search using the Google search engine may well disclose common law uses, such as businesses using the mark or other products offered under the mark both throughout the nation and internationally. Even a quick USPTO and Google-type search are better than no search. However, if a mark is important to a company and will be key to its future, a comprehensive search should be conducted.

Step Two: The Comprehensive Search

The most complete analysis of potentially conflicting marks is provided by professional trademark search firms. These companies review the records of the USPTO for existing registrations and pending applications, review state trademark office records for state trademark registrations, and they perform a "common law" search of various journals, directories, press releases, domain names, and Internet references to locate unregistered names and marks. Such a search is called a **comprehensive,** or *full,* **search.** Because there are literally thousands of journals, directories, telephone books, and other publications in which names and marks may appear, these professional search firms can save considerable time and money and, more importantly, provide a more thorough search than that which an individual can conduct on his or her own. Some of these companies advertise that their databases include more than one million marks that can be checked against the client's mark for potential conflicts. These companies will check for identical and phonetically equivalent marks for similar goods and services and will also check for foreign equivalents. Thus, a search for KARCOAT will disclose marks such as CARCOAT and CARKOAT. Marks with design elements also must be searched; these searches are usually a bit more expensive than searches for marks comprising solely words due to the time-consuming task of comparing other design marks to the proposed mark. Professional search firms can also customize searches and conduct investigations as to how a potentially conflicting mark is used in the marketplace.

Costs for full availability searches can run from $500 for results available in four business days to approximately $1,100 for same-day searches. These costs do not reflect an attorney's time in evaluating the results and providing a report to a client, but rather reflect only the costs of obtaining a report that discloses potentially conflicting marks. Some companies will send the report by express mail or other overnight service or may send it via facsimile (although due to the voluminous nature of many reports, this is not a common practice). Another more recent alternative is that the report may be sent to an office via electronic transmission or e-mail. The search company will post the report to a bulletin board server, and the law firm then retrieves the search. The report is typically divided into three sections: results gained from reviewing USPTO registrations and applications; results gained from reviewing state trademark records; and the common law results (references to marks in magazines, telephone directories, Internet domain names, and so forth).

Most of the professional searching firms will tailor the search to specific requirements, so that they will conduct only common law searches, or only an Internet domain name search, an international search, and so forth. Intellectual property practitioners who engage the professional searchers on a routine basis often obtain volume discounts.

Although the Internet makes thousands of common law uses of trademarks accessible, the sheer volume of sources makes weeding out immaterial uses of a mark difficult. No search, no matter how thorough, can guarantee that a client may use or register a mark.

International Searching

A client interested in protecting his or her mark in foreign countries should conduct a search of the records of each country in which an application will be filed. Although the U.S. search firms can conduct such searches, interpreting the results and predicting how a foreign trade-

mark office would view the application is very difficult for U.S. practitioners who typically are not experts in foreign trademark law. Therefore, most law firms that do trademark work have established relationships with their counterparts in foreign countries and rely upon these **associates** to conduct a search and report the results. The foreign associate then files the trademark application and prosecutes it, while the U.S. attorney generally supervises the process and communicates the progress of the application to the client.

In a recent development, some foreign countries have been allowing free searching of their trademark office databases, much the way one can search for U.S. marks through the USPTO's TESS or TARR systems.

The International Trademark Association (INTA) offers direct linking to the databases of trademark offices for Australia, Canada, the European Union, Japan, and the United Kingdom (among other countries) through its Web site at http://www.inta.org. The USPTO'S Web site also offers linking to foreign IP offices.

Professional Search Firms.

Some of the better-known search firms include the following.

- Thomson CompuMark, 500 Victory Road, North Quincy, MA 02171-3145; (800) 692-8833 (http://www.thomson-thomson. com). Thomson & Thomson is a well-known trademark services firm, offering a full line of service, from trademark searching to monitoring of trademarks to protect them from infringement, to investigations to retrieving documents at the USPTO. Thomson CompuMark is the owner of the TRADEMARKSCAN, DIALOG, and SAEGIS products described earlier in this chapter. In a recent development, Thomson CompuMark will not only mail the results of a trademark search but also posts them to a user's inbox, allowing colleagues to share trademark results and cut and paste search results into letters to clients.

- MicroPatent 250 Dodge Avenue, East Haven, CT 06512; (800) 648-6787 (http://www.micropat.com). MicroPatent offers full professional searching as well as access to its TRADEMARK.COM database described earlier.
- Government Liaison Services, Inc., 200 North Glebe Road, Suite 321, Arlington, VA 22203; (800) 642-6564 (http://www .trademarkinfo.com).

    Government Liaison Services offers full professional searching as well as document preparation and retrieval services.

- CT Corsearch, 345 Hudson Street, New York, NY 10014; (800) 732-7241 (http://www.ctcorsearch.com). CT Corsearch offers a full suite of trademark searching services, including professional searching, document retrieval, and monitoring services to ensure a client's trademark is not infringed.

Evaluating Trademark Search Reports

Once the results of the search have been obtained, they must be evaluated so that the fundamental questions whether the mark is available for use and registration can be answered. The evaluation begins with an analysis of each mark or name provided in the report and a comparison of it to the proposed mark to determine whether they are confusingly similar. This analysis requires one to take into account the overall commercial impressions presented by the marks; their similarity in regard to sight, sound, and meaning; the relative strength or weakness of the marks based on their descriptiveness or suggestiveness; and the goods or services offered under each mark.

A typical search entry will appear as follows:

Mark	BITTY BEAR
Reg. No.	1,990,314
Reg. Date	July 30, 2001
Filing Date	June 2, 1999
Date of first use	September 11, 1998
Goods	Toys and stuffed animals
I.C.	28
Owner	Pleasant Company Corp. 8400 Fairway Place Middleton, WI 53562

Assume a client wished to introduce a new line of children's books called BUDDY BEAR. The existence of BITTY BEAR for toys and stuffed animals may present a conflict. The marks are similar in appearance (with only a few letters being different) and similar in sound, and children's books may be viewed as related to children's toys. Consumers who encounter the BUDDY BEAR books might believe they are somehow connected with BITTY BEAR or that BUDDY BEAR is a new line of books sponsored by the makers of BITTY BEAR. On the other hand, if there are numerous other marks including BEAR for related goods (as in fact there are, such as BUBBLE BEAR and BOOMER BEAR), this is likely a sign that marks including BEAR for toys and related goods are weak and they have been allowed to coexist. If numerous similar marks for similar goods or services coexist, it is less likely that a mark will be refused or attacked. Consumers become adept at distinguishing similar marks for related products as seen by the coexistence of MICROSOFT®, MICRO STRATEGY®, and MICRO CENTER® for related goods and services. In many instances, paralegals provide the initial review of the search report and flag potential problems or "hits" for an attorney's later evaluation. Paralegals also play a key role in investigating some of the sources revealed in the report. By contacting the owner of a mark, it may be discovered the mark is no longer in use or that the company has ceased doing business. Marketing materials can be reviewed to determine the actual manner in which the mark is used. The file for a conflicting mark can be obtained from the USPTO (or perhaps viewed electronically through TDR) to determine what objections were made to the application by the USPTO and how the owner overcame them.

Reporting the Results to the Client

A formal written report will then be prepared for the client. The letter, often called an "availability" or "clearance" report, typically includes the following elements:

- a description of the mark that was the subject of the search;
- a description of the method of the search, the databases that were checked, and the dates applicable to the search parameters;
- a section describing limitations on the search report, such as a disclaimer or statement that the results of the search cannot be guaranteed and that, due to errors in cataloging records and files and time delays in entering marks into databases, some marks might not be disclosed in the search;
- a discussion of potentially conflicting marks;
- the opinion in regard to availability of the mark for use and registration; and
- recommendations for further action or investigation, if needed.

The heart of the report is the attorney's opinion in regard to whether the mark is available. Because this is the portion of the report in which the client is most interested, the opinion should be stated clearly and should outline any risks in using the mark. The attorney may state, "We believe the BUDDY BEAR mark is distinguishable from the references disclosed in the report and may be available for use and registration in connection with children's books," or, conversely, may state, "Based on our review of the results, we do not recommend that you use or apply for registration of BUDDY BEAR." The attorney may even go so far as to inform the client that use of BUDDY BEAR could subject the client to risk of an infringement action.

Providing the opinion is often a difficult and time-consuming task. Clients are often in a rush to launch a new product or service and are eager to adopt a mark. They may have already begun an advertising campaign. There may be significant pressure from the client to obtain a favorable response. All of these factors, coupled with the uncertainty inherent in subjective comparisons of marks, makes trademark opinion work difficult and stressful.

ETHICS EDGE: Paralegals May Not Provide Legal Advice

Although paralegals play an active and vigorous role in nearly all IP-related activities, there are a few activities in which paralegals may not engage:

- Paralegals may not establish a client relationship or set fees.
- Generally, they may not appear in court on behalf of clients.
- They may not provide legal advice.

Thus, while paralegals perform trademark searches, investigate conflicts, and write first drafts of opinion letters to clients regarding trademark availability, all letters to clients that provide legal advice must be signed by attorneys. Similarly, be careful not to respond to a client's request for advice. If a client asks what the results of a trademark search show, respond that the attorney will provide an opinion after the evaluation is complete. Alternatively, paralegals may relay information to clients, such as the following, "Mr. Lopez has asked me to tell you that his preliminary opinion is that the mark is available for use, and he will be in touch with you shortly."

Investigating and Resolving Conflicts

The report of the trademark search results may disclose several potential conflicts, and the IP team may seek the client's permission to investigate these conflicts further. Alternatively, some investigation may be done before the report is provided to the client. If the client is wedded to a mark that may be barred by another mark, several options can be explored.

- **Investigation and Research.** Further investigation can be conducted using other databases, such as Dun & Bradstreet, to determine the amount of business conducted by the potential opposer. Private trademark investigators may be hired to go to the place of business and see how the mark is being used by obtaining the toys bearing the BITTY BEAR mark. A search can be conducted of records at the TTAB or through *Shepard's Citations* to determine if the owner of BITTY BEAR has aggressively protected its mark through litigation. It is possible that while a conflicting mark is registered with the USPTO, it is no longer in use. Under the Lanham Act, there is a presumption that a mark has been abandoned if it is not used for three years. Similarly, failure to file various maintenance and renewal documents with the USPTO will result in cancellation of a registration. Thus, an investigation into how or whether the conflicting mark is used may reveal that the mark has been abandoned and is now available to the client to use. As discussed earlier, many of the professional search firms identified in this chapter will conduct investigations to determine how a mark is actually being used in the marketplace.
- **Consent to Use.** The owner of BITTY BEAR can be contacted to obtain consent to use and register the client's mark. The client may pay some money for this consent or may agree to display the mark only in connection with specified goods or in a certain typeface and format.
- **License and Assignment.** The client might seek to obtain a license from another to use a mark or might seek to acquire the other mark through an assignment for a certain sum of money.
- **Revising the Mark.** If none of these alternatives are fruitful, the client might revise its mark, in which case a new search must be conducted for the new mark.

Trivia

- Among the marks registered by celebrities for entertainment services or sound recordings are BON JOVI®, DIXIE CHICKS®, and JIMMY BUFFETT®.
- The USPTO has registered more than two million trademarks since the first trademark law was passed in 1870. Approximately one million of these are still in effect.
- Microsoft introduced its Excel spreadsheet program in 1985 but did not apply for trademark protection for the mark until 2004.
- Some marks that have celebrated their 100th anniversaries include Nabisco's CREAM OF WHEAT logo and General Electric's "GE medallion."

Trivia (cont'd)

- In 1921, Elmer Cline of the Taggart Baking Company was preparing to launch a new brand of bread. As he watched an international balloon race, he said to a friend, "What a wonder," and the name WONDER BREAD with its distinctive red, blue, and yellow balloons was born.
- Elvis Presley Enterprises has more than 130 pending applications and registrations for marks related to Elvis Presley, including registrations for JAILHOUSE ROCK®, BLUE SUEDE SHOES®, and HEARTBREAK HOTEL® for a variety of goods (including cigarette lighters and shot glasses).

CHAPTER SUMMARY

Once a client has selected a mark, the mark should be subjected to a search to ensure that no other party has secured rights to the mark or to a confusingly similar mark. Failure to conduct a search or failure to conduct an adequate search may be characterized by a court as carelessness and weigh in favor of a party who alleges infringement, although, standing alone, it is not evidence of bad faith and there is no legal requirement to conduct a search. Reviewing search results and reporting results to clients is difficult and time-consuming. Often, follow-up investigation is needed to determine whether potentially conflicting marks remain in use or are in use with related goods or services. Conducting a search, however, will result in a snapshot of the marketplace, providing information about competitors, conflicting marks, and how the USPTO has handled applications for similar marks.

If the search "clears" the mark, an application should be filed promptly with the USPTO for registration of the mark if the mark has been used in commerce or the client has a bona fide intent to use the mark in commerce.

CASE ILLUSTRATION—EFFECT OF FAILURE TO PERFORM TRADEMARK SEARCH

Case: *Savin Corp. v. Savin Group*, 391 F.3d 439 (2d Cir. 2004)

Facts: Plaintiff owned the mark SAVIN in connection with photocopy equipment, copy paper, and related goods. Nearly 30 years after plaintiff adopted the mark, defendant's founder adopted the mark SAVIN, which was his nickname, "Nivas," spelled backwards, in connection with professional engineering consulting services. Plaintiff sued for trademark infringement and alleged that defendant's failure to conduct a trademark search before adopting the mark SAVIN was evidence of bad faith. The trial court found no infringement.

CASE ILLUSTRATION—EFFECT OF FAILURE
TO PERFORM TRADEMARK SEARCH (CONT'D)

Holding: The appellate court affirmed. One factor in determining infringement is the defendant's good faith or bad faith in adopting a mark. In this case, even if the defendant had conducted a search, he would have discovered plaintiff's mark was registered in connection with photocopiers and would have had no reason to believe that using the same name for professional engineering services would infringe. Moreover, failure to perform an official trademark search, standing alone, does not prove that a party acted in bad faith.

CASE STUDY AND ACTIVITIES

Case Study.   Vision has decided to introduce a variety of new services and products, each of which will bear a different trademark or service mark. One mark is VISION CHALLENGE: GOLF PROS, which will be used for a one-time charity golf tournament. Other marks include SUNVISION, to be used in connection with skin care products, which will be sold in hotel spas, and VISIONTREK, to be used in connection with guided tours of the localities in which Vision's hotels are located. Finally, Vision will market a line of accessories for the home under the mark VISIONHOME.

Activities: Describe the types of searches that should be conducted for each mark. Assume that the search for VISIONHOME discloses an expired trademark registration for VISIONHOUSE for candles, pillows, and vases.

ROLE OF PARALEGAL

Paralegals play a significant role in the clearance and availability stage of a trademark application. Although legal advice can be given only by attorneys, there are numerous activities in which paralegals will be involved:

- obtaining information about the client's proposed mark;
- conducting a preliminary in-house knockout search to eliminate bars to registration;
- ordering and reviewing a comprehensive search;
- consulting with the IP team regarding potentially conflicting marks disclosed in searches; and
- conducting investigations of potentially conflicting marks.

INTERNET RESOURCES

USPTO TESS and TARR databases: http://www.uspto.gov (select "Trademarks" and then select either "Search TM database (TESS)" or "Check Status (TARR)")

Trademark search tips: http://www.clpgh.org/locations/reference/ptdl/tradetips.html
http://www.bpmlegal.com/howtotmsrch.html

Searching trademarks on the Internet: http://www.ubc.ca/scieng/patents/about_trademarks.html.

DIALOG tutorial: http://training.dialog.com/tours

Translation site (to translate foreign terms): http://babelfish.altavista.com

DISCUSSION QUESTIONS

1. Assume that a client intends to use the mark SUPERSAVE SPRING for a month-long sales promotion for its grocery store in Dayton. Discuss the kind of search that should be conducted.

2. Assume that SUPERSAVE SPRING will be used for a month-long sales promotion for a chain of grocery stores across the nation. Discuss the kind of search that should be conducted.

3. Assume that a client wishes to use the mark SPA LOTION for a skin moisturizer. A search of the USPTO records discloses that a previous registration for SPA LOTION for hand cream has expired. Discuss the risks to the client of using SPA LOTION without further investigation.

4. If a client wishes to use the mark SPA LOTION for skin moisturizer and discovers the marks SUN LOTION, LOTION AID, and GLOW LOTION for related goods, what does this suggest?

5. If a search of the USPTO records for SPA LOTION discloses a reference for SPA TREATMENT LOTION for moisturizers, what should the client do?

USING INTERNET RESOURCES

1. Give the name and address of the Patent and Trademark Depository Library nearest your school.

2. Access the Web site for the Arkansas Secretary of State and conduct a search to locate the mark SPARKY'S ROADHOUSE CAFÉ. When will this state registration expire?

3. Assume a client wishes to use the mark PEU DE TAVERNE for restaurant and café services. Use "Babelfish" and translate the mark, and then indicate what likely objection the USPTO would make to an application for this mark.

USING INTERNET RESOURCES (CONT'D)

4. Access the USPTO Web site and use the New User search form. Locate the application for DIPPIN' DOTS ICE CREAM.
   a. When was the application filed?
   b. Access TARR. When was the Final Refusal written?
   c. Access TDR. What is the date on the Notice of Publication?
5. Access the USPTO Web site and use the Structured Form. Insert "Cube" into one field and select "Non-Punctuated Word Mark." Then insert "Target" into the other field and select "Owner Name and Address." Select the connector "And."
   a. What is the name of the mark for the most recent registration you are given?
   b. Access TARR. Was this application filed in paper form or was it filed using the TEAS electronic system? What law office was this application assigned to?
   c. Access TDR. How much time elapsed between the Notice of Publication and registration of this mark? Review the Certificate of Registration. What notice is given about the use of the word "wine" in this mark?

Chapter **4**

The Trademark Registration Process

CHAPTER OVERVIEW

From the discussion in chapter 2, it is clear that federal registration of a mark offers a trademark owner distinct advantages over mere reliance on common law or state trademark rights. There are two primary paths to registration for U.S.-based applications: a use-based application (alleging use in interstate commerce) and an intent-to-use application (alleging a bona fide intent to so use the mark in the future). Both types of applications share many common features and progress through the registration process in a fairly similar fashion. The process for federal registration of a mark can be expensive and can take as long as 12 to 18 months, even if there are no significant problems or delays. Registrations based on foreign applications or foreign registrations are discussed in chapter 8.

PREPARING THE APPLICATION

Introduction

Once a mark has been selected and evaluated for use and registrability, an application for fed-

eral registration of the mark should be prepared and filed. The written application comprises a request for registration, the name of the applicant, the citizenship of the applicant, the address of the applicant, an identification of the goods and/or services offered under the mark, a drawing of the mark, a verification or declaration signed by the applicant or agent or attorney, a filing fee, and, usually, the basis for filing the application, namely, whether the application is based on actual use of the mark or the owner's intent to use the mark. The process of moving an application through the USPTO is called **prosecution**.

The application must be in English. Forms for electronically filed applications are provided by the USPTO. If the form provided by the USPTO is not used, the application should be on letter-size (namely 8½ inches by 11 inches) paper, typewritten, double-spaced, with margins of at least 1½ inches at the left and top of the pages. The application should be written on only one side of the paper. (See Appendix D, Form 1, Trademark Application.) The USPTO "strongly discourages" such self-created forms and prefers that applicants use its electronic application system or its pre-printed form.

The USPTO does not generally require that the documents submitted be originals. Photocopies may be submitted (except for foreign registrations and certain other special documents for which certified copies are required). Thus, if a client signs an application and returns it to your office by facsimile (fax), you may photocopy the signature page, attach it to the application, and file it with the USPTO, as long as the signature is legible.

The USPTO permits the filing by fax of most papers and documents; however, trademark applications are not acceptable by fax. They must be hand-delivered to the USPTO, filed by mail, or submitted electronically.

All of the requirements relating to the filing and prosecution of trademark applications are governed by the *Trademark Manual of Examining Procedure (TMEP)*, an excellent source of materials with numerous examples and case citations. Most trademark practitioners keep the TMEP handy at all times. The TMEP is also available on the USPTO Web site at http://tess2.uspto.gov/tmdb/tmep.

The USPTO introduced an electronic filing system in 1998. **The Trademark Electronic Application System (TEAS)** permits applicants to file numerous documents electronically. For example, applicants can now fill out a trademark application form electronically and submit it directly to the USPTO over the Internet, paying by credit card or USPTO deposit account. In addition to trademark applications, documents relating to renewals of trademarks and responses to USPTO inquiries and office actions can be filed electronically. Documents can be transmitted electronically or prepared using the USPTO online forms, printed out, and then mailed to the USPTO.

When a document is filed electronically, the USPTO receives it within seconds after filing and immediately issues a confirmation of filing via e-mail. These electronically filed documents are examined more quickly than their paper counterparts. Documents submitted electronically using TEAS are considered filed on the date the USPTO receives the transmission.

Documents requiring signatures use a symbol adopted by the applicant as a signature, for example, /john h. taylor/, or /jht, or a scanned pen and ink signature. Similarly, if a drawing, image, or specimen is required, the applicant must submit a digitized image in .jpg form.

The USPTO prefers that applicants file documents electronically using TEAS, and in 2006, 94 percent of initial applications were filed electronically. The USPTO almost exclusively communicates with customers electronically. The TEAS system can be accessed at http://www.uspto.gov/teas.

The Applicant

An application to register a mark can be made only by the owner of the mark or, in the case of an intent-to-use application, by a person who has a bona fide intent to use the mark in commerce. Applicants may be natural persons or business entities such as corporations, partnerships, associations, unions, or other organizations. Government entities such as nations, states, municipalities, and other governmental bodies also can apply to register marks that they own. For example, the U.S. Army Recruiting Command is the owner of the registered mark BE ALL YOU CAN BE®, and the New York State Department of Economic Development is the owner of the famous mark I LOVE NY® (with a heart design replacing the word "love").

The applicant's name must be in correct legal form. Thus, a corporation that owns a mark should be identified in the application by the name set forth in its articles of incorporation. Clients often abbreviate their corporate names or make mistakes in the punctuation of their corporate names. Because the certificate of registration will issue in the name of the applicant as set forth in the application, errors in an owner's name will result in errors in the certificate of registration. Therefore, the secretary of state in the state in which the corporation was incorporated may need to be contacted to verify the precise spelling and punctuation of the corporate name. All states allow online verification.

If the applicant is a person or business that conducts business under a fictitious business name, for example, "Sam Smith, doing business as 'Sam's Cheesecake Factory,'" the application should include the assumed name.

If the applicant is a partnership, for example, "Balboa Gardens Partnership," the application should be made by the partnership itself and should identify the state in which the partnership was organized.

Identifying an applicant as a "company" will result in rejection of an application because the term *company* does not have a specific meaning; the applicant must be expressly identified as a corporation, a partnership, a joint venture, a limited liability company, and so forth.

A trademark or service mark application is usually filed in the name of one party. Historically, the USPTO has been reluctant to accept applications by joint applicants because ownership by more than one party seems to be contrary to the function of a trademark to identify a single commercial source. Although an application by joint applicants is acceptable in some instances, for example, by a husband and wife who share joint ownership of a mark, an examining attorney at the USPTO will carefully scrutinize applications by joint applicants to ensure that both parties own the mark in common. A joint venture or a partnership cannot be joint applicants. A joint venture or a partnership is a single business applicant that owns a mark.

The application must specify the applicant's citizenship. For an individual, it is sufficient to state that the applicant is a citizen of the United States, France, or some other country. For a corporation or other business entity, the state or country of organization must be identified. Thus, a statement that the applicant is "ABC Inc., a corporation organized under the laws of the State of California" is acceptable.

The written application must provide the address of the applicant, including the zip code number. An individual may identify a residence or business address. Corporations and other business entities should set forth their business addresses.

Identification of Goods or Services

The application must identify the goods and/or services offered or to be offered under the mark that is the subject of the application. Careful consideration must be given to drafting this part of the application. Goods and services are categorized by the USPTO into 45 separate classes, called **International Classes** because most other nations use this same classification system established by WIPO. Until 1973, the USPTO used a different classification scheme, called the United States Classification Scheme. Each class requires a filing fee (presently $325 for electronic filing). Thus, an electronic application for the mark RALPH LAUREN® to be used in connection with paint in International Class (I.C.) 2, cosmetics in I.C. 3, stationery in I.C. 16, beverage glasses in I.C. 21, and clothing in I.C. 25, for a total of five classes, would require a filing fee of $1,625. A registered mark only receives protection for those classes in which it is registered. Thus, if in an effort to save $325, the application for the RALPH LAUREN mark does not include beverage glasses in I.C. 21, there will be no registration for the mark for those goods. Preparing the application requires careful analysis of all of the goods/services for which the mark will be used to ensure that the mark receives all the protection it needs. A detailed listing of the international classes with numerous examples is found in Chapter 1400 of TMEP, available on the USPTO's Web site. Alternatively, the USPTO offers its Trademark Acceptable Identification of Goods and Services on its website, providing a single alphabetical list of goods and services from abacuses to zwieback or allowing a search by key word. Thus, if you enter "baseball mitts" in the open field, you will be informed that these goods are in I.C. 28. (See Exhibit 4–1 for a list of the international classes and explanation of the goods/services in each class.)

If a mark is used for more than one class of goods or services, the applicant may either file a combined (or multiple class) application, listing all of the goods and services in the same application, or file entirely separate (or single) applications for each class of goods/services. The filing

fees will be identical. Some attorneys prefer to file separate applications, believing that a defect in regard to one class of goods or services in a combined application will hold up registration for the mark in all classes. For example, if three separate applications are filed for goods in I.C. 3, 21, and 25, and there is a delay with regard to the goods in I.C. 25, the other two applications may proceed to registration, thereby allowing the applicant to secure a registration for the mark at

EXHIBIT 4–1
List of International Classes

International Class	Goods/ Services	Explanatory Note
Goods		
1	Chemicals	Includes chemicals used in industry, science, photography, manures, adhesives used in industry
2	Paints	Includes paints, varnishes, lacquers, raw natural resins
3	Cosmetics and cleaning preparation	Includes bleaching preparations and other substances for laundry use, soaps, cleaning preparations, perfumery, cosmetics, hair lotions
4	Lubricants and fuels	Includes industrial oils and greases, lubricants, candles, and wicks
5	Pharmaceuticals	Includes pharmaceuticals and other preparations for medical use, disinfectants, materials for dressings, food for babies
6	Metal goods	Common metals and their alloys, metal building materials, pipes and tubes made of metal, safes
7	Machinery	Machines and machine tools, motors and engines (except for land vehicles), agricultural implements
8	Hand tools	Hand tools, cutlery, razors
9	Electrical and scientific apparatus	Scientific, nautical, surveying, photo-graphic, optical apparatus and instruments, cash registers, apparatus for recording, transmission, or reproduction of sound or images, magnetic data carriers, recording discs, calculating machines, data processing equipment and computers, computer games, discs, and cassettes, computer software

(continues)

EXHIBIT 4–1
List of Inter-
national
Classes
(continued)

International Class	Goods/ Services	Explanatory Note
10	Medical apparatus	Surgical, medical, dental, and veterinary apparatus and instruments, suture materials
11	Environmental control apparatus	Apparatus for lighting, heating, steam generating, cooking, drying, refrigerating, water supply, and sanitary purposes
12	Vehicles	Vehicles, apparatus for locomotion by land, air, or water, engines for land vehicles
13	Firearms	Firearms, ammunition and projectiles, explosives, fireworks
14	Jewelry	Precious metals and goods in precious metals, jewelry, precious stones, clocks, watches
15	Musical instruments	Includes mechanical pianos, musical boxes, electrical and electronic music instruments
16	Paper goods and printed matter	Paper, cardboard, printed matter, photo-graphs, stationery, artists' materials, typewriters and office requisites (except furniture), instructional and teaching material, magazines, books
17	Rubber goods	Rubber, gum, plastics in extruded form, packing material, flexible pipes (not of metal)
18	Leather goods	Leather and imitations of leather, trunks, traveling bags, umbrellas, whips, saddlery
19	Nonmetallic building materials	Building materials (nonmetallic), asphalt, pitch, nonmetallic rigid pipes for building
20	Furniture and articles not otherwise classified	Furniture, mirrors, picture frames, goods of wood, cork, wicker, bone, shell, amber, and substitutes for all these materials
21	Housewares and glass	Household or kitchen utensils and containers (not of precious metal), combs and sponges, brushes, articles for cleaning purposes, glassware, porcelain, earthenware
22	Cordage and fibers	Ropes, string, nets, tents, awnings, tarpaulins, sails, sacks
23	Yarns and threads	Yarns and threads, for textile use
24	Fabrics	Textile goods not in other classes, bed and table covers
25	Clothing	Clothing, footwear, headgear

(continues)

EXHIBIT 4–1
List of International Classes (continued)

International Class	Goods/ Services	Explanatory Note
26	Fancy goods	Lace and embroidery, ribbons, braid, buttons, pins, needles, artificial flowers
27	Floor coverings	Carpets, rugs, mats, linoleum, wall hangings (nontextile)
28	Toys and sporting goods	Games and playthings, sporting goods, decorations for Christmas trees
29	Meats and processed foods	Meat, fish, poultry, game, preserved and cooked fruits and vegetables, jams and jellies, eggs, milk and milk products, edible oils and fats
30	Staple foods	Coffee, tea, sugar, rice, flour and preparations made from cereals, bread, pastry and confectionery, honey, mustard, salt, yeast, spices
31	Natural agricultural products	Agricultural, horticultural, forestry products, and grains not in other classes, living animals, fresh fruits and vegetables, seeds, natural plants and flowers
32	Light beverages	Beers, mineral and aerated waters, and other nonalcoholic drinks, fruit drinks and juices, syrups
33	Wine and spirits	Alcoholic beverages (except beers)
34	Smokers' articles	Tobacco, smokers' articles, matches

Services

International Class	Goods/ Services	Explanatory Note
35	Advertising and business	Advertising, business management, business administration, office functions
36	Insurance and financial	Insurance, financial affairs, monetary affairs, real estate affairs
37	Building construction and repair	Building construction, repair, installation services
38	Telecommunications	Includes services allowing at least one person to communicate with another by sensory means
39	Transportation and storage	Transport, packaging and storage of goods, travel arrangement
40	Treatment of materials	Includes mainly services rendered by the mechanical or chemical processing or transformation of objects or substances, for example, dyeing a garment or destruction of trash

(continues)

International Class	Goods/ Services	Explanatory Note
41	Education and entertainment	Education, providing of training, entertainment, sporting, and cultural activities
42	Computer, scientific, and legal	Scientific and technological services and research and design relating thereto, industrial analysis and research services, design and development of computer hardware and software, legal services
43	Hotels and restaurants	Services for providing food and drink, temporary accommodations
44	Medical, beauty, and agricultural	Medical services, veterinary services, hygienic and beauty care for human beings or animals, agriculture, horticulture and forestry services
45	Personal	Personal and social services rendered by others to meet the needs of individuals, security services for the protection of property and individuals

EXHIBIT 4–1
List of International Classes
(continued)

least in regard to some goods. The final decision on whether to file a combined application or a separate application is one of tactics and strategy.

The USPTO requires that the identification of goods or services be as clear, accurate, and concise as possible. The accuracy of identification language is of particular importance because, while an identification may be limited or clarified, no addition to, or expansion of, an identification is permitted after an application is filed. Thus, if an application is filed on January 1 for women's clothing in I.C. 25 and the applicant later wishes to add perfume (in I.C. 3) to the application, such an amendment would not be allowed. The applicant would be required to file an additional application that would then have a later filing date than the first application filed January 1. The applicant may, however, amend the original application to clarify that the clothing to be offered consists of blouses, skirts, and pants. An applicant cannot attempt a blanket filing for "all the goods in I.C. 9." Such an application would be refused by the USPTO. If an applicant incorrectly classifies clothing in I.C. 26 rather than in I.C. 25, the USPTO will allow correction of this error.

Typically, the USPTO requires that the applicant use terms such as *namely* and *consisting* of when identifying goods. Thus, an identification of "cosmetics, *namely* lipstick and deodorant" is acceptable, while an identification of "cosmetics, *including* lipstick and deodorant" will be refused as indefinite and overbroad inasmuch as a reader cannot tell with specificity all of the goods that will be offered under the mark from reading the identification.

Finally, due to the increased volume of applications for computer-related goods in I.C. 9, the USPTO expressly requires that identifications of goods for computer software or comparable goods must specify the purpose or function of the program. For example, the following descriptions would be acceptable to the USPTO: "computer software for word processing" or "database management software for use by financial advisers." A broad description such as "computer programs in the field of medicine" is not acceptable. See Exhibit 4–2 for examples of identifications of goods and services.

Computer services are identified according to the class in which the underlying service is classified. Thus, banking services are in I.C. 36 (financial services) whether they are provided in a "brick and mortar" bank or online, and online bulletin boards and chat rooms are classified in I.C. 38 (telecommunications services) regardless of the content or subject matter.

Basis for Filing Application and Method of Use

The application submitted to the USPTO usually specifies one of the following bases for the application (and usually states the manner in which the mark is used, such as indicating that

the mark is affixed to goods or used in advertisements offering services):

- actual use of the mark in commerce, specifying a date of first use in commerce (15 U.S.C. § 1051(a));
- a bona fide intent to use the mark in commerce (15 U.S.C. § 1051(b));
- a bona fide intent to use the mark in commerce and a claim that the mark is the subject of a prior foreign application (15 U.S.C. § 1126(d)); or
- a bona fide intent to use the mark in commerce and a claim that the mark is

EXHIBIT 4–2
Samples of Identifications of Goods and Services

Type of Mark	Mark	International Class	Goods/ Services	Other Data
Trademark	POLO RALPH LAUREN	I.C. 14	Watches	Registration notes that "the name 'Ralph Lauren' identifies a particular living individual whose consent is of record."
Trademark (with disclaimer)	RAISIN BRAN CRUNCH	I.C. 30	Processed cereal	Registration notes the following disclaimer: "No claim is made to the exclusive right to use 'Raisin Bran' apart from the mark as shown."
Service mark	PARAMOUNT (& DESIGN)	I.C. 41	Entertainment services, namely production of motion pictures	Registration notes, "The mark consists of the word 'Paramount' in stylized letters about five shadow mountain with an arc of stars surrounding it all."
Design mark	[Design of Hat] registered to Walt Disney Company	I.C. 25	Hats	The registration notes, "The mark consists of the configuration of round mouse ears attached to a beanie."

(continues)

EXHIBIT 4–2
Samples
of Identifications
of Goods and
Services
(continued)

Type of Mark	Mark	International Class	Goods/ Services	Other Data
Service mark (with disclaimer)	JURASSIC PARK RIVER ADVENTURE	I.C. 41	Amuse-ment park services	The registration notes the following dis-claimer: "No claim is made to the exclusive right to use 'River Ad-venture' apart from the mark as shown."
Certification mark	U2 (& DESIGN)	I.C. A (previous classification for certification marks)	Pressure vessels intended for high-pressure application	The registration notes, "The certifica-tion mark is used by persons authorized by applicant to certify that the products on which the certification mark is stamped meet applicant's standards for the material, de-sign, construction and workmanship of said products."
Sound mark registered to Harlem Globetrotters	Sound mark	I.C. 41	Entertain-ment ser-vices in the nature of basketball exhibitions	Registration notes, "The mark consists of the melody 'Sweet Geor-gia Brown.'"
Collective membership mark	AMERICAN BAR ASSO-CIATION	I.C. 200 (previ-ous classifica-tion system for collective marks	Indicating member-ship in applicant	No other data noted

the subject of a prior foreign registration (15 U.S.C. § 1126(e)). Applications based on foreign applications and registrations are discussed in chapter 8.

If the basis for filing the application is not set forth in the application, it can be supplied during examination of the application.

DRAWING OF MARK

One of the most critical parts of the ap-plication is the **drawing** or the display of the mark. Because the drawing is entered into the automated records of the USPTO and is available to the public through TESS and TARR (discussed in chapter 3) and because the drawing is used when the mark is ultimately published in the USPTO publication *Official Gazette* and is reproduced in the actual certificate of registration, the drawing must conform with specific USPTO requirements.

There are two types of drawings: standard character drawings and special form drawings. A *standard character drawing* is simply a typewritten display of the mark. For example, the word KRAFT® constitutes a standard character drawing. In reality, the display is not a "drawing" at all. A standard character drawing is used when the mark consists solely of words, letters, or numbers with no pictorial or graphical element. The application must include a statement that the mark is in standard characters and no claim is made to any particular font style, size, or color, which statement will appear in the *Official Gazette* and on the certificate of registration. The applicant may use any font, bold or italicized letters, and uppercase or lowercase letters. Prior to late 2003, "standard character" drawings were called "typed" drawings and were always displayed entirely in uppercase letters.

A *special form drawing* is used when applicants seek to register a mark that includes a two- or three-dimensional design, color, and/or words, letters, or numbers or a combination thereof in a particular font style or size. For example, the well-known display of actor Paul Newman on various food products is an example of a special form or design mark.

Most trademark applications are now filed electronically through TEAS; thus, most drawings are submitted through TEAS. For standard character drawings, the applicant must enter the mark in the appropriate field or attach a digitized image of the mark. For special form drawings, the applicant must attach a digitized image of the mark in .jpg format.

If the trademark application is filed in paper form, there are numerous requirements relating to the type of paper used and the size of the drawing.

The precise and exacting requirements for the drawing correlate to the method for searching trademarks. If individuals could display marks in any format they desired, searching the USPTO records to determine if a confusingly similar mark exists would be nearly impossible. Moreover, the USPTO ultimately publishes the marks in the *Official Gazette*. Conformity in display of marks allows for ready review of the published marks.

Because applications filed under 15 U.S.C. § 1051(b) are based on an intent to use the mark in the future, an applicant may not have made a final determination on the exact appearance of a mark at the time an application is filed. For intent-to-use applications, the USPTO will allow some minor variation between the drawing submitted at the time the application is filed and the mark as actually used. Nevertheless, the drawing must be a substantially exact representation of the mark as it will eventually be used.

If an applicant wishes to claim color as a feature of the mark, the application must so specify. For example, the applicant will be required to state "the color yellow is claimed as a feature of the mark." If color is not claimed, the mark may be displayed in any color. Generally, therefore, color is claimed only when such a feature is critical to recognition of the mark, such as the golden color of McDonald's "golden arches" mark or the yellow color of the "Livestrong" bracelets used by the Lance Armstrong Foundation.

No drawing is required if the mark consists only of a sound, scent, or other nonvisual matter. For these types of marks, the applicant must submit a detailed written description of the mark.

Specimens

If the application is made under 15 U.S.C. § 1051(a) and alleges that the mark has been used in commerce, the USPTO will require that the applicant submit proof of such use by providing a **"specimen"** of the mark showing exactly how the mark is seen by the public. One specimen must be filed for each class of goods named in the application. Thus, if the application is for HELENA (& SWAN DESIGN) for soap in I.C. 3 and sweaters in I.C. 25, two specimens must be submitted.

For applications filed electronically, the applicant must submit a digitized image of the specimen in .jpg format. Most law firms use digital cameras to take pictures of their clients' specimens and then download them and attach them to the electronic application.

For paper applications, actual tags, bags, labels, and other similar items are highly preferred over photocopies. For example, the best specimen for the soap just described would be a wrapper for the soap, clearly showing the mark HELENA (& SWAN DESIGN). An appropriate specimen for the sweaters would be an actual tag that is sewn into the back of the garments. If the mark appears on a bulky item, such as a refrigerator or park bench, it would be ludicrous to send in the refrigerator or bench itself. Even its packaging would be cumbersome. In such cases, the USPTO will accept a photograph as long as the mark can be readily seen as being affixed to the item.

Advertising material is generally not acceptable as a specimen for *goods*. Thus, merely including a brochure or ad about products such as soap or clothing is insufficient. Similarly, letterhead displaying the mark and other similar materials such as invoices and business cards are not acceptable. The USPTO wishes to ensure that the mark is in actual use on the goods in question. Thus, mere promotional materials do not show use of goods.

Such advertising materials may, however, be sufficient to show use of a mark in connection with *services*. Thus, if the mark CHUCKY'S FUN TIME is used for restaurant services, an advertisement, coupon, brochure, direct-mail leaflet, and menu would be acceptable specimens inasmuch as there will be no actual product or good displaying the CHUCKY'S FUN TIME mark. An

audiocassette or compact disc is submitted as a specimen for a sound mark. A Web page that displays goods and their trademarks and provides for online ordering of such goods is an acceptable specimen.

A specimen need not be submitted at the time of filing an application. An appropriate specimen must be submitted, however, during the examination process for an application based on actual use of mark after the USPTO approves the application and when a statement alleging use is submitted by an applicant whose application is based on an intent to use the mark. Until October 30, 1999, the USPTO required three specimens for each class to be submitted at the time of filing of a use-based application. At present, one specimen per class is required, and although applicants may submit specimens during examination, most applicants continue to submit the specimen with their use-based applications. (See Exhibit 4–2.)

Declaration and Signature

The application must be signed by and include a declaration or verification by the applicant or its agent or attorney. The **declaration** is a statement placed at the end of the application whereby the signatory acknowledges that the statements in the application are true and that the signatory understands that willful false statements are punishable by fine or imprisonment and may jeopardize the validity of the application or any registration resulting from the application. (See Exhibit 4–3 for form of declaration.)

The declaration is intended to impress upon the signatory the seriousness of the trademark application procedure to ensure that applicants do not claim earlier use dates than those to which they are entitled and do not attempt to "lock up" marks for the purpose of reselling them to others. The applicant or its agent or attorney must then sign the application. For applications filed electronically through TEAS, the filer may use

EXHIBIT 4–3
Declaration
for Trademark
Application

> The undersigned being warned that willful false statements and the like are punishable by fine or imprisonment, or both, under 18 U.S.C. § 1001, and that such willful false statements and the like may jeopardize the validity of the application or document or any registration resulting therefrom, declares that all statements made of his/her own knowledge are true; and that all statements made on information and belief are believed to be true.
>
> _____
> (Signature)
>
> _____
> (Print or Type Name and Position)
>
> _____
> (DATE)

a symbol as a signature (such as /jane smith/). Alternatively, the application is completed online and then printed and given to the signatory who signs it in pen and ink. The document is then scanned to create a .jpg image and is transmitted electronically to the USPTO.

If the application is one made by an individual, this individual will sign the document. If the applicant is a corporation or partnership, the application is usually signed by an officer of the corporation or a general partner, respectively. Joint applicants should each sign the application. Applicants not domiciled in the United States usually appoint a "domestic representative" in the United States, namely, a party, typically a law firm, who will receive documents and notices affecting the mark.

Although an owner of a trademark may file and prosecute his or her own application for registration of a mark, trademark owners are often represented by attorneys familiar with trademark practice. Any attorney licensed to practice may practice before the USPTO, and there is no requirement for any special trademark registration with the USPTO. When attorneys represent applicants, the application may contain a power

of attorney designating the attorney to represent the applicant regarding all matters related to the mark. A power of attorney is no longer required, however, for an attorney to sign a declaration on behalf of an applicant.

The Principal and Supplemental Registers

The application should designate whether the application seeks registration on the **Principal Register** or the Supplemental Register. Registration on the Principal Register is preferred because it offers a wider scope of protection for a mark. A mark not eligible for registration on the Principal Register—for example, a descriptive mark that has not yet acquired secondary meaning—may be registered on the **Supplemental Register.** Registration on the Supplemental Register is an indication that a mark does not yet distinguish, but ultimately is capable of distinguishing, the applicant's goods or services from those of another. Once the mark has acquired distinctiveness, a new application can be filed seeking registration on the Principal Register. In fact, after five years of substantially continuous and exclusive use of a mark, there is a presumption that it has acquired the necessary distinctiveness to allow for registration on the Principal Register, and the registrant may file a new application for registration of the mark on the Principal Register.

The distinctions between registrations on the Principal Register and Supplemental Register are as follows:

- While a registration on the Principal Register is *prima facie* evidence of the registrant's exclusive right to use of the mark, registration on the Supplemental Register has no such evidentiary effect.
- A registration on the Principal Register is constructive notice of a claim of ownership so as to eliminate a defense of good faith in an infringement suit, but a Supplemental Registration has no such effect.
- While a registration on the Principal Register may become incontestable after five years of registration, a Supplemental Registration may never achieve that status.
- Registration on the Supplemental Register cannot be used to stop importations of infringing goods into the United States.

On the other hand, registration on the Supplemental Register does afford some protections:

- An action for infringement of the mark can be brought in federal court.
- The registration will be on file with the USPTO and can be cited by the USPTO against another's subsequent application to register a confusingly similar mark.
- The registration will be located through standard searches of USPTO records, thus possibly deterring others from using or applying for a similar mark.
- The registrant is entitled to use the registration symbol (®).

FILING THE APPLICATION, DOCKETING CRITICAL DATES, AND INITIAL ROLE OF THE UNITED STATES PATENT AND TRADEMARK OFFICE

Filing the Application

The application must be filed with the USPTO within a reasonable time after it has been signed by the applicant, generally within one year after signature. The application must be accompanied by a filing fee for each class of goods and/or services.

The amount of the trademark application fee varies depending on whether the application is filed on paper or electronically. To encourage electronic filing, the USPTO reduces fees for applications filed electronically through TEAS. A newer system called TEAS Plus reduces application fees even further. To qualify for TEAS Plus, an applicant must use a description of goods and services from the USPTO Manual (rather than some customized description), agree to file other documents electronically, and agree to receive communications from the USPTO by e-mail.

As an alternative to including a check for the filing fee, some applicants establish **deposit accounts** with the USPTO and deposit a certain amount of money (at least $1,000) into an account against which fees can be drawn. Alternatively, the USPTO accepts payment of fees by credit card. Trademark fees are set forth at the USPTO Web site at http://www.uspto.gov. (See Exhibit 4–4 for a schedule of USPTO filing fees.)

The application can be filed in person at the USPTO or can be mailed using either first-class or express mail of the U.S. Postal Service. Documents mailed to the USPTO should be addressed to Commissioner for Trademarks, P.O. Box 1451, Alexandria, VA 22313-1451, and include a certificate of mailing, verifying the date the correspondence was placed in the U.S. mail. When the USPTO receives a paper application, it will

EXHIBIT 4–4
Schedule of
USPTO Filing
Fees (Trademark
Matters)

Application for registration, per class (paper filing)	$375
Application for registration, per class (electronic TEAS filing)	$325
Application for registration, per class (electronic TEASPlus filing)	$275
Filing an amendment to allege use, per class	$100
Filing a statement of use, per class	$100
Filing a request for extension of time to file a statement of use, per class	$150
Application for renewal, per class	$400
Additional fee for late renewal or late section 8 affidavit, per class	$100
Issuing a new certificate of registration	$100
Filing an amendment or correction to registration certificate	$100
Filing section 8 affidavit of use of mark, per class	$100
Filing section 15 affidavit to achieve incontestability, per class	$200
Petition for cancellation, per class	$300
Notice of opposition, per class	$300
Dividing an application, per each new application (file wrapper) created	$100
Certified copy of registered mark	$15
Copy of trademark file wrapper	$50
Recording a trademark assignment (for first mark)	$40
For subsequent marks in the same document	$25 each

perform a cursory review to ensure that the minimum required elements of the application (and the filing fee) are present. The mailroom will then stamp the application with a serial or filing number that will accompany the application throughout the entire application process. The serial number is critical because the USPTO responds to inquiries only if a serial number is known. At present, most applications begin with the two-digit number "76" or "79," although the series code is "78" for applications filed electronically, using TEAS.

Most applicants who file by paper include either a duplicate copy of the application with a self-addressed stamped envelope or a postcard or "come-back card," requesting that the USPTO place a label on the duplicate application or the postcard with the date of filing and application filing number so the applicant can verify filing. Otherwise, the USPTO may take several weeks to send the applicant the official filing receipt verifying filing of the application.

An advantage of filing electronically through TEAS is that the USPTO immediately issues a confirmation of filing via e-mail that includes the serial number and date of receipt.

The filing date of the application is critical because it initiates various time limits. For example, applicants have a duty to inquire about the status of an application if they do not hear from the USPTO within six months of any filing. Thus, the filing date should be calendared or docketed so that you can ensure the USPTO has provided you with the official filing receipt within six months of the filing date. Similarly, if the application is filed based on an applicant's intent to use the mark in the future, the filing date constitutes **constructive use** of the mark. For example, if an intent-to-use application is filed on June 1, 2007, and the mark is ultimately registered, the date for determining priority between conflicting parties is June 1, 2007, even though the mark may not have been actually used until December 1, 2007, and may not have achieved registration until

February 1, 2008. Finally, if an applicant wishes to file an application for the mark in a foreign country that is a member of the Paris Convention (discussed in chapter 8), it has six months from the filing date within which to do so and thereby claim the date of the filing in the United States.

Docketing Critical Dates

Many law firms and offices that do a significant amount of trademark work have sophisticated computer programs that automatically docket critical dates. Such systems will automatically flag a file and provide notification that no action has been taken on an application in nearly 12 months so the applicant may investigate the problem. Nevertheless, most firms (and some malpractice carriers) also require that trademark practitioners maintain their own dockets, whether by means of an independent computerized system or a simple tickler file composed of index cards and divided into monthly categories, to serve as reminders of needed action in the coming months. The very nature of trademark work is deadline-sensitive. Failure to take certain actions on a timely basis may result in abandonment of a mark or application unless the delay was unintentional. Therefore, the utmost care must be taken to protect a client's interests. Develop a docketing system that works effectively and maintain it diligently. Failure to do so may be malpractice.

Initial Role of the United States Patent and Trademark Office: The File Wrapper and the Official Filing Receipt

When the USPTO receives a paper application, it scans the documents and creates an electronic file, called a **file wrapper,** which is the official USPTO file, and it contains the application, drawing, specimens, and all communications with the USPTO. Documents in these electronic file wrappers can be viewed and downloaded using the USPTO's system called **Trademark Document Retrieval (TDR).** Nearly all applications are available through TDR, and the USPTO is in the process of converting older paper files into digitized formats so they may be accessed via TDR. The USPTO no longer creates and maintains paper file copies of trademark applications and now relies exclusively on data submitted or captured electronically. Applications submitted electronically through TEAS are accessible nearly immediately through the USPTO's Web site.

Within several weeks after a paper application is filed or immediately after an electronic application is filed, the USPTO will issue an **Official Filing Receipt** or e-mail confirmation of filing, respectively. TEAS applications are assembled in an e-commerce office that creates an electronic file wrapper.

The filing receipt will confirm the filing date of the application, provide a serial number, and confirm all details of the application, including dates of first use, basis for filing, applicant's name and address, the goods or services offered under the mark, and the international class. Because the filing receipt reflects what the USPTO believes to be the pertinent details of the application, it should be carefully scrutinized for correctness. If there are any errors, even minor spelling mistakes, the applicant should immediately inform the USPTO. Failure to notify the USPTO of some discrepancy may result in the certificate of registration including the erroneous information. Once the filing receipt or e-mail confirmation is received, the docketing system should be updated to ensure that additional action is taken on the application within six months thereafter.

THE EXAMINATION PROCESS

Examination Procedure

After the USPTO issues the official filing receipt or e-mail confirmation, the application is assigned for review to an examining attorney, typically new attorneys employed by the USPTO.

Many move into private practice after a few years with the USPTO. Examining attorneys are assigned to "law offices" within the USPTO, each of which has responsibility for certain types of applications. For example, all applications relating to computer programs may be assigned to Law Office 106, while all applications dealing with business services may be assigned to Law Office 114. Concentrating similar applications in a given law office allows examining attorneys to become expert with certain types of applications, thereby facilitating the registration process. It is the function of an examining attorney to review the application, search the USPTO files to determine if the mark applied for is confusingly similar to another, make a determination on whether the mark is registrable, and ultimately either refuse registration of the mark or approve it for publication. Examination is the least predictable stage of the prosecution process. Applications by the same party for identical or similar marks, called **companion applications,** will be handled by the same examining attorney. Conversely, applications by different parties for conflicting marks, called **conflicting applications,** are not handled by the same examining attorney, although the actions of the examining attorneys should be consistent.

Office Actions and Refusals to Register Marks

Approximately five months after the application is filed, the examining attorney assigned to the application will issue a "first action" or **Office Action** regarding the application if there are any defects in the application. If there are no defects in a use-based application, the USPTO will approve the application for publication in the *Official Gazette.* The office action is a written communication sent by the examining attorney to the applicant (or, more likely, to the applicant's attorney) that states that the mark has been refused registration and explains why registration has been refused. All office actions must be re-

sponded to within six months to avoid abandonment of the application. To monitor pending applications, either use TARR (by entering a serial number) or TESS, through the USPTO Web site.

Curing Informalities and Technical Defects in the Application.   In many instances, the application may contain deficiencies that must be corrected before the application may be approved. For example, the applicant's name may be identified as "Lee Inc.," in the application itself and yet be signed by an officer on behalf of "Lee Co." The state of incorporation may need to be specified for a corporate applicant. The identification of goods or services may lack specificity, and the examining attorney may require clarification to the identification. In many instances, the office action suggests that the applicant telephone or e-mail the examining attorney to resolve the issue (within the six-month period for response) and often suggests a remedy for the defect. The applicant and the examining attorney are often able to resolve the issue in such a telephone or e-mail communication. Thereafter, the examining attorney will issue an **Examiner's Amendment** setting forth the agreed-upon correction or clarification, thereby eliminating the need for the applicant to file a formal written response to the office action. A use-based application will proceed to publication after the examiner's amendment has corrected any technical informality in the application. The USPTO encourages such telephonic and e-mail communications because they expedite the application process.

Substantive Refusals.   In many instances, the refusal to register is not due to some minor or technical error in the application that can be readily corrected but is due to a more significant or substantive defect or due to a statutory provision that would preclude registration. In these cases, the examining attorney will set forth the reason the mark has been refused registration. The applicant will then have six months to respond in writing to the office action and present arguments supporting registration. Some of the more common substantive or statutory refusals to register are as follows:

- The mark is immoral or scandalous.
- The mark is deceptive.
- The mark disparages a person or a national institution or displays the flag or insignia of a nation.
- The mark displays a portrait of a living person without his or her consent.
- The mark is primarily merely a surname.
- The mark is geographically deceptively misdescriptive.
- The mark is primarily merely descriptive.
- The mark is confusingly similar to another registered or applied-for mark at the USPTO.

Applicants who receive an office action refusing registration on one of these grounds generally submit written arguments to persuade the examining attorney to allow the mark for registration. Case law and other evidence may be cited. For example, if the mark is refused on the basis that it is primarily merely a surname, the applicant may submit telephone book evidence to show the name is so rare that consumers who encounter the mark would not perceive it to be primarily a surname. If a person's consent is needed, the applicant should secure it.

Refusals on the Basis of Descriptiveness. One of the most serious refusals occurs when the examining attorney refuses registration on the basis that the mark is merely descriptive and is thus barred under 15 U.S.C. § 1052(e)(1). The applicant will then submit a response to the office action arguing that the mark is not descriptive. Common arguments asserted by the applicant are as follows.

- The applicant may argue that the mark is not descriptive but is rather suggestive and therefore entitled to registration. To support such an assertion, the applicant may cite marks in case law that have been found to be suggestive and analogize them to the mark at issue. The applicant

may also conduct a search of USPTO records to locate other similar marks that were allowed to proceed to registration. The USPTO, however, is not bound by its past actions and may characterize the earlier allowed marks as mistakes that it need not repeat.

- The applicant may argue that the cases cited by the examining attorney in support of the refusal to register are inapplicable, and attempt to distinguish the present situation from that presented in the case law relied upon by the examining attorney.
- If the mark has been in commerce for five years, there is a presumption that it has acquired distinctiveness. In such a case, the USPTO will allow the applicant to claim distinctiveness under 15 U.S.C. § 1052(f) and the mark can proceed to registration. The wording for a claim of acquired distinctiveness is as follows:

  > The mark has become distinctive of Applicant's goods [or services] through the Applicant's substantially exclusive and continuous use in commerce for at least the five years immediately before the date of this statement.

- If the mark has not acquired distinctiveness through continuous use for five years, the applicant may attempt to introduce evidence to show the mark has acquired distinctiveness or secondary meaning through its significant use, sales, and advertising such that consumers associate the mark with the applicant. The applicant typically submits evidence consisting of sales and advertising data, survey evidence, and declarations from customers and consumers who confirm they are familiar with the mark and recognize the applicant as the source of the goods offered under the mark.

If none of these arguments are successful, the applicant may be allowed to amend the application to seek registration on the Supplemental Register *if* use of the mark has begun. Applications based solely on intent to use cannot be transferred to the Supplemental Register until after the applicant has shown actual use of the mark, because registration of U.S.-based trademarks is dependent on use in commerce.

If only a portion of the mark is descriptive or generic, that portion may be *disclaimed*. The purpose of a **disclaimer** is to allow registration of a mark that includes nonregistrable matter. For example, in the mark BOLERO TASTY COFFEE (used in connection with coffee), the words *tasty coffee* would likely have to be disclaimed because they merely describe something about the goods offered under the mark. A disclaimer is an acknowledgment by an applicant that he or she does not claim exclusive rights in the matter disclaimed (in this case, the wording *tasty coffee)*, apart from the mark as a whole. Disclaimers preserve the rights of other businesses to use needed terms such as *tasty* and *coffee*. Some marks, called **composite marks,** consist of both wording and design elements. If the wording in a composite mark is descriptive or generic, the applicant may have to disclaim exclusive rights to all of the wording, leaving the applicant with exclusive rights only to the design component. An applicant may not disclaim an entire mark.

A disclaimer does not affect one's common law rights; neither does it mean that the mark as a whole is not protectable. In the hypothetical, use by another company of VOLERO TASTY COFFEE could likely be enjoined on the basis of confusing similarity; however, a mark such as SUNRISE TASTY COFFEE would likely be allowable, inasmuch as the marks can be distinguished on the basis of their nondescriptive components.

The proper wording for a disclaimer is as follows:

No claim is made to the exclusive right to use "tasty coffee" apart from the mark as shown.

(See Exhibit 4–2 for examples of disclaimers.)

Refusals on the Basis of Confusing Similarity. In addition to refusing to register a mark on the basis that it is merely descriptive, another substantive or statutory ground for refusal to register is that the mark applied for so resembles a mark registered or applied for with the USPTO that, when used in connection with the goods or services of the applicant, it would be likely to cause confusion, mistake, or to deceive consumers. 15 U.S.C. § 1052(d).

In determining whether a mark applied for is confusingly similar to a prior registered or applied-for mark, a variety of factors, identified in *In re E. I. du Pont de Nemours & Co.*, 476 F.2d 1357 (C.C.P.A. 1973), are considered:

- the similarity of the marks in their entireties in regard to appearance, sound, connotation, and commercial impression;
- the similarity and nature of the goods or services offered under the respective marks;
- the similarity of the channels of trade in which the goods or services are offered, for example, whether the goods or services offered under the mark are offered through retail or wholesale channels of trade;
- the buyers to whom sales are made and the conditions of such sales, for example, whether purchases are made on impulse or after due care and deliberation;
- the fame of the prior mark (sales, advertising, length of use, and so forth);
- the number and nature of similar marks in use on similar goods or services; and
- the nature and extent of actual confusion.

The goods or services need not be identical for confusion to be found, as long as they are related in some manner. Thus, MARTIN'S for bread was held likely to be confused with MARTIN'S for cheese on the basis the marks were used in connection with related food products. *In re Martin's Famous Pastry Shoppe, Inc.*, 748 F.2d 1565

(Fed. Cir. 1984). If the item is purchased by consumers on "impulse," such as an inexpensive beverage, confusion will be more likely than if the item is expensive, is purchased by sophisticated consumers, and is purchased only after great thought and care. The USPTO does not use a mechanical approach in determining whether confusion is likely to occur; rather, an examination is made of all the factors. If there is any doubt about whether there is a likelihood of confusion, doubt will be resolved against the newcomer. Additional information relating to likelihood of confusion analysis is found in chapter 6 in the discussion of trademark infringement. (See Exhibit 4–5 for a comparison of some marks alleged to be confusingly similar.)

An applicant whose mark is rejected on the basis of confusing similarity will attempt to overcome the refusal to register by citing case law and analogizing cases in which confusion was not found, submitting evidence showing that the goods are not in the same channels of trade and that they are offered to different or sophisticated purchasers, and by submitting copies of other registered marks that have been allowed to coexist.

Alternatively, the applicant may contact the owner of the cited mark and seek a license to use the mark or seek its consent to coexistence and registration. The applicant may need to pay the prior user some amount of money to secure the consent. Although the USPTO is not bound to accept such a coexistence or consent agreement, generally the USPTO does so, believing that the owners of marks are in the best position to evaluate whether conflicts might exist and that if they believe no confusion would result from coexistence of the marks, the USPTO should affirm their decision. See chapter 6 for further discussion of consent agreements.

If there is a conflicting mark in a pending application, action on the application with the later filing date will be suspended until the mark in the conflicting application with the earlier filing date is either registered (in which case the later-filed application will be refused) or abandoned (in which case, the later-filed application can proceed to registration).

Responses to Office Actions. An applicant has six months to respond to an office action. Failure to respond within the appropriate time period will result in abandonment of the application unless the delay was unintentional (in which case an abandoned application may be revived).

As soon as an office action is received, its response date should be docketed. The client should then be informed in writing of the basis for the USPTO's refusal to register the mark. The law firm typically recommends a course of action and provides an estimate of the costs and fees the client can expect to incur in responding to the office action along with some assessment of the likelihood of success. The IP professional should continue to monitor the matter to ensure the client provides appropriate and timely instructions so the law firm can respond to the office action.

In some instances, a second office action may be issued after the applicant's response to the initial office action. Ultimately, the application will either proceed to the next step (publication) or will be subject to a "final refusal." Once a final refusal has been issued, the applicant's only recourse is to comply with the examining attorney's requirements, request reconsideration by bringing new matter before the examining attorney, or appeal the refusal to the Trademark Trial and Appeal Board (TTAB). Adverse decisions of the TTAB are reviewable by the U.S. Court of Appeals for the Federal Circuit and then by the U.S. Supreme Court if it decides to take the case. The Federal Circuit can set aside USPTO findings only when the findings are arbitrary, capricious, an abuse of discretion, or unsupported by substantial evidence. *Dickinson v. Zurko,* 527 U.S. 150 (1999). Alternatively, the applicant can initiate an action in federal district court where the issues will be determined *de novo* (literally, "anew").

Generally, an appeal may be taken to the TTAB for any final decision of an examining attorney. An appeal is taken by filing a notice of

EXHIBIT 4–5
Comparison of Marks Alleged to be Confusingly Similar and Action Taken by USPTO and Courts

Mark #1	Mark #2	Result
CONFIRM (for medical-related goods)	CONFIRMCELLS (for blood reagents)	Confusingly similar due to related goods
LAREDO (for land vehicles)	LAREDO (for pneumatic tires)	Confusingly similar due to related goods
LITTLE PLUMBER (for liquid drain opener)	LITTLE PLUMBER (for advertising services)	Not confusingly similar because goods/services not related
BIGG'S (for grocery and general merchandise store)	BIGGS (& DESIGN) (for furniture)	Confusingly similar due to related goods
GOLDEN GRIDDLE PANCAKE HOUSE (with "Golden Griddle" disclaimed) for restaurant services	GOLDEN GRIDDLE (for table syrup)	Confusingly similar due to related goods
CAREER IMAGE (STYLIZED) (for women's clothing and store services)	CREST CAREER IMAGES (for uniforms)	Confusingly similar due to related goods
TMM (for computer software)	TMS (for computer software)	Confusingly similar due to similarity in appearance
COBBLER'S OUTLET (for shoes)	CALIFORNIA COBBLERS (STYLIZED) (for shoes)	Not confusingly similar due to weakness of common element "COBBLERS"
BEST JEWELRY (& DESIGN) (for jewelry store services)	JEWELERS' BEST (for jewelry)	Not confusingly similar because marks create different commercial impression
TRUCOOL (for synthetic coolant)	TURCOOL (for cutting oil)	Confusingly similar due to similarity in appearance

appeal and by paying the appeal fee of $100 (per class) within six months of the mailing date of the action the party wishes to appeal.

An applicant who wishes to contest a refusal based on substance (such as a rejection of an application because the mark is merely descriptive) should file an appeal to the TTAB. If, however, the only issue in dispute is a question regarding the applicant's compliance with a technical provision of trademark rules, the applicant should file a petition to the Director rather than appeal.

For example, if a trademark application is refused on the basis that the mark is confusingly similar to that of another, an appeal should be taken to the TTAB. If a question arises as to whether a disclaimer was properly printed in standardized format, a petition to the Director should be filed.

POSTEXAMINATION PROCEDURE

Publication in the *Official Gazette*

Assuming the applicant responds satisfactorily to the office action, the examining attorney will approve the mark for publication in the weekly *Official Gazette* (sometimes called the *OG*; see Exhibit 4–6). The mark as applied for (wording, design, or some combination thereof) will be reproduced as the applicant set it forth in the drawing page together with an identification of the owner, the filing date, the goods or services offered under the mark, and the filing date and serial number of the application. The purpose of publication is to afford interested parties the opportunity to review the mark and oppose its registration, usually on the basis that the mark is confusingly similar to another mark. Opposition actions are discussed in chapter 6. Marks on the Supplemental Register are not published for opposition, but are issued as registered marks on the date that they are printed in the *Official Gazette.*

A notice of opposition (or request for extension of time to oppose) must be filed with the TTAB within 30 days of publication of the mark in the *Official Gazette.* Extensions of time to oppose may be granted as follows:

- A first request for a 30-day extension will be granted without a showing of good cause. Alternatively, a first request for a 90-day extension will be granted upon a showing of good cause.
- If the first request was for 30 days, a second request for a 60-day extension will be granted upon a showing of good cause.
- After receiving extensions totaling 90 days, a final request for a 60-day extension will be granted if the trademark applicant consents or if there is a showing of extraordinary circumstances. The time for filing an opposition may not be extended beyond 180 days from the date of publication in the *Official Gazette.*

Once again, docketing of dates is critical. A law firm not only should docket the date of its own clients' applications (so it can confirm that no one has opposed the clients' marks and, thus, the marks will proceed to registration), but also should review the *Official Gazette* to search for marks that may conflict with clients' marks and then notify the clients so they can have the opportunity to oppose other applications.

Because thousands of marks are published in the *Official Gazette* each week, it is virtually impossible for a firm with an active trademark practice to devote the effort needed to reading each week's *Official Gazette*. Most law firms suggest their clients authorize one of the professional search firms (identified in chapter 3) to conduct a **watch service** to review the *Official Gazette* and notify the firm of potential conflicts on a timely basis so the law firm can then inform the client that a conflicting mark may need to be opposed. Watch services can also monitor all applications filed at the USPTO after a client's application so immediate action can be taken against a conflicting mark. The cost of the watch services is approximately $400 per year per mark, although costs can be higher if several international classes need to be watched or if the mark includes unique design features. The five most recent issues of the *Official Gazette* are available online at the USPTO's Web site.

Intent-to-Use Applications and Statements of Use

If the application was based upon the applicant's actual use of the mark in commerce, the **actual use application** will proceed to registration after the publication period (assuming a notice of opposition is not filed). If the application was based on the applicant's intent to use the mark in commerce in the future, the mark cannot proceed to registration until actual use has been shown.

Thus, for intent-to-use (ITU) applications, after publication (and no opposition), the USPTO

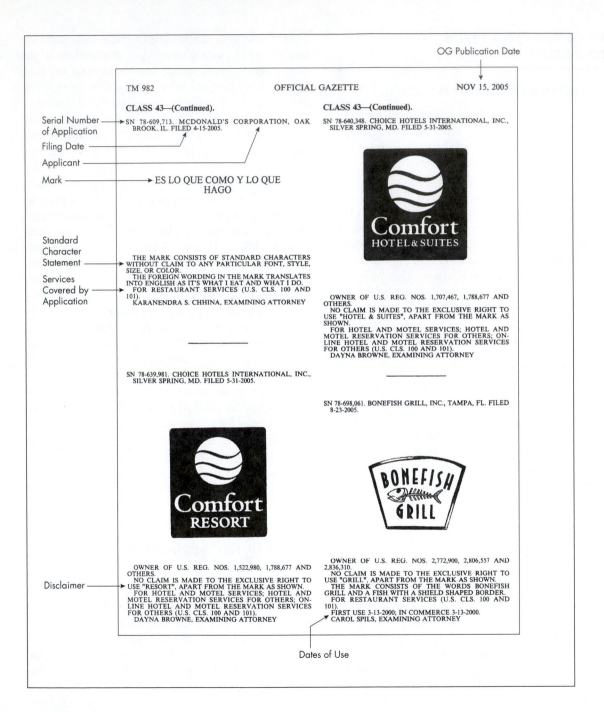

EXHIBIT 4–6
Official Gazette

will issue a **Notice of Allowance,** notifying the applicant that the ITU application has been allowed and granting the applicant six months (which may be extended for five additional six-month periods, up to a total of three years) within which to commence use of the mark and submit a statement and specimen verifying such use and the dates of first use. For example, if an ITU application has been published for opposition (with no one filing an opposition) and a notice of allowance is issued on June 1, 2006, the applicant will have until December 1, 2006, to file its **Statement of Use** (together with a specimen). If use is not commenced by December 1, 2006, the applicant may request an additional six-month period by alleging that it continues to have a bona fide intent to use the mark. Additional six-month extensions may be granted if the applicant alleges its continued good faith intent to use the mark and shows good cause for the extension, namely, ongoing efforts to make use of the mark in commerce, such as stating the additional time is needed to conduct market research and promotional activities.

Some applicants file a request for an extension of time to file a statement of use *with* a statement of use, sometimes called an "insurance" extension, for the purpose of securing additional time in case there are any deficiencies in the statement of use. Such a course of action may be well advised if the applicant believes that the statement of use might be rejected (e.g., the applicant may be concerned that the specimen submitted with the statement of use materially varies from the original drawing). Then if the statement of use is rejected, the applicant will have additional time to correct any deficiency.

Note that the first request for extension of time is granted automatically; subsequent extensions must show good cause why the extension should be granted. If no statement of use is submitted by June 1, 2009, the application will be deemed abandoned (unless the delay was unintentional). Filing fees of $100 are required for a statement of use and $150 for each request for extension of time to file a statement of use for each

class of goods/services covered by the application. (See Appendix D, Form 2, Statement of Use, and Form 3, Request for Additional Extension of Time to File Statement of Use.)

The statement of use verifies that the mark is in use in commerce, specifies the date of first use, and is accompanied by a specimen (label, packaging, and so forth for goods or promotional material for services) showing actual use of the mark. If the application was a combined application (e.g., for pens in I.C. 16 and clothing in I.C. 25), and the applicant can only show use in regard to goods in one class, the application can be divided by filing a formal **Request to Divide** (with the appropriate fee), with one class proceeding to registration and one lagging behind in a separate application.

If use of a mark was actually commenced during the application process of an ITU application, the applicant may file an amendment to its original application (called an **Amendment to Allege Use**) alleging that use has occurred and providing a specimen showing such use. The only significant difference between an amendment to allege use and a statement of use is the time of filing. The amendment to allege use may be filed during the initial examination phase, while the statement of use is not filed until after the USPTO issues a notice of allowance. An amendment to allege use or statement of use filed after the examining attorney approves the application for publication and before a notice of allowance is issued will be rejected. The period within which these documents cannot be filed is called the **blackout period.**

Statements of use and amendments to allege use can be filed electronically through TEAS, with a digitized image of the required specimen. Once a mark that is the subject of an ITU application achieves registration, the filing date of the application is deemed to be the date upon which the owner first used the mark. This "constructive use" date is important to the trademark owner because it will allow the owner to defeat an intervening user who may have actually used the mark before the ITU owner but after the ITU owner's application filing date. For example, using our case study, assume the following dates for an application by Vision for SUNVISION for skin care products.

- Intent to use application filed by Vision for SUNVISION on February 1, 2005.
- Actual use by Smith Co. for SUNNY VISION for skin care products on June 1, 2005.
- Use-based application filed by Smith Co. for SUNNY VISION on July 1, 2005.
- Notice of allowance issued for SUNVISION on February 1, 2006.
- Statement of use filed by Vision for SUNVISION on May 1, 2006, alleging actual use began on April 15, 2006.
- Registration issues for SUNVISION on August 1, 2006.

Given these dates, SUNVISION has priority over SUNNY VISION because once SUNVISION achieved registration, it was as if Vision had actually used the mark on the date it filed its application, namely, February 1, 2005, a date prior to June 1, 2005, the date of Smith's actual first use of SUNNY VISION. See Exhibit 4–7 for timeline and Exhibit 4–8 for application checklist.

Abandonment and Revival of Applications

Trademark applications are deemed abandoned by the USPTO if a timely response is not made to an office action or to a notice of allowance, and the USPTO will issue a formal notice of abandonment to the applicant. The USPTO, however, allows for revival of abandoned applications if a petition to revive is filed within two months of the mailing date of the notice of abandonment. The applicant's petition must state that the delay in responding to the office action or notice of allowance was unintentional.

Generally, it is not necessary to explain the circumstances that cause the unintentional delay. If an application was inadvertently abandoned

due to a USPTO error, an applicant may file a request to reinstate the application, instead of a formal petition to revive. For example, if the applicant can show e-mail confirmation that its response to an office action was filed through TEAS, a request to reinstate the application should be made.

An application can also be expressly abandoned, as when the applicant simply decides it does not wish to pursue registration.

REGISTRATION

For a use-based application, a registration will issue about 12 weeks after publication in the *Official Gazette* if no notice of opposition is filed to the application. For an ITU application, registration will occur after publication in the *Official Gazette*, notice of allowance of mark, and submission of the statement of use and requisite specimen and fee. The application process for use-based applications can take 12 to 18 months or longer, and the process for ITU applications can take from 18 to 42 months, or longer.

Eventually, however, the USPTO will issue a **Certificate of Registration** for the mark. The term of the registration is presently 10 years from the date the mark is registered (for registrations issued before November 16, 1989, the term is 20 years). The certificate will include all of the pertinent information about the mark and the owner and will set forth a registration number and a registration date. The mark as applied for will be reproduced. The law firm should carefully review the certificate and request a correction of any errors. Once the mark is registered, the owner (now called the **registrant**) can use any of the following registration notices in connection with the mark (assume the mark is SUNVISION):

- SUNVISION Registered in U.S. Patent and Trademark Office
- SUNVISION Reg. U.S. Pat. & Tm. Off.
- SUNVISION® (the letter *R* enclosed in a circle is the most common notice)

2/1/05	6/1/05	7/1/05	2/1/06	5/1/06	8/1/06
ITU application filed by Vision for SUN-VISION	Actual use by Smith of SUNNY VISION	Smith files application for SUNNY VISION	USPTO issues notice of allowance for SUN-VISION	Vision files statement of use for SUN-VISION alleging date of first use of 4/15/06	Registration issues for SUN-VISION. Vision has priority due to date of constructive use of 2/1/05

EXHIBIT 4–7
Timeline for ITU Application

Application Checklist

An application for trademark registration must include the following:
- written application with the following elements:
  - applicant's name;
  - applicant's legal entity (individual, corporation, and so forth) and identification of country of which applicant is citizen or country or state of business organization;
  - applicant's address;
  - basis for use of mark, namely, a statement that applicant has used the mark (and, if so, dates of first use and first use in commerce) or statement that applicant has bona fide intent to use the mark in the future;
  - identification of goods and services offered under the mark; and
  - identification of international class (if known by applicant)
- declaration by applicant (or person authorized by applicant) and signature
- one specimen for each international class
- drawing of mark
- appropriate filing fee

EXHIBIT 4–8
Trademark Application Checklist

The federal registration symbol or language cannot be used with a mark unless it has been registered with the USPTO. Until that time, trademark owners and applicants often use the designation "TM" (for trademark) or "SM" (for service mark) placed alongside the mark to notify others the owner claims rights in the mark, although these are not official symbols. A registrant is not required to use any registration notice; however, in an infringement suit based on

ETHICS EDGE: Computer Literacy

Part of the ethical duty of competent representation owed to a client is the duty to provide legal services as efficiently and cost-effectively as possible. Thus, all IP professionals should be familiar with the USPTO's Web site and its electronic tools for searching, filing documents, and checking status. Practitioners who engage in volume trademark work for clients can save their clients a great deal of money by filing trademark applications through TEAS or TEAS Plus. Take advantage of USPTO Web site tutorials, take training classes, or seek advice from colleagues to make sure clients are provided with cost-effective and efficient representation through all stages of trademark prosecution.

the mark, no monetary damages can be recovered by the registrant unless the defendant had actual notice of the registration. Using the registration notice provides such actual notice such that the registrant can later recover damages for infringement of the mark.

Once the law firm receives the certificate of registration, it will forward the certificate to the client along with pertinent information about monitoring the mark, using the registration notice, and pertinent dates to maintain the mark. Once again, the law firm must be certain to docket the critical dates to avoid abandonment of the registration. For example, between the fifth and sixth years after registration, and within the year before the end of every 10-year period after the registration date, the registrant must file a continued use affidavit with the USPTO verifying the mark is still in use or the registration will be canceled (to clear the USPTO files of **deadwood** and allow unused marks to be used by others). Additionally, the registration must be renewed at the end of each 10-year period following the registration date. The affidavit of continuing use and renewal document can be filed electronically through TEAS with a digitized image of the required specimen.

See Exhibit 4–9 for a Certificate of Registration, Exhibit 4–10 for a trademark prosecution flowchart that shows each step of the prosecution process, and Exhibit 4–11 for a list of documents that may be filed using TEAS.

The United States Patent and Trademark Office's TARR Monitoring System.

The USPTO's TEAS system has been remarkably successful; nearly all trademark applications are filed electronically using TEAS. Following are the documents that may be submitted through TEAS:

- applications for registration of marks
- amendments to allege use
- statements of use
- requests for extensions of time to file a statement of use
- affidavits of continued use
- affidavits of incontestability
- combined affidavits
- responses to office actions (in most cases)
- preliminary amendments
- notices of change of correspondence or owner's address
- petitions to revive abandoned applications
- appointment or revocation of attorney or domestic representative

Exhibit 4-9
Trademark Registration Certificate

The United States of America

CERTIFICATE OF REGISTRATION
PRINCIPAL REGISTER

The Mark shown in this certificate has been registered in the United States Patent and Trademark Office to the named registrant.

The records of the United States Patent and Trademark Office show that an application for registration of the Mark shown in this Certificate was filed in the Office; that the application was examined and determined to be in compliance with the requirements of the law and with the regulations prescribed by the Director of the United States Patent and Trademark Office; and that the Applicant is entitled to registration of the Mark under the Trademark Act of 1946, as Amended.

A copy of the Mark and pertinent data from the application are part of this certificate.

This registration shall remain in force for TEN (10) years, unless terminated earlier as provided by law, and subject to compliance with the provisions of Section 8 of the Trademark Act of 1946, as Amended.

Nicholas P. Godici

Acting Director of the United States Patent and Trademark Office

---

Int. Cl.: 35

Prior U.S. Cls.: 100, 101, and 102

Reg. No. 2,502,926

United States Patent and Trademark Office   Registered Oct. 30, 2001

SERVICE MARK
PRINCIPAL REGISTER

GROWTH ARCHITECTURE

SCHULER, ANDREW J. (UNITED STATES CITI-
ZEN)
6300 STEVENSON AVE., SUITE 916
ALEXANDRIA, VA 22304

FIRST USE 8-1-2000; IN COMMERCE 8-1-2000.

SN 75-857,060, FILED 11-24-1999.

FOR: BUSINESS MANAGEMENT CONSULTING
SERVICES, IN CLASS 35 (U.S. CLS. 100, 101 AND 102).

GEOFFREY FOSDICK, EXAMINING ATTORNEY

EXHIBIT 4–10
Trademark
Presentation
Flowchart

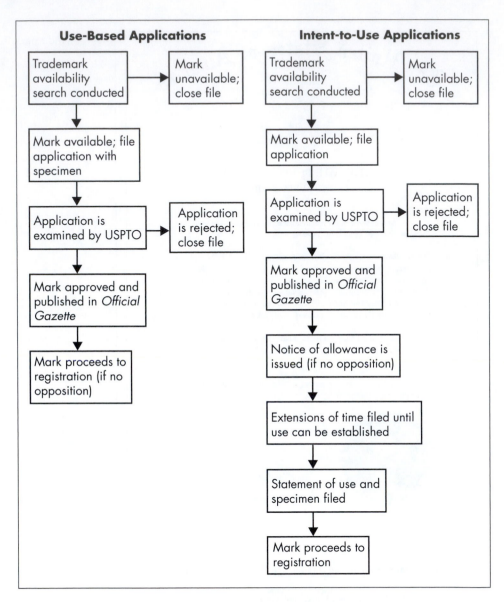

withdrawal of attorney in pending application

requests for express abandonment (withdrawal) of applications

The advantages of using TEAS include the following:

• When a document is filed electronically, the USPTO receives it within seconds

after filing, and immediately issues a confirmation of filing via e-mail that includes the date of receipt and a summary of the submission. This confirmation is evidence of filing should any question arise as to the filing date of the document.

• Electronic filing creates an automatic entry of receipt of this filing into the USPTO's automated system, helping

EXHIBIT 4-11
The TEAS System

The USPTO's TEAS system has been remarkably successful; nearly all trademark applications are filed electronically using TEAS. Following are the documents that may be submitted through TEAS:

- Applications for registration of marks;
- Amendments to allege use;
- Statements of use;
- Requests for extensions of time to file a statement of use;
- Affidavits of continued use;
- Affidavits of incontestability;
- Combined affidavits;
- Responses to Office Actions (in most cases);
- Preliminary amendments;
- Notices of change of correspondence or owner's address;
- Petitions to revive abandoned applications;
- Appointment or revocation of attorney or domestic representative;
- Withdrawal of attorney in pending application; and
- Requests for express abandonment (withdrawal) of applications.

The advantages of using TEAS include the following:

- When a document is filed electronically, the USPTO receives it within seconds after filing, and immediately issues a confirmation of filing via e-mail that includes the date of receipt and a summary of the submission. This confirmation is evidence of filing should any question arise as to the filing date of the document;
- Electronic filing creates an automatic entry of receipt of this filing into the USPTO's automated system, helping to avoid improper abandonment or cancellation; and
- Applications filed electronically are less expensive and are examined much faster than their paper counterparts.

to avoid improper abandonment or cancellation.
- Applications filed electronically are less expensive and are examined much faster than their paper counterparts.

THE UNITED STATES PATENT AND TRADEMARK OFFICE'S TARR MONITORING SYSTEM

Once you receive a filing receipt or e-mail confirmation containing the serial number of your application, you may check on the status of your application through the Trademark Applications and Registrations Retrieval (TARR) database on the USPTO's Web site at http://tarr.uspto.gov. TARR can also be used to check the status of any registered mark. If you do not have access to the Internet, you can call the Trademark Assistance Center at 1-800-786-9199 (or 571-272-9250 if you live in Northern Virginia) to request a status check. Applicants should check on the status of their pending applications at least every six months.

Trivia

- The public initiates more than one million queries per month through TESS (the online trademark search system).
- The top trademark applicants in 2006 were Mattel, Inc., Victoria's Secret Store Brand Management, and Disney Enterprises, Inc.
- In 2006, the USPTO issued more than 140,000 registrations on the Principal Register and just a little more than 6,000 registrations on the Supplemental Register.
- In January 2007, the one-millionth trademark application was filed electronically with the USPTO via TEAS.
- More than 20 different types of forms may be filed with the USPTO using TEAS.
- Nearly 150 countries, including the United States, use the International Classification system (classifying goods into 34 classes and services into 11 classes) administered by WIPO.

CHAPTER SUMMARY

After searching and clearance of a mark for availability, an application should be filed with the USPTO for registration of the mark. If the mark has actually been used in interstate commerce, the application should be accompanied by a specimen showing how the mark is actually used.

The application will be carefully reviewed by an examining attorney to determine if it meets the statutory requirements and whether any marks similar to the proposed mark have been registered or applied for in the same or related industries. The examining attorney's objections are enumerated in an office action. An applicant has six months to respond to an office action. The process continues until either the application is finally refused or it is allowed for publication in the *Official Gazette*, a weekly government publication. Individuals who believe they may be injured by the proposed registration have a statutory period within which to oppose registration of the mark. If no opposition is filed, the mark will proceed to registration.

If the applicant has not yet engaged in actual use of the mark, the procedure is essentially the same. The application will be reviewed by an examining attorney, who will approve it, publish it for opposition in the *Official Gazette*, and issue a notice of allowance. The applicant will then have six months to begin use of the mark in commerce and file a statement of use verifying such use with an actual specimen attached. Extensions of time may be granted. After review of the statement of use and specimen, the mark will be registered. Registration is a complex and lengthy process even if there are only minimal problems.

CASE ILLUSTRATION—LIKELIHOOD OF CONFUSION

Case: *In re Opus One, Inc.,* 60 U.S.P.Q.2d 1812 (T.T.A.B. 2001)

Facts: Applicant applied for the federal registration of OPUS ONE for restaurant services. The examining attorney refused registration on the basis that the mark was likely to be confused with the mark OPUS ONE, registered for wine. Applicant appealed to the Trademark Trial and Appeal Board.

Holding: The refusal to register was affirmed. The two marks are identical. Moreover, registrant's mark OPUS ONE used for wine is an arbitrary and strong mark and thus entitled to a broad scope of protection. Although the applicant argued that the services offered under the mark were not related, the TTAB disagreed, noting that the greater the similarity between marks, the lesser the degree of similarity between the goods and services is required to support a finding of likelihood of confusion. Thus, where marks are identical, as was the case here, there need only be a viable relationship between the respective goods and services are complementary goods and services that may be encountered together by the same purchasers. Thus, applicant's mark OPUS ONE for restaurant services was likely to be confused with registrant's mark OPUS ONE for wine.

CASE STUDY AND ACTIVITIES

Case Study.   Vision has operated well-known gift and souvenir shops called Treasure Trove in its hotels for several years. The shops offer a variety of hats, T-shirts, mugs, and toys that display the mark CLUB KID, which is also the name of Vision's child care camp that it offers to its hotel guests. Within the next year, Vision intends to expand its child care offerings and use the mark SAFARI EXPLORER for younger campers and VISIONTREKKERS for its older campers. Vision recently filed trademark applications for TREASURE TROVE. The first office action issued by the USPTO has stated that the mark is merely descriptive of gift store services. Vision intends to file applications for CLUB KID, SAFARI EXPLORER, and VISIONTREKKERS.

Activities.   You may need to access the USPTO Web site or the TMEP to answer some of these questions.

- Describe the arguments Vision should advance in its response to the office action rejecting the application for TREASURE TROVE.
- Draft an identification of goods and services for the goods and services offered under CLUB KID (and identify the international classes applicable to the mark), identify the

CASE STUDY AND ACTIVITIES (CONT'D)

filing fee Vision will need to pay in connection with the application(s), and describe any potential challenges the USPTO may raise to registration of the mark.
- Describe the type of applications that Vision would file for SAFARI EXPLORER and VISION TREKKER, and draft the identification of services and identify the international class applicable to the marks.

ROLE OF PARALEGAL

Paralegals typically have significant responsibility in the prosecution stage of a trademark application. In many law offices, primary responsibility may be assigned to paralegals, with attorney involvement limited to supervising and advising the paralegal and providing advice to the client on suggested strategies to overcome refusals to register. Among the many tasks IP professionals assume responsibility for are the following:

- gathering information from clients to assist in preparing applications
- preparing the trademark application
- reviewing specimen that supports use of a mark for consistency and proper display of marks
- filing the application and confirming same to client
- reviewing the official filing receipt or e-mail confirmation
- reviewing office actions and reporting same to client
- performing research for responses to office actions
- assisting in preparing responses to office actions
- reviewing the *Official Gazette* to ensure client's mark is accurately reproduced
- reviewing notice of allowance for ITU applications
- preparing statement of use and gathering specimen for ITU applications
- reviewing certificate of registration for accuracy
- assisting in reporting registration to client
- docketing all critical dates throughout the prosecution process
- monitoring the progress of the application

INTERNET RESOURCES

USPTO Web site:	http://www.uspto.gov
Trademark Manual of Examining Procedure (TMEP):	http://tess2.uspto.gov/tmdb/tmep
USPTO's Acceptable Identification of Goods and Services Manual:	http://tess2.uspto.gov/netahtml/tidm.html

TEAS information and forms: http://www.uspto.gov/teas/index.html

Official Gazette: http://www.uspto.gov (access USPTO Web site
                                          and select Trademarks Main Page
                                          and then select *Official Gazette* for online
                                          access to last five issues of the *Official Gazette*)

General trademark information: http://www.megalaw.com
                                          http://www.findlaw.com
                                          http://www.ipmall.fplc.edu (intellectual
                                          property resource Web site offered by Pierce
                                          Law school)

DISCUSSION QUESTIONS

1. Would an identification of "leather goods, including handbags and belts" be acceptable to the USPTO? Discuss.
2. Describe the type of specimen that would support use of the following marks:
   > OCEANA for restaurant services
   > JACK & JILL for children's books
   > AQUAKISS for bottled water
3. If an application for BRAINIAC COMPUTERS (for computer repair services) is refused registration on the basis that the mark is merely descriptive, how should the applicant respond?
4. Assume that a notice of allowance is issued on May 1, 2006, for a mark that is the subject of an ITU application. Discuss the deadlines applicable to the mark to ensure the application is not abandoned.
5. Assume that a mark is published in the *Official Gazette* on December 15. When should a notice of opposition be filed if one intends to oppose registration of the mark?
6. Assume the owner of the registered mark MORNING GLOW CREAM (for skin lotion and cream) disclaimed "Cream." Later users have applied for the marks EVENING GLOW CRÈME and SUGAR GLOW LOTION, both for skins lotions and creams. Discuss whether the marks are confusing similar.

USING INTERNET RESOURCES

1. Use the USPTO's Web site and identify the owner of Trademark Registration 2,961,563. Give the owner's full name.
2. Would a description of goods such as "Toys in I.C. 28, such as. . ." be acceptable? What section of the TMEP governs your answer?
3. Use the glossary on the USPTO's Web site and give the definition of "blackout period."
4. Use the TMEP. If a paper drawing is used in a paper trademark application, what size must the drawing be?

USING INTERNET RESOURCES (CONT'D)

5. The trademark AVALON is registered to Toyota. Access the USPTO's TDR system and review the specimen submitted for this mark. How is the mark displayed by Toyota?

6. Review the registered trademark WESTERN ENERGETIX.
   a. What is the "mark statement" given for this mark?
   b. Access the TDR system and review the signature on the application. When was the application signed and by whom was it signed? Is the signature legible?

7. Use the "New User" Search form on the USPTO Web site. Do you think you could file an application for the mark DE MILO for bracelets? Discuss fully. Review the Assignment Status records for the mark you located. Who is the current owner of the mark?

8. Access the USPTO Web site and locate the TDR documents for U.S. Application No. 78/844870. Review the Office Action issued by the USPTO. What were the two primary objections raised to the registration of the mark by the USPTO?

For additional resources, go to www.paralegal.delmar.cengage.com.

Chapter **5**

Postregistration Procedures, Trademark Maintenance, and Transfer of Rights to Marks

CHAPTER OVERVIEW

The Lanham Act imposes various requirements on registrants after registration of marks to ensure that only marks in use remain on the registers. Thus, registrants must file an affidavit between years five and six after registration and in the year before the end of each successive 10-year period after registration to allege continued use of the mark and file an application for renewal within one year before the end of the initial registration term and every 10 years thereafter. Failure to file the appropriate documents will result in cancellation of the registration for a mark.

Rights to marks can be lost by other means as well, primarily when the mark becomes generic or when the mark is abandoned by nonuse. Trademark owners often institute trademark use and compliance policies to ensure marks are not lost through genericide or abandonment.

Because a trademark is a form of property, it can be transferred or assigned to another if the goodwill symbolized by the mark is assigned with it. Similarly, a mark may be licensed to another party to use, as long as the trademark owner controls the nature and quality of the goods or services offered by the licensee.

THE AFFIDAVIT OF USE

Background

Although a registration is valid for 10 years, between years five and six after a registration is issued, and in the year before the end of each 10-year period after registration, the registrant is required to file an **Affidavit** (or *Declaration*) **of Use** with the USPTO, verifying that the mark is still in use in commerce in connection with the goods or services identified in the registration. Failure to submit the affidavit of use, called a "Section 8 affidavit," within the appropriate deadline (or within a six-month grace period) will lead to cancellation of the registration. Requiring registrants to notify the USPTO that marks are still in use allows the USPTO to clear its files of deadwood, making unused marks available for others. Nevertheless, the mark may still be used by its owner who will continue to have common law rights to the mark even though the federal registration for the mark has been canceled.

If the registration covers goods or services in several classes, the registrant must verify that the mark is in use in connection with all of the goods or services. If the mark is in use with regard to some items but not for others, the registrant must indicate such. The registration will be canceled as to any goods for which the mark is not in use. The USPTO filing fee is $100 per class of goods or services. Filing during the grace period results in additional fees of $100 (per class). If the Section 8 affidavit is not filed before the expiration of the grace period, the registration will be canceled. The USPTO prefers that the document be filed electronically through TEAS.

Changes in Ownership of the Mark

The Section 8 affidavit must be filed by the owner of the registration. Often, marks are transferred or assigned to other new owners who fail to notify the USPTO of the change in ownership. Although the Section 8 affidavit is filed by the new owner, USPTO records may continue to reflect the original registrant. In such cases, the Section 8 affidavit is refused until the appropriate changes are made to the USPTO records showing proper continuity of title, called the **chain of title,** to the party now filing the Section 8 affidavit. Even a change in the state of incorporation is a change of legal entity. Thus, if a Virginia corporation dissolves its status in Virginia so it can become a Delaware corporation, unless the USPTO has received formal notification of such change, as well as documentary evidence (such as certified copies of the Delaware incorporation documents), a Section 8 affidavit will not be accepted.

Changes in the Mark

When filing the affidavit, the owner must attach a specimen showing the mark as it is presently used for each class of goods or services identified in the registration. Thus, if the mark is used in connection with coffee creamer in I.C. 29 and coffee in I.C. 30, a specimen (generally labels, tags, packaging materials, or containers, or digitized images in .jpg format) for each class must be provided. If the mark as presently used differs from the mark as registered, the USPTO must determine whether the change is material. If the change is determined to be a material alteration, the Section 8 affidavit will be refused.

Because trademarks evolve over time (e.g., consider the periodic updating of the BETTY CROCKER® portrait mark and the TACO BELL bell design), alterations in marks are common. The USPTO will review the original mark as registered and compare it with the current specimen; if they are substantially the same, the affidavit will be accepted. A material alteration will result in a refusal on the basis that the mark currently in use is a new mark and that the registered mark is no longer in use. Generally, a mere pluralization in wording or a slight change in nonessential background design may be acceptable. Thus, if wording in a mark appears in a different typeface or script, it will likely be accepted. The addition of wording or design elements, however, will likely result in a refusal, requiring the registrant to file a new application and begin the registration process anew.

If the USPTO agrees that a change is not material and accepts the Section 8 affidavit, the registrant will usually be encouraged to amend the registration so it conforms to the mark as presently used.

If the registered mark is not in use in commerce, the owner may provide facts to the USPTO showing that nonuse is excusable due to special circumstances rather than any intent to abandon the mark. The owner must also state the date use of the mark stopped and when it is expected to resume. Merely stating that the applicant does not intend to abandon the mark is not sufficient. Additionally, reduced demand for the product or service does not excuse nonuse; ordinary economic or social conditions that result in nonuse of the mark cannot be excused, because these are exactly the types of marks the USPTO wants to eliminate. On the other hand, if there is some governmental regulation that precludes the owner from using the mark (e.g., a trade embargo against the sale of insecticides or certain chemicals), nonuse would be acceptable. Similarly, if the mark is temporarily not being used because of sale of a business, plant retooling (and production is scheduled to resume at some point), fire, illness, or other catastrophe, the nonuse might be excused. As soon as the external cause passes, the owner must resume use within a reasonable amount of time. Finally, if sales of a product are sporadic because the product is so expensive that few sales are customary in the particular industry, such is excusable nonuse.

THE AFFIDAVIT OF INCONTESTABILITY

Section 15 of the Trademark Act permits owners of registrations on the Principal Register to file affidavits whereby the right to use the registered marks for the goods or services set forth in the affidavit becomes **incontestable.** A Section 15 affidavit, also called an **Affidavit of Incontestability,** may not be filed until the mark has been in continuous use in commerce for at least five consecutive years after the date of registration. Thus, the Section 15 affidavit is often combined with the first Section 8 affidavit in one submission to the USPTO. The filing fee for the Section 15 affidavit is $200 per class of goods or services identified in the registration. The USPTO prefers that the owner file the document electronically through TEAS.

The benefit to filing a Section 15 affidavit is that it significantly reduces the challenges that may be made to a mark. Generally, a mark that is incontestable cannot be attacked unless it has become generic, has been abandoned, is being used to misrepresent the source of goods or services, is functional, or was procured by fraud. Although incontestability does not preclude all challenges to a mark, it does preclude two key challenges: that the mark is merely descriptive or that it is confusingly similar to a mark owned by a prior user.

In addition to verifying that the mark has been in continuous use for the five-year period, the Section 15 affidavit must state that there has been no final decision adverse to the registrant's claim of ownership of the mark, or to the registrant's right to register the mark, or to keep the mark on the Principal Register. The affidavit must also state that there is no proceeding involving these rights pending in the USPTO or any court.

No registrant is required to file a Section 15 affidavit; however, for obvious reasons, if the mark has been in continuous use for at least five years and satisfies the other conditions, a registrant should be strongly encouraged to do so to immunize the mark from various challenges. Only marks registered on the Principal Register (not the Supplemental Register) may become incontestable under Section 15. (See Appendix D, Form 4, for a combined affidavit under Sections 8 and 15.)

RENEWAL OF REGISTRATIONS

Any trademark registration issued after the Trademark Law Revision Act (namely, November 16, 1989) has a duration of 10 years. Before that date, registrations were valid for 20 years. Within one year before expiration of each pertinent period, the registrant must renew the registration or it will be automatically canceled (although common law rights to the mark may still exist if the mark is in use). The new **renewal** period for all marks is 10 years. Although the application for renewal (often called a "Section 9 renewal application") must be filed within a one-year period before each expiration date, there is a grace period of six months following the expiration of a registration during which an application for renewal may be filed. For example, for a registration issued November 1, 2003, the first application for renewal can be filed as early as November 1, 2012, and as late as November 1, 2013, before entering the six-month grace period. The filing fee for an application for renewal is $400 per class of goods or services. Filing during the grace period results in additional fees of $100 per class. If the renewal application is not filed before the end of the grace period, the registration will expire. The Section 8 affidavit required every 10 years can be combined with the renewal application in a single document filed every 10 years. The form for the combined filing is available through TEAS. (See Appendix D, Form 5.)

The requirements previously discussed for Section 8 affidavits (filed between years five and six after registration and every 10 years after reg-

istration) and applications for renewal are somewhat similar.

- The document should be filed by the owner of the mark. If the owner identified for the application for renewal is different from the one identified in the registration itself, renewal will issue in the name of the party who is shown as owner in the original registration.
- If the renewal application lists only some of the goods/services in the registration, it will be presumed that the renewal is sought for only the goods/services listed (and the goods/services omitted from the renewal application will be omitted from the registration).

No specimen is required, and there is no requirement of showing that any nonuse is due to special circumstances that excuse nonuse, generally because a specimen or showing of excusable nonuse are covered by Section 8 affidavits of continuing use, usually filed at the same time and in the same document as the renewal application under Section 9. (See Appendix D, Form 5, Application for Renewal of Trademark Registration Combined with Declaration of Use under Section 8 of Lanham Act.) (See Exhibit 5–1 for chart showing due dates for postregistration documents.)

DOCKETING REQUIREMENTS

As discussed, certain actions must be taken to maintain a trademark or service mark registration. Failure to take the appropriate action in a timely fashion will result in cancellation or expiration of a registration. Although an owner can petition the Director to review refusals of Section 8 affidavits and applications for renewal, such refusals are seldom reversed, and the decision of the director is final (unless the registrant appeals to the U.S. Court of Appeals for the Federal Circuit within two months). The registration will then be canceled.

Document	Statutory Requirement	Due Date for EXPLORE® (registered 6/01/04)	Grace Period	Specimen Needed
Section 8 Affidavit of Continued Use	Due between fifth and sixth year after registration and within the year before the end of every ten-year period	Due between 6/01/09 and 6/01/10; due between 6/01/13 and 6/01/14 (and every ten years thereafter)	Yes (six-month grace period)	One specimen needed
Section 15 Affidavit of Incontestability	Filing is optional; affidavit may be filed only after mark is in use in commerce for at least five consecutive years (for any five-year period)	May be filed at any time after 6/01/09	No grace period is needed because section 15 affidavit can be filed at any time after five years of consecutive use	No
Section 9 Application for Renewal	Must be filed within one year before ten-year anniversary of registration and every ten years thereafter	Renewal can be filed between 6/01/13 and 6/01/14 and every ten years thereafter	Yes (six-month grace period)	No (specimen not required because section 9 renewal application is usually filed with section 8 affidavit, which is accompanied by specimen)

EXHIBIT 5–1
Dates for Maintenance of Trademarks

Because cancellation is such an extreme result, the utmost care must be given to docketing critical dates. While many IP professionals maintain their own docketing systems, others use the services of one of the professional search firms (identified in chapter 3) to docket these critical dates. Because ownership of companies is in flux, marks evolve, and contact between the law firm and the registrant may have been intermittent in the years following registration, trademark maintenance (namely, handling affidavits of use under Section 8, affidavits of incontestability under Section 15, and applications for renewal under Section 9) can be difficult and time-consuming.

ETHICS EDGE: Docketing Duties

Although a statement noting the requirement for filing the Section 8 affidavits of use and renewal documents is noted on each certificate of trademark registration, this is the only notice that the USPTO provides regarding these requirements. The USPTO does not provide any reminders of the due dates for these critical documents. Thus, failure to calendar the due dates, grace periods, and so forth may likely be malpractice. Use computerized systems such as Microsoft's OUTLOOK® computer program, conventional calendars, or any other system that works for you. To calculate dates, use http://www.timeanddate.com.

LOSS OF TRADEMARK RIGHTS

While registrations can be canceled due to failure to file appropriate documents with the USPTO, as discussed earlier, rights to marks can also be forfeited due to **abandonment** of marks, failure to protect marks, or improper assignment or licensing of the mark.

The Lanham Act (15 U.S.C. § 1127) provides that a mark will be deemed to be abandoned when either of the following occurs:

- the mark has become a generic name; or
- use of the mark has been discontinued with intent not to resume use. Nonuse for three consecutive years is *prima facie* evidence of abandonment.

Genericide

As discussed in chapter 2, a mark can become generic (referred to as **genericide**) when consumers begin to call the product or service offered under the mark by the mark. Examples of once-valid marks that have become generic terms are *aspirin, yo-yo, cellophane, thermos,* and *escalator.* Once a mark becomes generic, it may be used by anyone. XEROX Corporation has always been worried that its famous mark would become generic due to consumers' misuse of the mark in saying, "I'm going to make a xerox of this document." XEROX Corporation has therefore expended substantial amounts of money in attempting to ensure consumers use the mark correctly by consistently saying in advertising copy, "XEROX® brand copiers are . . ." Similarly, Kimberly-Clark's promotional materials always refer to "KLEENEX® brand tissues" to ensure the mark does not become generic through consumers saying, "I need a kleenex."

Similarly, while ROLLERBLADE® is a registered trademark for in-line skates, it is in danger of becoming generic due to consumer misuse, as in "Let's go rollerblading" or "I need a new pair of rollerblades." Such use of a trademark as if it is the actual name for the product can cause a loss of trademark rights. Thus, while owners of marks want consumers to know and recognize their marks, the danger of a mark becoming too popular is that it can be misused, leading to genericide.

In mid-2006, *The Washington Post* noted that the word "Google" had been added to the Merriam-Webster's Collegiate Dictionary, and questioned whether the term had become generic. Within weeks, trademark counsel for Google Inc. wrote the newspaper, warning that the *Post*'s characterization might constitute genericide, and provided a list of appropriate and inappropriate uses of GOOGLE®. Similarly, Adobe Systems Inc. warns users not to use the term "photoshopped," but rather to use the phrase "ADOBE® PHOTOSHOP® software." In sum, marks that become generic are victims of their own success, as consumers become so familiar with a company's goods that they use the trademark as the name of a kind of product.

Abandonment by Nonuse

The more common means by which a mark becomes abandoned is through nonuse. One of the most famous trademark doctrines is "use it or lose it." Mere cessation of use is insufficient; the nonuse must be coupled with an intent not to resume use for abandonment to occur. There is a presumption that a mark has been abandoned if it has not been used for three years. 15 U.S.C. § 1127. Once a party can demonstrate such nonuse for three years, the trademark owner has the burden of rebutting the presumption of abandonment by proving that mark has not been abandoned (either by producing evidence of actual use during the relevant period or intent to resume use).

In determining whether abandonment due to nonuse has occurred, courts have concluded that "intent to resume use" means an intent to resume use within the reasonably foreseeable future. In one famous case, CBS stopped using the AMOS AND ANDY mark due to civil rights objections. When a third party began using the mark 20 years later, CBS sued for infringement, arguing that it intended to resume use of the mark when social policies permitted. The court held the mark had been abandoned because CBS did not have an intent to use the mark in the reasonably foreseeable future. *Silverman v. CBS Inc.,* 870 F.2d 40 (2d Cir. 1989).

The trademark owner need not use the mark everywhere in the United States; use anywhere is usually sufficient. However, trademark owners cannot make sporadic and token sales merely for the purpose of reserving rights in a mark. Moreover, minor activities will not suffice. Press releases and other similar announcements by a company that it is discontinuing a product line associated with a mark likely show an intent not to resume use from which abandonment will be inferred. Because abandonment leads to a complete forfeiture of rights to a mark, courts are reluctant to find abandonment unless there is clear and convincing evidence of such.

A trademark owner challenged with an allegation that his or her mark has been abandoned through nonuse may attempt to show special circumstances that would justify nonuse. These special circumstances are similar to those that excuse nonuse when a registrant files a Section 8 affidavit. For example, a labor strike that results in inability to ship products or government regulation precluding importation or shipping of goods bearing the mark will usually excuse nonuse. Similarly, the sale of few products bearing the mark when the products are extremely expensive may excuse nonuse. However, mere economic conditions that make selling the product or service unprofitable do not excuse nonuse.

It is possible that the mark has been so changed by the owner over time that the original mark has become abandoned. As discussed, minor changes will not result in loss of rights, but a material alteration in the mark may result in abandonment of the original mark. For protection, owners should register each version of a mark.

Marks can also be expressly abandoned, such as when a trademark owner cancels or surrenders his or her registration, perhaps as a result of a settlement agreement with another.

Abandonment causes a loss of common law rights as well as rights under the Lanham Act. Resumption of use by the owner after abandonment does not revive the mark but merely establishes a new use date for the new mark. On the other hand, if an applicant inadvertently abandons an application (perhaps because the applicant failed to timely respond to an office action) or a registration (because the registrant forgot to renew the registration), but continues to use a mark, rights to the mark continue and the owner retains common law rights from its date of first use and can reapply for trademark registration.

TRADEMARK USE AND COMPLIANCE POLICIES

Because misuse of a mark by allowing it to become generic or alteration of a mark can cause loss of rights, trademark owners should initiate compliance policies to ensure use of marks is proper. Failure to monitor and actively police a mark may result in abandonment of all rights to the mark. A **trademark compliance policy** will help to ensure that a company's marks continue to enjoy protection both under the Lanham Act and common law.

Following are some guidelines for proper trademark usage.

- A trademark should be displayed prominently in comparison with its surroundings and should clearly stand out on a label, advertisement, in text, and so forth. Thus, many owners capitalize their marks, display them in some prominent style or larger-than-average typeface, place them in quotation marks, or use distinctive lettering, colors, or the word *brand* after the mark, as in "VASELINE® brand petroleum jelly" to remind consumers that VASELINE is the brand name of or trademark for a certain product from a certain source and not the name of the product itself.
- Marks should be used in connection with the appropriate goods and services. Companies that have numerous similar marks for similar products and services must exercise care that a mark does not become abandoned because it is no longer used in correlation with the product or service for which it was registered. For marks used in connection with goods, the mark should be placed on the goods or on labels attached to the goods or packaging for the goods.
- Appropriate designations and notices should be used to inform the public that trademark rights are claimed in the mark. The federal registration symbol (®) is most often used for registered marks while the initials "TM" or "SM" are often used in connection with marks that are not yet registered. The symbols are generally placed to the right of and slightly above (or below) the mark, such as in "CAMPBELL'S® condensed cream of chicken soup." The symbol should be large enough to be easily spotted but need not be obtrusive. If a mark is repeated several times in an advertisement or brochure, the symbol may be displayed with the first or most prominent use of the mark. Alternatively, the mark can be displayed with an asterisk. A corresponding footnote at the bottom of the page can provide the information that the mark is a registered trademark owned by the company.
- Marks should be used consistently. The addition of words or symbols to a mark may lead to the conclusion that the company has abandoned its original mark and is now using some nonregistered form of the mark.
- The owner of the mark should be identified. For example, a notice may state "SOUTHRISE® is a federally registered trademark of Hutchins Associates, Inc."
- The mark should not be used in the plural form or possessive form, such as "Excedrins are great pain relievers" or "Shout's spot-removing power is improved." Such uses may result in the mark becoming generic.
- Marks should be used as adjectives rather than nouns to ensure the mark does not become generic. The mark should not be used to refer to the general type of a

product or service or to the owner. Use of a mark as a noun, rather than an adjective, suggests that the mark is the generic name for a product or service rather than a unique trademark for a particular product or service of a particular company. To avoid genericide, follow each use of a mark with the generic name for the product identified, as in "ROLLERBLADE® in-line skates" or "KLEENEX® tissues." Using such a term after the mark (or using the word *brand* as in "BAND-AID® brand adhesive strips") makes a mark an adjective rather than a noun.

Correct: SOUTHRISE® juices are refreshing.
            SOUTHRISE® cranberry juice is the juiciest.
            I used the GOOGLE® search engine to get directions.
            She ran a GOOGLE® search to check John's background.
Incorrect: Southrise refreshes you.
            Southrise is a sparkling beverage.

Southrise contains real cranberries.
I googled the directions.
She googled John.

Famous marks such as COKE® and FORD® are exceptions to this rule, and their owners do not always follow the noun-adjective rule. For example, advertising copy may read, "Have you driven a Ford lately?" This copy would be using the mark as a noun rather than an adjective. Other than these extraordinary cases, marks should always be used as adjectives rather than nouns.

To ensure that trademark use is proper and consistent, many companies use trademark handbooks and provide detailed information sheets to their employees, advertisers, suppliers, vendors, and licensees to instruct them in proper use of trademarks. When marks comprise color or design components rather than mere wording, companies usually supply advertising "slicks" as well so users can faithfully reproduce the mark. Many companies designate a responsible person to regulate use of the company's marks and verify compliance with guidelines and policies regarding use of the marks. (See Exhibit 5–2 for a chart showing examples of trademark usage.)

Guideline	Trademark Do	Trademark Don't
Display mark prominently.	VISIONTREK®, VISIONTREK®	Visiontrek
Use mark as registered and use in consistent manner.	**VISIONTREK®**	Vision-Trek, Vision Trek, VisionTrek
Use trademark registration notice.	VISIONTREK®	VISIONTREK
Identify owner of mark.	VISIONTREK® is a registered mark of Vision Corp.	Visiontrek
Do not use mark in plural form.	VISIONTREK® guided tours will thrill you.	Visiontreks offer a guided tour.

EXHIBIT 5–2
Trademark Usage Guide

(continues)

EXHIBIT 5–2
Trademark
Usage Guide
(continued)

Guideline	Trademark Do	Trademark Don't
Do not use in possessive form.	VISIONTREK® guided tours provide you with a full sight-seeing experience.	Visiontrek's guided tours provide you with a full sight-seeing experience
Use mark as an adjective rather that a noun.	VISIONTREK® guided tours are fully supervised.	Visiontrek is fully supervised.
	The VISIONTREK® tours will amaze you.	Visiontrek will amaze you.

TRADEMARK POLICING AND MAINTENANCE

In addition to ensuring that marks are used properly to avoid genericide or abandonment, trademark owners should initiate active policing and maintenance procedures to avoid infringement of their marks. The classic trademark rule is "police it or lose it." Among the steps trademark owners should take to protect their marks from infringement are the following.

- Critical dates for required actions with the USPTO should be docketed to ensure marks, applications, and registrations are not inadvertently abandoned and then used by others.
- Owners should subscribe to watching or tracking services to monitor marks for potential infringement. Professional service companies will review a number of trademark resources, including applications filed at the USPTO, the *Official Gazette*, state trademark registers, Internet domain names, and common law sources. Worldwide watching is also available for marks used internationally. Early notification of potential conflicts allows an owner to take aggressive action to protect a mark. The companies identified in chapter 3 (Thomson CompuMark, CT

Corsearch, and so forth) perform these watching services at varying rates. The most comprehensive watch of all resources previously described might cost more than $1,000 per year per mark per class. However, for a company like McDonald's Corporation that has spent years and substantial amounts of money in building goodwill in its marks, such as its GOLDEN ARCHES® mark, such a sum represents a very reasonable investment. Some trademark owners conduct an annual intellectual property "audit" to review the status of their intellectual property and detect potential infringing uses (see chapter 24). More limited watches, such as one only of new applications filed at the USPTO, might cost approximately $200 per year per mark.

- Company employees should be asked to be alert to competing uses in the marketplace. Trade publications, business press, and marketing materials of competitors should be monitored to ensure that marks that may be confusingly similar to the company's marks are not being used.
- Trademark owners should review Internet uses to locate infringing marks or misuses of a mark. Policing the Internet is a double-edged sword, however; while a few simple

keystrokes may reveal numerous uses, the trademark owner then runs the risk that ignoring infringers may lead
to a loss of trademark rights. Some companies with famous marks use a team to review Internet uses and then send e-mails explaining their trademark rights and asking the user to stop use of the owner's mark. If such a strategy is not successful, a more formal **cease and desist letter** is sent (see discussion later in this chapter).

USE OF MARKS OWNED BY THIRD PARTIES

Parties often use their competitors' marks in promotional materials comparing and contrasting the respective goods or services of the parties. A trademark owner does not have an absolute right to prohibit any and all uses of its trademarks. A **collateral use** of another party's marks may be acceptable in some circumstances. For example, it is not trademark infringement for a party to inform consumers truthfully that its products will "fit with" the trademark product of another. Thus, a seller of sponges was able to advertise that its sponges fit as replacements in the "O-CEDAR® 76 mop." Many parents are familiar with the announcements that certain blocks "work with LEGOS®."

Statements that one's products are "superior to" or "better than" another's, however, may be actionable as false advertising if the statement is untrue. Courts tend to examine language in advertising to ensure there is no misleading use, product disparagement, or confusion caused to the public. To reduce confusion, a party should always place the registration symbol (®) next to another party's registered mark and provide the announcement, "XYZ® is a federally registered trademark owned by XYZ Corp." This will help ensure that consumers are not confused about the source and origin of goods or services offered under the respective marks. The law of unfair competition is discussed in chapter 23.

TRANSFER OF OWNERSHIP OR RIGHTS IN TRADEMARKS

Assignment of Marks

A trademark or service mark may be transferred or assigned to another *if* the goodwill symbolized by the mark is assigned with it. TMEP 501.06 provides that partial assignments are permissible. Thus, a sole owner may assign 50 percent of his or her interest in a mark to another. The more common approach is an assignment or transfer of all of one's rights in a mark to another.

Because a mark is used to identify the source of goods and services, rather than existing as an independent object of property, it is inseparable from the goodwill of the business to which it applies. Thus, an arrangement by which a mark is assigned without the business goodwill that the mark symbolizes, called an **assignment in gross,** is ineffective to transfer trademark rights, and the new owner who begins using the mark cannot claim the original owner's use date for purposes of establishing priority in the mark. The new owner, the "assignee," will establish its own first use date upon using the mark. Thus, valuable trademark rights could be lost if a third party begins using a mark *after* the assignor's original use date but *before* the date of an assignment in gross to the assignee. This third party would have priority over the assignee and could prevent use of a confusingly similar mark by the assignee. To prevent such a situation, the parties should enter into a written **assignment** agreement that recites that the mark is being transferred together with the goodwill of the portion of the business associated with the mark. A recitation that goodwill is transferred with the mark is usually sufficient to ensure the assignee can capture or retain the original date of first use. Assignments of marks in which federal rights are claimed must be in writing (15 U.S.C. § 1060(a)).

The transfer of common law rights to a mark does not require a written agreement. If the assignment is oral, its existence may be proven by clear and uncontradicted testimony. However, while an oral agreement to transfer a common law mark is valid, a written agreement lends certainty and should always be used. Moreover, the assignment document should recite that the mark and the goodwill symbolized by the mark are being transferred to ensure there is no loss of trademark rights. The assignment document itself may be a relatively simple agreement (see Exhibit 5–3).

An entire business need not be transferred with a mark. A trademark owner may assign a mark used in connection with specific goods or services and retain other marks used in connection with other goods or services. If all of the assets of a business are sold, however, it is assumed that all marks and their goodwill pass with the other assets, even if they are not specifically mentioned in the sales documents.

In many cases, owners prepare written assignments on a later date to reflect an assignment that actually occurred earlier. For example, if Vision transferred or assigned its common

EXHIBIT 5–3
Assignment of
Trademark

WHEREAS, Hollis & Sanders Co., a corporation organized under the laws of the State of California, located and doing business at 890 Second Avenue, San Diego, CA 92117 ("Assignor"), is the owner of U.S. Trademark Registration No. 1,908,457 for the mark VISIONTREK issued December 14, 1996, for travel and tour services in I.C. 39 in the United States (the "Mark"); and

WHEREAS, Vision Corp., a corporation organized under the laws of the State of Delaware, located and doing business at 885 Third Avenue, 24th Floor, New York, NY 10022 ("Assignee"), desires to acquire all of Assignor's rights in and to the Mark and the goodwill symbolized thereby;

NOW, THEREFORE, for good and valuable consideration, the receipt and sufficiency of which are hereby acknowledged, Assignor hereby sells, assigns, transfers, and conveys to Assignee all of its right, title, and interest in and to the Mark, together with the goodwill of the business associated with the Mark, the same to be held and enjoyed by Assignee, its successors, assigns, and other legal representatives.

Assignor further assigns to Assignee all right to sue for and receive all damages accruing from past infringements of the Mark herein assigned.

Assignor represents it is the legal owner of all right, title, and interest in and to the Mark and has the right to assign the Mark and that there are no pending legal proceedings involving the Mark.

This Assignment shall be binding upon the parties, their successors and/or assigns, and all others acting by, through, with, or under their direction, and all those in privity therewith.

The parties agree to take any further action and execute any documents required to effect the purposes of this Assignment.

Hollis & Sanders Co.   Vision Corp.

By: _____   By: _____

Title: _____   Title: _____

Date: _____   Date: _____

law rights in a mark to another party but the parties neglected to prepare the actual assignment document at the time of transfer, Vision might later prepare a document reflecting such an event. Called a **Nunc Pro Tunc Assignment** (literally, "now for then"), the document merely recites that the assignment occurred on an earlier date and reflects an earlier transfer or assignment.

If the mark assigned has been registered or is the subject of a pending use-based application at the USPTO, the assignment must be in writing and should be filed or "recorded" with the USPTO. Although there is no requirement that the assignment be recorded to be effective, **recordation** is a relatively simple procedure that affords several advantages:

- It clarifies the records of the USPTO and affords notice to all of the identity of the owner of the mark.
- It allows the new owner to commence and defend actions at the USPTO in its name.
- It ensures that documents and notices issued by the USPTO will be sent to and will identify the correct owner.
- It simplifies postregistration procedures inasmuch as Section 8 affidavits will be rejected unless their identification of the trademark owner is consistent with the USPTO records.
- It provides public notice of the fact of the assignment such that later purchasers of the mark are bound by it.

In fact, an assignment is void against a later bona fide purchaser unless the assignment is recorded with the USPTO within three months after the assignment or before the subsequent purchase. 15 U.S.C. § 1060(a)(4).

Although common law marks, registered marks, and marks that are the subject of pending use-based applications can be assigned, marks that are the subject of intent-to-use (ITU) applications cannot be assigned prior to filing an amendment to allege use or a statement of use with the USPTO verifying that the mark is in use in commerce, unless the mark is being assigned to a successor of the business of the applicant to which the mark pertains and the business is ongoing and existing (15 U.S.C. § 1060(a)(1)). The purpose of the prohibition against assignment of marks not yet in use is to prevent the sale or trafficking of ITU applications. Additionally, permitting assignment of an application before a mark is used would conflict with the principle that a mark may be validly assigned only with some of the business or goodwill attached to use of the mark. There can be no goodwill attached to a mark that has not been used. An assignment of an ITU application prior to the filing of the verified statement of use is not only invalid but also voids the underlying trademark application or any resulting registration.

Recording documents at the USPTO requires that a party file a specific USPTO cover sheet or form (Form 1594, Recordation Form Cover Sheet; see Exhibit 5–4) identifying the conveying and receiving parties, the marks affected by the transfer, and a correspondent to whom the USPTO can send notices. The fees for recording are $40 for the first mark being assigned and $25 for each subsequent mark identified in the form. Form 1594 is also used to inform the USPTO that a mark has been acquired by a party through a merger (as when a corporation that owns a mark is acquired by another corporation) or in the event the trademark owner changes its name or state of incorporation.

To expedite recordation, the USPTO encourages recording electronically through its **Electronic Trademark Assignment System (ETAS).** Documents filed electronically are recorded much faster than paper documents. Using ETAS, a party can create and submit the recordation cover sheet by completing an online form and attaching the supporting legal documentation in PDF format for submission via the Internet. Fees can be paid by credit card, electronic funds transfer, or deposit account.

EXHIBIT 5-4

Form **PTO-1594** (Rev. 07/05)
OMB Collection 0651-0027 (exp. 6/30/2008)

U.S. DEPARTMENT OF COMMERCE
United States Patent and Trademark Office

RECORDATION FORM COVER SHEET

TRADEMARKS ONLY

To the Director of the U. S. Patent and Trademark Office: Please record the attached documents or the new address(es) below.

1. Name of conveying party(ies):

☐ Individual(s)   ☐ Association
☐ General Partnership   ☐ Limited Partnership
☐ Corporation- State:_____
☐ Other _____

Citizenship (see guidelines)_____

Additional names of conveying parties attached? ☐ Yes ☐ No

2. Name and address of receiving party(ies):

Additional names, addresses, or citizenship attached?   ☐ Yes   ☐ No

Name:_____
Internal Address:_____
Street Address:_____
City:_____
State:_____
Country:_____ Zip:_____

☐ Association   Citizenship _____
☐ General Partnership   Citizenship _____
☐ Limited Partnership   Citizenship _____
☐ Corporation Citizenship_____
☐ Other_____ Citizenship _____

If assignee is not domiciled in the United States, a domestic representative designation is attached: ☐ Yes   ☐ No
(Designations must be a separate document from assignment)

3. Nature of conveyance)/Execution Date(s) :

Execution Date(s)_____

☐ Assignment   ☐ Merger
☐ Security Agreement ☐ Change of Name
☐ Other_____

4. Application number(s) or registration number(s) and identification or description of the Trademark.

A. Trademark Application No.(s)

B. Trademark Registration No.(s)

Additional sheet(s) attached? ☐ Yes ☐ No

C. Identification or Description of Trademark(s) (and Filing Date if Application or Registration Number is unknown):

5. Name & address of party to whom correspondence concerning document should be mailed:

Name:_____
Internal Address:_____
_____
Street Address: _____
_____
City:_____
State:_____ Zip:_____
Phone Number: _____
Fax Number: _____
Email Address: _____

6. Total number of applications and registrations involved:

7. Total fee (37 CFR 2.6(b)(6) & 3.41) $_____

☐ Authorized to be charged by credit card
☐ Authorized to be charged to deposit account
☐ Enclosed

8. Payment Information:

a. Credit Card   Last 4 Numbers _____
                  Expiration Date _____

b. Deposit Account Number _____

   Authorized User Name _____

9. Signature:

_____   _____
            Signature   Date

_____
       Name of Person Signing

Total number of pages including cover sheet, attachments, and document: _____

Documents to be recorded (including cover sheet) should be faxed to (571) 273-0140, or mailed to:
Mail Stop Assignment Recordation Services, Director of the USPTO, P.O. Box 1450, Alexandria, VA 22313-1450

Licensing of Marks

A party may allow another party to use a mark and yet retain ownership rights in the mark. Such a form of limited permission is called a **license.** License agreements may be written or oral, although most are written. Some of the most common license arrangements occur in franchising. For example, McDonald's Corporation will grant a franchise to a party to open a McDonald's restaurant in a certain territory. In connection with the franchise, McDonald's will grant the party a license to use McDonald's marks on the cups, packaging, signs, and in advertising. McDonald's continues to own the marks; it has merely granted a license to its franchisee to use its marks for certain specific purposes.

The licensor will lose its rights to the mark, however, if it does not control the nature and quality of the goods or services offered by the licensee under the mark. Thus, license agreements must include "quality control" provisions whereby the licensor protects the mark by ensuring the goods and services offered under it by the licensee are consistent with those offered by the licensor. Failure of the licensor to exercise quality control will result in a **naked license** and a loss of the licensor's rights in the mark. Failure to monitor the goods and services offered under the license may result in abandonment of the mark and may preclude or estop the trademark owner/licensor from challenging use of the mark by the licensee during the period of unsupervised use. License agreements should therefore allow the licensor to conduct periodic inspection of the licensee's facilities and its use of the mark. The licensor may require the licensee to submit samples of how the mark is being applied to the goods or how it is used in advertising or may require testing of products offered under the mark. Such measures ensure that the licensee's products and services are of the same level of quality that consumers have come to associate with the licensor's mark. Failure to control and supervise the mark by the owner so as to ensure quality and consistency in the goods or services offered

under the mark leads to public deception inasmuch as the function of a mark is to identify the source of goods or services. Thus, a naked license (one without quality control provisions) results in loss of trademark rights.

In one famous example, for years a well-known trademark lawyer, Julius R. Lunsford Jr., traveled the country going to bars and restaurants to order COCA-COLA® drinks to determine if the establishments were actually serving COCA-COLA® and not another cola beverage. Lunsford would secretly retain a sample of the beverage and have it tested by company chemists. If necessary, Coca-Cola Co. would then prosecute the establishments for unfair competition.

The licensor may grant the licensee exclusive rights to use the mark. Alternatively, the licensor may limit the licensee's rights by allowing the licensee to use the mark only in specific geographic areas or may allow others to use the mark. Similarly, the licensor may retain rights to use the mark itself. The license agreement should specify whether the license is an **exclusive** or **nonexclusive license,** indicate whether use is restricted to any specific goods or services, or to any geographic territory, and must include adequate quality control provisions. Most license agreements also recite that the licensee acquires no ownership rights in the mark and cannot challenge the licensor's rights to the mark. A one-time fee may be paid by the licensee for the privilege of using the mark, or the licensee may make periodic royalty payments to the licensor based upon sales of the products. For example, the licensee may be required to pay the licensor 4 percent of its net profits arising out of its use of the mark as **royalties** or to achieve certain levels of sales. On occasion, a trademark owner may assign the entire mark to a party who then "licenses back" to the original owner the right to use the mark for some purpose. Litigation between trademark claimants is often resolved by such licensing arrangements. Although actions for infringement of federally registered marks are brought in federal court, actions involving the terms and conditions of licenses are governed by state laws relating to the general interpretation of contracts.

Although a license can be recorded with the USPTO (using Form 1594), there is no requirement of recording, and most parties in the United States do not do so, believing the license is a private agreement of which the public need not be informed. Moreover, license agreements do not involve a change of ownership or affect the chain of title to a mark. In most foreign countries, however, as discussed in chapter 8, there is usually a statutory duty to record a license agreement with the appropriate governing body.

The dates relating to trademark licenses should be docketed or calendared so that the license is terminated or renewed at the appropriate time. (See Exhibit 5–5 for a sample trademark license agreement.)

Trademarks as Collateral

Trademark owners may use their marks as collateral to secure their promise to perform some obligation. For example, a trademark owner may wish to borrow $400,000 from a bank. The bank may insist that certain property be pledged as collateral so that in the event of a default in payment by the owner, the bank can seize the assets pledged. Trademarks can be used as such collateral. Typically, the parties enter into an agreement called a security agreement that contains the terms and conditions of their arrangement. The security agreement will identify the marks being pledged as collateral. The security agreement is typically recorded at the USPTO (using Form 1594) to afford notice to the public that the marks are subject to the security interest. When the trademark owner satisfies its obligations, the security interest is released, again by using Form 1594. During the existence of the security agreement, the owner retains all rights in the mark. Granting a security interest in a trademark is not a transfer of any present rights in a mark. It allows a party to seize the marks (and then exercise all rights of ownership) only in the event of a default by the owner in regard to some promise

---

EXHIBIT 5–5
Trademark
License
Agreement

> This Trademark License Agreement (the "Agreement") is entered into and is effective as of this _____ day of _____, 20 _____, by and between Vision Corp., a Delaware corporation with its principal offices at 885 Third Avenue, 24th Floor, New York, NY 10022 ("Licensor") and _____, a corporation with its principal offices at _____ ("Licensee").
>
> WHEREAS, Licensor is the owner of the trademark V (and Eagle Design) (the "Mark") and U.S. Registration No. 1,789,746 therefor for children's books in I.C. 16, metal key chains in I.C. 6, and a variety of houseware items in I.C. 21, all as specified in the registration and Licensor has the right to license use of the Mark to others;
>
> WHEREAS, Licensor is desirous of licensing and Licensee is desirous of obtaining a license to use the Mark in connection with its business;
>
> NOW, THEREFORE, in consideration of the above, and for other good and valuable consideration, the receipt and sufficiency of which are hereby acknowledged, the parties agree as follows:
>
> 1. GRANT OF LICENSE AND LICENSE FEE
> Licensor grants to Licensee an exclusive, nontransferable, worldwide license to use the Mark in its name in connection with the goods covered by the registration of the Mark.

(continues)

Upon execution of this Agreement, Licensee shall pay Licensor the sum of _____ _____ Dollars ($_____) as consideration for the grant of license to use Licensor's Mark as described herein.

2. TERM OF LICENSE

Unless sooner terminated as provided in Section 8 hereof, the grant, as specified in Section 1, shall continue for a period of three (3) years from the date of this Agreement. This Agreement may be renewed for additional terms of three (3) years by mutual written agreement of the parties, which agreement may specify a license fee greater than the license fee provided in Section 1, not less than six (6) months prior to the expiration of the initial or any renewal term of this Agreement. Upon expiration of this Agreement:

    a. All rights of the Licensee to the Mark shall terminate and the Licensee shall have no further rights with respect thereto;

    b. Licensee shall not offer any goods in connection with the Mark or any confusingly similar mark and shall cease all use of the Mark or any confusingly similar mark; and

    c. Licensee shall cease any activity that suggests that it has any right to the Mark or that it has any association with the Licensor.

3. OWNERSHIP OF MARK

Licensee acknowledges the ownership of the Mark in Licensor, agrees that it will do nothing inconsistent with such ownership and that all use of the Mark by Licensee shall inure to the benefit of and be on behalf of Licensor, and agrees to assist Licensor in recording this Agreement with any appropriate domestic or foreign government authorities. Licensee agrees that nothing in this Agreement shall give Licensee any right, title, or interest in the Mark other than the right to use the Mark in accordance with this Agreement, and Licensee agrees that it will not challenge the title of Licensor to the Mark or challenge the validity of this Agreement.

4. QUALITY CONTROL STANDARDS AND MAINTENANCE

    a. Licensee agrees that the nature and quality of all goods offered or sold by Licensee in connection with the Mark shall be of high quality, manufactured free from defects and in full compliance with all laws, and of such style and appearance to be adequately suited to their exploitation to the best advantage and enhancement of the Mark and consistent with the quality control standards established by Licensor.

    b. At reasonable times during the term of this Agreement, Licensor may request Licensee to submit samples of any advertising or promotional materials and specimens of all uses of the Mark. If any such materials fail to meet with Licensor's approval, Licensee shall cease using such disapproved materials or items until such times that it modifies such materials and items and receives approval in writing from the Licensor of such materials and items, as modified.

    c. Licensor shall have the right to review the Licensee's use of the Mark and Licensee's business operations at any reasonable time and upon reasonable notice. Upon notice of defects given by Licensor, Licensee shall cure such defects in the use of the Mark or the goods offered thereunder. In the event that Licensee does not take reasonable steps to cure such defects within thirty (30) days after

EXHIBIT 5–5
Trademark License Agreement (continued)

(continues)

EXHIBIT 5–5
Trademark
License
Agreement
(continued)

notification by Licensor, Licensor shall have the right to require that Licensee re-move the Mark from any products or materials or, at the sole discretion of Licensor, to terminate this Agreement.

    d. Licensee shall operate its business in a manner that reflects favorably at all times on the Mark.

5. FORM OF USE

Licensee agrees to use the Mark only in the form and manner and with appropriate legends and notices as prescribed herein and from time to time by Licensor and not to use any other trademark or service mark in combination with the Mark without prior writ-ten approval of Licensor.

6. PROPRIETARY RIGHTS AND GOODWILL

    a. Licensee acknowledges that the Mark is owned by Licensor, which has the sole and exclusive right to license the Mark. The parties intend that Licensee shall use the Mark only under the terms and conditions of this Agreement. Licensor has the sole and exclusive right to deal with the U.S. Patent and Trademark Office in connection with the Mark, and Licensee will perform any acts reason-ably required by Licensor in connection with same. All costs associated with maintenance of the Mark shall be borne by Licensor.

    b. Licensee shall use all reasonable precautions and take all necessary steps to prevent the Mark from being acquired or duplicated or used by unauthorized persons. Licensee shall take appropriate action, by instructions, agreements, or otherwise, with any persons permitted access to the Mark to ensure that Licensee satisfies its obligations under this Agreement.

    c. Any goodwill arising out of Licensee's use of the Mark shall inure solely and exclusively to the benefit of Licensor, and Licensee shall have no rights therein or claims thereto. Licensee acknowledges that this Agreement does not confer any goodwill or other interest in or to the Mark except the right to use the same in accordance with the terms hereof.

7. INFRINGEMENT BY THIRD PARTIES

Licensee agrees to notify Licensor of any unauthorized use of the Mark by others promptly as it comes to Licensee's attention. Licensor shall have the sole right and discre-tion to bring infringement or unfair competition proceedings involving the Mark.

8. DEFAULT AND TERMINATION

Licensee shall be deemed to be in default and Licensor may, at its option, terminate this Agreement and all rights granted hereunder, without affording Licensee any oppor-tunity to cure the default, effective immediately upon receipt of notice by Licensee, upon the occurrence of any of the following events:

    a. If Licensee ceases to do business or otherwise forfeits the right to do or transact business in any jurisdiction where its business offices are located.

    b. If a threat or danger to public health or safety results from the management and operation of Licensee's business conducted in connection with the Mark.

(continues)

EXHIBIT 5–5
Trademark
License
Agreement
(continued)

   c. If Licensee is convicted of a crime of moral turpitude or similar felony or is convicted of any other crime or is the subject of any civil action that Licensor reasonably believes is likely to have an adverse effect on the Mark, the goodwill associated therewith, or Licensor's interest therein.
   d. If Licensee purports to transfer any rights or obligations under this Agreement to any third party without Licensor's prior written consent.
   e. If Licensee fails to maintain any of the quality control standards prescribed by Licensor in this Agreement or otherwise in writing.
   f. If Licensee engages in any business or markets any service or product under a name or mark which, in Licensor's opinion, is confusingly similar to the Mark.

9. MISCELLANEOUS
   a. This Agreement shall be construed in accordance with the law of the State of New York.
   b. Licensee shall not assign, sublicense, encumber, or otherwise transfer its rights and obligations under this Agreement without the prior written consent of Licensor.
   c. This Agreement contains the entire agreement between the parties with respect to licensing of the Mark. It supersedes and cancels any prior oral or written understandings or negotiations and may not be modified in any respect except in writing signed by both parties.
   d. The terms of this Agreement shall be severable such that if any term hereof is held to be illegal, invalid, or unenforceable, such holding shall not affect the validity of any of the other provisions of the Agreement, unless the severing of such term would defeat the purpose of this Agreement.
   e. The failure of any party to exercise any right or option given to it by or to insist upon strict adherence to the terms of this Agreement shall not constitute a waiver of any terms or conditions herein with respect to any other or subsequent breach.
   f. Any notice, payment, or statement required by this Agreement shall be either personally delivered or sent by registered or certified mail, postage prepaid, to the addresses indicated above and shall be effective when placed in the U.S. mail, properly addressed and containing the proper postage.
   g. This Agreement shall be binding on and shall inure to the benefit of the parties to this Agreement and their successors and assigns, if any.
IN WITNESS WHEREOF, the parties hereto have caused this License Agreement to be executed as of the date provided herein.

LICENSEE   LICENSOR

By: _____   By: _____

Name: _____   Name: _____

Title: _____   Title: _____

Trivia

- Words that were once valid trademarks but have become genericized include *cornflakes, dry ice, kerosene, linoleum, nylon, shredded wheat,* and *trampoline.*
- Someone registers a trademark every five minutes.
- In 1772, George Washington asked to use his name as a trademark for flour.
- In late November 2006, *The Washington Post* reported that Ford Motor Co. arranged $18 billion in bank loans, for the first time using company assets as collateral, including trademarks.

or obligation. Because the grant of a security interest is conditional (because it has no effect unless there is a default), a trademark that is the subject of an ITU application can be used as collateral.

CHAPTER SUMMARY

Merely obtaining a federal trademark registration does not guarantee an owner unlimited and perpetual rights to a mark. Because rights to a mark stem from use (rather than mere registration), the Lanham Act imposes certain requirements on registrants to ensure that only active marks remain on the USPTO rolls.

Thus, a registration will be canceled unless, between the fifth and sixth year after registration, and in the year before the end of each 10-year period after registration, the owner files a Section 8 affidavit with the USPTO alleging its continued use of the mark and submitting a specimen showing the mark as presently used.

If the mark is registered on the Principal Register, has been in continuous use for five years, and has not been the subject of any adverse action, the owner may file a Section 15 affidavit and thereby obtain incontestability status for the mark, severely limiting the grounds upon which attacks on the mark may be made.

At the end of the registration period, and every 10 years thereafter, an application for renewal must be filed to maintain the registration in force.

In addition to losing rights to federal registration, a trademark owner can lose rights to the mark if the mark becomes generic or if it is abandoned with intent not to resume use. Nonuse for three years creates a presumption of abandonment.

To ensure rights to marks are maintained, many trademark owners develop compliance policies that set forth guidelines for proper use and display of the mark. Additionally, many owners monitor use of marks in the marketplace to detect potentially infringing marks.

Finally, rights to marks can be lost by acts that cause the mark to lose significance, such as by an assignment of a mark that does not include its goodwill or a license of a mark without quality control provisions to ensure that a licensee's use will be consistent with the standards of quality the public has come to expect of a mark. Trademarks can be used as collateral to secure a party's obligation to perform a promise. In the event of a party's default, the marks are then seized by the secured party, who is usually a lender of money.

CASE ILLUSTRATION–GENERIC TERMS

Case: *America Online, Inc. v. AT & T Corp.,* 243 F.3d 812 (4th Cir. 2001)

Facts: America Online (AOL) brought an action for trademark infringement against AT & T for, among other items, infringing its common law mark "You Have Mail." The lower court held the phrase was generic.

Holding: The Court of Appeals affirmed. In the context of computer-based electronic communications, the phrase "You Have Mail" has been used for the common, ordinary purpose of informing users of the arrival of electronic mail in their electronic mailboxes. The phrase does not describe a service but simply informs subscribers, employing common words to express their commonly used meaning of the ordinary fact that they have new electronic mail messages in their electronic mailboxes. Thus, "You Have Mail" is generic and AT & T did not infringe.

CASE STUDY AND ACTIVITIES

Case Study.   Vision has obtained trademark registrations for several marks, including one for VISIONTREK, which was registered on May 8, 2006. Vision recently purchased all of the assets of a smaller company that operated a resort whose main attraction was a luxury spa called SUNSPA, the trademark for which was registered to the now defunct company. Two problems that Vision is struggling with are decreased sales for the hats offered under the mark SUNVISION (although another company has expressed interest in the mark) and a labor strike that has prevented it from making bracelets displaying Vision's registered mark "V" with its eagles' wings, which was registered five and one-half years ago for jewelry in I.C. 14.

Activities.
1. Give all dates relating to maintenance for the VISIONTREK mark.
2. What activities should be undertaken with regard to SUNSPA?
3. Vision would like to file the Section 8 affidavit of use for its V mark for its jewelry. What difficulties might it encounter?
4. What type of arrangement might Vision consider with regard to the SUNVISION mark?

ROLE OF PARALEGAL

Paralegals play a significant role in trademark maintenance. Some law firms with large trademark practices maintain separate departments for trademark prosecution and maintenance, with IP

ROLE OF PARALEGAL (CONT'D)

professionals taking an active role in every aspect of both. Among the activities participated in are the following:

- docketing dates for the Section 8 affidavits of use and the Section 9 applications for renewal;
- corresponding with (and often locating) clients to notify them that their registrations will be canceled unless the Section 8 affidavit or the renewal application is filed;
- ensuring the chain of title is continuous so that the party who files the postregistration documents with the USPTO is "of record" with the USPTO as the owner of the mark and recording changes in ownership of the marks, if required;
- comparing a specimen of the mark as presently used with that in the original registration to ensure a material alteration has not occurred that would preclude the filing of a Section 8 affidavit;
- conducting due diligence to determine whether a mark has been in such continuous use that the owner can file a Section 15 affidavit to obtain incontestable status of its mark;
- preparing, filing, and monitoring Sections 8 and 15 affidavits and applications for renewal;
- communicating USPTO action on affidavits and renewal applications to clients and docketing new date for renewal;
- docketing the fifth anniversary after registration of a mark on the Supplemental Register so a new application can be filed for registration on the Principal Register (due to the presumption that after five years of exclusive and continuous use of a mark, it has acquired distinctiveness);
- assisting clients in drafting trademark compliance policies;
- assisting clients in conducting monitoring of marks to detect possible infringing uses;
- reviewing clients' advertising copy and other materials to ensure display and use of marks is proper and that there is no misuse of another party's marks;
- drafting assignments and licenses;
- docketing dates for renewals and expiration of license agreements; and
- recording assignments, mergers, changes of name, and security interests with the USPTO.

INTERNET RESOURCES

USPTO Web site: http://www.uspto.gov (offers form for recordation cover sheet for assignment of trademarks)

Trademark Manual of Examining   http://tess2.uspto.gov/tmdb/tmep (see chapter
    Procedure (TMEP):   16 for information on trademark maintenance and chapter 5 for information on assignments)

Forms for assignments: http://www.allaboutforms.com and
                                          http://www.siccode.com/forms.php3

Guide to proper trademark use: http://www.inta.org
General information: http://www.ipmall.fplc.edu and
                                          http://www.megalaw.com

DISCUSSION QUESTIONS

1. What is the latest possible date to file a Section 8 affidavit for a trademark registered on July 15, 2007?
2. Over the years, the registered trademark EGG-NOG, used for bath products, has changed in appearance to EGGNOG. Discuss whether such a change might preclude the owner from filing a Section 8 affidavit for the mark.
3. Assume that a Section 15 affidavit of incontestability was filed for the mark PRECODA for computer software. ABC Inc. has recently alleged that the registration for PRECODA was procured through a fraud on the USPTO and that PRECODA is confusingly similar to ABC's mark. Discuss the effects of the Section 15 affidavit on these allegations.
4. A registrant has allowed its registration to expire but continues to use its mark. What rights does the mark owner have to the mark?
5. What are the dangers of consumers saying, "I love my Jacuzzi" or "I always play Frisbee on the weekends"? What should consumers say?
6. XYZ Inc. offers an extremely expensive automobile under the mark ESSARO. Last year it only sold 10 of the automobiles, and this year it has sold none. What effect does this type of use have on XYZ's ability to file Section 8 affidavits?
7. LMN Inc. has granted permission to another party to use LMN's mark in any manner it chooses. What are the dangers of such a permission, and what type of permission has been granted?
8. A franchisor has granted a license to a franchisee to offer hamburgers and other deli-style foods under its mark. What types of quality control provisions should a license agreement include?

USING INTERNET RESOURCES

Use the USPTO Web site to answer the following questions.

1. What is the status of U.S. Reg. No. 976,020?
2. Review U.S. Reg. No. 3,181,795. Locate the assignment records. When was the assignment for this mark recorded? Identify the assignor and assignee. Why was an assignment recorded?
3. Review U.S. Reg. No. 1,903,596. Identify the maintenance documents (and give their dates) that have been filed for this registration.

USING INTERNET RESOURCES (CONT'D)

4. Review U.S. Reg. No. 1,626,021. What is this mark and what is its status?
5. Review U.S. Reg. No. 789,009. What is the mark? Why was it assigned? What does the "Conveyance" language state?
6. Access the TMEP and review the materials relating to examples of special circumstances that excuse nonuse of a mark (such that a Section 8 affidavit alleging such nonuse would be allowed). Does decreased demand for a product excuse nonuse? Does the sale of business excuse nonuse?

For additional resources, go to www.paralegal.delmar.cengage.com.

Chapter 6

Inter Partes Proceedings, Infringement, and Dilution

CHAPTER OVERVIEW

Disputes often arise between parties regarding use and ownership of marks. Some proceedings occur at the USPTO, and others may be initiated in federal court. There are four categories of actions involving disputes over trademark rights: inter partes proceedings, trademark infringement cases, actions alleging dilution, and actions alleging unfair competition.

Inter partes (literally, "between parties") proceedings fall into four categories: oppositions, cancellations, interferences, and concurrent use proceedings. All of these matters are adjudicated by the Trademark Trial and Appeal Board (TTAB).

A person who believes a mark is being used so as to create a likelihood of confusion in the marketplace with his or her registered mark may initiate an action for trademark infringement under the Lanham Act. Infringement actions are brought in federal court.

The Federal Trademark Dilution Act protects famous marks by prohibiting uses that are not confusingly similar under conventional trademark analysis but may nonetheless cause a likelihood of diluting the strength of or tarnishing another's rights in a mark.

Finally, the Lanham Act provides broad sweeping protection for nearly all forms of unfair competition, including false advertising and infringement of trade dress, which protection is available to those who do not own a registered mark.

INTER PARTES PROCEEDINGS

Inter partes (literally, "between parties") **proceedings** are those involving disputes between parties regarding rights, use, and ownership of marks. These actions are heard before the TTAB, a department of the USPTO. Generally, the Federal Rules of Civil Procedure govern these proceedings, making the proceedings substantially similar to actions brought in federal courts. There are four types of inter partes proceedings: oppositions, cancellations, interferences, and concurrent use proceedings.

Oppositions

Timing Requirements. An **opposition** is a proceeding initiated by a person who believes that he or she would be damaged by registration of a mark on the Principal Register. Oppositions may not be initiated against marks sought to be registered on the Supplemental Register—those marks may be objected to by way of cancellation proceedings, discussed later. The document initiating the proceeding is called a **Notice of Opposition**. The time for initiating an opposition is triggered by the publication of a mark in the Official Gazette. Publication occurs after the examining attorney at the USPTO has approved the mark and is intended to provide notice to the public of the pending application so interested persons can oppose the registration.

An opposition must be filed prior to the expiration of the 30-day period after publication of the mark in the *Official Gazette* for opposition, or within an extension of time to oppose.

A potential opposer may file a first request for a 30-day extension without a showing of cause, followed by a request for a 60-day extension for good cause. Alternatively, the potential opposer may file a single request for a 90-day extension of time for good cause. After one or

two extensions of time totaling 90 days, the potential opposer may request one final extension of time for an additional 60 days with the consent of the applicant or upon a showing of extraordinary circumstances. No further extensions of time to oppose will be permitted. The time for filing an opposition will not be extended beyond 180 days from the date of publication. To be sure dates are calculated correctly, use an electronic calculator such as http://www.timeanddate.com. Typically, alleging that the potential opposer needs additional time to investigate whether the applied-for mark may conflict with his or her mark or that the parties are engaged in settlement negotiations is sufficient to demonstrate good cause.

There is no fee required for filing a request for extension of time to oppose. (See Appendix D, Form 6, for a sample form for request for extension of time to oppose.)

Notice of Opposition. If the parties themselves cannot reach some resolution, an opposition proceeding will be initiated by the filing of a notice of opposition. Requests for extension of time to oppose and oppositions may be filed by mail or electronically through the TTAB's Electronic System for Trademark Trials and Appeals.

The Lanham Act requires only that the notice of opposition set forth a "short and plain statement" of the reasons why the opposer believes it will be damaged by registration of the mark and the grounds for opposition. When the TTAB receives the notice of opposition, it forwards it to the applicant for response, much as a defendant in a civil action is provided with a copy of a complaint so the defendant may answer its allegations. The filing fee for a notice of opposition is $300 per class of goods/services identified in the application. (See Appendix D, Form 7, for a notice of opposition.)

Even if the parties ultimately reach resolution of the matter, the filing of a notice of opposition or even a request for extension of time to oppose seriously delays the application process. Thus, IP professionals should use TARR, the USPTO's online status reporting system, to monitor applications to determine if such documents have been filed, and alert clients of such an impediment to registration.

Grounds for Opposition. In brief, an opposer wishes to prevent registration of a mark. The most common reason a person might believe he or she will be damaged if the mark applied for proceeds to registration is that the mark is confusingly similar to the opposer's mark. Opposers are not, however, limited to asserting confusing similarity as a basis for opposition. The opposer is only required to state why he or she believes registration of the mark in question would result in damage. Thus, oppositions can also be initiated on the basis of descriptiveness or that the mark is a surname, contains immoral or disparaging matter, has been abandoned, is likely to dilute another's trademark, and so forth. Nevertheless, the vast majority of oppositions allege that the mark in an application should be refused because it is likely to cause confusion with the opposer's mark. In one novel case in 1999, the Federal Circuit held that an individual was entitled to come before the TTAB to oppose registration of the trademarks O. J. SIMPSON, O.J., and THE JUICE on the grounds that the marks disparaged his values, were scandalous because they would attempt to justify violence against women, and that others in the public shared his views. *Ritchie v. Simpson,* 170 F.3d 1092 (Fed. Cir. 1999). The court held that the opposer had asserted a reasonable belief of damage and thus had standing to oppose registration of the marks. A strongly worded dissent expressed concern that the ruling would open the USPTO up to oppositions or cancellations from any member of the public who found a mark to be offensive. The applications were eventually abandoned by the applicant, O. J. Simpson.

Nature of Proceeding. As soon as either a notice of opposition or a request for extension of time to oppose is filed, the examining attorney at the USPTO relinquishes the file to the TTAB, which will handle the matter until its conclusion.

The TTAB can suspend an opposition proceeding to allow the parties to engage in settlement discussions. Opposition proceedings are somewhat like trials. The notice (and a duplicate copy) of opposition (equivalent to a complaint) is filed, and a copy is forwarded to the applicant; within 30 or 40 days (as set by the TTAB) the applicant will file a response to the notice of opposition (equivalent to an answer in civil litigation); a discovery schedule will be issued by the TTAB and will occur by way of interrogatories, depositions, and the like; briefs are filed by each party; and the TTAB will render a decision. However, the entire opposition proceeding is done by filing of documents with the USPTO; no trial or oral presentations of evidence occur, unless the parties request to present oral argument. The schedule in an opposition is faster than that for most trials and the issue is narrow: Should the mark be allowed to register? Damages are not awarded and the opposer cannot force the applicant to stop using the mark. A successful opposition merely results in denial of registration of a mark in a pending application.

Just as most civil cases do not go to trial and conclude by voluntary settlement, opposition proceedings are overwhelmingly concluded by voluntary agreements. Generally, the opposer and the applicant enter into a written **consent agreement** (called a consent to use agreement) whereby they agree on the scope and nature of each party's use of its mark, submit the agreement to the TTAB, and then ask for dismissal of the opposition proceeding. The consent to use agreement is the equivalent of a settlement agreement in a civil action. Until relatively recently, the USPTO accorded such agreements little weight; however, since the decision in *In re Four Seasons Hotels Ltd.,* 987 F.2d 1565 (Fed. Cir. 1993), such agreements have been given great weight in determining whether confusion is likely to result from coexistence of marks. While the USPTO or TTAB can always refuse such an agreement on the basis that the public interest is not served thereby, *Four Seasons* makes it clear that if those parties who have the greatest interest in reducing confusion agree that confusion is unlikely, their decision should be respected by the USPTO. If an agreement is reached, the applicant's file wrapper will be returned to the USPTO for further processing, namely, registration (if the application was use-based) or allowance (if the application was based on the applicant's intent to use the mark). (See Appendix D, Form 8, for a consent to use agreement.)

Cancellations

As discussed, an opposition can be initiated only within a very limited time period. In fact, if no action is taken within 30 days of publication of the mark in the *Official Gazette,* an opposition proceeding may not be instituted. Because reading the *Official Gazette* and filing a timely notice of opposition can be extremely difficult, the Lanham Act recognizes that additional opportunity to object to registration of a mark should be afforded to those who might be injured by it. Thus, **cancellation** proceedings may be initiated after a mark is registered. The primary difference between oppositions and cancellations relates to their timing: Oppositions must be initiated before registration of a mark, while cancellations are initiated after registration. Additionally, cancellation actions are the only appropriate challenge to marks registered on the Supplemental Register.

Timing Requirements.   Any person who believes that he or she will be damaged by the continued existence of a registration (whether on the Principal or Supplemental Register) may petition to cancel the registration. If the mark is registered on the Supplemental Register, a **petition to cancel** can be filed at any time. If the mark is on the Principal Register, the petition to cancel must be filed within five years of the registration date if the grounds are those that would have justified denial of registration to begin with (such as descriptiveness, that the mark is confusingly similar to that owned by another, and so forth).

After five years, the Lanham Act narrows the grounds for cancellation and the registration may be canceled only if certain grounds are proven, typically that the mark has become generic, the registration was obtained through fraud, the mark is functional, or the mark has been abandoned through nonuse. 15 U.S.C. § 1064.

The Petition to Cancel.   The petition to cancel must set forth a "short and plain statement" of the reasons for the petitioner's belief that he or she will be damaged by continued registration of the mark, state the grounds for cancellation, and identify the owner of the registration so a copy of the petition can be forwarded to the owner. The filing fee for a petition to cancel is $300 per class of goods or services covered by the registration, and a duplicate copy must be forwarded to the TTAB so it can be forwarded to the owner of the registration.

Grounds for Petition to Cancel.   Just as with notices of opposition, petitions to cancel must be brought by one who believes he or she will be damaged by registration of the mark. Similar to the allowance of an opposition to the various O. J. Simpson marks described above, the rules relating to those who may petition to cancel a registration appear to have been relaxed in recent years. For example, in *Harjo v. ProFootball Inc.,* 30 U.S.P.Q.2d 1828 (T.T.A.B. 1994), it was held that Native Americans had the right to petition to cancel various registered trademarks relating to the Washington Redskins football team on the basis that the marks were disparaging to them as Native Americans. On appeal, the decision was reversed on procedural grounds. Thus, at present, there is no determination whether the marks disparage Native Americans.

Although a variety of grounds may be asserted in a petition to cancel (the mark comprises a flag of another nation, it is primarily merely a surname, it dilutes the mark of another, it contains immoral or scandalous matter, it includes the name of a living person without consent, or it is disparaging), the most common grounds asserted in a petition to cancel are the ones that must be brought within five years of registration: that the mark is merely descriptive, it is confusingly similar to another mark, or it has been abandoned.

Nature of Proceeding. The proceedings at the TTAB relating to cancellations are nearly identical to those involving oppositions. The petition to cancel will be filed at the TTAB, which will then forward a copy to the registrant. Within 30 or 40 days (as set by the TTAB), the registrant will file an answer to the petition (typically denying the grounds asserted in the petition and raising various defenses). Discovery will commence and depositions may be taken, interrogatories served, and documents requested. The TTAB will set dates for submission of written briefs and will review those briefs and render a decision.

As with oppositions, the vast majority of cancellations are settled voluntarily by the parties (who will enter into a trademark settlement agreement that is highly similar to the consent to use agreement shown in Appendix D, Form 8) rather than by TTAB decision. (See Exhibit 6-1 and Appendix D, Form 9, Petition to Cancel Trademark Registration.)

Interferences

If two pending applications conflict or if a pending application conflicts with an existing registration (that is not yet incontestable), the USPTO may declare an **interference.** Interferences are rare proceedings and occur only upon a showing of "extraordinary circumstances." Typically, if marks conflict, the parties resolve their differences by way of an opposition (if the potentially conflicting mark is not yet registered) or cancellation (if registration has occurred). Generally, only when an opposition or cancellation proceeding is unavailable to a party or will not adequately protect a party may a party request an interference proceeding. The TTAB will then determine the rights of the parties if they cannot reach a voluntary settlement arrangement. Interference actions are so rare that none were filed in 2006.

Concurrent Use Proceedings

If parties use similar marks in different geographical areas, a **concurrent use proceeding** may be initiated. Generally, these parties have used their marks in their respective areas in good faith and without knowledge of the other's existence. In a concurrent use application, a party requests that the registration that will ultimately issue be restricted geographically, so that on its face the registration will state that the owner has the right to use the mark in certain identified states, cities, or regions in the United States. Once the applicant files an application for concurrent use, the matter is referred to the TTAB. In most instances, the concurrent use proceeding is initiated after an application for registration is refused on the basis the mark is confusingly similar to another. The applicant then often approaches the other party in an effort to reach an accord whereby they each agree to use the mark in certain designated geographic markets. The applicant will then amend its original application to seek concurrent use by stating, "The Applicant claims the exclusive right to use the mark in the area comprising [specifying the geographic area]." The TTAB will allow concurrent use only if confusion is not likely to result.

In brief, in a concurrent use proceeding, the parties "carve up" the United States and each agrees to use his or her mark only in a specific geographical area. Concurrent use proceedings are relatively rare. Only about 40 were filed in 2006.

You may now view all TTAB proceedings by using the TTAB's system **TTAB Vue,** which allows users to review documents relating to oppositions, cancellations, and so forth, by entering a proceeding number, application number, registration number, or mark.

Appeals from TTAB Decisions

If a party is dissatisfied with the decision of the TTAB in an opposition, cancellation, interference, or concurrent use proceeding, an appeal may be taken to the Court of Appeals for the Federal Circuit (CAFC), located in Washington, DC. The Federal Circuit can set aside USPTO findings only when the findings are arbitrary, capricious, an abuse of discretion, or unsupported by substantial evidence. *Dickinson v. Zurko*, 527 U.S. 150

Suggested Format for Petition to Cancel

This is a suggested format for preparing a Petition to Cancel a trademark registration. This document is not meant to be used as a form to be filled in and returned to the Board. Rather, it is a suggested format, which shows how the petition should be set up. Petitioners may follow this format in preparing their own petition but need not copy those portions of the suggested format which are not relevant.

IN THE UNITED STATES PATENT AND TRADEMARK OFFICE
BEFORE THE TRADEMARK TRIAL AND APPEAL BOARD

In the matter of trademark Registration No..................................

For the mark...

Date registered.............................

(Name of petitioner)

v.

(Name of registrant)

PETITION TO CANCEL

State petitioner's name, address, and entity information as follows:[1]

(Name of individual as petitioner, and business trade name, if any;
Business address)
_____

OR   (Name of partnership as petitioner; Names of partners;
Business address of partnership)
_____

OR   (Name of corporation as petitioner; State or country of incorporation;
Business address of corporation)
_____

To the best of petitioner's knowledge, the name and address of the current owner of the registration are _____ *(provide if known)* _____

The above-identified petitioner believes that it/he/she will be damaged by the above-identified registration, and hereby petitions to cancel the same.[2]

The grounds for cancellation are as follows:
[Please set forth, in separately numbered paragraphs, the allegations of petitioner's standing and grounds for cancellation][3]

By ____Signature[4]____   Date _____
(Identification of person signing)[5]

OMB No. 0651-0040 (Exp. 5/31/04)

ETHICS EDGE: Contact with Other Parties

Although proceedings at the TTAB may seem informal because all appearances are by "paper" rather than in person, ethical rules governing parties' behavior still apply. The most important of these is that once a party is represented by counsel, the party may not be contacted directly; all contacts must be made with the party's attorney (unless the party's attorney agrees otherwise). Thus, in an opposition or cancellation proceeding, once the adverse party has retained counsel, you may not contact the party himself or herself. Be sure to work directly with the attorney involved.

(1999). Thereafter, an appeal may be taken to the United States Supreme Court if the Court, in its discretion, decides to hear the appeal. As an alternative to appealing to CAFC, the party may institute a civil action in federal district court that will determine the issues *de novo,* meaning that it can determine the issues anew and new evidence may be presented.

INFRINGEMENT OF TRADEMARKS

Introduction

Section 32 of the Lanham Act (15 U.S.C. § 1114) provides that the owner of a federally registered trademark may bring a civil action in federal court against any person who uses, without the registrant's consent, a mark that is likely to cause confusion with the registrant's mark. Such an action is for "trademark infringement." To prevail on a trademark infringement claim, a mark's owner must prove two things: that its mark has priority and that the infringer's mark is likely to cause confusion.

The central inquiry in an **infringement** action is whether there is a likelihood that an appreciable number of ordinarily prudent purchasers are likely to be misled or confused about the source, affiliation, or sponsorship of goods or services. If consumers, upon encountering the defendant's goods or services, would believe they are produced by or somehow affiliated with a plaintiff's goods or services, the defendant's mark infringes the plaintiff's.

The standard for determining whether there is a likelihood of confusion in an infringement action is the same as that used in the application process when an examining attorney refuses registration of a mark on the basis that it is likely to be confused with that of another prior mark. The standard is also identical to that used in opposition and cancellation proceedings when a party alleges registration of another mark should be denied or canceled because the mark is likely to be confused with that of the opposer or petitioner.

In the typical infringement action, a prior user alleges that a subsequent user is causing confusion in the marketplace by using a confusingly similar mark. In essence, the later or junior user is attempting to get a "free ride" on the reputation and renown of the senior user by adopting a similar mark. In some instances, however, the second user may become so well known and famous that it dwarfs the prior user and allegedly causes consumers to believe that the prior user's goods come from the subsequent user. The prior owner can then initiate an infringement action for "reverse confusion." Generally, reverse confusion occurs when the later user is a large, powerful company that uses its economic power to saturate the market with advertising, thereby causing confusion. (See Appendix D, Form 10, Complaint for Trademark Infringement.)

Standard for Determining Likelihood of Confusion

Various courts in various circuits have enumerated tests for determining whether one mark is likely to be confused with another. Generally, no one factor is determinative; courts examine the totality of circumstances in attempting to determine whether infringement has occurred. In general, the following factors are considered in determining whether trademark infringement exists:

- the similarity of the marks in regard to appearance, sound, connotation, and commercial impression
- the similarity of the goods or services offered under the marks
- the similarity in the channels of trade in which the goods or services are offered
- the conditions under which sales are made, namely, whether the purchases are made on impulse or after careful consideration by sophisticated purchasers
- the strength or fame of the prior mark
- whether there has been any actual confusion
- the number and nature of similar marks on similar goods
- the length of time during which there has been concurrent use with no confusion

See, e.g., E.I. du Pont de Nemours & Co., 476 F.2d 1357 (C.C.P.A. 1973); Restatement (Third) of Unfair Competition § 21 (1995).

Courts also consider the defendant's intent in adopting the mark when testing for likelihood of confusion. This list of factors is not exhaustive, and other factors that may be relevant to a likelihood of confusion may also be considered. Moreover, the factors are not applied in a rigid or mechanical approach. The significance of any one factor depends upon the facts of a particular case.

Sight, Sound, Meaning, and Connotation. With dissimilar marks, there is little likelihood of confusion. The more similar marks are, the more likely it is that confusion will occur. The single most important factor in determining likelihood of confusion is the similarity of the marks. Generally, marks are compared in their entireties rather than on the basis of a side-by-side comparison or a dissection of their respective elements inasmuch as courts cannot assume consumers would have the opportunity to make a side-by-side comparison when making a purchase. Some general rules have emerged.

- Marks may be confusingly similar in appearance notwithstanding the addition, deletion, or substitution of letters. Thus, TRUCOOL for synthetic coolant was held likely to be confused with TURCOOL for cutting oil. *In re Lamson Oil Co.,* 6 U.S.P.Q.2d 1041 (T.T.A.B. 1987).
- Similarity may occur due to sound or pronunciation. For example, BONAMINE was held confusingly similar to DRAMAMINE when both were used for medical goods. *G.D. Searle & Co. v. Charles Pfizer & Co.,* 265 F.2d 835 (7th Cir. 1959).
- Similarity in meaning may result in a finding of confusion. Thus, AQUA-CARE (STYLIZED) was held likely to be confused with WATERCARE when both were used for water conditioning products. *Watercare Corp. v. Midwesco Enter. Inc.,* 171 U.S.P.Q. 696 (T.T.A.B. 1971). Similarly, BUENOS DIAS for soap was held likely to be confused with GOOD MORNING for shaving cream, *In re Am. Safety Razor Co.,* 2 U.S.P.Q.2d 1459 (T.T.A.B. 1987), and CYCLONE and TORNADO were held confusingly similar for wire fencing because their connotations were the same.
- If the marks include compound words, some courts consider whether there is a dominant portion of the mark and give less weight to common or descriptive elements. Thus, there was no likelihood of confusion between SOLVENTOL and SOLVITE. *Solventol Chem. Prods. v. Langfield,* 134 F.2d 899 (6th Cir. 1943).

Because the descriptive prefixes *solvent* and *sol* are so commonly used, the court held that the remaining portions of the marks were distinguishable.

- When marks comprise both words and designs, greater weight is sometimes given to the wording, which would be used by consumers in requesting the goods or services.

- If an owner has a famous mark or a "family" of marks that has achieved public recognition, such as the family of "Mc" marks owned by McDonald's, the mark may be more likely to be infringed. Courts have held that marks with extensive public recognition and renown deserve more protection than obscure or weak marks. Thus, due to the strong association by the public of the "Mc" prefix with McDonald's, many attempted uses of a mark including "Mc" have been found to infringe McDonald's marks. For example, McPRETZEL was held to infringe McDonald's family of "Mc" marks. *J & J Snack Foods Corp. v. McDonald's Corp.,* 932 F.2d 1460 (Fed. Cir. 1991).

Similarity of Goods or Services. Generally, the more similar the goods or services are that are offered under the marks, the less similar the marks need be for confusion to be found, and vice versa. The goods or services need not be identical; confusion may be found if they are related in some manner in that they serve the same purpose, relate to the same activities, or are likely to be encountered by the same types of purchasers. Thus, LAREDO for vehicles was held likely to be confused with LAREDO for tires because both relate to vehicles, In re Jeep Corp., 222 U.S.P.Q. 333 (T.T.A.B. 1984), while LEXUS for vehicles was allowed to register over LEXIS for computer-assisted legal research services (because the goods are unrelated).

In 1996, Kellogg Company sued Exxon Corporation for trademark infringement, alleging that the energy company's tiger character was likely to be confused with Kellogg's "Tony the Tiger" character used to promote food products. Although the two characters had peacefully coexisted for more than 30 years, when Exxon began selling food products at its gasoline/convenience outlets, Kellogg sued for infringement. The parties ultimately settled their dispute.

This type of infringement is often referred to as **progressive encroachment,** meaning that a once permissible use gradually becomes an infringing use. Some departure in business practices or use of the mark has changed a once acceptable use into an infringement. For example, for several years the World Wildlife Fund allowed World Wrestling Federation Entertainment to use the initials WWF for certain purposes. After a period of time, the wrestling group, through extensive television and Internet exposure, began such widespread use of WWF and departure from the parties' original agreement that infringement occurred. After an adverse decision in London, the wrestling group agreed to cease use of WWF and refer to itself as WWE.

In many instances, in infringement lawsuits, when the plaintiff is accused of an undue delay in protecting its mark (the defense of laches, discussed later in this chapter), the plaintiff responds by alleging progressive encroachment, namely, that it had no duty to initiate an action until the defendant's use moved from the permissible realm to a squarely competitive use.

Courts also consider that parties may extend their product lines at some future time. Thus, the mark THE PALM for pasta would likely be refused on the basis of confusing similarity to THE PALM®, already registered for restaurant services, because restaurants often sell their food products, and consumers, upon encountering THE PALM for pasta, might believe it was associated with the restaurant of the same name.

Channels of Trade. In determining likelihood of confusion, courts consider to what extent the parties' respective goods or services are distributed through the same trade channels and advertised in the same media. Thus, if products offered under one mark are marketed to wholesalers while those under the other mark are marketed to retailers, there may be little likelihood of confusion because the goods are offered to different classes of purchasers. For example, no likelihood of confusion was found where one party sold computer services under the mark E.D.S. while the other sold power supplies and battery chargers under EDS. Although the marks were nearly identical and both parties sold in the medical field, the plaintiff sold its E.D.S. data processing services to medical insurers while the defendant sold its EDS batteries to makers of medical equipment. Because purchases would be made by different persons in different departments, coexistence of the marks was unlikely to cause confusion. *Elec. Design & Sales Inc. v. Elec. Data Sys. Corp.*, 954 F.2d 713 (Fed. Cir. 1992).

Consumer Care and Sophistication. In determining trademark infringement, everything hinges on whether there is a likelihood of confusion in the mind of an appreciable number of reasonably prudent buyers. The price level of the goods or services is an important factor in determining the amount of care the buyer will use. If the goods or services are relatively expensive, more care is taken, and buyers are less likely to be confused. Thus, purchasers of inexpensive items such as snack foods and sodas, which are purchased on impulse, do not give much care to such purchases and are more likely to be confused by items that bear similar marks. If the goods are expensive, however, the discriminating purchaser does not purchase casually or on impulse but only after thoughtful consideration. Thus, confusion is less likely than where the goods are inexpensive.

Strength of Marks. "Strong" marks are afforded greater protection than weak marks. Thus, marks that are coined, fanciful, or arbitrary are given greater weight than marks that are suggestive, descriptive, or generic. MUCKY DUCK (& DESIGN) for mustard was held confusingly similar to MUCKY DUCK for restaurant services

primarily because MUCKY DUCK was viewed as a unique and memorable mark. *In re Mucky Duck Mustard Co.*, 6 U.S.P.Q.2d 1467 (T.T.A.B. 1988). Thus, the marks EXXON® and XEROX® are given a broad scope of protection inasmuch as these coined or made-up marks had no meaning before their owners built up or developed goodwill in them. Nevertheless, even weak marks are entitled to protection against similar marks for closely related goods or services.

Actual Confusion. Actual confusion is not required to support a case for trademark infringement; the standard is likelihood of confusion. It is unnecessary to show actual confusion to establish likelihood of confusion. However, plaintiffs who can demonstrate that some significant level of actual confusion has already occurred in the marketplace generally prevail in trademark infringement cases. Conversely, if the marks have coexisted for a number of years with no confusion, such is strongly suggestive that confusion is not likely.

Plaintiffs establish actual confusion in two ways: through testimony by consumers who have been confused about the products and by survey evidence. In the first instance, a party's initial knowledge that a competing mark is in the marketplace and is causing confusion may come about through complaint letters from consumers, misdirected orders, or inquiries and e-mail and telephone calls sent to the wrong party. If, however, evidence shows that only a few purchasers were confused, such supports a finding that confusion may be unlikely. For example, when determining that SCOTT® (for paper products) and SCOTT'S LIQUID GOLD® (for furniture polish) were unlikely to be confused, the court noted that only 19 misdirected letters had been received even though some 50 million cans of the furniture polish had been sold during the relevant period. *Scott Paper Co. v. Scott's Liquid Gold*, 589 F.2d 1225 (3d Cir. 1978).

A plaintiff may also demonstrate actual confusion by survey evidence, namely, surveys conducted by experts to determine whether confusion of consumers is likely. However, flaws in survey methodology, the types of questions asked, and the failure to survey the proper universe of purchasers may weaken the effect of a survey.

Existence of Other Similar Marks. If numerous other marks that are similar to the alleged infringer's mark coexist with the plaintiff's mark, this may be evidence that confusion is unlikely. Defendants thus often conduct comprehensive searches to demonstrate that the field is crowded and that numerous other marks all coexist with the plaintiff's mark. For example, in Arizona, marks including the term *Desert* are common, and the owner of a restaurant operating under the mark DESERT SUN might have a difficult time persuading a court that a bar called the DESERT STAR infringes his or her mark. When numerous similar marks coexist, consumers often become adept in distinguishing those marks from each other. Thus, even the slight differences between DESERT STAR and DESERT SUN may be sufficient to obviate confusion when numerous "Desert" marks coexist. In fact, in *Sun Banks of Florida, Inc. v. Sun Federal Savings & Loan Ass'n,* 651 F.2d 311 (5th Cir. 1981), the court gave special weight to the fact that 25 competing financial institutions used the word *sun* in their titles and that more than 4,400 businesses in Florida used the term, thus making it weak in that locality.

Coexistence of Marks with No Confusion. If the allegedly infringing mark has coexisted with the plaintiff's mark for a period of time and there is no evidence of confusion in the marketplace, courts often find that confusion is unlikely. For example, when STEAMEX DELUXE 15 XL coexisted with Oreck's XL mark for 17 months with no instances of confusion, the court held there was no infringement. *Oreck Corp. v. U.S. Floor Sys., Inc.,* 803 F.2d 166 (5th Cir. 1986).

Intent of Alleged Infringer. Proving an alleged infringer's intent or lack of good faith is not required to sustain an action for trademark infringement. However, if a party adopts a confusingly similar mark with the intent of reaping the benefits of the prior user's goodwill, such tends to weigh in favor of confusing similarity; the infringer would not have willingly adopted a similar mark unless he or she intended to trade off another's established reputation and divert customers.

When the alleged infringer had actual knowledge of the plaintiff's mark or had a prior business relationship with the plaintiff, such tends to suggest an intent to cause confusion. On the other hand, conducting a comprehensive search and relying on advice of counsel tend to rebut any inference of an intent to cause confusion. In fact, in *Frehling Enterprises, Inc. v. International Select Group, Inc.,* 192 F.3d 1330 (11th Cir. 1999), *cert. denied,* 531 U.S. 944 (2000), the court held that failure to conduct a trademark search was "intentional blindness" and evidence of improper intent. Further, the court held that if it can be shown that a defendant adopted a plaintiff's mark with the intention of deriving a benefit from the plaintiff's business reputation, *this fact alone* might be enough to justify the inference that there is confusing similarity. Id. at 1340.

(See Exhibit 6-2, Anatomy of an Infringement Case.)

Defenses to Infringement

There are a variety of defenses that may be raised by one accused of trademark infringement. They include the following:

- The defendant may assert that an *abandonment* of plaintiff's rights in the mark has occurred through nonuse prior to the time the defendant began using the mark or through a naked license.
- The defendant may allege that the plaintiff's mark has become *generic* and is thus undeserving of exclusive appropriation by the plaintiff; thus, for example, because the word *bundt* has been held to be generic for a certain type of ring cake, anyone can use this word without fear of infringement.

EXHIBIT 6-2
Anatomy of an
Infringement
Case

Case:	*Phat Fashions, L.L.C. v. Phat Game Athletic Apparel, Inc.*, No. CIV. S-01-1771, 2002 WL 570681 (E.D. Cal. Mar. 20, 2002).
Background:	In 1992, Russell Simmons, the cofounder of Def Jam Records, founded Phat Fashions, a manufacturer and distributor of urban and athletic apparel offered under the registered mark PHAT FARM® and other marks, including PHAT® and BABY PHAT®. In 1998, defendants began to sell athletic apparel and accessories bearing the mark PHAT or PHAT GAME. Defendants filed a trademark application to register PHAT GAME, and plaintiff brought an action for trademark infringement, unfair competition, and dilution.
Marks:	Plaintiff's Marks: PHAT FARM® and PHAT® Defendants' Mark: PHAT GAME
Analysis:	After stating that to prove trademark infringement a plaintiff must show he or she has a valid, protectable trademark and that the defendant's mark created a likelihood of confusion, the court analyzed the various infringement factors as follows:

Factor	Court Analysis	Court Conclusion
Strength of the Mark	The plaintiff's PHAT mark was arbitrary and thus strong and was well known by the purchasing public.	First factor weighs heavily in plaintiff's favor.
Similarity of Marks	First word (*phat*) in each mark is dominant feature and consumers would conclude that the word *phat* in defendants' mark refers to plaintiff.	Second factor weighs in plaintiff's favor.
Similarity of Goods	Marks are both used on identical goods (namely, wearing apparel).	Third factor weighs in plaintiff's favor.
Channels of Trade	Goods are sold for similar prices and there is similarity in marketing channels used for distribution.	This factor weighs in plaintiff's favor.
Purchaser Care	Both parties market to young people, and prices for many goods are under $30. These young consumers are often not careful purchasers, especially when prices are low.	Because of youth of defendants' market and relatively low prices, this factor weighs in plaintiff's favor.
Actual Confusion	Actual confusion is not necessary to find trademark infringement.	Lack of actual confusion weighs only slightly in defendants' favor, if at all.
Intent of Defendants	Defendants knew of plaintiff's marks and had conducted some research and trademark searches. Thus, defendants deliberately adopted their mark to obtain a business advantage.	This factor weighs heavily in plaintiff's favor.

(continues)

Holding:	Defendants have infringed plaintiff's trademarks and have engaged in unfair competition. Defendants were ordered to cease using PHAT GAME, disable their Internet web site (http://www.phatgame.com), and transfer their domain name to the plaintiff.	**EXHIBIT 6-2** Anatomy of an Infringement Case

- A defense may be raised that the mark is *merely descriptive* and that it has not acquired secondary meaning, and, thus, it is undeserving of protection.

- The defendant might assert that the plaintiff's registration was procured by *fraud*, is thus invalid, and cannot support an action for infringement.

- The accused infringer might assert **estoppel,** that is, that the plaintiff is *estopped* or precluded from asserting trademark infringement because it led the defendant to believe that it could use the mark (e.g., by allowing numerous other similar uses to go unchallenged).

- The defendant might assert **acquiescence,** a defense that alleges that words or conduct on the plaintiff's part amounted to an assurance to the defendant-infringer that plaintiff would not assert its trademark rights against the defendant.

- The defendant might assert that the plaintiff has **unclean hands** and has committed such a serious wrongful act (such as wrongfully using a trademark notice when it had no right to do so) that relief should not be awarded to it.

- The defendant might assert **laches,** namely, that the plaintiff delayed an unreasonable amount of time to bring the action and this delay has prejudiced the defendant (who, for example, during the period of delay, expended significant time and money in promoting the mark and thus should be allowed to continue using the mark).

- The defendant may allege the mark is *functional* and thus unprotectable.

- The defendant might allege that its use is a mere *parody* and is protected by the First Amendment.

- The defendant may assert that its use was a **fair use,** meaning that it did not use the plaintiff's name or mark as a trademark but merely to describe its goods in a general fashion.

There is no statute of limitations for actions brought under the Lanham Act for trademark infringement, and typically laches is the defense raised to assert that an action is time-barred.

One of the more interesting modern defenses is a free speech defense. Recently, artist Tom Forsythe was sued by Mattel Inc. (owner of the famous BARBIE® mark) for posing BARBIE dolls in inappropriate positions, such as mooning the camera. Forsythe prevailed in a suit by Mattel on the basis that his work was legitimate social commentary protected under the First Amendment and was not a commercial use of Mattel's mark. *Mattel Inc. v. Walking Mtn. Prods.,* 353 F.3d 792 (9th Cir. 2003).

Monitoring and policing for misuse of trademarks is critical because a failure to assert an infringement claim promptly might give rise to successful defenses based on acquiescence or laches. As discussed in chapter 5, policing trademarks has become more complicated due to the thousands of misuses that can appear on the Internet. Simply enter "Jell-O" into any search engine and you will be presented with hundreds of misuses of Kraft's registered trademark. Because trademark owners must vigorously enforce their marks or they risk loss of trademark rights, the Internet presents special problems for trademark owners. A number of companies have hired agencies to scour the Internet for misuses of their marks and then send e-mail requests asking the user to cease use of the registered mark. (See Exhibit 6-3.)

Trademark owners should thus maintain a consistent level of enforcement and protection

EXHIBIT 6-3
Case Study: Food Fights

In 1969 the Kern family registered the trademark DERBY-PIE® for their chocolate and walnut pie first served in their restaurant in Kentucky. Since then, the family has challenged a variety of users of its registered mark, including church cookbooks, *Bon Appetit* magazine, and the *Washington Post* newspaper, all of which published recipes for "Derby Pie." In fact, the family has hired an individual to scour the Internet to find offending uses of its mark. The users are then sent an e-mail request to cease using the registered trademark. If the misuse persists, the family has often sued, instituting about thirty lawsuits over the years to protect the mark, including a lawsuit against the Public Broadcasting Service, which featured actress Annie Potts baking her grandmother's "Derby Pie" on a televised broadcast. Thus, there's only one DERBY-PIE®. Everyone else is baking chocolate nut pie.

Similarly, Unilever has hired an agency to review the Internet to find infringing uses of its marks POPSICLE®, CREAMSICLE®, and FUDGSICLE®, and Pillsbury has a registration for BAKE-OFF® and will not allow other baking contests to use the name. Finally, your recipes can call for "hot sauce" or "chocolate chips" but not TABASCO® or TOLL HOUSE® morsels.

for their marks; however, the need for active enforcement should be balanced by the reality that it may be impossible to detect and stop all infringing uses, especially insignificant and minor uses of the mark. Some experts suggest using an initial warning letter, informing the user of the owner's rights and stating that the trademark owner will continue to monitor the user to ensure infringement does not occur. In any event, courts seem to be recognizing this dilemma, and at least one judge has remarked that a trademark owner is not bound to "take on" more than one infringer at a time.

Remedies for Infringement

A plaintiff who is successful in proving trademark infringement might obtain a variety of remedies, including the following:

- an **injunction** preventing the defendant from further use of the confusingly similar mark, ordering an infringer to disable an offending Web site, or ordering the defendant to print a notice (called a *disclaimer*) on its goods that it is not affiliated with the plaintiff (e.g., in one case, the publisher of *Polo* magazine was ordered to issue a disclaimer stating, "not affiliated with Polo Ralph Lauren," to avoid consumer confusion)

- *monetary damages* to compensate the plaintiff for the damage it has suffered, including actual damages due to lost sales and injury to its reputation and goodwill (which damages may be trebled, if necessary to compensate the plaintiff), and an accounting of the profits earned by defendant (however, no profits and no damages may be recovered unless the defendant had actual knowledge of the trademark registration—thus, a registrant should always use the registration symbol (®) to afford such notice)

- *seizure or destruction* of the infringing articles and related marketing materials

- *costs* of the action, including attorneys' fees (in exceptional cases) and actual expenditures

Courts have noted that injunctive relief is the "remedy of choice" for infringement because stopping the infringing use is usually the trademark owner's primary goal. If an infringing use is for a similar good or service, a broad injunction is especially appropriate. As to monetary relief, the largest trademark verdict to date is $143 million awarded against Pfizer Inc. for use of the mark TROVAN® registered to another, although the case was reversed on appeal. *Trovan Ltd. v. Pfizer Inc.*, No. CV-98-0094 2000 WL 709149 (C.D. Cal. May 24, 2000).

Resolving an Infringement Dispute

Because an infringement action, like any civil action, is expensive and time-consuming, parties often try to resolve trademark disputes between themselves before or during the pendency of litigation. Typically, a party who believes its mark is being infringed will send a cease and desist letter (see Exhibit 6-4) to the alleged infringer, notifying the infringer of its rights to the mark and demanding that the infringer cease any further use of the confusingly similar mark. Even if the cease and desist letter does not achieve the goal of convincing the infringer to stop use of the mark, it puts the infringer on notice of the prospective plaintiff's rights and thus serves to cut off any defense of good faith or lack of knowledge of the existence of the prior mark the infringer may later attempt to assert. Moreover, as discussed previously, informing another of a registration allows one to recover damages for infringement. Investigation should be conducted before sending a threatening letter to ensure the alleged infringer is the junior user. Otherwise, the alleged infringer may turn the tables on the sender of the letter.

The accused infringer typically responds to the cease and desist letter by denying its allegations, asserting various defenses, or suggesting a compromise. A compromise might be reached by the parties agreeing to use their marks only in certain geographic areas. The accused infringer might agree to place a prominent notice on its goods that it is not affiliated in any way with the prior user (although called a *disclaimer*, this notice is different from the disclaimer used in the prosecution process when an applicant disclaims or agrees it has no exclusive rights in a descriptive term in a mark). The parties might agree that the defendant should modify its mark in some way or gradually phase out use of the infringing mark. They may enter into a monetary arrangement whereby the infringer pays a sum of money to the senior user to license the mark. One party may acquire the other's mark by outright purchase. One party might agree to assign its interest in the mark to the other, who then permits or licenses the original assignor to use the mark. They may agree to have an arbitrator resolve the dispute rather than going to federal court.

Typically, the arrangement between the parties is set forth in a written agreement, usually called a "trademark settlement agreement." (See Appendix D, Form 11, for a sample trademark settlement agreement.)

Trademark Infringement Litigation

If the dispute cannot be resolved, the plaintiff will file an action for infringement in federal district court. The action will be governed by the Federal Rules of Civil Procedure relating to federal civil actions generally; these rules set the times for responding to the complaint, matters pertaining to motions and discovery, and any other litigation-related matters. Within one month after the action is commenced (and upon its conclusion), the clerk of the court must provide notice thereof to the USPTO so notice of the action and its conclusion can be published in the file wrappers relating to the marks.

If the defendant has a cause of action relating to the trademark to assert against the plaintiff, it must be asserted by way of a counterclaim in the litigation so that all disputes between the parties affecting the mark can be resolved at the same time.

A claim may also be made for **contributory infringement** when one party aids another

June 24, 2007

Mr. Michael Taylor
InterSys Products, Inc.
2957 Fifth Avenue
New York, NY

   Re: Trademark BENSON BEAR
       U.S. Reg.. No. 1,423,293

Dear Mr. Taylor:

   Watson Inc. ("Watson") is the owner of U.S. Trademark Registration No. 1,423,293 for the mark BENSON BEAR used by Watson since 1988 in connection with its well-known stuffed plush animal toy. A copy of Watson's registration certificate for BENSON BEAR is enclosed. This trademark is a valuable asset of Watson, which has expended a great deal of time and effort in establishing and maintaining consumer recognition of the mark.

   Watson recently became aware that InterSys Products, Inc. ("InterSys") is using the mark BENSON BEAR in connection with stuffed toys. Your use of the mark BENSON BEAR is likely to cause confusion, mistake, or deception of the purchasing public and the trade as to the source and origin of the goods offered under the respective marks, thereby causing damage and irreparable injury to Watson and diminishing the valuable goodwill associated with Watson's mark. Consequently, InterSys's conduct is an infringement and violation of Watson's proprietary rights in its mark, unfair competition, false advertising, and false designation of origin under applicable state laws and the U.S. Trademark Act.

   Watson therefore demands that InterSys immediately cease and desist from using the mark BENSON BEAR or any other mark confusingly similar to Watson's mark, and cease and desist from marketing, selling, or distributing any goods or materials bearing the mark or any confusingly similar name or mark.

   Because this matter is of significant importance to Watson, we request that you respond within ten days of the date of this letter to confirm your intention to cease and desist from any further use of BENSON BEAR or any other mark confusingly similar to any of Watson's marks. If we do not receive a satisfactory response within this time period, we will consider all available remedies under state and federal law, including requesting injunctive relief and the recovery of damages for trademark infringement, which damages may be trebled by a court, and attorneys' fees and costs incurred by Watson in protecting its mark.

   We sincerely desire a quick and amicable resolution to this matter. Therefore, we look forward to your timely reply.

                                                    Sincerely,

                                                    _____

to infringe a party's mark. Thus, assisting in infringement or inducing infringement is also actionable.

   After the complaint, answer, and counterclaim have been filed, various motions may be made. Discovery will commence. The plaintiff and defendant will take depositions to obtain testimony of those who may have information about the case (e.g., the plaintiff may depose individuals in the defendant's marketing department to determine how the defendant came to adopt its mark); interrogatories may be served on either party to obtain information, such as to inquire about experts either side may intend to call or the existence of documents; and each party may ask the other to produce relevant documents, such as surveys or complaints by consumers indicating confusion.

Ultimately, if the matter cannot be resolved by private agreement, it will proceed to trial. Either party may request a jury trial: otherwise, a judge will render the decision. The decision in the case may be appealed to the United States Court of Appeals for the circuit in which the district court is located. Thereafter, the matter may be appealed to the United States Supreme Court, if the Court decides, in its discretion, to hear the appeal.

Alternative to Infringement

As an alternative to suing for trademark infringement in the United States for another's act of importing the trademarked invention, a trademark owner may bring a proceeding before the International Trade Commission to block the infringing device from entry into the United States. The International Trade Commission (ITC) is an independent quasi-judicial federal agency with broad responsibilities in matters of trade. Under Section 337 of the Tariff Act of 1930 (19 U.S.C. § 1337), the ITC conducts investigations into allegations of unfair practices in import trade, including trademark infringements. Typically, a party files a complaint with the ITC alleging an act of trademark infringement. The ITC then examines the complaint and determines whether an investigation, called a Section 337 investigation, should be conducted. If an investigation is ordered, an administrative law judge is assigned to conduct it. A Section 337 investigation is somewhat similar to a trial in that motions will be made, discovery will occur, parties will testify, and an evidentiary hearing will be held. The administrative law judge will render an initial decision as to whether Section 337 has been violated.

If Section 337 has been violated, the ITC may issue an **exclusion order,** which bars the products from entry into the United States (which order is enforced by the U.S. Customs and Border Protection) or may issue a cease and desist order, which directs violators to cease certain actions. An award of money damages is not available as a remedy for violation of Section 337.

In recent years, Section 337 investigations have become increasingly popular with trademark holders, primarily because of the strong remedies the ITC can order and because the proceedings are far less expensive and more expeditious than infringement trials in U.S. courts. For example, ITC investigations are almost always completed within 12-15 months, while getting to trial in the U.S. district courts generally takes nearly three years. In an era of growing globalization and outsourcing, the ITC has become an increasingly popular forum for blocking imported goods that infringe U.S. trademarks. Decisions may be appealed to the Court of Appeals for the Federal Circuit.

In addition to enforcing exclusion orders issued by the ITC, the U.S. Customs and Border Protection also allows owners of U.S. trademarks to order an **import survey** to provide the trademark owner with the names and addresses of importers of merchandise that appears to infringe the trademark. The customs survey does not stop infringement or importation, but it does provide information relating to the importer, who can then be sued for infringement or named in a complaint filed with the ITC to initiate a Section 337 investigation.

DILUTION OF TRADEMARKS

Introduction

In January 1996, the long-awaited Federal Trademark Dilution Act (15 U.S.C. § 1125(c)) was enacted to provide special protection to "famous" marks when the owners of those marks are unable to establish likelihood of confusion and thus avail themselves of the many avenues afforded to protect marks from confusingly similar uses. Moreover, the Act was intended to bring uniformity to the protection of famous marks, which were previously protected on an inconsistent basis in the various states.

Dilution refers to unauthorized acts that tend to blur the distinctiveness of a famous mark or to tarnish the mark by using it in a disparaging or unsavory way. For example, use of the mark TIFFANY® by a restaurant in Boston was found not to be likely to be confused with TIFFANY for jewelry store services in New York, inasmuch as no reasonable consumer would believe the uses were related or that the restaurant services were sponsored by or originated with Tiffany jewelers. Nevertheless, use by the restaurant was held to be a dilution of Tiffany jeweler's famous mark and was enjoined because of the erosion of the public's identification of a very strong trademark with Tiffany jeweler's alone. *Tiffany & Co. v. Boston Club, Inc.,* 231 F. Supp. 836 (D. Mass. 1964).

Another well-known case involved the use of DOGIVA in connection with dog biscuits. Clearly, consumers would not be confused upon encountering the mark and believe that the dog biscuits were related to GODIVA® brand chocolates. However, use of DOGIVA on such a product tended to injure or tarnish the plaintiff's business reputation and was enjoined. *Grey v. Campbell Soup Co.,* 650 F. Supp. 1166 (C.D. Cal. 1986).

Finally, use of a bottle in the shape of that protected by Coca-Cola Company for white bubble gum resembling cocaine was held to tarnish Coca-Cola's well-known and famous marks and was enjoined even though, under traditional likelihood of confusion analysis, there would have been no infringement.

The primary focus of the Dilution Act is to preserve a trademark owner's property rights and goodwill in its famous mark, which might evaporate if junior users were allowed to use the mark even on unrelated goods. Dilution is generally defined as the lessening of the capacity of a famous mark to identify and distinguish goods and services.

The chief distinction between an infringement claim and a dilution claim is that one can prove dilution without a showing of likelihood of confusion. Moreover, injunctive relief is available once dilution is proved, but monetary damages are awarded only on a showing of willfulness.

To prevail on a dilution claim, a plaintiff must show four things.

1. Its mark is famous (either inherently or through acquired distinctiveness).
2. The defendant is making a commercial use of its mark in commerce.
3. The defendant's use began after the plaintiff's mark became famous.
4. The defendant's use of the mark is likely to cause dilution by blurring or tarnishing the famous mark, whether or not there is actual confusion or actual economic injury to the plaintiff.

In October 2006, Congress enacted the Trademark Dilution Revision Act to provide that injunctive relief can be obtained against use of a mark that is *likely to cause dilution* by blurring or tarnishing a famous mark. This amendment to the Federal Trademark Dilution Act eliminated the need to prove *actual dilution,* which had been required under the U.S. Supreme Court case *Moseley v. V Secret Catalogue, Inc.,* 537 U.S. 418 (2003). As discussed in chapter 23, under the Act, famous trade dress can also be diluted.

Blurring and Tarnishment

Generally, there are two types of unauthorized use that constitute dilution: blurring and tarnishment. **Blurring** is the whittling away of an established trademark's selling power through its unauthorized use upon dissimilar products. Examples might include STARBUCKS PENS, SHELL COFFEE, PEPSI VIDEO, or the use of TIFFANY for restaurant services as described earlier. Such uses would eventually drain away the distinctive power of the original mark even if they did not cause consumer confusion. **Tarnishment** is an association arising from the similarity between a mark and a famous mark that harms the reputation of the famous mark. Generally, tarnishment occurs when a mark is linked to products of an inferior quality or when the mark is portrayed in an unwholesome or embarrassing context (such as a poster reading "Enjoy Cocaine" in a script and color identical to that used by Coca-Cola Company or the substitution of an expletive for "Dunkin" in the mark DUNKIN' DONUTS®). Tarnishment is often found when the senior mark is linked to sexual activity, obscenity, or illegal activity. For example, General Electric's mark was found to be tarnished by GENITAL ELECTRIC, and Anheuser-Busch (owner of the famous BUDWEISER beer mark) was able to enjoin the distribution of BUTTWEISER T-shirts.

Federal Remedies for Dilution

The Act provides a remedy for owners of famous marks in federal court. Under the Act, a mark is famous if it is widely recognized by the general consuming public. Thus, marks that are famous only in a niche market are not protected against dilution. Marks are distinctive whether they are inherently distinctive or whether they have acquired distinctiveness. In determining whether a mark possesses the requisite degree of recognition, a court may consider the following factors: the duration, extent, and geographic reach of advertising and publicity of the mark; the amount, volume, and geographic extent of sales of goods or services offered under the mark; the extent of actual recognition of the mark; and whether the mark is federally registered. An owner who prevails is entitled to injunctive relief, destruction of all diluting goods, and, if willful intent to dilute is shown, actual damages, treble damages, the violator's profits, and costs.

Some types of conduct are exempt from liability, such as fair use of a famous mark in comparative advertising, parody, noncommercial use, and news reporting. These uses are protected under the First Amendment.

Many of the newer cases discussing dilution relate to the use of Internet addresses that dilute famous marks. Thus, the address "candyland. com" for sexually explicit goods and services was held to dilute the famous CANDYLAND® mark owned by Hasbro Toys, *Hasbro Inc. v. Entm't Group Ltd.*, 40 U.S.P.Q.2d 1479 (W.D. Wash. 1996), and the address "adultsrus.com" for sexual paraphernalia was held to dilute the famous TOYS R US® mark owned by Toys "R" Us, Inc. *Toys "R" Us. Inc. v. Akkaoui,* No. C 96-3381 CW, 1996 WL 772709 (N.D. Cal. Oct. 29, 1996).

RELATED TRADEMARK CLAIMS

Trademark owners often assert additional claims in actions for trademark infringement. For example, in *Phat Fashions* (see Exhibit 6-2), the plaintiff alleged trademark infringement, dilution, and unfair competition, all arising out of the same course of conduct. Thus, there is an array of various causes of action a trademark owner might assert.

Importation of Gray Market Goods

In many instances, U.S. trademark owners grant rights to those in foreign countries to manufacture goods that bear their U.S. trademark. After the goods are distributed in the foreign markets, other parties buy them (often in bulk) and import them back into the United States to resell to others, in competition with the U.S. trademark owner. These goods are called **gray market goods** or **parallel imports**. The law relating to the permissibility of such importation is unsettled, with most courts holding that the import and sale of genuine gray market goods is not infringement, because once a mark owner sells goods bearing its mark, it cannot prevent subsequent owners from reselling the goods if there is no deception or consumer confusion; the goods are physically the same as those sold by the U.S. trademark owner and the U.S. registrant and the foreign manufacturer are the same or related entities. The situation is analogous to resales in the United States. For example, a consumer who purchases a baby stroller bearing the APRICA® mark can later resell it to another. This doctrine is referred to as the **exhaustion theory** inasmuch as once the first lawful sale is made, the trademark owner's rights are exhausted or extinguished in regard to subsequent sales. Allowing importation of genuine gray market or parallel goods is consistent with the exhaustion theory. As discussed in chapter 16, recent holdings in the copyright field are also consistent with this theory.

However, if the gray market goods are materially different from the authorized imports, then there is likelihood of confusion and the imports may be banned. For example, imports of TIC TAC® breath mints were banned when they were materially different in size and caloric content from the authorized products sold in the United States. *Ferrero U.S.A. Inc. v. Ozak Trading, Inc.*, 753 F. Supp. 1240 (D.N.J.), *aff'd*, 935 F.2d 1281 (3d Cir. 1991). In sum, as in any trademark infringement case, the central inquiry in a gray market goods import case is whether the goods create a likelihood of confusion of U.S. consumers.

Counterfeiting

Trademark **counterfeiting** is a particularly specious type of infringement. A counterfeiter applies the trademark owner's mark to goods or services that do not originate with the owner. Perhaps the best examples of counterfeiting or "black market" activities involve the unauthorized sale of scarves bearing the HERMES® mark, handbags bearing the KATE SPADE® or LOUIS VUITTON® marks, watches bearing the ROLEX® mark, and other high-end or designer items that are sold at flea markets, corner stands, and "on the street." The items sold and which bear the mark are not genuine and are intentionally sold for the express purpose of trading off the owner's established goodwill and reputation.

Universities, athletic teams, and rock bands that own valuable marks often have their marks counterfeited and placed on black market goods, primarily T-shirts, sweatshirts, and jackets. To

deter counterfeiters, statutes allow for the immediate impoundment and destruction of the "knockoff" goods; awards of treble damages, actual damages, and attorneys' fees; and criminal penalties. It has been reported that in just the few months prior to the 1996 Atlanta Olympics, $2.5 million worth of infringing merchandise was seized, mostly in the Atlanta area. Similarly, the night of game four of the 2000 baseball World Series, Major League Baseball Properties Inc. assembled a squad of 25 in-house investigators and, accompanied by court-ordered marshals and lawyers, served 150 complaints and seized 15,000 T-shirts and other unauthorized apparel from counterfeiters around the stadium. Unfortunately, however, seizing the goods provides little long-term benefit, inasmuch as the counterfeiter simply moves its stall or stand to some other location the next day.

Even the wine industry has been recently plagued by counterfeits. Fake French labels have been placed on wine produced in China. To combat counterfeit products, many winemakers and luxury goods-makers are now embedding holograms and microchips on their products, which can be read with optical scanners.

In recent years, counterfeiting has taken on an even darker side, with fake medicine, baby formula, and airplane parts sold as genuine, causing not only consumer confusion but also actual harm and injury. The United States works with various countries to attempt to curb counterfeits, and a recent government-wide initiative, "Strategy Targeting Organized Piracy (STOP!)" aims to stop trade in pirated and counterfeit goods. The USPTO has developed a Web site (http://www.stopfakes.gov) and maintains a hotline for reporting of IP theft. Additionally, criminal penalties for counterfeiting have been increased; however, the problem of bogus goods continues to plague both governments and IP owners. In one novel approach, some trademark owners now bring lawsuits not only against those who sell the fake products, but also against their landlords. In 2006, 18 landlords in New York agreed to post signs saying store owners were not authorized to see Louis Vuitton merchandise and to evict those who do.

Unfair Competition

Section 43 of the Lanham Act (15 U.S.C. § 1125) provides that any person injured by a false designation of origin or false representation may bring a civil action against the offending party. This statute is often used as a catchall because it is so broadly worded that it prohibits nearly all forms of **unfair competition,** including false advertising and infringement of trade dress. Moreover, a party need not have a registered trademark to invoke its protections. Thus, it affords even broader protection than section 32 of the Lanham Act (15 U.S.C. § 1114), which prohibits infringement of a registered mark. In most instances, parties alleging trademark infringement under section 32 of the Lanham Act also include a cause of action for unfair competition under section 43 (and state consumer protection or unfair competition statutes, if they exist). In fact, in Phat *Fashions* (see Exhibit 6-2), the court stated that because the plaintiff had demonstrated infringement, *it followed that* the plaintiff had equally established unfair competition. Unfair competition is fully discussed in chapter 23.

Customs Regulation

Additional protection is provided to trademark owners through section 42 of the Lanham Act (15 U.S.C. § 1124), which allows owners of registered trademarks to deposit their certificates of registration with the U.S. Customs and Border Protection Service in order to block importation of offending goods. The trademark owner files an application with the Intellectual Property Rights Branch of the U.S. Customs and Border Protection Service (CBP) in Washington, DC, to have its marks recorded with CBP, deposits one certified copy and five additional copies of its registration certificates with CBP, and pays an application fee of $190 per class. The form may now be submitted electronically. CBP will then "post its ports." **Posting of ports** means that CBP will monitor ports of entry into the United States and will seize any unpermitted goods bearing the owner's mark. Criminal sanctions may be imposed on the offending party.

Trivia

- In July 2006, the TTAB imposed sanctions against Leo Stoller, who had filed more than 1,800 requests for extensions of time to oppose registration of various marks with the TTAB over less than two years. The sanctions imposed included vacating pending approvals of extension requests, a two-year prohibition on filing extension requests, and a requirement that Stoller be represented by an attorney in any extension request.
- In 2004, Microsoft agreed to pay Linux seller Lindows $20 million to settle a long-standing trademark dispute. Lindows (which had claimed that "Windows" was a generic computing term) agreed to surrender the name LINDOWS in favor of LINSPIRE and to drop any references to "Lindows."
- Ninety-five percent of all TTAB proceedings are resolved prior to trial.
- In 2006, 6,581 oppositions were filed, 1,426 cancellations proceedings were filed, 43 concurrent use proceedings were filed, and no interferences were filed.

Trivia (cont'd)

- In 2001, the maker of the nougat treat offered under the NUTELLA® mark forced the owner of the domain names GNUTELLA.DE and NEWTELLA.DE (used in connection with music) to cease use of the names on the basis that the latter marks infringed the NUTELLA® mark.
- Uncle Milton Industries still owns the trademark-ANT FARM®. "Everyone else can call it a 'formicarium,'" says a company spokesperson.

CHAPTER SUMMARY

Disputes over use and ownership of trademarks are common. Such disputes typically fall into one of four categories: inter partes proceedings, infringement actions, actions for dilution, and actions alleging unfair competition.

An inter partes proceeding is one brought before the Trademark Trial and Appeal Board and may be categorized as follows:

- an opposition by a party to registration of a mark
- a petition to cancel an existing registration of a mark
- an interference
- a concurrent use proceeding, whereby parties each agree to use their respective marks in specifically designated geographical areas

An action for trademark infringement can be brought in federal court if a defendant's use of a mark is likely to cause confusion with a registered mark to an appreciable number of reasonably prudent consumers about the source, origin, affiliation, or sponsorship of goods or services. Courts consider a variety of factors in determining whether there is a likelihood of confusion, including the similarity of the marks, the similarity of the goods/services offered under the marks, the similarity of trade channels, the strength of the senior mark, whether the sale is made on impulse or only after careful deliberation, and whether actual confusion has occurred. A trademark infringement action proceeds much like any trial: a complaint is filed, an answer is filed, motions may be made, discovery occurs, and a trial is held. Relief may include injunctions, monetary damages, and destruction of infringing articles.

An action for dilution may be brought if another uses a famous mark in a way that is likely to cause confusion by blurring the distinctiveness of a famous mark or tarnishing its reputation and goodwill.

If a mark is not registered, an action for unfair competition may be brought against a party who is using a false designation of origin or is engaged in false advertising. Additional protection is afforded by depositing a certificate of trademark registration with U.S. Customs and Border Protection to prohibit offending goods from entering the United States.

Thus, securing a federal registration for one's mark enhances the level of protection for a trademark owner who may then bring a civil action for infringement of the registered mark and may obtain the assistance of CBP in blocking offending goods from entry into the United States. Owners of unregistered marks may seek protection under section 43 of the Lanham Act for unfair competition, but the remedies specifically provided for infringement actions and posting of ports are not available to them.

CASE ILLUSTRATION–LIKELIHOOD OF CONFUSION

Case: *J & J Snack Foods Corp. v. McDonald's Corp.,* 932 F.2d 1460 (Fed. Cir. 1991).

Facts: Plaintiff, a snack food company, attempted to register McPRETZEL and McDUGAL McPRETZEL for frozen soft pretzels. The U.S. Patent and Trademark Office denied registration and the company appealed.

Holding: The court affirmed the denial of registration because there was a likelihood of confusion with the family of marks owned by McDonald's. The plaintiff argued that McDonald's was not entitled to all "Mc" marks for all purposes. The court, however, held that because of its extensive advertising and use, McDonald's had created public recognition of a family of marks, wherein the prefix "Mc" is combined with the generic name of a food product, and the public has come to associate such marks with McDonald's. McDonald's presented survey evidence showing that 30 percent of consumers believed McPRETZEL originated with McDonald's. It is the perspective of the consumer that is critical. Moreover, preference is accorded to the prior user as against a newcomer. In this case, ordinary purchasers would be likely to be confused as to the source of the pretzels.

CASE STUDY AND ACTIVITIES

Case Study. In reviewing the *Official Gazette* for March 15, Vision noticed a pending application for EXPRESS ESPRESSO for ground coffee beans. One of Vision's popular products in its gift stores is ESPRESSO EXPRESSO® used for ground coffee beans. Vision is also planning to build tot lots at its resorts to be called KID CITY. In conducting its trademark search, Vision has discovered that while Disney Co. owns a registration for KID TOWN®, the sections within its amusement parks that used the mark KID TOWN® were dismantled two years ago. Vision recently discovered that another resort company is marketing its golf courses under the mark GREEN DREAMS. Vision owns a registered trademark for DREAM GREENS® for its golf courses. Finally, Vision, which offers a well-known line of candy in its gift stores under the mark CANDY EXPRESS®, recently discovered that a company is using the name CANDY XPRESS in connection with adult pornography.

Activities. Discuss the appropriate actions Vision should take to protect it marks ESPRESSO EXPRESSO®, DREAM GREENS®, and CANDY EXPRESS®. Additionally, if Vision wishes to use KID CITY for its tot lots, what should it do with regard to the registration issued to Disney Co.?

ROLE OF PARALEGAL

Paralegals are typically involved in a variety of interesting and challenging tasks related to trademark protection, including the following:

- reviewing the *Official Gazette* to locate marks that may need to be opposed or reviewing reports from watching services relating to publication of marks that may need to be opposed
- docketing relevant dates for filing a notice of opposition, request for time to oppose, or petition to cancel
- preparing or responding to cease and desist letters
- preparing notices of opposition, petitions to cancel, complaints for infringement, or responses or answers thereto
- docketing all relevant dates in opposition, cancellation, and infringement proceedings, such as dates for close of discovery, submission of written briefs, and so forth
- assisting in the discovery process by drafting interrogatories, reviewing documents produced, summarizing depositions, reviewing surveys, and so forth
- conducting searches and investigations to determine the number and use of other similar marks
- drafting consent to use or trademark settlement agreements
- providing general assistance for infringement trials, such as locating witnesses, organizing exhibits and documents, conducting research, and preparing jury instructions
- preparing applications to U.S. Customs to record trademark registrations to block importation of offending goods

INTERNET RESOURCES

USPTO Web site:	http://www.uspto.gov (offers basic forms for notice of opposition and petition to cancel registered marks) Additionally, select TTAB and then TTAB Manual of Procedure for rules relating to inter partes proceedings.
Trademark Manual of Examining Procedure (TMEP):	http://tess2.uspto.gov/tmdb/tmep (offers information on standards for likelihood of confusion of marks in Chapter 12)
U.S. Customs and Border Protection:	http://www.cbp.gov (provides information about filing requests with U.S. Customs and Border Protection to post ports and prevent importation of infringing goods)
General information:	http://www.megalaw.com
	http://www.ipmall.fplc.edu

Sample cease and desist letters: http://www.chillingeffects.org (offers sample and actual cease and desist letters and general information about trademark infringement)

DISCUSSION QUESTIONS

1. If a mark is published in the *Official Gazette* on July 3, and a party wishes to oppose registration of the mark, when must it do so?
2. Assume a registration is issued on the Principal Register on June 1, 2005. What are the time limits for petitioning to cancel the registration based on the following grounds:
   a. The mark has been abandoned.
   b. The mark is descriptive.
   c. The mark is confusingly similar to another's mark.
3. What are the time limits for petitioning to cancel a registration issued on the Supplemental Register on the basis that the mark is confusingly similar to another's mark?
4. The trademark POLAROID® is a coined mark. In an infringement action brought by the owner of the mark, why is the mark entitled to a strong scope of protection?
5. Assume that the owner of POLAROID® has known of the use of a mark POLARIDE used in connection with an amusement park ride for two years. The owner of POLARIDE has recently begun offering photographic supplies under the mark POLARIDE. The owner of POLAROID® has decided to sue for trademark infringement. What defenses is POLARIDE likely to assert? What response is POLAROID® likely to make?
6. A client of your law firm is writing an exposé of certain business practices of Nike Corp. The article will be published in the *New York Times* and will use several of Nike's trademarks. May Nike object to this use of its marks? Discuss.
7. In a trademark infringement action, the plaintiff would like to introduce evidence that an intern in the company asked individuals who passed by the plaintiff's office building whether they were confused by the defendant's mark and 60 percent of the respondents answered affirmatively. What might the defendant assert with regard to such evidence?
8. Discuss whether the following might constitute blurring or tarnishment.
   PEPSI (for pasta)
   OLD CROW (for bird seed)
   APPLE (for pornographic materials)

USING INTERNET RESOURCES

1. Use TTAB Vue and locate information about U.S. Reg. No. 1931937. Who was the plaintiff in the proceeding filed on November 25, 2003? Who was the defendant? What mark had the defendant applied for? Review the status of this matter. What was the result?
2. Use TTAB Vue and locate information about the mark THE BUCK STARS HERE. Who is the plaintiff?

USING INTERNET RESOURCES (CONT'D)

3. Review Sections 101.01 and 101.02 of the Trademark Trial and Appeal Board Manual of Procedure. What laws, regulations, and rules govern TTAB proceedings?
4. Review chapter 12 of the TMEP. In case of doubt as to whether marks are confusingly similar, how is that doubt resolved? What section governs your answer?
5. Use the USPTO's glossary and give the definition for "cancellation."
6. Access the TTAB's site and locate a decision mailed November 7, 2006, in which the petitioner was Mattel, Inc. and its mark was U.S. Reg. No. 2,397,901. What was the TTAB's decision?

Chapter 7

New Developments in Trademark Law

CHAPTER OVERVIEW

New issues have arisen in trademark law that were entirely unanticipated just a few years ago. The emergence of the Internet as a tool for electronic communication and commerce has resulted in complex intellectual property issues; chief among them are the assignment of Internet domain names and attendant disputes over such domain names. Companies that have invested significant amounts of time and money in their marks have been surprised when they have attempted to use their marks as part of their domain names, only to find the names have been taken by cybersquatters or electronic pirates who register famous domain names in the hopes of ransoming them back to their rightful owners. The issue of domain name assignment and dispute resolution is one that has caused great controversy and cries for reform. The passage of the Anticybersquatting Consumer Protection Act in 1999 has resulted in far fewer acts of cybersquatting in recent years.

Use of marks on the Internet has also led to various First Amendment issues, especially with

regard to the practice of using another party's mark on one's Web site as a link to another site. Finally, courts have struggled with the issue whether merely operating a passive Web site should expose a party to jurisdiction in all states where the Web site can be accessed. Generally, courts have held that passive Web sites offering information should not subject the Web site operator to personal jurisdiction in other states.

As use of the Internet continues to increase in ways not yet imagined, intellectual property rights are likely to continue to be affected, requiring courts to be imaginative and flexible in dealing with emerging technologies.

THE INTERNET

Introduction

Trademark owners throughout the world are struggling with new issues presented by increased electronic communication, primarily that occurring through the Internet. The Internet derives from a network set up in the 1970s by the Department of Defense to connect military and research sites that could continue to communicate even in the event of nuclear attack. In the 1980s, the National Science Foundation expanded on the system, and its first significant users were government agencies and universities. In the early 1990s, however, it became apparent that the system could provide a global communication network, allowing people from all over the world to talk with each other; send written messages (electronic mail or "e-mail"), pictures, and text to each other; and establish Web sites to advertise their wares and provide information to their customers. Thus, the Internet has become a channel of commerce with more than 1 billion users worldwide. In the United States alone, retail commerce on the Internet exceeded $71 billion in 2004.

To communicate on the Internet, businesses and individuals are assigned addresses called domain names, for example, "ford.com." To consumers, these domain names function much like a trademark in that they identify a source of goods or services.

Assignment of Domain Names

The rapid explosion of the Internet has presented two novel trademark issues: how should domain names be registered for use on the Internet and how should disputes over domain names be resolved? As marks are used more frequently on the Internet, trademark owners need to ensure that their marks continue to serve their key functions of distinguishing an owner's goods and services from those of others and protecting the public from deception and confusion. Moreover, businesses desire domain names that are easy to remember and that relate to their name, products, or services. Owners of famous trademarks, such as Nestlé Co., typically register their primary trademark as their domain name, as in "nestle.com." Additionally, consumers who do not definitely know a company's domain name often merely type in the company name, such as "ibm.com," in the hope of locating the company's site. This method is often successful.

A company's presence on the Internet begins with its address or **domain name.** A domain name not only serves as a locator for a company but also may function as a designation of origin and a symbol of goodwill—a trademark. There are two portions to a domain name: the **generic top-level domain,** which is the portion of the name to the right of a period (such as .gov or .com), and the **secondary level domain,** which is the portion of the name to the left of a period (such as "kraft" in "kraft.com"). Disputes frequently arise between owners of registered marks and owners of domain names who use domain names similar or identical to the registered marks. While several parties might have identical trademarks because their products or services are not confusingly similar (e.g., DOVE® for soap can coexist with DOVE® for ice cream), it is not possible for two parties to have identical Web addresses. For example, a company might register the mark SHOEBIZ® for its shoes. Another party might adopt the domain name "shoebiz.com." When consumers encounter the domain name, they may go to the site seeking information on the shoe products and instead be presented with information from an entirely unrelated company. Moreover, the owner of the SHOEBIZ mark might not be able to secure the domain name for its business even though it has a valid trademark registration because the domain name has already been taken by someone else.

Domain names are appearing as assets in sales of businesses and in bankruptcies. The name "business.com" sold for $7.5 million, and "sex.com" sold for $12 million in 2006. The art of establishing a value for a domain name is a burgeoning business. After a drop in price for Internet addresses (likely due to the "dot bomb" recession after 2002), market interest has recently increased. In many instances, a speculator buys names and then hopes to sell them later for a windfall. Internet REIT, a Texas company, aggressively acquires Internet domain names and currently has an inventory of more than 400,000 domain names.

Domain names are registered on a first-come, first-served basis, thus allowing anyone to register a domain such as ford.com, even if the registrant has no connection with Ford Motor Co. The organizations that register domain names, called **registrars,** generally do not prescreen potentially troublesome names (although they typically require domain name applicants to represent that they believe they have a right to use the name and the registration is in good faith). Federal law (15 U.S.C. § 1114(d)) specifically provides a safe harbor for domain name registrars; thus, they are not liable for merely registering an infringing domain name absent a showing of bad faith intent to profit from such registration or maintenance of the domain name.

Internet Corporation for Assigned Names and Numbers (ICANN)

To help resolve the problems in the domain name registration and use process, the U.S. government created the **Internet Corporation for Assigned Names and Numbers (ICANN)** in 1998 to oversee naming policies. ICANN, a nonprofit corporation, has assumed responsibility for overseeing the domain name system in the United States. ICANN is governed by an international board of directors elected in part by various members of the Internet community.

Domain names such as www.ford.com can be registered through more than 100 different registrars that compete with each other. Only registrars accredited by ICANN are authorized to register domain names ending with certain suffixes, such as .com, .org, and .net. Registrations usually last one year, at which time they can be renewed or will expire. Registration requires a representation that the person seeking to register the name is not doing so for an unlawful purpose and does not know of any infringement that will result from his or her registration.

ICANN recently added new top-level domains, including .biz (for businesses), .info (for all uses), and .travel (for travel-related uses).

PROTECTING A DOMAIN NAME

Introduction

Over the past several years, one of the biggest issues facing domain name users has been the infringement of their names. In many cases, people register well-known marks as domain names to prey on consumer confusion by misusing the domain name to divert customers from the legitimate mark owner's site. This practice is commonly called **cybersquatting.** The cybersquatter's own site is often a pornography or gambling site that derives advertising revenue based on the number of visits (called "hits") the site receives. In other cases, the cybersquatters offer to ransom back the domain name to the true owner for unreasonable amounts of money.

Victims of hijacked trademarks can pursue a variety of remedies against cybersquatters. An action for trademark infringement can be brought if likelihood of confusion and use in commerce can be shown. Most victims, however, rely on one of the following three approaches because proving use in commerce by the cybersquatter can be difficult (because the cybersquatter often merely registers the domain name and doesn't use it but rather hopes to sell it to the rightful owner):

1. an action can be brought under the Federal Trademark Dilution Act;
2. a civil suit can be instituted under the recent Anticybersquatting Consumer Protection Act; or
3. van administrative quasi-arbitration proceeding can be instituted through ICANN's dispute resolution process.

Cybersquatters and the Dilution Doctrine

If the domain name owner uses its site to promote or offer goods or services confusingly similar to those offered by a trademark owner with prior rights, and the domain name and mark are confusingly similar, the trademark owner can bring an action for infringement under the Lanham Act just as it would for any act of infringement. More difficult issues have arisen, however, when domain names have been registered and are used merely for an e-mail address with no Web site associated with them (making the name unavailable as a domain name for the rightful owner) or are used in connection with goods or services that are unrelated to those offered by the trademark owner. In such cases, the trademark owner cannot bring an action for infringement inasmuch as the owner cannot show likelihood of confusion or commercial use. Enter the dilution doctrine.

When the Federal Trademark Dilution Act (15 U.S.C. § 1125(c)) was being considered, Senator Patrick J. Leahy (D. Vt.) expressed his hope that it would be useful in prohibiting the misuse of famous marks as domain names on the Internet. Since the passage of the act, many trademark owners have in fact relied on the Act in disputes over domain names.

In *Intermatic v. Toeppen,* 947 F. Supp. 1227 (N.D. Ill. 1996), one of the most famous cybersquatting cases, the owner of the well-known mark INTERMATIC® (used on a variety of electronic products) sued Dennis Toeppen, an individual who had registered the domain name "intermatic. com" with NSI. Toeppen did not offer any goods or services on his "intermatic.com" site and acknowledged he intended to "arbitrage" the name, along with more than 240 other names he had registered as domains, including "deltaairlines. com" and "neiman-marcus.com," which he then offered to sell to their owners for sums ranging between $10,000 and $15,000. The district court held that the act of registering a domain name with the intent to resell it constituted "use in commerce" and was therefore covered by the Federal Trademark Dilution Act. Toeppen's acts were held to have diluted the famous INTERMATIC mark by decreasing the owner's ability to identify and distinguish its goods on the Internet because the domain name registration system does not permit two entities to use the same domain name (unlike marketplace conditions in which similar or identical marks may coexist), and it de-

creased Intermatic's ability to control the association that the public would make with its mark. In mid-1998, the Ninth Circuit Court of Appeals upheld a summary judgment ruling against Toeppen for trademark dilution arising out of similar acts, namely, attempting to sell Panavision's domain name to it for $13,000. *Panavision Int'l, L.P. v. Toeppen,* 141 F.3d 1316 (9th Cir. 1998).

Similarly, in *Hasbro Inc. v. Internet Entertainment Group Ltd.,* 40 U.S.P.Q.2d 1479 (W.D. Wash. 1996), Hasbro, the owner of the CANDYLAND® mark used in connection with the famous children's board game, was able to enjoin the defendant's use of the domain name "candyland.com" for a Web site featuring sexually explicit material. The court held that the defendant's use tarnished the famous CANDYLAND mark under the Federal Trademark Dilution Act.

Just as in any dilution case, a prevailing plaintiff is entitled to an injunction against another person's commercial use in commerce of its mark (and, if willful intent is proven, monetary damages may be awarded). To prevail, a plaintiff must show that the defendant has commenced use in commerce of a mark that is likely to cause dilution of a famous mark or a distinctive mark (either inherently distinctive or that has acquired distinctiveness) by blurring or by tarnishment. There is no need for the plaintiff to show actual confusion, competition, or any actual economic injury; proving likelihood of dilution is sufficient.

Cybersquatters and the Anticybersquatting Consumer Protection Act

In 1999 Congress enacted the **Anticybersquatting Consumer Protection Act (ACPA)** to bring additional uniformity to the problems associated with domain name registration and cybersquatting. The Act (located at 15 U.S.C. § 1125(d)) makes it illegal for a person to register, traffic in, or use a domain name of another if the domain name is identical to or confusingly similar to the trademark of another, and the person has a bad faith intent to profit from the mark. ACPA is the world's first law on domain names. Note that there is no requirement under ACPA that a party have a *registered* mark.

A registrant's bad faith must be shown for a plaintiff to prevail under ACPA. In determining whether a person has a bad faith intent, a court may consider a number of factors, including whether the person intends to divert consumers from the mark owner's online location either for commercial gain or with the intent to disparage the mark, whether the person has offered to sell the domain name to another for financial gain without having used the domain name, and whether the person has acquired multiple domain names that are identical or confusing to those of others. Without such a showing of bad faith, recovery will be denied. For example, in *Hasbro Inc. v. Clue Computing, Inc.*, 66 F. Supp. 2d 117 (D. Mass. 1999), the court held that the defendant's domain "clue.com" did not infringe Hasbro's famous Clue mark because the defendant computing firm had its own trademark rights in the word *clue* and was a legitimate first user.

To prevail in a civil action under ACPA, a plaintiff must prove three things:

1. the plaintiff's mark is a distinctive or famous mark deserving of protection;
2. the defendant has used, registered, or trafficked in a domain name that is identical to or confusingly similar to the plaintiff's mark; and
3. the defendant registered the domain name in bad faith.

Parties who prevail in actions under ACPA can obtain actual damages and lost profits as well as attorneys' fees. For plaintiffs who have difficulty proving actual damages, the Act provides for statutory damages in an amount of up to $100,000 per domain name. Additionally, a court can order the wrongful domain name canceled or transferred to the plaintiff.

A standard trademark infringement case requires a plaintiff to prove that the defendant wrongfully used a mark in commerce. ACPA, however, allows recovery if the defendant either wrongfully used or registered the mark. Thus, recovery under ACPA is easier in cases in which the wrongdoer simply registers the domain name and attempts to sell it back to the mark owner without having actually used it.

Cases under ACPA are just starting to emerge from the nation's appellate court system. One of the most famous is *Shields v. Zuccarini*, 254 F.3d 476 (3d Cir. 2001), in which the defendant registered several misspelled versions of the popular Web site http://www.joecartoon.com owned by the plaintiff, a well-known cartoonist named Joe Shields. This practice is a variation of cybersquatting called **typosquatting.** When visitors attempted to access the plaintiff's site and mistyped a letter or two, they would become **mousetrapped** in Zuccarini's site and need to click on a number of advertisements before they could exit the site. Zuccarini received payment for each click on one of these advertising sites. Shields was awarded damages in the amount of $10,000 for each infringing domain name and nearly $40,000 in attorneys' fees. It was later found that Zuccarini had been making $800,000 to $1 million each year by charging advertisers whose ads appeared after an Internet user mistyped names such as Victoria's Secret or *Wall Street Journal*. In many cases, the advertisers were promoting gambling and pornography.

Just months later, Zuccarini was still at it and had registered additional misspelled domain names. The court stated that he was a "notorious cybersquatter" and had "boldly thumb[ed] his nose" at the court. Zuccarini was ordered to pay $500,000 in damages and more than $30,000 in attorneys' fees. The Federal Trade Commission later ordered him to stop his scheme and pay almost $1.9 million to victims. Altogether, Zuccarini lost 53 state and federal lawsuits and has had about 200 domain names taken from him. In 2004, Zuccarini was sentenced to 30 months in prison for luring children to pornographic Web sites by misspelling Internet domain names such as Britney Spears and Disneyland.

A new development in cybersquatting is registration of domain names of fledgling celebrities and athletes in the hope they will become famous. These "soft squatters" hope that when fame occurs, they will then develop a business relationship with the celebrity, offering Web site design services or Web site hosting.

ACPA has proven to be a potent weapon for trademark owners. Recovery of money damages (and attorneys' fees) and cancelation of the domain name are available under the Act. Its popularity is demonstrated by the fact that in just one six-month period in 2001, over 700 federal lawsuits had been filed seeking relief under ACPA.

Resolving Disputes through the Uniform Domain Name Dispute Resolution Policy

In 1999, after assuming control of the domain name registration process, ICANN adopted a **Uniform Domain Name Dispute Resolution Policy (UDRP),** an international policy for resolving controversies relating to domain names. All ICANN-accredited registrars must follow UDRP, and ICANN designated four approved providers to oversee disputes. Of the four, the World Intellectual Property Organization (WIPO), headquartered in Geneva, has emerged as the most popular forum for domain name disputes. About one-half of all cases filed seeking relief under the UDRP are filed with WIPO. The UDRP provides a quick and inexpensive alternative to bringing a formal lawsuit under ACPA.

The UDRP establishes an administrative procedure for efficient and inexpensive resolution of a specific category of disputes: those arising from abusive, bad faith registrations of domain names, namely, cybersquatting. Under the UDRP, the holder of a trademark files an online complaint with one of the four approved dispute resolution service providers (often WIPO, as discussed previously). Providers set their own fees, which average about $1,500. A decision is usually rendered by a neutral arbitration panel (either one panelist or three panelists) in about two months. Remedies are limited to canceling a wrongful

domain name or transferring it to its rightful owner. Neither money damages nor injunctive relief can be obtained under the UDRP. Nevertheless, if the trademark owner seeks a quick and inexpensive resolution of a domain name dispute, the UDRP provides an excellent forum for cancelation or transfer of a domain name.

To prevail under the UDRP, the trademark owner must establish three things:

1. the allegedly wrongful domain name is identical or confusingly similar to the complainant's trademark;
2. the domain name registrant has no legitimate interest in the domain name; and
3. the domain name is being used in bad faith.

The UDRP resolution process is perceived as complainant-friendly, and statistics show that the panels rule in favor of trademark owners about 80 percent of the time. A party who is unhappy with the result under UDRP can appeal to court; thus, UDRP decisions are not final.

ICANN and its registrars allow those registering domain names a five-day grace period within which to return those names without incurring fees. In a new practice, speculators often register thousands of names, and use the five-day period to conduct research to determine if the domain name is likely to make more than the $6 annual registration fee. Advances in technology allow these speculators to register hundreds of thousands of domain names and "taste" them. If the names are not desired, the domain tasters return them, causing an enormous amount of administrative processing for ICANN. Some experts estimate that more than 90 percent of domains are returned within the grace period. In April 2006, out of 35 million registrations, only a little more than 2 million were permanently purchased. ICANN is considering allowing registrars to impose a return fee when one of these "domain tasters" returns more than 90 percent of the domains initially registered.

The Future of Cybersquatting

As discussed, there are a variety of dispute mechanisms available to trademark owners whose marks are hijacked by cybersquatters (see Exhibit 7–1). With the success of the UDRP and increasing awareness that abusive practices will no longer be tolerated, coupled with the quick and simple UDRP process, many cybersquatters have abandoned their practices.

Many experts also note that the unscrupulous practice of cybersquatting is on the wane as evidenced by the fact that the number of proceedings initiated under the UDRP declined 22 percent in 2005 from 2000 (although there was a slight increase in 2006). The track record of cybersquatters has been dismal, and thus the potent combination of ACPA and the UDRP may well make domain name piracy a thing of the past, resulting in reliability of domain names on the Internet.

HYPERLINKING AND THE FIRST AMENDMENT

Web page owners frequently provide symbols, called **hyperlinks** (or "links"), that designate other Web pages that may be of interest to a user. Thus, a trademark owner's mark may be displayed on thousands of different Web sites, allowing users to "click" on the symbol and be transported to a different location, either to a different page within that same Web site or to an entirely different Web site on the Internet. Links are location pointers and are often shown in blue underscoring.

Most companies have no objection to linking, rightfully believing that linking allows more individuals to visit their sites and thus increases commercial use. Thus, most Web site owners have not sought permission from others to link to their site.

A recently enacted Georgia statute prohibited the use of any trademark on the Internet that falsely implied that permission to use the symbol

had been granted. In striking down the statute as unconstitutional, the United States District Court for the Northern District of Georgia held that the First Amendment protects the linking function as free speech. *ACLU v. Miller*, 977 F. Supp. 1228 (N.D. Ga. 1997). Moreover, in *Knight-McConnell v. Cummings*, No. 03 CIV 5035 (NRB), 2004 WL 1713824, at *2 (S.D.N.Y. July 29, 2004), in which the plaintiff claimed that the defendant violated federal law by linking to her site without her permission, the court held that the "mere appearance on a website of a hyperlink will not lead a web-user to conclude that the owner of the site he is visiting is associated with the owner of the linked site."

Many experts analogize linking with library card files or footnoting in written documents, namely, a signal to users that additional information can be sought elsewhere. Linking, however, is not permissible if it points to material with the purpose of disseminating illegal material. Moreover, linking to unsavory Web sites could result in liability.

At this time, however, the permissibility of **deep linking,** which allows a user at one site to proceed directly to certain information at another site, bypassing the home page of the second site, is open to debate. Because home pages often provide background information and their owners sell advertising on their home pages, arguments have been made that deep linking that bypasses a home page deprives the second site owner of advertising revenue and is thus impermissible. Most experts, however, believe that deep linking, by itself, without causing confusion, should be permissible. In *Ticketmaster Corp. v. Tickets.Com Inc.*, No. 99-7654 HLH, 2000 WL 525390, at *3 (C.D. Cal. Mar. 27, 2000), in which the defendant deep linked users into interior pages of the plaintiff's Web site, the court stated that "deep linking by itself (i.e., without confusion of source)" does not necessarily infringe another's rights.

Another unresolved issue somewhat related to linking is **framing,** the retrieval by one Web site of content from another site that is incorporated into the original Web site within a frame,

EXHIBIT 7–1
Remedies for
Cybersquatting

Form of Action	What Plaintiff Must Show	Permitted Recovery	Disadvantages
Infringement Action	Likelihood of confusion and use in commerce must be shown.	Injunctive relief and money damages (including attorneys' fees in exceptional cases) are recoverable.	Plaintiff must show use in commerce, which may be difficult if domain name is only registered and not used.
Action under Federal Trademark Dilution Act	Plaintiff must show likelihood of dilution of a famous or distinctive mark; use in commerce is shown by mere registration of a domain name with "bad intent."	Injunctive relief may be obtained, and if willful intent is shown, money damages (and attorneys' fees in exceptional cases) may be recovered.	Plaintiff must show some commercial use; damages may be hard to recover; domain name cannot be canceled or transferred.
Anticybersquatting Consumer Protection Act	Plaintiff must show bad faith in registration of a confusingly similar or identical domain name; acts such as "ransoming back" name constitute commercial use. Famous personal names may be protected. Plaintiff need not have registered mark.	Cancelation of domain name is possible as well as money damages; if money damages are difficult to prove plaintiff may opt for statutory damages. Injunctive relief may also be ordered.	Court proceeding may be expensive and time-consuming
Uniform Domain Name Dispute Resolution Policy	Complainant must show identical or confusingly similar domain name (including personal name) is being used in bad faith.	The only possible remedies are cancelation or transfer of domain name to rightful owner.	Money damages are not recoverable; however, process is quick and inexpensive.

often obscuring advertisements and content. Some courts have suggested that because framing "captures" content from another's site and stores it in the user's hard drive, there may be infringement.

At this time, due to the uncertainty relating to deep linking or framing, many commentators believe that permission of the original Web site owner should be sought by those wishing to deep link and bypass a home page or those

ETHICS EDGE: Staying Current

The intersection of the Internet with trademark law presents novel and interesting issues. Case law changes rapidly as courts grapple with developing trends in cyberspace. To fulfill your professional duty to maintain competency, subscribe to an intellectual property–related listserv, which will e-mail you bulletins about new cases, trends, and issues. Although there are many legal newsletters, two of the best are offered by FindLaw (subscribe to a weekly IP newsletter at http://newsletters.findlaw.com/nl) and GigaLaw.com (subscribe to a daily e-mail newsletter at http://www.gigalaw.com).

wishing to incorporate others' material by framing. However, those challenged with infringement or other intellectual property violations on the Internet should strongly consider asserting that their acts are protected by the First Amendment. In sum, liability for linking and framing rests on where the linking leads, the content of the linked or framed site, and the likelihood of consumer confusion.

OTHER CYBERSPACE TRADEMARK ISSUES

Asserting Jurisdiction over Web Site Owners

One of the questions that has troubled courts over the past several years is whether by operating a Web site accessible in all 50 states, a Web site operator becomes subject to the jurisdiction of courts in each state such that it can be sued in that state. In general, a state can only subject a party to personal jurisdiction if the party has had some minimum contacts with the state such that subjecting him or her to jurisdiction does not offend traditional notions of justice. Thus, for example, a company doing business only in Atlanta cannot be sued in Boston.

The most recent analyses of this issue typically use a sliding scale approach in determining whether jurisdiction can be asserted over a nonresident defendant. At one end of the spectrum, if a party merely posts information or advertises its products and services on a passive Web site, jurisdiction cannot be exercised over a nonresident defendant. At the other end of the spectrum, if the defendant is actively conducting business or entering into contracts, jurisdiction can likely be exercised. The middle ground, in which a Web site owner engages only in some limited interaction with users, is closely scrutinized by courts to determine the specific nature of the interactions. If interaction is significant, jurisdiction can be imposed. *Zippo Mfg. Co. v. Zippo Dot Com, Inc.*, 952 F.Supp.1119 (W.D. Pa. 1997).

Thus, once a defendant "purposefully avails" itself of the privilege of conducting business in the forum state by directly targeting its Web site or electronic activity into the state, knowingly interacting with residents of the forum state via its Web site or with the intent of engaging in business or other interactions in the state, or through sufficient other related contacts, personal jurisdiction may be imposed.

Clandestine Trademark Misuse, Metatags, Keying, and Phishing

Another area of growing concern is that of clandestine trademark abuse. This involves embedding a trademark into a Web site such that it is not visible to the viewer. The search engine, however, registers the presence of the hidden or clandestine trademark and lures the viewer to another Web site, generally that of a competitor. The practice is usually accomplished by the use of "metatags," which are special codes whose function is to emphasize key words, making it easier for search engines to locate the Web site.

In *Playboy Enterprises, Inc. v. Welles*, 279 F.3d 796 (9th Cir. 2002), the defendant, a former Playboy Playmate of the Year, used the plaintiff's registered trademarks PLAYBOY® and PLAYMATE OF THE YEAR® on her Web site both visibly and invisibly through the use of metatags that drew visitors to her site when they entered the term "playboy" into a search engine. The court held that the plaintiff's registered trademarks were being used merely to describe the defendant in an accurate fashion. Because the defendant did not suggest that Playboy Enterprises sponsored or endorsed her, such use was acceptable; however, the court cautioned that its decision might be different if the metatags were so numerous that the defendant's Web site would appear before Playboy Enterprises' in searches. While allowing the metatags, the court refused to allow Welles to use the plaintiff's marks as "wallpaper," or background content on her site, because there was no descriptive purpose for such use.

Many cases dealing with cutting-edge issues relating to use of trademarks on the Internet consider whether a party uses another's trademark in a manner calculated to cause initial interest confusion (attracting another's potential customers by misleading use of a trademark). Diversion of consumers' initial interest is actionable under the Lanham Act (whether or not an actual sale is made). Thus, when one party placed another's trademark in the metatags of its Web site thereby creating initial interest confusion (and not merely using the mark in a fair use or purely descriptive manner), trademark infringement was found. *Brookfield Commc'ns, Inc. v. W. Coast Entm't Corp.*, 174 F.3d 1039 (9th Cir. 1995).

Perhaps the most recent issue relating to Internet trademark use relates to **keying,** an advertising practice in which a preselected banner ad pops up when certain search terms are used. For example, in yet another case involving Playboy Enterprises, when a searcher entered "playboy" as a search term, banner ads for pornography companies were displayed. The court held that such a practice (called "keying" because the banner ad that appears is matched to certain "key" search words) was acceptable and was similar to a store selling one name-brand perfume on the shelf next to another. *Playboy Enters., Inc. v. Excite, Inc.*, 55 F. Supp. 2d 1070 (C.D. Cal. 1999). Some experts believe the case is somewhat narrow and hinges on the fact that "playboy" is a common word in the English language. Thus, the ruling may not be applicable if a coined trademark such as KODAK® were used to stimulate pop-up ads.

In sum, use of another's trademark in a metatag can constitute infringement if the use is not a fair use or a merely descriptive use and is likely to cause confusion or initial interest confusion (purposefully steering or diverting potential customers away).

Keyword advertising occurs when companies pay to have their ads displayed when a computer user performs a search for a particular product name or word, including the name of a competitor. Cases considering the issue generally hinge on their particular facts; however, it is clear that keyword advertising that causes consumer confusion can constitute trademark infringement.

Trademark owners have also sued for trademark infringement when pop-up ads of their competitors appear on a user's computer screen when the user accesses the trademark owner's Web site. Courts have generally held that these pop-up ads do not constitute trademark infringement for two reasons: there is no use of the trademark owner's mark (because it is not displayed as part of the pop-up ads) and the situation is similar to a store's placement of its own generic products next to trademarked products to induce consumers to consider the store's less expensive product.

Another new trademark issue raised by the Internet relates to **phishing,** the act of using sophisticated lures to "fish" for sensitive financial information by e-mails or Web sites. For example, you may receive a legitimate-looking e-mail from what purports to be a bank, displaying an accurate reproduction of the bank's logo or trademark, notifying you that your account has been breached and asking you to verify your account number. If you "bite," the phisher has your account number and may steal your identity. Because these schemes fraudulently use others' trademarks in a manner likely to cause deception or confusion, they are acts of trademark infringement. Because it is difficult to determine the identity of the phishers (especially if they are offshore), most financial institutions rely on educating their customers not to respond to such requests for financial or sensitive information. The database Whois (http://www.whois.net) may supply some information about the party hosting the originating e-mail site.

In sum, domain-name decisions, linking and framing decisions, and keyword, pop-up advertising, and phishing decisions rely on well-established trademark principles: If the defendant's conduct constitutes use in commerce and is likely to cause consumer confusion, infringement may be as readily found in cyberspace as in a conventional setting.

Trademark Policing on the Internet

Although many companies conduct annual or periodic audits and searches to review possible conflicting marks, the proliferation of use of marks and domains on the Internet adds yet another level of complexity to a trademark owner's duty to monitor and protect its marks. Many search companies review lists or databases of domain names, but further investigation may be called for due to the use of hyperlinking and embedded use of marks on others' sites. To access information about registered domains, go to http://www.whois.net, which provides information about parties who register domain names, host Web sites, or provide connectivity to sites. Another company, Markwatch (http://www.markwatch.com) provides Internet monitoring services, blog tracking, and monitoring of eBay auctions.

While most search engines (such as Google and Yahoo!) can search only for words or text, new software tools claim they can "see" images and logos in order to locate infringing uses of design marks. Finally, a company called Cyveillance Inc. (http://www.cyveillance.com) will scour the Internet looking for false and defamatory statements made about companies and their trademarked products as well as protect against phishing schemes and counterfeiting.

In addition to disclosing potential conflicts, periodic monitoring will reveal deadwood domains, namely, those not in actual use, so they may then be applied for and used by others. Although monitoring is well advised, no court has yet required trademark owners to constantly scour the Internet looking for offending trademark uses.

Internet Complaint Sites

Irate consumers have frequently set up their own Web sites, often called gripe sites, to complain about certain products or services. In one case, Bally Total Fitness claimed that its BALLY® mark was infringed by a defendant's "Bally Sucks" Web site. The court held there was no infringement because consumers would not be confused in as much as the addition of the word *sucks* clearly distinguished the defendant's site from Bally's registered mark. The court also held that the Web site did not dilute Bally's mark in as much as the defendant's use was not commercial, and the federal dilution statute was not intended to prohibit noncommercial expression such as parody and satire. There was no tarnishment because the defendant's use was consumer commentary. *Bally Total Fitness Holding Corp. v. Faber*, 29 F. Supp. 2d 1161 (C.D. Cal. 1998). Thus, the use of another's mark on a Web site to complain about a product or service is permissible as long as there is no consumer confusion, the remarks are protected parody or noncommercial expression, and the content is neither false nor defamatory. Visitors to the site should know at a glance that the site is a criticism page. If so, the site is likely protected so long as it doesn't tarnish another's mark by associating it with unsavory activity such as sexual conduct or drug use.

Some gripe sites include links to competitors. Although this may render the use "commercial," generally a likelihood of confusion cannot be found because no reasonable viewer would believe that the company "griped about" would endorse such a site or message. Nevertheless, if the gripe site is used to deceive others into believing they are accessing a plaintiff's site or causes initial interest confusion, such transforms otherwise protected speech into commercial speech. There is no right to confuse viewers into thinking they are entering the target's site. In sum, only legitimate, noncommercial speech is protected.

If it can be shown that actual harm has occurred from cyber-slander, judges often order Internet service providers to divulge the identity of the "speaker." Unless such harm is shown, the identity of Internet users is generally confidential. Otherwise, valid criticism and free speech would be chilled.

Trivia

- The first lawsuit brought under ACPA was filed by actor Brad Pitt against two domain name holders. Mr. Pitt was successful.
- J. Crew International Inc. won a decision under the UDRP after an individual registered "crew.com" and attempted to sell it to J. Crew. Other successful complainants include NASDAQ, Madonna, Tom Cruise, and Spike Lee.
- A federal court has held that an Internet domain name registrar cannot be sued for civil rights violations for refusing to register domain names that included obscene terms.
- By mid-2005 Internet users had registered more than 76 million domain names.
- In October 2006, WIPO handled its 25,000th domain name dispute.
- Sales of 5,851 domain names generated $29 million in 2005.
- "Dot com" is the most popular domain suffix.

CHAPTER SUMMARY

The Internet has dramatically changed communication. Along with that change, however, has come conflict over use of domain names and trademarks. The assignment of domain names, or Internet addresses, has resulted in disputes between the owners of domain names and the owners of trademarks. Courts have protected the rights of trademark owners against "cybersquatters," those who register domain names in bad faith, for example, for the purpose of selling them to their rightful owners rather than for some bona fide use or purpose.

If a dispute arises between parties claiming rights to domain names, the aggrieved owner has a variety of avenues in which to pursue relief. Under the new Anticybersquatting Consumer Protection Act, money damages can be obtained in court. Under the Uniform Domain Name Dispute Resolution Policy, a streamlined and inexpensive process, a panel can cancel an abusive domain name or order it transferred to its rightful owner.

Use of the Internet also implicates First Amendment rights to freedom of speech. At present, courts have held that merely providing links to another party's Web site is permissible. Deep linking (allowing a party to bypass a home page and proceed directly to relevant material) by itself (i.e., without confusion of source) is likely permissible, as is the use of a metatag or "hidden" mark or message used in a descriptive manner or fair use. If such use is likely to cause confusion, infringement may be found. Using another's trademark in a phishing scheme, designed to obtain personal information from Web users, is actionable. Merely having a passive presence or Web site on the Internet will likely not subject a party to personal jurisdiction; however, if goods are offered for sale or contracts are entered into through a Web site, a court may subject the Web site owner to personal jurisdiction. Finally, use of another's mark on a noncommercial Web site for the purposes of satire, parody, or consumer commentary is likely permissible as long as there is no likelihood of confusion.

CASE ILLUSTRATION—INTERNET GRIPE SITES

Case: *Bihari v. Gross*, 119 F. Supp. 2d 309 (S.D.N.Y. 2000)

Facts: After a dispute with the plaintiff, an interior designer doing business as "Bihari Interiors," the defendant set up a number of Web sites, all of which used "bihari interiors" as metatags and all of which were critical of the plaintiff's design services. These sites included hyperlinks to other sites offering services competing with those of the plaintiff. The plaintiff sued for trademark infringement.

Holding: Defendant's use of hyperlinks to other sites transformed otherwise protected speech into commercial speech and constituted commercial use of a mark. Nevertheless, there was no likelihood of confusion and thus no trademark infringement because no reasonable viewer would believe that the criticism was sponsored by the plaintiff. As to whether there was initial interest confusion, the court held that the defendant's use of metatags was not a bad faith attempt to trick users into visiting his Web site and divert them from the plaintiff. Far from diverting people looking for information on Bihari Interiors, the defendant's Web sites provided users with information about Bihari Interiors. Prohibiting the use of "Bihari Interiors" in the metatags of any Web sites not sponsored by Bihari would effectively foreclose all comment about Bihari Interiors, including fair comment. Courts must be particularly cautious of overextending the reach of the Lanham Act and intruding on First Amendment values.

CASE STUDY AND ACTIVITIES

Case Study.   Vision, the owner of the registered trademarks VISION QUEST® for hotel services and VISION® for a variety of goods and services (and the owner of the domain name www. vision.com) recently discovered that Bob Russell has registered the domain name

CASE STUDY AND ACTIVITIES (CONT'D)

www.vizion.com for gambling-related activities and that an eye-care center has registered www.vision.net for its services. Russell has made a significant amount of money from visitors or "hits" to his site, and he has offered to sell the domain name www.vizion.com to Vision for $45,000. Vision's own Web site allows prospective vacationers to make hotel reservations at any of Vision's hotels and resorts. Finally, Vision has a link on its Web site to www.pga.com so prospective golfers can obtain information about golf handicaps and equipment.

Activities.   What should Watson do, if anything, to protect its mark from Russell and the eye-care center? What practice has Russell engaged in? May Vision bring an action against the eye-care center under ACPA? Finally, discuss the permissibility of Vision's link and whether Vision can be sued throughout the United States.

ROLE OF PARALEGAL

Paralegals can assist in enhancing protection for trademark owners in a variety of ways:

- monitoring new developments in cyberspace by reading articles of interest and visiting Web sites devoted to areas of trademark concern;
- filing applications for domain name registrations;
- assisting in periodic audits or reviews of uses of conflicting marks in cyberspace;
- reviewing sites of the competitors of clients for embedded marks; and
- checking links from and to clients' Web sites to ensure that neither the clients' nor third parties' marks are being infringed.

INTERNET RESOURCES

WIPO:	http://www.wipo.int (site of World Intellectual Property Organization, offering information and statistics about proceedings under the UDRP)
ICANN:	http://www.icann.org (site of Internet Corporation for Assigned Names and Numbers, offering information about domain name registration and the full text of the UDRP)
Information on Internet and First Amendment–related issues:	http://www.chillingeffects.com (site devoted to examining issues relating to trademark use and the First Amendment and offering sample cease and desist letters and general information

about issues such as deep linking and the use
of metatags)
http://ww w.citizen.org/litigation (site offering
information on Internet free speech and gripe
sites)

DISCUSSION QUESTIONS

1. Ann operates a Web site in California that provides information about her gift baskets. Gift baskets cannot be ordered through the site, but the site shows pictures of the baskets and allows viewers to send comments and suggestions to Ann. May Ann be sued in Missouri? Discuss.

2. Dan is unhappy with the service he received from Roto-Rooter Corporation, and has established a domain name called www.rotorooterscam.com. The Web site offers critical commentary about Roto-Rooter and asks users to submit their opinions about Roto-Rooter. Is Roto-Rooter, the owner of a federal registration for ROTO ROOTER® likely to prevail in a trademark infringement case? In a suit brought under ACPA? Discuss. What if Dan used the site to promote his own drain and plumbing services? Discuss.

3. Your firm's client, Marriott International, Inc. has received complaints from customers that its Web site is pornographic. In investigating the issue, Marriott discovered that several misspellings of its name (for example, Mariott or Marriot) lead users to unsavory Web sites. The person who registered the domain names, Phil, has offered to sell the domains to Marriott. What is this practice called? What is the most efficient avenue for Marriott to pursue to obtain rights to these sites? Is the registrar of the site liable to Marriott? Why or why not?

4. Your firm's client, Toys R Us, Inc., has discovered a Web site www.adultsrus.com that provides pornographic pictures. What type of action might Toys R Us bring against the operator of the site?

5. Your firm's client, Bank of America, recently discovered that its customers have been receiving e-mails that display Bank of America's trademark and logo and that inform customers that the bank needs to verify their account status and ask for account numbers. What is this practice called? Will an action for trademark infringement lie? Discuss.

6. Your firm's client King Corp. is a well-known real estate company in your locality. When King Corp. attempted to register the domain name www.King.com, it discovered that an individual in New York, Jenna King, who operates King Design Services, Inc. had already registered www.King.com. Will King Corp. be successful in attempting to recover the name www.King.com? Discuss.

USING INTERNET RESOURCES

1. Access the Web site for Whois and locate information about the Web site http://www. paralegals.org.
   a. Who is the registrant?
   b. Who is the sponsoring registrar?
   c. When will the domain name expire?

USING INTERNET RESOURCES (CONT'D)

2. Access WIPO's site, and review its index of UDRP Panel Decision. Locate the cases relating to individuals, specifically individuals in the entertainment industry. Locate Case D2006-0402.

   a. What domain name was involved?

   b. Who was the complainant?

   c. Review paragraph 7 of the decision. What were the three results or conclusions reached by the panel?

3. Locate California Business & Professions Code § 22948. What is the name of this statute? Review § 22948.3. What remedy is a trademark owner who is damaged by a violation of this section entitled to?

4. Access ICANN's Web site and locate the Uniform Domain Name Dispute Resolution Policy. What does Section 4(i) provide?

For additional resources, go to www.paralegal.delmar.cengage.com.

Chapter 8

International Trademark Law

CHAPTER OVERVIEW

Foreign nationals who wish to offer their products and services under a trademark or service mark in the United States can seek registration under the Lanham Act. While foreign applicants can seek federal registration on the same bases as U.S. applicants, namely, based on actual use of a mark in commerce, or based on a bona fide intent to use the mark in commerce, two additional bases are available. First, the foreign applicant may apply for registration of a mark in the United States based on a pending application in a foreign country, and if the application was filed in the foreign country within the previous six months, the applicant will be able to use the earlier filing date as its priority date in the United States. Second, the applicant may apply for registration of a mark in the United States based upon a registration issued by a foreign country. The advantage of using either of these latter two bases for registration is that neither requires use in commerce, thus allowing foreign applicants to secure federal registrations for marks that are not in use in commerce in the United States.

Just as foreign nationals may apply for trademark protection in the United States, U.S. trademark owners should give serious consideration to protecting their marks in foreign countries. Because the trademark laws of various foreign countries are complex and often rapidly changing, most U.S. law firms work in tandem with attorneys in the foreign countries who will prosecute the application on behalf of the U.S. trademark owner. The priority date afforded to foreign applicants in the United States is also available to U.S. trademark owners who wish to seek trademark protection in various foreign countries. If the foreign application is filed within six months of the U.S. application, it will retain the earlier filing date for priority purposes.

A new system, called the Community Trademark System, allows U.S. trademark owners to file one single application for the member nations of the European Union, thereby saving considerable time, effort, and money.

Similarly, the Madrid Protocol, an international treaty, allows a trademark owner to seek registration in any of the more than 70 countries that are members of the Madrid Protocol by filing a single application.

U.S. trademark owners who are considering foreign expansion should consider filing trademark applications in the countries in which they intend to do business to protect their marks and to ensure their marks are not "pirated" by unscrupulous third parties who register marks owned by others and then attempt to sell the marks to the rightful owners.

APPLICATIONS IN THE UNITED STATES BASED ON FOREIGN APPLICATIONS AND REGISTRATIONS

As discussed in chapter 4, in the United States, application for federal registration of trademarks can be made by anyone based on actual use of the mark or a bona fide intent to use the mark in commerce in the future. In addition to these bases, the United States has assumed certain obligations under international agreements in the trademark field, principally the Paris Convention for the Protection of Industrial Property of 1883, briefly mentioned in chapter 1. The Paris Convention seeks to afford citizens of each member nation protection against unfair competition and trademark infringement and requires that member nations provide the same trademark protection to citizens of other member nations as they do for their own citizens. More than 170 countries are member nations of the Paris Convention, including Canada, Mexico, most of South America, Europe, and many African and Asian countries. (See Appendix A for a table of treaties and identification of members of the Paris Convention.)

Section 44 of the Lanham Act (15 U.S.C. § 1126) implements these agreements. Section 44 provides significant benefits to any person whose country of origin is a party to a treaty relating to trademarks to which the United States is also a party by allowing the party to file an application for registration of a trademark with the USPTO based upon one or both of the following.

- The applicant filed an *application* in his or her country of origin or a member nation within the previous six months and has a bona fide intent to use the mark in the United States (called a **Section 44(d) application** after section 44(d) of the Lanham Act).
- The application in the United States is based upon a *registration* already secured in the applicant's country of origin or in a member nation and the applicant has a bona fide intent to use the mark in the United States (called a **Section 44(e) application**).

One of the significant benefits of the Section 44(d) application is that it affords the applicant a priority filing date; that is, if the applicant files an application in the United States within six months after filing the application in the foreign country, the applicant's priority date in the United States will relate back to the earlier foreign filing date. For example, if Compagnie Le Chat of France files an application in France on March 1, 2007, and files an application under section 44(d) with the USPTO anytime before September 1, 2007, the critical date for determining Compagnie Le Chat's priority in the United States with regard to conflicting marks is the foreign filing date of March 1, 2007.

A significant benefit of the Section 44(e) application is that it allows those who have secured registrations in a member nation to use that registration as a basis for securing a U.S. registration *even if the mark has not been used in the United States*. The U.S. principle is that the *first to use* a trademark has rights, while most foreign countries provide that the *first to register* a trademark has rights. Thus, many foreign countries allow registration of marks even though the marks have not been used. Once a registration is secured in the foreign country, it may then serve as a basis for securing a U.S. registration, with no use whatsoever of the mark anywhere in the world (although an intent to use the mark in commerce must be alleged to ensure marks are not warehoused). In this way, foreign applicants receive more favorable treatment than U.S. applicants who can never secure a U.S. registration without a showing of use in commerce. All applicants under section 44, however, must verify that they have a bona fide intent to use the mark in commerce in the United States.

Contents of Applications Made under Section 44

Applications made under section 44 must comply with a variety of requirements, some of which are identical to those imposed on other applications and some of which are in addition to those imposed on other applications. One additional requirement is that an applicant who relies on a foreign application under section 44(d) must specifically assert its claim of priority by stating either in the application or before the end of the priority period, "Applicant has a bona fide intention to use the mark in commerce on or in connection with the above-identified goods/ services, and asserts a claim of priority based upon a foreign application in accordance with 15 U.S.C. § 1126(d), as amended. The application was filed in [country] on [date] and was assigned the serial number [application filing or serial number]."

An applicant who relies on an existing foreign registration under section 44(e) must submit a certified copy of the foreign registration during the prosecution process and state in the application, "Applicant has a bona fide intention to use the mark in commerce on or in connection with the above-identified goods/services and will submit a certification or certified copy of a foreign registration in accordance with 15 U.S.C. § 1126(e), as amended. The mark was registered in [country] on [date] and was assigned the registration number [registration number]." Typically, a certified copy of the foreign registration (not merely a photocopy) must be submitted before the USPTO will issue a registration. If the foreign registration is not in English, a translation must be provided together with a signature by the translator.

Applications filed under section 44 (for applicants not domiciled in the United States) may also include a "Designation of Domestic Representative," which designates some person in the United States, typically a law firm, as the **domestic representative** to whom the USPTO can direct notices and correspondence regarding the mark. (See Exhibit 8–1.) In many instances, law firms in the United States have developed relationships with law firms in foreign countries, generally referred to as "foreign associates." Each firm sends applications and business to the other to assist its own clients in securing trademark protection in foreign countries. Because U.S. lawyers are not experts in the trademark laws and procedures of foreign nations, these relationships allow U.S. law firms to refer business to respected attorneys in other countries. Similarly, the U.S. law firms usually expect that the foreign associates will refer trademark matters to them as well. The Trademark Data Sheet found in Exhibit 3–1 that is used to gather information from domestic applicants can be easily modified to gather information from foreign clients who wish to register their marks.

Applicants under section 44 must submit a drawing of the mark applied for in the United States, just as is required of other applicants, and the drawing must conform to the drawing shown in the foreign application or registration. Applicants under section 44 also must identify the goods and services applied for and specify the international class for the goods or services. Many foreign countries allow applicants to claim all goods in an entire class or allow broad identifications of goods (such as "computer goods in I.C. 9"), but that would not be permissible in the United States, and the examining attorney at the USPTO may request a more specific identification in accordance with general USPTO policy. Because an application filed under section 44 does not require use of the mark in commerce, such an application will generally not state a date of first use. Similarly, because the mark need not be in use, specimens are not usually filed with the applications.

EXHIBIT 8–1
Designation of Domestic
Representative

The law firm of Bailey & Bailey, L.L.P., 4890 Terrace Place, Minneapolis, MN 09847, is designated the Applicant's representative upon whom notices or process in proceedings affecting the mark may be served, and all prior appointments in connection herewith are hereby revoked.

MAISON BLANC, L.C. of the
United Kingdom _____

By: _____

Title: _____

Date: _____

Examination of Applications Made under Section 44

Although applications made under section 44(d) (based upon a pending application in a member nation) and section 44(e) (based upon an existing registration in a member nation) are exempt from the actual use requirements of the Lanham Act, they must meet all other requirements for registration set forth in the Lanham Act. Securing registration in the country of origin does not guarantee registration in the United States because section 44 applications are subject to the same review as other applications and may be refused on the basis they are scandalous or immoral, merely descriptive, or confusingly similar to a registered mark or a mark in a pending application. Office actions may be issued and must be responded to in six months, just as is required for other applications. If a mark that is the subject of a section 44 application is refused registration on the basis that it is merely descriptive, the section 44 applicant may assert (just as its U.S. counterpart would) that the mark has acquired distinctiveness or secondary meaning through its long-standing and continuous use such that consumers, upon encountering the mark, recognize it as the applicant's mark and have come to associate the mark with the applicant. However, such a claim of acquired distinctiveness must be based upon use in commerce in the United States; the applicant may not rely on use solely in

a foreign country to show the mark has acquired such distinctiveness or secondary meaning that it is not merely descriptive.

For applications filed under section 44(d) (based upon a pending foreign application), the applicant will eventually be required to submit a certified copy of the resulting registration issued by the foreign country before the mark can be published in the *Official Gazette* and then registered by the USPTO. A translation may be necessary if the registration is in a foreign language. If the foreign application is subject to delays, the USPTO may suspend action on the U.S. application until the foreign registration is issued. The USPTO generally requires that the applicant submit written status reports every six months informing the USPTO of the status of the pending application and when registration in the foreign country is expected. Failure to respond will result in abandonment of the U.S. application.

Registration of Marks Applied for under Section 44

After publication of the mark in the *Official Gazette*, and assuming there is no opposition made to registration of the mark, the mark will proceed to registration. Once issued, the U.S. registration exists independently of the underlying foreign application or registration and is subject to all provisions of the Lanham Act that apply to all other registrations, such as affidavits of use, renewals, assignments, and similar matters. Thus, although the applicant need not have actually used its mark in the United States to obtain a U.S. registration, actual use must occur thereafter because the Section 8 affidavit (due between the fifth and sixth years after registration and every 10 years) must verify that the mark is in use in commerce in the United States. When submitting any other documents, the foreign applicant or registrant should designate a domestic representative in the United States upon whom notices and documents affecting the mark may be served (see Exhibit 8–1).

SECURING TRADEMARK PROTECTION IN FOREIGN COUNTRIES

Introduction

The globalization of the world economy and ever-expanding markets in other countries for goods and services from the United States has made trademark protection abroad an increasing interest of many U.S. companies. In many instances, a vital part of a company's market strategy includes penetration of foreign markets with a concomitant need to protect the trademarks and service marks under which goods and services will be offered. Similarly, a trademark owner may need to consider registering its marks in countries in which trademark piracy is common so that if and when it decides to enter a foreign market, its name is available to it.

One of the first treaties or "conventions" designed to address trademark protection in foreign countries was the Paris Convention of 1883, adopted to facilitate international patent and trademark protection. The Paris Convention is based on the principle of reciprocity so that foreign trademark owners may obtain in member countries the same legal protection for their marks as can citizens of those member countries.

Perhaps the most significant benefit provided by the Paris Convention is that of priority. An applicant for a trademark has six months after filing an application in a member nation to file a corresponding application in other member countries and obtain the benefits of the first filing date. The text of the Paris Convention is available at http://www.wipo.int.

Initial Considerations

Once a decision has been made to adopt a mark, consideration should be given to whether the mark should be applied for in any foreign countries. One of the first factors to consider is the meaning of the mark in various foreign languages. One of the classic international trademark stories is that of Chevrolet's adoption of the mark NOVA in various foreign countries for a compact car. While NOVA connotes "new" or perhaps "star" in English, the literal translation in Spanish of "no va" is "it does not go," immediately dooming the product to ridicule or failure. Thus, if a trademark owner intends to "go global," the assistance of trademark experts in foreign countries is necessary even before a mark is adopted to ensure the mark's translation into the respective foreign language is acceptable.

Once a mark, or perhaps several alternatives, has been selected, international searches should be conducted. Although the search companies identified in chapter 3 are capable of conducting extensive international searches, many law firms prefer to ask their foreign associates to conduct the search, believing they are most capable of reviewing the results, interpreting the results of the search, and providing an opinion regarding availability of the mark for registration. Once again, the relationships between U.S. trademark counsel and their foreign counterparts can be long-standing and intimate. Some trademark firms have established relationships with foreign law firms that date back for several generations and are based on mutual respect and business interests.

ETHICS EDGE: Working with Foreign Associates

Paralegals must always ensure that those with whom they work understand that they are not attorneys. To ensure that foreign associates/counsel (who may not be familiar with law firm position titles) understand your role and position, make sure that all of your correspondence is clearly marked not only with your name but your position. Signing documents as "Marissa Peters, Paralegal to Hillary Parks" should be sufficient to clarify that you are a paralegal and not an attorney.

The Foreign Application

Just as foreign applicants can file an application with the USPTO and claim priority based on a pending foreign application, so too can U.S. applicants claim such benefits afforded by the Paris Convention. Therefore, upon filing an application for a client, many U.S. law firms confirm the filing particulars and inform the client that if protection for the mark is desired in any foreign country, such a decision should be made within six months from the USPTO filing date in order to claim priority in the member nation and secure the benefit of the earlier U.S. filing date. (See Exhibit 8–2.) Similarly, just as foreign applicants can use a foreign registration as a filing basis in the United States, U.S. companies can use registrations issued by the USPTO as a basis to secure registration of marks in any of the more than 170 member nations of the Paris Convention.

Trademark owners who are considering global expansion should file trademark applications in any countries in which they anticipate they may do business. Because most countries do not require that a mark be in use to be registered, filing applications in foreign countries allows U.S. trademark owners to protect their marks in anticipation of future expansion and may deter others from using similar marks for similar goods or services. In many countries, because use is not required to secure a registration, third parties often attempt to register marks in anticipation of the entrance of a trademark owner. These "trade-

mark pirates" then attempt to sell the marks to their true owners. Alternatively, pirates register copycat marks, such as registrations secured for "Pizza Hot" and "Sharaton Hotels" in Cambodia. Thus, filing applications in foreign countries preempts trademark piracy and reserves the mark for its rightful owner. Recently, the United States has been pressing its trading partners to strengthen their laws to prevent such acts of piracy and provide stronger protection to the intellectual property rights of U.S. citizens.

The progress of an application filed in a foreign country varies dramatically based upon the country. Some countries have an expeditious procedure, and others take several years. A few countries do not yet recognize service marks. Therefore, if a client is engaged in hotel or restaurant services, rather than forego the opportunity to secure any trademark protection in such a country, the owner may seek registration in I.C. 16 for its printed matter, menus, and brochures relating to the hotel or restaurant services. Some countries, such as Saudi Arabia, have nearly prohibitive filing fees. Others, such as Italy, have more reasonable fees but take nearly three years to process the application. Searching can be speculative inasmuch as some countries lack sophisticated databases and are unable to search for phonetic equivalents of marks and the like. Just as learning the rules and processes of the USPTO requires patience and determination, learning the vagaries of international trademark offices requires the same. In almost

EXHIBIT 8–2
Letter to Client Advising
of Foreign Priority Date

March 30, 20xx
Mr. John R. Taylor
Vision Corp.
885 Third Avenue, 24th Floor
New York, NY 10022

Re: Mark: VACATION WITH VISION
     Serial No.: 79/034,598
     Filing Date: January 3, 20xx

Dear Mr. Taylor:

We are pleased to enclose the official filing receipt issued by the United States Patent and Trademark Office (USPTO) in connection with the application filed for VACATION WITH VISION on January 3, 20xx. We have reviewed the official filing receipt and it appears to be correct; however, if you notice any errors, please inform us so we can ensure the USPTO records are corrected.

In view of the backlog of applications at the USPTO, no action in connection with this application should be expected for approximately four to six months.

If protection for this mark is desired in any foreign country, or if you plan to expand your business and offer products and services in any foreign country, please notify us immediately. In many countries, it is possible to obtain the benefit of the U.S. application's filing date if the foreign application is filed within six months of the U.S. filing date. In your case, applications in foreign countries must be filed by July 3, 20xx in order to claim priority.

We will continue to keep you informed of any further developments in connection with this application.

Sincerely,

David N. Bailey
Bailey & Bailey, L.L.P.

all instances, the services of reputable foreign counsel should be retained. To locate counsel with experience in trademark matters, consult *Martindale-Hubbell Law Directory,* which provides information and biographical sketches of foreign counsel, or contact the International Trademark Association (INTA), an association of approximately 5,000 trademark owners and practitioners from all over the world, at http://www.inta.org.

The nature and type of examination of an application pending before a foreign trademark office vary greatly, with some countries subjecting the mark to strict scrutiny and issuing refusals similar to the office actions issued by the USPTO, while other countries merely review the form of

the application and then issue a registration unless there is a prior identical mark or nearly identical mark. Registrations are usually valid for 10 years and may be renewed for like periods. Proof of use often must be submitted after the third or fifth year of registration in many foreign countries. If use is not proved, the registration will be canceled, similar to the U.S. practice of canceling registrations if the Section 8 affidavit of continued use is not submitted between the fifth and sixth years and every 10 years after registration.

If the owner of a foreign trademark registration allows or licenses another to use the registered mark, many countries require that a **registered user agreement** be filed with the foreign trademark office, providing information about the owner of the mark, the licensee, and various other license terms. Recall from chapter 5 that in the United States licensing arrangements are viewed as private agreements between the concerned parties, and are therefore seldom recorded with the SPTO.

The European Community Trademark

In 1996, a new **Community Trademark (CTM) System** was established by the then 15 member countries of the European Union (Austria, Belgium, Denmark, Finland, France, Germany, Greece, Ireland, Italy, Luxembourg, Netherlands, Portugal, Spain, Sweden, and the United Kingdom). The new system makes it possible for an applicant to file an application for one trademark or service mark that can be protected in each of the member countries of the **European Union (EU).** A single application in a single language may cover any number of classes of goods or services, although the initial fee (900 euros) covers up to only three classes of goods/services. The CTM blanket application covering the member nations of the EU (a market of more than 480 million consumers) provides significant protection at a considerable savings over filing separate applications in the member nations. Consistent with the philosophy of many foreign countries, actual use is not required to secure a registration. The CTM System does not replace the trademark offices in the member nations but coexists with them.

The primary European trademark office for the filing of the CTM application is the Office for Harmonization in the Internal Market, located in Alicante, Spain. An application may, however, also be filed with any one of the national offices of the European Union countries or in the Benelux trademark office, in which case it will then be transmitted to Alicante for prosecution. There is no requirement to be domiciled in any EU member nation or to have actually used the mark anywhere in order to file a CTM application.

Another distinct advantage to the new CTM application is that there is no need to perform a search prior to filing the application. An examining attorney at the central office in Alicante, Spain, is charged with the responsibility of clearing the mark in each of the member countries, providing additional savings of time and money. After examination, the mark will be published for opposition purposes. If there is no opposition, the mark will proceed to registration. Once registered, the CTM registration is valid for 10 years from the date of filing and may be renewed for successive 10-year periods by filing one renewal application that keeps the registration in force in all member countries. Although the mark need not be in use in order to be registered, it must be in use by five years after registration to avoid cancellation by a third party; however, use in any member country constitutes use of the mark for all member countries.

Among the advantages afforded by the CTM System are the following:

- An attractive fee structure is provided, both in terms of the official fees and the reduction in the number of trademark attorneys required.
- The unitary filing simplifies licensing or assigning the mark.
- A single infringement action may be brought to cover all countries in the European Union, and a decision is enforceable in all EU countries.
- Priority can be claimed in the CTM application if another trademark application was filed within the previous six months in a member nation of the Paris Convention, allowing the CTM application to capture the earlier priority date.
- Protection of a mark is possible throughout all of the EU countries that may not have previously been possible due to some countries' strict examination of marks (e.g., surnames are considered to be *prima facie* distinctive in a CTM application, while these are generally refused registration in the Scandinavian countries).

- Use in any one of the member nations of the EU constitutes use of the mark for all member countries and will protect a CTM registration throughout the EU against cancellation of a registration due to nonuse of a mark.
- A user-friendly filing system allows applications to be filed by facsimile or electronically (in which case, fees are reduced).

A disadvantage of the CTM System is that a CTM application can be refused if a ground for refusal exists in just one member country or if a confusingly similar or identical registration already exists in any one member country. In such a case, the CTM application fails completely, in an all-or-nothing scenario. As a safety net, however, a party may then convert the CTM application into separately filed applications in the desired countries. The converted applications have the same filing date as the earlier-filed CTM application.

Notwithstanding any disadvantages, in just the short period of time since the CTM System was established, it has proven to be enormously successful, and more than 50,000 CTM System applications are filed each year.

The EU enlarged its membership and accepted 10 new member states in mid-2004 (Cyprus, Czech Republic, Estonia, Hungary, Latvia, Lithuania, Malta, Poland, Slovakia, and Slovenia), and two more in 2007 (Bulgaria and Romania). Negotiations with Turkey, Croatia, and the Republic of Macedonia are in process. If a party had a CTM registration in force at the time of enlargement, protection was automatically extended to the territories of the new member states.

In sum, the CTM System allows a trademark owner to achieve uniform trademark protection in all 27 member countries of the EU by filing only one trademark application. A single filing fee, one application, one registration, one renewal, and simplified use and licensing requirements make the CTM System an attractive way to achieve significant protection for a trademark throughout the EU.

The Madrid Protocol

In April 1996, the Madrid Protocol came into existence at the instigation of the World Intellectual Property Organization (WIPO), allowing trademark protection for more than 30 countries and all of the European Union countries by a single trademark application. The United States became a party to the Madrid Protocol in late 2003.

Under the Protocol, the owner of a mark that is registered or applied for with the USPTO can file a single trademark application (usually called an international application) in a single language with a single set of fees with the USPTO designating in which of the more than 70 Madrid Protocol countries it desires protection. Applications may be filed on paper or electronically. The international application may claim priority rights under the Paris Convention if it is filed within six months of the underlying application. The USPTO then certifies and forwards the application to WIPO's offices in Geneva, which conducts a review of the application to ensure it complies with certain formalities. WIPO then publishes the mark and transmits the application to each country designated in the application. Each country conducts a substantive examination of the application, and each has the independent right to refuse protection. When registered, the international registration under the Protocol is effective only in those countries where the application was not refused or successfully opposed. The registration is valid for 10 years in all other designated countries and has one renewal date, making it easy to manage renewal of the registration every 10 years.

The Madrid Protocol thus facilitates a one-stop, low-cost, efficient system for the international registration of trademarks by permitting a U.S. trademark owner to file for registration in any or all Madrid Protocol member nations by filing one application with the USPTO, in English, with one fee. The previous system required the filing of individual trademark applications in different languages in multiple trademark offices (with different renewal dates as a result).

Developments in Eastern Europe

The disintegration of the Communist bloc into independent republics greatly changed trademark practices in Eastern Europe and the former Soviet Union. The Soviet Union, once a single nation, has now become 15 countries, each of which is attempting to achieve some degree of free market economic development. Many of these countries have their own trademark offices, and it is now possible to file applications in each country.

The breakup of Czechoslovakia led to the creation of two trademark offices, one in the Czech Republic and one in the Slovak Republic. Each has adopted its own trademark laws, and each accepts trademark applications. It is also possible to file trademark applications in Croatia, Slovenia, and the Republic of Macedonia. Some countries such as Cuba are presently subject to U.S. embargo, and U.S. citizens are not permitted to file applications there.

EFFECTS OF NEW INTERNATIONAL AGREEMENTS (NAFTA AND TRIPS)

The North American Free Trade Agreement (NAFTA) came into effect on January 1, 1994, and is adhered to by the United States, Canada, and Mexico. The most significant change in U.S. trademark law resulting from NAFTA is that trademarks that are primarily geographically deceptively misdescriptive cannot be registered in the United States, even if they have acquired secondary meaning.

The World Trade Organization (WTO) is located in Geneva and is a global international organization dealing with rules of trade between nations. Its primary function is to oversee and administer various agreements entered into by most of the world's trading nations. The agreements are created through a series of negotiations, called "rounds." The WTO was formally created by the Uruguay Round negotiations and was established in 1995, although it is a successor to the General Agreement on Tariffs and Trade (GATT), which

itself was established after World War II. One hundred and fifty one countries are members of the WTO, and the United States has been a member since January 1, 1995. GATT was both an organization (which was replaced by the WTO) and an agreement (which still exists but has been amended and incorporated into TRIPs, discussed later).

The Uruguay Round negotiations brought intellectual property rights into the GATT-WTO system for the first time through an agreement called the Agreement on Trade-Related Aspects of Intellectual Property Rights (TRIPs). TRIPs is the most comprehensive multilateral agreement on intellectual property. The first of two key changes to U.S. trademark law resulting from TRIPs is that nonuse of a mark for three years must be shown for a registration to be canceled for such nonuse (prior to TRIPs, the United States followed a rule that two years of nonuse of a mark resulted in a presumption of abandonment). The second change is that TRIPs provides that all signatory countries must prevent the use of a trademark that misleads consumers as to the geographical origin of goods. Even stronger protection is provided for geographical indications for wines and spirits, in that TRIPs precludes registration of marks for wines and spirits that contain misleading geographical indicators. For example, a wine bearing the mark SONOMA must originate in that region of the United States.

INTERNATIONAL ASSOCIATIONS

There are a variety of international associations devoted to protecting the rights of trademark owners. The best known are the International Trademark Association (INTA) and WIPO.

International Trademark Association (INTA)

INTA was founded in 1878 as the United States Trademark Association and is dedicated to the advancement and support of trademarks as valuable items of world commerce. It is a not-for-profit association that serves its members and actively pursues private and public policy matters concerning trademarks. More than 5,000 trademark owners and professionals from more than 190 countries belong to INTA, together with others interested in promoting trademarks such as law firms practicing in the field of trademarks and advertising agencies that deal with trademarks.

INTA has played a significant role in trademark legislation, including promotion of the passage of the U.S. Trademark Act in 1946 and the 1988 Trademark Law Revision Act, designed to bring U.S. trademark law into conformity with that of the international community. INTA presently advocates that all WIPO member nations adhere to the Madrid Protocol. In 1993, a name change from United States Trademark Association to International Trademark Association was effected to reflect the association's worldwide focus. INTA offers a variety of educational seminars and publications, including many worthwhile materials available for free on the Internet (see INTA's home page at http://www.inta.org). INTA is located at 655 Third Avenue, 10th floor, New York, NY 10017-5617 (212/642–1700).

World Intellectual Property Organization (WIPO)

WIPO, founded in 1883, is an intergovernmental organization headquartered in Geneva, Switzerland. Since 1974, WIPO has been a specialized agency of the United Nations. Its purposes are to promote intellectual property throughout the world through cooperation among nations and to administer 24 multilateral treaties dealing with intellectual property, including the Paris Convention, Madrid Agreement, the Trademark Law Treaty, and the Berne Convention. WIPO encourages new treaties and modernization of national legislative bodies, disseminates information, and provides technical assistance to developing nations. More than 180 nations are members of WIPO. (See Appendix A for identification of WIPO members.)

Additionally, WIPO has an Arbitration and Mediation Center whose purpose is to offer binding arbitration or nonbinding mediation services to resolve intellectual property disputes between parties. These services are available to any person, regardless of nationality. As discussed in chapter 7, WIPO is the leading dispute resolution service provider for cybersquatting disputes.

WIPO promotes protection of all aspects of intellectual property (trademarks, copyrights, and patents), while INTA is devoted exclusively to promoting trademarks. WIPO offers a variety of useful information on the Internet including the list of international classifications for trademarks, texts of treaties administered by WIPO, and information on publications offered by WIPO (see WIPO's home page, located at http://www.wipo.int).

Trivia

- A CTM application may be filed in any one of the 22 languages of the EU nations.
- Approximately 64 percent of all CTM registrations from 1997–2005 issued to non-EU nations were issued to U.S. registrants.
- In 2006, more than 77,000 CTM applications were filed.
- More than 60 percent of all CTM applications are filed electronically.
- INTA was established more than 100 years ago by 17 merchants and manufacturers to protect and promote the rights of trademark owners.
- WIPO administers 24 treaties related to intellectual property.

CHAPTER SUMMARY

A foreign national may file an application for trademark registration with the USPTO on the basis of actual use of the mark in commerce in the United States, a bona fide intent to use the mark in commerce in the United States, or on the bases of a pending application or existing registration in a foreign country. If the application is filed with the USPTO within six months of its filing in the foreign country, it will retain its earlier foreign filing date for purposes of determining priority rights in the mark. Once filed, the application will proceed similarly to other applications, although to secure a U.S. registration, the applicant must submit to the USPTO a certified copy of the registration issued by the foreign country. One significant difference is that while U.S. applicants can receive a registration only upon a showing of actual use, foreign nationals can obtain registrations without ever using the mark (inasmuch as their U.S. registration is based upon their foreign registration, which may not have required use).

Just as foreign nationals may seek protection for their marks in the United States, U.S. trademark owners may seek protection for their marks in various foreign countries. The assistance of a foreign associate who is expert in trademark law in the relevant country is nearly always required. As with applications filed by foreign nationals in the United States, applications filed in countries that are members of the Paris Convention within six months of the date of a U.S. application retain the earlier U.S. filing date for priority purposes. U.S. trademark owners should file applications in countries in which they intend to do business and in any countries that have a history or tradition of trademark piracy, namely, countries in which third parties attempt to register marks for goods or services they will not be offering in anticipation of the entrance of a foreign trademark owner to whom they can then sell the mark.

A new system called the Community Trademark System allows trademark owners in the United States to file one single trademark application and receive a single registration covering all 27 member nations of the European Union, resulting in significant savings of time and money.

Similarly, the Madrid Protocol allows a trademark owner to seek registration in any of the more than 70 Madrid Protocol member nations by filing a single application with a single set of fees, in English.

CASE ILLUSTRATION—MAINTENANCE REQUIREMENTS FOR FOREIGN REGISTRANTS

Case: *Imperial Tobacco Ltd. v. Philip Morris, Inc.*, 899 F.2d 1575 (Fed. Cir. 1990)

Facts: Imperial Tobacco, a United Kingdom corporation, obtained a registration for the mark JPS for cigarettes based on section 44(e). After obtaining its registration, it did not use the mark for more than five years, and Philip Morris petitioned to cancel the registration on the basis that the mark had been abandoned. The Trademark Trial and Appeal Board cancelled the registration.

Holding: The Court of Appeals for the Federal Circuit affirmed. Section 44(e) gives foreign applicants an advantage because they can obtain a registration without proving use in this country; however, it gives no similar advantage regarding *maintenance* of a registration. After registration, a section 44(e) registrant is subject to U.S. law and to the same treatment and conditions that prevail in connection with domestic registrations. After registration, there is no dispensation of any requirements relating to use. In this case, the foreign registrant failed to use the mark in the United States for more than five years after obtaining its registration. Thus, it abandoned its rights to the mark, just as would be the case for a U.S. registrant.

CASE STUDY AND ACTIVITIES

Case Study.   Vision filed an application in the United States for its mark VACATION WITH VISION on June 19. Vision is considering opening resorts in the Czech Republic, Spain, Portugal, and France and would like to ensure it can use the VACATION WITH VISION mark in those countries in the future. Vision is also considering opening a resort in Australia.

Activities.   What kind of trademark application should Vision file to protect the VACATION WITH VISION mark for future use in the Czech Republic, Spain, Portugal, and France? When should the application be filed? Why? What happens if the application is refused in Spain? Assume the mark achieves registration in the four countries. If Vision uses the mark only in France, may the registration be cancelled in Portugal due to nonuse? Is there a way for Vision to apply for registration in Australia at the same time that it applies for registration in the other four countries? Discuss.

ROLE OF PARALEGAL

International trademark work can be interesting and challenging. Working with clients and attorneys from foreign countries provides an international perspective on trademark law. Individuals with fluency in other languages should emphasize such skills to potential employers, who are often in need of translations of foreign documents and correspondence.

Among the tasks IP paralegals will undertake in the area of international trademark law are the following:

- assisting clients and foreign associates in completing a trademark data worksheet to determine what marks should be protected in the United States
- preparing applications based on section 44 and securing either filing particulars about a pending foreign application or a certified copy of the foreign registration
- monitoring the progress of section 44 applications and corresponding with foreign associates regarding the same

ROLE OF PARALEGAL (CONT'D)

- notifying U.S. clients of the advantages of filing applications in Paris Convention nations within six months of the date an application is filed with the USPTO
- working with foreign associates in filing applications for marks in foreign countries
- maintaining dockets to track the progress of foreign applications
- providing status reports to clients regarding the progress of foreign applications
- reviewing registration certificates and docketing same for maintenance and renewal

INTERNET RESOURCES

Information on section 44 applications: See TMEP at http://tess2.uspto.gov/tmdb/tmep (see chapter 11).

Information on the Madrid Protocol: The USPTO offers detailed information about the Madrid Protocol, including basic facts, FAQs, and a link to chapter 19 of the TMEP, which deals with the Madrid Protocol at http://www.uspto.gov/web/trademarks/madrid/madridindex.htm

Texts of Paris Convention and Madrid Protocol: WIPO's Web site at http://www.wipo.int includes basic information about the Paris Convention and the Madrid Protocol, their full texts, and identifications of contracting parties.

Information about CTM applications: See Web site of Office for Harmonization in the Internal Market at http://www.oami.europa.eu/en/default.htm

World Trade Organization: http://www.wto.org (Web site offers information about the WTO and full text of TRIPs and Uruguay Round agreements)

International Trademark Association: http://www.inta.org

World Intellectual Property Organization: http://www.wipo.int

DISCUSSION QUESTIONS

1. Pierre, a French citizen, filed an application in the United States based on a registration issued in France. Peter, a U.S. citizen, filed an application in the United States based on his intent to use his mark in the United States. In what way will the application process for these marks differ?

2. If Filippo, an Italian citizen, files an application in Italy on March 10, when should a corresponding U.S. application be filed? Why?

3. Eamon, a citizen of Ireland, obtained a U.S. registration based on his registration in Ireland. When must Eamon use the mark in the United States?

4. Tim, the owner of a CTM registration, discovered that his mark was being infringed in Ireland by TechCo and prevailed in an infringement action against TechCo. Tim has recently discovered that TechCo is now using the mark in Austria. What is the effect, if any, of Tim's previous infringement action?

5. Flagg Winery, Inc. intends to offer two wines under the marks SAPPHIRE RESERVE and MONTEREY RED. Both wines are made in New York. Discuss whether there are any problems with the intended marks.

6. Suzanne, a French citizen, has obtained a French registration for APPLE GALETTE (meaning "apple wafer") for apple desserts and wafers. Suzanne applied for registration of the mark in the United States based on section 44(e), and the USPTO refused registration on the basis that the mark is merely descriptive. Suzanne has argued that the USPTO must register the mark because it is registered in France. Is this a valid argument? Discuss.

USING INTERNET RESOURCES

1. Access WIPO's Web site.
   a. Review the fees related to the Madrid Protocol. What is the fee to renew a registration (for one class)?
   b. When was the Madrid Protocol entered into force in China, New Zealand, and the United States?
   c. Review the summary for the Trademark Law Treaty. May signatory countries require that signatures on documents be authenticated or attested?

2. Use the TMEP and locate information about the Madrid Protocol. What happens to an international registration registered under the Madrid Protocol if the corresponding U.S. registration is cancelled within five years?

3. Access the USPTO Web site. What is the fee for certifying an international application based on one registration with three classes?

4. Access the Web site for the Office for Harmonization in the Internal Market. What is the full address of the office in Alicante?

For additional resources, go to www.paralegal.delmar.cengage.com.

PART
III

The Law of Copyrights

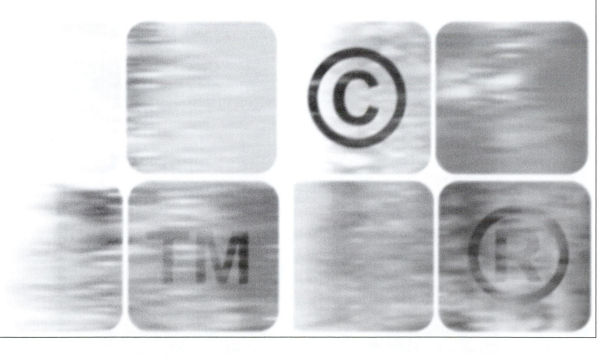

Chapter 9

Foundations of Copyright Law

CHAPTER OVERVIEW

Copyright is a form of protection arising from the Patent and Copyright Clause of the U.S. Constitution. Copyright protects the works of authors and artists to ensure their products are not unlawfully reproduced, distributed, performed, or displayed, acts that would deprive them of revenue and discourage further creative work. As new technologies have developed, copyright law has evolved to keep pace, thereby affording protection to works not originally contemplated by the framers of the Constitution, such as computer programs.

The present act governing copyrights in the United States is the Copyright Act of 1976, which provides protection upon creation of a work in a fixed form rather than requiring publication of a work as a prerequisite to protection as did the previous Copyright Act of 1909. Rights arise automatically upon creation of a work, and no publication or registration with the Copyright Office is required to secure copyright, although there are several advantages to registration.

INTRODUCTION

Just as medieval merchants in guilds in England used trademarks on their wares to indicate the source of those products, mercantile interests in England prompted the first insistence upon protection for publication of books. When the invention of the printing press in about 1440 resulted in the ability to produce books by machine rather than by hand, bookbinders and printers demanded protection from copying of books. Authors also began to demand protection from unauthorized copying and demanded to share in the financial rewards the publishers were winning. Finally, in 1710, Parliament enacted the first copyright statute, the Statute of Anne, which limited the formerly perpetual rights publishers enjoyed to a period of 14 years. Under the statute, damages for infringement were set at one penny for every sheet found in the infringer's custody, one-half to go to the author and one-half to go to the Crown. Authors were thus granted the right to control copying of their books. This grant of rights was called a *copyright*.

Just as trademark law protects the investment by merchants in the marks under which their goods are sold, copyright law protects the creators of books, music, and art by providing them with the exclusive right to reproduce their works and derive income from them. Protecting these rights fosters creative effort—there would be little to be gained from investing and pouring effort into composing a song or writing a novel if others could reproduce the song or book at will without compensating its creator.

Not only is copyright at the center of the creative soul of artists, but it has a significant financial impact in the United States as well. Approximately 7 percent of the gross domestic product in the United States derives from copyright industries, including software, films, music, and television shows. Additionally, copyright piracy costs U.S. businesses an estimated $30–35 billion each year in lost revenues.

Copyright law in the United States stems from the Patent and Copyright Clause of the Constitution, which provides that Congress shall have the power "to promote the progress of science and useful arts, by securing for limited times to authors and inventors the exclusive rights to their respective writings and discoveries." U.S. Const. art. I, § 8. Under this clause, Congress has the power to enact legislation to provide copyright protection for authors for limited periods. Over time, the wording in the clause has been liberally interpreted to incorporate new technologies and protect new forms of expression such as films and video games as varieties of "writings."

Congress enacted the first copyright act in 1790, and the first federal copyright registration was issued that same year to author John Barry for *The Philadelphia Spelling Book.* Since 1790, the act has been subject to major revision on four occasions: in 1831, 1870, 1909, and 1976. The 1790 act provided copyright protection to maps, charts, and books, and set damages for infringement of published works in the sum of 50 cents for every sheet found in the infringer's possession, one-half of the damages to go to the copyright owner and one-half to the federal government. Subse-

quent revisions to the 1790 act reflect a gradual expansion of the categories of works or "writings" that are entitled to protection. Thus, musical compositions, dramatic compositions, photographs, paintings, and sculpture were eventually included within the definition of copyrightable material. The present act provides protection to nearly anything that can be expressed in tangible form, including sound recordings, videotape, and computer software.

Copyright rights are governed exclusively by federal law. Pursuant to 17 U.S.C. § 301, the federal government has preempted all rights relating to copyright. Thus, the individual states cannot grant copyright, and there is no such thing as a state copyright registration. The federal government regulates copyright in two ways: by providing a method of registration of copyright and by allowing access to the federal courts for copyright infringement claims. All cases alleging copyright infringement must be brought in federal court. On the other hand, for example, an allegation that a contract by which one party licensed a copyright to another was procured by fraud would be a matter of standard contractual interpretation and would be governed by state law because copyright issues themselves would not be involved in such a case.

Copyright law strives to balance two competing interests: the interests of authors in protecting their works from unauthorized copying and the interest of the public in having the greatest possible access to works of authorship. U.S. copyright law is intended to stimulate the creation of new works of art, literature, music, sculpture, and other tangible forms of expression.

COMMON LAW RIGHTS AND RIGHTS UNDER THE 1976 COPYRIGHT ACT

Until January 1, 1978 (the effective date of the 1976 Copyright Act), the United States had a dual system of copyright protection in that a distinction was drawn between unpublished works and

ETHICS EDGE: **Leading by Example**

Although it is tempting to think that no one is hurt if you download a song or a software program from the Internet, remember that such acts are, in fact, acts of theft, just as reaching into someone's pocket and taking his or her money would be. Creators of songs and software programs have invested significant effort and time in creating their works and thus deserve to be compensated for their efforts. Resist the temptation of thinking, "Everyone is doing it." As a valued member of the legal profession, lead by example. Educate others, and explain to them why such downloading is illegal.

those that were published. Until 1978, authors had a perpetual common law right to their unpublished works. Thus, the author of an unpublished manuscript could exclude others from copying the material forever. Once the work was published, however, the common law perpetual copyright was extinguished and protection was afforded by virtue of the 1909 act, which then provided a period of protection up to 56 years. **Publication** is the distribution of copies of a work to the public for sale or other transfer of ownership, by rental, lease, or lending.

Because this dual nature of copyright protection was complex, and the point at which works became published often led to controversy, the 1976 act eliminated the distinction between unpublished and published works and provides simply that a work is protected from its **creation,** that is, as soon as it is created or fixed in some tangible form. Thus, even an unpublished manuscript is governed by the 1976 act inasmuch as it is created when the author sets the words down onto paper or types them into a computer.

Works published before the 1976 act, for example, Ernest Hemingway's *A Farewell to Arms* (published in 1929), are governed by the act in existence on the date of their publication. Hemingway's book would thus be governed by the 1909 act.

Just as trademark rights arise from use and not from registration with the USPTO, copyright rights arise from the creation of a work in fixed form and not from publication or registration or

other action in the United States. No permission or application with the U.S. Copyright Office is required to secure copyright protection; however, just as securing a trademark registration from the USPTO provides certain advantages to trademark owners, securing a copyright registration from the Copyright Office provides certain advantages to authors of works, including the following:

- Registration establishes a public record of the copyright claim.
- Before an infringement suit may be filed in court, registration is necessary for works of U.S. origin.
- If made before or within five years of publication, registration will establish *prima facie* evidence in court of the validity of the copyright and of the facts stated in the certificate.
- If registration is made within three months after publication of the work or prior to an infringement of the work, statutory damages and attorneys' fees will be available to the copyright owner.
- Registration allows the owner of the copyright to record the registration with the U. S. Customs and Border Protection for protection against the importation of infringing copies.

The copyright registration process is far simpler than either the trademark or patent registration process. The application fee is only $45 (for a paper application), and the process takes about three months.

Copyright protection generally lasts until 70 years from the death of the author. The 1976 Copyright Act is found at 17 U.S.C. §§ 101–1101. (See Appendix E.)

The 1976 Copyright Act has been amended several times. In 1980, specific protection was afforded to computer programs as works entitled to copyright protection. In 1989, the United States joined the Berne Union, an organization now comprising more than 160 nations, by entering into an international treaty called the Berne Convention for the Protection of Literary and Artistic Works. Just as the Paris Convention requires member nations to treat citizens of member nations as they do their own citizens with regard to trademarks, the Berne Convention requires member nations to treat citizens of member nations as they do their own citizens with regard to copyrights. To satisfy our obligations under the Berne treaty, Congress once again amended the 1976 Copyright Act by eliminating any requirement for a copyright notice (©) to be used with a work (although use of the notice is recommended) and by requiring copyright applicants to submit two copies of a published work in which copyright is claimed when they apply for copyright registration. In 1990, the Copyright Act was again amended to bring U.S. copyright law more into conformity with that of other Berne Union members, particularly with respect to rights of attribution and integrity for certain works of visual arts (see chapter 11).

The most recent significant amendment to the 1976 Copyright Act was enacted in late 1998, pursuant to the Sonny Bono Copyright Term Extension Act, when Congress extended the duration of copyright to 70 years from an author's death rather than 50 years from death as was previously the case.

Another 1998 amendment to copyright law is the Digital Millennium Copyright Act, which updates copyright law for the digital age by including provisions forbidding individuals from circumventing copyright protection systems and limiting the liability of Internet service providers (such as AOL) for copyright infringement. A number of experts believe that the Digital Millennium Copyright Act of 1998 is the most comprehensive updating of copyright law in a generation. The Act is discussed in detail in chapters 15 and 16. References in this text to the Copyright Act are references to the 1976 act (with its later amendments).

THE UNITED STATES COPYRIGHT OFFICE

The U.S. Copyright Office is a division of the Library of Congress and is located in Washington, DC. Its address and telephone number are as follows: Register of Copyrights, Copyright Office, Library of Congress, 101 Independence Avenue SE, Washington, DC 20559-6000 (202/707-3000). Its chief officer is the Register of Copyrights, and its powers and procedures are established in the 1976 Copyright Act. The primary function of the Copyright Office is to issue copyright registrations and serve as a depository for materials in which copyright is claimed. The Copyright Office is not permitted to give legal advice and will not offer guidance on matters such as disputes over the ownership of a copyright, suits against possible infringers, or other matters related to copyrights. It does, however, provide a variety of information, publications, circulars (information packets), and forms related to copyright, most of which are provided free of charge. Among the more useful publications and materials are the following:

- forms for copyright registration
- Circular 1, "Copyright Basics"
- Circular 2, "Publications on Copyright"
- Circular 3, "Copyright Notice"
- Circular 4, "Copyright Fees"
- Circular 15, "Renewal of Copyright"
- Circular 15a, "Duration of Copyright"
- Circular 38a, "International Copyright Relations of the United States"

- Circular 61, "Copyright Registration for Computer Programs"

To order copyright publications, write to:

Library of Congress
Copyright Office
Publications Section, LM-455
101 Independence Avenue SE
Washington, DC 20559-6000

Alternatively, you may call the Copyright Office's Forms and Publications Hotline at (202) 707-9100 (24 hours a day). Orders are recorded automatically, and materials will be mailed to you as quickly as possible, usually within two weeks.

Frequently requested Copyright Office circulars, announcements, application forms, and the most recent proposed and final regulations are now available for free through the Copyright Of-fice's Web site at http://www.copyright.gov. This Web site gives you access to information created by the Copyright Office and links to a wide variety of other copyright resources.

Finally, the Copyright Office provides a free electronic mailing list, "NewsNet," that issues periodic e-mail messages on copyright issues. These messages alert subscribers to hearings, deadlines for comments related to copyright rules and regulations, new and proposed rules and regulations, and other copyright-related matters. To subscribe, access http://www.copyright.gov and then select "News" and follow the instructions.

The Copyright Office has implemented a limited electronic system to accept applications for registration online, but only about 20,000 applications annually are accepted electronically at present.

Trivia

- According to the Department of Commerce, combined copyright and trademark industries represent the second-fastest-growing segment of the U.S. economy (behind Internet-related electronic commerce).
- The Business Software Alliance has reported that in 2005, of 97 countries, the United States had the lowest rate of software piracy (21 percent). Vietnam had the highest rate (90 percent).
- It has been estimated that nearly 70 percent of college students may be using software illegally.
- The total number of copyrights registered in the United States, through 2006, was more than 32 million.

CHAPTER SUMMARY

In the United States, copyright law arises under the Patent and Copyright Clause of the Constitution. The U.S. copyright laws have been amended several times, and the current governing statute is the Copyright Act of 1976. Copyright ensures that an author or creator of a work will derive benefits from his or her creation and will be protected from unauthorized use or copying of a work. Under the Copyright Act of 1909, a work had to be published to be protected under the act. The 1976 act eliminated the requirement of publication and provides that copyright is secured automatically when the work is created in a fixed medium. No publication or registration is necessary to secure copyright protection, although there are certain advantages to registration of a copyright with the U.S. Copyright Office.

CASE ILLUSTRATION—PURPOSE OF COPYRIGHT LAW

Case: *Fox Film Corp. v. Doyal*, 286 U.S. 123 (1932)

Facts: The plaintiff was engaged in Georgia in licensing copyrighted motion pictures and brought suit to restrain the collection of taxes by the State of Georgia on the ground that copyrights are granted by the federal government and should not be subject to state tax. The plaintiff's suit was dismissed and it appealed.

Holding: The judgment was affirmed. The sole interest of the United States and the primary object in conferring copyright rights lies in the general benefits derived by the public from the labor of authors. The federal government grants a limited monopoly to authors in return for the benefits bestowed on the public by the genius and skill of authors and creators. Copyright law encourages further such creative efforts. Although the property of the United States is not subject to state taxation and copyrights are granted by the federal government, copyrights are owned by private individuals and are thus subject to state tax.

CASE STUDY AND ACTIVITIES

Case Study.   Vision Inc. has decided to issue a series of children's books based on its well-known cartoon character spokesman, Vee. Additionally, Vision employees have prepared a series of scripts for prospective advertising campaigns and commercials. A computer game is also being developed for guests' children. Finally, Vision employees have written a song for the company's recent ad campaign.

Activities.   Which of the foregoing items is protectable under copyright law? What advantages does Vision secure by registering any copyrights?

ROLE OF PARALEGAL

At this stage of copyright protection and prosecution, IP paralegals will typically be engaged in general legal research relating to copyrightability of clients' works. Additionally, paralegals should contact the Copyright Office and begin creating form files for forms and publications related to copyrights. The files should be maintained in a central location, and indexes to the forms and publications should be circulated to all other IP professionals. Finally, paralegals should routinely monitor the Copyright Office Web site to keep informed of new developments in copyright law, check fee schedules, and determine whether the Copyright Office has implemented new procedures.

INTERNET RESOURCES

Federal laws relating to copyright:	http://www.law.cornell.edu http://www.findlaw.com http://www.copyright.gov/title17/circ92.pdf
Copyright Office:	http://www.copyright.gov
General information:	http://www.law.cornell.edu/wex/index.php/ Copyright (site of Cornell Law School) http://www.findlaw.com http://www.megalaw.com http://www.csusa.org (site of Copyright Society of the United States, a nonprofit corporation organized in 1953 to foster interest in and study of copyright law)

DISCUSSION QUESTIONS

1. In what way does copyright law encourage artistic expression?
2. Why is the term of a copyright limited to a certain period of time? Why shouldn't authors enjoy copyright rights forever?
3. Sue enters her thoughts and feelings in her daily journal. She has no intent to publish this journal and intends to pass it along to her children. Is this work protected under the 1976 Copyright Act? Would it be protectable under the previous 1909 Copyright Act?
4. Ron finished writing a novel in 2005. How long will copyright protection for the book last?
5. Are Webcasts protectable under the current Copyright Act? What language in 17 U.S.C. § 102 governs your answer?

USING INTERNET RESOURCES

Access the Web site of the U.S. Copyright Office to answer the following questions.

1. Who is the current Register of Copyrights?
2. Review "Copyright Basics." When was the requirement of using a copyright notice eliminated? Why was it eliminated?
3. Review "FAQs." May the following be protected by copyright?
   a. Web site
   b. domain name
   c. recipe
   d. name of a band

For additional resources, go to www.paralegal.delmar.cengage.com.

Chapter 10

The Subject Matter of Copyright

CHAPTER OVERVIEW

To be eligible for copyright protection, matter must be original, it must be fixed in some tangible form, and it must qualify as a "work of authorship." The requirement of originality does not mean the work must be new or novel; it must merely be created independently by its author. The most common subjects of copyright protection are literary works; musical works; dramatic works; choreographic works; pictorial, graphic, and sculptural works; motion pictures and other audiovisual works; sound recordings; and architectural works. Not all printed or communicable matter can be the subject of copyright protection. For example, useful articles, facts, ideas, titles, and U.S. government works cannot be copyrighted. In some instances, however, material that itself is not copyrightable (such as facts) may be subject to protection if it is arranged or compiled in such a way that shows creativity, for example, arrangement of facts into a book of lists.

INTRODUCTION

The limits of copyrightability are dictated by federal statute. According to 17 U.S.C. § 102, copyright protection exists in original works of authorship fixed in any tangible medium of expression, now known or later developed. Thus, there are three basic requirements for copyrightability.

1. A work must be original.
2. A work must be fixed in a tangible form of expression.
3. A work must be a work of authorship.

Each of these requirements will be discussed in this chapter.

ORIGINALITY OF MATERIAL

To be eligible for copyright protection, material must be original, meaning that it must have been independently created and must possess a modicum of creativity. The requirement of **originality** should not be confused with novelty, worthiness, or aesthetic appeal. The requirement is rather that the material must be an independent product of the author and not merely some copy or minimal variation of an existing work.

A work can be original even if it is strikingly similar or identical to that of another. The Copyright Act only requires originality, meaning independent creation by the author. Thus, if two photographers each take photographs of the Washington Memorial, each will have copyright protection for the work (as long as one did not copy another). Similarly, if two authors independently write novels that are strikingly similar, each will have copyright protection (again, assuming there was no copying). In a famous copyright case, *Feist Publn's, Inc. v. Rural Tel. Serv. Co.*, 409 U.S. 340, 345–46 (1991), the Supreme Court held:

> Originality does not signify novelty; a work may be original even though it closely resembles other works so long as the similarity is fortuitous, not the result of copying. To illustrate, assume that two poets, each ignorant of the other, compose identical poems. Neither work is novel, yet both are original, and, hence, copyrightable.

"Originality" thus does not mean "first"; it merely means "independently created."

In regard to the level of creativity required for copyright protection, the threshold is quite low. Even a slight amount of "creative spark" will suffice. In order to be protected by copyright, however, a work must contain at least a certain minimum amount of original expression. Thus, copyright does not extend to blank forms, column headings, names, titles, or lists of ingredients. In *Feist*, the Supreme Court held that telephone white page listings did not satisfy the requirement inasmuch as they lacked minimal creativity. The Court held that the names, towns, and telephone numbers were all merely facts arranged in alphabetical order, an age-old practice, and thus were uncopyrightable. Although facts are not copyrightable, an author's original selection and arrangement of those facts may be copyrightable as a compilation. (See the section in this chapter entitled "Compilations, Collections, and Derivative Works.")

FIXATION OF MATERIAL

The Copyright Act protects works of authorship that are "fixed in any tangible medium of expression." A work is "fixed" when it is embodied in a copy or phonorecord and is sufficiently permanent or stable to permit it to be perceived, reproduced, or communicated for a period of more than transitory duration. 17 U.S.C. § 101.

There are thus two categories of tangible expression in which works can be fixed: "copies" and "phonorecords." A **copy** is a material object (other than a phonorecord) from which a work can be perceived, reproduced, or communicated, either directly by human perception or with the help of a machine. Thus, according to the Copyright Act, a famous photograph by Ansel Adams that appears on a book cover, a calendar, a T-shirt, a tie, and a coffee mug is a "copy" in each case. The photograph, calendar, and so forth are copies because they are material objects from which an image can be perceived. The scope of "material object" is broad enough to encompass writings on paper, images on marble, and even designs on fabric.

A **phonorecord** is a material object in which sounds (other than those accompanying a motion picture or other audiovisual work) are fixed and from which the sounds can be perceived, reproduced, or communicated either directly by human perception or with the help of a machine. Thus, a record, a cassette tape, and a CD recording of a song by the Rolling Stones are all considered to be "phonorecords." Thus, for example, a song (the "work") can be fixed in sheet music ("copies") or in a CD (a "phonorecord"), or both.

Because the definition of **fixation** requires that a work be embodied in some sufficiently stable or permanent form to be perceived, an oral presentation, lecture, or live performance is not fixed (unless it is reduced to writing or placed on film or tape). However, by virtue of 17 U.S.C. § 101, which defines the word *fixed,* a live broadcast of a television or radio show is viewed as fixed *if* it is recorded simultaneously with its broadcast transmission. Thus, an impromptu stand-up comedy routine by Jerry Seinfeld is not fixed; however, a recording and transmission of the same routine is fixed. Fixation occurs when a work is reduced to words, numbers, sounds, or shapes and placed on some permanent or stable medium. Thus, literary works are fixed when they are typed or processed into a computer or put onto a disk; sound recordings are fixed when they are recorded and placed on tape; and photographs are fixed when they are captured on film. Although live performances are thus not protected because they are not "fixed," a special statute (17 U.S.C. § 1101) provides civil and criminal remedies for "bootlegging" sound recordings of live musical performance and music videos to ensure that concertgoers do not surreptitiously record live concerts.

Prior to the 1976 act, works were protected only if they were fixed in a form that was perceptible to the human eye (although special rules existed for sound recordings, protecting records). One famous case held that the rolls of music for a player piano were not subject to copyright protection because they could not be read by humans as sheet music could. *White-Smith Music Publ'g Co. v. Apollo Co.,* 209 U.S. 1 (1908). The 1976 act (17 U.S.C. § 102), however, provides that copyright protection subsists in original works of authorship fixed in *any* tangible medium of expression, now known or later developed, from which they can be perceived, reproduced, or otherwise communicated, either directly or with the aid of a machine or device, thus allowing protection for works that are perceived by machines as well as humans, such as CDs, video games, and videotapes.

WORKS OF AUTHORSHIP

The Copyright Act provides that copyright protection subsists in original works of authorship fixed in any tangible medium of expression, *now known or hereafter developed,* from which they can be perceived, reproduced, or otherwise communicated, either directly or with the aid of a machine. 17 U.S.C. § 102. Section 102 then lists eight categories of protectable works. The list is preceded by the phrase that works of authorship "include" those categories, demonstrating that the listed categories are not the only types of works that can be protected, but are illustrative only. Thus, it has been held that fabric designs and toys are copyrightable even though they are not specifically listed in section 102. Moreover, the provision that copyright protection exists in works "now known or hereafter developed" indicates congressional intent to protect new forms of expression that are not yet existent. The eight enumerated categories are as follows:

1. literary works
2. musical works (including accompanying words)
3. dramatic works (including accompanying music)
4. pantomimes and choreographic works
5. pictorial, graphic, and sculptural works
6. motion pictures and other audiovisual works
7. sound recordings
8. architectural works

Literary Works

A **literary work** is one expressed in words, numbers, or other verbal or numerical symbols, regardless of the nature of the material objects, such as books, periodicals, manuscripts, phonorecords, film, tapes, discs, or cards, in which they are embodied. This broad category includes works of fiction and nonfiction, poetry, catalogs, reports, speeches, pamphlets, and manuscripts. Works such as computer programs, databases, and Web sites (if text predominates) are also treated as literary works because they are expressed in letters and numbers. Literary works can include dictionaries, an employee handbook, an instruction manual, or an advertisement. The fact that many people would not regard an advertisement or an instruction manual to be *literary* in the sense the word is usually used is of no significance. If the material is original, in fixed form, and can be expressed in letters or numbers, it is "literary" even though it may be entirely lacking in artistic merit to most people.

Musical Works (Including Accompanying Words)

A **musical work,** together with its accompanying words, is copyrightable. A musical work or composition may be in the form of a notated copy (such as sheet music) or in the form of a phonorecord (such as a record, a cassette tape, or a CD). The author of a musical work is usually the composer, and the lyricist, if any.

The lyrics or words to a musical composition are not protected as a literary work, but rather as a musical work. Both elements of a composition are separately protected. Thus, if someone writes the lyrics to "Yesterday" in a novel, without permission, it is a violation of the author's copyright. Similarly, an unauthorized performance of the musical arrangement for "Yesterday" on stage, even without singing of lyrics, is also a copyright violation.

Dramatic Works (Including Accompanying Music)

A **dramatic work** is usually a theatrical performance or play performed for stage, movie, television, or radio. Dramatic works usually include spoken text, plot, and directions for action. The music accompanying a dramatic work is protected as a dramatic work rather than as an independent musical work. Examples of dramatic

works include the well-known plays *Phantom of the Opera, Cats,* and *Death of a Salesman.*

Pantomimes and Choreographic Works

Pantomime or *mime* is a performance using gestures and expression to communicate with no accompanying sound. An impromptu street performance of mime would not be protected (because it is not fixed in some stable or permanent medium of expression), but a filmed performance of the famous mime Marcel Marceau or a precise description of the pantomime in text would be protected.

The 1976 act was the first statute to include choreography as a copyrightable work. Choreography is the composition and arrangement of dance movements and patterns. Simple dance routines and social dance steps such as the waltz, the fox trot, and the second position of classical ballet are not copyrightable in and of themselves; however, once these steps are incorporated into an otherwise choreographic work, they are protected, much like words are protected once they are incorporated into a work of fiction or nonfiction. A **choreographic work** does not need to tell a story in order to be protected by copyright; however, the work must be fixed in a tangible medium of expression from which the work can be performed, such as a recorded or notated choreographic work. In one case, still photographs of a George Balanchine ballet performance were held to infringe his copyrighted choreographic work *The Nutcracker. Horgan v. MacMillan, Inc.,* 789 F.2d 157 (2d Cir. 1986).

Pictorial, Graphic, and Sculptural Works

Pictorial, graphic, and sculptural works include two-dimensional and three-dimensional works of fine, graphic, and applied art. This category of copyrighted works is extremely broad and includes the following: photographs; prints, posters, and art reproductions; maps; globes;

charts; diagrams; artwork applied to clothing; bumper stickers; cartoons and comic strips; dolls; toys; jewelry designs; mosaics; patterns for sewing; record jacket artwork; tapestries; quilts; fabric, floor, and wall-covering designs; games; puzzles; greeting cards, postcards, and stationery; stencils; sculptures (including carvings, figurines, and molds); models; and technical drawings, including architectural plans and blueprints. A minimal threshold of creativity is required. Thus, a simple shape such as a drawing of a circle or square may not be protected; however, even a drawing of a bowl of chili on the label of a can is copyrightable as a pictorial work.

Copyright law does not protect useful articles. A **useful article** is one having an intrinsic utilitarian function. Examples of useful articles are clothing (including costumes), vehicular bodies, furniture, machinery, appliances, dinnerware, and lighting fixtures. Toys, dolls, and stuffed animals are not useful articles and can be copyrighted, even if they portray a utilitarian product. Thus, a toy airplane was held not to be a useful article in *Gay Toys, Inc. v. Buddy L. Corp.,* 703 F.2d 970 (6th Cir. 1983). The intent of Congress was to exclude from copyright protection industrial products such as cars, appliances, and electronic products. Many of these useful objects are protected under patent law. In one case, the court of appeals affirmed that automobile wire-spoke wheel covers were useful and were not subject to copyright protection. The creator argued that the wheel covers were ornamental and were intended to beautify and embellish the wheels, but the court held that the wheel covers were mere utilitarian articles serving to protect lug nuts, wheels, and axles from damage. *Norris Indus. v. Int'l Tel. & Tel. Corp.,* 696 F.2d 918 (11th Cir. 1983).

The Copyright Act provides, however, that the design of a useful article shall be considered a copyrightable pictorial, graphic, or sculptural work if such design incorporates pictorial, graphic, or sculptural features that can be identified separately from and are capable of existing independently of the utilitarian aspects of the article. Thus, the famous statuette that adorns the hood of a Rolls Royce can be protected by copyright inasmuch as it can exist as a sculpture independently from the hood and the car. Similarly, a carving on the back of a chair, animal foot slippers, or a floral relief design on silver flatware is protectable by copyright, but the design of the chair, slipper, or flatware itself is not because these are useful articles.

Motion Pictures and Other Audiovisual Works

A **motion picture** is an audiovisual work consisting of a series of related images that, when shown in succession, impart an impression of motion, together with accompanying sounds. These works are typically embodied in film, videotape, or videodisc. Music accompanying a movie (the motion picture soundtrack) is protected as part of the motion picture.

An **audiovisual work** is a work that consists of a series of related images that are intended to be shown by the use of machines or devices such as projectors, viewers, or electronic equipment, together with accompanying sounds. Thus, a photograph of a mountain is protected as a pictorial work. If the photograph is made into a slide, it remains a pictorial work; however, when the photograph is made into a slide that becomes part of a presentation about mountains of the world, the resulting slide show is an audiovisual work.

Sound Recordings

A **sound recording** is a work that results from the fixation of a series of musical, spoken, or other sounds, regardless of the nature of the material objects, such as discs, tapes, or other phonorecords in which they are embodied. Thus, a sound recording could be a narration by Meryl Streep of a book played on a CD or cassette tape, a CD by Fergie, or an album by Kanye West. Sound recordings, however, do not include the sounds accompanying a motion picture or other audiovisual work. A *song* is the notes and words;

a *sound recording* is what you hear when you play the radio or a CD.

There is a distinction between a "musical work" and a "sound recording." A musical work consists of music, including any accompanying words. The author of a musical work or composition is generally the composer, and the lyricist, if any. A musical composition may be in the form of sheet music or a cassette tape, album, or CD. A sound recording results from the fixation of a series of musical, spoken, or other sounds. The author of a sound recording is the performer whose performance is fixed, or the record producer who processes the sounds and fixes them in the final recording, or both.

For example, the song "You Are the Sunshine of My Life" by Stevie Wonder is frequently recorded by other artists. The original music and lyrics are copyrighted by Stevie Wonder as a musical work. If Celine Dion performs the song "You Are the Sunshine of My Life," she cannot claim copyright in the lyrics and music because she did not create them. However, her particular and unique arrangement of the lyrics and song is copyrightable as a sound recording by her and her record producer. If a later artist wishes to perform "You Are the Sunshine of My Life," permission must be sought from Stevie Wonder (or the present copyright owner). Permission need not be sought from Celine Dion or her record company because the new artist will not be copying Celine Dion's particular arrangement (unless the new artist wishes to extract or "sample" some of the Celine Dion arrangement into the new version, in which case permission must be sought from Celine Dion and/or the record company for the part sampled).

As discussed earlier, sound recordings are embodied in phonorecords (meaning cassette tapes, CDs, LPs, and so forth), not copies.

Architectural Works

An **architectural work** is the design of a building as embodied in any tangible medium of expression, including a building, architectural plans, or drawings. The work includes the overall form and arrangement and composition of spaces, but not individual standard features such as windows, doors, and other standard components of buildings, which cannot be registered. The term *building* includes not only permanent and stationary structures for human occupancy (such as houses and office buildings) but also gazebos, churches, and garden pavilions. Structures other than buildings (such as bridges, tents, and mobile homes) are not subject to protection.

Before 1990 and the United States's adherence to the Berne Convention, architectural plans and models were protected only as graphic and sculptural works. Because buildings were useful articles, they could not be protected. Protection was allowed only for nonuseful portions, such as decorative moldings, murals, friezes, and so forth.

In 1990, however, Congress passed the Architectural Works Copyright Protection Act and expressly amended the 1976 Copyright Act to provide copyright protection to "architectural works." A claim to copyright in an architectural work is distinct from a claim in technical drawings of the work. If registration is sought for both an architectural work (such as a building) and technical drawings of the work, separate applications must be submitted to the Copyright Office.

If the building is ordinarily visible to the public, anyone can take pictures of it or display it in a painting or movie. 17 U.S.C. § 120(a). One recent case demonstrates the difficulties inherent in protecting architectural works. The 1997 movie *The Devil's Advocate* with Al Pacino and Keanu Reeves displayed a frieze placed over the doorway of the National Cathedral in Washington, DC. A noted sculptor claimed this was an infringement of his work. The sculptor sued, alleging copyright infringement. The producers of the movie claimed the frieze was independently created and was merely part of a building ordinarily visible to the public. The case settled out of court, and thus there was no determination of the rights of the parties.

Destruction and alteration of works of fine arts are discussed further in chapter 11. Under 17 U.S.C. § 120(b), the owner of a building may alter or destroy it without the consent of the author or copyright owner of the architectural work.

EXCLUSIONS FROM COPYRIGHT PROTECTION

Not all works are protected by copyright. In addition to articles that are purely useful and that cannot be copyrighted, a number of other works are not protected under copyright law, including ideas, blank forms, short phrases, slogans, titles, works in the public domain, facts, and computing devices.

Ideas, Methods, or Systems

Section 102 of the Copyright Act not only lists eight categories of works that are protected by copyright, but also states that the following are specifically excluded from copyright protection: ideas, procedures, processes, systems, methods of operation, concepts, principles, and discoveries, regardless of the form in which they are described, explained, or illustrated. This statutory prohibition sets out in long form a well-established copyright principle: copyright protects expression, not ideas.

The rule that copyright protection extends only to the expression of ideas, and not to ideas themselves, derives from a famous Supreme Court case, *Baker v. Selden*, 101 U.S. 99 (1879). In that case, Selden published a book explaining a bookkeeping system that included blank forms with ruled lines and columns for using the new system. Baker later published a book with additional forms for using Selden's system. Selden sued for copyright infringement. The Court denied relief, holding that a copyright on a book explaining a system does not prevent another party from explaining the same system; otherwise, the bookkeeping system or method itself would be monopolized by the first to explain it. The Court held that Baker had copied only Selden's unpro-

tectable idea and not any protectable expression of the idea. The discussion by the Court is often referred to as the **idea-expression dichotomy** and results in a well-known copyright principle: Ideas are not protectable, although the expression of those ideas is subject to copyright protection. The Court also held that the forms were not writings and were thus unprotectable, thereby giving rise to the rule that mere blank forms are not copyrightable.

The Copyright Office itself states that copyright protection is not available for the following: ideas or procedures for doing, making, or building things; scientific or technical methods or discoveries; business operations or procedures; formulas of mathematical principles; algorithms; business operations or procedures; or any other concept, process, or method of operation.

Generally, if there are a number of ways of explaining a topic or subject, the original expression will be protected against copying; however, if there are no or few alternative ways of expressing something, only literal copying (rather than mere paraphrasing) will likely result in infringement. In such cases, it is said that the expression merges with the idea, and copyright protection is denied to the merged expression because ideas are not copyrightable. This principle is known as the **merger doctrine.** Thus, in a case involving alleged infringement of contest rules, the court held that because there were a limited number of ways of expressing the rules, given their straightforward nature, only exact copying was prohibited. Otherwise, the first to express the idea in writing would be able to prohibit all later users. *Morrissey v. Procter & Gamble Co.*, 379 F.2d 675 (1st Cir. 1967).

Blank Forms, Titles, Short Phrases, and Common Property

In order to be protected by copyright, a work must contain at least a certain minimum amount of original literary, pictorial, or musical expression. Copyright does not extend to names, titles, short phrases, slogans, clauses such as column headings, or simple checklists. Thus, many books and even movies may share the same title. For example, there are numerous textbooks that share the title *Introduction to Mathematics.* If one person could appropriate a title to the exclusion of others, creativity would be hindered rather than encouraged. Similarly, neither a title nor a slogan such as "You deserve a break today" may be copyrighted (although they may qualify for protection as a trademark or under the law of unfair competition).

Mere variations in typeface, familiar symbols or designs, lettering or coloring, and mere lists of ingredients or contents are not protected by copyright. Similarly, blank forms (such as forms for bank checks, time cards, account books, diaries, scorecards, report forms, address books, and order forms) that are used primarily for recording information rather than conveying information lack sufficient creativity to be copyrightable. Although mere listings of ingredients or contents as in recipes, formulas, or prescriptions are not subject to copyright protection, when the recipe or formula is accompanied by substantial literary expression (such as advice on wine pairings or table settings) or when there is a combination of recipes (as in a cookbook), there may be a basis for copyright protection.

Finally, copyright protection does not extend to works consisting entirely of information that is common property containing no original authorship, such as standard calendars, height and weight charts, tape measures and rulers, schedules of sporting events, and lists or tables taken from public documents or other common sources. Thus, a Sierra Club calendar or Far Side calendar would be protected to the extent of the photographs or cartoons accompanying the calendars, but the calendars themselves with their standard and readily ascertainable information are not copyrightable.

Public Domain Works

A variety of works are not subject to appropriation by copyright inasmuch as they are said to be in the **public domain,** meaning they are free for all members of the public to use and

exploit. The two primary types of works in the public domain are those that arise from expired copyrights and works of the U.S. government.

Expired and Forfeited Copyrights. Copyrights have always been subject to some period of limited duration. Once a copyright expires, or it is forfeited by its owner, it resides in the public domain and is free for all to use. Under the 1909 act, copyrights were subject to an initial period and a period of renewal. Failure to renew the copyright at the appropriate time resulted in a forfeiture of the copyright with the work being placed in the public domain. For works created on or after January 1, 1978, the copyright duration is the life of the author and an additional 70 years. If the work is the product of corporate authorship, it will last for 95 years from publication, or 120 years from its creation, whichever occurs first. These time periods have recently been changed. Until October 1998 and the passage of the Sonny Bono Copyright Term Extension Act, each period of duration was 20 years shorter. In addition to expired or forfeited works being available for all to use, some works are dedicated to public use by their authors. For example, an author could elect not to pursue copyright protection for a work and expressly allow anyone to use it. Some Internet Web sites expressly indicate that certain material on the site is available for all to freely use.

United States Government Works. Pursuant to section 105 of the Copyright Act, copyright protection is not available for any work of the U.S. government or any of its agencies if that work is prepared by an officer or employee of the U.S. government as part of that person's official duties. Thus, federal laws and cases may be freely reproduced and distributed, together with federal regulations, and information and forms from agencies such as the Internal Revenue Service, USPTO forms, and forms provided by the Copyright Office. There is one exception to the rule that the works of the federal government are not copyrightable. Under 15 U.S.C. § 290(e), the

Department of Commerce's standard reference data (consisting of databases for scientists and engineers for use in technical problem solving, research, and development) are copyrighted.

If the U.S. government commissions special work by an independent contractor, for example, a sculpture for a national park commissioned by an artist not employed by the federal government, the independent contractor will retain copyright in the work (unless he or she agrees that the government can own the copyright). The U.S. government is not precluded from receiving copyrights transferred to it by a third party. Thus, the artist could assign or transfer the copyright to the government.

Works produced by state governments and local governmental bodies are not covered by the Copyright Act, although they may be covered under relevant state law. Thus, because the Copyright Act only refers to the federal government, states and municipalities may own copyrights. Nevertheless, certain information such as cases, statutes, regulations, and ordinances are not copyrightable inasmuch as the public needs free access to such information. In a recent case, however, it was held that Suffolk County, New York, held a copyright in tax maps, even though those maps were compiled and maintained at taxpayer expense. *County of Suffolk v. First Am. Real Estate Solutions*, 261 F.3d 179 (2d Cir. 2001).

Facts

Facts are not protected by copyright because one who uncovers a fact is not an author or creator. Facts are viewed as "discoveries" and are thus excluded from copyright protection under section 102 of the Act. Moreover, according to *Feist,* facts are not original to a researcher and are not created by a researcher, even if the researcher is the first to reveal them. For example, statistics relating to population, dates of birth and death, and other ascertainable matters cannot be protected by copyright. Thus, the protection afforded to purely factual works, such as books that merely

gather statistics or that provide biographies consisting primarily of factual information, is relatively narrow. Although a newscast content may be protected by copyright, the facts recited by newscasters themselves cannot be appropriated by one party to the exclusion of others.

Computing and Measuring Devices

Devices and similar articles designed for computing and measuring cannot be copyrighted. Examples of such uncopyrightable works are slide rules, wheel dials, and perpetual calendar systems. The printed material on the device (numbers, symbols, calibrations, and their arrangements) is not capable of copyright protection because the material is dictated either by the underlying idea (which is uncopyrightable) or some standard formula (which is uncopyrightable). Moreover, a computing or measuring device does not contain a minimum amount of creative authorship—it is merely a means for arriving at a result or reading and does not communicate facts or ideas in and of itself.

Other Copyright Issues: Characters, Scenes a Faire, and Immoral Works

A variety of interesting issues have arisen in copyright law regarding the protectability of characters (both graphical and literary), scenes a faire, and immoral works.

Characters and Scenes a Faire. Generally, graphical characters, such as cartoon figures like Superman, Mickey Mouse, Dick Tracy, Tarzan, and Doonesbury, are protectable separate and apart from the cartoon strips, films, and books in which they appear. Thus, in one case, a party was enjoined from using a "Wonderman" character on the basis that it infringed the copyright in Superman when the only significant difference between the two characters was the color of their uniforms. *Detective Comics Inc. v. Bruns Publ'ns, Inc.,* 111 F.2d 432 (2d Cir. 1940). On the other hand, the concept of a hero who bravely saves people and the planet from destruction and peril is merely an idea that cannot be protected by copyright. Other heroes with similar characteristics would be permissible as long as they did not appropriate the details of Superman's persona. Cartoon strips, films, and books are also protectable as pictorial works, motion pictures, and literary works, respectively.

In regard to literary characters or characters depicted in a television series or movie, such as James Bond in the Ian Fleming books and movies, Jack Ryan in the Tom Clancy novels, or the Terminator in the *Terminator* movies, if those characters are specifically described and presented, they may be protectable. In 1988, the Ninth Circuit was called upon to determine whether the television series *The A-Team* infringed a screenplay called *Cargo.* Noting that both shared a common approach (adventure actions portraying Vietnam veterans), the court held that this idea alone was unprotectable. There was little similarity in terms of plot, dialogue, or setting. The fact that both involved action-adventure heroes was not sufficient to show infringement. *Olson v. Nat'l Broad. Co.,* 855 F.2d 1446 (9th Cir. 1988). This reasoning is a further illustration of the rule that ideas are not protectable, while the expressions of those ideas are. In sum, basic character types are not copyrightable; characters that are uniquely developed and display some level of novelty, however, such as Rocky Balboa, are copyrightable.

Certain standard or stereotypical characters and incidents, called **scenes a faire** (literally, "scenes which must be done"), are generally excluded from copyright protection. For example, stock characters, standard literary devices, common expressions, and common incidents are viewed as uncopyrightable scenes a faire. For example, in one case involving police fiction, a court held that foot chases, morale problems of police officers, and the "familiar figure of the Irish cop" are common themes in such works and are thus unprotectable scenes a faire. Similarly, the mazes, scoring table, tunnels, and dots of the "Pac-Man" computer game have been held to be scenes a faire, protectable only from identical copying.

Immoral Works. Although the Trademark Act forbids registration of immoral, disparaging, or scandalous works, no such prohibition exists in the Copyright Act. Generally, Congress has been reluctant to place restrictions on the copyrightability of certain matter believing it would chill First Amendment rights. Thus, even offensive and immoral books, plays, and songs are copyrightable.

COMPILATIONS, COLLECTIONS, AND DERIVATIVE WORKS

Compilations

An author often selects certain items and groups them together in a new presentation. For example, a book may be published that presents lists of Oscar winners or tables of statistics and data that are not themselves copyrightable. Such a work is called a **compilation.** According to section 101 of the Copyright Act, a compilation is a work formed by the collection and assembling of preexisting materials or of data that are selected, coordinated, or arranged in such a way that the resulting work as a whole constitutes an original work of authorship. Compilations are protected by copyright if there is original authorship in the selection or arrangement of the material.

Thus, although the material that makes up the compilation is usually not original (and therefore is not copyrightable), the manner of its selection and arrangement results in an original work. For example, a type of day planner that consists of calendars, blank forms for appointments, entries, maps, lists of area codes, and time zones may be copyrightable as a compilation due to its unique arrangement, even though the parts that comprise it (calendars, blank forms, and so forth) are not copyrightable because they lack originality or are standard devices. As another example, a book of lists or an information-based almanac likely consists of mere facts or raw data that are not copyrightable in and of themselves; however, the unique arrangement of those facts into a select and coordinated system is copyrightable. The author has reviewed certain facts, selected the particular facts to include, and then arranged or presented the facts so that they are interesting or useful to the reader. It is this selection that shows sufficient creativity and originality that copyright protection is provided for that arrangement or selection. The underlying facts themselves, however, remain uncopyrightable.

As seen in *Feist*, in which an alphabetically arranged telephone directory was held not copyrightable, not every selection of facts or compilation will pass muster. As always, a certain level of creativity, namely, "originality," is required. In *Feist*, the Supreme Court recognized that while the requirement of originality is not stringent, the arrangement of facts cannot be so mechanical and routine as to demonstrate no creativity whatsoever. The Court noted that taking data and listing telephone subscribers alphabetically by surname resulted in "a garden-variety white pages directory, devoid of even the slightest trace of creativity." 499 U.S. at 360.

Collections

According to section 101 of the Copyright Act, the term *compilation* includes collective works. A **collective work** is a work, such as a periodical issue, anthology, or encyclopedia, in which a number of contributions, constituting separate and independent works in themselves, are assembled into a collective whole. Thus, a CD containing musical compositions by various artists and called *The Golden Age of Rock* would be a collective work, as would a book of selected short stories dealing with sports, an anthology of poems by 20th-century American poets, or selected film clips showing the greatest comedy routines

of the 1980s. Even when the works assembled into the collection are public domain works (e.g., folk songs or spirituals), the resulting work qualifies for protection as a collection. In the cases in which works that comprise the collection are copyrighted (e.g., individual poems or songs), permission must be obtained from the individual copyright owners to reproduce their works by assembling them in the new collection. The new authorship in the collection extends to the particular selection and arrangement of the poems and songs but not to the poems or songs themselves.

The difference between a compilation and a collection is that the matter making up the compilation is usually not copyrightable (think lists of facts, such as found in an almanac), while the matter comprising the collective work (think short stories, photos, or poems) is copyrightable.

Derivative Works

A **derivative work** is one that is based on (or derived from) one or more already existing works, such as a translation, dramatization, fictionalization, or any other form in which a work may be recast, transformed, or adapted. Thus, the author of a derivative work transforms or somehow changes a preexisting work (while the author of a compilation or collective work assembles or arranges preexisting materials). The resulting work is copyrightable if it includes original work of authorship and if the original material was not used unlawfully.

Derivative works, also known as *new versions*, include such works as musical arrangements, motion picture versions, abridgments, and condensations. Additionally, any work consisting of editorial revisions, annotations, elaborations, or other modifications that, as a whole, represent an original work, is a derivative work subject to copyright protection.

The following examples show some of the many different types of derivative works.

ETHICS EDGE: Seeking Permission to Reprint

As noted in the text, collections involve bringing together other's copyrighted works (such as collecting the best short stories of author Alice Munro). Derivative works are those based on other works (such as a movie based on a book). You may not prepare a collective work or derivative work unless you have permission from the copyright holder of the underlying work(s), unless the material is in the public domain. When in doubt, always seek written permission from the copyright owner for any use of his or her material. Some information and sample permission letters may be found at Purdue University's Copyright Management Center at http://www.copyright.iupui.edu/_permitintro.htm.

- A television drama of *The Glass Menagerie* based on the earlier play by Tennessee Williams.
- A motion picture of *Flags of Our Fathers* based on the earlier book by James Bradley.
- A play of *In Cold Blood* based on the work by Truman Capote.
- AOL version 9.0 based on earlier versions.
- A television dramatization of *The Gambler* based on the song by Kenny Rogers.
- A novel in English, such as *Doctor Zhivago* (translated from a book originally published in Russian).
- The movie *Chicago* based on the earlier play.
- The movie *Rocky II* based on the original *Rocky* movie.

To be copyrightable, the derivative work must be different enough from the original to be regarded as a new work or must contain a substantial amount of new material. Making minor changes or additions of little substance to a preexisting work will not qualify the work as a new version for copyright purposes. The new material must be original and copyrightable in itself.

The copyright in a derivative work covers only the additions, changes, or other new material appearing for the first time in the work. It does not extend to any preexisting material and does not imply a copyright in that material. The copyright in the derivative work relates only to the new, independent work and does not affect or extend the nature, scope, or duration of copyright protection for the original work. Thus, if a new preface or foreword is prepared for a new printing of John Grisham's novel *The King of Torts*, only the new material is independently protected and owned by the new author. John Grisham retains the rights in the original work. One cannot extend the length of protection for a copyrighted work by creating a derivative work. A work that has fallen in the public domain (i.e., one that is no longer protected by copyright) may be used for a derivative work, but the copyright in the derivative work will not restore or revive the copyright of the public domain material; neither will it prevent anyone else from using the same public domain material for another derivative work.

Only the owner of copyright in a work has the right to prepare or to authorize someone else to create a new version of that work. The owner is generally the author or someone who has obtained rights from the author

Trivia

- Approximately 4 percent of all employment in the United States is in copyright-related industries.
- The core copyright industries were responsible for nearly 13 percent of the U.S. economy's growth in 2005.
- In *Arden v. Columbia Pictures Industries, Inc.*, 908 F. Supp. 1248 (E.D.N.Y. 1995), the court considered whether plaintiff's novel of a man trapped in a repeating day, forced to live the same day over and over, was infringed by the famous movie *Groundhog Day*, produced 12 years later. The court held that there was no infringement because the works were not substantially similar. While the *ideas* expressed were the same, the *expression* of those ideas was quite different because the novel was dark and introspective and featured witchcraft while the movie was a romantic comedy. Any similarity between the two related only to unprotectable ideas, concepts, or abstractions.
- Even silence may be copyrightable. Artist John Cage, now deceased, recorded "4'33'" (an entirely silent piece lasting 4 minutes and 33 seconds). Whenever "4'33'" has been recorded by other artists, as it was by Frank Zappa in 1993 (for a tribute album to Cage), royalties have been paid to use the silent work.

CHAPTER SUMMARY

Copyright protects original works of authorship that are fixed in a tangible form of expression such that they can be perceived, communicated, or reproduced either directly or with the aid of a machine or device. The requirement of originality means that the work must be independently created by the author; it need not be the only work of its kind. Copyrightable works include the following categories: literary works; musical works (including any accompanying words); dramatic works (including any accompanying words); pantomimes and choreographic works; pictorial, graphic, and sculptural works; motion pictures and other audiovisual works; sound recordings; and architectural works.

Some matter is uncopyrightable, such as ideas, useful articles, blank forms, titles, short phrases, common property (such as height and weight charts), lists of ingredients, facts, and matters in the public domain, including works whose copyrights have expired and works of the U.S. government.

A compilation of otherwise uncopyrightable material may be protectable (such as a book of lists). Similarly, a collection of other copyrightable material (such as the collection of film clips that made up the movie *That's Entertainment*) may itself be copyrightable as a new work. Finally, a work that is recast (such as a movie made from a book) is copyrightable, in regard to the new material, as a derivative work.

CASE ILLUSTRATION—EXTENT OF COMPILATION COPYRIGHT

Case: *Publications International Ltd. v. Meredith Corp.,* 88 F.3d 473 (7th Cir. 1996)

Facts: Defendant Meredith obtained a copyright for a compilation of recipes using Dannon yogurt. Plaintiff published many of the recipes in its own books and magazines. Plaintiff sued Meredith for unfair trade practices, and Meredith counterclaimed, alleging that the plaintiff infringed its copyright. The lower court enjoined the plaintiff from further publishing the recipes, and plaintiff appealed.

Holding: The court vacated the injunction. A compilation protects only the order and manner of presentation of the compilation's elements. When the elements that compose a compilation are not themselves copyrightable, the only protectable expression is the manner in which the compiler has selected and arranged the elements. A list of recipe ingredients lacks the requisite element of originality for copyright protection and is merely a statement of facts. These recipes lacked any instructive and valuable narration. Thus, the compilation copyright does not extend to cover the individual recipes themselves, but only extends to the order and manner in which they are presented. Because the plaintiff offered the recipes in a manner and order different from Meredith, there was no copyright infringement.

CASE STUDY AND ACTIVITIES

Case Study.   Vision's gift shops at its resorts offer originally designed jewelry, original guidebooks with maps and suggestions for touring surrounding areas, cookbooks featuring recipes from the hotel restaurants, and DVDs featuring information about the resorts. Its lounges offer live concert and comedy routine performances. As patrons leave the resort, they are given survey cards to "rate" their satisfaction with Vision's services. Vision has recently retained a new architecture firm to develop plans for new resorts, and this firm has prepared technical drawings and models of planned resorts. Finally, Vision has developed a new system for "check out" for its hotel guests.

Activities.   Discuss the copyrightability of each of the above works.

ROLE OF PARALEGAL

The role of paralegals prior to preparing a copyright application will likely be limited to legal research relating to copyrightability so that clients can be advised about whether works created by them qualify for copyright protection and to ensure clients do not infringe the rights of others. Research may focus on any of the following topics:

- whether a work is an original, fixed work of authorship
- what type of work of authorship an author's work is, for example, a literary work, dramatic work, musical work, or pictorial work
- whether the work is subject to protection as an expression rather than a mere idea, system, or process
- whether the work is excluded from copyright protection because it consists of blank forms, titles, slogans, common property, or facts
- whether the work is excluded from copyright protection as a work of the U.S. government
- whether the author's work is a compilation, collective work, or derivative work

INTERNET RESOURCES

Federal laws relating to copyright:	http://www.law.cornell.edu http://www.findlaw.com http://www.copyright.gov/title17/circ92.pdf
Copyright Office:	http://www.copyright.gov
General information:	http://www.law.cornell.edu/wex/index.php/ Copyright (site of Cornell Law School) http://www.findlaw.com http://www.megalaw.com http://fairuse.stanford.edu (Stanford University's excellent site providing general information about copyright law)

DISCUSSION QUESTIONS

1. Classify the following as likely copyrightable or not copyrightable.
   - the lyrics to the Macarena song
   - the dance steps and moves to the Macarena song
   - the filmed television performance of celebrities on *Dancing with the Stars*

- a PowerPoint presentation by the board of directors of Ford Motor Co.
- a speech written for the chairman of Ford Motor Co.
- a law firm's sheets for keeping time
- a list of Supreme Court Justices
- GEICO's slogan "Even a caveman can do it"
- the scripts for the GEICO "caveman" commercials
- a knife
- an engraved rose on a knife
- an idea for a method of online banking
- federal regulations relating to banking
- a novel that includes highly offensive language and racist content

2. A photographer takes a picture of the Washington Monument. The next day, another photographer takes an identical picture of the Washington Monument. Which picture is entitled to copyright protection? Discuss.

3. A writer has written a script for a new sitcom based upon a colorful and glamorous group of housewives living in a suburb and their marriages, friendships, and relationships. Would such a script infringe the well-known sitcom *Desperate Housewives*? Discuss.

4. Identify each of the following as a compilation, collection, or derivative work.
   - the Broadway play *Spamalot* based on the earlier Monty Python sketches
   - a chart entitled *Fast Facts about U.S. Presidents* that provides a listing of the presidents' birth dates and birthplaces and information about their personality traits and families
   - a book of photographs titled *Nature Photography* and showing various artists' photographs of landscapes, parks, and other natural scenes
   - a cookbook entitled *Betty Crocker's Diabetes Cookbook*
   - the movie *The Da Vinci Code* based on the book of the same name
   - a book listing the 200 best movies
   - a directory listing the best hotels in the United States according to several criteria, including location, amenities, cleanliness, and so forth
   - the movie Ocean's Thirteen (based upon the earlier movies Ocean's Eleven and Ocean's Twelve)
   - a book entitled *Best Short Stories of 2007*

USING INTERNET RESOURCES

1. Use the Web site of the Copyright Office to answer the following questions.
   a. Review Circular 32. Is typeface or typography of a work protected under copyright law? Would a sports schedule showing the schedule of the L.A. Lakers be protected under copyright law?
   b. Review Fact Sheet 109. What form should be used if a person desires to secure a copyright registration for a dissertation? May one submit a handwritten manuscript to the Copyright Office?

USING INTERNET RESOURCES (CONT'D)

     c. Review Circular 40. Is a sewing kit copyrightable? Is a stained glass design copyrightable? Is the "smiley face" symbol copyrightable?

     d. Review Circular 56. What three examples are given of sound recordings?

     e. Review Form TX. What does Section 6 require the copyright claimant to identify?

2. Review Stanford University's Copyright and Fair Use site. Review Copyright FAQs, question 1. Are scribbled notes on the back of an envelope copyrightable?

For additional resources, go to www.paralegal.delmar.cengage.com.

Chapter 11

The Rights Afforded by Copyright Law

CHAPTER OVERVIEW

Under the Copyright Act, a copyright owner has a "bundle" of rights: the right to reproduce, adapt, distribute, perform, and display the work to the exclusion of others. Thus, copyright owners have a full complement of ways to commercially exploit their works. There are, however, some limitations on these exclusive rights. For example, once certain works have been distributed, under the "first sale doctrine," the subsequent owner is free to use or resell the item without liability for infringement. Similarly, some activities do not constitute infringement, for example, some uses for certain educational activities, noncommercial fundraising, or for religious worship. Rights for sound recordings are considerably more limited than rights for other works, such as literary or musical works. Authors of fine arts such as paintings and sculptures may also have "moral rights," meaning rights personal to themselves that survive the sale of their work so that authorship of the work is forever attributed to them and the work is not mutilated or altered, which would prejudice their reputation as artists and creators.

INTRODUCTION

Section 106 of the Copyright Act provides that, subject to certain exceptions, the owner of a copyright has the exclusive rights to do and to authorize any of the following:

- to reproduce the copyrighted work in copies or phonorecords
- to prepare derivative works based on the copyrighted work
- to distribute copies or phonorecords of the copyrighted work to the public
- to perform the copyrighted work publicly (in the case of certain works)
- to display the copyrighted work publicly (in the case of literary, musical, dramatic and choreographic works, pantomimes, and pictorial, graphic, or sculptural works)
- to perform the copyrighted work publicly by means of a digital audio transmission (in the case of sound recordings)

Unless exemptions exist, unauthorized exercise of any of these rights by another is an infringement of the owner's copyright in the work, whether or not the owner has secured a copyright registration and whether or not the owner has published the work. Any of these exclusive rights may be transferred and they may be owned separately. For example, the composer of a song may authorize one person to perform it publicly and another to create a television show based on the song. Each right is separately transferable.

These exclusive rights, usually referred to as a "bundle," will be examined in this chapter.

RIGHTS OF REPRODUCTION

The most fundamental of the rights granted to copyright owners is the right to reproduce the work, thereby excluding others from reproducing the work. A violation of the Copyright Act occurs whether or not the violator profits by the reproduction. Consider the warning displayed at the beginning of every video you rent that reproduction is a violation of the Copyright Act. Thus, making a copy of the movie *Lord of the Rings* violates the owner's right to reproduction, even if you only intend to view the movie privately.

Only the owner has the right to reproduce the work. Secretly taping a concert, taking pictures at a filmed performance, or recording a simultaneously recorded speech all violate the owner's right to reproduce the work even if there is no later sale or distribution of the work.

At the suggestion of Congress, in 1978 a group of authors, publishers, and users established a not-for-profit entity called Copyright Clearance Center (CCC) to serve as a clearinghouse granting rights to reproduce and distribute books and periodicals. Authors register their works with the CCC, which then grants licenses to academic, government, and corporate users to copy and distribute the works. The CCC grants permission or licenses to use works and then collects royalty fees, which are distributed to the authors. Companies that photocopy articles from journals and magazines often enter into licensing arrangements with the CCC so they can make copies of articles for internal distribution within the company and remain in compliance with copyright

law. The CCC is located at 222 Rosewood Drive, Danvers, MA 01923. Its telephone number is (978) 750-8400, and its Internet address is http://www.copyright.com.

A new trend among some copyright owners is to expressly grant licenses for others to use their works in limited ways. Creative Commons, a nonprofit organization, allows musicians and authors to grant licenses to others to borrow or adapt their works under a "some rights reserved" policy. Authors may either grant limited rights or total access by using free license agreements available through Creative Commons' Web site (http://www.creativecommons.org). For example, one type of license allows others to sample, tweak, or remix a musical work as long they credit the original composer.

RIGHTS TO PREPARE DERIVATIVE WORKS

Section 106 of the Copyright Act provides that the owner of a copyright has the exclusive right to prepare derivative works based upon the copyrighted work. This right is often referred to as the right to adapt the original work.

As discussed in chapter 10, a derivative work is broadly defined as a work based upon one or more preexisting works, such as a translation, dramatization, fictionalization, motion picture version, abridgment, condensation, or any other form in which a work may be recast, transformed, or adapted. A work consisting of editorial revisions, annotations, elaborations, or other modifications is also a derivative work, if the new material represents original work of authorship.

The copyright owner thus has the right to exclude others from adapting his or her work or creating works based on the owner's work. For example, George Lucas has the right to exclude others from making sequels to his *Star Wars* works. Stephen King can exclude others from making a play or a television movie based upon his books. John Mellencamp can prevent another from making a movie based upon his songs. Of course, if the authors of the works consent, others

ETHICS EDGE: Avoiding Copyright Infringement

One of the easiest ways to violate the copyright rights of others is by reproducing or distributing materials without permission. The following are all copyright violations that are commonly committed by students (assuming there are no exceptions):

- copying more than an insubstantial portion of a book or article, for example, copying an entire chapter of a textbook
- making unauthorized copies of posters, photos, or other copyrighted artwork
- distributing multiple copies of an interesting article to friends and colleagues
- downloading music or movies without paying the necessary license fees
- uploading copyrighted material to the Internet

may be granted rights to adapt a work. Thus, many of author Danielle Steel's works of fiction have been made into television movies, and the novel *The Da Vinci Code* was made into a motion picture. The new derivative work is separately copyrightable in regard to its new elements. Copyright in the derivative, however, does not affect the copyright in the original. Thus, the new elements, lines, characters, and so forth that are added to the movie *The Da Vinci Code* are separately copyrightable as a derivative work, while the original author retains rights to any material in the novel *The Da Vinci Code*.

In a new twist on derivative rights, fans of certain movies, television shows, books, and other works now write **fan fiction,** unauthorized works about preexisting characters and settings authored by those other than original authors. For example, devoted fans now write fanzine articles or post blogs on the Internet detailing new adventures of their favorite Harry Potter or Star Trek characters. Although these writings nearly always violate the copyright owners' rights to create derivative works, some authors tolerate or even encourage such fan fiction because it enhances interest and encourages sales of their original works. Other copyright owners zealously scour the Internet for infringements and then attempt to enjoin fan fiction. Fan fiction is not only likely a copyright violation (unless it is

a protected fair use, such as a parody), but may also constitute a trademark violation or dilution of a mark if the fan fiction tarnishes a mark.

RIGHTS OF DISTRIBUTION AND THE FIRST SALE DOCTRINE

Section 106(3) of the Copyright Act provides that the owner of a copyright has the exclusive right to distribute copies or phonorecords of the work to the public by sale or other transfer of ownership, or by rental, lease, or lending. A violation of the distribution right can arise solely from the act of distribution itself even if the distributor did not make an unlawful copy or know the copy being distributed was unauthorized. Thus, Blockbuster Video stores can be liable for violating an owner's right to distribute a movie, even if Blockbuster does not know that the movie was placed on videocassette or DVD without the owner's authority. Authors often grant permission to others to distribute their works, including granting licenses through entities such as the CCC, discussed earlier.

One limitation on a copyright owner's sole right of distribution is found in section 109 of the Copyright Act, which provides that once the author has parted with ownership of a copy or phonorecord, the new owner of a lawfully made copy can treat the object as his or her own and can then freely use, sell, lease, or lend the work to another. Just as in trademark law (see chapter 6), where the first sale "exhausts" the trademark owner's right to a mark, in copyright law, the copyright owner's sale of an item exhausts his or her exclusive right to distribute the work. Thus, purchasing a copy of the book *Seabiscuit* or purchasing a DVD of the movie *The Devil Wears Prada* gives the new owner the right to lend the book or movie to a friend, re-sell the work at a garage sale, or even destroy it. The **first sale doctrine** does not apply to or limit the author's exclusive rights to prepare derivative works or rights of public performance and dis-play, but only to distribution rights. The first sale doctrine rests on the principle that once the copy-right owner sells the initial physical copy, he or she has received full economic value for the work and should not be able to restrict future sales.

The copyright owner, however, while hav-ing parted with distribution rights, retains other rights, such as the right to reproduce the work, perform it, adapt it, and prepare derivative works based on it. Thus, in the previous example, the purchaser of the book *Seabiscuit* does not have the right to make a movie of the book or to pre-pare a second updated version of the book based upon the original. The original owner, the au-thor, retains such derivative rights, having lost only the right to distribution through the first sale doctrine.

Courts have struggled with the question whether the first sale doctrine applies to goods imported into the United States. Section 602 of the Copyright Act provides that importing copies or phonorecords of a work acquired abroad into the United States without the copyright owner's authorization is an infringement of the copy-right owner's exclusive right to distribute his or her works. In a 1998 decision, the U.S. Supreme Court held that once a first sale of a domestically manufactured product occurs, even if the sale is made abroad, the copyright owner's right to dis-tribute is exhausted. Thereafter, the owner of the work or product can resell the item freely, with-out permission of the copyright owner. *Quality*

King Distribs. v. L'anza Research Int'l Inc., 523 U.S. 135 (1998). See chapter 16 for further discussion of this topic.

Exceptions to the First Sale Doctrine

There are some exceptions or limitations to the doctrine that once a copyright owner parts with ownership of a copy or phonorecord he or she has lost the right to distribute his or her work.

- The first sale doctrine applies only to lawfully made copies and phonorecords. Thus, if Borders bookstore comes into possession of a pirated or unauthorized version of *Memoirs of a Geisha*, resale to others would violate the author's rights of distribution, even if Borders did not know it possessed a pirated version of the book.
- Due to a special statutory exception, enacted largely at the urging of the music industry, the first sale doctrine does not apply to commercial rentals of records and certain computer programs. Those works cannot be commercially rented. Prior to the enactment of 17 U.S.C. § 109(b), record stores would rent records and CDs to customers who then went home and made copies of the record or CD on a blank tape for a fraction of the price of buying the original. Because of the threat to the music industry, this rental practice is now banned. Thus, Shania Twain can prohibit the purchaser of her records or albums from renting those works commercially, generally because commercial renting of sound recordings would seriously undermine creativity and deprive copyright owners of revenue. Nonprofit libraries and other similar institutions may, however, lend or rent out sound recordings and computer programs. Additionally, if the computer program is incapable of being copied, it can be rented. Thus, Blockbuster Video can rent out computer video games

to consumers because consumers are generally unable to duplicate or copy the video games. Finally, this limitation does not apply to computers that are part of other machines or products. Thus, a car can be rented by a consumer inasmuch as the computer programs, such as an onboard navigational system that makes up part of the car, cannot be readily copied and are integrated into the car itself. In sum, however, the author of a sound recording or computer program can prevent owners of lawfully made copies from renting, leasing, or lending their copies of the sound recording or computer program to others for direct or indirect commercial advantage.

The Droit de Suite Doctrine

Droit de suite (literally, "right of continuation"), is a doctrine recognized in many foreign countries, but not generally in the United States, that allows authors of works of fine art to share in the appreciation of the value of a work. Under this doctrine, if a painter sells a painting for $25,000 and the painting is later sold for $100,000, the painter would be able to share in the $75,000 appreciation of the work. California has enacted a statute called the California Resale Royalties Act (Cal. Civ. Code § 986), which accomplishes the same goal by allowing artists residing in California to collect 5 percent of any resale price for their works, if the work (which must be an original painting, sculpture, drawing, or an original work of art in glass) is sold for at least $1,000 and is sold for more than the reseller paid for it.

Thus, in California, the first sale of a work of fine art does not exhaust the owner's distribution right because the original owner can share in the proceeds of a later sale. Some experts have questioned the constitutionality of the California statute inasmuch as the Constitution provides exclusive authority to Congress (not the individual states) to promote science and arts through copyright law. Moreover, the California law may ultimately damage the California art market if buyers avoid purchasing art in California in order to circumvent the 5 percent royalty they may later need to pay an artist.

RIGHTS TO PERFORM THE WORK PUBLICLY

Section 106(4) of the Copyright Act provides that in the case of literary, musical, dramatic and choreographic works, pantomimes, and motion pictures and other audiovisual works, the copyright owner has the exclusive right to perform the copyrighted work publicly. The word *perform* means to recite, render, play, dance, or act a work, either directly or by means of a device or process to show its images in any sequence or to make the sounds accompanying it audible. Thus, if an individual reads the copyrighted novel *Bridget Jones's Diary* on the *Oprah Winfrey Show*, there have been two performances: one in the reading of the work before the live audience and the other in the transmission of it by the television show.

The copyright owner's right to perform is limited to public performances. To perform a work publicly means to perform the work at a place open to the public or at any place where a substantial number of persons outside of a normal circle of a family and its social acquaintances is gathered or to transmit or communicate the work to the public or to a place open to the public (again, outside of a small family or social setting), whether the performance is live or recorded. Performances at places such as clubs, lodges, schools, and summer camps are "public performances" subject to copyright protection. Thus, if Van Morrison sings a song copyrighted by Bob Dylan at a nightclub, theatre, in concert, on Howard Stern's radio show, or on the *Tonight Show,* he has violated Bob Dylan's right of public performance. Note that if Howard Stern's radio show is live in New York City but taped for later transmission in Los Angeles, there have been two separate public performances. The transmission by radio or television broadcast is a public performance even though listeners receive the transmission at different times and places and in the privacy of their own homes or cars. If Van Morrison sings the same song for a small group of friends and family gathered at his home, there is no violation because there has been no public performance.

If a room or facility is open to the public and a copyrighted movie or song is performed therein, there has been a violation of the owner's exclusive right to public performance of his or her work. Courts have held, however, that a private viewing or transmission of a rented movie in a guest's hotel room is not a public performance, and such a viewing is treated the same as rental of a movie for home viewing. *See Columbia Pictures Indus., Inc. v. Prof'l Real Estate Investors, Inc.,* 866 F.2d 278 (9th Cir. 1989).

Exception for Sound Recordings

The exclusive right of a copyright owner to perform his or her work publicly does not extend to sound recordings. 17 U.S.C. § 114 (a). Recall from chapter 10 that a sound recording usually protects the arrangement or production of a song, while a musical work is a musical composition and its accompanying words. There are two separate rights in music: the right protecting the notes and lyrics (this is the *musical work*) and the right protecting what you hear, such as the performer singing, the musicians playing, and the entire production and recordation of sound (which is the *sound recording*).

For example, when a radio station plays or transmits a record of Frank Sinatra singing "My Way," a song written by Paul Anka, there is no violation of Frank Sinatra's or the record company's rights; however, there has been a violation of Paul Anka's right to perform the work publicly because he is the author of the underlying musical composition (assuming Paul Anka did not authorize the performance). The likely rationale for this rule is to ensure that radio stations are not burdened by paying double royalties in order to play most songs.

Other Exceptions

According to section 110 of the Copyright Act, the following performances, many of which relate to nonprofit educational or charitable activities, do not violate a copyright owner's exclusive right to perform his or her work publicly.

- **Face-to-face teaching.** The Copyright Act protects performances or displays of a work by instructors or pupils in the course of face-to-face teaching activities of a nonprofit educational institution and certain instructional or educational broadcasting by governmental bodies or nonprofit educational institutions engaged in systematic instructional activities. Thus, students in a drama class can perform a copyrighted play without liability. The Copyright Office has recommended to Congress that this provision be amended to allow for distance learning as well as face-to-face instruction (see chapter 15).
- **Religious services.** Performances of a nondramatic literary or musical work in the course of services at a place of worship or other religious assembly are permissible.
- **Promotion of records.** The Copyright Act allows performances of nondramatic musical works (namely, the playing of recorded music) at retail stores, such as record stores and stores that sell CDs and CD players, to promote sales.
- **Nonprofit performances.** Live (not transmitted) performances of nondramatic literary or musical works for noncommercial purposes are permissible if there are no admission charges or, if there are charges, the net proceeds are used for charitable purposes and the author is notified so he or she can object prior to the performance (this exception promotes benefit and fundraising concerts for educational, religious, or other charitable purposes).

- **Veterans and fraternal organizations.** The Copyright Act allows performances of nondramatic literary or musical works at social functions organized by a nonprofit veterans' organization or a nonprofit fraternal organization to which the public is not invited and the proceeds of which are used for charitable purposes and not for financial gain.

- **Agricultural and horticultural fairs.** Performances of a nondramatic musical work by a governmental body or nonprofit agricultural or horticultural association in the course of an annual agricultural or horticultural fair or exhibition are permissible.

- **Small commercial establishments.** The Copyright Act (17 U.S.C. § 110(5)) allows transmissions of radio and television broadcasts in small businesses, restaurants, and bars (less than 2,000 square feet for non-eating establishments and less than 3,750 square feet for eating establishments), thus allowing such establishments to play radios and televisions for the enjoyment of their customers without obtaining licenses, as long as no direct fee is charged and there is no further retransmission. Note that this exception applies only to radio and television transmissions—setting up a CD player and playing a CD would be prohibited as a violation of the copyright owner's exclusive rights. Businesses whose square footage exceeds the stated amounts also qualify for the exemption if they use six or fewer speakers or four smaller televisions.

- **Transmissions for handicapped persons.** The Copyright Act allows certain transmissions for the benefit of blind and deaf persons, if the performance is for nonprofit.

- **Homestyle exemption.** Under 17 U.S.C. § 110(5), communication of a transmission of a performance or display by the public reception of the transmission on a single receiving apparatus of a kind commonly used in a private home (hence the term "homestyle") is permissible, unless there is a direct charge or a retransmission. Often called the homestyle exemption, this provision allows one to receive a transmission in public. For example, turning on your radio on the beach or watching an ordinary television in a public park is not a performance for which you need permission.

As you can readily see, the foregoing exceptions share certain common characteristics. Generally, they either accommodate a particular public interest type of use, or they otherwise cause minimal economic impact on the copyright owner. Thus, several relate to specific nonprofit, educational, or charitable uses; others narrowly limit the circumstances of the use to ensure that there is no meaningful commercial exploitation.

Note that many of the exceptions relate to "nondramatic literary or musical works," meaning books, songs, and records and excluding plays, motion pictures, and operas. Thus, showing a motion picture at a religious service (even if it is related to religion) violates the owner's rights of performance and is prohibited.

Performing Rights Societies

Because the playing of music by CDs and radio in theatres, clubs, or large establishments is a public performance (requiring permission of the copyright owner of the music) and because the copyright owner of the music would have a difficult time keeping track of each time his or her musical work is publicly performed to enforce his or her copyright rights, performing rights societies came into existence to reduce the administrative burdens for both those seeking to perform the work and copyright owners.

Composers, lyricists, and publishers usually join one of three performing rights societies that grant licenses to others to publicly perform the works of their members. The societies then collect and distribute royalty fees for the licenses granted.

A **performing rights society** acts as an agent for musical copyright owners and issues licenses in their behalf. The best known of the performing rights societies are ASCAP (American Society of Composers, Authors, and Publishers) and BMI (Broadcast Music, Inc.). ASCAP and BMI are the dominant organizations in the field, and together their repertoires include nearly all the world's copyrighted music. A smaller society is SESAC (formerly, the Society of European Stage Authors & Composers). These societies issue blanket licenses to commercial establishments, radio and television stations, and clubs, allowing them to play any of the works in the societies' repertoires or inventories for a fixed fee, thus eliminating the need for a large commercial establishment or radio station to negotiate thousands of separate licenses to play music owned by others. The societies charge license fees and then distribute the collected royalty fees to the thousands of composers, authors, and publishers they represent. ASCAP and BMI monitor and visit radio stations, clubs, restaurants, skating rinks, conventions, shopping malls, gyms, and other commercial establishments to ensure that copyrighted works are not being publicly performed without license. ASCAP, BMI, and SESAC function in granting licenses to perform music the way the Copyright Clearance Center does in granting licenses to others to reproduce and distribute written works. Information about the societies can be found at their Web sites: www.ascap.com, www.bmi.com and www.sesac.com.

Commercial establishments such as hotels, stores, and other businesses may also be engaged in public performances when they "pipe in" music throughout the establishment or play music when callers are placed on hold, whether the music is from the owner's own record or CD or is music being simultaneously played on the radio. Although smaller commercial establishments are exempt, as discussed earlier, if larger enterprises pipe in such music, there has been a public per-

formance for which permission or a license must be sought. Thus, in *Sailor Music v. Gap Stores, Inc.*, 516 F. Supp. 923 (S.D.N.Y.), *aff'd*, 688 F.2d 84 (2d Cir. 1981), the Gap stores were held to have publicly performed musical works in violation of the owners' copyrights where two stores had several speakers recessed in their ceilings that broadcast songs, and the stores encompassed an average of 3,500 square feet of space.

Generally, fees charged by ASCAP and BMI are determined by square footage, room capacity, revenue generated by the license, or the number of trunk lines a company has coming into its offices that play music on hold.

RIGHTS TO DISPLAY THE WORK PUBLICLY

Section 106(5) of the Copyright Act provides that in the case of all copyrighted works other than sound recordings and works of architecture, the copyright owner has the exclusive right to display the work publicly. A display is "public" under the same circumstances in which a performance is "public," namely, if it occurs at a place open to the public or at a place where a substantial number of persons outside of the normal circle of a family and its social acquaintances is gathered or if it is transmitted or communicated to the public or to a place open to the public (again, outside of a small family or social setting), whether the display is live or recorded.

Exception for Owners of Lawful Copies

Just as the first sale doctrine allows the owner of a lawful copy of a book to sell it or lend it to another, a similar right allows the owner of a lawful copy of a work (other than a sound recording or architectural work) to display that copy publicly, either directly or by the projection of no more than one image at a time, to viewers present at the place where the copy is located.

17 U.S.C. § 109(c). Thus, a museum or gallery that has purchased a painting or sculpture may display that work in the museum or gallery but may not display it by multiple displays, such as displays on multiple computer screens, or by some other method of transmission (e.g., closed-circuit television transmission) to viewers at another location. By way of illustration, a department store cannot have a bank of screens that display several multiple slide projections of a painting even if it has purchased the painting. Only one image at a time can be displayed to viewers present at the place where the copy is located (likely to ensure that movies are not shown or performed without the owner's permission). Thus, as an exception to the first sale doctrine, the original painter, sculptor, or other author or copyright owner retains the right to display the copy publicly.

Other Exceptions

Other exceptions to the copyright owner's exclusive right to display are similar to certain of the exceptions to the copyright owner's exclusive right to perform discussed earlier, such as the following:

- displays in face-to-face teaching activities of nonprofit educational institutions and certain transmissions that are part of systematic instructional activities of a governmental body or nonprofit educational institution
- displays in the course of religious worship and services
- "homestyle"-type displays

RIGHTS TO PERFORM COPYRIGHTED SOUND RECORDINGS

The rights in sound recordings (the author of which is the performer whose performance is fixed or the record producer, or both) are quite limited and are far different from the rights in musical works (composed music including words, on sheet music, in records, or on CDs). The exclusive rights given to owners of copyrighted works in section 106 of the Copyright Act to perform and display their works do not extend to sound recordings. Once a sound recording exists, others may perform the recording without liability. Thus, radio and television stations can play sound recordings without liability (although they undoubtedly have entered into blanket licenses with ASCAP and BMI so that the composers and authors of the underlying musical works are being compensated inasmuch as the owners of copyright in musical works are granted exclusive unlimited rights to perform their works).

Although the owner of a sound recording has the exclusive right of reproduction, this right is quite limited and allows the owner merely to produce actual physical copies and thereby prohibits pirates from making bootleg copies of a record.

Some experts believe these limited rights available to the owners of copyrighted sound recordings are meant to relieve those who would pay royalties (such as radio and television stations) from the multiple burdens of having to pay royalties to the composer or author of the underlying musical work as well as to the record companies that produce the sound recording and the performer who performs the work.

In 1995, Congress granted a new and sixth exclusive right to copyright owners, relating strictly to sound recordings. The Digital Performance Right in Sound Recordings Act, 17 U.S.C. § 106(6), provides that owners of sound recordings have the exclusive right to perform their works publicly by means of digital audio transmission. This grant recognized that new technologies, whereby one can easily download a digital transmission of a song and never pay for a tape, record, or CD, needed to be addressed. Thus, the new protection afforded to the owners of copyright in sound recordings is protection against public performances of their sound recordings by subscription services (such as transmission by a cable service that charges recipients for the service) and interactive services (such as services that allow a person to request by telephone or e-mail and then receive a digital transmission of a sound recording). Although there are several exemptions, in brief, digital music services must now pay recording companies and performers when they transmit sound recordings.

However, the owner of a sound recording cannot preclude others from publicly performing the work (other than by digital audio transmission) because the owner does not have rights of performance. Additional issues relating to the downloading of music through the Internet and music file sharing are discussed in chapter 15.

OTHER LIMITATIONS ON EXCLUSIVE RIGHTS

In addition to the exemptions to copyright owners' exclusive rights already discussed (namely, exemptions for use of works for certain educational purposes, religious worship, noncommercial charitable purposes, limited transmission for small establishments, performances at fairs, and performances for the handicapped), there are a few other limitations on a copyright owner's exclusive rights to his or her work:

- Libraries or archives may reproduce and distribute one copy of a copyrighted work and maintain three copies for preservation if there is no commercial advantage, the library is open to the public, and a copyright notice is placed on the work.
- Libraries and archives are not liable for infringement for unauthorized photocopying of copyrighted works by their patrons as long as a notice is placed on the equipment warning that the making of copies may be subject to copyright law.
- Secondary transmissions whereby hotels and other similar establishments relay radio and television transmissions to

private guest rooms without charge are acceptable.
- Radio and television stations that have entered into lawful arrangements to perform works may make one temporary or "ephemeral" recording of the work so that it is easier for them to transmit it and may preserve it for archival purposes (e.g., a radio station may copy a compact disc onto a cartridge so it can be readily played).
- An owner of a computer program may make a copy of it for archival or backup purposes.

In addition to the exceptions described, certain uses of copyrighted works are not infringement, for example, quoting lyrics of a song or narrative from a book in reviews of the material, using a work in news reporting or teaching, or parodying works. Such a use is called "fair use" and is discussed in chapter 14 as a defense to copyright infringement.

MORAL RIGHTS AND THE VISUAL ARTISTS RIGHTS ACT

Introduction

Many countries recognize certain personal and noneconomic rights of authors in their works to protect their honor and reputation, even after they have sold their work. Such personal rights are referred to as **moral rights.**

There are two primary moral rights: the right of **attribution** (sometimes called the right of paternity), which ensures the author's right to be known as the author of a work, and the **right of integrity,** which ensures that the work not be distorted, mutilated, or misrepresented in a way that would injure the author's reputation.

The Berne Convention, to which the United States is a signatory, requires that member nations protect authors' moral rights of attribution and integrity. In 1990, Congress enacted the Visual Artists Rights Act (17 U.S.C. § 106A) in order to comply with its Berne Convention obligations.

Prior to this legislation, authors generally protected their moral rights through actions for breach of contract, defamation, misrepresentation, or unfair competition.

Definition of Visual Arts

The Visual Artists Rights Act is quite limited and applies only to works of visual arts, namely, paintings, drawings, prints, photographs (produced for exhibition purposes), or sculptures that exist in a single copy or in a limited edition of 200 or fewer copies, if those copies are signed and consecutively numbered. Works of visual art do not include posters, maps, globes, charts, technical drawings, motion pictures, books, magazines, newspapers, electronic information services or publications, or merchandising, promotional, packaging material, works made for hire, and works not subject to copyright protection (such as useful articles). Thus, the term *visual arts* generally refers to what is commonly called *fine art*.

Rights of Attribution and Integrity

The author of a work of visual art has the following rights of attribution:

- to claim authorship of the work
- to prevent the use of his or her name as the author of any work of visual art that he or she did not create
- to prevent the use of his or her name as the author of a work of visual art that has been distorted, mutilated, or otherwise modified such as to prejudice his or her honor or reputation

The author of a work of visual art has the following rights of integrity:

- to prevent intentional distortion, mutilation, or other modification that would be prejudicial to his or her honor or reputation
- to prevent any destruction of a work of recognized stature, whether through intentional or gross negligence

Thus, authors of fine arts have the right to be identified as the creator of their works and to prevent mutilation of their works, such as intentional distortions of their paintings or removal of limbs from sculptures. Modifications that are the result of the passage of time (such as chipping and fading), conservation, or presentation to the public (such as occurs when paintings in museums fade due to exposure to light) are not violations of the statute. The California statute discussed earlier also prohibits the destruction or mutilation of works of fine art and recognizes the right of attribution. Other states, including Massachusetts and New York, also have versions of moral rights statutes.

The removal of works of visual arts from buildings presents special problems. If the works (e.g., murals) can be removed without destruction or distortion, removal can proceed if the owner of the building provides notice to the artist and the artist fails to remove or pay for removal of the work. If removal will cause destruction, the owner of the building and the artist must sign a written consent to remove the work. 17 U.S.C. § 113. In a recent case in San Francisco, a famous four-story mural called *Lilli Ann* was whitewashed by the new owners of the building on which it was painted. After more than a year of litigation, the artists were paid $200,000 by way of settlement for the destruction of their work.

Extent and Duration of Moral Rights

The artist who creates the covered work owns the moral rights in it, even after selling the work to another. The moral rights reside with the author and, because they are personal rights, cannot be assigned or transferred to another, although the owner can waive his or her moral rights if the waiver is in writing.

In the case of a joint work prepared by two or more authors, a written waiver by one author waives rights for all authors.

For works created after June 1, 1991, moral rights endure for the author's life. Moral rights in works created jointly last until the death of the last surviving author.

Other Ways to Protect Moral Rights

Because the Visual Artists Rights Act applies to such a narrow category of works, namely, fine arts, authors of other works often use other remedies to achieve a level of protection equivalent to moral rights. Authors can agree by contract when they sell their works that they are entitled to future attribution and integrity rights. If the purchaser later removes the author's signature from the work or destroys it, a breach of contract has occurred. Authors may also be able to bring an action for violation of their exclusive right to prepare derivative works if a subsequent owner of a work defaces it or edits it. Finally, section 43 of the Lanham Act prohibits persons from making a false designation about the origin of goods. Thus, failure to give attribution by naming the author of a work or implying that an author is the creator of a revised or edited work likely violates this prohibition.

COMPULSORY LICENSES

In the early days of music recording, under the 1909 Copyright Act, once a composer authorized a sound recording, the composer was automatically entitled to a compulsory license or royalty fee of two cents per copy. Another producer was free to copy the sound recording as long as the statutorily set fee was paid. This arrangement, known as a **compulsory license,** allowed certain copyrighted works to be used by others, provided that the fixed fees were paid, eliminating the need for the user to contact each and every copyright owner for permission to use works. Compulsory licenses are governed by 17 U.S.C. § 115.

The provisions of section 115 of the Copyright Act do not prohibit a party from entering into a voluntary license arrangement with a copyright owner but rather provide a method of licensing when voluntary arrangements are not pursued, the copyright owner is unwilling to negotiate, or the copyright owner cannot be located. In such a case, the person intending to record the work may use the compulsory licensing provisions of the copyright law. The compulsory license is limited to distributing the sound recordings.

Once a nondramatic musical work (such as a song) has been distributed to the public on a phonorecord under the authority of the copyright owner, any other person may make or manufacture other phonorecords for distribution to the public as long as notice is given and the set fees are paid. A compulsory license may be obtained only if the primary purpose in making the phonorecords is to distribute them to the public for private (not commercial) use. A compulsory license is not available for phonorecords intended for use in background music systems, jukeboxes, broadcasting, or any other public use. Proprietors of establishments that allow patrons to make selections on coin-operated jukeboxes are encouraged to enter into voluntary (rather than compulsory) license agreements and typically do so through one of the performing rights societies, such as BMI or ASCAP.

At present, licenses for coin-operated jukeboxes are available from the Jukebox License Office, a joint venture of ASCAP, BMI, and SESAC, by which all of the songs in their repertories may be performed by the jukebox operator. If music is performed at an establishment by some means other than a jukebox (e.g., a band or DJ), a separate license from one or more of these performing rights societies is needed.

Other compulsory licenses relate to secondary transmission by cable television systems (17 U.S.C. § 111), noncommercial broadcasting (17 U.S.C. § 118), and secondary transmissions of superstations and network stations for private home viewing (17 U.S.C. § 119). The Copyright Office's Licensing Division also collects and administers royalties for these compulsory licenses.

Generally, compulsory licensing requires that users register with and pay the royalty fees established by the Copyright Office to the copyright owner or to the Licensing Division of the Copyright Office, which then remits the payments to the Copyright Royalty Board within the Copyright Office that determines and distributes the royalty fees to the copyright owners.

The Copyright Office and the music industry are in agreement that section 115 (governing compulsory licenses for sound recordings) should be modernized to reflect the realities of online music distribution and music piracy; however, at the time of writing of this text, there is no relevant legislation pending, although the Register of Congress has testified before Congress on the need for reform.

In a recent development, the Copyright Office determined in 2006 that cell phone ringtones are subject to the compulsory license provisions of section 115. See chapter 15 for additional discussion.

Trivia

- According to the Recording Industry Association of America (RIAA), the year 2004–2005 saw an 8 percent drop in music sales units in the United States, probably due to high-tech piracy and CD burning.
- In fiscal year 2005, the Copyright Office collected and deposited approximately $214 million in royalty fees for various copyright owners.
- The largest source of revenue for copyright owners is public performances of their works.
- ASCAP represents more than 275,000 U.S. composers, songwriters, and lyricists.
- ASCAP's repertory is more than 8 million works; BMI's repertory is 4.5 million copyrighted musical works.
- The performing rights societies (such as ASCAP and BMI) return to their members about $0.84 of every dollar collected.
- John Philip Sousa, Jerome Kern, Irving Berlin, and Victor Herbert were among the first members of ASCAP.

CHAPTER SUMMARY

Owners of copyright are granted a bundle of exclusive rights:

- rights to reproduce the work
- rights to prepare adaptations or derivative works based on the original work
- rights to distribute the work
- rights to perform the work
- rights to display the work

Exercise of any of these rights without permission of the copyright owner will constitute infringement of copyright, even if there is no intent to infringe and the use is innocent. There are, however, certain exceptions to the exclusive rights granted to copyright owners, such as rights to use certain copyrighted works in certain instructional and educational activities, during religious worship services, for noncommercial fundraising, for the handicapped, and for transmission of works in small commercial establishments. Moreover, according to the first sale doctrine, once a copyrighted work (excluding sound recordings and certain computer programs) has been lawfully distributed by the owner, the new purchaser is free to further distribute the work by sale or lending.

A copyright owner's rights in sound recordings are significantly more limited than rights granted to authors of other works.

Finally, authors of fine arts such as paintings and sculptures are granted "moral rights" in those works, allowing them to be identified as the author of the work and prohibiting destruction or alteration of the work, even after the creator has sold it.

CASE ILLUSTRATION—AUTHORS' DERIVATIVE RIGHTS

Case: *Anderson v. Stallone,* 11 U.S.P.Q.2d 1161 (1989)

Facts: Sylvester Stallone wrote scripts for the movies *Rocky I, Rocky II,* and *Rocky III* and played the role of Rocky Balboa in each. In 1982, after viewing *Rocky III*, plaintiff Anderson wrote a 31-page treatment entitled *Rocky IV* that he hoped would be used by Stallone and MGM movie studio as a sequel to *Rocky III*. Some meetings between the parties were held but no agreements were reached. After Stallone released *Rocky IV*, Anderson sued for compensation for the alleged use of his treatment.

Holding: The court first noted that the Rocky characters were protected by copyright because they were among the most highly developed characters in modern American cinema and not mere stock characters. The character Rocky Balboa is thus protected by copyright and from bodily appropriation into a sequel that builds upon the relationships and characteristics of the first three *Rocky* movies. Because Stallone owned the exclusive copyright to the first three *Rocky* movies, he has the exclusive right to prepare derivative works based on the Rocky character. Anderson's treatment was thus an unauthorized derivative work.

CASE STUDY AND ACTIVITIES

Case Study.   Vision allows its guests to select popular DVDs to be played in their rooms. Vision also plays music throughout its lobby and common areas and in the elevators. Vision has also purchased some artwork that is placed in its lobby and reproduced the artwork on postcards that it sells in its gift shops. Lounges in the hotels feature live music performances, with singers performing various well-known "easy listening" songs. Its 50s-style diner allows guests to use coin-operated jukeboxes to select songs to be played throughout the diner. Finally, Vision is hosting a charity function next week in one of its largest conference rooms to raise money for diabetes research. Well-known singers will sing songs from hit Broadway plays.

Activities.   Consider each activity and determine whether any of the exclusive rights of copyright owners have been violated.

ROLE OF PARALEGAL

Paralegals may need to participate in copyright audits to ensure that clients are not infringing copyrighted works, even innocently. Common activities include the following:

- surveying clients to determine if music is played on hold for telephone callers or if music is piped into clients' business establishments
- contacting ASCAP and BMI and obtaining sample license agreements and royalty fee schedules so arrangements can be made for performance of copyrighted works
- preparing newsletters and copyright fact sheets for distribution to clients advising them of possible copyright violations in the photocopying and distribution of literary works (such as magazine and journal articles), use of copyrighted materials including songs and movie clips in presentations, and playing of music on hold or throughout the clients' places of business

INTERNET RESOURCES

Federal laws relating to copyright:	http://www.law.cornell.edu
	http://www.findlaw.com
Copyright Office:	http://www.copyright.gov (for information on compulsory licenses)
Performing rights societies:	http://www.ascap.com
	http://www.bmi.com
	http://www.sesac.com
Copyright Clearance Center:	http://www.copyright.com
General information:	http://www.findlaw.com
	http://www.megalaw.com

DISCUSSION QUESTIONS

1. The owner of your local coffee shop, Bill, has brought in some of his CDs from home, including several by Carrie Underwood, to play in the shop for the enjoyment of his customers. Have any copyright rights been violated? Discuss.
2. The ABA is holding its annual convention next week and intends to play music in various conference rooms before the beginning of seminars. Have any copyright rights been violated? Discuss.
3. If you recently purchased a DVD of the movie *The Pursuit of Happyness*, may you later sell it at a garage sale? What principle governs your answer?
4. Given the facts in question 3, may you show the film in your home at a private party?

DISCUSSION QUESTIONS (CONT'D)

5. Given the facts in question 3, may you show the film at your local church's annual fundraiser?
6. A high school drama class is rehearsing the play *Cats*. Is this a violation of any copyright laws? What if the high school performs the play in its auditorium and charges an admission fee? Discuss.
7. John, a well-known artist, does not like the way a local art museum is displaying his paintings. John believes that the lighting for the display is inappropriate to show the paintings at their best. Is this a violation of any copyright laws? Discuss.
8. Given the facts in question 7, what if the museum has framed one of John's paintings in a way that covers up his signature. Have any copyright rights been violated? Discuss.
9. Your cousin has hired a local DJ to play music at her wedding. Is this a public performance such that a license would be needed to play the music? Discuss.
10. You are driving a carpool with four people and turn the radio on in your car. Is this a public performance? Discuss. What if you drive a tour bus that charges admission to the passengers? Is this a public performance? Discuss.

USING INTERNET RESOURCES

1. Access the Copyright Office Web site. Review the materials relating to licensing.
   a. What is the fee to record a notice of intent to make and distribute phonorecords under 17 U.S.C. § 115?
   b. What is the term of the Copyright Royalty Judges?
2. Access ASCAP's Web site and search for works written by Billy Joel.
   a. How many songs or works are identified?
   b. Select *New York State of Mind*. Has Tony Bennett ever performed this work?
   c. Search for works performed by Beyonce Knowles. Locate the song *Irreplaceable*. Is Beyonce the writer of the song?
3. Access BMI's Web site.
   a. Search for works by the rap artist Ludacris. How many titles are listed?
   b. Review "About" BMI. How many compositions does BMI represent?
4. Access the Web site of the Copyright Clearance Center and review "About Us" and then "Corporate Overview." How many works are managed by the Copyright Clearance Center?

For additional resources, go to www.paralegal.delmar.cengage.com.

Chapter 12

Copyright Ownership, Transfers, and Duration

CHAPTER OVERVIEW

Copyright ownership vests in the author of a work. Special issues arise when more than one person creates a work, when a derivative work based upon an underlying work is created, or when existing works are combined into a collection, such as an anthology. Determining ownership is critical because the exclusive rights of reproduction, performance, display, and so forth belong to the copyright owner. The person who creates a work is the author; however, if a work qualifies as one "made for hire," the employer or commissioning party, not the author, is the creator. A work qualifies as a work made for hire if the work is created by an employee within the scope of employment or if the work falls within one of nine enumerated types of works and the parties agree in writing that the work is one made for hire. In such cases, the exclusive rights ordinarily granted to the work's creator will instead be owned by the employer or commissioning party.

Copyright rights may be transferred. A transfer of exclusive rights must be in writing, while a nonexclusive grant, or license, need not be in writing. To protect copyright authors, even absolute or exclusive transfers can be set aside by the author or certain heirs during a five-year period beginning in the 36th year after a transfer.

Duration of copyright rights for works created after the 1976 act is for the author's life plus 70 years. For joint works, the duration is for 70 years after the last survivor's death. For works made for hire, the duration is generally 95 years from first publication or 120 years from creation, whichever is shorter. Works copyrighted before the 1976 act are subject to special rules.

COPYRIGHT OWNERSHIP ISSUES

Copyright in a work protected under the Copyright Act initially vests in the **author** or authors of the work. 17 U.S.C. § 201(a). Issues about ownership arise when more than one person creates a work, when the work has multiple parts (such as a song consisting of a melody composed by one person and lyrics composed by another), or when work is created by an employee. Determining ownership is critical because it affects other rights, such as the ability to transfer or license a work and the duration of the copyright in a work.

Ownership of a physical object is separate and distinct from ownership of the copyright embodied in the material object. 17 U.S.C. § 202. Thus, the purchaser of choreographic notations for a ballet written by Mikhail Baryshnikov acquires only the written document. Baryshnikov, as the copyright owner, retains the exclusive rights granted under section 106 of the act, such as rights to perform the work and prepare derivative works based on it. Similarly, purchasing a manuscript, handwritten lyrics to a song scratched on an envelope, or letters written by a famous person gives the purchaser ownership only of those physical objects. Unless copyright has been explicitly conveyed with those physical articles, the original authors generally retain all other rights associated with the works, including the rights to reproduce them, create derivative works based on them, and any other exclusive rights granted to copyright owners under section 106 of the Copyright Act (subject, of course, to the first sale doctrine).

JOINT WORKS

Intent to Create a Unitary Whole

A **joint work** is a work prepared by two or more authors with the intention that their contributions be merged into inseparable or interdependent parts of a unitary whole. 17 U.S.C. § 101. Only one copyright exists in the created work. Examples of joint works are books that are coauthored by individuals; plays that are composed of narrative written by one party, music by another, and lyrics to the music by a third; songs such as "Don't Cry for Me Argentina," in which the music was written by Andrew Lloyd Webber and the lyrics by Tim Rice; and books that consist of narrative written by one person and illustrations by another.

It is the intent of the parties at the time a work is created that determines whether it is a joint work. Thus, if two persons sit at a piano and collaborate on a melody and lyrics, the resulting song is a joint work. More difficult issues arise when parts to a work are created at different times, for example, when a melody is composed by itself and lyrics are added later. The parties' intent governs. If the first composer intended the work to be complete at the time he or she composed it, the copyright in the melody is owned solely by him or her. Merely changing one's mind at some later date and allowing another to add lyrics to a completed work does not convert the work into a joint work. In such a case, the first composer owns the copyright to the melodic composition, and the lyricist has created a derivative work based on the first and owns rights in the newly created lyrics alone. Unless both parties intend at the time they make their contributions that the parts be combined or absorbed into an integrated unit, there is no joint work. Joint works also result when a copyright owner transfers rights to more than one person or a copyright passes by will to two or more persons.

Merely making suggestions or giving directions to one creating a work is not sufficient to make one a joint author. For example, giving an architect instructions that a house to be designed by the architect should have a certain amount of living space does not make one a joint author. Although the contributions of coauthors need not be equal, each must make some significant contribution.

In *Aalmuhammed v. Lee,* 202 F.3d 1227 (9th Cir. 2000), a case involving contributions made by an individual to the movie *Malcolm X,* the court held that to be a joint author, it is not enough to make a valuable contribution to a work; joint authors are those who "mastermind" or "superintend" the creative effort. Otherwise, nearly anyone who contributes to a movie or Web site design could claim to be a joint author. While the plaintiff made important contributions to the movie, neither Warner Brothers nor the director, Spike Lee, were bound to accept them. Thus, because he had no control over the work, the plaintiff was not a joint author.

In regard to dividing profits arising out of joint works, courts presume the parties contributed equally unless they provide otherwise. Thus, if three individuals coauthor a book, the profits or royalties will be divided in equal thirds unless the parties agree to some other division. Equal division of profits occurs even when the contributions of the coauthors are not equal. Agreements regarding division of revenue among joint authors should thus be in writing to avoid later disputes.

Ownership Rights in Joint Works

If individuals are authors of a joint work, each owns an equal undivided interest in the copyright as a tenant in common, meaning that each has the right to use the work, prepare derivative works based on it, perform it, display it, and so forth, without seeking the other coauthor's permission. Because each coauthor has rights in the work, one cannot exclude another from using the work or exercising the rights of copyright ownership. Nevertheless, if profits arise out of such uses, an accounting must be made so that each author shares in the benefits or proceeds.

Any coauthor may grant a *nonexclusive* license to another party to use the joint work without permission from the other coauthors; however, the granting of an *exclusive* license (one in which rights are granted solely to one party with no other party having any rights to use the work) requires consent from all coauthors of a joint work. Similarly, a joint owner cannot transfer all interest in the work without the written consent of the other coauthor(s).

Upon the death of a coauthor, his or her rights pass to heirs who then own the rights in common with the other coauthor(s). Joint ownership of a work often arises in this fashion. A book may be authored by one person. Upon that person's death, the copyright may pass to several heirs who now own the work jointly.

Duration of Works of Joint Ownership

A copyright generally lasts for the author's life plus 70 years. 17 U.S.C. § 302. If the work is a joint work, however, the copyright lasts until 70 years after the last surviving coauthor's death. Additionally, as discussed in a later section in this chapter entitled "Termination of Transfers of Copyright," each joint author has the ability to terminate his or her transfers.

OWNERSHIP IN DERIVATIVE OR COLLECTIVE WORKS

If a work such as a book is created by one person who intends it to be complete at the time and illustrations are later added to it by another, the work cannot be a joint work because there was no intention of the parties to create a unitary whole at the time of their creation. In such a case, the new work, consisting of text and illustrations, is a derivative work (assuming the original author authorized the illustrator to use the earlier work).

The author of the original book has rights only to his or her work and cannot reproduce or perform the derivative work without permission. Similarly, the author of the derivative work cannot create further works based on the original book without permission and cannot reproduce the original work (or exercise other copyright rights) without permission. Each author owns nothing more than his or her original contribution.

Copyright to the first work (the book alone) will last until 70 years after its author's death, and copyright to the derivative work (book and illustrations) will last until 70 years after its author's death.

Multiple ownership rights may also arise if separately copyrightable works are compiled into a collection. For example, if essays written by Jerry Seinfeld, Ellen DeGeneres, and Steve Martin are collected into a humor anthology by Bill Jones (with permission of the original authors), the original authors retain their exclusive rights (such as rights to reproduce, distribute, and perform) in their respective essays. No joint work is created because there was no intent at the time the separate essays were created to merge them into a unitary whole. No derivative work is created because the original works have not been transformed in any way and nothing new has been added to them. The anthology by the compiler, Bill Jones, is a collective work and, pursuant to section 201(c) of the act, Jones acquires only the right to reproduce and distribute the contributions as part of the particular collective work or any revision of the collective work. Jones does not have any ownership interest in the original essays.

WORKS MADE FOR HIRE

Introduction

Although the general rule is that the person who creates a work is the author of that work and the owner of the copyright therein, there is an exception to that principle: The copyright law defines a category of works called **works made for hire.** If a work is "made for hire," the author is considered to be the employer or commissioning party and not the employee or the actual person who created the work. The employer or commissioning party may be a company or an individual.

There are two types of works that are classified as works made for hire: works prepared by an employee within the scope of employment and certain categories of specially ordered or commissioned works.

Works Prepared by Employees in the Scope of Employment

Copyright in works prepared by employees is presumptively owned by their employers. For example, if an employee is tasked with creating a computer program by his or her employer, the resulting work is owned by the employer who is treated as the author of the work for purposes

of copyright law. Unless the parties have agreed otherwise in writing, the employer owns all of the rights pertaining to the works created by an employee on the job. Oftentimes, however, questions arise whether the person creating the work is an "employee" (such that his or her creations belong to the employer) or whether the person is an **independent contractor** (such that his or her creations belong to him or her as the owner/ author). This question often arises when freelance artists prepare works for others.

In *Community for Creative Non-Violence v. Reid*, 490 U.S. 730 (1989), the Supreme Court held that the term *employee* for purposes of determining authorship of works made for hire should be interpreted according to general common law agency principles. If the person doing the work is an employee under common law agency principles and the work was done in the scope of employment, the employer (not the employee) is the copyright owner/author.

The Court identified certain factors that characterize an employer-employee relationship:

- **Control by the employer over the work.** If the employer has a voice in how the work is done, has the work done at the employer's location, and provides equipment and tools to the person to create the work, such tends to show an employer-employee relationship.
- **Control by the employer over the worker.** If the employer controls the worker's schedule in creating work, has the right to have the worker perform other assignments, determines the method of payment, and/or has the right to hire the worker's assistants, such evidences an employer-employee relationship.
- **Status of employer.** If the employer is in business to produce such works, provides the worker with benefits similar to those received by other workers, and withholds taxes from the worker's compensation, such is supportive of an employer-employee relationship.

These factors are not exhaustive; for example, courts can also consider the duration of the relationship of the parties (a long-term relationship is indicative of employment) and the skill level of the employee. Moreover, no one factor is determinative. All or most of these factors, however, characterize a regular, salaried employment relationship, and works created by employees in the course and scope of such a relationship are works made for hire, authorship and copyright of which vests in the employer (unless the parties agree in writing otherwise).

The Copyright Office has provided the following examples of works made for hire:

- a software program created by a staff programmer for Creative Computer Corporation
- a newspaper article written by a staff journalist for publication in a daily newspaper
- a musical arrangement written for XYZ Music Company by a salaried arranger on its staff

Note that the work must be created *within the scope of employment* to be a work made for hire. Thus, if the software program was created by a person before joining Creative Computer Corporation, the company has no rights to the work. Similarly, if an employee employed by Creative Computer Corporation writes a book about computers in the evenings and weekends, the work is likely not a work made for hire because it was not created in the course of the employee's duties.

Many employers demand that employees sign agreements acknowledging that works created by the employees will be works made for hire. Such agreements may be considered by courts, but an agreement alone is not controlling. Other factors may be considered in determining the nature of the parties' relationship. One approach to ensure ownership vests in the employer may be to recite in an agreement that the relationship is one of employer-employee, that works created by the employee are works made for hire

owned by the employer, and that in the event it is later determined by a court that the work is not one made for hire, the employee irrevocably and automatically assigns all rights to the work to the employer. Such an agreement will likely be given effect by a court. If the employee desires to retain ownership of works created in the course of employment that otherwise would be works made for hire, the parties must expressly agree in a written instrument signed by both parties. (See Appendix D, Form 12, for sample provisions in employment agreements relating to works made for hire.)

Specially Commissioned Works

If the work is not one prepared by an employee but, rather, is one prepared by an independent contractor, it can be deemed a work made for hire and thus owned by the commissioning party if three conditions are met: it is a specially ordered or commissioned work; the parties agree in writing that the work is one made for hire; and the work falls into one of nine specially enumerated categories. 17 U.S.C. § 101. All three of these elements must be satisfied if the work is to be one made for hire. The nine categories of works are as follows:

1. a contribution to a collective work
2. part of a motion picture or other audiovisual work
3. a translation
4. a supplementary work (a work prepared for publication as a secondary adjunct to a work by another author for the purpose of introducing, illustrating, or explaining the work, such as forewords, pictorial illustrations, tables, editorial notes, bibliographies, appendices, and indexes)
5. a compilation
6. an instructional text (a literary, pictorial, or graphic work prepared for publication with the purpose of use in systematic instructional activities)
7. a test

ETHICS EDGE: **Looking out for the Client**

Inherent in the duty of competence imposed on all legal professionals is to be proactive in protecting clients' interests. As you review client materials, look for ways to ensure clients' rights are protected. For example, as you review employee manuals or agreements with vendors, check to ensure that appropriate provisions exist to protect intellectual property. Employment manuals and agreements with vendors should include clauses reciting that intellectual property created by employees or vendors is owned by the client/employer and that if for some reason the clause is ineffective, the employee or vendor automatically assigns intellectual property rights to the client/employer. Protecting clients' interests in such a way is not "looking for business," but is rather part of an overall strategy designed to ensure clients have the widest possible scope of protection for their IP assets.

8. answer material for a test
9. an atlas

Although the parties can agree in writing that the commissioning party owns the work, this agreement will not convert a work that does not fit within one of the nine statutorily designated categories into one made for hire. Therefore, the safest approach for the commissioning party is for the parties to agree in writing that the work is one made for hire and that if for some reason the work is determined not to be one made for hire, by the same document, the work is automatically assigned and transferred to the person who commissioned the work.

For example, assume that a museum hires a freelance graphic artist to create a painting and an audiovisual slide presentation for a museum opening, and the parties agree in writing that the works are to be owned by the museum and are to be considered works made for hire. While the audiovisual slide presentation is a work made for hire (it was specially commissioned, the parties agreed in writing it would be considered a work made for hire, and it fits the statutory definition), the painting is not a work made for hire despite what the parties agreed because it does not fit the statutory definition. Thus, a safety net clause should be added in written agreements conveying all of the author's rights in the painting in the event it is not a work made for hire. This would allow the museum to create derivative works based on the painting, display it, and so forth.

Effects of Works Made for Hire

There are several effects if a work is classified as one made for hire:

- **Ownership.** The owner/author of a work made for hire is the employer or commissioning party. The artist who created the work has no more rights in the work than any stranger, and the artist cannot reproduce, distribute, or perform the work, or prepare derivatives based on it, without being liable for copyright infringement.
- **Duration.** Copyrights in works made for hire endure for 95 years from publication or 120 years from creation, whichever is shorter. Copyrights in other works generally endure for the author's life plus 70 years thereafter.
- **Reversion of transfers.** Rights in works that are not made for hire can be

recaptured by the author after 35 years, even if there has been an unconditional transfer or sale to another. (See the section entitled "Termination of Transfers of Copyright" later in this chapter.)

- **Moral rights.** There are no moral rights (rights of attribution and integrity) in works made for hire because they are not defined as works of "visual arts." 17 U.S.C. § 101.

TRANSFERS OF COPYRIGHT

Divisibility of Ownership

Any or all of the exclusive rights of the copyright owner (rights to reproduce, prepare derivative works, distribute the work, and perform and display the work publicly) can be transferred or licensed to another party. 17 U.S.C. § 201(d). Thus, the author of a book may grant the right to prepare derivative works based on the book to one party and yet transfer the rights to distribute the book to another party. The grants or licenses can be perpetual or for limited terms. Similarly, they can be limited to certain geographic areas, such as when one party is granted the right to distribute a work in the western region of the United States and another party is granted the right to distribute the work in the eastern region of the United States.

Copyright rights are divisible, meaning they can be subdivided, such as occurs when the copyright owner of a book carves up his or her rights to prepare derivative works by granting one party the right to translate the book, granting another party the right to make a motion picture based on the book, and granting a third party the right to prepare a sequel to the book.

Granting rights to others is a way for copyright owners to exploit their works to the fullest extent. The copyright owner will grant rights and generally require payment therefor, such as by negotiating a flat fee or by continuing and periodic royalties on the sales of each book or song exploited by the licensee.

Requirement of Writing for Transfer of Exclusive Rights

A transfer of copyright ownership other than a transfer by operation of law is not valid unless the transfer is in writing and signed by the owner of the rights conveyed (or his or her exclusive agent). 17 U.S.C. § 204(a). This requirement of a writing protects copyright owners from inadvertently transferring their copyrights. Granting rights on a nonexclusive basis (e.g., allowing several parties to reproduce the work) is not considered a "transfer" under the Copyright Act and thus need not be in writing. Such an arrangement is generally called a license, and although there is no requirement that there be a written document, such is advised because it lends certainty to the terms of the transaction. (See Exhibit 12–1, Assignment of Copyright.)

Like other property rights, copyrights can be transferred by operation of law, generally meaning the law can require a transfer. For example, transfers by operation of law occur when, in a bankruptcy, the bankrupt's property is transferred to the bankruptcy trustee or to a creditor; when a court orders the sale or transfer of a copyright in a divorce proceeding; or when an owner dies without leaving a will and the laws of intestate succession govern who acquires the decedent's property. Copyrights can also pass by will to one's specified beneficiaries.

Just as trademarks can be used to secure obligations, copyrights can serve as secured property. If Sheryl Crow wishes to borrow money from a bank, the bank may require her to pledge certain copyrights in her songs as security for repayment of the debt. If she fails to repay the debt, the bank can seize the copyrights and all rights therein. In fact, some entertainers, including David Bowie and the group Iron Maiden, have sold bonds backed by predicted revenues from future recordings and performances. Bowie

EXHIBIT 12–1
Assignment of Copyright

WHEREAS, Kathryn Sherman ("Assignor"), an individual residing at 1010 Canyon Glen Terrace, Phoenix, AZ 22098, is the owner of all copyrights in that literary work entitled The Challenge (the "Work") and is the author of such Work; and

WHEREAS, Blake Publishers, Inc. ("Assignee"), a corporation organized under the laws of the State of New York, located and doing business at 555 Avenue of the Americas, New York, NY 96607, desires to acquire all of Assignor's rights in and to the Work;

NOW, THEREFORE, for good and valuable consideration, the receipt and sufficiency of which are hereby acknowledged, Assignor hereby irrevocably sells, assigns, transfers, and conveys to Assignee the entire right, title, and interest in and to the Work, including any copyrights and registrations, the same to be held and enjoyed by Assignee, its successors, assigns, and other legal representatives.

Assignee shall have the right to register the copyright in the Work in its own name and shall have the exclusive rights to develop, exploit, publish, reproduce, distribute, perform, display, and prepare derivative works based thereon throughout the world.

Assignor represents and warrants that she created the Work independently, the Work is the result of her original effort, and that she is the owner of all copyrights and other rights in the Work and that no other party has any rights in or to the Work.

Assignor further assigns to Assignee all right to sue for and receive all damages accruing from past, present, and future infringements of the Work herein assigned.

This Assignment shall be binding upon the parties, their successors and/or assigns, and all others acting by, through, with, or under their direction, and all those in privity therewith.

Assignor agrees to cooperate with Assignee and take any further action and execute any documents required to effect the purposes of this Assignment.

Kathryn Sherman   Blake Publishers, Inc.

_____   By: _____

Date: _____   Title: _____

                                            Date: _____

financed one of his tours with the money raised from the sale of such bonds.

Recordation of Transfers

There is no requirement that transfers or licenses of copyright or grants of security interests in copyright be recorded with the U.S. Copyright Office. Recordation is prudent, however, because it provides notice of rights in copyrights and may establish priorities of conflicting transfers. The Copyright Office does not make or participate in the transfer but merely records the document in its files. Recordation can be made whether the work is published or unpublished and whether or not it has been registered with the Copyright Office. Other documents pertaining to copyrights can also be recorded. For example, a will that bequeaths a copyright can be recorded with the Copyright Office. The Copyright Office provides a form for a cover sheet, which is designed to facilitate recordation of documents. The current basic fee for recording a document covering one work is $95. An additional charge of $25 is made for each group of 10 additional titles or fewer. In certain circumstances (generally when litigation is pending or threatened), special handling may be requested and recordation will be expedited (usually within five business days) upon the payment of an additional fee and a showing of the necessity for special handling.

TERMINATION OF TRANSFERS OF COPYRIGHT

Introduction

In many instances, young artists, songwriters, and other creators transfer or license rights in their copyrighted works at a time when they do not truly have an idea about the value of the works transferred. The works may be exploited by the new owners who may collect astounding amounts of money, and yet the original creators of the works may not realize any economic gain whatsoever from these early works and may not be able to exercise any control with regard to reproduction, distribution, preparation of derivative works, performance, or display of the works. To remedy this situation, section 203 of the Copyright Act provides that transfers of copyrights can be terminated after 35 years so that the original author can recapture his or her works.

The Copyright Act's termination of transfer provisions are highly unusual and are contrary to general principles of contract law, which hold that once a valid contract has been entered into, it cannot be set aside (except in extreme cases, such as those involving fraud). When an individual sells a house, he or she is not allowed to cancel the sale and reclaim the house if it later appreciates. Bad decisions made on the stock market cannot be set aside. Yet transfers of copyrights can be set aside or terminated, reflecting Congress's intent to protect artists and authors from exploitation.

Grants Executed after January 1, 1978

Statutory Authority. Section 203 of the Copyright Act sets forth the procedures for terminating grants or transfers of copyrights that occurred after the 1976 Copyright Act became effective on January 1, 1978. Section 203 refers to transfers that occur after January 1, 1978, regardless of when the work was created. Thus, termination of these grants will begin in 2013.

According to section 203(a), in the case of any work *other than a work made for hire,* an exclusive or nonexclusive grant of a transfer or license of a copyright or of any right under a copyright, executed by an author after January 1, 1978, and other than a grant made by will, is subject to termination. Grants of copyright that occur by way of a will cannot be terminated, apparently because Congress saw no exploitation of the author in such cases. The author's right to reach back in time and terminate an earlier transfer cannot be waived, and any provision attempting to waive the protections afforded by section 203 is void.

Who May Effect Termination. In the case of grants by a single author, the author may terminate. If the author has died, his or her termination rights may be exercised by the surviving spouse and his or her children and grandchildren. These successors may terminate in the author's place if they hold more than 50 percent of the author's termination rights.

Section 203(a)(2) sets forth an elaborate scheme for determining who may exercise the termination rights of a deceased author. In brief, the following apply:

- If a spouse survives the death of the author, and there are no children or grandchildren, the spouse owns all of the termination rights.

- If the author leaves both a spouse and surviving children or grandchildren by a deceased child, the spouse owns one-half of the termination rights and the surviving children and grandchildren share the remaining one-half.
- If there is no surviving spouse, the author's living children and any children of a deceased child own all of the termination rights.
- Each surviving child gets his or her percentage share. Children of a deceased child of the author take the share that would have gone to their parent and, in casting their votes to effect a termination, must act as a unit. A majority vote controls. Children of surviving children have no rights.
- If the author leaves no surviving spouse, children, or grandchildren, his or her executor owns the author's termination interest.

Example: Author Smith dies, leaving a widow (*W*), one living child (*LC*), and four grandchildren (*GC*) by way of a deceased son. Their termination rights are as follows: *W* owns 50 percent; *LC* owns 25 percent; and the *GC*s collectively own 25 percent. To terminate a transfer, more than 50 percent approval is needed. *W* must be joined either by *LC* or the *GC*s (three of whom must approve the transaction) in order to terminate.

In the case of a transfer by joint authors of a work, the transfer may be canceled by a majority of the authors who made the transfer. If any of the joint authors has died, his or her termination rights are exercised according to the scheme just described.

Effecting a Termination. Generally, termination of the prior grant may be effected at any time during a period of five years beginning in the 36th year after the date of execution of the grant. To effect the termination, those who own the rights of termination (or their authorized

agents) must sign and serve a written notice to the grantee no less than 2 and not more than 10 years before the transfer is to be terminated. The notice must set forth the date of termination (which date must fall within the five-year period) and must describe the grant being terminated. A copy of the notice must be recorded with the Copyright Office. Upon the effective date of the termination, the rights in the work automatically revert to the author or the author's successors (including those who voted against the termination). The author (or successors) must follow this statutory procedure in order to effect a termination. If the author or his or her surviving family fail to take the necessary steps within the appropriate time periods, the original transfer cannot be set aside and it will continue for the remaining term of the copyright.

After the effective date of termination, the author who recovered the copyright (or successors who have recovered his or her rights) may make a new grant of rights to a different party. If the author (or successors) wishes to regrant rights to the original grantee, such can be done once the notice of termination has been served. In fact, once the notice of termination is served, the grantee will often commence negotiations with the author (or successors) so the grantee can continue to exercise the rights originally granted to him or her. Typically, new fee payments are negotiated. The new grant or regrant must be signed by the same number and proportion of owners as are required to terminate the grant.

Grants Prior to January 1, 1978

Grants or transfers made by copyright authors prior to January 1, 1978, the effective date of the 1976 Copyright Act, are governed by section 304 of the Act. Most of the rules and procedures relating to termination of transfers granted after the Copyright Act of 1976 also apply to transfers granted under the previous 1909 act. One difference, however, is that under the 1976 act, only grants made by the author of a work in his or her lifetime may be terminated. Under section 304, grants made by the author, or certain of his or her beneficiaries or executor if the author was dead, may be recaptured. Most other rules relating to notice, recordation of the notice with the Copyright Office, effect of termination, inability to waive termination rights, and so forth remain the same.

Under section 304, termination can be effected of rights (other than copyrights in works made for hire or those transferred by will) at any point during a five-year period that begins at the end of 56 years from the date copyright was originally secured (or beginning on January 1, 1978, whichever is later). For a copyright in its renewal term, if a termination right had expired, under the new Sonny Bono Copyright Term Extension Act, a termination of a transfer may be effected at any time during the five years beginning at the end of 75 years from the date copyright was secured. Identical to rights terminated under the 1976 act, rights that have been recaptured may be granted to a new party after the termination is effective, and an agreement to regrant rights to the original transferee may be effected as soon as the notice of termination is served.

DURATION OF COPYRIGHT

Introduction

The duration of a copyright depends upon whether the copyright was created after January 1, 1978, the effective date of the 1976 Copyright Act, or before that date. Under the Copyright Act of 1909, federal copyright protection commenced upon publication of the work. Prior to publication, common law copyright principles controlled. Under the 1976 act, federal copyright protection commences upon creation of the work in a fixed form, whether the work is published or not. Because works under the 1909 act may still be subject to copyright protection, it is important to understand the periods of duration for works created under both acts.

Duration under the 1909 Copyright Act

Under the 1909 act, the copyright in a work lasted for a first term of 28 years from the date it was secured. During the last year of the term, the copyright was eligible for renewal either by the author or specified heirs. If renewed, the copyright was extended for a second term of 28 years. If not renewed, the copyright expired at the end of the first 28-year term. Thus, the maximum allowable length of copyright protection under the 1909 act was 56 years.

Duration under the 1976 Copyright Act

For works that are created and fixed in a tangible medium of expression after January 1, 1978, the Copyright Act of 1976 (17 U.S.C. § 302) does away with the burdensome renewal requirements and establishes a single copyright term. There are three basic categories of works:

- For works created after January 1, 1978, copyright extends for the lifetime of the author plus 70 years (this term is similar to that of many foreign countries).
- For joint works, the term lasts for 70 years after the last surviving author's death.
- For works made for hire and for anonymous works (those in which no natural person is identified as the author on the copies or phonorecords of the work) and pseudonymous works (those in which the author is identified by a fictitious name on the copies or phonorecords of the work), the duration of copyright is 95 years from the first publication of the work or 120 years from creation, whichever is shorter (although if the anonymous or pseudonymous author discloses his or her name to the Copyright Office, the duration will convert to life plus 70 years).

Until 1998, duration of each of these copyrights was 20 years shorter. To harmonize U.S. law with that of many foreign countries, Congress passed the Sonny Bono Copyright Term Extension Act in late 1998, which extended the duration of copyright terms as set forth herein. This legislation was subject to much debate, with critics complaining that extending the duration of copyright protection benefits only copyright owners and deprives the public of having works enter the public domain for ready dissemination at the earliest possible date. To respond to fears by libraries and archives that the extended copyright duration would inhibit their educational functions, a provision was added to allow, during the last 20 years of any term of copyright of a published work, a library or archive to make certain uses of copyrighted materials for preservation, scholarship, or research purposes, if those works are not commercially available.

A recent U.S. Supreme Court case considered whether the continual extensions to the term of copyright protection (and, in particular, the additional 20-year term granted under the Sonny Bono Copyright Term Extension Act) violated the U.S. Constitution, which clearly provides that authors shall have copyright rights for "limited times." In *Eldred v. Ashcroft*, 537 U.S. 186 (2003), the petitioners were those whose products depended on copyrighted works that have entered the public domain. Thus, they objected to an extension of the term of copyright protection an additional 20 years. The Court held that the extension of copyright terms did not exceed Congress's power under the Constitution. The extension reflected a rational judgment of Congress in harmonizing U.S. law with that of most European countries.

Effect of 1976 Copyright Act on Preexisting Works

Any copyright still in its renewal term on October 27, 1998 (the date the new Sonny Bono Copyright Term Extension Act became effective) now has a copyright term of 95 years from the date copyright was originally secured (the original 28-year term and a 67-year second term)

Works that were in existence but were not published or copyrighted on January 1, 1978 (e.g., an unpublished manuscript that had no copyright protection under the 1909 act and was governed by common law principles), are automatically given protection as if they were created after January 1, 1978 (the life-plus-70 or the 95- and 120-year terms, as applicable), or until December 31, 2002, whichever occurs last. To encourage publication, Congress provided that if the work was published before December 31, 2002, an additional 45 years of protection would be granted, until December 31, 2047.

In many instances, owners of copyrights that were in their first terms on January 1, 1978, did not apply to renew their copyrights and their copyrights expired after only 28 years. To avoid similar situations, in 1991 Congress amended the Copyright Act of 1976 to provide for automatic renewals for works in their first term. There is now no requirement to file a renewal application to extend the original 28-year copyright term to the full term of 95 years. Although the renewal term is automatically extended, there are, however, a number of incentives that encourage the filing of a renewal application (using Copyright Office Form RE), especially during the 28th year of the copyright term (e.g., the Copyright Office will issue a renewal certificate that constitutes *prima facie* evidence of the validity of the facts stated in the renewal certificate and the copyright in the extended term).

(See Exhibit 12–2 for a chart illustrating duration of copyright.)

Calculating Dates for Copyright Duration

The act provides that all terms of copyright will run through the end of the calendar year in which they would otherwise expire. For example, if an author of a work created in June 1980 died in

Date of Work	Duration of Copyright
Works created on or after 1/1/1978	Author's life plus 70 years (or if a joint work, 70 years after last survivor's death); if work is "work made for hire" (or anonymous or pseudonymous work), copyright lasts for 95 years from publication or 120 years from creation, whichever is shorter
Works created before 1/1/1978, but not published or registered	Author's life plus 70 years or until 12/31/2002, whichever is longer (if work is published before 12/31/2002, copyright extended until 12/31/2047)
Copyright secured under 1909 act and in first or renewal term on 1/1/1978	Term automatically extended to give a total length of copyright of 95 years from the year copyright secured
Works published before 1923	Work is now in the public domain

EXHIBIT 12–2
Copyright Duration

June 1990, protection would extend until December 31, 2060.

Restoration of Lost Copyrights

Neither the 1976 act nor any amendments provide for revival or restoration of lost copyrights in works of U.S. origin. If a U.S. work fell into the public domain because its author failed to renew the work under the 1909 act, it is not restored by any statutory provision. However, copyright in foreign works whose U.S. copyright protection had been lost because of noncompliance with formalities of U.S. law were restored as of January 1, 1996, under the provisions of the Uruguay Round Agreements Act. Additional information on these restored foreign copyrights can be found in Copyright Office Circular 38b, available at http://www.copyright.gov.

Trivia

- In 2006, the Copyright Office received 594,125 claims of copyright and recorded more than 13,000 documents.
- *To Kill a Mockingbird*, the movie, a derivative work based on Harper Lee's earlier novel, was copyrighted in March 1963.
- The Copyright Office employs approximately 500 staff. Its fiscal year 2006 budget was more than $58 million, approximately $30 million of which was funded by fees charged by the Copyright Office.

CHAPTER SUMMARY

Determining ownership of a copyright is critical because a wide variety of rights flow from copyright ownership, including rights to reproduce, adapt, distribute, perform, and display the work. Moreover, the duration of copyright depends upon its ownership. When two or more people create a work with the intent that their separate contributions be merged into the completed work, the work is a joint work, and the authors each have rights to distribute, perform, reproduce, or display the work. A derivative work is one based upon an underlying work. The author of the underlying work has exclusive rights in his or her work, and the author of the derivative work has rights in his or her newly created work that exist independently from any rights in the original work.

Although the general rule is that the person who creates a work is the author of that work, there is an exception to that rule: The copyright law defines a category of works called "works made for hire." If a work is one "made for hire," either the employer or commissioner of the work is the author for copyright purposes and possesses the exclusive rights of a copyright owner. A work made for hire is one prepared by an employee in the scope of employment or one of nine specially enumerated types of commissioned works that the parties have agreed in writing will be a work made for hire.

Because copyrights are property, they may be transferred. Moreover, the rights of a copyright owner (including rights to reproduce, adapt, distribute, perform, and display the work) are divisible, meaning that the author may transfer some rights and retain others. Transfers of exclusive rights must be in writing. Transfers of copyright can be terminated either by the author or certain of his or her heirs during a statutorily defined period beginning the 36th year after the transfer. This unusual provision in copyright law is intended to protect authors who transfer rights before they fully understand the value of their works.

Copyrights created after the 1976 act last for the author's life plus 70 years or 70 years from the last survivor's death, in the case of joint works. For works made for hire and anonymous and pseudonymous works, the duration of copyright is 95 years from first publication of the work or 120 years from its creation, whichever first occurs.

CASE ILLUSTRATION—INDEPENDENT CONTRACTORS

Case: *Kirk v. Harter,* 188 F.3d 1005 (8th Cir. 1999)

Facts: A business owner brought an action for copyright infringement against an individual, Harter, who developed certain computer programs used by the business. The district court found that Harter was an employee and was liable for copyright infringement.

Holding: The court of appeals reversed. When there is no written employment contract, courts look to common law rules of agency to determine when a party is an employee or an independent contractor. In this case, although there were some factors that suggested that Harter was an employee (he spent time at the plaintiff's offices, the plaintiff furnished equipment and directed the hours and days he would work, and he wore the plaintiff's uniform), a review of several factors used to determine employment status showed that Harter was an independent contractor. In particular, the fact that Harter's pay was reported to the IRS as payment to an independent contractor, Harter received no employee benefits, and Harter hired his own assistants showed that Harter was an independent contractor and not an employee. Thus, Harter was the owner of the computer program he developed and cannot be liable for infringement.

CASE STUDY AND ACTIVITIES

Case Study.   Vision has asked two of its in-house marketing employees to create a jingle for a new ad campaign. There is no agreement as to who will own the copyright in the finished jingle. In 2000, Vision purchased all of the assets (including the intellectual property) of Ronald Hanson. The asset purchase agreement was in writing, but no documents were recorded at the Copyright Office.

Activities.   What are the rights of Vision or its employees or others in the jingle? Discuss ownership rights and the duration of the copyright for the work. What are the rights, if any, of Ronald Hanson? Should the copyrights acquired by Vision in 2000 be recorded with the Copyright Office? Discuss.

ROLE OF PARALEGAL

There are numerous tasks for paralegals to be involved in relating to ownership, transfer, and duration of copyrights. Commonly performed tasks are as follows:

- conducting legal research to determine whether a work is a joint work, derivative work, or collective work
- drafting agreements between or among joint authors in regard to divisions of royalties and other rights
- investigating circumstances of employment to determine whether an individual is an employee or an independent contractor
- drafting provisions for employment agreements relating to ownership of works created by employees
- drafting agreements relating to specially commissioned works confirming the works are "made for hire," and providing that if they are later determined not to be works made for hire, the creator assigns all rights to the commissioning party
- drafting agreements transferring or assigning copyright rights to others
- drafting agreements subjecting copyrights to security interests
- recording transfers of copyright ownership with the Copyright Office
- docketing transfers of copyright so dates for termination of transfers can be tracked
- drafting notices for termination of transfers of copyright and recording notices with the Copyright Office

ROLE OF PARALEGAL (CONT'D)

- docketing dates for duration of copyright so owners can be informed that copyright protection will terminate
- renewing copyrights for works protected under the 1909 act to obtain benefits of voluntary renewal

INTERNET RESOURCES

Federal laws relating to copyright:	http:/www.law.cornell.edu http://www.findlaw.com
Copyright Office:	http://www.copyright.gov (for forms, circulars, and information on copyright ownership, works made for hire, transfers, termination of transfers, and duration)
General information:	http://www.findlaw.com http://www.megalaw.com
Forms:	http://www.lectlaw.com http://www.allaboutforms.com (forms for assignments, employment agreements, and independent contractor agreements)

DISCUSSION QUESTIONS

1. Sue has purchased the John Grisham novel *An Innocent Man.* What copyright rights, if any, has Sue acquired when she purchased the book? What statute governs your answer?
2. Joanna and Kat are working together on a children's book. Joanna is writing the story and Kat is doing the illustrations for the book. Kat's husband has occasionally offered suggestions to Kat on the drawings. Who owns the copyright in the finished book? Discuss the rights of all parties, and indicate how long copyright in the work will last.
3. Use the facts in the preceding question. After the children's book is published, Joanna asks Pam to compose a song about the characters in the book. Is Pam a joint author? Discuss fully.
4. ABC Inc. has asked its in-house computer programmers to create a program for the company that will help it track and locate documents. Who owns the copyright in the computer program? What principle governs your answer?
5. ABC Inc. has entered into a written agreement with an independent film company to produce a short film to celebrate the 100th anniversary of the company. The written agreement states that the finished product is one made for hire. Who owns the copyright in the

film? What if there had been no written agreement between the parties? Who would own the copyright? Discuss.

6. Sam and Bill are joint authors of a book relating to the Vanderbilts, although Sam did substantially more work on the book than Bill did. They had no agreement relating to dividing profits arising from the work. Sam has granted the right to a motion picture company to make a film based on the book. Must the agreement be in writing? How will profits from the film be divided? Discuss.

7. Assume Sam and Bill transferred the copyright in the book to the motion picture company. Would such an agreement need to be in writing? Would Sam and Bill have any rights to the work after the transfer? Discuss.

8. Indicate the duration of copyright for the following:
   a. a novel written by Carlos in 2003
   b. a book of poems written by Randy and Russell in 2007
   c. an employee manual written by the employees of XYZ Inc. (created in 2000 and published in 2003)
   d. a song written by Phil, who died in January 2000 (give exact date of expiration of copyright)

USING INTERNET RESOURCES

1. Access the Web site of the Copyright Office.
   a. Review Circular 12. What information should appear in Space 1 of the Document Cover Sheet?
   b. Review Factsheet SL 4d. What is the fee for special handling of recordation of a document?
   c. Review Circular 9. What is the effect of a work made for hire on termination rights?
   d. Review Circular 10. When may special handling be requested when recording a document?
2. Access the Web site of the Copyright Office. Assume you need to record a document reflecting the transfer of 12 copyright titles. What fee will be assessed by the Copyright Office?

For additional resources, go to www.para.legal.delmar.cengage.com.

Chapter 13

Copyright Registration, Searching Copyright Office Records, and Notice of Copyright

CHAPTER OVERVIEW

In the United States, copyright protection exists from the time a work is created. Thus, applying for and securing a copyright registration is not a condition of copyright protection. Nevertheless, copyright registration provides several benefits, such as establishing a public record of the claim of copyright, allowing a claim of infringement to be brought in federal court, and resulting in availability of statutory damages and attorneys' fees if a registered work is infringed. The Copyright Office provides all forms necessary for registration, and the process typically takes about 12 weeks. The Copyright Office also is open for searching of records, and its information specialists will help conduct searches of records for a fee. Although notice of copyright is optional since March 1, 1989, use of a notice is recommended. A copyright notice consists of the symbol © (or the word "Copyright" or the abbreviation "Copr."), the year of first publication of the work, and the name of the copyright owner.

INTRODUCTION

As discussed in chapter 9, neither publication of a work nor registration or other action in the U.S. Copyright Office is required to secure copyright protection under federal law. Copyright is secured automatically when the work is created. A work is "created" when it is fixed in a copy or phonorecord for the first time. Although not required to provide copyright protection for a work, registration of copyright with the Copyright Office is inexpensive, easy, and provides several advantages, chiefly, that registration is a condition precedent for bringing an infringement suit for works of U.S. origin. The relative ease with which works may be registered is chiefly due to the fact that there is no substantive examination of applications for registration of copyrights (as there is for trademarks and patents). To register a work, the applicant must send the following three elements to the Copyright Office: a properly completed application form, a filing fee, and a deposit of the work being registered. Registration may be made at any time within the life of the copyright.

THE APPLICATION FOR COPYRIGHT REGISTRATION

Parties Who May File Applications

The following persons are entitled to submit an application for registration of copyright:

- the author (either the person who actually created the work or, if the work is one made for hire, the employer or commissioning party)
- the copyright claimant (either the author or a person or organization that has obtained ownership of all of the rights under the copyright originally belonging to the author, such as a transferee)
- the owner of exclusive rights, such as the transferee of any of the exclusive rights of copyright ownership (e.g., one who prepares a movie based on an earlier book may file an application for the newly created derivative work, the movie)
- the duly authorized agent of the author, claimant, or owner of exclusive rights (such as an attorney, trustee, or anyone authorized to act on behalf of such parties)

Application Forms

Types of Forms. The Copyright Office provides forms for applications for copyright registration. Each form is one 8½-by-11-inch sheet, printed front and back. An applicant may use photocopies of forms. Because the Copyright Office receives approximately 600,000 applications each year, each application must use a similar format to ease the burden of examination. The type of form used is dictated by the type of work that is the subject of copyright. For example, one form is used for literary works, while another is used for sound recordings. Following are the forms used for copyright applications.

- **Form TX.** Form TX is used for registration of published or unpublished nondramatic literary works, excluding periodicals or serial issues. This class includes a wide variety of works: fiction, nonfiction, essays, poetry, textbooks, reference works, catalogs, advertising copy, compilations of information, and computer programs.
- **Form PA.** Form PA is used for works of the performing arts (namely, those to be performed before an audience), including plays, pantomimes, choreographic works, operas, motion pictures and other audiovisual works, musical compositions, and songs.
- **Form VA.** Form VA is used for registration of published or unpublished works of visual arts, including two- and three-dimensional works of fine, graphic, and applied art, such as cartoons, comic strips, dolls, toys, fabric and wall-covering

designs, games and puzzles, greeting cards, jewelry designs, maps, original prints, photographs, posters, sculptures, and technical drawings including architectural plans and blueprints.

- **Form SR.** Form SR is used for sound recordings.
- **Form SE.** Form SE is used to register each individual issue of a serial, such as periodicals, newspapers, magazines, newsletters, annuals, and journals.
- **Short forms.** The Copyright Office offers a short version of some of its application forms to make registering a copyright claim easier. The information requested is minimal and the instructions are brief. Short forms may be used if the application is by a living author who is the sole author and owner of the work, the work is completely new, and the work is not one made for hire. The following forms are available in short form: Short Form PA (for works of the performing arts), Short Form TX (for literary works), and Short Form VA (for works of the visual arts).
- **Group forms.** Group forms may be used for certain applications comprising several parts, such as the following: Form Group/DN (for registering copyrights in a group of daily newspapers or newsletters); Form Group/CP (for submission with Forms TX, PA, or VA when a group of works such as short stories or a series of sculpture figurines is being applied for); and Form Group/SE (for applying for a group of serials, such as several issues of a magazine).

The Copyright Office provides other forms as well, namely, forms for renewals for works under the 1909 act (Form RE); forms for continuation when, due to length, the application cannot be completed on one page (Form CON); and a form to correct or amplify information given in the Copyright Office record of an earlier registration (Form CA).

Obtaining Application Forms. There are a variety of ways to obtain application forms from the Copyright Office. Application forms are provided free of charge.

- **Forms and circulars hotline.** A person can call the Copyright Office (202/707-9100) and leave a recorded message asking for forms by name and leaving a mailing address. The forms will be sent within a week or two.
- **Ordering by mail.** Copyright applications can be obtained by mailing a request to Library of Congress, Copyright Office, Publications Section LM-455, 101 Independence Avenue SE, Washington, DC 20559-6000.
- **Internet.** All Copyright Office application forms are now available on the Internet. They may be downloaded and printed for use in registering or renewing copyrights. You may connect through the Copyright Office home page at http://www.copyright.gov. You must have Adobe® Acrobat® Reader installed on your computer to view and print the forms. Print the forms head to head (the top of page 2 must be directly behind the top of page 1) on a single sheet of 8½-by-11-inch white paper. Applications may be typewritten or printed by hand in black ink. Applications can also be viewed and filled in on the Copyright Office Web site and then printed and mailed in. The Copy-right Office began accepting some forms electronically (on a limited basis) in 2007.

Preparing the Application Form. Although there are a variety of application forms to be used in applying for registration, the information required of an applicant and the format of the forms are nearly identical from form to form. Generally, there are several sections or "spaces" that must be completed. In order to obtain the information needed for the copyright application, many law firms ask clients to complete copyright questionnaires so information will be complete and accurate (see Exhibit 13–1 for a sample questionnaire).

Space 1: Title.   Every work submitted for copyright registration must be given a title to identify it. If the copies or phonorecords of the work bear a title or any identifying phrase that could serve as a title, this wording should be used in its exact and complete form. Indexing of the registration and future identification of the work depends on its title. If the work is a collective work (such as a collection of songs), the overall title of the collection should be given.

The applicant must also indicate if the work has been known under a previous title or if there is an additional title under which someone searching for the registration might be likely to look. For example, if a movie title is changed in the course of filming, the previous title should be given. Similarly, the song "My Heart Will Go On" is also known as the "Theme Song from Titanic." Both titles should be given.

Space 2: Author(s).   A variety of information must be given about the author(s) of the work. The fullest form of the author's name should be given, unless the work is a work made for hire, in which case the name of the employer or commissioning party should be given as author. If there is more than one author (such as may be the case in a joint work consisting of a book and its accompanying illustrations), all should be identified.

The application must indicate if the author's contribution is anonymous or pseudonymous. An author's contribution to a work is **anonymous** if a natural person is not identified on the copies or phonorecords of the work. An author's work is **pseudonymous** if the author is identified under a fictitious name, such as the books written by Stephen King under the pseudonym Richard Bachman.

If the author is dead, the application requires that the date of death be given (because copyright protection for most works lasts for life plus

70 years, the author's date of death determines copyright duration). The author's birth date is requested, although it is not required. If the work is one made for hire, the date of birth space should be left blank. The author's citizenship or domicile must be given in all cases.

Finally, a brief description of the nature of authorship must be given. For example, the following terms are usually acceptable: *entire text, illustrations, computer program, words and music, sculpture, photographs, lyrics,* and *motion picture.* Conversely, the following terms should be avoided because they suggest lack of copyrightable material: *idea, concept, typeface, title, system, method,* and *layout.*

Space 3: Creation and Publication.   Space 3 of each copyright application requires an identification of the year in which creation of the work was completed. Under the Copyright Act, a work is "created" when it is fixed in a tangible form for the first time. Generally, when a work is prepared over a period of time, as is the case with a novel, the date of creation is the date of completion of the finished project.

If the work has been published, space 3 requires that the month, day, and year of the first publication be provided together with an identification of the country in which publication first occurred. "Publication" of a work is the distribution of copies or phonorecords of a work to the public by sale, transfer of ownership, or by rental, sale, or leasing. A work is also published if there has been an offering to distribute copies or phonorecords to a group of persons for purposes of further distribution, public performance, or public display. Thus, a novel is published when it has been offered to bookstores for further sale to the public.

Space 4: Claimant(s).   The names and addresses of the copyright claimant(s) of the work must be given even if they are the same as those of the author(s). The copyright claimant is either the author of the work or a person or organization to whom the copyright has been transferred. For

EXHIBIT 13–1
Copyright
Questionnaire

The following questions are intended to help determine whether a work is entitled to copyright registration and the particular form to be used in applying for registration. Complete the questions to the best of your knowledge. If you do not know the answer to a question, indicate such and we can address outstanding issues together.

1. Describe your work. Is it a book? A short story? A song? A painting?
2. What is the title of your work?
3. Has the work had any previous or alternative titles? If so, list the titles.
4. Is the work part of a contribution to a periodical, such as a magazine or other serial? Has it been published in the magazine or is it scheduled to be published?
5. Who created the work? Give full name(s). Did anyone else participate in creating the work as a joint effort? If so, identify all joint authors. What part did each author play in the creation of the work? For example, one author may create text and another illustrations for a book, or one author may compose a melody and another the lyrics for a song?
6. Did you create the work in the scope of your employment as an employee of another?
7. Are you an employer whose employee created the work in the scope of employment? Was the creator of the work your employee or was the creator acting as an independent contractor for you?
8. Was the work created as a result of a special order or commission? If so, describe.
9. Give the date(s) of birth, and if applicable, date(s) of death of the author(s) of the work. What is the nationality or domicile of the author(s)?
10. Will the author be identified on the work or is the author anonymous? Is the author known by a pseudonym or fictitious name?
11. In what year was the work created (what year was it fixed in a tangible form)?
12. Has the work been published? ("Publication" refers to distribution of the work to the public by sale, transfer, sale, lease, or lending, or an offering to distribute it to a group of persons for purposes of further distribution, public performance, or display)? If the work has been published, give the exact date and nation in which it was first published.
13. Who is the owner of the copyright in the work? Has it been transferred by its author to anyone?
14. Have any licenses been granted to others to use the work, reproduce it, distribute it, or perform it? If so, are these licenses exclusive or nonexclusive? Were the licenses in writing?
15. Has registration for this work or an earlier version of this work already been sought in the Copyright Office? If so, please provide a copy of the earlier registration and describe how this version of the work differs from the earlier version.
16. Does the work include contributions by others, such as photographs or text by others? Does the work include any material owned by the U.S. Government?
17. Is this work based upon another work? For example, is this work a translation of another work? Is it based upon another work such as a book, song, movie, or play? Is it a condensation or abridgment of another work? Does it consist of revisions or editorial modifications? Describe.
18. If the work contains both original and preexisting material, identify and describe the new material.
19. Identify any oral or written agreements relating in any way to the work.

Give the full name, address, and telephone number of the individual completing this questionnaire.

example, if Beverly Young is the author of a novel who has sold all rights to the novel to ABC Inc., Beverly Young would be listed as "author" and ABC Inc. would be identified as the claimant. If the claimant is not the author, a brief statement of how the claimant obtained ownership must be given. It is sufficient to state that the claimant obtained ownership "by written contract," "by transfer of all rights by author," "by assignment," or "by will."

Space 5: Previous Registration. The questions in space 5 are intended to show whether an earlier registration has been made for the work and, if so, whether there is any basis for a new registration inasmuch as only one basic copyright registration can be made for the same version of a particular work.

If the version of the work subject to the application is substantially the same as the work covered by a previous registration, a second registration is generally impermissible.

If the work has been changed and a new registration is being sought to cover the additions or revisions, a new registration can be sought for these changes. Thus, if a movie is published in 2006 and a new version of it with additional scenes and footage is published in 2007, a second registration can be sought for the new version. Similarly, a new version of a computer program is eligible for copyright registration. The applicant must briefly describe the changes made to the work and give the number and date of the latest registration, if any.

Space 6: Derivative Work or Compilation. Space 6 requires the applicant to indicate if the work is a derivative work or compilation. A derivative work is a work based on a preexisting work (such as a movie based on a novel, a translation, editorial revisions, or a condensation). A compilation is a work formed by collecting and assembling preexisting materials or data that are selected and arranged in such a way that they constitute an original work (such as an almanac or a collection of short stories). If the work is a derivative work, the applicant must identify the preexisting work upon which the derivative work is based, for example, by stating "French translation of *The Departed.*" Whether the work is a derivative work or a compilation, the applicant must give a brief description of the new material covered by the copyright claim. For example, the applicant may state "foreword, editing, and annotations" for a derivative work or "compilation of short stories by 20th-century feminists" for a compilation.

Remaining Spaces. The remaining portions of copyright application forms ask for a variety of information.

- **Deposit account.** Individuals who file many copyright applications (at least 12 transactions each year) can establish a deposit account with the Copyright Office by depositing at least $450, eliminating the burden of sending in a fee with each application filed. If a deposit account is established, the applicant indicates the deposit account number on documents submitted to the Copyright Office so fees can be automatically withdrawn from the account. The Copyright Office sends monthly statements showing charges so individuals can replenish the account. If no deposit account has been established, the applicant merely sends in the fee with the application.

- **Correspondence.** The applicant should provide a name, address, telephone number, fax number, and e-mail address of a person to be consulted in the event correspondence about the application is necessary.

- **Certification.** The application cannot be accepted unless it bears the date and handwritten signature of the author or other copyright claimant or of the owner of exclusive rights or the duly authorized agent of such. The signature certifies to the Copyright Office that the information provided in the application is correct to the best of the applicant's knowledge.

Making a false representation of a material fact can subject the signatory to a fine up to $2,500.

- **Address for return of certificate.** The address to which the certificate of registration should be sent must be given. The address space should be completed legibly because the certificate will be sent in a window envelope and this information will appear in the window.

(See Exhibit 13–2 for a sample of a completed copyright application.)

Filing Fee

17 U.S.C. § 708 authorizes the Copyright Office to charge fees. Effective July 1, 2007, the non-refundable fee for filing a paper application is $45. Check the Copyright Office Web site or call (202) 707-3000 for the latest fee information. The fee for a copyright application may be paid by deposit account or by check or money order payable to Register of Copyrights. Cash is not accepted. Electronic transfers and credit card charges are generally not permissible. Effective in mid-2007, the Copyright Office reduced the basic filing fee to $35 for electronically filed applications; however, the electronic filing system was still being beta-tested at the time of writing of this text, and thus, only a limited number of applications are accepted electronically at present.

DEPOSIT MATERIALS

Introduction

Section 407 of the Copyright Act requires that the owner of copyright or of the exclusive right of publication in a work published in the United States deposit, within three months after publication, two complete copies of the best edition of the work or, if the work is a sound recording, two complete phonorecords of the best edi-

tion. Deposits are to be made into the Library of Congress so that it can continue its tradition of cataloguing and collecting works published in the United States by ensuring that it receives copies of every copyrightable work published in the United States. The Copyright Act presumes that individuals will make the deposit voluntarily.

Although this deposit requirement can be fulfilled through application for copyright registration (because deposit materials are required to be submitted with the application), the requirement is mandatory whether or not an application is ever filed (although certain works including greeting cards, postcards, stationery, speeches, sculptures, technical drawings, and advertising materials are exempt). Failure to deposit the materials does not cause a loss of copyright protection, but it may subject a party to a fine (presently, $250) if the Copyright Office requests the deposit and the copyright owner fails to supply the materials within three months. The deposit requirements in the United States are similar to those in other countries.

Deposit Materials Accompanying Copyright Applications

An application for a copyright registration must be accompanied by a nonreturnable deposit of the work being registered. Although the deposit requirements vary in particular situations, the general requirements are as follows:

- if the work is unpublished, one complete copy or phonorecord
- if the work was first published in the United States on or after January 1, 1978, two complete copies or phonorecords of the best edition

The "Best Edition" Requirement

The Copyright Act requires that copies or phonorecords deposited be of the **best edition** of the work. The "best edition" requirement is intended to discourage inferior deposit materials and encourage deposit materials of high

Copyright Office fees are subject to change. For current fees, check the Copyright Office website at *www.copyright.gov*, write the Copyright Office, or call (202) 707-3000.

Form TX
For a Nondramatic Literary Work
UNITED STATES COPYRIGHT OFFICE

EXHIBIT 13–2
Completed
Copyright
Application

REGISTRATION NUMBER

TX   TXU

EFFECTIVE DATE OF REGISTRATION

Month   Day   Year

DO NOT WRITE ABOVE THIS LINE. IF YOU NEED MORE SPACE, USE A SEPARATE CONTINUATION SHEET.

1

TITLE OF THIS WORK ▼
The Summer Vacation

PREVIOUS OR ALTERNATIVE TITLES ▼
None

PUBLICATION AS A CONTRIBUTION If this work was published as a contribution to a periodical, serial, or collection, give information about the collective work in which the contribution appeared.   **Title of Collective Work ▼**

If published in a periodical or serial give: **Volume ▼**   **Number ▼**   **Issue Date ▼**   **On Pages ▼**

2   **a**

NAME OF AUTHOR ▼
Stacy P. Andrews

DATES OF BIRTH AND DEATH
Year Born ▼   1965   Year Died ▼   NA

Was this contribution to the work a "work made for hire"?
☐ Yes
☑ No

AUTHOR'S NATIONALITY OR DOMICILE
Name of Country
OR { Citizen of ▶ United States of America
     Domiciled in ▶

WAS THIS AUTHOR'S CONTRIBUTION TO THE WORK
Anonymous?   ☐ Yes ☑ No
Pseudonymous? ☐ Yes ☑ No

If the answer to either of these questions is "Yes," see detailed instructions.

NATURE OF AUTHORSHIP Briefly describe nature of material created by this author in which copyright is claimed. ▼
Entire text

NOTE
Under the law, the "author" of a "work made for hire" is generally the employer, not the employee (see instructions). For any part of this work that was "made for hire" check "Yes" in the space provided, give the employer (or other person for whom the work was prepared) as "Author" of that part, and leave the space for dates of birth and death blank.

b

NAME OF AUTHOR ▼

DATES OF BIRTH AND DEATH
Year Born ▼   Year Died ▼

Was this contribution to the work a "work made for hire"?
☐ Yes
☐ No

AUTHOR'S NATIONALITY OR DOMICILE
Name of Country
OR { Citizen of ▶
     Domiciled in ▶

WAS THIS AUTHOR'S CONTRIBUTION TO THE WORK
Anonymous?   ☐ Yes ☐ No
Pseudonymous? ☐ Yes ☐ No

If the answer to either of these questions is "Yes," see detailed instructions.

NATURE OF AUTHORSHIP Briefly describe nature of material created by this author in which copyright is claimed. ▼

c

NAME OF AUTHOR ▼

DATES OF BIRTH AND DEATH
Year Born ▼   Year Died ▼

Was this contribution to the work a "work made for hire"?
☐ Yes
☐ No

AUTHOR'S NATIONALITY OR DOMICILE
Name of Country
OR { Citizen of ▶
     Domiciled in ▶

WAS THIS AUTHOR'S CONTRIBUTION TO THE WORK
Anonymous?   ☐ Yes ☐ No
Pseudonymous? ☐ Yes ☐ No

If the answer to either of these questions is "Yes," see detailed instructions.

NATURE OF AUTHORSHIP Briefly describe nature of material created by this author in which copyright is claimed. ▼

3   **a**

YEAR IN WHICH CREATION OF THIS WORK WAS COMPLETED   This information must be given in all cases.
2006 ◀ Year

b   **DATE AND NATION OF FIRST PUBLICATION OF THIS PARTICULAR WORK**
Complete this information ONLY if this work has been published.
Month ▶ August   Day ▶ 18   Year ▶ 2006
◀ Nation

4

See instructions before completing this space.

COPYRIGHT CLAIMANT(S) Name and address must be given even if the claimant is the same as the author given in space 2. ▼
Stacy P. Andrews
1101 Cedar Ridge Road
Springfield, MO 65721

TRANSFER If the claimant(s) named here in space 4 is (are) different from the author(s) named in space 2, give a brief statement of how the claimant(s) obtained ownership of the copyright. ▼

APPLICATION RECEIVED

ONE DEPOSIT RECEIVED

TWO DEPOSITS RECEIVED

FUNDS RECEIVED

DO NOT WRITE HERE
OFFICE USE ONLY

MORE ON BACK ▶   • Complete all applicable spaces (numbers 5-9) on the reverse side of this page.
• See detailed instructions.   • Sign the form at line 8.

DO NOT WRITE HERE

Page 1 of _____ pages

EXHIBIT 13–2
Completed
Copyright
Application
(continued)

EXAMINED BY	FORM TX
CHECKED BY	
☐ CORRESPONDENCE Yes	FOR COPYRIGHT OFFICE USE ONLY

DO NOT WRITE ABOVE THIS LINE. IF YOU NEED MORE SPACE, USE A SEPARATE CONTINUATION SHEET.

PREVIOUS REGISTRATION Has registration for this work, or for an earlier version of this work, already been made in the Copyright Office?

☐ **Yes** ☑ **No** If your answer is "Yes," why is another registration being sought? (Check appropriate box.) ▼

a. ☐ This is the first published edition of a work previously registered in unpublished form.

b. ☐ This is the first application submitted by this author as copyright claimant.

c. ☐ This is a changed version of the work, as shown by space 6 on this application.

If your answer is "Yes," give: **Previous Registration Number** ▶   **Year of Registration** ▶

5

DERIVATIVE WORK OR COMPILATION

Preexisting Material Identify any preexisting work or works that this work is based on or incorporates. ▼

NA

Material Added to This Work Give a brief, general statement of the material that has been added to this work and in which copyright is claimed. ▼

6 **a** **b**

See instructions before completing this space.

DEPOSIT ACCOUNT If the registration fee is to be charged to a Deposit Account established in the Copyright Office, give name and number of Account.

Name ▼   **Account Number** ▼

7 **a**

CORRESPONDENCE Give name and address to which correspondence about this application should be sent.   Name/Address/Apt/City/State/Zip ▼

Stacy P. Andrews
1101 Cedar Ridge Road
Springfield. MO 65721

Area code and daytime telephone number ▶ (314) 455-1999   Fax number ▶ Same

Email ▶ StacyP11@verizon.net

b

CERTIFICATION* I, the undersigned, hereby certify that I am the

Check only one ▶ {
☑ author
☐ other copyright claimant
☐ owner of exclusive right(s)
☐ authorized agent of _____
}

of the work identified in this application and that the statements made by me in this application are correct to the best of my knowledge.

Name of author or other copyright claimant, or owner of exclusive right(s) ▲

8

Typed or printed name and date ▼ If this application gives a date of publication in space 3, do not sign and submit it before that date.

Stacy P. Andrews   Date ▶ September 10, 2006

Handwritten signature ▼

9

Certificate will be mailed in window envelope to this address:	Name ▼ Stacy P. Andrews
	Number/Street/Apt ▼ 1101 Cedar Ridge Road
	City/State/Zip ▼ Springfield. MO 65721

YOU MUST:
• Complete all necessary spaces
• Sign your application in space 8

SEND ALL 3 ELEMENTS IN THE SAME PACKAGE:
1. Application form
2. Nonrefundable filing fee in check or money order payable to *Register of Copyrights*
3. Deposit material

MAIL TO:
Library of Congress
Copyright Office
101 Independence Avenue SE
Washington, DC 20559-6222

*17 *USC* §506(e): Any person who knowingly makes a false representation of a material fact in the application for copyright registration provided for by section 409, or in any written statement filed in connection with the application, shall be fined not more than $2,500.

Form TX – Full Rev: 11/2006 Print: 11/2006 — 30,000 Printed on recycled paper   U.S. Government Printing Office: 2006-xx-xxx/60,xxx quality. Generally, the best edition is one that is larger rather than smaller; in color rather than black and white; and printed on archival-quality rather than less permanent paper. For example, for books, hardcover rather than softcover copies are the best edition, and sewn rather than glue-only binding is preferred; for photographs, unmounted rather than mounted photographs are the best edition; for phonorecords, compact digital discs rather than vinyl discs are the best edition; for motion pictures, films rather than videotape formats are the best edition. Copyright Office Circular 7b fully describes the best edition requirements.

If the depositor cannot deposit the best edition, a request for special relief may be made, stating why the applicant cannot send the required deposit and what the applicant wishes to submit in place of the required deposit.

Deposit Requirements for Specific Works

Following are the deposit requirements for specific works.

- **Visual arts materials.** Because it would be impracticable or impossible to submit large sculptures, paintings, and posters, photographs are generally acceptable for these works. For fabrics and wall coverings, swatches showing the design repeat are acceptable. For games, a complete copy of the game must be submitted unless it is large, in which case a photograph is permissible.
- **Literary works.** Copies of the text, book, advertising copy, and so forth must be submitted.
- **Performing arts works.** For plays, cinema, radio, and television scripts, the scripts themselves should be deposited. For pantomimes and choreographic works, a film or video recording showing the work is permissible, or the works may be described in written text.

- **Architectural works.** The required deposit for an architectural work, whether or not the building has been constructed, is one complete copy of an architectural drawing or blueprint. If the building has been constructed, the deposit must also include photographs showing the work (preferably 8-by-10-inch photos showing interior and exterior views).
- **Motion pictures.** For motion pictures, one copy of the work as first published is required (one of the first prints or tapes made from the master, clear, undamaged, and unspliced). Additionally, a separate description of the work is required, such as a script or summary.
- **Musical compositions.** For vocal and instrumental music, generally the sheet music or full score must be submitted.
- **Sound recordings.** The deposit for sound recordings is two complete phonorecords of the best edition plus any text or pictorial matter published with the phonorecord (compact discs, albums, or cassettes). Examples of the textual material include all phonorecord packaging, record sleeves, and separate leaflets or booklets enclosed with the phonorecords.
- **Computer programs.** Generally, the first and last 25 pages of source code must be submitted as the deposit for computer programs; however, as discussed in Copyright Office Circular 61 and in chapter 15, the Copyright Office permits authors to "block out" portions of the source code if it constitutes a trade secret.
- **Multimedia works.** A multimedia work is a work that combines forms of authorship, such as a book including charts or a slide presentation to be shown with accompanying narration or music on a cassette tape. A single application can be used if the copyright claimant is the same for each element of the work and the elements of the work, if published, are

published as a single unit. Generally, the deposit should be a complete multimedia kit containing all elements covered by the registration.

Recall that in the case of published works, two copies of the best edition are required. For unpublished works, one copy is required. In special cases claimants may obtain relief from the deposit requirements (usually due to cost).

THE APPLICATION PROCESS AND REGISTRATION OF COPYRIGHT

Filing the Application

After the correct application form has been selected and completed and the correct deposit materials have been identified, the application may be filed with the U.S. Copyright Office. The application may be sent by regular or express mail. Despite the apparent complexity of the numerous forms and deposit requirements, for those with familiarity with copyright law and procedure, completing the application form often takes 30 minutes or less.

Although not required, it is a good idea to send a cover letter accompanying the application. The cover letter can confirm the contents of the package and provide a name and phone number of a person to contact in the event the Copyright Office has questions. Many applicants also include a "come-back" card, a self-addressed and stamped postcard so the Copyright Office can confirm the filing of the application because the Copyright Office itself does not issue any acknowledgment that an application has been received.

Examination of the Application and Copyright Registration

The Copyright Office will assign the application to a specialist; however, the examination of the application is not substantive, as is the case with trademark and patent applications. Gener-

ally, a copyright application is examined only to ensure that the material in which copyright is claimed is copyrightable (e.g., a copyright claim in facts, a recipe, or a blank form will be refused) and that the material deposited complies with statutory requirements.

There are four major examining sections in the Copyright Office: one for literary works, one for works of the performing arts, one for works of visual arts, and one for renewals. The examiner will review the application to ensure all information is complete and compare the application and deposit for consistency.

It is nearly impossible to determine the status of an application that has been filed. The Copyright Office Certifications and Documents Section (202/707-6787) may have information, but such information is provided only upon payment of applicable fees. Due to the volume of applications filed each year (approximately 600,000), the Copyright Office does not provide free information about the status of an application.

Nevertheless, within approximately 12 to 16 weeks of filing the application, the Copyright Office will either issue a certificate of registration or contact the applicant by letter or phone asking for additional information or explaining why the application has been rejected. If the Copyright Office has questions, the applicant usually has 120 days to respond. Failure to respond within the time required generally results in closing of the file without further notification. If registration is later desired, a new application, deposit, and fee must be submitted.

If the application is acceptable, the Copyright Office will register the copyright by returning a certificate of registration, namely, a copy of the application stamped with a seal, a registration number, and date of registration. A copyright registration is effective on the date the Copyright Office receives a complete application package in acceptable form, regardless of how long it may take to process the application. In general, Copyright Office policy is to resolve questionable cases in favor of the applicant under its **rule of doubt,** meaning that although the Copyright Office has doubts about copyrightability, it will resolve doubts in favor of the applicant and allow a court to make a final determination in the future if questions arise regarding copyrightability.

The Copyright Office is in the process of implementing an electronic filing system called the Copyright Office Electronic Registration, Recordation, and Deposit System (CORDS). The CORDS project aims to develop and implement a totally electronic system of receipt and processing of copyright applications, deposited works, and related documents over communications networks such as the Internet. The CORDS system will enable the Copyright Office to complete its review and processing and issue a registration certificate within a few days or weeks rather than the four-month period usually experienced. Testing and implementation will continue over the next several years. At present, the Copyright Office accepts only literary texts, serials, and musical works in electronic form from a limited number of participants. The Copyright Office recently began referring to the CORDS system as "eCO" (Electronic Copyright Office).

In mid-2007, the Copyright Office began beta testing online filing of applications. Those who file online will be given a reduced application fee ($35 rather than the paper application fee of $45), will benefit from a faster processing time, will be able to track the status of their applications online, and will be able to make payment by credit card or deposit account. For published works, hard copies of the deposit material (e.g., books) must still be submitted to the Copyright Office to comply with the best edition requirements. As mentioned earlier, the system was still in its infancy at the time of writing of this text, and few applications are being filed electronically.

Refusal of Registration

If registration is refused by the Copyright Office, reconsideration can be requested. The applicant "appeals" the adverse decision by making a written request for reconsideration and paying the fee of $250 within three months after refusal. A response in writing will be made by the exam-

ining division. Further reconsideration may be requested of the Copyright Office Board of Review upon payment of an additional fee of $500. If registration is still refused, the applicant may seek judicial review in the United States District Court for the District of Columbia.

Because copyright registration is a prerequisite for an infringement suit for works originating in the United States, refusal of registration would put a party who believes his or her work has been infringed in the untenable situation of being unable to initiate action in federal court for infringement. Thus, if registration has been applied for and refused, the applicant may still file an infringement action but must provide notice of the action and a copy of the complaint to the Register of Copyrights. The Register may become a party to the court action but only with regard to registrability of the work.

The Copyright Office can cancel a registration if it is determined that a work is not copyrightable or the check for the filing fee is returned for insufficient funds. Prior to cancellation, the Copyright Office will provide notice to the registrant so the registrant has an opportunity to respond to the cancellation procedure.

Special Handling

In some instances, applicants may not be able to wait 12 to 16 weeks to receive notification that a copyright has been registered. For example, before a copyright infringement suit may be filed in court, registration is necessary for works of U.S. origin. Thus, a party who wishes to commence an infringement action upon short notice must have assurance that a copyright has been registered. To expedite the processing of applications for registration (or the recordation of documents relating to copyrights), the Copyright Office has established **special handling** procedures.

Special handling is granted only in special circumstances. These are:

- pending or prospective litigation
- customs matters

- contract or publishing deadlines that necessitate the expedited process

Special handling is typically requested by a letter stating the reasons why special handling is needed. The request must also include a signed statement certifying that the information contained in the request is correct to the best of the requestor's knowledge. Once a request for special handling is approved, every effort is made by the Copyright Office to process the application or request for recordation within five working days. The present fee for a special handling request for an application is $685 (plus the usual application filing fee of $45 or, for expedited recording of documents, $435 plus the usual fee for recording documents).

Supplementary Copyright Registration

If information in a registration is incorrect or incomplete, an application may be filed for **supplementary copyright registration** to correct the error or amplify the information given. Supplementary registration can be made only if a basic copyright registration for the same work has already been issued. Form CA is used, and the filing fee is $115. No deposit materials should be included.

Supplementary registration is not necessary for minor typographical errors or omission of articles, such as the word *the*. Some of the more common reasons a supplementary copyright registration is requested are the following:

- the original application identified an incorrect author
- the work was registered as published when publication had not yet taken place
- a coauthor was omitted
- a change in the name or title of the work has occurred (e.g., a book or movie title has been changed)

If the supplementary registration is issued, there will be two registrations on file with the Copyright Office. The original registration will not be expunged or canceled, but the supplementary registration will direct the public's attention to an error or omission in the basic registration and will place the correct facts or additional information on official record.

Benefits of Securing Registration

Because copyright protection exists from the time a work is created, securing a registration from the Copyright Office is not necessary to protect copyright material. Nevertheless, federal copyright law provides several inducements to encourage copyright owners to secure registration. Among these advantages are the following:

- Registration establishes a public record of the claim of copyright.
- Before an infringement suit may be filed in courts, registration is necessary for works of U.S. origin (except for a suit alleging a violation of the right of attribution or integrity under the Visual Artists Rights Act) and for foreign works not originating in a Berne Union country.
- If made before or within five years of publication, registration constitutes *prima facie* evidence of the validity of the copyright and of the facts stated in the certificate.
- If registration is made within three months after publication or prior to an infringement of an unpublished work, statutory damages and attorneys' fees will be available to the copyright owner in court actions. Otherwise, only an award of actual damages and lost profits is available to the copyright owner.
- Registration allows the owner of the copyright to record the registration with the U.S. Customs and Border Protection for protection against the importation of infringing copies.

ETHICS EDGE: **Staying Current**

A legal professional's duty of competency requires that he or she be sufficiently familiar with Copyright Office procedures that the client's work can be performed as efficiently and economically as possible. Periodically visit the Copyright Office Web site; understand that using short forms when possible saves the client time and money. Be ready to use the online registration procedure when it is fully implemented. Understand when special handling is necessary and how to obtain deposit materials.

Preregistration

A new procedure in the Copyright Office (pursuant to the 2005 Family Entertainment and Copyright Act, 17 U.S.C. § 408(f)) allows **preregistration** for certain classes of works that have a history of prerelease infringement. Preregistration allows a copyright owner to sue for infringement while a work is still being prepared for commercial release. To qualify for preregistration, the work must be unpublished, it must be in the process of being prepared for commercial distribution, and it must be a certain type of work (namely, a motion picture, sound recording, musical composition, literary work, computer programs including video games, or advertising or marketing photographs). Preregistration is not a substitute for regular registration but is simply an indication of an intent to register a work once it is completed or published. If a work has been preregistered, the copyright owner must register the work within one month after the owner becomes aware of infringement and no later than three months after first publication in order to be able to sue for infringement in federal court.

To preregister, the copyright owner must apply online (no paper application form is available). Only an application and fee are required. No deposit is required; however, a more detailed description of the work is required. For example, for a movie, the applicant should describe its subject matter, provide a summary of the plot, identify the director and principal actors, and

so forth. In fiscal year 2006, the Copyright Office handled about 300 preregistrations.

SEARCHING COPYRIGHT OFFICE RECORDS

It may become necessary to determine whether copyright for a work has been registered or what copyrights are registered to a company or individual. For example, if a company is selling all of its assets to another, the buyer will typically conduct **due diligence** and review records of the USPTO and the Copyright Office to determine what patents, trademarks, and copyrights are registered in the seller's name so these can then be transferred to the buyer.

Conducting searches prior to applying for copyright registration is not nearly as critical as conducting searches prior to applying for trademark or patent protection. Because copyright protection exists once a work is created and independent creation is permissible, the fact that another party has a copyright registration for a work will not preclude registration for another similar or identical work (as long as the works do not copy from each other). Moreover, although titles are not copyrightable, an author may wish to select a unique title for a book or movie, and a search would reveal similar or identical titles, which might confuse consumers.

There are a variety of ways to search Copyright Office records.

- The records of the Copyright Office are open for inspection and searching by the public. The Copyright Office, however, cannot give legal advice, answer questions on possible infringement, recommend publishers, or enforce contracts. The records freely available to the public include an extensive card catalog (for registrations from 1870 through 1978) and an online catalog (for registrations since 1978) that provide an index to more than 40 million registered copyrights. Searching can be done by the title of the work, author(s), claimant(s), date of publication, or registration number.

- The Library of Congress card catalog can be searched; however, only a portion of the works deposited for copyright are selected for inclusion in the Library's collections, and the Library does not always fully catalog those works it selects. Some searching of Library of Congress records can be done through the Library's Web site at http://www.loc.gov. Select "Library Catalogs" and follow the instructions given.

- Most copyright records since 1978 can be searched over the Internet. The Internet site address for the Copyright Office files is http://www.copyright.gov/records. This is an experimental system best used for short and simple searches.

- The Copyright Office itself will conduct searches for $150 per hour. The Reference and Bibliography Section of the Copyright Office will conduct a sear ch and provide a factual report on the results of the search. Searches can be initiated by writing to this section or by calling (202) 707-6850. The Copyright Office will estimate the total search fee (for a fee of $100) and initiate the search upon receiving the fee. Upon payment of additional fees, the search can be expedited. A search request form is provided in Copyright Office Circular 22.

- Private companies can conduct searches. Just as companies will search USPTO records and provide reports of trademarks, they will conduct searches of Copyright Office records, file applications and other documents, and provide copies of documents. Contact Thomson CompuMark, 500 North Quincy, MA 02171 (800/692-8833, http://thomsoncompumark. com) or CT Corsearch, 345 Hudson Street, New York, NY 10014 (800/732-7241, http:// www.ctcorsearch.com).

OBTAINING COPYRIGHT OFFICE RECORDS AND DEPOSIT MATERIALS

Upon request, the Certificates and Documents Section of the Copyright Office will prepare certified or uncertified copies of certain public records. Applications, registrations, assignments, licenses, and other documents pertaining to copyrights can be obtained. Generally, these records can be obtained for minimum fees (e.g., $40 for an additional copy of a certificate of registration). Certified copies are usually requested as evidence of the authenticity of a document when litigation involving the copyright is involved. Upon payment of additional fees, expedited service is possible.

Obtaining copies of deposit materials is considerably more difficult than obtaining copies of records. Moreover, not all deposits are retained. The Copyright Office policy is to retain deposits for published works for five years (10 years for works of visual arts). Unpublished deposits are generally kept for the full copyright term. Registrants who wish to ensure the Copyright Office retains their published deposits for the duration of a copyright term must pay a fee of $425 to cover storage costs.

Assuming the material is available, the Copyright Office will provide certified or uncertified copies of the actual works deposited with the Copyright Office only when one of the following three conditions has been met:

1. Written authorization is received from the copyright claimant of record or his or her agent (or the owner of any of the exclusive rights upon written documentation of the transfer).
2. A Copyright Office Litigation Statement Form is completed and received from an attorney or authorized representative stating there is actual or prospective litigation involving the copyrighted work, giving assurance that the material will be used only in connection with the litigation, and providing detailed information about the parties, the controversy, and the court.
3. A court order is issued for reproduction of a deposited article that is the subject of litigation.

Rather than providing the actual deposit material, the Copyright Office may provide a reproduction, such as photographs or photocopies or a reproduction of a sound recording. A fee will be quoted by the Copyright Office when the request for deposit material is made.

COPYRIGHT NOTICE

Introduction

Since March 1, 1989 (the date of adherence by the United States to the Berne Convention), use of a **notice of copyright** (usually the symbol © together with the year of first publication and copyright owner's name) is no longer mandatory, although it is recommended and offers some advantages. Use of the notice informs the public that the work is protected by copyright, identifies the copyright owner, and shows the year of first publication. Furthermore, if a work is infringed, if a proper notice of copyright appears on a published work to which the defendant had access, the defendant cannot assert that infringement was innocent. (A successful innocent infringement defense may result in a reduction of damages.) Use of the notice is the responsibility of the copyright owner and does not require advance

permission from or registration of copyright with the Copyright Office.

Works published before January 1, 1978, are governed by the 1909 Copyright Act. Under that act, if a work was published under the copyright owner's authority without a proper notice of copyright, all copyright protection for that work was permanently lost in the United States. Many works fell into the public domain merely because the owner failed to include the copyright notice. To align the United States with the laws of most other foreign countries, the United States joined the Berne Convention in 1989 and agreed to eliminate any requirement for copyright notice. With regard to works published between January 1, 1978, and March 1, 1989, omission of a notice was generally excused if the notice was omitted from a small number of copies, registration was made within five years of publication, and a reasonable effort was made to add the notice after discovery of its omission. See Exhibit 13–3.

Form of Notice for Visually Perceptible Copies

The form of notice used for visually perceptible copies—those that can be seen or read either directly (such as books) or with the aid of a machine (such as movies)—is different from the form used for sound recordings (such as CDs or cassettes).

Under 17 U.S.C. § 401, the form for visually perceptible copies includes three elements that should appear together or in close proximity. The elements are the following:

1. the symbol © (the letter C in a circle), or the word "Copyright," or the abbreviation "Copr."; and
2. the year of first publication (the year can be omitted when a pictorial, graphic, or sculptural work is reproduced on greeting cards, stationery, jewelry, dolls, or toys); and
3. the name of the owner of copyright in the work, or an abbreviation or alternative

EXHIBIT 13–3
Copyright Notice
Requirements

For works published before 1/1/78	Failure to include notice on published work invalidates copyright, and work will go into the public domain.
For works published between 1/1/78 and 3/1/89	Notice required for all published works. If notice omitted, copyright valid if notice only omitted from a small number of copies, registration is sought within five years, and a reasonable effort is made to add notice.
For works published after 3/1/89	Use of copyright notice is optional. Lack of notice, however, may allow a defendant to assert infringement was innocent and may affect damages.

designation by which the name can be recognized.

Recall that *publication* is defined as the distribution of copies or phonorecords of a work by sale, transfer, rental, lease, or lending or an offering to distribute copies or phonorecords to a group of persons for purposes of further distribution, public performance, or display. If there are joint owners, all of their names should be given. The Copyright Act does not specify the actual order of the elements of the copyright notice but only requires that the notice be placed in such a manner and location as to give reasonable notice of the claim of copyright.

Examples of acceptable copyright notices are "© 1995 John Andrews," "© 2007 ABC Inc.," and "Copr. 1997 Madonna."

Form of Notice for Sound Recordings

Because audio recordings such as audiotapes and phonograph discs are not "copies" but are "phonorecords" under the Copyright Act, the form of copyright notice is different from that used for visually perceptible copies. Copyright in

a sound recording protects the particu-lar series of sounds fixed in the recording against unauthorized reproduction, revision, and distribution. Phonorecords may be records (such as LPs and 45s), audiotapes, cassettes, or discs. Notice for phonorecords should contain the following three elements:

1. the letter "P" placed inside a circle; and
2. the year of first publication; and
3. the name of the owner of copyright or an abbreviation or alternative designation by which the owner can be recognized.

Special Notice Requirements

Questions about the form of copyright notice arise in a variety of cases. Some commonly encountered problems are as follows:

- **Contributions to collective works.** A single copyright notice applicable to the collective work (such as an anthology of poems or a magazine) as a whole is sufficient protection for all the contributions in the collective work (except advertisements). Nevertheless, the separate contributions to the collective work may bear their own notices of copyright (primarily to inform the public of the identity of the owner of the contribution).

- **Publications incorporating U.S. government works.** Any work published before March 1, 1989, that included government works was required to include a special notice identifying the portions of the work that incorporated government works. Thus, if a 1985 textbook reproduced the U.S. Constitution, the notice should state "© 1985 Penguin Books. Copyright is not claimed as to the U.S. Constitution reproduced in chapter 14." For works published after March 1, 1989, the notice is not required but is recommended, because including the notice will preclude a defendant from alleging his or her infringement was innocent.

- **Derivative works.** In the case of a derivative work (one based on an underlying work, such as a sequel to a preexisting book), the information in the notice should relate to the new work, not the underlying work. The symbol © (or the word "Copyright" or the abbreviation "Copr."), the year of first publication of the new work, and the name of the copyright owner of the new work should be given. Only the new material is owned by the new author, and one cannot extend the length of copyright protection by creating a derivative work. On occasion, a copyright notice will indicate a range of years for a work, for example, "© 1998, 1999, 2002 Jane Doe" to indicate the years of publication of the original work and later derivative works.

- **Unpublished works.** There has never been a requirement for use of a copyright notice for unpublished works, although a notice may be used. An example would

be "Unpublished work © 2007 Daniel Donoghue."

Location of Notice

The Copyright Act does not dictate exact placement of the copyright notice but requires only that it be placed in such a way that it gives reasonable notice of the claim of copyright. According to 37 C.F.R. § 201.20, the following placements are acceptable:

- **Works published in book form.** The notice may be placed on the title page, the page immediately following the title page, either side of the front or back covers, or the first or last page of the work.
- **Single-leaf works.** The notice may be placed anywhere on the front or back of the leaf.
- **Contributions to collective works.** The notice may be placed under the title or elsewhere on the same page if the contribution consists of one page. If the contribution spans more than one page, the notice may be placed under the title, on the first page of the contribution, or at the end of the contribution.
- **Works published as periodicals or other serials.** The notice may be placed at any of the locations acceptable on books, near the masthead or on the same page as the masthead, or adjacent to a prominent heading near the front of the issue.
- **Computer programs and works produced in machine-readable copies.** The notice may appear with or near the title or at the end of the work, on visually perceptible printouts, at the user's terminal at sign-on, on continuous display on the terminal, or reproduced durably on a label securely affixed to the copies or to a container used as a permanent receptacle for the copies.

- **Motion pictures and other audiovisual works.** The notice may be placed with or near the title, with the credits information, at or immediately following the beginning of the work, or at or immediately preceding the end of the work. If the work is distributed to the public for private use (such as rental of videotaped movies or DVDs), the notice can also be placed on the permanent container for the videotape or DVD.
- **Pictorial, graphic, and sculptural works.** For works embodied in two-dimensional copies (such as paintings and posters), the notice may be affixed to the front or back of the copies or any backing or mounting material. For works reproduced in three-dimensional copies (such as sculptures, globes, and dolls), the notice may be affixed to any visible portion of the work or any base or mounting for the work. If it is impracticable to affix a notice to the copies directly (such as is the case with jewelry), a notice may be placed on a tag or label. For sheeting such as fabrics and wall coverings, the notice may appear on the margin selvage or reverse side of the material in frequent and regular intervals. For games and puzzles, the notice may be reproduced on the container.
- **Sound recordings.** The notice may be placed on the surface of the phono-record or on the phonorecord label or container.

When a notice does not appear in one of the precise locations prescribed by 37 C.F.R. § 201.20, but a person looking in one of those locations would be reasonably certain to find the notice in another somewhat different location, that notice will be acceptable.

Omission of and Errors in Notice

Under the 1909 Copyright Act (and until March 1, 1989), copyright notices were mandatory; failure to give the notice resulted in permanent loss of copyright. There were no provisions to cure omissions of notice. The 1976 act attempted to lessen the harshness of prior law and allowed for cure of omissions of notice or certain errors as long as cure occurred within five years of publication. For works published after March 1, 1989 (the effective date of the Berne Convention Implementation Act), use of the notice of copyright is optional, and omissions and errors in the notice are less important. Nevertheless, the 1909 act still applies to works published while it was in effect. For example, if copies of a work first published in 1987 omit or have errors in the copyright notice, the owner risks losing copyright protection if the defect is not cured.

Some errors are considered so serious that they are viewed as equivalent to omitting the notice entirely. These errors include failing to include the symbol ©, the word "Copyright," or the abbreviation "Copr."; dating a notice more than one year later than the date of publication; giving a notice without a name; and locating a notice so that it does not give reasonable notice of the claim of copyright. Omission of a notice does not affect copyright protection and no corrective action is required if the work was published after March 1, 1989.

Under section 406, if an error in the date occurs for works distributed after January 1, 1978, and before March 1, 1989, it may affect copyright duration. For example, if a work for hire is published in 1985 and yet the copyright notice gives the year as 1984, the term will be measured from 1984 and the copyright will last until 2079 (95 years from 1984). If the year date in the notice is more than one year later than the year of publication, the work is considered to be published without any notice.

Surplusage in Copyright Notice

Many copyright owners and publishers place notices or information in addition to the three elements of a copyright notice. For example, the following information is often seen: "Not for reproduction," "All Rights Reserved," and "No portion of this work may be reproduced, displayed, broadcast, or disseminated in any form without prior written consent." Such additional information may be included on the copyrighted work; however, it is mere surplusage and provides no rights beyond those already provided for by the Copyright Act. The phrase *all rights reserved* is often seen inasmuch as it is commonly used in many foreign countries. Surplusage should never take the place of the actual copyright notice and serves primarily to offer a certain level of comfort to the author or copyright owner.

Restoration of Copyright in Foreign Works

Pursuant to the Uruguay Round Agreements Act, effective January 1, 1996, copyright in foreign works whose U.S. copyright protection had been lost due to noncompliance with notice requirements in U.S. law (e.g., if the work were published in the United States without a copyright notice) was automatically restored. Works of U.S. origin are unaffected, but foreign works that fell into the public domain in the United States were automatically restored as of January 1, 1996. Additional information is available in Copyright Office Circular 38b at http://www.copyright.gov.

Trivia

- The song "White Christmas" was registered by Irving Berlin in 1942. The song is said to be the most valuable music copyright in the world.
- Total copyright registrations in 2006 were 520,906. The total number of copyright registrations issued by the Copyright Office is more than 32 million.
- During 2005, the Copyright Office received only 241 first requests for reconsideration of the refusal of copyright registration.
- In fiscal year 2005, the Copyright Office Web site logged 29.5 million hits.
- More literary works are copyrighted than any other type of work. In 2006, 243,778 literary works were copyrighted, 124,410 works of performing art were copyrighted, and 90,749 works of the visual arts were copyrighted.

CHAPTER SUMMARY

Copyright protection exists from the time a work is created in fixed form. No publication or registration or other action in the Copyright Office is required to secure copyright. There are, however, several advantages to securing registration, namely, the ability to initiate suit in federal court for copyright infringement, the ability to recover statutory damages and attorneys' fees in infringement actions, and the creation of a public record of one's claim to copyright.

Because there are many advantages to copyright registration, copyright owners should be encouraged to complete an application for copyright registration. Three elements are required to register a work: a properly completed application form; a nonrefundable filing fee of $45; and supporting deposit materials. The Copyright Office provides forms for applications. The registration process takes approximately 12 weeks, although it can be expedited if certain conditions are met. Existing registrations can be corrected or amplified if needed.

Searches of Copyright Office records can be conducted at the Copyright Office, online, or by requesting search assistance from the Copyright Office or a private company. The Copyright Office provides copies (both certified and uncertified) of records upon request and payment of fees.

Although use of a copyright notice is optional for works created on or after March 1, 1989, use of the notice is recommended. The notice consists of three elements: the symbol © (or the word "Copyright" or abbreviation "Copr."); the year of first publication of the work; and the name of the copyright owner. The notice should be affixed to copies or phonorecords in such a way as to give reasonable notice of the claim of copyright.

CASE ILLUSTRATION—EFFECT OF COPYRIGHT REGISTRATION

Case: *Saenger Organization, Inc. v. National Insurance Licensing Ass'n*, 119 F.3d 55 (1st Cir. 1997)

Facts: Plaintiff, a company that published insurance licensing texts and manuals, brought an action for copyright infringement against a former officer of the company. The officer claimed that the copyright registrations for the materials were invalid because they did not list him as an author. The district court granted summary judgment for the plaintiff.

Holding: The First Circuit Court of Appeals affirmed. Because the former officer admitted that he had copied substantial portions of the manuals, the only issue was whether the copyrights were valid. In judicial proceedings, a certificate of copyright registration constitutes prima facie evidence of copyrightability and shifts the burden to the defendant to demonstrate why the copyright is not valid. In this case, the copyrights were valid despite the failure to include the former officer's name as a coauthor; the manuals were prepared during the course and scope of his employment with the company and were thus works made for hire, the copyrights of which were owned by the company.

CASE STUDY AND ACTIVITIES

Case Study.   Vision is in the process of preparing copyright applications for a variety of works that it will offer its guests, including maps of the locales near its hotels, a game developed for sale in the hotel gift shops, and a new advertising jingle, now entitled "InVision It" but originally entitled "VisionNext." Additionally, Vision has learned that one of its chief competitors is building a variety of new hotels, and Vision would like to view the architectural plans and any models or other deposits on file with the Copyright Office. Finally, Vision's creative team is developing certain photographs to be used in a commercial advertising campaign, and Vision has learned that an employee "leaked" the photos to a competitor, and the competitor plans to publish the photographs.

Activities.   Identify the particular copyright form that Vision should use to register each copyright, the location of copyright notice for each item, and the deposit material that must accompany each application. Is there anything Vision can do to stop infringement of the photographs that are still being created? May Vision obtain its competitor's deposit materials? Discuss fully.

ROLE OF PARALEGAL

Paralegals are more actively involved in applying for copyright registration than in any other aspect of copyright law. Among the many activities in which IP professionals are engaged are the following:

- obtaining forms and circulars from the Copyright Office so the office has a ready supply of application forms and information
- assisting copyright owners in completing copyright questionnaires so applications can be prepared
- preparing applications and sending them to clients for review and signature
- assisting clients in collecting deposit materials to accompany copyright applications
- establishing deposit accounts with the Copyright Office and monitoring those accounts to ensure they are routinely replenished
- filing copyright applications with come-back postcards
- filing copyright preregistrations online
- working with clients to determine if special handling is needed for applications
- docketing dates of filing of applications and monitoring progress of the typical 12- to 16-week application process
- responding to requests for information or clarification from the Copyright Office
- reviewing certificates of registration for errors and preparing supplementary registration to correct or amplify information in copyright records
- preparing letters confirming registration, indicating duration of copyright, and giving instructions for providing notice of copyright
- searching or requesting searches of Copyright Office records
- requesting copies, certified and uncertified, of Copyright Office records
- arranging to review deposit materials in litigation matters
- reviewing client materials to ensure copyright notices are in compliance with law and are placed properly
- monitoring the Copyright Office Web site to keep abreast of changes in copyright law and procedure

INTERNET RESOURCES

Federal laws relating to copyright: http://www.law.cornell.edu
http://www.findlaw.com

Copyright Office: http://www.copyright.gov (for forms, circulars, and instructions and information on filing copyright applications, fee schedules, information on special handling, requesting deposit materials, and other information)

General information: http://www.findlaw.com
http://www.megalaw.com

DISCUSSION QUESTIONS

1. Owen, an employee of ABC Inc. was hired to create a computer program for ABC Inc. Who owns the resulting computer program? What form should be used in registering the copyright for the program? May a short form be used? How should the work be described in space 1? Discuss.

2. Henry Young, now deceased, is the author of a book, the copyright for which was not registered during his lifetime. Henry's sole heir, his son Steven, is preparing a copyright application for the work. Who will be identified as the author and who will be identified as the copyright claimant? What special statement should be included in the copyright application form in space 4?

3. In what way does the "rule of doubt" help copyright applicants?

4. Paramount Pictures Corp. intends to release its big blockbuster movie next summer and is concerned that someone in the studio may be bribed to release the movie on the Internet prior to its commercial release. What may Paramount do to protect its rights in the movie?

5. Betsy's new novel will be published next month. Neither Betsy nor her publisher has yet applied for copyright registration for the book. What approach should Betsy or the publisher take to ensure a copyright registration is secured before the book is published?

6. Jon and James composed a song together. By mistake, the copyright registration identifies only James as the author. What should the parties do to correct this situation?

7. Jon and James intend to sue another for infringement of their song. They would like to review the infringer's deposit materials to compare the two versions of the song. May they review the deposit material? Discuss.

8. Give the form for copyright notice for the following:
   a. a book written in 1965
   b. a CD of country music songs published in 2000
   c. a computer program published in 2004

USING INTERNET RESOURCES

1. Access the Web site of the Copyright Office.
   a. Review Circular 7b. If there are two hardbound books, one on acid-free paper and one on average paper, which is the best edition?
   b. Review Factsheet SL 8. What short forms are available in fill-in format?
   c. What is the fee for copyright preregistration?
2. Access the Copyright Office Web sites for searching copyright records.
   a. Select "Books, Music, etc." Search for items relating to Oprah Winfrey. Review Item 2, a book entitled *Make the Connection.* How many pages is the book? What is its registration number?
   b. Select "Books, Music, etc." Search for the original motion picture score for the movie *Legally Blonde.* Who was the claimant? Was this a work made for hire? What is the registration number?
   c. Search the Preregistration Records. Locate the information for the movie *Failure to Launch.* What is the preregistration copyright number? When did creation of the work begin? What is the date of preregistration?
3. Locate the current edition of the Code of Federal Regulations (use Google to locate "GPO Access"). Review 37 C.F.R. § 202.19.
   a. Are automated databases exempt from the deposit requirements of the Library of Congress? Give your answer and the subsection that governs your answer.
   b. Would a J. Crew catalog be exempt from the deposit requirements of the Library of Congress? Give your answer and the subsection that governs your answer.

Chapter **14**

Copyright Infringement

CHAPTER OVERVIEW

A copyright owner who has a registered copyright may bring an action for infringement when any of his or her exclusive rights have been infringed by another. Generally, to prevail in an infringement action, a plaintiff must show ownership of copyright and impermissible copying. Copying is generally proven by demonstrating that the defendant had access to the work, and the defendant's work is substantially similar to that of the copyright owner.

There are various defenses a defendant may assert in an infringement action. One of the most common defenses is that the defendant's use of the work is a "fair use." A fair use is generally a use for scholarly, research, or educational purposes. Courts examine four factors in determining whether a defendant's use of a copyrighted work is a fair use: the purpose and character of the use, including whether the use is of a commercial nature or is for nonprofit educational work; the nature of the copyrighted work (with factual works receiving less protection than works of fiction or fantasy); the amount and

substantiality of the portion taken by the defendant; and the effect of the defendant's use on the market for the plaintiff's work. Other defenses include laches, unclean hands, and the statute of limitations, which is three years from the infringing act. Remedies available to a plaintiff include injunctive relief, impoundment of the infringing goods, actual damages and the defendant's profits, statutory damages, costs, and attorneys' fees. Criminal sanctions can be imposed for certain willful infringements.

INTRODUCTION

Registration (or preregistration) of a copyright is a requirement for initiating an action for infringement, 17 U.S.C. § 411, although registration is not required for works not originating in the United States. Moreover, prompt registration is a prerequisite for certain remedies for infringement. 17 U.S.C. § 412. Thus, although registration is not required to obtain copyright protection for a work, the failure to register will preclude a copyright owner from seeking redress for infringement. If registration of a work is refused by the Copyright Office, an action for infringement may still be brought if the author notifies the Copyright Office of the action. The Register of Copyrights then has the right to become a party to the action with respect to the issue of registrability of the copyright claim. 17 U.S.C. § 411.

Section 501 of the Copyright Act provides that anyone who violates any of the exclusive rights of a copyright owner (rights of reproduction, adaptation, distribution, performance, and display), or of the author (as provided in the Visual Artists Rights Act), or who imports copies or phonorecords into the United States in violation of copyright law, is liable for direct infringement of the copyright or right of the author. For example, the following may constitute infringement: playing copyrighted music in a large department store without permission; failing to provide attribution for a painting or other work covered by the Visual Artists Rights Act; and photocopying material from a copyrighted book.

ELEMENTS OF INFRINGEMENT

Ownership of Copyright

To prevail in an infringement action, a plaintiff must prove two things: his or her ownership of the copyright and copying or some other impermissible invasion by the defendant of one of the exclusive rights afforded to copyright owners. Ownership is usually more easily established than copying. A party may prove ownership by demonstrating that he or she is the author of the work or that the copyright in the work has been transferred to him or her. A certificate of copyright registration (made before or within five years of first publication of the work) will establish *prima facie* evidence in court of the validity of the copyright and of the facts stated in the certificate, including identity of the author or copyright owner. Ownership issues often arise in the context of work made for hire disputes, particularly when a party claims he or she is not an

employee and thus a work cannot be owned by an employer or when a party claims there was no written agreement relating to the status of a specially commissioned work and thus he or she has retained copyright ownership.

If the copyright has been transferred to another, that party is now the owner of the transferred rights and has the right to protect the work by an infringement action. For example, if a copyright author has transferred (in writing) exclusive rights to perform a work to another and the work is infringed by impermissible performance, the transferee's rights have been infringed. If there has been unauthorized reproduction rather than unauthorized performance, the original copyright author's rights have been infringed, and he or she may initiate an infringement action. Courts will insist the plaintiff prove the transfer, and show how the plaintiff acquired rights. Additionally, the plaintiff must have been the owner at the time his or her rights were infringed. If a copyright owner has transferred a work to another and yet retains some connection with the work, for example, by receiving periodic royalty payments, the owner as well as the transferee's rights have been infringed because both are affected by an infringement that would reduce the value of the work; therefore, both have standing to initiate an infringement suit.

Upon introduction of the registration (or transfer of copyright) into evidence, the court will presume that the work is protected under copyright law (although that presumption can be rebutted or defeated by the defendant) and that the plaintiff has ownership rights in the work such that he or she is the proper party to bring the infringement action.

Copying

Introduction. Proving copying generally requires that the plaintiff in an infringement action show that there is substantial similarity between his or her work and that of the defendant and that the defendant had access to the copyrighted work. The infringing work must derive from the copyrighted work. An independently created work cannot infringe even if it is identical to the copyrighted work.

Innocent Infringement Is Not a Defense.   Infringement does not require an intent to infringe; even **innocent infringement** gives rise to liability. For example, assume *A* is given a book that *B* claims *B* wrote. The book was actually the creation of *C*. If *A* copies the book, *A* has infringed *C*'s copyright even though *A* did not intend to infringe and did not know *C* had any copyright interest in the book. Thus, neither intent to infringe nor knowledge of copyright is required for infringement to occur, although innocence may have a bearing on the amount of damages for which a defendant is liable. Moreover, merely attributing the material copied to the owner by stating that copies of chapters of a text are the product of their author will not protect an infringer. Attribution may reduce damages, but a party cannot escape liability for infringement by merely acknowledging the work is owned by another.

Additionally, infringement can be "subconscious," as was the case in *Bright Tunes Music Corp. v. Harrisongs Music, Ltd.*, 420 F. Supp. 177 (S.D.N.Y. 1976), *aff'd*, 722 F.2d 988 (2d Cir. 1983), in which a court held George Harrison's song "My Sweet Lord" infringed the song "He's So Fine" recorded by The Chiffons. In that case, the court held that Harrison did not deliberately plagiarize the earlier song but that he subconsciously recollected the copyrighted song when he composed "My Sweet Lord." On appeal, the Second Circuit reaffirmed that intent to infringe is not essential and that to allow a defense of innocent infringement would undermine the protections Congress intended copyright owners to possess.

Access.   **Access** is generally interpreted to mean that a party had the opportunity to perceive or review a work, either directly or indirectly. Access can be inferred if the copyrighted work has been widely disseminated. Moreover, if the two works are identical or nearly so, it may be presumed that the defendant had access to the plaintiff's work. Generally, the greater the similarity between two works, the less access must be shown. Conversely, if the works are entirely dissimilar, no amount of access will result in a finding of copying.

In some cases, where there has been no evidence of access, courts have nevertheless found infringement if the two works are strikingly similar. Access may be inferred where the works are so similar that the possibility of independent creation or coincidental creation is precluded.

Access has been shown where copies of the plaintiff's work have been sent to the defendant, where the defendant has visited the plaintiff's place of business, where the plaintiff's works have been displayed at events attended by the defendant, and where access occurred through a third party, such as a manufacturer, connected to both the plaintiff and the defendant.

Substantial Similarity of Works.   Because it is seldom possible to prove copying by direct evidence (such as testimony from a witness who saw the defendant copy from the plaintiff's book), copying is usually proven through circumstantial evidence. Thus, infringement is usually shown by demonstrating that the allegedly infringing work is substantially similar to the copyrighted work. In some instances, map makers and directory authors purposely include fictitious entries in their works; when the same erroneous matter is found in a defendant's work, copying is generally found to exist.

The test used, often referred to as the ordinary observer test, focuses on whether the accused work is so similar to the copyrighted work that an ordinary reasonable person or lay observer would recognize that the copyrighted work was appropriated by the defendant.

The lay observer test has been refined to take into account the intended market for the works.

Thus, where infringement of a video game was alleged, and the target market was young men, a court found that the intended purchasers (17½-year-old males) were a knowledgeable and discerning group and would not regard the works as substantially similar. *Data East USA, Inc. v. Epyx, Inc.*, 862 F.2d 204 (9th Cir. 1988). Another refinement of the lay observer test occurs when the works are complex, such as computer programs. In such cases, expert testimony is often used to prove or disprove substantial similarity inasmuch as computer programs are highly technical and unfamiliar to most of the general public.

Many courts use a two-step analysis to determine if infringement has occurred. The first step analyzes whether there has been copying. Once copying has been established, the second step requires that a determination be made whether the copying constitutes an impermissible appropriation, namely, whether the copying of the protected material was so extensive that it rendered the offending and copyrighted works substantially similar. In the first stage, some courts compare the works element by element and create lists of similarities and dissimilarities, in essence, "dissecting" the works. Other courts criticize dissection and prefer to focus on the overall similarities or the "total concept and feel" of the works, especially when only some of the work is protectable. For example, *Boisson v. Banian, Ltd.*, 273 F.3d 262 (2d Cir. 2001), a case involving infringement of quilt patterns, some of which included nonprotectable elements such as alphabet letters, the court relied on the "more discerning observer" test and stated that determining substantial similarity required examination of the total concept and feel of the two works, as instructed by common sense.

Courts have continually struggled in assessing "substantial similarity." In *Nichols v. Universal Pictures Corp.*, 45 F.2d 119 (2d Cir. 1930), Judge Learned Hand commented that copyright protection cannot be limited literally to the text; otherwise a plagiarist would be able to make immaterial variations with impunity. Thus, a party need not copy the entire work to be an infringer.

When only a part of a work is taken, such as one scene from a play, Judge Hand stated that the question is whether the part taken is substantial. Even more difficult questions, however, arise when the plagiarist does not copy a block of material but rather abstracts the whole work. In these two instances (**literal copying** of some of a work and nonliteral copying of an entire work), Judge Hand remarked that "Nobody has ever been able to fix that boundary [of protection], and nobody ever can." *Id*. at 121.

If part of a work is copied or taken, courts usually examine not only the quantity of the work taken but also its characteristics and the nature of the work itself. Infringement has been found even if language is not identical when recognizable paraphrases have been taken. There is no precise answer to the question "how much is too much?" In one case, the taking of fragments from three sentences in a book of more than 200 pages was found to be infringement. Moreover, if the part taken is the "heart" of the material, there may be an infringement. Thus, a love story about lovers from different economic classes with a tragic ending might not infringe the book *Love Story*; however, using the well-known line, "Love means never having to say you're sorry," might well constitute an infringement because the statement is a substantial portion of or the "heart" of the work copied.

Once copying is shown, examination must focus on whether the elements taken were protected by copyright. It is permissible to take ideas but impermissible to appropriate expression of those ideas. Works in the public domain may be examined, and the defendant may attempt to prove that both the plaintiff's work and the defendant's work share elements and similarities with works in the public domain. If all similarities arise from use of common ideas or works in the public domain, there can be no substantial similarity and no infringement.

Some courts use a test known as the "abstraction-filtration-comparison" test to separate protectable expression from unprotectable ideas in copyright infringement cases. First, a court dissects the allegedly infringing work and isolates each level of abstraction in it. Second, unprotectable elements, such as ideas, processes, facts, and public domain information, are filtered out. Third, a comparison is made of the remaining protectable elements to determine if the second work misappropriates substantial elements of the first. *Gates Rubber Co. v. Bando Chem. Indus., Ltd.,* 9 F.3d 823 (10th Cir. 1993). The abstraction-filtration-comparison test is used most frequently in determining whether infringement of computer programs has occurred and is discussed further in chapter 15. See Exhibit 14–1 for copyright infringement myths.

Some of the newer issues involving copyright infringement relate to the Internet. For example, in March 2007, entertainment giant Viacom sued Google's YouTube for copyright infringement, alleging that the video Web site does little or nothing to prevent users from posting copyrighted videos on its site. Viacom has asked for $1 billion in damages, noting that clips from popular shows such as *South Park* are routinely posted on YouTube, which in the past has removed offending clips upon a "takedown" request by copyright owners. Thus, YouTube alleges that because it complies with the DMCA's takedown provisions, it is shielded from liability. Most experts believe that digital infringement should be treated no differently from conventional infringement and that the likely resolution is that the two companies will enter into an arrangement whereby YouTube licenses the right to show Viacom's content. In the interim, Google has

EXHIBIT 14–1
Copyright
Infringement
Myths

There are a number of myths or misconceptions regarding copyright infringement. Some of the more common myths include the following:

- **I can use anything without a copyright notice.** False. Placing a copyright notice on a work is optional since March 1, 1989, and works are protected under copyright law from the time of their creation in a fixed form.
- **If I give credit or attribution to another, there is no infringement.** False. While indicating that material is the product of another may show innocent infringement and help to reduce damages, infringement is not cured by reciting that another is actually the author of a work.
- **I'm only using a little bit, so there can be no infringement.** False. Copyright infringement does not depend on how much is taken. This myth is similar to a common misunderstanding that a musician can use four bars of another's song before infringement will be found. If the amount taken is qualitatively significant, infringement will exist. In one case, the taking of two bars of music was held to be an infringement.
- **If I don't charge for what I took, there can be no infringement.** False. Although a noncommercial use of a work may affect the damages awarded in an infringement case, unauthorized taking constitutes infringement whether or not it is for profit-making purposes.
- **I'm only paraphrasing, so there can be no infringement.** False. Infringement is not limited to exact copying. If two works are substantially similar, copying may be shown.
- **I mailed it to myself and thus copyrighted the work.** False. For some reason, a myth persists that if one mails a copy of one's work to oneself, the work is now protected by copyright. The mailing of the work has no relationship to copyright protection. The work is protected from the time it is created in a fixed form.

unveiled a filtering system that gives the owners of copyrighted materials the option of promoting or blocking their content on the YouTube site.

CONTRIBUTORY INFRINGEMENT AND VICARIOUS INFRINGEMENT

Courts have held persons and companies liable for the infringing acts of others. If a person, with knowledge of an infringing activity, induces, causes, or contributes to infringing conduct, he or she will be liable for infringement as a contributory infringer. **Contributory infringement** occurs when photo shops reproduce or duplicate photographs bearing a copyright notice, when copy shops reproduce or allow customers to photocopy books and other protected materials, when operators of flea markets or swap meets allow pirated works to be sold, or when an individual sells specially formatted blank cassettes and tape duplicating equipment to pirates with knowledge they are engaging in acts of infringement.

Generally, contributory infringement requires either personal conduct that furthers the infringement or contribution of goods or machinery that provide the means of infringement. If the equipment supplied is capable of significant noninfringing uses, no contributory infringement will be found.

In the famous case *Sony Corp. of America v. Universal City Studios Inc.*, 464 U.S. 417 (1984), the Supreme Court was called upon to determine whether home videotaping of copyrighted works for later private viewing (e.g., taping the movie *Shakespeare in Love* shown on television so one can watch it at a more convenient time, commonly referred to as "time-shifting") constituted infringement and whether the defendant Sony was contributorily liable for making the videocassette recorders used to make the allegedly infringing copies. The Court held that time-shifting did not constitute infringement and that the sale of copying equipment, like the sale of other articles of commerce, does not consti-

tute contributory infringement if the product is widely used for legitimate and unobjectionable purposes. Sony was held not liable for contributory infringement. By contrast, in *Elektra Records Co. v. Gem Electric Distributors, Inc.*, 360 F. Supp. 821 (E.D.N.Y. 1973), the defendant stores sold blank tapes and for a fee loaned customers prerecorded tapes containing copyrighted songs. Customers would then duplicate the entire tapes on the defendants' Make-A-Tape systems at the stores. The defendants were held liable for contributory infringement because they supplied all means necessary to infringe. Moreover, the defendants had a financial interest in the infringement.

Vicarious infringement occurs when one party is responsible for infringement conducted by another when the two parties share a special relationship, such as that of employer-employee. One who is in a position to control the use of copyrighted works by others and has a financial interest in exploitation of the copyrighted works will be liable for vicarious infringement, even if he or she had no knowledge the infringement was occurring. For example, universities may be held liable for the infringing activities of teachers who photocopy copyrighted materials for distribution to students. The universities are in a position to control and direct the activities of teachers and should implement policies refusing photocopying unless the teachers obtain copyright releases or permission forms from the authors. Similarly, the operator of a swap meet was held vicariously liable for the sale of counterfeit recordings by a vendor who rented space from the operator on the basis that the operator had the right and ability to supervise the direct infringer and derived a financial benefit from the infringer's activities. *Fonovisa, Inc. v. Cherry Auction, Inc.*, 76 F.3d 259 (9th Cir. 1996).

DEFENSES TO INFRINGEMENT

There are a variety of defenses a defendant charged with copyright infringement may assert. As stated, however, the infringer's intent is not relevant, and infringement can be found whether or not the defendant intended to infringe copyrighted works. Intent, however, may be relevant in assessing damages.

Fair Use

Section 107 of the Copyright Act provides that the fair use of a copyrighted work for purposes such as criticism, comment, news reporting, teaching, scholarship, or research is not an infringement. Fair use is thus a privilege to use copyrighted material without permission of the copyright owner. The rationale for allowing certain uses of copyrighted material is to benefit the public and promote the arts and sciences. The fair use defense is the most important defense to an allegation of copyright infringement.

The Copyright Office has given examples of activities that courts have regarded as fair use, including the following:

- quoting excerpts from copyrighted materials in a review or criticism of the work
- quotation of short passages in scholarly or technical works for illustration or clarification of the author's observations
- use in a parody of some of the parodied work
- reproduction of a small portion of a work by a teacher to illustrate a lesson
- a summary of an address or article, with brief quotations, in a news report

Thus, reviewers critiquing a song may quote lyrics from it, and parodies may be made of other works.

The act identifies (and courts consider) four factors in determining whether a use is fair and is thus permissible:

1. the purpose and character of the use, including whether such use is of a commercial nature or whether it is a nonprofit educational use
2. the nature of the copyrighted work

3. the amount and substantiality of the portion used in relation to the copyrighted work as a whole
4. the effect of the use upon the potential market for or value of the copyrighted work

None of the four factors identified in section 107 is meant to be conclusive. Courts will examine each factor and weigh all considerations in determining whether a use is a permissible fair use or an infringing use. No one test is applied, and each case is determined on its own merits.

The Purpose and Character of the Use. One factor considered by courts focuses on the purpose for which reproduction, adaptation, distribution, performance, or display of a copyrighted work is undertaken and the use that is made of it. Generally, use for comment, criticism, and so forth is acceptable because it benefits the public and advances the public good; however, if a for-profit motive underlies any of these purposes, a different conclusion may be reached. Although commercial use will not automatically defeat a defense of fair use, use of another's work for a commercial purpose is less likely to be permitted than use for a noncommercial purpose. According to *Harper & Row Publishers, Inc. v. Nation Enterprises*, 417 U.S. 539 (1985), every commercial use is presumptively an unfair exploitation of the copyright owner's rights. Thus, commercial use tends to weigh against a finding of fair use.

Courts also examine whether the defendant's use adds something new with a new purpose or different character. Addition of new material or a productive use benefits the public. Failure to transform a work in any way weighs against a finding of fair use.

Finally, a use that is merely incidental is more likely to be determined to be a fair use. For example, if a CNN news reporter stands in front of a copyrighted painting while reporting on theft of works of art, such a use is incidental and may support a finding of fair use, even though the use is commercial and it violates the copyright owner's right to display the work.

The Nature of the Copyrighted Work.   Courts consider the degree of creativity in the copyrighted work in determining whether a use is fair. Generally, the more creative the work, the more protection it is afforded. Conversely, the more informational or factual the work, the less protection it receives. Thus, the fact that a second work is factual or informational in nature tends to support a finding of fair use. Once again, use and dissemination of factual and informational material tends to advance research and scholarship and is thus encouraged.

Whether the work is published or unpublished is important. Unauthorized use of an owner's work prior to publication severely affects the owner's right to determine the timing of entry into the market and be the first "on the scene." Thus, works that are unpublished generally receive more protection than those that have been published. Nevertheless, 17 U.S.C. § 107 specifically provides that the fact that a work is unpublished shall not itself bar a finding of fair use.

Amount and Substantiality of the Portion Used.   In determining whether use of another's copyrighted work is fair, courts consider the quantitative as well as the qualitative portion of the work that is reproduced. Generally, it is not a fair use to reproduce an entire work. When less than all of a work is reproduced, whether the use is fair depends on the importance of the portion used, namely, whether the reproduced portion is the essence or "heart" of the copyright owner's work. Even when the amount taken is quantitatively small, the use may still be impermissible if what is taken is the central or pivotal portion of the work. For example, in *Harper & Row,* although the portion taken was small (only about 300 words out of 200,000 words), the verbatim copying was the essence of the copyrighted work. This amount was considered excessive.

The Effect of the Use on the Market for the Copyrighted Work.   Most courts agree that the effect of the defendant's use on the potential market for the copyright owner's work is the most important of the four factors considered in determining whether a use of another's work is a permissible fair use. If the defendant's use causes or will cause a loss of revenue to the copyright owner, such argues against a finding of fair use. If the work will supplant the market for the copyright owner's work or diminish the potential market, the use is likely not a fair one.

Overview of Fair Use Cases.   A brief review of some fair use cases will help demonstrate the balancing of the fair use factors engaged in by courts.

- *Sony Corp. of America v. Universal City Studios, Inc.,* 464 U.S. 417 (1984). In this case, Universal alleged that use of VCRs sold by the defendants violated the 1976 Copyright Act and that sale of the VCR machines constituted contributory infringement. The Court focused on the fourth factor of the fair use doctrine (the effect of the use on the potential market for the copyrighted work). The Court held that the practice of using a VCR to record a program for later private viewing ("time-shifting") was a fair use because it was noncommercial, and there was little likelihood of harm to the potential market for the copyrighted works. Moreover, the VCRs had substantial noninfringing uses.
- *Harper & Row Publishers, Inc. v. Nation Enterprises,* 471 U.S. 539 (1985). In this case, former President Ford granted Harper & Row exclusive rights to publish his memoirs and to license prepublication serialization of those memoirs. *Time* magazine then purchased

from Harper & Row the right to publish certain excerpts from the book before its publication. Before *Time* could publish the excerpts, someone provided a copy of the manuscript to *Nation* magazine, which then published an article about the forthcoming book and included approximately 300 words of direct quotes from the book. Because it had been "scooped," *Time* abandoned its plans to publish excerpts from the book and refused to pay the balance of its license fee to Harper & Row. Harper & Row sued *Nation* for copyright infringement. The Court held that the use was not a fair one: The publication in *Nation* was commercial in nature; the amount copied, though small quantitatively, captured the "heart" of the book; and the publication had an adverse effect on the potential market for the book.

• *Basic Books, Inc. v. Kinko's Graphics Corp.,* 758 F. Supp. 1525 (S.D.N.Y. 1991). For many years, Kinko's, a copy shop, had prepared course packets consisting of photocopies of assigned reading for college students. Publishing houses sued Kinko's, alleging that Kinko's practice of copying portions of books without permission and without payment violated the publishers' copyrights. The court found that Kinko's use was not fair use. Although the students' use of the materials was educational, Kinko's purpose in copying them was commercial. The amount and substantiality of the portions copied also weighed against a finding of fair use, and the potential market for the copyrighted materials was harmed in that Kinko's offered the materials at a lower cost and thus students refrained from buying the books.

• *Consumers Union of United States, Inc. v. General Signal Corp.,* 724 F.2d 1044 (2d Cir. 1983). In *Consumers Union,* the defendant's commercials included excerpts from the magazine *Consumer Reports,* which favorably rated the defendant's product. The court held the use was fair and concluded that the purpose of the use was to report factual information and that the commercials made relatively insignificant use of the work. Use of reviews containing significant original analysis and conclusions from the first work rather than primarily factual material, however, might not be a fair use.

• *American Geophysical Union v. Texaco, Inc.,* 60 F.3d 913 (2d Cir. 1994). In this case, publishers of several scientific journals brought suit against Texaco, alleging that the company's practice of copying articles from journals and then routing or distributing the articles to its more than 400 researchers was infringement. The researchers placed copies of the articles in their files for later use and reference. The publishers alleged the practice infringed their rights in the articles. The court held that Texaco's copying was not a fair use. Although the for-profit motive of Texaco was relevant, the court stated the focus should be on the use of the material itself rather than the user. The fact that the materials were used for an archival purpose—they were merely placed in files and not transformed in any way— weighed against a finding of fair use. On the second factor (the nature of the work), the court found the articles were scientific and factual, and this weighed in favor of Texaco. The third factor (amount of work copied) weighed against Texaco because entire separately copyrighted articles were copied. In regard to the last factor (effect of the copying on the potential market for the copyrighted materials), the court found against Texaco because the publishers lost subscription revenue and because Texaco could have entered into a license with the Copyright Clearance Center (CCC), a central clearinghouse established by publishers at the suggestion of Congress to license the copying of materials, much like ASCAP and BMI license the performance of music. By bypassing CCC, Texaco's copying caused a loss of licensing revenue to the publishers. Texaco appealed to the United States Supreme Court, which granted *certiorari;* however, before the Court heard the case, the parties entered into a settlement with Texaco agreeing to pay more than $1 million and an additional retroactive license fee to CCC. Texaco also agreed to enter into a five-year licensing arrangement with CCC.

The *Texaco* case has caused much consternation inasmuch as it has been common practice for many companies to purchase only a limited number of subscriptions to journals and then copy articles as needed for distribution to employees. Without a ruling by the Supreme Court, users are left with the Second Circuit's holding that the practice is infringement. Many issues remain unresolved, including whether there is a difference between the archiving of articles by researchers funded by government grants and archiving by those funded by private company grants, and what result should be reached when copying is done by an institution that serves both the commercial sector and the educational sector. The safest course appears to be to enter into private licensing arrangements with the publishers or to obtain a license through CCC. The CCC also offers guidelines for creating copyright compli-ance policies. Call (978) 750-8400 or access CCC's Web site at http://www.copyright.com.

Parody

Parodies of works of literature, art, and music are viewed as a productive form of social commentary and criticism. Because copyright owners are highly unlikely to grant permission to another to parody their work, parodists often rely on the fair use defense when infringement is alleged by the owner of the parodied copyrighted work. Generally, no more than is necessary to accomplish the parody may be taken from the original work. The parodist's work must "conjure up" the copyright owner's work and link the parody with that of the original to make social comment or criticism. If the parodist merely copies a work to make social comment on some other topic, fair use is not available.

In *Campbell v. Acuff-Rose Music, Inc.,* 510 U.S. 569 (1994), Acuff-Rose, a music company, brought suit against the rap group 2 Live Crew claiming that the group's rap version of the song "Pretty Woman" infringed its copyright in the famous Roy Orbison song, "Oh, Pretty Woman." The Supreme Court held the parody was a fair use. In regard to the first fair use factor, the Court held that although the use was commercial, the new work added something new with a new expression and meaning. The second factor (the nature of the copyrighted work) was held to be of little use in the context of a parody because a parody, by definition, almost always copies known works such as the Orbison song. As for the amount and substantiality of the work copied, the Court stated that even if 2 Live Crew copied the "heart" of the Orbison song, it is the heart that most readily conjures up the original for the parody. Regarding the fourth factor, there was no evidence that the 2 Live Crew song had any impact on the market for nonparody or nonrap versions of the original Orbison song. Persons interested in the original song were unlikely to purchase the parody version in its place.

Conversely, in *Dr. Seuss Enterprises, L.P. v. Penguin Books USA, Inc.,* 109 F.3d 1394 (9th Cir, 1997), the court held that a poetic account of the O. J. Simpson double murder trial presented in the style of the famous *Cat in the Hat* rhyming book was not protected parody inasmuch as it did not target or parody that book itself but merely copied its general style to make comments regarding society as a whole. Thus, a parody must comment in some way on the original material in order to satisfy the fair use requirement of criticism.

Reproduction of Copyrighted Works by Librarians and Educators

Pursuant to Section 108 of the Copyright Act, libraries can reproduce a work for distribution and for preservation purposes. Similarly, libraries are protected from liability for infringement for unpermitted photocopying by their patrons as long as a notice is displayed on the photocopy equipment that the making of copies may be subject to copyright law.

In 1975, Congress urged educators and publishers to meet to reach an agreement regarding permissible educational uses of copyrighted material. The result was the "Agreement on Guidelines for Classroom Copying in Not-for-Profit Educational Institutions with Respect to Books and Periodicals." These guidelines were made part of the legislative history of the 1976 act. Some of the more notable provisions of the guidelines follow.

- Single copies of copyrighted materials (such as chapters from books, short stories, charts, or articles from a journal) may be made by teachers for scholarly research or use in teaching.
- Multiple copies (not to exceed more than one copy per pupil in a course) may be made if the copying meets specified tests for brevity (the guidelines include stated criteria for the amount of work

that may be copied, for example, a poem may be copied if it is fewer than 250 words) and spontaneity (the decision to use the material is made so close to the time the material is needed that it would be unreasonable to expect a reply to a request to the author to use the material); each copy includes a copyright notice; and the cumulative effect of the copying is limited (e.g., no more than nine instances of multiple copying for one course during one class term can be made).

Similarly, music teachers and publishers met and developed "Guidelines for Educational Use of Music" to state the standards of educational fair use of music. The guidelines for books and for music are available as Circular 21 from the Copyright Office (http://www.copyright.gov).

Other Defenses to Infringement

Although fair use is one of the most widely asserted defenses in actions for infringement, a number of other defenses are also available.

Invalidity of Copyright or Fraud. A defendant may assert that the material sought to be protected by the plaintiff is uncopyrightable. Even if a certificate of copyright registration has been issued, the defendant may rebut the presumption of validity arising from registration and prove that the work lacks sufficient originality to be protectable and that the Copyright Office erroneously registered the work. Thus, the defendant may assert that the works are useful articles, public domain matter, common facts not subject to copyright protection, or scenes a faire (common or stock themes) that flow naturally from a premise or setting and are thus unprotectable. Moreover, works are not protected merely because they result from hard work. To be protectable, works must contain copyrightable expression. Thus, in *Feist Publications, Inc. v. Rural Telephone Service Co.,*

499 U.S. 340 (1991), the Supreme Court held that although a telephone company had invested a great deal of hard work or "sweat of the brow" into compiling its telephone directory, the directory was unprotectable because it was merely factual. A similar result was reached in 1998 when the Second Circuit held that West Publishing Company's addition of certain features, such as attorney information, parallel citations, and star pagination, to cases in the public domain did not result in original copyrightable work entitled to protection. *Matthew Bender & Co. v. West Publ'g Co.*, 158 F.3d 674 (2d Cir. 1998). A defendant may also show that the plaintiff intentionally failed to disclose certain facts to the Copyright Office (such as that the plaintiff's work was a derivative work or a useful article), thus rendering the registration invalid.

Estoppel.   A copyright owner who knows of an infringing use and acquiesces in it may be estopped or precluded from later claiming the use is an infringement, particularly when the defendant has expended sums in marketing the work.

Misuse or Unclean Hands.   A plaintiff may be precluded from obtaining relief in an infringement action if it is guilty of inequitable conduct, unclean hands, or **misuse** of its copyright. For example, requiring a defendant who licenses one copyrighted work to license another or coupling a copyright license with a restrictive covenant precluding a party from developing its own original copyrighted works may be such misuse as to preclude the licensor from later asserting infringement of copyright (at least until the misuse is cured).

Improper Copyright Notice.   Section 406 of the Copyright Act provides a complete defense to infringement if the alleged infringer is misled by a pre-Berne copyright notice (meaning, be-fore March 1, 1989) that misidentifies the copyright owner. In one case, the plaintiff created a video and licensed it to another, the licensee, for use in schools. The video contained a copyright notice that improperly identified the licensee as the copyright owner (rather than the plaintiff, the true owner). The licensee sold copies of the video to the defendant. The defendant successfully defended the action on the basis that the copyright notice identified the licensee as the owner and that he therefore had the right to assume that such party could sell the video to him. The court agreed and found no infringement by the defendant.

Statute of Limitations and Laches.   Section 507(b) of the Copyright Act provides a three-year statute of limitations on civil copyright infringement actions. The time period may be tolled or suspended if the defendant has fraudulently concealed his or her copyright infringement from the plaintiff such that the plaintiff did not know to bring an action. The three-year period is measured from the time the copyright owner knows of the violation or is chargeable with such knowledge. If the infringement is continuing in nature, the plaintiff may obtain relief for any infringing activity that occurred within the three-year limitation period.

Even if the plaintiff is within the three-year statute of limitations, the defendant may assert a defense of laches, namely, that the plaintiff unjustifiably delayed in bringing suit and this delay caused prejudice to the defendant. Laches typically does not excuse infringement but may preclude a plaintiff from obtaining injunctive relief.

De Minimis Defense.   Another defense that may be successfully asserted is that what was taken was so small that its use should be excused. Called the **de minimis defense** (based on the Latin maxim "de minimis non curat lex," meaning "the law does not concern itself with trifles"), it makes certain infringements nonactionable, generally because what is taken falls below the quantitative threshold of substantial similarity to the copyrighted work. For example, the movie *Seven* displayed 10 copyrighted photographs for a few seconds. The court held that because the photographs appeared fleetingly, were severely out of focus, and virtually unidentifiable, the use of those photographs was de minimis. *Sandoval v. New Line Cinema Corp.*, 147 F.3d 215 (2d Cir. 1998).

INFRINGEMENT ACTIONS

Generally, a party who believes its copyrighted work has been infringed will send a cease and desist letter to the other party (much like the cease and desist letter used in trademark infringement matters shown in chapter 6, Exhibit 6–4). If the parties cannot resolve their dispute amicably, they may proceed to arbitration or litigation.

The federal courts have exclusive jurisdiction over copyright infringement cases and any cases arising under the Copyright Act. Thus, infringement cases can be brought only in federal district courts and not in state courts. Some cases, however, might be heard in state court because they do not "arise under" the Copyright Act. For example, if *A* agrees to pay a license fee to *B* for use of *B's* copyrighted song but fails to make the required payments, the matter may be heard in state court as a straightforward breach of contract matter.

Like any civil action, a copyright infringement proceeding is initiated by the filing of a complaint by the plaintiff. The clerk of the court must report the action to the Register of Copyrights. The defendant typically answers the complaint and asserts various defenses or challenges to the complaint. If the defendant has claims against the plaintiff relating to the matter at issue, they must be made in the same action. This promotes judicial economy because the court can resolve all differences between the parties at the same time.

The action is governed by the Federal Rules of Civil Procedure. The plaintiff has the burden of proving all elements of an infringement action: ownership of copyright; copyrightable subject matter; and unauthorized use, copying, reproduction, adaptation, performance, or display of material expression by the defendant. Discovery will be scheduled by the court, and the parties may take depositions, propound interrogatories to each other, and request that various documents and other materials be produced. If settlement is not reached, the matter will proceed to trial. Either party may demand a jury trial. Expert witnesses may testify. Ultimately, the fact finder (either the jury or the judge) will render a decision. Within one month after any final judgment, the clerk of the court must notify the Register of Copyrights of the judgment or order. An appeal may be filed in the appropriate U.S. Court of Appeals by the losing party if a prejudicial error of law occurred at the trial. Further review may be sought in the U.S. Supreme Court, although it has discretion to deny certiorari and refuse to hear the case. See Exhibit 14–2 for some highlights of recent entertainment-related infringement issues.

As is the case for trademarks and patents (see chapters 6 and 20, respectively), as an alternative to suing for copyright infringement in court, a party whose copyrighted work has been infringed may bring a Section 337 proceeding before the International Trade Commission to block infringing goods from entering the United States. If section 337 has been violated (determined after an investigation and a hearing), the ITC may issue an exclusion order barring the infringing products from entry into the United States or may issue a cease and desist order. Although money damages are not available, the proceedings are less expensive and far more expeditious than court proceedings.

ETHICS EDGE: **Maintaining Your Calendar**

Like all litigation matters, copyright infringement litigation requires careful docketing and calendaring of dates. Use your office's computerized calendar to maintain dates for discovery, court appearances, and other critical deadlines. Use a secondary system (e.g., Microsoft Outlook or a conventional calendar) as a backup. Use colored markers or sticky flags to provide visual cues of critical dates. For example, use red markers or flags for final action dates, yellow markers or flags for interim dates, and so forth. Use http://www.timeanddate.com to help calculate due dates.

EXHIBIT 14–2
That's Entertainment!

Some of the more interesting infringement cases often arise in the entertainment industry. Consider the following show business battles:

- In 2005 a federal court ruled that the best-selling book *The Da Vinci Code* did not infringe the copyrights of a book published by another author. The court noted that although both books were mystery thrillers, the details in each book were quite different from each other and that "ideas and general literary themes themselves are unprotectable" under copyright law.
- The much-awaited blockbuster "Spider-Man 3" was available on the streets of Beijing prior to its 2007 official studio release.
- After an Apple iTunes commercial aired featuring a child singing along to "Lose Yourself," rapper Eminem's Oscar-winning song, Eminem immediately sued for copyright infringement. The parties later reached an undisclosed financial settlement.
- When an author claimed that Twentieth Century Fox's 2005 film "Kingdom of God" infringed his book "Warriors of God," a spokesman for Fox responded, "You cannot copyright the Crusades."
- The following works "hit" the Internet prior to their official release dates:
  - U2's album "How to Dismantle an Atomic Bomb";
  - "Star Wars" Episode III–Revenge of the Sith" (which was posted to BitTorrent, a file-sharing network); and
  - Mel Gibson's movie "Passion of the Christ" (which became the most-pirated movie on Internet file-sharing networks in April 2004, prior to its release in DVD versions).

Remedies for Infringement

Plaintiffs in infringement actions may seek both monetary and nonmonetary relief. In some instances, the plaintiff may be more interested in ensuring the infringing activity ceases than in recovering damages. Courts can use a variety of remedies to ensure the copyright owner is adequately protected:

- **Injunctive relief.** Section 502 of the Copyright Act provides that a court may grant both temporary and final injunctions to prevent or restrain infringing activities. To secure an injunction before trial, generally a plaintiff must prove that it is likely to succeed on the merits of its case, that it will suffer irreparable injury unless injunctive relief is ordered, that the threatened injury to it outweighs possible damage to the defendant, and that monetary damages will not provide sufficient relief. If a plaintiff has delayed in seeking injunctive relief, such tends to show that there is no irreparable harm occurring and injunctive relief may be denied.

- **Impoundment.** Courts can order the **impoundment** of infringing copies during the pendency of an infringement action and may order their destruction as part of a final judgment. The plaintiff usually must post a bond so that if no infringement is found, the defendant is recompensed for the pre-trial seizure of the goods.

- **Compensatory damages and profits.** Plaintiffs may recover **compensatory damages**—the actual damages suffered as a result of the infringement—and any additional profits received by the defendant arising out of the infringing activities. Actual damages should compensate the plaintiff for lost sales and revenues. To recover the infringer's profits, the plaintiff must present proof of the infringer's gross revenue, and the infringer may then prove deductible expenses and profits attributable to factors other than the infringing work. Even indirect profits may be recovered. For example, in one case, a plaintiff recovered a portion of the defendant's hotel and gambling revenue on the basis that the performance of an infringing show in the hotel drew additional business to the hotel and casino.

- **Statutory damages.** In lieu of actual damages, if the copyright owner has secured registration within three months after publication or, for unpublished works, before the defendant's infringement, a plaintiff may elect an award of **statutory damages** under section 504(c) of the act. The statutory damages are set by the judge or jury in their discretion in a sum of not less than $750 and not more than $30,000 for infringement of one work (all the parts of a compilation or derivative work are viewed as one work). If willful infringement is shown, statutory damages may be awarded in an amount not exceeding $150,000. If the court finds that infringement was innocent (the infringer was not aware his or her acts were infringing and had no reason to know such), the court can reduce statutory damages to an amount not lower than $200. The election to seek statutory damages rather than actual damages and profits can be made at any time prior to entry of final judgment and is usually made in cases in which the plaintiff has difficulty proving actual damages. In one case, it was held that each unauthorized airing of a television series episode by a different station controlled by the defendant was a separate act of infringement. Because the defendant's acts were willful, damages were fixed at just over $70,000 per act multiplied by 440 separate airings, for a total damage award to the copyright owner of $31.7 million (plus costs and attorneys' fees). This award was made by a jury in April 1999 and is believed to be the second-highest ever award of statutory damages. *Columbia Pictures Television v. Krypton Broad. of Birmingham, Inc.*, 259 F.3d 1186 (9th Cir. 2001). The Supreme Court has held that under the Seventh Amendment, if a party demands, there is a right to a jury trial on all issues pertinent to an award of statutory damages, including the amount itself. *Feltner v. Columbia Pictures Television, Inc.*, 523 U.S. 340 (1998).

- **Costs and attorneys' fees.** If registration has been secured within three months after publication of a work (or, for un-published works, before the defendant's infringement), a court may award re-asonable attorneys' fees to the plaintiff. The plaintiff may also recover costs (e.g., expert witness fees, court filing fees, photocopy charges). If the defendant prevails, reasonable attorneys' fees and costs may be awarded to him or her in the discretion of the court.

- **Criminal sanctions.** Under the No Electronic Theft Act (the NET Act) signed into law in late 1997 (17 U.S.C. § 506 and 18 U.S.C. § 2319), various criminal penalties can be imposed (with jail terms up to five years) for infringers who reproduce or distribute by electronic means copyrighted works of a certain value (generally, over $1,000). Subsequent offenses can result in jail terms of up to 10 years. Fines up to $250,000 can also be imposed under the NET Act. The NET Act strengthens prior criminal provisions to make serious copyright piracy subject to criminal penalties even if there is no profit motive. Its primary purpose was to close the "LaMacchia Loophole," named for David LaMacchia, a student at MIT who set up an electronic bulletin board from which users downloaded approximately $1 million of free software. A copyright piracy case against LaMacchia was dismissed because LaMacchia had received no monetary compensation for the software he distributed. The NET Act also extended the statute of limitations in which criminal action may be brought from three years to five years. The Register of Copyrights testified before Congress in support of enhancing criminal penalties for copyright violations, stating that advances in technology increased the potential for copyright piracy because it is easy and inexpensive to make and distribute pirated copies without a major investment in equipment and facilities. Thus, more serious penalties were needed to deter infringers. Additionally, as discussed in chapter 15, those who circumvent measures designed to protect certain works (e.g., by thwarting computer encryption programs) may be subject to both civil and criminal penalties.

- **Fines.** A fine up to $2,500 may be imposed when a copyright notice is fraudulently used or removed. Making a knowingly false statement of a material fact in a copyright application may subject a person to a fine up to $2,500.

Trivia

- In September 2000, a district court allowed presidential candidate Ralph Nader to continue to criticize the fundraising tactics of the major parties by parodying MasterCard's "Priceless" ad campaign. The court held that the ad was a protected parody of the MasterCard ad and that Nader had made fun of MasterCard to make a political comment.
- In *Sun Trust Bank v. Houghton Mifflin Co.*, 268 F.3d 1357 (11th Cir. 2001), the Court of Appeals reversed a lower court's injunction that prohibited the publication of *The Wind Done Gone*, a parody of *Gone with the Wind*. The appellate court held that the use was highly transformative and provided social benefit and thus the author of *The Wind Done Gone* was entitled to a fair use defense. After the decision, the parties reached a private settlement and *The Wind Done Gone* was published.
- In 1991, singer Michael Bolton was ordered to pay $5.4 million in damages for infringing a 1964 song called "Love Is a Wonderful Thing" by the Isley Brothers. The court found that Bolton had access to the earlier work and that the two works (which shared the same name) were substantially similar; a judgment of $5.4 million was affirmed. *Three Boys Music Corp. v. Bolton*, 212 F.3d 477 (9th Cir. 2000).
- Lawsuits for infringement of architectural works are increasing. In 2001, a Virginia jury awarded $5.2 million to an architectural firm whose home designs were used to construct more than 300 homes. The award represented the defendant's profits in the approximate amount of $17,000 for each of the 300 infringing houses.
- The largest copyright infringement verdict was handed down by a jury in California in 2002, which found a defendant liable in the amount of $136 million in statutory damages for willfully infringing copyrights in CDs.

CHAPTER SUMMARY

An infringement action may be brought by an owner of a registered copyright whenever any of his or her exclusive rights have been violated. Infringement requires that a plaintiff prove copyright ownership and impermissible copying. Copying is usually demonstrated by showing that the defendant had access to the copyrighted work and that there is substantial similarity between the copyrighted work and defendant's work.

A defendant in an infringement action may assert a variety of defenses. The most common defense raised is that the defendant's use was a "fair use" of the copyrighted work. The fair use doctrine was developed to promote scholarly and educational use of certain works. Courts examine four factors in determining whether a defendant's use is fair: the purpose and character of the use, including whether the use is for commercial or nonprofit purposes; the nature of the work (with factual and scholarly works receiving less protection than works of fiction or fantasy); the amount and substantiality of the portion of work taken by the defendant (even a small taking may constitute infringement if it is the heart of the work); and the effect of the defendant's activities on the potential market for the copyrighted work. No one factor is conclusive; courts examine and weigh all factors in reaching a conclusion about infringement. Parody is a form of fair use, as are certain uses by libraries and educators.

Other defenses to infringement are invalidity of the plaintiff's copyright; estoppel to allege infringement due to the plaintiff's acquiescence in infringement; misuse or unclean hands by the plaintiff; and the statute of limitations, which provides that a civil infringement action must be brought within three years of the infringing activity.

Remedies available to a plaintiff include injunctive relief, actual damages and the defendant's profits, statutory damages (in lieu of actual damages and profits), costs, and attorneys' fees. Criminal penalties may be imposed in the case of certain willful infringements.

CASE ILLUSTRATION—FAIR USE

Case: *Twin Peaks Productions, Inc. v. Publications International, Ltd.*, 996 F.2d 1366 (2d Cir. 1993)

Facts: The defendant published a book about the plaintiff's popular television show, *Twin Peaks*. The book contained detailed plot summaries of the television series; two chapters consisted of extensive direct quotations from the show's dialog. The lower court held that the use was not a fair use and constituted copyright infringement. The defendant appealed.

Holding: The court affirmed, holding that the defendant's book was an unauthorized derivative work and infringed the plaintiff's right to adapt its work and create derivative works. Examining the four fair use factors, the court concluded the following: (1) although the defendant's book provided commentary about the plaintiff's television show, it reported the show's plots in extraordinary detail and went far beyond what was required to serve any legitimate purpose and was commercial in character; (2) plaintiff's television show was a creative and fictional work entitled to a high level of protection; (3) the amount taken was "plainly substantial"; and (4) the book competed in a market in which the copyright owner had a legitimate interest because it might want to capitalize on its work and create derivative works. Thus, because all four fair use factors favored the copyright owner, the court rejected the fair use defense.

CASE STUDY AND ACTIVITIES

Case Study. Vision published a book about its founder, Victor Niles, which includes biographical information about Niles and the history of the founding of the Vision hotel chain. The book is offered for sale in Vision's hotel gift shops. Vision has discovered that

CASE STUDY AND ACTIVITIES (CONT'D)

an author has published a very unflattering book about Niles, which includes biographical information about Niles and information about Niles's founding of the hotel chain. Some of the information is identical to that in Vision's book. Additionally, Vision has discovered that a competitor is using the "tune" or melody of one of Vision's featured television advertisements to promote its own hotel chain. Finally, an economist has published a poem in the *New Yorker* featuring Vision's character Vee and mocking Vision and its hotels as greedy corporate exploiters of labor.

Activities.   Discuss whether these three incidents constitute copyright infringement and what defenses the alleged infringers are likely to assert.

ROLE OF PARALEGAL

The role of paralegals in infringement matters is similar to the role played by paralegals in other litigation matters. Intellectual property practitioners may be engaged in the following activities:

- obtaining certified copies of certificates of registration or other documents to prove a plaintiff's ownership of copyright
- obtaining certified copies of applications for registration of copyrights to examine applications for misstatements to prove misuse of the copyright application procedure by a plaintiff
- conducting research regarding defenses that may be asserted by a defendant, especially the fair use defense
- preparing a cease and desist letter (or response to same)
- drafting complaints, answers, motions, and other pleadings in infringement actions
- assisting in the discovery process in infringement actions (summarizing depositions, drafting interrogatories and responses to interrogatories, reviewing documents produced, examining statements related to defendant's revenues, and so forth)
- assisting at the trial (preparing and maintaining exhibits and lists of witnesses, preparing a trial notebook, preparing jury instructions, and assisting in preparing motions and trial briefs)

INTERNET RESOURCES

Federal laws relating to copyright: http://www.law.cornell.edu
                                          http://www.findlaw.com

Copyright Office:	http://www.copyright.gov (for forms, circulars, information on fair use, Guidelines for Classroom Copying, and other materials)
Information on fair use:	http://fairuse.stanford.edu (for links to cases, regulations, treaties, and articles on copyright and fair use) http://www.chillingeffects.org/copyright (Chilling Effects Clearinghouse, providing information on copyright, fair use, and parody)
Crash Course in Copyrights:	http://www.utsystem.edu/ogc/intellectualproperty/ cprtindx.htm (information on copyright and fair use)
General information:	http://www.findlaw.com http://www.megalaw.com

DISCUSSION QUESTIONS

1. Luis is the copyright owner of a novel. He authorized Dave to produce a derivative work based on the original novel, in return for which Dave pays Luis royalties based on Dave's sales. The parties have discovered that the derivative work is being infringed. Who is a proper plaintiff in an action alleging infringement?

2. Franklin Computer Software exhibited at an industry-wide trade show in Las Vegas last year, where it introduced its new software program. Franklin has discovered that Harrison Computer Software is marketing a highly similar program. In fact, a deliberate error that Franklin inserted into its program appears in Harrison's program as well. Discuss whether Harrison likely "copied" Franklin's work.

3. Barbara is a well-known author of a series of romance novels, featuring an English heroine, Candace, who is routinely saved from various perilous events by a strong, handsome hero. Barbara has discovered that another author, Ann, has written a book featuring an English heroine who falls in love with a handsome hero who saves her from financial ruin. Have Barbara's works been infringed? Discuss.

4. The owner of a shopping mall has licensed a space within the mall to Al, who is selling counterfeit copies of CDs and DVDs. Which of the parties have liability for copyright infringement? Discuss. What principle governs your answer?

5. An Internet blogger obtained a copy of a planned blockbuster book about Anna Nicole Smith and posted several chapters, verbatim, online. The blogger has asserted that the use was a fair use because she was providing valuable commentary about our culture of celebrity. Discuss whether such a defense is likely to succeed. Discuss whether a story on *NBC Nightly News* about the blogger and quoting some passages from the book is fair use.

DISCUSSION QUESTIONS (CONT'D)

6. Tim, a songwriter, has discovered that four years ago James sang one of Tim's songs on a live television show. May Tim bring an action for infringement? Discuss.

7. Tom published his novel in January of this year and registered his copyright seven months later. May Tom elect to pursue statutory damages rather than compensatory damages for infringement that occurred between the two dates? Discuss.

USING INTERNET RESOURCES

1. Access the Copyright Office Web site. Review Circular 21 relating to "Classroom Guidelines" and the definition of brevity.
   a. Would a teacher's reproduction of a complete article of 2,000 words be permissible?
   b. Would a teacher's reproduction of three charts from a book be permissible?
2. Access the Copyright Office Web site. Review Factsheet FL 102.
   a. Would the reproduction of an article in a Congressional report be a fair use of that work?
   b. May a library photocopy one chapter in a book to replace a damaged portion of the book and rightly claim fair use of that work?
3. Access Stanford's Copyright and Fair use Web site. Review the materials relating to fair use, specifically "Measuring Fair Use."
   a. What is the "de minimis defense"?
   b. Why were certain copyrighted photographs allowed to be displayed in the movie *Seven*?

Chapter 15

New Developments in Copyright Law and the Semiconductor Chip Protection Act

CHAPTER OVERVIEW

Technological advances have created new forms of copyright authorship that in turn have created new issues relating to protection and dissemination of these new works. Although it is clear that computer programs and automated databases are copyrightable literary works, issues relating to copying computer programs continue to present challenges to the courts. The literal portions of computer programs (source code and object code) are protectable, but the nonliteral portions are often viewed as unprotectable useful articles, scenes a faire, or merged ideas and expressions. Reverse engineering of computer pro-

grams to create compatible programs may be acceptable, but creating identical or substantially similar programs may be infringement.

No subject in copyright law is subject to as much debate as copyright in the electronic age. The ease with which works can be viewed, copied, manipulated, reproduced, displayed, and transmitted using electronic means, particularly the Internet, has given rise to serious concern by authors that their works will be subject to wholesale infringement and piracy. Although some advocate that there should be no restrictions on information on the Internet, others are furiously working to develop encryption and metering devices that can track and monitor electronic use of works and charge for that use. The protection and infringement of songs and movies is of critical interest to their authors and industries. For example, just 12 hours after the release of the long-anticipated book *Harry Potter and the Half-Blood Prince* in June 2005, it could be obtained illegally online. Legislation is routinely introduced in Congress to address these issues. Nevertheless, many experts believe the solutions to technology-related issues lie with technology rather than the courts or the legislature and that copyright protection on the Internet will be advanced by encryption and coding devices rather than piecemeal legislation or court decisions.

In 1998, the **Digital Millennium Copyright Act (DMCA)** became effective to promote electronic commerce and the distribution of digital works by providing tools and remedies to combat copyright piracy and to impose penalties on those who circumvent technological protection measures. This new act has spawned a series of court decisions and significant controversy with regard to whether the act chills innovation and free speech. The DMCA also provides for registration of the designs of original boat vessel hulls.

Protection for semiconductor chips stems from the Semiconductor Chip Protection Act of 1984. The act establishes a new form of intellectual property protection for the stencils or "masks" used to create the electronic circuitry of semiconductor chips. Although this form of protection is said to be *sui generis* (literally, "one of a kind"), mask protection draws upon many copyright principles.

INTRODUCTION

Developments in technology create new industries and opportunities for reproduction and dissemination of works of authorship. A number of new issues have arisen relating to the growth of electronic publishing, distribution, and viewing of copyrighted works. Along with new and expanded markets for works comes the ever-increasing challenge of protecting works from piracy or infringement. For example, in 2006, rapper Jay Z's album *Kingdom Come* was leaked onto the Internet six days before its release date. Similarly, in mid-2002, bootlegged versions of the movie *Star Wars: Attack of the Clones* appeared on the Internet within hours of movie house premieres.

Both the courts and Congress continue to be faced with issues that were unimagined just a decade ago. "High-tech" legislation continues to be introduced in Congress. Courts struggle with the complexity and balance between protecting the rights of authors and promoting the progress of science and useful arts as is mandated by the Constitution. This chapter is intended to introduce some of the copyright cutting-edge and bleeding-edge issues presently confronting authors, users, legislators, and judges.

COPYRIGHT PROTECTION FOR COMPUTER PROGRAMS

Protectable Elements of Computer Programs

Computer programs have been accepted for copyright registration since the mid-1960s. In 1974, Congress created the Commission on New Technological Uses of Copyrighted Works (CONTU) to analyze various technology-related issues and report to Congress on several topics, including copyrightability of computer programs. The CONTU recommended that the 1976 Copyright Act be expressly amended to make clear that computer programs are copyrightable. In 1980, Congress followed CONTU's recommendations and added a definition in the Copyright Act for the term *computer program* and a limitation on the exclusive rights of computer program authors in order to allow users to make certain adaptations to program and to make archival copies of programs.

According to section 101 of the Copyright Act, a **computer program** is a set of statements or instructions to be used directly or indirectly in a computer in order to bring about a certain result. Copyright protection extends to all of the copyrightable expression embodied in the program. Copyright protection is not available for ideas, program logic, algorithms, systems, methods, concepts, or layouts. Computer programs are copyrightable as literary works, and applicants seeking registration of computer programs should generally use application Form TX (the same form used for books and other literary materials). However, if pictorial or graphic authorship predominates, registration may be made using Form PA (for audiovisual works).

Computer languages are written in specialized alphanumeric languages (such as Basic, C, or Java), called **source code,** that are human-readable. In order to operate a computer, source code must be translated into machine-readable **object code,** consisting of only two symbols, 0 and 1, which represent the alphanumeric characters of the source code. Object code cannot be read by humans. Both source code and object code are copyrightable.

Copyright protection extends to screen displays as well, if they possess copyrightable material. Screens consisting of mere menus or blank forms usually are not protectable, either because they lack original expression or because they are useful articles. In *Lotus Development Corp. v. Borland International, Inc.,* 49 F.3d 807 (1st Cir. 1995), *aff'd,* 516 U.S. 233 (1996), the First Circuit held that the menu command hierarchy of the Lotus 1-2-3 spreadsheet was uncopyrightable subject matter inasmuch as it was a mere method of operation. The court noted that highlighting a "p" for "print" on a computer screen was really no different from pressing a "play" button on a VCR. Such was not protectable expression.

A single registration is sufficient to protect the copyright in a computer program, including related screen displays, without a separate registration for the screen displays or a specific reference to the displays in the application. Acceptable identifications of the work include "computer program," "entire text of computer program," "entire program code," and "text of user's manual and computer program." These identifications will cover any copyrightable authorship contained in the computer program and screen displays. The Copyright Office will refuse registration if the claim of authorship is based only on "encrypting," "firmware," "formatting," "functions," "printout," "software methodology," or "system."

Because most computer programs are accompanied by user manuals, the manuals may be included as part of the computer program registration, thus eliminating the need for a separate application for the manuals.

Deposit Requirements for Computer Programs

For published or unpublished computer programs, the first 25 and last 25 pages of source code should be submitted in a form visually perceptible without the aid of a machine or a device. If the program is less than 50 pages in length, all of the source code should be deposited.

Because computer programs often contain proprietary information and trade secrets, the Copyright Office has developed alternative deposit requirements for such works. Where a computer program contains trade secret material, a cover letter should accompany the application, stating that the claim contains trade secrets. One of the following must then be deposited:

- first 25 and last 25 pages of source code with portions containing trade secrets blocked out; or
- first 10 and last 10 pages of source code alone, with no blocked-out portions; or
- first 25 and last 25 pages of object code plus any 10 or more consecutive pages of source code, with no blocked-out portions; or

- for programs less than 50 pages in length, entire source code with trade secret portions blocked out.

Some applicants are reluctant to deposit even blocked-out portions of source code. They may therefore apply for a registration under the Copyright Office's "rule of doubt" by submitting object code together with written confirmation that the material does contain copyrightable authorship. The Copyright Office will issue a registration on the basis of the information given by the applicant even though it is unable to examine the deposited material and determine the existence of ccpyrightability. If questions arise later regarding copyrightability, a court will determine whether the material is copyrightable.

Notice of Copyright

Although the form of copyright notice is the same for computer-related works as for other works (the symbol ©, the year of first publication, and the name of the owner), the location of the notice presents special problems. The Copyright Office has stated the following are acceptable placements of the notice:

- a notice embedded in the copies in machine-readable form in such a manner that on visually perceptible printouts it appears either with or near the title, or at the end of the work
- a notice that is displayed at the user's screen or terminal at sign-on
- a notice that is continuously on the screen or terminal display
- a legible notice on a label securely affixed to the copies or to a box, reel, cartridge, cassette, or other container used as a permanent receptacle for the copies

Video Games

Although the ideas underlying some video games (such as a solitaire game) are not copy-rightable, certain elements of video games, such as a sequence of sounds and images, are copyrightable as audiovisual works apart from the underlying computer program. Some infringers alleged early on that video games were not copyrightable inasmuch as player participation causes variations in games and different outcomes, and thus the works are not "fixed," but courts have held that many of the game elements remain constant and that the memory devices of games satisfy the requirement of fixation.

Revisions and Modifications to Computer Programs

Computer programs are frequently updated and revised by their authors, generally to provide additional features to users. Substantive revisions will result in a new work for which a new copyright registration should be sought. Thus, each separately published version of a computer program should be separately registered, assuming each contains a sufficient amount of new or revised authorship to sustain a claim of copyright. The Copyright Office will accept the following claims of authorship: "new modules," "revised modules," "revised program," "new routines," and "revised routines."

Copyright owners have the exclusive right under section 106 of the Copyright Act to reproduce their works and to prepare derivative works based on their copyrighted works. Section 117 of the act, relating exclusively to computer programs, limits these exclusive rights by allowing a backup copy to be made and allowing some modifications of programs for an owner's own use, such as improving the program or increasing its speed of performance.

Generally, a computer program is copied onto a computer every time it is used. Section 117 was added to the copyright act to ensure that merely loading and using a computer program after one purchased the program was not an infringement of its author's rights to reproduce a work. Section 117 provides that notwithstanding the otherwise exclusive rights of a copyright owner, it is not an infringement for the owner of a copy of a computer program to make an additional copy of the program to use it or to make an archival or backup copy. Additionally, it is not an infringement to adapt a program if the new copy or adaptation is created as an essential step in the utilization of the computer program. Thus, section 117 authorizes some modifications to computer programs for a purchaser's own use under the theory that having paid for a computer program, the consumer may experiment with the product and create new variations of play, for personal enjoyment, without creating an infringing derivative work. *Lewis Galoob Toys, Inc. v. Nintendo of Am., Inc.*, 964 F.2d 965 (9th Cir. 1992). In *Lewis Galoob*, the defendant manufactured a device called Game Genie to be used with Nintendo's video games that could increase the speed of a character's moves and increase the number of lives of a player's character. The court held that these were merely permissible enhancements to the copyrighted work. The device was not an unauthorized derivative work and did not physically incorporate a portion of the copyrighted work. The Game Genie was useless by itself and did not supplant demand for a component of Nintendo's works. Additionally, converting a program from one language to another to facilitate its use or adding features to a computer program for one's own needs is permissible. *Foresight Res. Corp. v. Pfortmiller*, 719 F. Supp. 1006 (D. Kan. 1989). Section 117 applies to "owners," and thus courts have held that its provisions are inapplicable to licensees of software or those who are in possession of software unlawfully.

Infringement of Computer Programs

Some of the most complex copyright cases involve the extent of protectability for computer programs. A number of litigants have asserted that computer operating systems are not protectable inasmuch as they are uncopyrightable "processes" or "systems," expressly excluded from protection according to section 102 of the Copyright Act. Courts generally have held otherwise, reasoning that if other programs can be written or created that perform the same functions, then an operating system is an expression of an idea and is therefore copyrightable. If the idea cannot be expressed in any other way, however, then it is purely necessary to the purpose and is functional, and hence not copyrightable. This is the merger doctrine, discussed in chapter 10, that provides that if an idea in a work can be expressed in only one way or a very limited number of ways, it is unprotectable inasmuch as it would be unfair to allow one party to appropriate an idea and exclude all others from using it. When an idea and its expression are so merged or inseparable that the unprotectable idea cannot be used without also using protectable expression, then use is not infringement.

Courts have struggled with infringement issues in computer-related cases in part because the issues are often technical, unfamiliar, and complex. Thus, experts are often relied upon rather than the "ordinary observer" commonly referred to in other infringement actions. Moreover, unlike songs and books, which are highly creative, computer programs are usually task-oriented, performing very specific and utilitarian functions. Historically, "useful articles" are excluded from copyright protection.

Some courts have expressly recognized that many computer programs are by nature utilitarian articles inasmuch as their purpose is to accomplish tasks. See *Computer Assoc. Int'l, Inc. v. Altai, Inc.*, 982 F.2d 693 (2d Cir. 1992). Thus, functional commands and aspects are unprotectable. Based on the merger doctrine, courts have held that when specific instructions are the only means of accomplishing a given task, another may use them without infringing the original work.

Moreover, many cases involving computer-related works have held that certain elements are unprotectable inasmuch as they are standard or stock scenes a faire (literally, "scenes which must be done"). Thus, hardware and software standards, mechanical specifications, industry programming practices, and compatibility requirements have been held to be unprotectable scenes a faire since they are expressions dictated by external factors and their creation is the natural product of such external considerations.

Most courts have used the "abstraction-filtration-comparison" test discussed in chapter 14 in determining whether infringement of computer programs has occurred. A court will abstract or dissect the allegedly infringed program's structure, filter out the unprotectable elements (such as processes, facts, merger material, and scenes a faire), and then compare the remaining protectable elements of the two works to determine whether infringement exists. *Gates Rubber Co. v. Bando Chem. Indus., Ltd.*, 9 F.3d 823 (10th Cir. 1993). Other courts focus on the idea-expression dichotomy and hold that only those elements not necessary to the purpose or function of the work are protectable expression.

Early cases often involved nearly identical copying of code (often referred to as "literal copying"), and courts found it easy to determine that in such cases infringement had occurred. Analogizing computer programs to other textual works, such as books, which could be infringed even without literal copying (namely, by paraphrasing), courts then extended copyright protection to the structure, sequence, and organization of programs, namely the nonliteral elements of a program.

Later cases have involved less clear-cut issues, such as copying functional elements of programs. Many of these cases involve **reverse engineering,** or disassembling a computer program to understand its functional elements. In *Sega Enters. Ltd. v. Accolade, Inc.*, 977 F.2d 1510 (9th Cir. 1993), the defendant reverse engineered Sega's video game programs in order to make its own video games that would be compatible with Sega's console into which the defendant's game cartridges were inserted. The Ninth Circuit held

that such was permissible because the defendant had copied Sega's software solely in order to discover the functional elements for compatibility with Sega's console, elements of Sega's programs that were not protectable by copyright. The court held that where disassembly is the only way to gain understanding and access to the ideas and functional elements embodied in a copyright program and where there is a legitimate reason for seeking such access, such disassembly is a fair use of the copyrighted work.

Many experts interpret *Sega* as part of a growing trend of courts to limit the scope of copyright protection for computer programs, particularly for the functional elements of programs. Thus, many owners are now seeking patent protection for their computer programs (see chapter 21). Nevertheless, although efforts can be undertaken to understand a work's ideas, processes, and methods of operation (all unprotectable functional aspects of a computer program), if the final program produced by the "engineer" is substantially similar to the original work, infringement may be found.

Under section 117 of the Copyright Act, owners of a computer program are specifically authorized to make backup copies of their programs and load the program onto a computer's hard drive from a floppy disk or CD-ROM. They cannot, however, make copies for purposes of commercial distribution.

Licensing of Computer Programs

Due to the ease of copying computer programs (allowing numerous users to share one purchased program) and due to the first sale doctrine (allowing the owner/purchaser of a copy to sell or rent it to others), makers of software programs became concerned over piracy and potential loss of revenues. To remedy the problem, they implemented the practice of licensing their programs. Software purchased over the counter is thus not typically "sold" by the maker but rather "licensed" by the maker to the user/purchaser.

Such a license is often called a **shrink-wrap license** because opening the plastic wrapping on the package immediately subjects the user/purchaser to the terms of the license agreement. A notice to this effect is placed on or in the box or packaging, and a method for returning the software is usually provided if the user/licensee objects to the license terms. Courts generally have held that such licenses are valid contracts enforceable under the principles of contract law unless their terms are objectionable on grounds applicable to contracts in general, for example, if they are unconscionable. *ProCD, Inc. v. Zeidenberg,* 86 F.3d 1447 (7th Cir. 1996).

The license agreements contain warranties and the terms and conditions under which the user/licensee can use the software and make it clear that violation of any of the terms, such as loading the software into more than one computer or decompiling it, constitutes infringement. Because the transaction is a license rather than a sale, no "first sale" concerns are implicated, and the user/licensee cannot resell or rent the software to another inasmuch as there was no sale to him or her in the first instance. In some cases, software is licensed electronically; this license agreement is referred to as a **click-wrap license,** since the license terms and conditions come into existence when the user/licensee clicks an icon displayed on a computer screen to indicate "purchase" or license of the work per the stated terms. Such click-wrap licenses may not be valid unless the computer screens display reasonably conspicuous notice of the existence of the contractual terms and require the user or licensee to unambiguously manifest agreement to those terms. Asking users to show assent by clicking "OK" or "I agree" before proceeding shows assent to an agreement; however, a process allowing users to download software without first viewing an agreement or even being made aware of its existence does not show assent.

Section 117 of the Copyright Act, allowing owners of copies of computer programs to make a new copy or adaptation if necessary to use the program or to make an archival or backup copy, is limited to "owners" and is thus not applicable to licensees under shrink-wrap or click-wrap license agreements. Most software makers/licensors, however, typically include as a term of the license a provision substantially similar to section 117, allowing the user/licensee to make a new copy or adaptation if necessary to enable the use for which the software was obtained or for archival purposes. The Digital Millennium Copyright Act (discussed later) allows software developers who have lawfully obtained the right to use a computer program to reverse engineer it to analyze the elements necessary to achieve interoperability of an independently created computer program. Additionally, either owners or licensees can make a copy of a computer program for purposes of maintaining or repairing the computer hardware.

Piracy of Software

In addition to the complex legal issues surrounding protection and infringement of computer-related works, there are significant economic issues as well. It has been estimated that software piracy caused a loss of revenue of nearly $7 billion in 2005 in the United States alone. One expert has estimated that there may be nearly 50,000 sites on the Internet that offer software illegally. Piracy of other content is also rampant. Just the day after the film *Titanic* won several Oscar awards, 50 separate Web sites offered illegal copies of the film. One of the most common types of software piracy is "softlifting," or making unauthorized copies of a licensed software program (often for a home computer, fellow employee, family, or friends). The economic effect of computer piracy is reportedly more than $12 billion worldwide per year, costing 111,000 jobs in the United States alone. Consequently, many companies, notably Microsoft Corporation, are stepping up their crusades against software piracy, both through educational programs and legal action. One counterfeiting operation in late 2001 in California resulted in a seizure of about $60 million of pirated MICROSOFT® software.

Software makers often join one of two associations, the Software & Information Industry Association (SIIA, formerly the Software Publishers Association) or the Business Software Alliance (BSA), that exist to educate businesses about copyrights in software and to locate infringers. The SIIA has more than 800 members and represents the software and digital content industries. The BSA was formed in the late 1980s, and some of its members are Apple, Borland, Dell, Intel, and Microsoft. Generally, it represents the interests of the leading makers of software for personal computers. It has filed hundreds of lawsuits for software infringement, asking for restraining orders and audits of a company's computers to locate pirated software. Most lawsuits are settled out of court, with the infringers paying the retail value of the software and replacing the pirated software. In other cases, damages have been assessed in the millions of dollars. Both BSA and SIIA have hotline numbers to report infringement, and in many instances, disgruntled former employees report infringement by their former employers. Both companies offer significant rewards to those who report verifiable instances of piracy. Visiting technicians to companies and temporary employees also tend to report infringement.

The BSA offers a publication to help businesses implement antipiracy programs. Call (800) 688-2721 (or access http://www.bsa.org) and ask for *Software Management Guide*. The SIIA offers a variety of educational materials and audit tools. Write to SIIA at 1090 Vermont Avenue NW, Washington, DC 20005.

Although software piracy is of great concern in the United States, it is estimated that most loss from computer piracy arises in foreign countries due to their lax enforcement practices and laws. For example, until 1998, software piracy was not a crime in Argentina or Brazil. The BSA has rated China as having a piracy percentage of 86 per-

cent, meaning that for every 100 programs sold, nearly 90 are pirated. The U.S. Trade Representative attempts to work with these countries to secure their commitment to protect copyrighted works by placing countries on intellectual property "watch lists," which can lead to trade restrictions and sanctions. Countries on the 2006 priority watch list include India, Russia, Vietnam, and China. Once a country is placed on a watch list, an investigation is initiated to determine whether tariffs or trade restrictions should be imposed on the offending country. In 2003, the U.S. Trade Representative imposed $75 million worth of sanctions on Ukraine exports for Ukraine's repeated failures to protect intellectual property. The sanctions were lifted in 2005 after efforts by the Ukranian government to stem illegal production and trading of CDs and DVDs.

COPYRIGHT PROTECTION FOR AUTOMATED DATABASES

According to the Copyright Office, an **automated database** is a body of facts, data, or other information assembled into an organized format suitable for use in a computer and comprising one or more files. An automated database is a compilation because it is formed by collecting and assembling preexisting materials or data. Although there is no specific reference to automated databases anywhere in the Copyright Act, they are viewed as types of literary works subject to copyright protection. An example of an automated database is WESTLAW's database of federal court cases. Although the cases themselves are government works in the public domain, Thomson/West's arrangement of those cases qualifies for copyright protection as a compilation.

Automated databases will not receive protection if there is no original authorship in the selection and ordering of the data, such as is the case in merely transferring data from hardcopy to computer storage. Registration is secured using Form TX. If the material in the database has been previously published, previously registered, or is in the public domain, the claim should be described as "compilation." If the material is original, the claim should be described as "text."

For a single-file database (one in which the data records pertain to a single common subject matter, such as bankruptcy cases), the deposit should consist of the first and last 25 pages or data records. For a multiple-file database (one in which there are separate and distinct groups of data records, such as bankruptcy cases, federal regulations, and state statutes), the deposit should consist of 50 data records from each file, or the entire file, whichever is less. The Copyright Office will consider requests for relief from the deposit requirements if the database contains trade secrets or the applicant is unable to deposit the materials.

The Copyright Office provides specific information about copyright registration for automated databases in its Circular 65, obtainable from the forms hotline (202/707-9100) and on the Internet at http://www.copyright.gov.

In April 1998, the United States sponsored a conference on database protection to discuss providing additional protection to databases. Additionally, on three occasions, Congress has considered legislation that would protect databases created through a substantial investment of time and money (a provision that would effectively overrule *Feist*, which held that a database work, namely, a telephone directory, was not protectable merely because it was the result of "sweat of the brow"). Thus, protection would be provided for realtors' home listings, stock quotations, and certain case reports. Certain databases containing information for educational, scientific, research, and news-gathering purposes (namely, fair uses) would be exempt. Such protection would harmonize U.S. law with that of many of the European Union countries, which provide some protection to noncreative compilations of material. As discussed in chapter 16, the issue of providing enhanced protection to databases is the subject of both national and international debate and dis-

cussion, with no present resolution in regard to the extent to which databases should be protected. Generally, however, companies that have been damaged because their databases were infringed have been successful in court, leading some experts to say this shows that no dramatic new legislation relating to database protection is needed.

The Copyright Office supports appropriate legislation to protect databases. In recent years, some experts have wondered whether owners of information have overreached in their efforts to protect information. For example, in 2005, Major League Baseball challenged a sports fantasy league's use of baseball statistics. In August 2006, the Eastern District of Missouri ruled that Major League Baseball could not prohibit a sports fantasy league from using player names and records because the information was purely factual.

COPYRIGHT IN THE ELECTRONIC AGE

Introduction

There is a dynamic tension inherent in copyright law: The rights of authors and creators to protect their works and reap the benefits of their creations must be balanced against the right of the public to have access to information. Nowhere is that tension more pronounced than in the discussion of copyright in cyberspace. It is amazingly easy to make electronic copies of works and then transmit those works to others using digital media. Using our computers, we are capable of retrieving, storing, revising, and disseminating vast amounts of information created by others with a single keystroke. There are few mechanical or economic restrictions precluding or restricting the free flow of information in cyberspace.

On one side of a vigorous debate are the adherents to the "Dyson model," named after Esther Dyson, former board member emeritus of the Electronic Frontier Foundation, who believe that "information wants to be free," meaning that the logical product of the Internet and our global communications capacities is unrestricted dissemination of information. Widespread access to information is beneficial to the research, educational, and scientific communities, all benefiting the public interest. On the other side of the debate are authors and creators of works who fear that unrestricted access to their works on the Internet will impair the value of their works, cause a loss of revenue to them, and ultimately discourage creation of work. If authors fear loss of protection, they will not create work, and the public will then receive no benefit.

The Copyright Act has been liberally written to encompass new technologies as seen in the reference in section 102 that copyright protection subsists in original works of authorship fixed in any tangible medium of expression, *now known or later developed*. Nevertheless, although the Copyright Act anticipates emerging technologies, developments of the past several years have been so unexpected and rapid that many experts believe additional amendments to the Copyright Act may be necessary.

Issues Confronting Cyberspace Users

Some of the issues presently facing authors, consumers, and Internet service providers (such as AOL or Verizon DSL) are the following.

- Should individuals browsing information offered on the Internet be required to obtain the author's permission before viewing the information; saving the information; transmitting it to others; revising the material; making a hardcopy of or printing the information; or reproducing the information in another form, such as in a newsletter? At least one court has held that a company that downloaded copyrighted material from a Web site to post on an internal intranet was liable for copyright infringement.

Marobie-FL v. Nat'l Ass'n of Fire Equip. Distribs., 983 F. Supp. 1167 (N.D. Ill. 1997).

- Should the owner of a digital version of a copyrighted work be permitted to disseminate that information to another under the "first sale" doctrine? At present, the first sale doctrine has not been expanded to permit digital transmission of copies of copyrighted works.
- Is placing information (or "uploading") on the Internet a dedication to the public domain such that anyone can thereafter use, reproduce, adapt, or display the information for any purpose?
- Is posting information on a bulletin board system a "performance" of a copyrighted work?
- Is quoting material from others in a chat room infringement?
- Should the U.S. government be able to restrict exports of the most powerful encryption software unless the maker of the software provides the government with a decoding key or "back door" so the government can fight organized crime and terrorism?

A common thread running through all of these issues is whether the Copyright Act should be amended to address these issues or whether the courts should resolve these questions on a case-by-case basis.

The National Information Infrastructure

In 1993, President Clinton formed the Information Infrastructure Task Force to study the complex issues posed by posting and disseminating information in cyberspace and to develop guidelines for a National Information Infrastructure (NII). The NII encompasses digital interactive services now available, such as the Internet, as well as those that may be developed in the future.

The NII is not restricted to copyright issues. The NII, combining computer technology and communications technology, can support our education systems by connecting students and educators all over the world, advance cultural and entertainment opportunities, and increase participation in the democratic process by making available speeches, bills, and other government works. However, the NII has a direct impact on copyrighted works. Two-dimensional works are easily converted to digitized form (a series of zeroes and ones) and can then be easily and rapidly reproduced (with each "copy" identical in quality to the original) and transmitted to others with just a few keystrokes. They may be posted on a bulletin board where thousands of individuals can have access to them. These works can be changed by modifications and by combining them with other works (such as the addition of lyrics written by one party to music written by another), blurring ownership rights. Just one unauthorized uploading of an author's work onto a bulletin board could have a devastating effect on the market for that author's work.

Thus, appropriate systems must be put into place to protect authors' rights. After holding hearings and examining a variety of issues, the task force determined that although some minor modifications and amendments would be needed to the 1976 Copyright Act to reflect the realities of the NII and to take account of current technology, the act was fundamentally adequate and effective. The task force also concluded that no revisions were needed to trademark, patent, or trade secret law at the time. Its final report, however, "The White Paper on Intellectual Property and the National Information Infrastructure" (available at http://www.uspto.gov) has engendered much criticism. Opponents of the recommendations set forth in the White Paper have formed the "Digital Future Coalition," which believes that the White Paper recommends far too much protection to authors at the cost of drying up information that should be freely accessible to the public. The Web site of the Digital Future Coalition (http://www.dfc.org) provides information about its activities

in the ongoing debate regarding intellectual property law in the digital network environment.

Copyright Notices in the Electronic Age

Authors concerned about unauthorized reproduction and dissemination of their works by electronic means can include notices with their works to remind users that further reproduction or transmission is unauthorized and may constitute infringement. Some notices are as follows:

- © 2007 John Doe. Copying, transmitting, reproducing, or archiving this work in any media or by any means for other than personal use without express permission of John Doe is prohibited and may constitute copyright infringement.
- Access to and use of this Web site is subject to the following terms and conditions: You may browse this site only for information and entertainment use; you may not modify, transmit, or revise the contents of this site without the owner's written permission; any communication you post to this site will be treated as nonconfidential; you may not post or transmit any unlawful or defamatory material; your use of the site constitutes acceptance of these terms.
- This Web site contains links to other sites. Such links are not affiliations with or endorsements of other sites or the products or services offered by or through such sites.
- © 2007 Jane Roe. The user or viewer of this work is hereby granted an express nonexclusive license to reproduce the work, display, transmit, and distribute it by all means and in any media.
- Those individuals who post messages or works to this list own the copyrights to the messages or works; however, they grant a nonexclusive license to the list

owner to reproduce, transmit, forward, and archive any messages or works posted to this list.

Although these notices will not preclude infringement, they may assist an author in obtaining damages for willful infringement or, alternatively, clarify that the work may be freely disseminated.

Digital Rights Management

Because it is impossible to sue every person who infringes copyright by downloading music, movies, or other content over the Internet or by using digital works, a number of technologies have been introduced to protect digital works (including music purchased online and DVDs) from unauthorized copying and reproduction. These technologies are generally referred to as **digital rights management** (DRM) or "copyright rights management." Some DRM methods are relatively benign (such as servers that are set to block offending e-mail, software that protects sensitive financial or private data from theft, or the sign you may encounter when you view material online that states, "Sorry, this file is read-only"). Other DRM techniques used to thwart piracy include the following:

- "metering" each use of a copyrighted work so that viewers are required to pay for viewing or distributing the work
- installing encryption devices that preclude copying or distribution of copyrighted works (unless authorized and "unlocked," usually by a "key," some of which are time-limited)
- making "one use" DVDs or DVDs that self-destruct after a period of time
- verifying the authenticity of a disc or other work by means of a seal, often a difficult-to-replicate hologram, which verifies the authenticity of the CD and alerts users to counterfeit copies
- placing "spoof" or dummy files on the Internet so that when would-be pirates

download content, they obtain a spoof, containing silence, repetitive loops of lyrics, spyware, or viruses, all intended to deter and annoy pirates
- installing digital watermarks to identify a file's copyright owner and its rights and prohibit copying
- releasing Web robots or spiders to scour the Internet to find and attack infringing uses
- protecting works through the use of passwords and requiring users to agree to certain terms and conditions before viewing materials
- installing devices that that monitor and track digital usage to ensure a work is not copied, altered, or disseminated to others

At the time of the writing of this text, one of the hottest copyright issues is that relating to the **broadcast flag,** a type of watermark or DRM code that would be required to be embedded into digital television receivers that would "flag" whether a program could be recorded or not. After the FCC mandated the use of broadcast flags in 2003, a court rejected the regulations. Most experts expect the battle over raising the broadcast flag to be played out in Congress with content owners arguing for the flags and others arguing that they would stifle innovative devices. Some critics have questioned whether content owners are overreaching, noting that a device that won't let you skip trailers when you rent a DVD has nothing to do with copyright protection (and everything to do with advertising).

The dark side of DRM was revealed in 2005 when it was discovered that Sony sold millions of music CDs with hidden files that could damage a user's operating system, install spyware, and render the user's computer vulnerable to attacks by third parties and viruses. After a class action lawsuit, Sony agreed to a settlement with consumers.

Specific proposals to deter piracy are discussed later in this chapter.

Practical Do's and Don'ts

Because of the uncertainty inherent in viewing, archiving, transmitting, reproducing, downloading, uploading, and otherwise using digital information on the Internet, following are some practical pointers and guidelines for copyright compliance in the electronic age.

- Even attributing quotes to their authors may not protect against a claim of infringement. When on the Internet, do not quote from, transmit, copy, archive, or reproduce others' works without permission (unless such use is a fair use).
- Review material placed on the Internet for permissions; in many cases, authors have already granted limited permissions or licenses for others to use and view the materials. Unless permission is given, all material on the Internet, especially software, should be considered copyrighted work. Therefore, software should not be downloaded or modified without permission from the copyright holder. Similarly, downloading and printing an article you find for your personal use may be appropriate; however, printing multiple copies of the article and distributing them to others without permission likely violates the owner's exclusive copyright rights. Although such acts are infringements, copyright violations are common. For example, the developer of the popular computer games "Quake" and "Doom" estimates that 50 percent of the versions of Quake now being played are unlicensed, having been downloaded from unauthorized Web sites.
- Do not place any documents or materials from clients or your employer on the Internet without permission and without including a copyright notice.
- Newsgroup and e-mail postings are not always in the public domain. The safest course may be to forward postings only with permission (although a number of people believe that posting messages is an implied license to either archive or to forward those messages to others).
- Do not copy material (whether text, music, or graphics) from another's Web page without permission, and do not combine items from others' Web pages to create a Web page.
- Ask permission before establishing links to others' sites, and indicate that links to unaffiliated sites are so unaffiliated to avoid presumed sponsorship of others.
- Place copyright notices on all Web sites and on all original works.

THE DIGITAL MILLENNIUM COPYRIGHT ACT

Introduction

In 1998, Congress enacted the Digital Millennium Copyright Act (DMCA), 17 U.S.C. § 1201 *et seq.*, to move the nation's copyright law into the digital age. Because piracy of digital content is so easily accomplished, Congress sought to expand copyright protection for digital works by ensuring that copyright protection tools (such as encryption technology) could not be circumvented. Additionally, the DMCA sought to update U.S. copyright law to prepare for ratification of various WIPO treaties (see chapter 16). Some experts have stated that the DMCA represents the most comprehensive copyright reform in a generation.

Some of the most significant provisions of the DMCA are as follows:

- prohibitions against acts that circumvent technological protection measures
- provisions forbidding trafficking in products or technology that are used in circumventing copyright protection measures

- provisions forbidding removal or tampering with copyright management information (e.g., removal of digital watermarks)
- safe harbor provisions insulating online service providers (such as AOL and Yahoo!) from liability for acts such as transmitting or linking to unauthorized content (if the provider meets certain criteria such as adopting policies to terminate service of copyright offenders and removing infringing material upon receiving a *takedown notice* from the copyright owner)

The most frequently used part of the DMCA relates to the safe harbors granted to online or Internet service providers (ISPs). Following is an example of how the takedown procedure works.

- Assume that Paramount Pictures believes that counterfeit DVDs of its movie *Dreamgirls* are being sold by Smith on eBay. Paramount must send a notice, under penalty of perjury, to an agent designated by eBay (filed with the Copyright Office) to receive the notice. The notice must comply with the requirements of 17 U.S.C. § 512(c)(3).
- If eBay blocks or removes access to the material, it is immune from liability under the safe harbor provisions. eBay will notify Smith that it has blocked access.
- If Smith believes that *Dreamgirls* was mistakenly removed or blocked, he or she may send a counter notice to eBay alleging such.
- Unless Paramount files an action seeking a court order against Smith, eBay must put the material back up within 10–14 business days after receiving the counter-notification.

The DMCA expressly authorizes reverse engineering of computer programs. Both civil and

criminal penalties can be imposed for violations of the DMCA.

The DMCA has met with a great deal of criticism from electronics manufacturers, computer scientists, researchers, and libraries that are concerned that the act may chill freedom of expression. For example, the American Library Association's Web site states that under the DMCA, "the doctrine of 'fair use' has never been more threatened . . . ."

Issues Arising under the DMCA

A number of interesting cases and issues have arisen under the newly enacted DMCA, including the following.

- **DeCSS technology.** DeCSS is a software program created by a 15-year old computer hacker that enables users to descramble the encryption code that prohibits the copying of DVDs. In *Universal City Studios v. Reimerdes*, 111 F. Supp. 2d 294 (S.D.N.Y. 2000), *aff'd*, 273 F.3d 429 (2d Cir. 2001), eight motion picture studios sued a journalist to enjoin him from using his Web site to make available the DeCSS software program. The court held that dissemination of DeCSS violated the DMCA. The defendant was not only enjoined from offering DeCSS on his own Web site but was enjoined from offering links to other sites where DeCSS could be found. Although the defendant argued that he had a First Amendment right to offer the software program, the court held that disseminating the program violated the antitrafficking and antidecryption provisions of the DMCA. Additionally, the court found that dissemination of DeCSS was neither a fair use nor acceptable reverse engineering under the DMCA.
- **First Amendment issues.** In 2001, a university professor at Princeton University planned to publish a paper explaining methods he had used to

defeat certain DRM schemes, and was threatened with litigation under the DMCA. The professor withdrew his presentation, a decision which arguably chilled free speech. Similarly, in 2003, a graduate student was threatened with a DMCA lawsuit after publishing a report documenting flaws in a DRM program. In response to a Copyright Office recommendation, in 2006 a regulation was promulgated which provides an exemption from liability under the DMCA for those who may circumvent DRM methods for the purpose of testing, studying, or correcting flaws. 37 C.F.R. § 201.40 (2007).

• **Online service providers.** In 2000, a San Francisco court held that the online service provider eBay was not liable for auctioning sound recordings on its Internet Web site that might infringe copyrights of others. The court held that imposing liability on eBay for the sale of bootleg recordings would place an unjustifiable burden on eBay and would likely force it to cease or restrict its operations. Similarly, in 2002, a California appeals court held that eBay was not liable for the sale of fake sports memorabilia on its auction site. These and other courts have ruled that eBay does not have the ability or right to control infringing activity, a standard required for liability to be imposed under the DMCA. Moreover, eBay generally qualifies for the "safe harbor" provisions of the DMCA because it will remove or block access to offers to sell infringing materials (including music, movies, and artwork) when it receives an appropriate takedown notice. Some online service providers, including eBay, engage in voluntary monitoring of their sites to locate infringing material.

• **Webcasts.** The DMCA requires radio stations to pay royalties to music per-

formers and their record labels when broadcasts or **webcasts** are transmitted over the Internet, a practice called **streaming**. In mid-2002, the Librarian of Congress established royalty fees for these Internet radio stations and webcasters. Thus, radio broadcasters that simultaneously offer Internet transmission of their radio programs must pay the statutorily set fees (presently set at $0.11 per song per listener). As discussed in chapter 11, radio stations pay royalties to composers and authors of songs (usually through ASCAP and BMI) but do not pay the record producers for sound recordings. Thus, webcasters have vigorously objected to what they perceive as "double royalty payments" and allege that requiring such fees to be paid will chill their ability to provide Internet webcasts and drive them out of business. Webcasters continue to submit proposals to the Copyright Office for decreased royalty fees.

Nearly 10 years after its passage, the DMCA continues to be a controversial piece of legislation. Court cases continue to challenge its provisions, and Congress has been asked to amend some of its provisions. Additionally, the DMCA mandates that various studies and reports be conducted by the U.S. Copyright Office on the effects of the DMCA. These reports are available at http://www.copyright.gov.

A number of scholars and experts have questioned whether the DMCA and DRM measures have gone too far. One 2004 study by economists concluded that the oft-cited decrease in CD sales was unrelated to piracy and that downloading tunes actually increased sales of popular CDs. The authors concluded that CD sales have been declining due to economic reasons, boring radio playlists, a reduction in the number of CDs released, and possible consumer backlash against the recording industry.

With critics asserting that the DMCA has been used to stifle competition and intimidate researchers and that digital file sharing has continued to increase even after passage of the DMCA, a number of experts have called for changes to the DMCA. Others are concerned about our "clearance culture," in which it is becoming increasingly difficult and expensive to obtain access or permission to use copyrighted material, squelching creativity. For example, one filmmaker has theorized that the History Channel shows a preponderance of World War II documentaries because the film footage is in the public domain and filmmakers need not obtain copyright clearances.

ENTERTAINMENT NOTES

Introduction

The music industry has likely been the hardest hit by technology that enables consumers to swap or share copyrighted songs over personal computers, thus eliminating the need to buy records or CDs. Surveys suggest that more blank CDs are sold in the United States than recorded ones. Sales of albums and CDs in the United States have continually decreased over the past several years. The International Intellectual Property Alliance reported than an estimated

20 million songs were illegally downloaded in 2006 alone and that the estimated loss in 2006 due to music piracy in 60 selected countries was more than $2 billion.

The battle to stop music piracy is fought principally by the Recording Industry Association of America (RIAA). Initially, the RIAA's strategy focused on peer-to-peer music swapping services, such as Napster, developed in 1999 by a college student. RIAA has since broadened its focus by pursuing companies, universities, and individual users while simultaneously seeking legislative assistance from Congress in stopping piracy. One of RIAA's chief obstacles, however, is that surveys continually show that users who download music from the Internet do not perceive it as "theft" and the widespread practice of music piracy may be nearly impossible to control.

In fact, a 2006 study revealed that more than one-half of all college students download music and movies illegally. The RIAA has thus strengthened both its deterrence and education efforts aimed at universities and students.

Napster and MyMP3.com

Napster's software enabled users to search the computer drives of thousands of other users for music files. The users could select songs from vast music repertories and download copyrighted

ETHICS EDGE: Tracking Legislation

Because bills are introduced each year that may affect clients' rights, you will need to monitor and track this pending legislation. Both Lexis and Westlaw not only provide the text of pending legislation but also can monitor developments and notify you by e-mail of updates and changes. Use Lexis's Eclipse service or Westlaw's WestClip service to track and keep informed of legislation relating to IP issues. Similarly, the Copyright Office's Web site allows you to select "Current Legislation" to link to legislation relating to copyright issues.

songs from one another's computers rather than by way of another's server, a practice often called **peer-to-peer file sharing.** Napster's popularity was immediate, and nearly every college student and teenager was easily able to download copyrighted songs and make their own CDs.

The RIAA and various record labels sued Napster in late 1999 in the U.S. District Court in San Francisco for copyright infringement. After a series of court skirmishes, most of which resulted in rulings against Napster, Napster's site was ordered shut down and it agreed to pay certain damages to some of the plaintiffs. Napster also entered into agreements with some of the record labels in an effort to launch a secure music subscription service. Napster ultimately filed for Chapter 11 bankruptcy in mid-2002 and its assets were later auctioned. Napster was officially shut down in September 2002. In late 2003, Napster was reestablished as a paid subscription service, and its stock is now sold on Nasdaq.

The RIAA and Universal Music Corp. also sued MP3 Board, Inc., which provided a service called "MyMP3.com," allowing subscribers to develop a digital music "locker" from which they could access sound recordings. In 2002, the U.S. District Court for the Southern District of New York ruled that the service was a violation of copyright law. Court cases involving Napster and MyMP3.com easily found that the services were not fair uses of copyrighted material and that the services were not entitled to the safe harbor provisions immunizing online service providers under the DMCA.

The Grokster Case

Although the RIAA prevailed in its cases against Napster and MyMP3.com, the offending services were immediately replaced by other music swapping services, among them, Kazaa, Morpheus, and Grokster, which gained millions of users. Shutting down these new song swapping services proved difficult, partly because these services do not route traffic through a central server. Instead, each user's computer becomes a "virtual server." Thus, there was no one central network that could be shut down.

In mid-2005, the U.S. Supreme Court settled the issue, unanimously holding defendants Grokster and StreamCast (the provider of Morpheus) liable for copyright infringement because they distributed devices with the object of promoting their use to infringe others' copyrights. *Metro-Goldwyn-Mayer Studios Inc. v. Grokster, Ltd.*, 545 U.S. 913 (2005). Although the programs were capable of lawful use, evidence showed that copyright infringement constituted 90 percent of the total use of the services. The defendants were thus contributorily or secondarily liable because they induced others to engage in copyright infringement as shown by the affirmative steps they had taken to foster infringement, such as marketing to Napster users, failing to develop filtering tools to diminish infringing activity, and thriving on infringement.

In the wake of *Grokster*, which was hailed by the Register of Copyrights as "one of the most significant developments in copyright law in the past twenty years," Grokster stopped distributing its peer-to-peer software and has shut down; like Kazaa and Napster, Morpheus was relaunched as a paid subscription service.

Our Post-Grokster World

After their success in closing down Napster and Grokster, content owners have engaged in a multipronged approach to reduce piracy, including the following.

- **Digital music services.** Recording and other companies have introduced subscription services allowing consumers to access music files for monthly or per-song fees. One of the best known is Apple's iTunes, which has about 75 percent of the online music market. There are more than 200 of these online music stores, showing that they are moving into the mainstream and gaining widespread consumer acceptance. Nevertheless, although online sales of singles from services such as iTunes increased 60 percent in 2006, revenue from CDs experienced its greatest one-year decline that year (principally because online sales remain a small percentage of all music sales). Some consumers continue to complain about the online stores because they often cannot find and purchase major acts. One consumer criticism (that DRM software was built into the song files to prevent piracy and unauthorized sharing) was largely eliminated in early 2007 when music label EMI Group agreed to make thousands of songs available on iTunes in a DRM-free version. Additionally, Apple's Steve Jobs has called for an open-music system that would allow songs to be played on any device (just as a DVD purchased from any store can be played on any DVD machine, regardless of its manufacturer). While iTunes has recently begun selling music that can be played on a PC device, music purchased on iTunes initially could be played only on iPod players, and music purchased elsewhere generally cannot be played on the iPod. Making music easier to buy than to pirate should reduce piracy.

- **New technologies.** Some experts have noted that the technology used by Grokster is nearly antique and has been largely supplanted by BitTorrent, a peer-to-peer protocol designed for transferring files legally. BitTorrent has more than 130 million users who enjoy both free movies and music, publish their own content, and purchase movies and music. Because BitTorrent encourages noninfringing uses of content and operates noncommercially (making its money through advertising and not through the trading of content), it should be immune from liability under *Grokster*.

Other new technological advances include content-recognition software, which makes it possible to identify copyrighted material even from poor-quality images. For example, Audit Magic's software was able to quickly identify a colorless and blurry video clip, with dialogue dubbed in Chinese, as a scene from the film *Kill Bill: Vol. 2*. Just as a human fingerprint identifies a person, these fingerprinting technologies quickly locate the unique characteristics of video content and identify them so they can be removed from sites such as YouTube.

- **Licensing arrangements.** Labels are entering into licensing arrangements with sites such as YouTube so that users can use such content in their homemade videos. Similarly, as discussed in chapter 11, content owners may use licenses available from Creative Commons, a nonprofit organization that helps people dedicate their creative works to the public domain or license them for certain uses, in a type of "some rights reserved" rather than "all rights reserved" approach.
- **Education.** Content providers continue to try to educate the public about the high costs of music and movie piracy. For example, the Motion Picture Association of America shows trailers before movies that inform viewers of the effects of copyright infringement, and various programs are aimed at reducing piracy on college campuses.
- **Enforcement.** Both the RIAA and MPAA have stepped up their enforcement efforts in recent years. These efforts range from working with law enforcement to seize illegal goods (such as discs manufactured illegally), to raids, to offering rewards to theatre employees who stop illegal camcorder recording of movies, to training law enforcement officials to recognize pirating operations. Litigation

is also used to combat piracy and deter infringers.

- **Legislation.** Content providers routinely educate and lobby Congress and have been successful in increasing penalties for pirates and in making camcorder recording in theatres a federal felony.

Legislative and Prosecutorial Efforts to Stop Piracy

Some of the persistent problems with countermeasures designed to stop piracy include the fact that as soon as the music industry introduces a form of protection technology, consumers figure a way to outwit it. For example, after one company released CDs with encryption technology that precluded copying, furious consumers figured out they could defeat the encryption with a felt-tip marker. Pay-for-play subscription services are growing, but some consumers have been unhappy with the catalogs offered and continue to illegally download music and movies. As a result, the entertainment industries have often turned to Congress for help. Bills introduced in Congress have ranged from those requiring manufacturers of computers and other electronic devices to incorporate technology that would prevent illegal copying to those that would disrupt or even attack a user's computer drive if a copyright holder has a reasonable basis to believe piracy is occurring on that computer.

One significant new law passed in 2005 is the **Family Entertainment and Copyright Act,** which affects the entertainment industries in several ways.

- It imposes criminal penalties for camcorder recording movies in a movie theatre.
- It criminalizes uploading a movie before its commercial release.
- It authorizes copyright preregistration of works being prepared for commercial distribution, such as movies (see chapter 13).

- It allows members of private households to filter out profanity, violence, and sexual content from movies and immunizes the makers of equipment used for such purposes.

The final law removed a section referred to as the "Pirate Act," which would have allowed federal prosecutors to file civil lawsuits against suspected copyright infringers. Critics successfully argued that such a law would use taxpayer dollars to fight the copyright battles of the music and movie industries.

The Department of Justice has established a Computer Crime & Intellectual Property Section to combat computer and intellectual property crimes worldwide. It prevents, investigates, and prosecutes computer and IP crimes. Additional information can be found at http://www.cybercrime.gov.

Conclusion

At the time of writing of this text, no one is sure how to prevent piracy of music and movies. The solution is likely a combination of education, enforcement, technology (including digital rights management methods), and legislation to protect valuable entertainment content.

RECENT DEVELOPMENTS IN COPYRIGHT LAW

As is apparent from the foregoing discussion, copyright law continues to evolve with technology. Some of the more recent and interesting developments are as follows.

- While acknowledging that clothing is a useful article and thus not subject to copyright protection, a New York federal court ruled that lace designs, copyrighted as writings and incorporated into wedding dresses, were protectable and enjoined another maker of wedding dresses from making or marketing copies. Similarly, detailed embroidery or some other two-dimensional drawing or graphic work affixed to a portion of a garment may be copyrightable. Haute couture fashion designers have been lobbying for some form of protection against piracy for their designs. The protection would not be a pure copyright protection (because such protection is not available for useful items) and would be for a limited period, perhaps only three years, because the demand for such designs is relatively short-lived. In August 2007, a bill was introduced in Congress that would extend copyright protection for three years for certain fashion designs. At the time of the writing of this text, no major action had been taken on the bill, and the Register of Copyrights had not yet taken a position on the issue.

- A federal court in California recently held that while type fonts themselves are not protectable under copyright law, a software program that generated and created the typefaces was protectable. The Copyright Office has ruled the same.

- As soon as Stephen King sold his book *Riding the Bullet* exclusively in an Internet format, an individual cracked the copyright protection software and posted free copies of the book on the Internet. The publishers responded by adopting stronger encryption technology. Similarly, in 2000, Mr. King suspended online publication of a serial novel because too many individuals were downloading the work without paying for it.

- As discussed in chapter 14, in late 1997, President Clinton signed into law the No Electronic Theft (NET) Act (amending 18 U.S.C. § 2319) to enhance criminal penalties for copyright infringement, even if the infringer does not profit from the transaction. The act also extends the statute of limitations for criminal copyright infringement from three to five years, and allows law enforcement officers to use federal copyright laws against online copyright violation, thereby extending the same copyright protection to the Internet that is provided to other media.

- In mid-2000, President Clinton signed the Electronic Signatures in Global and National Commerce Act, making digital executions, called **e-signatures,** as legally binding as their paper counterparts.

- As further evidence of the seriousness of IP piracy, the Department of Justice announced a 38 percent increase in criminal indictments between 2003 and 2005 for IP thefts and has secured criminal convictions against more than 60 people on criminal copyright infringement charges.

- In 2002, Milberg Weiss Bershad Hynes & Lerach, a well-known securities litigation law firm, noticed that other law firms were "copying" its complex class action complaints and other pleadings, and began to place copyright notices on the documents it filed with courts. Most experts believe that any such claim to copyright will fail because documents filed with courts are public records, there is a need for public access to such documents, and any use by others is likely a fair use.

- After Congress extended the term of copyrights (from the life of the author plus 50 years to the life of the author plus 70 years), a number of **orphan works** (works for which no copyright owner can be found) were created. This situation places a burden on those who wish to use the works and who thus risk infringement if they cannot locate a copyright owner from whom to seek permission to use the work. For example, some consumers have been unable to have old family photographs duplicated because the photo finishers could not verify whether the photograph was subject to copyright protection. The Register of Copyrights has recommended that Congress enact legislation so those who use orphan works are not subject to costly penalties if they have made a reasonable effort to find the owner. Legislation was introduced in the 109th Congress in 2006 but was not enacted.

- In late 2006, the Copyright Office issued a decision finding that ringtones used in cell phones that are excerpts of preexisting recordings (e.g., a portion of an existing song) are subject to the statutory licensing scheme of 17 U.S.C. § 115 (meaning that reproductions of musical works may be made or distributed without obtaining the consent of the copyright owner provided the maker or distributor pays the statutory license fee set by the Copyright Office). The ruling was a blow to songwriters who argued that ringtones were "new" and creative derivative works, and thus royalties should be negotiated for each use. The ruling clarifies that once the copyright owner of a musical work distributes it (either as a song or a ringtone) to the public, anyone can obtain a statutory license to use the musical work in that ringtone. Because most ringtones do not change the basic melody or character of a musical work, most will be subject to the statutory license, and thus anyone may use such as long as the standard royalty fee is paid. Statutory licenses are discussed in chapter 11.

- In August 1999, the National Conference of Commissioners on Uniform State Laws passed a model law, called the Uniform Computer Information Transactions Act (UCITA), to regulate electronic commerce, including shrink-wrap and click-wrap licenses. The act, the product of three years of work, is intended to provide a uniform law for software and other computer information transactions and is now being presented to the various state legislatures for consideration and adoption. The act, however, is subject to much dispute and controversy, with its opponents saying it favors the software, Internet, and banking industries. Attorneys General from 24 states oppose the act as presently written, and thus, its adoption in all states is highly uncertain. In fact, at the time of writing of this text, only Maryland and Virginia have adopted UCITA.

- In 2002, Congress amended section 110 of the Copyright Act to grant educators the right to transmit copyrighted works by Internet for distance learning if certain conditions are met (the educational institution must be nonprofit, only officially enrolled students may view the material, and so forth).

- In *New York Times v. Tasini*, 533 U.S. 483 (2001), the Court held that the conversion of articles that had appeared in the *Times* in print form to electronic form was a republication of the works such as would entitle authors to additional compensation when the individual articles were taken from various journals and offered in isolation and not in the same context as their print versions. Similarly, in a second victory for writers, in *Random House, Inc. v. Rosetta Books LLC*, 150 F. Supp. 2d 613 (S.D.N.Y. 2001), *aff'd*, 283 F.3d 490 (2d Cir. 2002), the court held that the right to print and sell works in conventional book form does not include the right to publish the work in digital or electronic formats (unless the author agrees to such). Note, however, that if a publisher reproduces an exact electronic replica of a magazine, such is permissible, and freelance writers and photographers are not entitled to additional compensation when their print material is simply digitally scanned and then appears electronically in the same format and order as the prior print edition. *Faulkner v. Nat'l Geographic Enters. Inc.*, 409 F.3d 26 (2d Cir. 2005). Note that parties are always free to agree on future use and publishing of their works in electronic form.

- In another publishing case, Google's massive plan to scan every book ever published and to make the full texts searchable has been objected to by the Authors' Guild and major publishers as a blatant violation of copyright law. Litigation was commenced in the Southern District of New York in 2005 and is still pending at the time of the writing of this text. Although Google allows copyright owners to "opt out" of the program and allows users to view mere excerpts rather than full books, copyright owners allege that the burden should be on Google to secure their permission to scan their works. Many experts expect that the litigation will ultimately be settled and that Google and the publishers will reach a licensing arrangement.

- One area of concern to the copyright industries is the piracy of optical disc products (such as CDs and DVDs). The International Intellectual Property Alliance has noted that because of the high profit margin (with a markup for DVD piracy higher than that for cocaine and heroin), organized and dangerous crime syndicates have moved into the "business" of optical disc piracy, establishing production plants and laboratories for creating and burning discs.

- The Second Circuit has ruled that West is not entitled to copyright protection for certain elements in its database of judicial opinions. The court held that West's star pagination system and additions of attorney information and parallel citations to cases in the public domain were not sufficiently original to qualify for copyright protection. *Matthew Bender & Co. v. West Publ'g Co.*, 158 F.3d 674 and 693 (2d Cir. 1998), *vacated and remanded on other grounds*, 240 F.3d 116 (2d Cir. 2001). As a consequence of this ruling, West and other database publishers are now looking toward Congress rather than the courts, hoping that Congress will pass some form of database protection law (see earlier discussion of "Copyright Protection for Automated Databases" in this chapter) that will result in protection for its compilations of judicial opinions.

- Copyright experts are debating whether file retrieval by "intelligent agents," akin to Web robots, that monitor the Internet, search for files on behalf of users, and copy the files for later viewing and use constitutes infringement.

- Many Internet service providers are now introducing privacy policies, allowing customers to prohibit or limit distribution of information about themselves to others and prohibiting collection of information relating to children unless parental permission is granted.

While many authors and copyright owners are justifiably concerned over infringement of their works by electronic means, a number of other experts compare the situation to that faced by the music industry several years ago when it became possible to make copies of tapes and CDs. For years people have been able to borrow books and tapes from friends and libraries, and yet there remains a strong market for the sale of books and music. Thus, many experts believe that although some measures and controls are needed to reduce electronic infringement and piracy, there is no need for panic, at least not yet.

TERMS OF THE TRADE

Following is a glossary of some terms currently used in discussing availability of works in the electronic age.

- **Softlifting.** Loading unauthorized copies of software into other computers, a practice frequently encountered in small businesses that do not wish to incur the expense of buying software for each computer and by consumers who share software with friends and family.

- **Copyhoarding.** Retaining all rights in a work, especially software, and refusing to allow others to view it, reproduce it, display it, or use it in any way.

- **Shareware.** Releasing copyrighted software under the condition that if the user likes what he or she sees, the user will pay a license fee.

- **Copylefting.** Licensing all users of software to have free and unfettered access and rights for any purpose and requiring that any improvements or adaptations they make to the work be similarly treated. This concept is even more permissive than that allowed for works in the public domain, which, although not protected, may serve as the source for derivative works that can then be copyrighted and protected from unauthorized use. Copylefting ensures that any derivative works based on the original work remain as freely available as the underlying work.

- **Freeware.** Allowing others to use software for free but retaining rights to ensure the work is not reverse engineered or disassembled.

- **Downstream infringement.** Infringement by users who obtain copyrighted items from legitimate users. Thus, if a licensee allows X to make an unauthorized copy of a software program, X is a downstream infringer (and the licensee may be liable for contributory infringement).

- **Warez.** The term "warez" typically refers to more than one piece of pirated software; warez sites allow distribution of pirated software over the Internet. Alternatively, the term is also a slang tern for all images, music, and content traded on the Internet.

VESSEL HULL PROTECTION

Title V of the DMCA, referred to as the Vessel Hull Design Protection Act (17 U.S.C. § 1301 *et seq.*), provides for protection for original designs of boat vessel hulls. Vessel hull design protection draws many of its concepts from both copyright and patent law but affords a new form of intellectual property protection. It is thus said to be *sui generis* (literally, "the only one of its kind"). The new law grants an owner of an original vessel hull design certain exclusive rights provided that an application for registration of the design is made with the Copyright Office within two years of the design first being made public. Registration is made using Form D-VH and the application fee is $200. Deposit material may consist of either drawings or photographs of the design. To ensure that protection is not granted for useful articles, protection is limited to those designs that make the article attractive and distinctive in appearance. Vessel hull design protection is not available for designs that have received patent protection.

Vessel hull design protection was prompted by a 1989 case in which the U.S. Supreme Court struck down a Florida statute that had protected the designs of boat hulls against copying. The new act affords protection for original vessel hull designs far more quickly and inexpensively than patent protection affords.

Protection of vessel hull designs is not the same as copyright protection, and the term of protection lasts 10 years. When any vessel hull embodying a protected design is publicly exhibited or distributed, the hull must carry a notice of the design's protection; omission of the notice would prevent the owner from recovering against a party who infringes before receiving notice of the protection. Generally, the notice consists of the words "Protected Design" or the symbol "D" together with the name of the owner and the year in which protection commenced. In 2006, the Copyright Office registered only 61 vessel hull designs under the new act.

SEMICONDUCTOR CHIP PROTECTION

Introduction to the Semiconductor Chip Protection Act

Semiconductor chips (or integrated circuits) are used in a wide array of products, including watches, cardiac pacemakers, microwave ovens, televisions, automobiles, and computers. Development and engineering of the complex chips can cost millions of dollars, yet once created, chips can be easily copied. Copyright law does not provide adequate protection for the chips inasmuch as they are useful products and cannot be copyrighted (although the design drawings of chips are copyrightable). Neither does patent law provide adequate protection because the chips generally do not meet the strict standards that patent-able material be nonobvious (see chapter 17). Furthermore, issuance of a patent typically takes two years, and given the rapidity of technological advances, chips are often nearly obsolete by the time a patent might issue.

In 1984, Congress fashioned a solution to the lack of protection for semiconductor chips by enacting the Semiconductor Chip Protection Act. The act creates an entirely new form of intellectual property right in semiconductor chips, one that is different from either copyright law or pat-

ent law. As such, and like vessel hull design protection, it is said to be *sui generis*. Nevertheless, many of the concepts relating to protection, registration, and infringement of chips draw from copyright law. The act is found in title 17 of the United States Code, after the copyright statutes (17 U.S.C. § 901 *et seq.*). The Copyright Office offers Circular 100, entitled "Federal Statutory Protection for Mask Works," to provide information about semiconductor chip protection and registration of mask works. The circular can be downloaded from the Copyright Office's Web site.

Protectable Matter

The act protects **mask works**, which are the stencils used to etch, pattern, or encode an electronic circuit on a semiconductor chip. A **semiconductor chip** is defined as any product "having two or more layers of metallic, insulating, or semiconductor material, deposited or otherwise placed on, or etched away or otherwise removed from, a piece of semiconductor material . . . and intended to perform electronic circuitry functions." 17 U.S.C. § 901(a)(1). Protection extends to the three-dimensional images or patterns formed on the layers of metallic or semiconductor material, that is, the topography of the wafer-thin chip.

To be protected, the mask work must be "fixed," meaning that it must be capable of being perceived or reproduced for more than some transitory period. Additionally, the mask work must be original or independently created and cannot consist of some commonplace variation of an already existing design.

Duration of Protection and Exclusive Rights

Eligibility for protection for a mask work commences on the date the mask work is registered with the Copyright Office or on the date on which it is first commercially exploited (gener-ally meaning the written offer, sale, or distribution to the public) anywhere in the world, whichever occurs first. Protection lasts for 10 years from the date protection begins (assuming the mask work is registered with the Copyright Office within two years after it is commercially exploited).

The mask work owner has the following exclusive rights:

- to reproduce the mask work
- to import or distribute a semiconductor chip product that embodies the mask work
- to induce or knowingly to cause another to do the foregoing acts

The mask owner's rights are infringed by copying of the work. The House Report relating to the act explicitly recognized that the concepts used to determine infringement of copyright (such as substantial similarity and the protection of expression rather than ideas) are applicable to mask works. Thus, a mask work that is substantially similar to a protected work infringes even if it is not an identical copy.

Limitations on the Rights of Mask Work Owners

There are several notable limitations on the exclusive rights granted to mask work owners.

- Similar to copyright law, there is no protection if another mask work is independently created. The act prohibits copying, not independent creation.
- It is not an infringement to reproduce a mask work for teaching, analyzing, or evaluating the concepts or techniques embodied in the mask work. Moreover, it is not an infringement to incorporate the results of this analysis in another original mask work. Thus, mask works can be lawfully reverse engineered.
- Also similar to copyright law, protection does not extend to ideas, systems, processes, or methods of operation, but only to the expression of those ideas in the mask work.

- In another borrowing from copyright law, the first sale doctrine applies such that a person who lawfully obtains a semiconductor chip product may later use, sell, or otherwise dispose of it (as long as the work is not reproduced). Thus, after lawfully purchasing the product, the owner may thereafter also sell, import, distribute, use, or dispose of the semiconductor chip product.

Registration and Notice of Protection

Registration of a mask work is highly similar to that of registration of copyrights. An application is made with the Copyright Office (using Form MW), and identifying matter must be deposited with the application. The fee is $95. However, an application must be made within two years after the work is first commercially exploited. Protection for a mask work terminates if an application is not made with the Copyright Office within that two-year period. Thus, registration is encouraged by providing a longer period of protection for registered works (10 years) than for nonregistered works (2 years).

The registration process for mask works is nearly identical to that for copyrights in that the examination by the Copyright Office is not exhaustive. If the application is correctly completed, the deposited materials are sufficient, and the fee is paid, the registration will be issued, generally within four months. Few refusals are made. In 2006, the Copyright Office issued 349 registrations for mask works.

The mask work owner may affix a notice of protection to the mask work and to masks and semiconductor chip products embodying the mask works. The notice is not a prerequisite for protection, although it constitutes *prima facie* evidence of notice of protection. The notice consists of the words "mask work," the symbol "M," or the letter "M" in a circle, and the name of the owner of the mask work. No date is needed. The notice is usually placed on a label attached to the packaging for the product.

Infringement of Mask Works

A person who violates any of the exclusive rights of a mask work owner may be sued for infringement. To bring an action in federal court for infringement, however, the owner must have registered the mask work (or been refused registration by the Copyright Office). The action must be brought within three years after the claim accrues. Actual damages and the infringer's profits may be awarded to the mask work owner. Alternatively, similar to copyright actions, the owner may elect statutory damages (up to $250,000). A court may enjoin further infringement and may impound and destroy infringing works and the drawings by which infringing chips are reproduced. Attorneys' fees and costs may be awarded.

Trivia

- The Business Software Alliance estimates that about one of every three software applications worldwide is pirated.
- Worldwide, about 500,000 movies are illegally downloaded each day.
- Sales of compact discs declined nearly 25 percent globally between 2000 and 2006.
- U.S. copyright industries lost more than $15 billion in 2006 due to piracy in 60 selected countries.
- Worldwide, the motion picture industry lost $18.2 billion in 2005 as a result of piracy.
- The MPAA says the typical movie pirate is male, between the ages of 16 and 24, and lives in an urban area.
- The MPAA seized 81 million illegally manufactured compact discs in 2005 and made nearly 43,000 raids.
- To deter movie piracy, studios have posted guards with night-vision goggles to locate pirates who are illegally recording movies in theatres.
- Twenty billion songs were illegally downloaded in 2006 alone.

CHAPTER SUMMARY

Computer programs and automated databases are copyrightable and may be registered with the Copyright Office as literary works. As original works of expression, computer programs are protectable against infringement. Nevertheless, a number of cases have held that purely functional elements of programs, stock or standard scenes a faire, and merged ideas and expressions cannot be protected. To hold otherwise would grant developers of computer programs a monopoly and would discourage creative expression. Computer programs may be reverse engineered in certain instances, for example, when it is necessary to gain access to unprotected elements of a program.

The ease with which works may be copied, stored, reproduced, and disseminated by electronic means, primarily the Internet, has caused much debate among authors and owners of works who are concerned about infringement of their works and those who believe that information "needs to be free." Some experts believe that technology itself can solve the challenges of the electronic age: devices can be constructed that would encrypt or protect works and prevent them from being copied or transmitted unless permission or royalties are first obtained. In the interim, the Copyright Act is sufficiently muscular to protect works from infringement by electronic means. Thus, copying, downloading, or transmitting works over the Internet is subject to risk.

The Digital Millennium Copyright Act of 1998 updated U.S. copyright law for the digital age by prohibiting circumvention of copyright protection systems and protecting online service providers from liability for copyright infringements on their services if they follow certain safeguards.

The music and movie industries remain concerned about piracy of songs and movies and continue to educate consumers about copyright piracy, prosecute infringers, and push for legislation to protect music and movies from rampant downloading over the Internet. The original designs of boat vessel hulls are protectable against infringement under the DMCA.

Because neither patent law nor copyright law afforded sufficient protection for complex and expensively developed semiconductor chips, Congress enacted the Semiconductor Chip Protection Act of 1984. The act creates an entirely new form of intellectual property protection for mask works, the stencils used to pattern or encode semiconductor chips. Mask works may be registered with the Copyright Office and are protected against infringement.

CASE ILLUSTRATION—THE SAFE HARBOR OF THE DMCA

Case: *Hendrickson v. Amazon.com, Inc.*, 298 F. Supp. 2d 914 (C.D. Cal. 2003)

Facts: Hendrickson, the owner of a copyright in a movie, *Manson*, had never released his movie in DVD format. Hendrickson wrote a letter to Amazon.com informing it that any copies of *Manson* in DVD format infringed his copyright. Nearly ten months later, Hendrickson observed that *Manson* was available for sale on Amazon.com. Hendrickson alleged that Amazon.com was liable for both direct and vicarious infringement.

Holding: Amazon.com was not liable for direct infringement because it was not a seller. Whether Amazon.com was liable for vicarious infringement depended on whether the notice sent by Hendrickson was sufficient under the DMCA. The court held that the DMCA places a burden on the copyright owner to monitor the Internet for infringing activity. A copyright owner cannot write one blanket letter that remains viable forever. In this case, Hendrickson's letter was not adequate to provide notice of infringing activities that occurred nearly ten months thereafter. Amazon.com was thus entitled to the safe harbor defense under the DMCA.

CASE STUDY AND ACTIVITIES

Case Study.   Vision has recently discovered that one of its advertising commercials has been posted on YouTube without its authority or permission. Vision has sent YouTube a notice identifying its rights and demanding that YouTube remove the commercial. Vision uses a software program (designed by a third party) to provide continued training to its staff. Vision licensed the program by a "shrink-wrap license." Vision would like to make multiple copies of the program and send them to its various hotels throughout the nation. Vision would also like to circumvent various copy protection measures built into the software program. Finally, Vision has discovered that in order to increase competition and motivation, employees of its competitors have been furnished cell phones that play several bars of Vision's well-known "theme song." Vision has not authorized this use.

Activities.   Discuss the copyrightability of the works discussed in the case study as well as any other copyright or infringement issues relating to the works.

ROLE OF PARALEGAL

Because copyright issues confronting users, authors, legislators, and judges are continuing to evolve, the primary task of IP paralegals may be simply to monitor the issues by continuing research. Specifically, practitioners may be involved in the following tasks:

- preparing and monitoring copyright applications for computer programs, Web sites, and automated databases
- tracking legislation relating to copyright using Lexis or Westlaw or the free and accessible Internet sites THOMAS (http://thomas.loc.gov), Government Printing Office Access offering access to public laws and various congressional documents at http://www.gpoaccess.gov, or the Senate and House home pages at http://www.senate.gov and http://www.house.gov
- monitoring articles, bulletin boards, and other postings on the Internet for information relating to copyrights in the electronic age
- reviewing legal periodicals and journals for articles relating to emerging copyright issues
- assisting in preparing newsletters and bulletins for clients to inform them of developments in the field
- assisting clients in developing copyright compliance policies to ensure their employees do not infringe copyrights of others
- reviewing clients' Web sites and other electronic materials to ensure copyright notices are displayed at those sites
- reviewing Web sites of competitors of clients to ascertain whether clients' copyrighted materials are being infringed or whether links to clients' sites are being improperly used

- preparing and responding to DMCA "takedown" notices
- preparing and monitoring applications for registration of mask works and vessel hull designs
- ensuring that clients' mask works (or the containers therefor) contain the proper mask work notice

INTERNET RESOURCES

Federal laws relating to copyright:	http://www.law.cornell.edu http://www.findlaw.com
Copyright Office:	http://www.copyright.gov (for forms, circulars on mask works, information on the DMCA, vessel hull protection, and new copyright developments and legislation)
National Conference of Commissioners on Uniform State Laws:	http://www.nccusl.org (for text of UCITA)
Business Software Alliance:	http://www.bsa.org (for information on antipiracy and technology policy)
Software Information & Industry Association:	http://www.siia.net (for information on protecting and promoting software and digital content)
Recording Industry Association of America:	http://www.riaa.org (for information on active music issues)
Motion Picture Association of America:	http://www.mpaa.org (for information on movie piracy)
Electronic Frontier Foundation:	http://www.eff.org (for information on cutting-edge technology issues and links to cases)
Chilling Effects Clearinghouse:	http://www.chillingeffects.org (joint project of EFF and various law schools regarding intellectual property and First Amendment issues)
Digital Future Coalition:	http://www.dfc.org (for information on active issues relating to digital and electronic copyright rights)
International Intellectual Property Alliance	http://www.iipa.com (for information and reports on international protection of intellectual property)

DISCUSSION QUESTIONS

1. Spectrum Corp. would like to register its new computer software program, which has only 40 pages of source code; however, it does not wish to deposit all of the pages with the Copyright Office because it believes that several pages include valuable trade secrets. What should it do?

2. Fred has purchased a new video game. He has made three backup copies for his own use and has improved the speed of the game to challenge his skill level. Discuss the permissibility of each of these actions.

3. Georgia owns a new version of the "Turbo Tax" software program, which she purchased at Best Buy and which came in a package with inserts labeled as "License Material." Why can't Georgia sell it or rent it to another under the first sale doctrine?

4. Helen is a professor of software engineering. In order to publish an academic paper for an upcoming conference, Helen circumvented the digital watermarks inserted into various copyrighted materials. Has Helen violated the DMCA? What if Helen circumvented the digital watermarks in order to make several copies of the film *Little Miss Sunshine* for her own use?

5. Sheryl Crow has observed that one of her copyrighted music videos has been posted on YouTube without her permission. What should Ms. Crow do? Is YouTube liable for copyright infringement?

6. Celia and Sam are concerned about the profanity and violence in a movie they have purchased for their children's viewing and are filtering it out. Is such a violation of the copyright owner's right to adapt its work? Is the maker of the equipment used by Sam and Celia to delete the objectionable scenes liable for infringement? Discuss.

7. What does it mean to say that protection for vessel hulls and semiconductor chips is "sui generis"?

USING INTERNET RESOURCES

1. Access the Copyright Office's Web site.
   a. What is the fee assessed by the Copyright Office for one to record a designation of an agent to receive a "takedown" notice under the DMCA?
   b. Review the FAQs. May one copyright a Web site? What circular provides information on this topic?

2. Access the Web site Webopedia.
   a. What is the definition given for "DRM"?
   b. What is a "torrent"?

3. Access the Web site for the Department of Justice. What is the telephone number for the Computer Crime and Intellectual Property Division?

4. Access the Web site for the Recording Industry Association of America. Select "Anti-Piracy." What is the difference between "pirate recordings" and "bootleg recordings"?

5. Access the U.S. Supreme Court's Web site and locate the *Grokster* case issued in the 2004 term. Review the Court's syllabus.
   a. How many files were shared across the peer-to-peer networks each month, as revealed by discovery?
   b. Did Grokster and StreamCast receive revenue from users?
   c. Did Grokster and StreamCast make any attempt to filter copyrighted works or to otherwise impede the sharing of copyrighted files?

For additional resources, go to www.paralegal.delmar.cengage.com.

Chapter 16

International Copyright Law

CHAPTER OVERVIEW

There is no international copyright law that protects copyrighted works in every country. More than 160 nations, however, adhere to the Berne Convention, the terms of which require members to treat nationals of other member countries like their own nationals for purposes of copyright. By joining the Berne Convention in 1989, the United States was required to make some changes to its copyright laws, notably, eliminating the requirement that works be accompanied by a copyright notice in order to receive protection and allowing owners of works not originating in the United States to sue in federal court for copyright infringement even if they did not possess a copyright registration. New treaties supplementing the Berne Convention ensure that copyrighted works are protected from infringement by any means, including electronic means, and prohibit attempts to defeat encryption or protection of copyrighted works. The United States is also a party to the Universal Copyright Convention and the Uruguay Round Agreements Act. Finally, in 2002, two international treaties adopted

by the World Intellectual Property Organization, and often called the "Internet treaties," entered into force to protect copyrighted works in the digital environment. The United States is a party to both of these new treaties, which are viewed as the most important updates to international copyright protection in a generation.

INTRODUCTION

Nearly 1 million books and other literary titles, 5,000 feature films, and 3 million songs are published worldwide each year. Yet there is no such thing as "international copyright" that will protect an author's work throughout the world. Protection generally is afforded on a country-by-country basis. However, most countries offer protection to foreign works under international conventions and treaties. There are two principal international copyright treaties or conventions: the Berne Convention for the Protection of Literary and Artistic Property (Berne Convention) and the Universal Copyright Convention (UCC). These treaties impose certain minimum requirements that each signatory or contracting nation must agree to implement. After instituting these minimum obligations, countries are free to enact other statutes and provide additional protection. Thus, protection for copyright around the world is far from uniform.

Authors who desire protection for their works in foreign countries should first determine the scope of protection available to works of foreign authors in that country. Determination should be done prior to publication of the work in any country inasmuch as the extent of protection afforded to a work may depend on facts existing at the time of first publication anywhere. The laws of most countries provide that copyright protection exists independently of any formalities and that it is not necessary to register a copyright to achieve protection for a work.

If the country in which protection is sought is a party to one of the international copyright conventions, the work generally may be protected by complying with the conditions of that convention. Even if the work cannot be protected under an international convention, protection may still be available under the specific laws of a foreign country. Some countries, however, offer little or no copyright protection to foreign works.

THE BERNE CONVENTION

The Berne Convention was created in 1886 under the leadership of Victor Hugo to protect literary and artistic works and has more than 160 member nations (see Appendix A for a table of nations adhering to the Berne Convention). In 1989, the United States became a party to the Berne Convention by entering into an international treaty called the Berne Convention for the Protection of Literary and Artistic Works. The Berne Convention is administered by the World Intellectual Property Organization (WIPO), an organization whose objective is to promote the protection of intellectual property throughout

the world. The Berne Convention is based on the precept that each member nation must treat nationals of other member countries like its own nationals for purposes of copyright (the principle of **national treatment**).

Moreover, the Berne Convention has established certain minimum levels of copyright protection to which all member nations must adhere (such as specifying that all members must recognize that authors have the exclusive rights to perform, broadcast, adapt, and reproduce their works), ensuring that copyright laws in the member nations will share many features. The Berne Convention also provides that copyright protection cannot be conditioned upon compliance with any registration formalities, thus clarifying that works are automatically protected without requiring notice of copyright or registration. Finally, the Berne Convention provides that works are protected independently of the existence of protection in the country of origin of the work. If a work originates in one of the more than 160 member nations of the Berne Union, it is entitled to protection in all other member nations. A work's "country of origin" is usually the place of its first publication. Generally, works are protected under the Berne Convention for a minimum of 50 years after the author's death, though member nations may provide for a longer term, as has the United States.

In order to fulfill its obligations under the Berne Convention, the United States made certain changes in its copyright laws, effective after March 1, 1989, the date the United States acceded to the Berne Convention. Perhaps the most significant change to U.S. copyright law was that the mandatory notice of copyright (e.g., © 1988 John Doe) that was previously required in the United States was abolished so that failure to place a notice on copyrighted works would no longer result in the loss of copyright. Thus, for all works published after March 1, 1989, use of a copyright notice is voluntary (although it is strongly recommended, because use of a notice will preclude a party from asserting its infringement was innocent, which claim might reduce damages in an infringement action).

The Berne Convention also recognizes "moral rights" (the rights of authors to claim authorship of their works and to object to any mutilation or modification of the work that would be prejudicial to the author's reputation or honor). In 1989, in order to become a party to the Berne Convention, the United States for the first time recognized moral rights; however, the scope of moral rights afforded in the United States is less extensive than in many other countries inasmuch as the Visual Artists Rights Act (17 U.S.C. § 106A) provides moral rights only to works of fine arts. (See chapter 11.)

As discussed in chapter 14, before a copyright infringement suit is brought for a work of U.S. origin, the work must be submitted to the Copyright Office for registration. Works originating in Berne Union countries are exempt from the requirement to register before bringing suit. Authors whose works originate in the United States, however, are still subject to the requirement of registering their work (or showing they attempted to register but registration was refused).

TREATIES SUPPLEMENTING THE BERNE CONVENTION: THE WIPO TREATIES

In December 1996, WIPO convened in Geneva, Switzerland, to work on the first amendment to international copyright laws in 25 years, action that was primarily spurred by concern over piracy of copyrighted works through the Internet. Authors, of course, are concerned that the value of their works will be diminished by unauthorized reproduction and transmission, and Internet service providers are concerned they may face liability for contributory or vicarious infringement based on the fact that their services are used to carry out infringing activities.

Two treaties, the WIPO Copyright Treaty and the WIPO Performances and Phonograms Treaty, were adopted at the Geneva conference and were then considered for ratification by individual countries. In order to fulfill obligations under the WIPO treaties, most countries, including the United States, were required to amend their copyright laws in several respects, chief among them to protect against the unlawful circumvention of technologies used by copyright owners to prevent electronic theft of their works. The passage of the Digital Millennium Copyright Act in the United States in 1998 (see chapter 15) accomplished this goal, and the WIPO treaties came into force in early 2002 when they were each ratified by 30 countries.

The WIPO Copyright Treaty expressly states that computer programs are protected by copyright as literary works and makes it clear that authors' rights of distribution extend to electronic distribution by granting authors the exclusive right to distribute, sell, or rent their works via electronic means. The Copyright Treaty also requires adhering nations to provide remedies against any person who removes or alters electronic rights management information (information about copyright works, authors, and owners that is appended or attached to works in electronic form) and to provide adequate legal protection against the circumvention of security or encryption devices used by authors to protect their works. The act prohibits both the use of circumvention methods and the manufacturing or offering of circumvention devices. Circumvention is permissible for computer security testing, encryption research, certain library uses, and for law enforcement activities. The WIPO Performance Treaty provides similar rights, granting protection to sound recordings first fixed in a treaty member country.

Neither treaty addresses liability of Internet service providers for copyright infringement using the Internet, although legislation passed in late 1998 in the United States (17 U.S.C. § 512(c)) as part of the Digital Millennium Copyright Act clarifies that Internet service providers are not liable for infringement if they do not know of such acts and if they do not profit from them. As discussed in chapter 15, upon receiving notification of claimed infringement, the service providers must expeditiously take down or remove access to the material. Finally, although much discussion occurred relating to whether databases resulting from a substantial investment of time and effort should be protected, the parties could not reach agreement; however, they did agree that databases consisting of original work could be protected. Recall that the United States expressly rejected the "sweat of the brow" doctrine in *Feist Publications v. Rural Telephone Service Co.*, 499 U.S. 340 (1991), holding that a telephone directory consisting merely of facts could not be copyrighted even if it was the result of much effort. The conference adopted a recommendation calling for another session to further discuss database protection inasmuch as many experts fear that extending database protection rights to compilations resulting from effort and time would result in sports statistics, weather information, stock market information, and transportation schedules all being monopolized by the first to compile the data. As discussed in chapter 15, Congress has considered extending copyright protection to databases produced through investment of substantial time and money (although databases generated with government funding would likely remain available for all to use, and the fair use of information in databases would be protected). If passed, such legislation would create an entirely new form of copyright protection for databases and would nullify *Feist* to some extent because it would protect collections of information or data that might not otherwise be copyrightable. To date, any proposed legislation relating to databases has been subject to much debate and an uncertain future.

THE URUGUAY ROUND AGREEMENTS ACT

In December 1994, President Clinton signed the **Uruguay Round Agreements Act** (URAA) that implements the Uruguay Round General Agreement on Tariffs and Trade (GATT), which itself includes an agreement on Trade-Related Aspects of Intellectual Property (TRIPs). TRIPs requires all members of the WTO to provide certain minimum standards of protection for trademarks, copyrights, patents, and trade secrets and requires countries to provide effective enforcement of these rights.

The URAA amended federal copyright law in several ways, including the addition of civil and criminal penalties to provide remedies for "bootlegging" sound recordings of live musical performances and music videos. Prior to this amendment, U.S. copyright law generally protected only the fixed work (such as the song being performed) rather than the live performance itself. The new provisions prohibit unauthorized recording or broadcasts of live performances and reproduction or distribution of unauthorized fixations of the work.

Equally important, the URAA also provided for the automatic restoration of copyright in certain foreign works (but not U.S. domestic works) that had fallen into the public domain in the United States but were protected by copyright in their countries of origin. Typically, works from eligible countries had fallen into the public domain because their authors failed to comply with formalities required by the United States, such as including a notice of copyright on the work or renewing the work (during the time when the United States required copyright notice and had a renewal period for copyrighted works).

Eligible copyrights are restored automatically and remain protectable for the term they would have enjoyed had they not entered the public domain. However, the URAA directs that the owner of a restored work notify "reliance parties"

(parties who, relying on the public domain status of the work, were using the work prior to its automatic restoration under the URAA) if the owner of rights in a restored work intends to enforce his or her rights. Either actual notice may be given to a reliance party, or constructive notice may be given through filing a "Notice of Intent to Enforce" with the Copyright Office. The reliance party then has a grace period of 12 months to sell off its existing stock, publicly perform the work, or phase out its reproduction, distribution, performance, or display of the work.

The **World Trade Organization (WTO)** was established in 1995 to implement the Uruguay Round Agreements, serve as a forum for trade negotiations, handle trade disputes, and monitor national trade policies. It has more than 150 members. (See Appendix A.) The United States has been a member of the WTO since 1995. The WIPO and the WTO cooperate to provide assistance to developing countries with respect to intellectual property rights and laws.

As discussed in chapter 8, GATT (the organization) was replaced by the WTO, which oversees various trade agreements.

THE UNIVERSAL COPYRIGHT CONVENTION

The United States became a party to the original **Universal Copyright Convention** (UCC) in 1955, more than 30 years before the United States became a party to the Berne Convention; thus, the UCC was the first international convention relating to copyright to which the United States was subject. Similar to the Berne Convention, the UCC is based on the principle of national treatment, requiring that works originating in a member nation must be given the same protection in each of the other member nations as is granted by the laws of the country of origin. The UCC imposes fewer minimum standards on its members than does the Berne Convention. The UCC provides that use of a copyright notice

in a prescribed form (the © symbol, accompanied by the year of first publication and the name of the copyright owner) will satisfy notice requirements in all other member nations. Because the Berne Convention imposes requirements that are stricter than those of the UCC, to ensure members would not drop out of the Berne Convention and rely strictly on the UCC, the UCC provides that no Berne member may withdraw from Berne and later rely on the UCC in its relations with other Berne members. Additionally, the Berne Convention takes precedence over the UCC inasmuch as the terms of the Berne Convention, rather than those of the UCC, apply to relationships among Berne members, even though those parties may also be members of the UCC. Some Berne member countries joined the UCC to establish relations with nations that are not members of Berne (such as British Virgin Islands, Gibraltar, and Saint Helena). The UCC is administered by UNESCO.

TRADE ASPECTS OF INTELLECTUAL PROPERTY LAW

There is a strong correlation between trade policies and intellectual property protection. The International Intellectual Property Alliance has concluded that countries with the poorest records of protecting intellectual property have slower rates of information technology growth.

Similarly, Jack Valenti, the former president of the Motion Picture Association of America, stated that "copyright industries are the jewels in America's trade crown." Thus, the United States favors strong international protection of intellectual property because theft of such intellectual property has a damaging effect on the U.S. economy.

The "Special 301" provisions of the Trade Act of 1974 require that the United States Trade Representative (USTR) identify "priority" foreign countries that deny adequate and effective protection of intellectual property rights. Once

ETHICS EDGE: Knowing What You Don't Know

Knowing what you don't know is every bit as important (if not more so) as knowing what you do know. International law in the copyright arena is a complex field of law and requires a great deal of expertise. You can't "dabble" in this field on a periodic basis and expect to understand its nuances and emerging developments. Part of the duty of competency to which you are subject requires you to disclose fully to your superiors when you are "in over your head." Ask for help or additional resources when you are tasked with a new or difficult international copyright issue. Know your limits.

countries are identified in the USTR's annual Special 301 review, the USTR can initiate an investigation. If the foreign country is determined to deny adequate protection to intellectual property, the USTR can impose trade sanctions. For example, in 2002, the USTR imposed $75 million in trade sanctions against Ukraine (which sanctions were terminated in 2005 after Ukraine amended its laws to strengthen IP). According to the USTR, "Although [2006's] Special 301 Report shows positive progress in many countries, rampant counterfeiting and piracy problems continue to plague both China and Russia, indicating a critical need for stronger intellectual property protection in China and Russia."

The full text of USTR reports is available at http://www.ustr.gov.

GRAY MARKET GOODS

Section 602(a) of the Copyright Act bars importation of copyrighted goods into the United States without the authority of the copyright owner (the goods are often referred to as "gray market" goods because they are lawfully made as opposed to pirated "black market" goods). In 1998, the Supreme Court held that a copyright holder loses control over subsequent sales of material produced in the United States once a first sale has occurred anywhere. In *Quality King Distributors, Inc. v. L'anza Research International*, 523 U.S. 135 (1998), hair care products affixed with copyrighted labels were manufactured in the United States and then exported for exclusive sale outside the United States. The products were then imported back into the United States without the copyright owner's permission. The copyright owner alleged that such importation violated its exclusive right to distribute the products. The defendant contended that once a first sale of the product occurred abroad, the copyright owner's exclusive right to distribute was exhausted. The Supreme Court agreed that once the first sale occurred, even abroad, the owner of a work or product manufactured in the United States could resell the item anywhere without permission of the copyright holder.

Copyright holders are concerned over this ruling, and some experts believe they will attempt to use provisions in their contracts barring importation of goods into the United States, move their manufacturing or production abroad, or lobby Congress for a change in the law to ensure their domestic revenues are not undercut by identical goods intended for export only.

Additionally, at least one court has stated that *Quality King* is limited to its facts and does not apply to goods manufactured and first sold abroad. *See Swatch S.A. v. New City Inc.*, 454 F. Supp. 2d 1245 (S.D. Fla. 2006).

SUMMARY OF UNITED STATES RELATIONS WITH FOREIGN NATIONS

The United States is a party to various copyright conventions, agreements, and treaties with other nations. Following is a summary of some of the agreements and treaties to which the United States is a party.

- **Berne Convention.** The United States is a party to the Berne Convention as of March 1989. The Berne Convention provides protection to literary and artistic works, including computer programs.
- **Universal Copyright Convention.** The United States has been a party to the Universal Copyright Convention since September 16, 1955.
- **WIPO Internet Treaties.** The United States implemented the WIPO Copyright Treaty and WIPO Performances and Phonograms Treaty in late 1998, and the treaties entered into force in 2002.
- **World Trade Organization**. The United States has been a member of the World Trade Organization, established to implement the Uruguay Round Agreements, since 1995.

Trivia

- The BSA estimates that 35 percent of all software programs worldwide are pirated.
- The BSA rates China's software piracy at 86 percent, Vietnam's software piracy at 90 percent, and the United States's software piracy at 21 percent.
- Lawmakers allege that China and Russia together were responsible for $4 billion in business losses in 2005 due to piracy of copyrighted materials.
- In 2007, the United States initiated two actions in the WTO against China to force it to stop blatant counterfeiting and drop restrictions on the distribution of U.S. films, books, and music.
- At the time of the writing of this text, the 2006 movie *The Departed* could be obtained in China for about $1, and the Microsoft Office suite could be purchased for about $3.

CHAPTER SUMMARY

There is no one treaty or agreement governing copyright throughout the world. More than 160 nations, however, belong to the Berne Convention, which is based on the principle of national treatment: Each member nation must treat works originating in other member nations as it does its own domestic works. Recent supplements to the Berne Convention clarify that computer programs are protectable literary works, that unauthorized reproduction or distribution of a work by electronic means is infringement, and that devices that defeat copyright security measures such as encryption are prohibited. The international copyright community is struggling with the issues presented by the ease and rapidity of electronic communications, just as is the United States.

To comply with its commitments under the Berne Convention, the United States was required to modify its copyright law, primarily to eliminate any requirement for a copyright notice for a work to be protectable and to allow owners of works not originating in the United States to sue in federal court for copyright infringement even if they did not possess a U.S. registration for their work.

The United States is also a party to the Universal Copyright Convention and the Uruguay Round Agreements Act (which required the United States to amend its copyright law to allow restoration of copyright for works that had fallen into the public domain due to lack of copyright notice or failure to renew the work during the time the United States required renewal).

Finally, the United States is a party to the WIPO Internet treaties, designed to fight Internet piracy by prohibiting devices and services that circumvent technological protection measures for copyrighted works. Both treaties entered into force in 2002. To comply with its obligations under the WIPO treaties, the United States amended its copyright law in 1988 by enacting the Digital Millennium Copyright Act, which imposes penalties for circumvention of copyright protection devices (see chapter 15).

CASE ILLUSTRATION—TERRITORIAL LIMITS OF COPYRIGHT ACT

Case: *Update Art, Inc. v. Modiin Publishing, Ltd.*, 843 F.2d 67 (2d Cir. 1988)

Facts: The plaintiff sued for copyright infringement arising out of unauthorized reproduction of its "Ronbo" poster (which mimicked the well-known "Rambo" character). The defendant published a full-page reproduction of plaintiff's poster in its Israeli newspaper. A magistrate held that copyright infringement had occurred.

Holding: The magistrate's ruling was affirmed. Although copyright laws do not generally have extraterritorial effect, there is an exception: When an act of infringement such as reproduction occurs in the United States and then a product is distributed in a foreign country, U.S. copyright law applies. In this case, the evidence showed that the "predicate" or initiating act of infringement (namely, illegal reproduction of the poster) occurred in the United States even though the poster was then distributed in Israel. In such a case, U.S. copyright laws apply and the magistrate correctly assessed damages against the defendants.

CASE STUDY AND ACTIVITIES

Case Study. Vision would like to use many of its advertising brochures and jingles in several foreign countries (all of which adhere to both the Berne Convention and the WIPO treaties). These materials have previously been used in the United States. Vision is concerned,

CASE STUDY AND ACTIVITIES (CONT'D)

however, because some of its recent brochures do not display a copyright notice. Vision is also concerned that some of its advertising jingles, which are protected with encryption technology, will be pirated and downloaded on the Internet in foreign countries. Finally, Vision needs to know the term of protection for copyrighted works in the foreign countries and would like to know if it can file a single application for copyright protection in the various countries (similar to a Madrid Protocol application for trademarks in foreign countries).

Activities.   Discuss the protection that Vision may be able to secure in these countries for its advertising materials.

ROLE OF PARALEGAL

Unless a client sells or distributes its products or works abroad, involvement by IP paralegals with international copyright issues will be minimal. Nevertheless, inasmuch as works can now be sold or distributed in foreign countries merely by the touch of a computer key, some familiarity with international copyright protection is needed. Intellectual property professionals will likely be involved in the following tasks:

- monitoring issues related to international copyright by reading journals, articles, and other materials
- gathering information and publications from the U.S. Copyright Office related to international copyright protection, such as Circular 38a entitled "International Copyright Relations of the United States" and Circular 38b entitled "Highlights of Copyright Amendments Contained in the Uruguay Round Agreements Act"
- retrieving the text of treaties to which the United States is a party either by locating them in conventional print form at law libraries or locating them on the Internet (the Berne Convention and the WIPO Internet treaties can be located through WIPO at http://www.wipo.int, and the Universal Copyright Convention can be located through the United Nations site at http://www.un.org or http://www.unesco.org)
- routinely monitoring various Web sites (see the resources at the end of this chapter and in Appendix C) related to intellectual property to keep abreast of new developments in the international arena

INTERNET RESOURCES

Federal laws relating to copyright: http://www.law.cornell.edu
http://www.findlaw.com

Copyright Office: http://www.copyright.gov (for Circulars 38a and 38b, relating to international copyright relations)

United States Trade Representative: http://www.ustr.gov (for annual reports and information on efforts by foreign countries to protect intellectual property rights; identification of foreign priority watch countries)

World Intellectual Property Organization: http://www.wipo.int (for information on international copyright law and the text of the Berne Convention and the new WIPO Internet treaties)

UNESCO: http://www.unesco.org (for text of Universal Copyright Convention)

World Trade Organization: http://www.wto.org (for information on trade and intellectual property issues)

International Intellectual Property Alliance: http://www.iipa.com (for information on international protection of copyrighted materials)

DISCUSS QUESTIONS

1. Robin, a U.S. citizen, has copyrighted her book in the United States. She would now like to copyright the book in Bolivia and Brazil, members of the Berne Convention. If those countries afford their nationals a copyright term of protection for the author's life plus 50 years, what will the term of protection be for Robin's book in Bolivia and Brazil? What principle governs your answer? May those countries require Robin to place a copyright notice on her book?

2. What policies might underlie the reluctance of the United States to provide full copyright protection for all databases? Discuss.

3. Ron is a national of the United Kingdom, which has been a Berne Convention member since before 1900. Ron distributed his book in the United States in 1985 without a copyright notice. The book has been protected by copyright in the United Kingdom. Is this book protected by U.S. copyright law? Discuss. What agreement governs your answer? What is the term of protection for the book?

4. Assume that in 1993 Cynthia began reproducing Ron's book in the United States. In 1995, what should Ron have done with regard to Cynthia to clarify his rights in the book in the United States?

5. Discuss whether the "Special 301" provisions imposed by the U.S. Trade Representative are a "carrot" or a "stick" to ensure that other countries vigilantly protect IP rights.

USING INTERNET RESOURCES

1. Access the Web site of the Copyright Office.
   a. Review Circular 38a. Identify the copyright relations or treaties for Hong Kong.
   b. What is the fee to record a notice of intent for three separate books?
2. Access the Web site of the WTO. When did Vietnam become a member of the WTO?

USING INTERNET RESOURCES (CONT'D)

3. Access the Web site of UNESCO. How many countries are parties to the Universal Copyright Convention?
4. Access WIPO's Web site. Review the lists of contracting states for the WIPO Copyright Treaty and the WIPO Performances and Phonograms Treaty. Have the treaties entered into force for Canada and the Czech Republic? If so, provide all dates.
5. When did France, Germany, and Saudi Arabia become members of the Berne Convention?

For additional resources, go to www.paralegal.delmar.cengage.com.

PART
IV

The Law of Patents

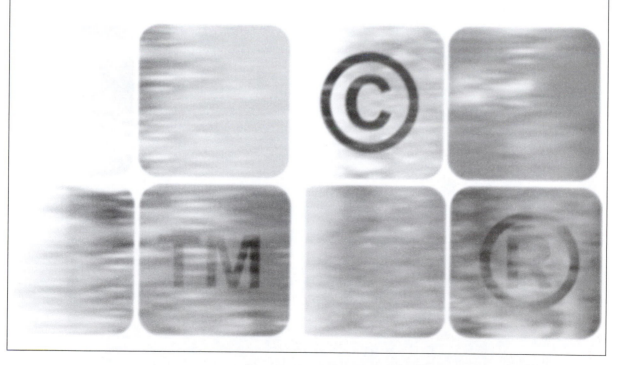

Chapter 17

Foundations of Patent Law

CHAPTER OVERVIEW

A patent is a legal right granted by the federal government that permits its owner to prevent others from making, using, selling, or importing an invention. There are three types of patents: utility patents, design patents, and plant patents. The great majority of patents are utility patents, granted for useful objects or processes. Patents are generally granted to the first to invent, assuming the invention or discovery is not known or used by others in the United States or patented or described in a printed publication in the United States or elsewhere.

Not all discoveries or inventions are eligible for utility patent protection. Patent protection is available only for a new and useful process, machine, manufacture, or composition of matter, or any new and useful improvement thereof. Thus, an inventor must demonstrate that the invention or discovery is useful, novel, and nonobvious. Generally, patent law prohibits the patenting of an invention that is merely an insignificant addition to or alteration of something already in existence or already known.

Some items are excluded from patent protection. For example, a mere arrangement of printed matter, naturally existing substances, some methods of doing business, and scientific principles are unpatentable subject matter.

Applications for patents are filed with the U.S. Patent and Trademark Office (USPTO), and protection begins only when a patent is issued by the USPTO (as opposed to trademark protection, which arises from first use rather than registration with the USPTO, and copyright protection, which arises from creation of a work in a fixed form rather than from registration with the Copyright Office).

INTRODUCTION

The word *patent* is a shorthand expression for "letters patent." A **patent** is a grant from the U.S. government to exclude others from making, using, selling, or importing another person's new, nonobvious, and useful invention in the United States for the term of patent protection. After this period of exclusive protection (20 years from filing for utility and plant patents and 14 years from grant for design patents), the invention falls into the public domain and may be used by any person without permission. This right of exclusion is far different from the rights provided under copyright law. Under patent law, inventors can enjoin the making, using, selling, or importing of an infringing invention *even if it was independently created*. In contrast, copyright law protects only original works of authorship. If two writers independently compose the same poem, both are protected under copyright law. A patent allows its owner to exclude others from using the owner's invention; it does not provide any guarantee that its owner can sell the invention.

To obtain a patent, an inventor must file an application with the USPTO, the same agency of the Department of Commerce that issues trademark registrations. The application must describe the invention with specificity. The application will be reviewed by a USPTO examiner, and, if approved, the patent will issue. The patent is a written document that fully describes the invention.

Just as U.S. copyright law derives from the Constitution, so does patent law. The U.S. Constitution provides that Congress shall have the power "to promote the progress of science and useful arts, by securing for limited times to authors and inventors the exclusive right to their respective writings and discoveries." U.S. Const. art. I, § 8, cl. 8. The wording applicable to patents is *science, useful arts, inventors,* and *discoveries*.

Patents promote the public good in that patent protection incentivizes inventors. If inventors of useful discoveries could not protect their works from use or exploitation by others, there would be little motivation to expend effort, time, and money in creating inventions. The introduction of new products and processes benefits society. In return for the full disclosure to the public of the specifics of the invention, thus advancing science and technology, the inventor is given a limited period of time within which to exploit his or her invention and exclude others from doing

so. Inventors are thus encouraged to create new products, and the public benefits from inventions that ultimately will fall into the public domain.

RIGHTS UNDER FEDERAL LAW

As stated, patent law derives from the Constitution. In 1790, pursuant to the direction provided in the Constitution, Congress passed the first patent statute, which in large part relied upon English law. Just three years later, the statute was replaced with a new act authored by Thomas Jefferson. These early acts provided the structural framework for U.S. patent law and specified the four basic conditions, still existing, that an invention must satisfy to secure patent protection.

1. The invention must be a utility, design, or plant patent.
2. It must be useful (or ornamental in the case of a design patent or distinctive in the case of a plant patent).
3. It must be novel in relation to the prior art in the field.
4. It must not be obvious to a person of ordinary skill in the field.

Revisions of federal patent statutes occurred in 1836 when the Patent Office was created and again in 1870 and 1897. Thereafter, in 1952, Congress enacted a new patent act, codified in title 35 of the *United States Code*. This was the last major revision to federal patent statutes, although the American Inventors Protection Act of 1999 (discussed in later chapters) resulted in the biggest changes to U.S. patent law since 1952. Issues relating to patents are resolved solely by federal law. Moreover, development of patent law has evolved primarily through federal court decisions rather than the legislature. Just as seen in copyright law, where the term *writings* has been held to be broad enough to cover emerging technologies such as computer programs, the language in the 1793 act relating to the protectability of machines, manufactures, art (later changed to *process*), and composition is broad enough to cover new developments such as computers and electronics. In 1982, Congress created a new court, the Court of Appeals for the Federal Circuit (CAFC), to exercise exclusive jurisdiction over all cases involving patent issues and to promote uniform interpretation of the U.S. patent statutes, which until then had been interpreted in often inconsistent ways by the various federal courts of appeals throughout the nation.

Unlike trademark and copyright law, both of which recognize common law rights in marks and works of authorship even without federal registration, patent law requires that an inventor secure issuance of a patent to protect and enforce his or her rights against infringers. Inventors, however, may also secure some protection for their works under trade secret law (see chapter 22). Moreover, some inventions, such as computer programs, are protectable under copyright law as well as patent law.

UNITED STATES PATENT AND TRADEMARK OFFICE

Patents exist only by authority of government grant. The department of the government responsible for granting patents is the Department of Commerce, acting through the USPTO. The USPTO receives applications, reviews them, and issues or grants patents. The USPTO also publishes and disseminates patent information, records assignments of patents, maintains files of U.S. and foreign patents, and maintains a search room for public use in examining issued patents and records. The present address for mailing and most patent-related documents is Mail Stop _____ (insert particular mail stop or box number per USPTO Web site instructions), Commissioner for Patents, P.O. Box 1450, Alexandria, VA 22313–1450. Correspondence sent via priority mail and express services must use another address. Because addresses may change, always

check the USPTO Web site before submitting documents or correspondence to the USPTO. Additionally, the USPTO Web site (http://www.uspto.gov) offers a wealth of general information, forms for downloading, patent statistics, news updates about issues affecting the USPTO and patent practice, schedules of patent fees, and other valuable information.

As secretary of state, Thomas Jefferson was the first head of the Patent Office. Legend has it that the reason the files in which patents are kept and maintained are called *shoes* is that the first patent applications were stored in Jefferson's shoeboxes.

The practices and procedures relating to examination and issuance of patents are found in the USPTO publication ***Manual of Patent Examining Procedure* (MPEP),** which most practitioners keep handy to serve as a reference tool for patent issues and questions. The entire text of the MPEP is available for viewing and downloading at the USPTO Web site.

Additionally, regulations relating to patents are found in title 37 of the Code of Federal Regulations. These rules and regulations explain how the patent laws are to be implemented, provide procedures to be followed at the USPTO, and generally govern the day-to-day situations that may arise at the USPTO.

A variety of methods for locating patents are available. Pierce Law's IP Mall (http://www.ipmall.fplc.edu) provides links to a variety of patent-related sites, including one listing famous patents, from Eli Whitney's cotton gin, to the application by Orville and Wilbur Wright for the airplane, to the first application for a computer program. Another site (http://www.colitz.com/site/wacky_new.html) identifies the "wacky patent of the month" and references issued patents for oddities such as hay fragrance and eye protectors for chickens.

Another way of locating and retrieving issued patents is through the USPTO patent database, which provides the full text of all patents issued since 1976 and full-page images of all patents issued since 1790. Patents from 1790 through 1975 are searchable only by patent number and the current patent classification system of identifying patents. Patents issued after 1975 are searchable through a variety of techniques, including patent number, inventor name, or topic (using Boolean connectors). The USPTO Web site offers search tips, and patent searching is discussed further in chapter 18.

More than seven million patents have been issued since the first patent in 1790. The patent office is increasingly busy. In 2006, 443,652 patent applications were filed, and 183,187 patents were issued. Many experts attribute the onslaught of filings to applications for software and Internet-related inventions.

(See Exhibit 17–1 for a list of famous patents issued in the United States.)

PATENTABILITY

An invention must satisfy four basic requirements to be eligible for patent protection.

1. The invention must be one of the types specified by statute as patentable subject matter (namely, a utility, design, or plant patent).
2. The invention must be useful.
3. The invention must be novel.
4. The invention must be nonobvious.

Patentable Subject Matter—Utility Patents

There are three distinct types of patents: utility patents, design patents, and plant patents. Utility patents are the most common and cover a wide variety of inventions and discoveries including the typewriter, the automobile, the sewing machine, the zipper, the helicopter, sulfa drugs, gene sequences, and genetically altered mice. Design patents cover new, original, and ornamental designs for useful articles such as furniture and containers. Plant patents cover new

and distinct asexually reproduced plant varieties, such as hybrid flowers or trees. Because the vast majority of patents are utility patents, they will be discussed first. Design and plant patents will be discussed later in this chapter.

Federal law establishes the subject matter that can be protected by a **utility patent:** "Whoever invents or discovers any new and useful process, machine, manufacture, or composition of matter, or any new and useful improvement thereof, may obtain a patent therefor . . . ".

Although ideas are not patentable, processes are. A **process** is a method of doing something to produce a given result. According to *Cochrane v. Deener*, 94 U.S. 780, 788 (1877), a process is "an act, or series of acts, performed upon the subject-matter to be transformed and reduced to a different state or thing. If new and useful, it is just as patentable as is a piece of machinery." A patent may be issued for a newly developed process or a new use of an already known process. Some examples of patented processes are the process for chrome plating; the process for making synthetic diamonds; processes for vulcanizing India rubber, smelting ore, tanning, and dyeing; Louis Pasteur's 1873 patented yeast process; and Clarence Birdseye's process for packaging frozen food. In fact, the first patent issued in the United States, to Samuel Hopkins in 1790, was entitled "improved potash process." In some instances, not only the process but also the result of the process is patentable, such as U.S. Patent No. 6,881,428 for the "process of making a lactose-free milk and the milk so processed," which combines a process (the method of manufacturing) with a product (the milk).

The other types of utility patents (machines, manufactures, and compositions of matter) are all products or items. A **machine** is a device with moving parts that accomplishes a result, such as a sewing machine or a typewriter. A **manufacture** includes anything under the sun that is made by humans; the term is broad enough to include a pitchfork and the patented Monopoly game. It is often said that the category of "manufactures" is

EXHIBIT 17–1
Famous U.S.
Patents

Patent Number	Inventor	Description	Date of Issuance
None	Samuel Hopkins	Improved potash process (first patent)	7/31/1790
None	Eli Whitney	Cotton gin	3/14/1794
None	Samuel Colt	Revolver	2/25/1836
1,647	Samuel F.B. Morse	Telegraph	6/20/1840
3,630	Linus Yale	Door lock	6/13/1844
6,281	Walter Hunt	Safety pin	4/10/1849
6,469	Abraham Lincoln	Buoying boats over shoals	5/22/1849
13,661	Isaac Singer	Sewing machine	10/9/1855
22,186	John Mason	Mason jar	11/30/1858
127,568	Richard Chesebrough	VASELINE® petroleum jelly	6/4/1872
140,245	Samuel Clemens	Scrapbook	6/24/1873
174,465	Alexander Graham Bell	Telephone	3/7/1876
182,346	Melville Bissell	Carpet sweeper	9/19/1876
223,898	Thomas Edison	Electric light	1/27/1880
388,850	George Eastman	Roll film camera	9/4/1888
473,653	Sarah Boone	Ironing board for sleeves	4/26/1892
504,038	Whitcomb Judson	Zipper	8/29/1893
644,077	Felix Hoffman	Aspirin	2/27/1900
686,046	Henry Ford	Automobile	11/5/1901
775,135	King Gillette	GILLETTE® safety razor	11/15/1904
821,393	Wilbur and Orville Wright	Airplane	5/22/1906
1,102,653	Robert Goddard	Two-stage rocket	7/7/1914
1,242,872	Clarence Saunders	Supermarket	10/9/1917
1,370,316	Harry Houdini	Diver's suit	3/1/1921
2,071,250	Wallace Carothers	Nylon	2/16/1937
2,177,627	Richard Drew	SCOTCH® cellophane tape	10/31/1939
2,682,235	Buckminster Fuller	Geodesic dome	6/29/1954
2,717,437	George de Mestrel	VELCRO® faster tape	9/13/1955
2,799,619	Seifter, Monaco, & Hoover	Tranquilizer	7/16/1957
4,270,182	Satya Asija	First computer program (software)	5/26/1981

a type of catchall category to encompass devices or items not easily classified as machines, compositions of matter, or processes. A **composition of matter** is a combination of two or more chemical or other materials into a product, such as a synthetic diamond or the fabric known as polyester. An invention can also consist of some new use of a process, machine, manufacture, or composition of matter as long as that new use demonstrates significant change from the original invention. Thus, new and nonobvious uses of old inventions and compositions are patentable.

Usefulness

The Constitution itself provides that patent protection is available for *"useful* arts," and 35 U.S.C. § 101, in defining what is patentable, states that patents are available for *useful* processes, machines, manufactures, and compositions of matter. Although **usefulness** is not a stringent standard, the invention must be of some benefit to humanity to be "useful." Mere novelties or inventions that conflict with scientific principles, such as a perpetual motion machine, are not patentable because they are not useful. In brief, such an invention has no usefulness because it does not work. Similarly, inventions whose only purpose is detrimental or dangerous or would promote illegal ends cannot be patented inasmuch as, by definition, they are not useful. For example, a patent was denied for a process of making a low-cost tobacco leaf that resembled a more select leaf on the basis that its only purpose was to deceive consumers. *Rickard v. Du Bon,* 103 F. 868 (2d Cir. 1900). Inventions that serve to amuse or entertain are considered useful. Generally, a small degree of utility is sufficient to show that an invention satisfies the requirement of usefulness. In fact, the commercial success of an invention is evidence of its utility.

The usefulness required of an invention must be present usefulness (determined at the time of invention), not usefulness purely for research purposes. Thus, patent protection will be denied to a drug whose usefulness cannot yet be shown or to a process, the result of which produces an article that has no current use. The fact that a drug, invention, or result of a process might show some benefit or usefulness at some time in the future is generally not sufficient and a patent therefor will be denied. Nevertheless, even if an invention or discovery shows no benefit to humans, it will be protected by patent law if usefulness for animals can be shown. Thus, drugs or compounds whose effectiveness has been demonstrated for animals can be patented even though their usefulness for humans cannot yet be shown. *In re Brana,* 51 F.3d 1560 (Fed. Cir. 1995). Applications that claim some drug or other substance is useful for humans must be accompanied by supporting evidence, usually results of tests or trials, and must show the substance is reasonably safe. To be patentable, an invention need not meet the stricter standards of regulatory agencies such as the Food and Drug Administration; it need only be "reasonably safe."

To ensure that the invention is useful, the application must disclose or specify the usefulness of the invention. To allow a patent that does not specify its utility would be to grant a patent on an entire range of unknown applications, thereby allowing an inventor to obtain a mono-poly on an entire field of knowledge. Thus, patent applications must describe their specific advantage or usefulness so the public can benefit from the invention. Similarly, a patent will be denied when an invention fails to operate as described or claimed in the application.

Novelty

Section 101 of the Patent Act requires that an invention (or any improvement to an invention) be "new" or novel. Section 102 of the Patent Act elaborates on the requirement of **novelty** by setting forth certain situations that demonstrate the invention is not novel. Most codify the basic principle that the first to invent will be granted a patent. If an invention is known or used by others, is the subject of an existing patent, or has been described or sold, then it is not novel and, accordingly, is not eligible for patent protection.

In such a case, it is deemed that the applicant's invention was anticipated and an application will be denied. Often called the **doctrine of anticipation,** this principle is intended to ensure that a second or junior inventor does not secure a monopoly on an invention that a senior inventor owns or that is in the public domain.

The seven subsections of Section 102 are as follows.

Section 102(a): Inventions Known or Used by Others. Section 102(a) provides that a person shall be entitled to a patent unless before the invention of the article by the applicant:

- the invention was known or used by others in this country; or
- the invention was patented or described in a printed publication in this or a foreign country.

Section 102(a) articulates the "first to invent" rule followed in the United States and is directed to the acts of others. If another has used the invention, patented it, or described it in a printed publication before the applicant invented it, the invention is not novel, and an applicant who is not the first to invent is not entitled to receive a patent for the invention.

An invention is "described in a printed publication" when it is printed in nearly any kind of document by any means (including electronic means) and has been made available to the public. Such availability can occur by circulating copies of a document at a conference, releasing advertising brochures, or by disseminating a thesis. Internal business documents or documents provided to others under conditions of confidentiality are not publications within the meaning of the statute.

Section 102(b): Invention Is in Use or on Sale. Any of the following acts occurring more than one year before the filing of a patent appli-

cation in the United States will preclude the applicant from obtaining a patent:

- The invention was patented in the United States or a foreign country;
- The invention was described in a printed publication in the United States or a foreign country;
- The invention is in public use in the United States; or
- The invention is on sale in the United States.

The requirements of section 102(b), typically called the **on sale bar,** are intended to ensure that inventors act promptly to secure protection for their inventions. Once an invention is in public use or offered for sale or sold in the United States or is patented or described in a printed publication anywhere, the inventor has a one-year **grace period** or statute of limitations to file an application. Failure to file an application in a timely manner will bar issuance of a patent.

An invention is "in use" if it is being used in the manner intended by the inventor without any confidentiality restrictions. An exception allows **experimental use** of the invention so that the inventor can perfect the invention or ascertain whether it will fulfill its intended purpose. Thus, such experimental use will not trigger the one-year grace period. Similarly, private use by the inventor or use for the inventor's own enjoyment will not trigger the one-year limitation period; however, an invention that is "ready for patenting" will start the one-year limitation period if there is a commercial offer for sale of the invention. *Pfaff v. Wells Elecs., Inc.,* 525 U.S. 55 (1998). In *Pfaff,* the one-year on sale bar applied although the inventor had made only engineering drawings and had not yet made the invention, although he had accepted an offer to sell the invention.

An invention is deemed "on sale" if it is offered for sale, even though no actual sales occur. Even a single sale may bar patentability. An invention is "described in a printed publication" if it has been printed by any manner (including electronic methods) and described in such a way that a person of ordinary skill in the art could make the invention, just as is the case under section 102(a), described previously.

Section 102(b) is often called a "statutory bar," and the one-year grace period is often triggered by the inventor's own acts, such as offering the article for sale, describing it in a promotional literature, and so forth. Thus, inventors should place confidentiality notices on documents to avoid triggering "publication" of the invention.

The on sale bar engenders many refusals by the USPTO. It is intended to encourage prompt action by inventors. It would be unfair to allow an inventor to use an invention for profit and delay filing for an application because such a delay has the effect of adding time to the term of protection for the patent and delaying its placement in the public domain.

Recall that the focus of section 102(a) is on the acts of those *other than* the inventor. The focus of section 102(b) is on the actions of both the inventor and others more than one year before the inventor files his or her patent application (although it is often the inventor's own acts that trigger the one-year time bar). Another distinction between the two subsections is that section 102(a) bars a patent if the invention was patented or described in a printed publication anywhere in the world before the *invention* by the applicant; section 102(b) bars a patent if the invention was printed or described anywhere in the world more than one year before an *application* is filed for the invention.

Section 102(c): Invention Has Been Abandoned.   A person cannot obtain a patent if he or she has abandoned the invention. Abandonment is shown when the inventor expressly or impliedly demonstrates an intent to abandon his or her right to a patent. Abandonment usually requires an intentional act. Delay alone in filing an application does not usually constitute abandonment.

Section 102(d): Invention Is the Subject of a Foreign Patent.   Section 102(d) establishes two conditions, which, if both are present, establish a statutory bar against the granting of a patent in this country:

1. an application has been filed in a foreign country more than 12 months before the U.S. application was filed; and
2. the foreign patent must be granted before the U.S. filing date

Assume that Jose, an inventor, invents a new type of disposable razor on January 1, 2005. He files a patent application for the invention in Spain on May 1, 2005, and the patent is granted by Spain on July 1, 2006. If Jose applies for a U.S. patent for this invention anytime after July 1, 2006, he will be barred. If the Spanish patent has not been granted at the time Jose files his U.S. application, Jose will not be barred. The policy underlying section 102(d) is to encourage prompt entry into the U.S. patent system once an inventor begins seeking foreign patent protection.

Section 102(e): Invention Is Described in a Prior Published Application or Patent.   Pursuant to section 102(e), an application will be denied if an invention was described in:

- another's published U.S. patent application before the invention by the applicant; or
- another's issued U.S. patent granted before the invention by the applicant.

An invention cannot be novel if it is described in an existing patent already granted or an application that has been published. Section 102(e) is meant to provide priority to senior parties.

Section 102(f): Inventor Did Not Invent the Invention.   Only the inventor is entitled to a patent for the invention or discovery. The inventor is the person who conceived the specific invention. If the inventor derived the invention from another, a rejection under section 102(f) is proper.

An employee who invents an item while on the job remains the inventor. Although the employer may have a contractual right to own any inventions created by employees, a patent application must be filed by the individual inventor. It can, however, be assigned to the employer or another concurrently with filing. Parties who work jointly on an invention may be joint inventors even though their contributions are not equal or simultaneous. An application for the resulting invention must name all inventors.

Section 102(g): Invention Was First Invented by Others.

A person is entitled to a patent in the United States if, before the applicant's invention:

- the invention was made in this country, and
- the prior invention was not abandoned, suppressed, or concealed.

Section 102(g) codifies and confirms that in the United States, a patent is awarded to the first to invent; however, the statute provides that this presumption can be overcome if the first inventor abandons, suppresses, or conceals the invention. In such a case, the first inventor forfeits his or her priority.

Sections 102(a), (e), and (g) are all intended to ensure patents are granted to the first inventor. The second or junior inventor's product or process is not novel in such circumstances.

Abandonment typically requires an express intention to relinquish rights to a patent. Merely failing to file a patent application does not constitute abandonment, suppression, or concealment. Similarly, use of the product under agreements with others to protect the invention as a confidential trade secret is not necessarily concealment or suppression as long as the public is receiving some benefit from the invention. Typically, inventors are required to engage in diligent efforts to bring the invention to the marketplace. Such efforts will help counter a claim the invention has been abandoned, suppressed, or concealed. Because abandonment, suppression, and concealment of information that could be valuable and beneficial to the public are contrary to patent law policy,

patent law punishes such acts by allowing the second inventor to secure a patent even though another previously invented the item or process.

In determining priority of invention, the statute provides that the dates the inventors conceived of the invention, the dates they reduced their inventions to practice, and their reasonable diligence in reducing the invention to practice will be considered. As discussed in chapter 19, reduction to practice can be actual (making or building the invention or a prototype) or constructive (filing an application for a patent after invention).

Summary of Novelty Standards and Statutory Bars

Section 102 codifies the basic patent principle that a patent cannot be granted unless an inventor creates something new. Note that the actual title of 35 U.S.C. § 102 is "Conditions for patentability; Novelty and loss of right to patent," thus indicating that the statute relates to two separate events: novelty of an invention and the loss or forfeiture of patent rights. Specifically, some of the subsections of section 102 (namely, subsections (a), (e), and (g)) relate to ensuring that an invention is novel and deal with acts by others that occur before the date the applicant allegedly *invented* the invention. Something cannot be new if another has known or used it or it has been described in another's patent application. Other subsections, namely, subsections (b), (c), and (d), are often referred to as **statutory bars** because they bar a patent or cause a loss of patent rights even if the invention is novel. These subsections relate to an inventor's forfeiture of patent rights, not because the invention is not novel, but usually because of the inventor's acts in delaying disclosing the invention by failing to file an application promptly or by abandoning the invention. The provisions of 35 U.S.C. § 102(f) (requiring the inventor to invent the invention) exist independently and cannot be classified as either novelty provisions or statutory bar provisions.

Note that the provisions of sections 102(a), (e), and (g) are all triggered by an event that takes place before the *invention* by the patent applicant. In contrast, the loss of rights that occur under the statutory bar provisions of sections 102(b) and (d) are triggered by a date that is one year before the *application date* by the patent applicant. (See Exhibit 17–2 for a summary chart of the various novelty and statutory bar provisions of 35 U.S.C. § 102.)

Nonobviousness

Merely because an invention is useful and novel does not automatically entitle it to patent protection. To qualify for a grant of patent, the invention must be nonobvious to those having skill in the field or art to which the subject matter pertains. 35 U.S.C. § 103. The subject matter sought to be patented must be sufficiently different from what has been used or described before that it may be said to be nonobvious to a person having ordinary skill in the area of technology related to the invention. For example, the substitution of one material for another in an invention and mere changes in size are ordinarily not patentable because they are obvious. A distinct improvement, however, is patentable even if the new invention improves matter in the public domain. Similarly, a new use of a known process is patentable.

Determining whether an invention is nonobvious is one of the most difficult tasks in patent law. After all, a disposable razor, a safety pin, and a retractable tape measure all seem obvious now, yet none of these items were obvious at the time they were invented.

Until the 1952 Patent Act, courts generally required that an invention result from a "flash of genius" or some sudden insight. The view was that an invention must have been so nonobvious that no amount of diligent research would

EXHIBIT 17–2
Novelty and Statutory Bars under 35 U.S.C. § 102

Statutory Provision	Condition for Patentability	Novelty or Statutory Bar
35 U.S.C. § 102(a)	Invention known, Described, or used by others before Date of Invention	Novelty
35 U.S.C. § 102(b)	Invention is Described or in Use or On Sale More than One Year Before Date of Application	Statutory Bar—One Year Grace Period
35 U.S.C. § 102(c)	Invention has been Abandoned	Statutory Bar
35 U.S.C. § 102(d)	Invention is the Subject of a Foreign Patent	Statutory Bar
35 U.S.C. § 102(e)	Invention is Described in Another's Prior Published Application or Patent before Invention by Applicant	Novelty
35 U.S.C. § 102(f)	Applicant did not Invent the Invention	Neither Novelty nor Statutory Bar
35 U.S.C. § 102(g)	Invention was First Invented by Others	Novelty

have produced it. The act now states that "patentability shall not be negatived by the manner in which the invention was made." 35 U.S.C. § 103. Thus, whether an invention is produced by dint of arduous research or a flash of genius does not determine whether it is nonobvious. The present method of determining **nonobviousness** is by reference to the prior art.

The *Graham* Factors. In *Graham v. John Deere Co.*, 383 U.S. 1 (1966), the Supreme Court articulated the following factors to consider in determining whether an invention is nonobvious and thus deserving of a patent.

Analogous prior art. One must review the scope and content of the prior art in the pertinent field to determine if an invention is nonobvious. The term **prior art** refers to the circumstances set forth in sections 102 and 103, namely, the generally available public knowledge relating to the invention for which a patent is sought and which was available prior to invention. Thus, information contained in existing patents, printed publications, and inventions that were known and used before the subject invention will be considered.

Prior art is pertinent or analogous if it is from the same field of endeavor or from a different field of endeavor but reasonably related to the same problem as that addressed by the invention. *Graham* involved a type of shock-absorber system for a plow shank. Thus, a review of the analogous prior art should consider other plow shanks as well as other shock-absorbing devices (regardless of the field, e.g., shock absorbers used for plow shanks, airplanes, or cars).

Differences between the prior art and the invention. In determining whether an invention is nonobvious, consideration must be given to differences between the prior art and the invention at issue. Applicants themselves may include statements in their applications in regard to how their inventions differ from and are improvements over prior art. An invention that achieves superior results is likely not obvious.

Level of ordinary skill in the prior art. If the invention would be obvious to a person having ordinary skill in the art to which the invention pertains, it cannot be patented. A person of "ordinary skill" is neither a highly sophisticated expert or genius in the art nor a layperson with no knowledge of the field of art but rather some hypothetical person who is aware of the pertinent prior art.

Secondary Considerations. In *Graham*, after enumerating the factors evaluated in determining whether an invention is nonobvious, the Court suggested that some **secondary considerations,** all of which are nontechnical and objective, could be considered in determining nonobviousness. Some of the secondary considerations include the following:

- **Commercial success.** An invention that is a commercial success may be nonobvious because acceptance by the marketplace tends to show that an invention is significant; moreover, if the invention were obvious, someone would already have attempted to commercialize it for his or her own financial gain.
- **Long-felt need and failure of others.** If there has been a longstanding need for a device or process that has gone unresolved despite the efforts of others to solve the problem, and the invention satisfies this need, it tends to show the invention is nonobvious. If the invention were obvious, others would have been able to discover it readily.
- **Commercial acquiescence.** If competitors seek to enter into licenses with the owner so they may use or sell the invention to others, such tends to show nonobviousness because otherwise the third parties would have challenged the patent as invalid based on nonobviousness.
- **Copying.** Copying or infringement of the patent by another suggests

nonobviousness because otherwise the infringer would have been able to independently develop the invention. Conversely, the independent and near-simultaneous invention of like products or processes tends to suggest obviousness.

If it is easy for a number of people in the field to invent the same product or process, it is likely obvious to those with ordinary skill in the art.

To ensure that courts do not overrely on the secondary considerations (commercial success, long-felt need, commercial acquiescence, and copying), the Federal Circuit requires that a party demonstrate some link, or *nexus*, between the secondary characteristic and the invention. For example, if an inventor argues that an invention is nonobvious because it is commercially successful, the inventor must demonstrate that commercial success is due to some property inherent in the invention, rather than due to some external factor such as aggressive marketing or the renown of the inventor.

Combination Patents.   One area that has caused debate over obviousness relates to new inventions consisting of a combination of older, known elements. The unique combination of the elements may make the invention novel, but the combination must be nonobvious to receive patent protection. A factor sometimes used in determining whether these patents, often called **combination patents,** are nonobvious is *synergism:* The newly combined elements must result in some different function or some result that is different or unexpected such that one who possesses ordinary skill in the art would not have predicted the result of the combination of the known elements. If there is such a new result, the invention is nonobvious and is patentable.

The Patent Act was amended in 1996 to provide preference to inventions relating to biotechnology processes. Section 103(b) expressly provides that a biotechnological process is nonobvious if it uses or results in a novel, non-obvious product or composition. Thus, the process as well as the composition is patentable in the biotechnology field.

There is overlap between the requirements of novelty and nonobviousness. Both depend on examination of prior art. To ensure novelty, one must examine the prior art (what others know, use, and publish) to determine if the invention could have been anticipated. To ensure nonobviousness, one must examine the scope and content of pertinent prior art to determine if the invention would be obvious to a person having ordinary skill in the field.

In one of the most important patent rulings in a generation, in 2007, the U.S. Supreme Court tightened the standards for obtaining patents on new products that combine elements of already existing inventions. In *KSR International Inc. v. Teleflex Inc.*, 127 S. Ct. 1727 (2007), a unanimous Court held that if the combination results from nothing more than "ordinary innovation" and does nothing more than yield "predictable results," the invention is obvious and is not entitled to patent protection. The Court held that the Federal Circuit's test (which had held that if there was a "teaching, suggestion, or motivation" to combine known elements, the resulting invention should be barred for obviousness) had been too strictly applied and often required third-party documentation. The Court endorsed a more "common sense" and flexible approach: If a person of ordinary skill in the art can implement a predictable variation of an invention and would see the benefit of doing so, then the invention should be barred for obviousness. While the "teaching, suggestion, motivation" test provides helpful insights, it cannot be used in a rigid and inflexible manner. In determining obviousness, one must thus ask whether the improvement is more than a predictable use of prior art elements according to their established functions. Accordingly, if at the time of invention there is a known problem for which there is an obvious solution, an invention should be barred for obviousness. Most experts predict that the ruling in *KSR* will have far-reaching implications and

ETHICS EDGE: **Competent Legal Research**

The duty to perform adequate legal research has been discussed in several cases. Legal professionals are expected to know common principles of law and to be able to discover other rules of law that may readily be found by standard research techniques. *Camarillo v. Vaage,* 130 Cal. Rptr. 2d 26, 32 (Ct. App. 2003). Thus, patent paralegals must be familiar with basic patent principles relating to novelty and nonobviousness.

will make obtaining patents more difficult (because patent examiners will reject applications for patents on the basis that the invention results from nothing more than ordinary innovation and is thus obvious). Paradoxically, this tightening of the obviousness test may stem the tide of junk patents but may also produce litigation challenging existing patents on the basis that they are obvious. In fact, less than two weeks after the *KSR* case was decided, it had spawned an allegation in a lawsuit that a patent was invalid for obviousness and thus could not be infringed.

Exclusions from Patent Protection

There are a variety of items, products, and processes that cannot be patented. The following are excluded from patent protection either by statutory prohibition or judicial interpretation.

- **Products of nature.** Only human-made inventions can be patented. Naturally occurring substances cannot be protected by patent even if they have previously been unknown to others. For example, a new plant or mineral that is discovered cannot be patented. On the other hand, genetically altered living organisms can be patented as "manufactures" or "compositions of matter." In *Diamond v. Chakrabarty,* 447 U.S. 303 (1980), the Court held that a live, human-made microorganism (in that case, a genetically engineered bacterium capable of break-

ing down crude oil) was patentable as a human-made "manufacture" or "composition of matter" and stated that "anything under the sun made by man" is patentable. Thus, genetically altered oysters and mice have been held patentable. The distinction is not between living and inanimate things but between products of nature (whether living or not) and human-made inventions. *Id.* at 313.

- **Laws of nature.** Laws of nature, physical phenomena, scientific truths, and abstract ideas cannot be patented. As the Court remarked in *Chakrabarty,* "Einstein could not patent his celebrated law that $E = mc^2$; nor could Newton have patented the law of gravity." *Id.* at 310. Generally, mere chemical or mathematical formulas or algorithms divorced from any tangible result cannot be patented; however, chemical substances can be patented, systems using formulas can be patented as processes, and items that are produced as the result of formulas can be patented. Thus, a machine or product that depends on some law of physics or the law of gravity can be patented. A process is not unpatentable merely because it contains a law of nature or a pure mathematical algorithm. Similarly, computer programs, although they consist of algorithms, can be patented in many instances. In *Diamond v. Diehr,* 450 U.S. 175 (1981), a patent was upheld for the process of molding rubber products with the aid of a computer. The Court noted that although mathematical formulas as such are not patentable, a process employing a well-known mathematical equation was patentable. Additionally, the use of a computer to improve an otherwise patentable process did not preclude the process from being patented. Thus, incorporating a computer program as a step in a process or as a component in a machine or manufacture may be acceptable. In sum, a disembodied mathematical concept that represents a law of nature or abstract idea is not patentable; however, if the principle is applied to produce a useful, concrete, and tangible result, it may be patentable. See chapter 21 for additional discussion on protection of computer programs under patent law.

- **Printed matter.** Printed forms cannot be patented.
- **Atomic weapons.** Under the Atomic Energy Act of 1954, atomic weapons cannot be patented.
- **Nonuseful business methods and mental steps.** Systems for the operation of businesses cannot be patented unless they produce a useful, tangible, and concrete result. A useful and novel business system or idea is not patentable unless there is a product or process to effect it. Similarly, processes consisting solely of mental steps, meaning human thought and deliberation, cannot be patented. For more than 100 years, the USPTO rarely granted a patent for any business method, reasoning that such methods were akin to abstract ideas. Since 1998, however, the USPTO has granted a record number of what are usually referred to as business method or software patents so long as the method or software is useful and produces a tangible result. See chapter 21 for additional discussion on this topic.

DESIGN PATENTS

The Patent Act provides that whoever invents any new, original, and ornamental design for an article of manufacture may obtain a patent. 35 U.S.C. § 171. Comparing the scope of this provision to that of section 101 relating to utility patents, it is clear that the requirement of "usefulness" for utility patents has been replaced by a requirement of "ornamentality." The design must be novel and nonobvious. Just as a person may obtain a patent for a chemical compound and one for the process utilizing the chemical compound, a person may obtain a utility patent and a design patent for one article of manufacture because a useful article may be ornamented with a design. A **design patent** can be obtained for articles as diverse as jewelry, furniture, trash receptacles, and clothing.

Recognizing that while authors could seek protection for their works under copyright law and inventors could seek protection for their works under patent law, no protection was afforded for the creators of decorative arts, Congress filled this gap and allowed design patents in 1842. One of the first design patent cases related to a claim by Gorham Manufacturing that its spoon and fork handle design patents had been infringed. *Gorham Mfg. v. White*, 81 U.S. (14 Wall.) 511 (1871). In *Gorham*, the Court noted that the intent of the design patent statute was to encourage the decorative arts.

To be protectable a design must satisfy the following four requirements:

1. **It must be an "article of manufacture."** An article of manufacture is nearly anything made by a human and may consist of a manufactured article's configuration (the particular shape of a chair), surface ornamentation (the design on the handle of tableware), or a combination of both (a uniquely shaped fork with two irregularly sized tines, embossed with a leaf design).
2. **It must be new.** The requirements of novelty for utility patents discussed in the

previous section on patentability under the heading "Novelty" apply equally to design patents.

3. **It must be original.** The requirement of originality is the equivalent of the requirement of nonobviousness for utility patents. A design cannot be patented if a designer of ordinary skill who designs articles similar to the one applied for would consider the design obvious in view of the prior art.

4. **It must be ornamental.** To be patentable, a design must be primarily ornamental rather than utilitarian. The article may serve a useful purpose (e.g., a spoon and a chair serve a useful purpose), but its primary purpose cannot be functional. A design or shape that is entirely functional, without ornamental or decorative aspect, does not meet the criteria for a design patent. If there are several ways that an item could be designed and yet still remain functional, then any one design is likely ornamental rather than functional. An article may qualify for design patent protection if at some point in its life cycle its appearance is a factor even if, when ultimately used, the article is hidden. Thus, caskets and artificial hip prostheses have been given design patent protection. Although both are primarily useful, the appearance of the article is of importance at some point even though when put to their intended use, the articles are hidden from view.

The bars to novelty set forth in section 102 and discussed earlier in this chapter apply equally to design patents. Most of the bars aim at ensuring that designs are promptly patented.

There is some overlap between design patents and copyright. It has been held that the same work can qualify for protection under both copyright law and patent law. For example, the drawing of a cartoon character can be protected under copyright law; when the character is embossed on some article, such as china plates, it may be protected under patent law. Similarly, the same item may qualify for protection under trademark law and patent law. For example, in a case involving the shape of a bottle of Mogen David wine, the court stated the design qualified for both patent and trademark protection. *In re Mogen David Wine Corp.,* 328 F.2d 925 (C.C.P.A. 1964). Finally, there is overlap between trade dress protection and patent law such that the ornamental appearance of an item may be protected under trade dress law and as a design patent.

Securing copyright protection is generally the easiest and least expensive method of protecting certain designs. Although copyright registration is not required, a copyright registration may be obtained for a filing fee of $45 within three to four months, and protection will last for the life of the author plus 70 years. Trademark registrations can last forever (if they are properly maintained and renewed), and patent protection comes into being only once the patent issues, a process that may take two to three years from the date of application. Moreover, the nonrenewable term of a design patent is 14 years from the date of issuance of grant. Practical matters should also be considered. If a design will likely be somewhat limited in its appeal or trendy, such as a piece of jewelry, it is far less expensive and far more expeditious to obtain copyright rather than patent protection for the item. Thus, a combination of intellectual property strategies may be needed to secure the broadest possible scope of protection for certain articles.

PLANT PATENTS

Patents for plants have been recognized only since the passage of the Plant Patent Act in 1930. Prior to that time, the philosophy was that plants were natural products not subject to patent protection. Section 161 of the Patent Act now provides that whoever invents or discovers and asexually reproduces any distinct and new variety of plant may obtain a patent therefor. Just as design patents substitute the requirement of "ornamentality" for the "usefulness" required of utility patents, plant patents substitute the requirement of "distinctiveness" in place of "usefulness."

Congress allowed patents for plants to provide the benefits of the patent system that were then available to manufacturing and industry to the agriculture business in order to incentivize growers and protect their plant products from infringement. Without patent protection, copies of plants could be produced by grafting techniques. Thus, a **plant patent** affords its owner the right to exclude others from asexually reproducing the plant. The term of protection is the same as that for utility patents, namely, 20 years from the application date. The term *plant* is construed in its ordinary meaning and does not include bacteria. The use of the term *discovery* means a discovery by asexual propagation; plants discovered in the wild cannot be patented; however, a plant discovered in a cultivated area and later reproduced asexually can be patented. Tubers, such as potatoes, are not eligible for protection under the Plant Patent Act.

There are four requirements that must be satisfied before a plant can be patented:

1. **The new variety must be asexually reproduced.** A grower or discoverer of a new and distinct variety of plant must be able to reproduce the plant by asexual means. Generally, this is accomplished by taking cuttings of the original plant and placing them in soil or by grafting so as to create a new plant. **Asexual reproduction** involves growing something other than from a seed.

2. **The plant must be distinctive.** The new plant must be clearly distinguishable from existing varieties. Features that show distinctiveness are color, odor, flavor, shape, ability of the plant to grow in a different type of soil, its productivity, its factors of preservation, or immunity to dis-

ease. The requirement of distinctiveness imposes only a requirement that the plant be different from, rather than superior to, other varieties. A new color of a rose may be different from other roses but may not be better than some other rose variety. Nevertheless, it may be patented. There is a great deal of overlap between nonobviousness for utility patents and distinctiveness for plant patents. One patent for a variety of bluegrass recites that the plant is a "new and distinct variety of Kentucky Bluegrass characterized by its excellent tolerance to drought, low fertilizer requirements, deep rooting system, excellent tolerance to Fusarium blight, and good to excellent shade tolerance. The plant tolerates a close cut, is highly resistant to most common bluegrass diseases, is extremely aggressive, has a medium to coarse leaf texture and consistently maintains excellent turf quality." U.S. Plant Patent No. PP4,704.

3. **The plant must be novel.** The new variety of plant must not have previously existed in nature. The bars to novelty set forth in section 102 and discussed in the earlier section on patentability under the heading "Novelty" apply equally to plant patents. For example, selling a plant in the United States more than one year prior to filing a patent application for it will bar issuance of a patent for it.

4. **The plant must be nonobvious.** Although section 161 of the Patent Act providing for statutory protection for plant patents does not specifically state that patents for plants must be nonobvious, the section does provide that the provisions of the act relating to utility patents apply equally to plant patents unless otherwise specified. Generally, the standards set forth in *Graham v. John Deere Co.,* discussed in the earlier section on patentability under the heading "Nonobviousness," apply equally with regard to plant patents.

See Exhibit 17–3 for comparison of utility, design, and plant patents.

Although the most common means of securing protection for plants is through application for a plant patent, two other methods of protection exist for plants. In 1970, Congress enacted the **Plant Variety Protection Act** (7 U.S.C. § 2321), allowing quasipatent protection for certain sexually reproduced plants, meaning plants bred through seeds. Sexually reproduced plants could not receive protection under the 1930 Plant Patent Act because new varieties could not be reproduced true-to-type through seedlings. The new variety was not always stable, and its new characteristics could not be passed uniformly from one generation to the next. By 1970, however, it was generally recognized that true-to-type sexual reproduction of plants is possible, and the Plant Variety Protection Act was passed.

These new varieties, produced through the use of seeds, are awarded "plant variety protection certificates" by the Department of Agriculture, rather than letters patent issued by the USPTO. The primary purpose of the Plant Variety Protection Act is to encourage the development of novel varieties of sexually reproduced plants. The certificate owner may exclude others from selling, offering, reproducing, or trading infringing plants. The term of protection is generally 20 years from date of issue of the certificate.

Finally, a plant may qualify for protection as a utility patent, even though it also qualifies for protection under the Plant Patent Act as a plant patent or under the Plant Variety Protection Act for patentlike protection. An application for a utility patent for a plant must satisfy the requirements for utility patents generally, namely, usefulness, novelty, and nonobviousness.

In some cases, matters of tactics and strategy may dictate whether an inventor seeks protection for a plant under the Plant Patent Act of 1930, the Plant Variety Protection Act of 1970, or as a general utility patent. Although the most significant determinant is how the plant can be reproduced (asexual reproduction is required under the Plant Patent Act while sexual plant reproduction is protected under the Plant Variety Protection Act), other factors should be considered. For example, the requirement that an invention be nonobvious applies to utility patents and plant patents reproduced asexually, but not to the Plant Variety Protection Act. Thus, an inventor who

	Utility Patent 35 U.S.C. § 101	Design Patent 35 U.S.C. § 171	Plant Patent 35 U.S.C. § 161
Inventions Covered	Processes, machines, manufactures, compositions of matter, or improvements thereof	Designs for articles of manufacture	Plant varieties
Usefulness Required	Yes	No	No
Novelty Required	Yes	Yes	Yes
Nonobviousness Required	Yes	Yes (referred to as "originality")	Yes
Ornamentality Required	NA	Yes	No
Asexual Reproduction Required	NA	NA	Yes
Distinctiveness Required	NA	NA	Yes

EXHIBIT 17–3
Comparison of Utility, Design, and Plant Patents

cannot demonstrate nonobviousness might seek protection under the Plant Variety Protection Act. Similarly, fees to maintain the patent are due on utility patents but not on plant patents. Assuming applications do not claim identical subject matter, it is possible that a patent could be obtained for a plant both under the Plant Patent Act and under the Patent Act as a utility patent. Each statute has different requirements and affords different protections.

DOUBLE PATENTING

The **double patenting** principle prohibits the issuance of more than one patent for the same invention or for an invention that is substantially the same as that owned by an inventor. The intent of this bar is to ensure that inventors do not make some insignificant change to an invention near the end of its term of existence in order to secure another 20-year monopoly on the invention or discovery. Nevertheless, design and utility patents may coexist because they relate to arguably distinct subject matter. A utility patent claims protection for the usefulness of the object while a design patent covers its ornamentality. Inventors often insert a **terminal disclaimer** into their applications, agreeing that the term of protection for a second invention will terminate upon expi-

ration of the patent for the first invention and that the patent claim to the second invention will be valid only as long as both inventions are owned by the same person or entity. Such a disclaimer will enable an inventor to overcome a rejection based on double patenting. Double patenting is discussed further in chapter 18.

THE ORPHAN DRUG ACT

Just as the Plant Variety Protection Act grants rights somewhat similar to patents, the Orphan Drug Act (21 U.S.C. §§ 360aa–360ee) provides rights for certain drugs that are similar to patent rights, namely, an exclusive right for seven years to market an **orphan drug** that is necessary to treat a disease that affects fewer than 200,000 people. Protection under the act is triggered when the Food and Drug Administration determines that unless such protection is granted, the drug would likely not be made or available to those in need of it. The act applies whether or not the drug can be patented (thus affording protection for drugs that may lack novelty or nonobviousness). The act thus provides incentives to pharmaceutical companies to develop drugs for rare diseases or conditions when otherwise they might not invest the time and effort in developing a drug for a small target group if patentability could not be assured.

Trivia

- Most experts attribute the modern concepts of patents to England where, in 1449, King Henry VI granted a patent for manufacturing stained glass to John of Utynam.
- In fiscal year 2006, the USPTO issued 183,187 patents.
- Between fiscal years 1997 and 2006, the number of patent applications filed increased 87 percent.
- More than 93 percent of the patent applications filed with the USPTO are for utility patents; approximately 6 percent are for design patents; and less than 1 percent are for plant patents.
- George Washington Carver invented more than 300 uses for peanuts.
- The inventor of VELCRO® reported that he thought of the invention while removing burrs from his pet's fur after walking in the woods.

CHAPTER SUMMARY

A patent is a grant from the federal government allowing an inventor to exclude others from producing, using, selling, or importing the inventor's discovery or invention for a limited period of time, generally 20 years from the filing date of a patent application. Patent laws are aimed at fostering and promoting discoveries. There are three types of patents: utility patents, design patents, and plant patents. The vast majority of patents are utility patents, which must satisfy the requirements of usefulness, novelty, and nonobviousness in order to secure protection. An invention or discovery that is merely an insignificant addition to or alteration of something already known or in existence is unpatentable. Protection is allowed for processes, machines, human-made articles of manufacture, and compositions of matter.

Not all inventions or discoveries may be patented. Generally, patents are awarded to the first to invent. Additionally, patents are not available for scientific or mathematical principles, some business methods (if they produce a useful, concrete, and tangible result), printed matter, or substances existing in nature.

Design patents protect original, new, and ornamental designs for articles of manufacture. Plant patents protect new and distinct varieties of asexually reproduced plants.

CASE ILLUSTRATION—REQUIREMENT OF USEFULNESS

Case: *Banning v. Southwestern Bell Telephone Co.,* 384 F. Supp. 831 (D. Tex. 1974)

Facts: Plaintiff Banning invented a push-button telephone number selector and sued defendant Southwestern Bell for infringement. The defendant alleged that it had not infringed because the plaintiff's patent was invalid for lack of usefulness and lack of novelty.

Holding: There was no infringement because Banning's patent was invalid for lack of utility and novelty. A patentable invention must be useful; a patented invention is useful if it is capable of performing a beneficial function claimed for it. Although it is not necessary that a patented invention function perfectly in all situations to be considered useful, it is necessary that the device be capable of a practical application in industry. In this case, the invention lacked a speed control and was thus inoperable and not useful.

CASE STUDY AND ACTIVITIES

Case Study.   Vision is renovating the grounds of one of its hotels in Los Angeles. Vision landscaping staff has managed to asexually reproduce a new type of grass that is highly resistant to various diseases and pests. Vision's in-house design team has also designed and made various detachable fanciful canopies shaped like flowers for the loungers in the pool areas. In an effort to reduce noise in the hotel, Vision's engineers have developed

CASE STUDY AND ACTIVITIES (CONT'D)

new insulation for the walls between hotel rooms. This insulation decreases noise far more successfully than the insulation currently used. Finally, about 18 months ago, Vision developed a new type of swing for the hotel's tot lot. Vision has been test-marketing the swing in the tot lot and allowing children to try it out to determine how well the children like the swing and thus whether it would be suitable for all tot lots in the Vision system.

Activities.   Discuss the patentability of the various items and products discussed.

ROLE OF PARALEGAL

Until patent searching begins and an application is filed, the role of an IP paralegal will be somewhat limited. Typically, tasks may consist of conducting research to help assess and satisfy the required elements of usefulness, novelty, and nonobviousness. If a law firm does not have a general information letter available that can be sent to clients who have basic questions about patent law, one should be drafted. Similarly, a "frequently asked questions" sheet can be prepared for distribution to clients. Flowcharts showing the patent process can be made, and charts comparing types of patents (e.g., plant patents and utility patents for plants) can be prepared.

An IP paralegal may also be involved in conducting some type of audit of clients to inquire whether they have invented any processes or products that may qualify for patent protection. A questionnaire should be prepared to assess whether clients' intellectual property is being fully protected. See chapter 24 for sample questions for an intellectual property audit.

INTERNET RESOURCES

Federal laws relating to patents:	http://www.law.cornell.edu http://www.findlaw.com
U.S. Patent and Trademark Office:	http://www.uspto.gov (general information about patents, frequently asked questions, forms, and filing fees)
Manual of Patent Examining Procedure:	http://www.uspto.gov/web/offices/pac/mpep/mpep.htm (Chapter 700 contains information on rejections based on lack of novelty, lack of usefulness, lack of nonobviousness, and double patenting)
National Inventors Hall of Fame:	http://www.invent.org (honoring inventors and their inventions)
General information:	http://www.ipmall.fplc.edu (Pierce Law IP Mall with excellent information and articles and links to other IP sources)

	http://www.megalaw.com
	http://www.findlaw.com
Glossary of IP terms:	http://www.uspto.gov/main/glossary
Absurd patents:	http://www.totallyabsurd.com (identifies odd and unusual patents)

DISCUSSION QUESTIONS

1. Classify each of the following as a utility, design, or plant patent.
   - a pen
   - a prosthetic hip joint
   - a chain for a watch
   - ornamental design for a trash can
   - portable trash compactor
   - skin moisturizer
   - method of manufacturing a golf ball
   - pharmaceutical composition for controlled drug delivery system
   - climber rose plant with a spicy scent
   - lipstick case with a design of a tulip
   - asparagus cutter
   - asparagus plant named "Jersey Jewel"

2. Discuss what policy reasons underlie the principle that products and items that occur naturally cannot be patented.

3. On May 1, 2006, Nick describes his new retractable pencil on his Web site. He includes pictures and diagrams. On June 1, 2007, he files a patent application for the invention. Is the patent likely to be granted? Discuss.

4. Tina has been working on her newly invented silicone potholder. Tina has invited several friends to her home each week for dinner to "test out" the potholder and to make sure the invention actually works. Fifteen months after Tina invents the potholder, she files a patent application for it. Is the patent likely to be granted? Discuss.

5. Maureen received a patent last year for a new type of stapler (which was always shown in painted pink metal). This year, Maureen would like to file a patent application for the stapler in painted blue metal. Does the new invention satisfy the statutory requirements for a patent? Discuss.

6. On July 1, 2007, Gerald filed applications for a utility patent, a design patent, and a plant patent. When will each patent expire?

7. Howard, a noted scientist, would like to patent the following items. Discuss whether the items are likely patentable.
   - a formula for improving time-release medications
   - an idea for improving traffic flow in urban areas
   - a genetically altered mouse
   - a mouse

USING INTERNET RESOURCES

1. Access Chapter 700 of the Manual of Patent Examining Procedure, available through the Web site of the USPTO. Review the section relating to rejections under 35 U.S.C. § 101. What three examples are given of subject matter that is not patentable under section 101?

2. Access the Web site for the National Inventors Hall of Fame. Who invented the Dolby noise reduction system, and what patent number relates to this invention?

3. Access the Web site for the USPTO. Who was the inventor of U.S. Patent No. 7,013,166 and what does the invention cover?

4. Access the Web site for the USPTO. When was PP17,233 issued, and what does the invention cover?

For additional resources, go to www.paralegal.delmar.cengage.com

Chapter 18

Patent Searches and Applications

CHAPTER OVERVIEW

Before an application for a patent is filed, a search should be conducted to ensure that the invention is novel and nonobvious. If the search results suggest that an invention may be patentable, an application is then prepared. An application consists of two parts: the specification (describing the invention) and the inventor's oath or declaration. Applications must be filed by individual inventors, although the application can be assigned to another at the same time it is filed. After the application is filed at the USPTO, it will be examined for patentability. Application proceedings at the USPTO are generally confidential until the application is published, 18 months after the application filing date. The examiner may issue office actions, requiring amendment of some of the claims of the invention. No new matter can be added to an application. When an application is allowed by an examiner, a notice of allowance is issued, and an "issue fee" must be paid to the USPTO for the patent to be granted. The term of utility and plant patents is 20 years from the date of filing of the application therefor. The term of design patents is 14 years from the date of grant. Maintenance fees must be paid at three intervals during the term of a utility patent to maintain it in force. Once the patent is issued, its owner may exclude others from making, selling, importing, or using the invention for the term of the patent.

PATENT SEARCHING

The Need for a Search

Patentability requires novelty and nonobviousness. The only predictable method of determining whether an invention is new and nonobvious is to conduct a search of the prior art (including patent records and printed publications). The patentability search, sometimes called a **novelty search** or prior art search, will help determine whether the differences in the subject matter sought to be patented and the prior art are such that the subject matter as a whole would have been obvious to a person having ordinary skill in the art. Moreover, because 35 U.S.C. § 102 excludes from patent protection inventions that have been known or used by others in the United States or patented or described in a printed publication in the United States or elsewhere, a search will disclose whether such bars to protection exist. Finally, if an invention has fallen into the public domain because its patent has expired, anyone can use it and no one can obtain a patent for it. Searching will disclose the existence of such expired patents. Thus, although not required prior to filing a patent application, a search is recommended to determine the feasibility of obtaining a patent. Otherwise, an inventor may incur costs of several thousand dollars in prosecuting a patent application only to have an examiner determine that the invention fails to satisfy the requirements of novelty and nonobviousness. An additional benefit of conducting a search is that it may provide ideas for drafting the application itself.

A novelty search is somewhat limited in scope and is designed to disclose whether an application will be rejected on the basis of lack of novelty or obviousness. A novelty search can usually be completed for less than $1,500. If an invention is intended for immediate commercial use or sale, an additional search, called a freedom to operate or infringement search, is often conducted concurrently with the novelty search. An invention may be patentable as a significant improvement over an existing invention and yet still infringe a patent.

Although the terms "freedom to operate search" and "infringement search" are often used interchangeably, there are differences between the two types of searches, although both focus on whether the client's invention is blocked by another's intellectual property rights. A **freedom to operate** search is usually conducted before the invention is brought to market and is intended to ensure that the invention does not infringe any patents. In contrast, an **infringement search** is usually conducted after the inventor has been informed that he or she is violating another's patent, and it focuses on examination of this specific and known patent.

An infringement search or full patentability search is far more extensive than a novelty search and is thus more expensive, often costing between $2,000 and $10,000. Conducting a search and obtaining an opinion relating to infringement is critical inasmuch as persons have affirmative duties of due care to avoid patent infringement. Obtaining advice of competent counsel may protect a person from having punitive damages imposed against him or her in an action for patent infringement because it demonstrates exercise of the duty of due care (see chapter 20).

Some inventors conduct their own searches. Others retain patent attorneys to perform the search or to engage the services of a professional search company. Naturally, the scope and breadth of the search depends on a variety of factors, including cost and importance of the invention. In many instances, paralegals conduct preliminary searches of the U.S. Patent Trademark Office (USPTO) databases and if this initial review indicates that the invention may be patentable, a more comprehensive search is conducted by professional patent searchers.

Patent Search Resources

There are several separate resources or facilities for patent searching.

USPTO Patent Search Room. The USPTO maintains a Patent Search Room at its Alexandria, Virginia offices. The search room is open to the public and houses all U.S. patents granted since 1790. Searching is usually accomplished by using state-of-the-art computer databases (described later). The USPTO also offers a Scientific and Technical Information Center at its offices, which offers more than 120,000 volumes of scientific and technical books as well as numerous journals and foreign patents.

Patent and Trademark Depository Libraries. Because many inventors do not have the resources to travel to the USPTO's Virginia offices, the USPTO has designated more than 80 libraries throughout the nation as **Patent and Trademark Depository Libraries (PTDLs).** Nearly every state has a PTDL, and larger states, such as California and New York, have several. About one-half of the PTDLs are academic libraries affiliated with universities, and the other one-half are public libraries. The PTDLs receive copies of patents and offer free public Internet access to all USPTO search tools, indices, and directories. The scope of the print collections varies from library to library. A list of all PTDLs is available on the USPTO Web site.

USPTO Online Database. The USPTO's online database includes all patents issued since 1790 and applications published since March 2001. The database of more than seven million patents includes information about all U.S. patents, offering the full text of patents granted since 1976, and the patent number and current U.S. classification for all patents granted from 1790 through 1975. Copies of patents may easily be ordered through the USPTO Web site or via telephone upon payment of a moderate fee.

USPTO Search Assistance. The USPTO public search facility staff conducts minimal searching for a fee. Specifically, the staff will conduct an inventor search and then provide a list of the patent numbers related to that inventor for $40 per hour.

Commercial Search Services. Although many paralegals and patent agents and attorneys (and some inventors) are skillful in conducting patent searches using the USPTO databases, most patent attorneys use or recommend the use of a professional commercial patent search company for the most accurate and complete patentability and infringement searches. In many instances, a combination approach is used: The paralegal or patent attorney performs a preliminary search using online databases, and if the results suggest that the invention is patentable, a more comprehensive search is then ordered from a commercial vendor. These vendors have numerous

databases at their fingertips and are highly experienced in locating the relevant prior art. Some search companies simply provide access to their vast databases for a fee charged to the inventor or law firm; others perform the search themselves and provide a full written report. Searches can be customized to the inventor's needs; for example, a search may focus solely on foreign patents. Some of the well-known commercial search companies include the following.

Delphion. Originally a product of IBM and now owned by the Thomson Corporation (the provider of Westlaw), Delphion (http://www.delphion .com) provides a full complement of patent searching options. It is highly popular and allows searching by patent number, inventor name, and a variety of other fields. It offers monthly subscriptions and a "one-day pass" for private inventors.

Dialog. Dialog is another Thomson business. It provides access to more than 900 databases and more than 15 million patents covering 60 countries. Dialog (http://www.dialog.com) offers access to IP firms and practitioners who then perform searches to determine patentability.

LexisNexis. LexisNexis (http://www.lexisnexis .com/patentservices) offers a Patent and Trademark Solutions service. You may obtain copies of U.S. and foreign patent documents, file histories from the USPTO, and other documents. Moreover, professional searchers at LexisNexis perform prior art searches and produce a written search report.

MicroPatent. MicroPatent (http://www .micropat.com) is yet another Thomson business. It provides inventors and law firms electronic access to tens of millions global patent documents. Searching can be done by keyword, patent number, and various other means.

PatPro, Inc. PatPro (http://www.e-pat.com/ index.htm) is located near the offices of the USPTO. It was founded by former USPTO examiners and it offers document retrieval and full search reports that list references found and discuss those references.

The previously mentioned commercial vendors are just a few of the many companies that perform patent searches and related services. Links to many professional search companies can be found at the "Patent Searching Academy" offered by Pierce Law School's IP Mall at http://ipmall.org/web_resources/record_request_pb_12.php. The IP Mall is one of the best-known IP sites on the Internet. It provides a wealth of IP resources, links to other useful IP sites, articles, information, and many other reliable and useful tools.

Patent Search Methods

There are two primary methods that can be used to search for prior art: the keyword search method and the classification search method.

Keyword Searching. The patent record databases (e.g., the USPTO's database of more than seven million issued patents) allow searching by keyword. This method matches words, phrases, and terms relating to the claimed invention to the words, phrases, and terms in the patents themselves. Patents from January 1976 to the present can be searched by a variety of fields or terms, such as the inventor's name, the patent's title, the full description of the invention, and the claims.

Most keyword searches rely on Boolean searching to formulate queries. The **Boolean search** method uses the terms and connectors *or*, *and*, and *and not* to construct searches. For example, a query of "mouthpiece and clarinet" would produce documents in a database only if both of those words were present in the document. The USPTO's "Quick Search" screens allow searchers to use the Boolean connectors to construct search queries.

Additionally, the USPTO database affords several elements or "fields" that can be searched, so that a search will retrieve only documents relating to the attorney representing an applicant, a specific patent examiner, issued patent number,

and so forth. The display of each patent's full-text includes a hyperlink to obtain full-page images of each page of the patent. Pre-1976 patents can only be searched by the patent number or the USPTO's classification number or code assigned to the invention; however, this limited display also includes a hyperlink to obtain full-page images of each page of the patent.

The USPTO database affords several methods to narrow a search and obtain precise results. For example, searchers may select a date range to obtain patents issued only after a specific date.

Keyword searches are fast and easy; however, the quality of a keyword search is highly dependent on the searcher's ability to anticipate the words an applicant used in an application. For example, a keyword search for a term such as "bird" will produce only patents with that specific word and no patents with the word "avian."

Introduction to Classification Searching. For more than 100 years, the USPTO has used a classification system, called the **United States Patent Classification,** for its patents. Although the system is primarily designed to be used by patent examiners in the course of examining patent applications, the system is also used by searchers. In fact, most commercial searchers use the classification method of searching. The system categorizes inventions according to the features of the invention. All relevant patents for a given technology are grouped together by class. There are separate classes for design and plant patents.

There are approximately 450 classes of inventions, from class 005 for beds, to class 102 for ammunition and explosives, to class 703 for data processing. Thus, any inventions relating to beds are found in class 005. Within each class are subclasses, which are smaller, more refined subsets within the main class. Thus, a designation such as 005/100 refers to the main class of beds and the subclass of cots; the designation 005/665 refers to the class of beds and the subclass of waterbeds. The USPTO uses three digits for all classes and three digits for all subclasses. Some inventions may be described by multiple classification numbers or codes. There are approximately 150,000 subclasses. Most classes have about 300 subclasses.

Searchers often begin with the Index to the U.S. Patent Classification, which functions much like the index at the back of this text. It is an alphabetical listing of technical and common terms from abacus (in class 435 for education and demonstration) to zwieback (in class 426 for food and edible material). The Index provides a useful introduction to the classification system.

Classification searches are useful because they retrieve all patents issued since 1790. Moreover, they do not require searchers to "guess" the words used to describe an invention as does the keyword technique. However, the classification system can be daunting for newcomers, who will need to spend some time learning how the system works. Moreover, as new technologies are developed, the USPTO assigns new classes and subclasses, which can make it difficult for new searchers to locate patents in cutting-edge technologies. Additionally, sometimes patents are misclassified. Finally, note that the classification system covers only U.S. patents; foreign patents cannot be obtained through the USPTO database.

Explanations of the U.S. Patent Classification system and suggestions for searching are provided on the USPTO's Web site at http://www.uspto.gov/go/classification/help.htm#5.

Using the Classification Method to Search Patents. The USPTO's Web site suggests the following four-step strategy to search for patents using the classification system (all steps may be accomplished online).

1. Begin with the alphabetical listing in the Index to the U.S. Patent Classification to "get your feet wet" and gain a basic understanding how the system works. Look for common terms describing the invention, its function, and use. Note the class and subclass numbers.

2. Use the U.S. Manual of Classification to access the classes and subclasses you located in the Index. The Manual provides lists of class titles in both numerical and alphabetical order. The titles are descriptive and suggestive of the technology involved and will further help refine the search parameters. The Manual's list of classes and subclasses is helpful in showing interrelationships between classes and subclasses.

3. Review the Classification Definitions (which are comprehensive descriptions of the class). These definitions establish the scope of the class and subclass and provide important search notes and suggestions for further research.

4. Click on the "P" icon to automatically search and retrieve patents for that particular classification code. Review the patents retrieved to make sure you are on the right track.

Other Search Methods. As described, patents in the USPTO database (and other databases) can be accessed by a variety of fields. Thus, for patents issued since 1976, searchers can locate all applications filed by a certain inventor or all patents owned by a certain individual or company. Searchers can also locate any patent by its patent number. Because many inventions and products are marked with their patent numbers and technical and scientific literature will note patent numbers, locating patents by number can be useful in reviewing similar or related prior art. Similarly, a product may be marked with the notice "patent pending." A searcher can then try to locate information about the invention by searching for its inventor or owner. Most applications are published 18 months after their filing dates; thus, information about these pending applications may be available.

Other Web sites offer highly specialized patent searching. For example, the U.S. Department of Agriculture offers searching of patents related solely to the intersection of agriculture and bio-technology at its Web site at http://www.nal.usda.gov/bic/Biotech_Patents.

Limitations on Patent Searches. Although a thorough search by an experienced searcher can provide invaluable information, there is no guaranteed way to predict whether an invention is novel, nonobvious, patentable, or likely to infringe another's patent. There are two primary limitations on patent searches.

- **Innumerable Resources.** Remember that an invention is not novel if it has been known or used by others in the United States or patented or described in a printed publication in this or a foreign country. Thus, there are literally millions of sources that might bear upon novelty, including more than seven million issued patents, magazine articles, books, academic papers, Web sites, and the like. It is not possible for any search to cover all of these resources.

- **Pending Patent Applications.** Patent applications are generally maintained in secrecy until 18 months after the date the application is filed with the USPTO (and some are kept secret until a patent issues). During this period, it is not possible to obtain any information about the pending application. Thus, it is possible that a review of USPTO records might lead a patent attorney to believe the client's invention is new, nonobvious, and noninfringing, and the attorney would then recommend that the client file a patent application. The USPTO might thereafter publish an existing patent application that would bar the client's application, and there would have been no absolute way to anticipate or predict the existence of such an application.

Patent Opinions

Once the appropriate search has been conducted, the results must be analyzed and communicated to the client. Typically, the results of a professional search company are provided to the law firm, which analyzes all materials and provides a formal legal opinion on patentability of the invention or the likelihood that an invention infringes another invention.

Although patent opinion letters will differ because they will address different issues (e.g., some address patentability, while others address freedom to operate or infringement), they usually include several common elements.

- The letter generally begins by reiterating the client's request for the opinion.
- Opinion letters include a description of the client's invention so that the client can correct any errors in the law firm's understanding of the invention.
- The letter will fully describe the search methodologies used by the firm, including a description of which databases were reviewed, the types of prior art that were examined, whether foreign publications were analyzed, and so forth.
- The letter will identify any relevant patents. Each patent will be fully analyzed and a conclusion will be given as to whether and how each patent located bears upon patentability, infringement, and so forth.
- A formal conclusion will be given indicating whether, in the law firm's professional opinion, the invention is patentable, whether the client has the freedom to operate and bring the invention to market, or whether the invention infringes any patents. The conclusions provided are not phrased as certainties but rather as probabilities. Thus, it is common to see language such as "It is more likely than not" or "Based

ETHICS EDGE: Avoiding the Unauthorized Practice of Law

Although paralegals are intimately involved in numerous patent-related tasks, they cannot provide legal advice. Thus, avoid giving any advice or opinion to a client regarding patentability, infringement, and so forth. While paralegals play a significant role in conducting searches and may assist in drafting opinion letters, only a licensed attorney can provide legal advice. Thus, an attorney must always sign the opinion letter.

upon our review, we believe that" and similar somewhat equivocal language.

- The letter will end with disclaimers reminding the client that apparently favorable results from a search do not necessarily guarantee that a patent can be obtained, that due to human error and mistakes in filing it is possible that not all relevant patents were disclosed, that the opinion is not a guarantee, and that the opinion is solely for the client's use and not for the use of others (such as bankers or investors).

THE PATENT APPLICATION PROCESS

Overview of the Application Process

The process of preparing, filing, and shepherding a patent application through the USPTO toward issuance is called "prosecution" (just as is the process of obtaining a trademark registration). An application may be filed by the inventor himself or herself or, as is more usual, by a patent attorney. Only 20 percent of all applications are filed by inventors without the assistance of attorneys. After the application is filed with the USPTO, it will be assigned to one of more than 4,700 patent examiners having experience in the area of technology related to the invention who will review the application and conduct a search of patent records to ensure the application complies with the statutory requirements for patents (including novelty, usefulness, and nonobviousness). Generally, there will be some objection made by the examiner, which will be set forth in a document called an office action. The applicant or attorney typically responds to the office action either by telephone or in writing. If the rejections cannot be overcome, the application may be abandoned or the examiner's refusal may be appealed to the Board of Patent Appeals and Interferences. Alternatively, the examiner will accept the response(s) to the office action(s) and allow the application. A Notice of Allowance will be sent to the applicant, which specifies an issue fee that must be paid to the USPTO in order for the patent to be granted. Until 2000, all patent applications were maintained in confidence. Since November 2000, however, most patent applications are published 18 months after their filing date (although the applicant can avoid publication by certifying that the invention disclosed in the application has not and will not be the subject of an application filed in another country). Once a patent issues, however, the entire application file (the "file wrapper") becomes a matter of public record. Patents are granted for roughly 65 percent of all applications filed.

It generally takes anywhere from one to three years to prosecute a patent (in fiscal year 2006, the average time was 31 months), and costs and fees can range from $5,000 to more than $30,000, with fees generally ranging from $10,000 to $15,000. Because of the time and the high costs involved in obtaining a patent, inventors should conduct a cost-benefit analysis to determine whether the invention merits the effort and expense of obtaining a patent. If the invention will have limited application, it may not be worth securing a patent for it. On the other hand, if the invention is likely to be a commercial success, the time and expense involved in obtaining patent protection will be a worthwhile investment.

Patent Practice

While preparing trademark and copyright applications is relatively straightforward, preparing a patent application requires skillful drafting as well as knowledge in the relevant field, whether that is biotechnology, chemistry, mechanical engineering, physics, computers, pharmacology, electrical engineering, and so forth. Because patent practice is highly technical, law firms that provide patent services to clients generally have a number of attorneys with different skill sets, and the patent department itself may be divided into different groups, such as a mechanical group, a biotech group, and an electrical group. Most **patent attorneys** possess both a law degree and an advanced degree in engineering, physics, chemistry, or the like. Due to the highly skilled nature of patent work, patent attorneys are highly marketable and often command salaries significantly higher than other attorneys. Similarly, other experienced IP professionals are also in high demand.

To represent patent applicants before the USPTO, an attorney must be registered to practice with the USPTO. An attorney must pass a registration examination (often called the "patent bar exam"), which requires the attorney to demonstrate he or she possesses the legal, scientific, and technical qualifications to represent patent applications. The examination is a six-hour 100-question multiple-choice test. The examination is computer-based and all questions are drawn from the *Manual of Patent Examining Procedure*. The examination is very difficult, and the pass rate tends to hover around 45 percent.

In addition to the inventor himself or herself and registered patent attorneys, individuals called registered **patent agents** can prosecute patent applications. Patent agents are not attorneys but rather skilled engineers and scientists who take and pass the patent registration examination. All are college graduates or must have the equivalent of such a degree. Although patent agents can engage in patent prosecution, they may not engage in activities that constitute the practice of law, such as representing parties in patent infringement actions or providing legal advice. Many paralegals are registered patent agents.

A list of attorneys and agents registered to practice before the USPTO is available from the Government Printing Office located in Washington, DC. Alternatively, the USPTO Web site (http://des.uspto.gov/OEDCI/index.jsp) provides an index to the more than 24,000 attorneys and 7,500 agents who are registered to practice before the USPTO. Many cities also have attorney referral services that can recommend patent attorneys or agents. Finally, a local or state bar association may have associations of patent attorneys and agents.

Confidentiality of Application Process and Publication of Patent Applications

For more than 200 years, all patent applications filed with the USPTO were maintained in strict confidence throughout the entire application process. Only when the patent issued was the file wrapper open to public inspection. Under the American Inventors Protection Act (AIPA) of 1999, however, which took effect in November 2000, the USPTO now publishes utility and plant applications 18 months after their filing unless the applicant requests otherwise upon filing and certifies that the invention has not and will not be the subject of an application filed in a foreign country. 35 U.S.C § 122. Applicants may request earlier publication. A fee of $300 is charged by the USPTO for publication. If the applicant later decides to apply for a patent in a foreign country, the applicant must provide notice of this foreign filing to the USPTO within 45 days or the application will be regarded as abandoned.

Basic information about the patent is published and the information is accessible through the USPTO's Web site.

The intent of the new law was to harmonize U.S. patent procedures with those of other countries, almost all of which publish patent applications after an initial period of confidentiality. Most commercial inventors supported the idea of preissuance publication because it indicates trends in patents and allows inventors to design their new inventions in ways to avoid infringement. The new act protects inventors from having their inventions infringed by providing that patentees can obtain reasonable royalties if others make, use, or sell the invention during the period between publication and actual grant of the patent. In any event, once a patent application matures into an issued patent, the entire file wrapper is available for review by the public.

Types of Applications

Although the prosecution of patents is essentially the same for any type of patent application, there are different types of applications. They are as follows.

- **Provisional application.** Effective in 1995, and as a result of the adherence of the United States to the General Agreement on Tariffs and Trade (GATT), it is possible to file a **provisional patent application** with the USPTO. A provisional application is less formal than a full utility patent application. It is intended as a relatively inexpensive and expeditious way of embarking on patent

protection. A provisional application need not include any claims, and the filing fee is inexpensive ($210 for large entities and $105 for small entities). The applicant must, however, file for a standard utility patent within 12 months of filing the provisional application or the provisional application will be deemed abandoned. A provisional application may be most useful when an inventor is in a race with a competitor and wishes to be the first to file an application. Filing a provisional application allows the inventor to mark the invention with the notice "patent pending." The 20-year term for a utility patent begins with the filing of the actual utility patent. Thus, filing a provisional application and then filing a corresponding nonprovisional application allows an inventor to delay the start of the 20-year period of patent protection. Moreover, it provides the inventor a simplified filing with a lower initial investment with one full year to assess the invention's commercial potential before committing to the higher costs of filing and prosecuting a standard utility patent. Although there are obvious advantages to filing a provisional patent application, there are disadvantages as well, primarily that the application will not be reviewed by an examiner during its 12-month pendency. Thus, the inventor is left without any indication regarding the ultimate protection for his or her invention.
- **Utility application.** An inventor may file a utility application for a new, useful, and nonobvious process, machine, article of manufacture, or composition of matter or some improvement thereof. If a provisional application has previously been filed by an inventor, a **utility application** must be filed within 12 months of the filing date of the provisional application.

- **Design application.** A **design application** seeks protection for new, original, and ornamental designs for articles of manufacture.
- **Plant application.** A **plant application** seeks protection for new and distinctive asexually reproduced plants.
- **Continuing application.** A **continuing application** claims priority from a pre-viously filed application. There are two types of continuing applications: continuation applications and continuation-in-part applications. The **continuation application** is a continuation patent filed when an examiner issues a final office action rejecting some claims in an application, and the inventor wishes to proceed with the allowed claims and then continue to pursue the rejected claims in a separate application. The continuation application must be filed before the original application is either abandoned or patented. The applicant and the patent examiner continue to discuss the rejected claims while the approved claims go forward toward issuance of a patent. The filing date for the continuation application is the same as the filing date of the original earlier-filed **parent application.** Thus, its effect is that it may shorten the term of existence of the later-issued patent (because the term of a patent is 20 years from the filing date of the original or parent application). On the other hand, by capturing the date of its parent, it may circumvent recent prior art. The other type of continuing application is the **continuation-in-part (CIP)** application, which contains significant matter in common with the original or "parent" application but also adds new matter not disclosed in the earlier parent, usually because an improvement to the invention was developed subsequent to the filing of the parent application. Claims that relate

to the later-filed CIP (e.g., the newly added matter) are entitled to the filing date of the CIP rather than the filing date of the original application. Claims that relate to the original application retain the original filing date.

- **Divisional application.** After an application is filed, the examiner may determine that the application covers more than one invention. Because each patent application can cover only one invention, a **divisional application** will be created to carve out a new application for the additional invention. The new divisional application typically retains the filing date of the original or parent application. The USPTO refers to divisional applications as a type of continuing application.
- **PCT application.** A **Patent Cooperation Treaty (PCT) application** allows an applicant to file one application that may be relied upon for later filing in countries that are members of the Patent Cooperation Treaty, to which more than 135 nations belong, including the United States. PCT applications are administered by the World Intellectual Property Organization (WIPO). Because section 102 of the Patent Act bars patents that are the subject of patents in foreign countries, an inventor wishing to protect a discovery or invention would be required to file simultaneous applications in every country in which he or she desires patent protection in order to avoid the statutory bar of section 102. Such filings would be an extremely expensive gamble inasmuch as the applications might be denied in various countries or the inventor might discover there is no market for the invention in some countries and might wish to abandon the process. The PCT application process allows an inventor to file one standardized application and then

postpone prosecuting the applications in other member nations for 30 months. The filing date for each foreign country is deemed to be the date identified in the original application. Although often called an "international application," the application does not automatically result in registration in member nations of the PCT. The application must still be prosecuted separately in each individual nation in which the inventor desires protection. The primary purpose of a PCT application is to allow an inventor to delay prosecution in foreign countries until a determination is made about whether protection is desirable in those countries. PCT applications are discussed in chapter 21.

Preparing the Application

Except where noted, the following discussion relates to regular utility patent applications rather than to provisional applications or to design, plant, or other patent applications. An application for patent must be in English, and it includes the following elements (which are shown later in Exhibit 18–6, an issued patent).

- a **specification** (the part of the application that describes the invention and the manner and process of making and using it) and the **claims** (separate paragraphs that distinctly claim the subject matter that the applicant regards as the invention)
- a drawing (when necessary for understanding of the invention)
- an oath by the applicant stating the applicant's belief that he or she is the original and first inventor of the invention

A filing fee must also accompany the application. Although these elements are few, their importance cannot be underestimated. Drafting the specification (describing the invention) is difficult and painstaking work. For a complex in-

vention, it may take 40 hours or more. The level of detail and specificity imposed on applicants is a trade-off: In return for obtaining a 20-year monopoly during which they may exclude others from selling, making, or using their inventions, inventors must fully disclose to the public what the invention is and exactly how it works.

Specification. The **specification** is the part of the application that describes the invention and the manner and process of making it and using it. It must be made in "such full, clear, concise, and exact terms as to enable any person skilled in the art . . . to make and use the same, and shall set forth the best mode contemplated by the inventor of carrying out his invention." 35 U.S.C. § 112.

Section 112 requires that the specification must be so complete as to enable one skilled in the art to make and use the invention. Thus, a general description such as "the invention is a high-speed drill" will be insufficient. In many instances, an application is rejected because of a **nonenabling specification,** meaning the specification is not sufficient to teach or enable another to make or use the invention. Simply put, stating what the invention is is insufficient; the application must describe how the invention works. A specification may incorporate by reference other materials such as pending or issued patents, publications, and other documents as part of the enabling requirement.

In addition to the enabling requirement, the application must set forth the "best mode" or preferred method contemplated by the inventor for making the invention. When the patent ultimately expires, competitors will then be able to compete with the former patentee on an equal footing because they will know how to make and use the invention.

The specification itself is composed of several distinct elements.

- **Title.** The invention must be given a short and specific title that appears as a heading on the first page of the application.

Examples of titles are "Bat for Baseball," "Nail Gun," and "Combined Refrigerator and Microwave Oven with Timed Overload Protection."

- **Cross-references to related applications.** If the application seeks the benefit of the filing date of a prior invention applied for by the same inventor or claims an invention disclosed in an earlier application by the same inventor, the second application must provide a cross-reference to the earlier application and identify it by serial number and filing date.

- **Background.** The **background** section of the specification should identify the field of the invention and discuss how the present invention differs from the known art. Generally, this section critiques other inventions and demonstrates the need and worth of the invention being applied for. A typical background section might discuss the shortcomings of existing similar inventions and itemize the benefits of the subject invention.

- **Summary of invention.** The summary section provides a short and general statement of the nature and substance of the invention. Because the summary and the background section are highly similar, some applications merge the two together into one called "Background and Summary of the Invention."

- **Brief description of drawings.** If drawings are included, they should be briefly described. The applicant must include a listing of all figures by number (e.g., Figure 1-A) with corresponding statements explaining what each figure depicts.

- **Detailed description of the invention.** In this section, the invention must be explained along with the process of making and using the invention in full, clear, concise, and exact terms. This description must be sufficient so

that any person of ordinary skill in the pertinent art or science could make and use the invention without involving extensive experimentation. The best mode contemplated by the inventor of carrying out the invention must also be set forth. Each element of the drawing should be mentioned. This section was previously called "Description of the Preferred Embodiments."

- **Claims.** A specification must include a least one **claim.** The claims define the scope of the invention. Although the language is precise and each claim is limited to one sentence, the inventor's goal is to draft the claims in such a way as to achieve the broadest possible scope of protection for the invention and yet comply with the statutory requirement of specificity. The claims are the most significant part of the application. The claims will be compared against the prior art to determine whether the invention is entitled to be patented. If the inventor later alleges another has infringed his or her invention, a court will compare the claims set forth in the patent with the alleged infringer's invention in determining whether infringement has occurred. Claims are often compared to the descriptions of real estate found in deeds that describe the "metes and bounds" of a parcel of property. A patent claim similarly describes the boundaries of the claimed invention. Each claim begins with a capital letter and ends with a period.

There are different types or formats of claims.

- **Independent claims.** *Independent claims* describe the invention in a general and broad manner. They stand by themselves and do not refer to any other claims.

- **Dependent claims.** *Dependent claims* are more narrowly stated and refer back to or incorporate all elements of the more broadly stated independent claims. Dependent claims cannot stand on their own; they must be read with one or more of the previously stated claims. For example, a dependent claim might read as follows: "The exercise device of claim 1, wherein the apparatus is a circular trampoline." Thus, each dependent claim is narrower and more specific than any preceding claim. Examples of independent and dependent claims can be seen in Exhibit 18–1.

- **Functional claims.** *Functional claims* define the invention by what it does rather than in terms of its structure. These types of claims are also referred to as "means-plus-function" claims or "means claims" and might read as follows: "A means for attaching the gadget described in Claim 1 to the panel described in Claim 2."

- **Product-by-process claims.** *Product-by-process claims* define a product by its process of preparation or manufacture and are often seen in chemical or pharmaceutical inventions. A product-by-process claim might read as follows: "A synthetic steel material prepared by a process comprising the steps of . . . ."

- **Jepson claims.** *Jepson claims* (named for the inventor who used this format) are used for improvements to existing inventions and identify what is new to the invention. They are useful for pointing out to the patent examiner's attention the specific novelty of an invention and might read as follows: "A locking fuel pump dispenser nozzle having a nozzle connected to a fuel pump, the improvement comprising a locking mechanism . . . ."

- **Markush claims.** *Markush claims* (also named after an inventor) are found in inventions relating to chemicals. A Markush claim recites alternatives in a format such as "An acid inhibitor selected from the group consisting of A, B, and C."

Design patent applications have only one claim, for example, "the ornamental design of a child's chair, as shown and described." Plant patents also have only one claim inasmuch as the entire plant is claimed as the inventive material. (See Exhibit 18–1 for a sample of claims.)

- **Abstract.** Strictly speaking, the abstract is not part of the specification but is rather a concise statement of the invention. The purpose of the abstract is to enable the USPTO and the public to determine quickly the nature of the technical disclosures of the invention. It points out what is new in the art to which the invention pertains. The abstract begins on a separate page and should not be longer than 150 words. The **abstract** should be a single short paragraph. The abstract for U.S. Patent No. 6,929,573 entitled "Bat for Baseball" is as follows:

> An improved baseball bat comprises a tubular core of rigid materials having a first section to support a handle and a second section to support a striking portion. The second section of the core has a diameter relatively larger than that of the first section of the core. A covering member of semi-rigid materials has a handle portion embracing the first section of the core and a striking portion embracing the second section of the core. Whereby, the baseball bat has a light weight, good equilibrium, and high structural strength for a good performance.

An abstract for a plant patent might read, "A hybrid tea rose having two-toned blossoms of pink with a white reverse."

Drawings, Models, and Specimens. If drawings are needed to understand the invention, they must be included. Nearly all patent applications are accompanied by drawings. The drawings must also be described so that the viewer knows whether the drawing is a cross-section, a side view, and so forth. For example, the drawings might be described as follows: "Figure 3 is a right-hand perspective view of the child's chair. Figure 2 is a front plan view thereof." The USPTO has stringent requirements relating to the size, symbols, and format of drawings, and usually a graphic artist or patent draftsperson is retained to prepare the drawings. Many law firms that practice patent law employ draftspersons on a full-time basis. Using new computer-assisted design and drawing software, some patent practitioners can prepare their own drawings. Informal drawings (photocopies) may be submitted if they are legible, but the examiner will usually impose a requirement that formal pen and ink drawings be submitted. The drawings must show every feature of the invention as specified in the claims.

Applicants were formerly required to submit a working model of the invention, but this requirement was eliminated in the late 1800s (although an examiner does have the authority to require that a working model be submitted). If the invention relates to a composition of matter, the USPTO may require the applicant to furnish specimens or ingredients for the purpose of inspection or experiment.

Oath of Inventor.   The applicant must sign an oath or declaration that he or she believes himself or herself to be the original and first inventor of the process, machine, manufacture, or composition of matter, or improvement thereof. The applicant must also identify his or her country of citizenship and provide an address. The applicant must acknowledge that he or she has reviewed and understands the contents of the application and understands the duty to disclose all information known to be relevant to the application. An oath is made before a notary public, while a declaration is a statement by the applicant

acknowledging that willful false statements are punishable by law. Either an oath or a declaration is acceptable.

The Patent Act requires that the person claiming the patent must be the actual inventor. 35 U.S.C. § 111. The applicant cannot be an assignee of the inventor. Thus, a review of the more than seven million applications on file with the USPTO will disclose that in nearly every case, the application has been made by an individual. Applications are not made by General Electric, Ford Motor Company, Microsoft Corporation, or any other corporation or business entity. Although these companies may employ the inventors and may, in fact, own the invention (due to agreement between the parties that the employer will own any invention made by the employee), the application itself must be signed by the individual inventor. This requirement helps to ensure that inventions are not stolen by others. If an inventor cannot be found or refuses to file an application, an assignee may file the application upon showing such facts. If an inventor has died or is subject to some incapacity, his or her estate or legal representative may file the application.

If an invention has been made by two or more persons jointly, they must file the application jointly. A **joint application** may be made even if the inventors did not physically work together at the same time, did not each make the same type or amount of contribution, or did not each make a contribution to the subject matter of every claim in the patent. Accurate records should be kept regarding each inventor's contributions so that if one inventor's contributions are refused or dropped from the claims he or she can be removed from the application.

An application can be assigned to another person or company concurrently with the execution of a patent application or at any time thereafter. Concurrent assignments usually take place when companies own the inventions created by their employees. All assignments should be recorded with the USPTO to provide public notice of the owner of the patent rights even though

EXHIBIT 18–1
Claims for Utility
Patent (U.S. Patent
No. 6,929,573)

What is claimed is:

1. An improved baseball bat comprising: a tubular core of rigid materials having a first section to support a handle and a second section to support a striking portion, said second section having a diameter relatively larger than that of said first section; a covering member of semi-rigid materials having a handle portion embracing said first section of said core and a striking portion embracing said second section of said core; wherein said first section and second section of said core are respectively made and connected by a connecting means; and wherein said connecting means is a ring like device inserted tightly into one end of said second section of said core.

2. The baseball bat as claimed in claim 1, wherein said core is made of a material selected from a group consisting of composite materials, metals, and plastics.

3. The baseball bat as claimed in claim 2, wherein said core is made of fiber-reinforced plastic materials.

4. The baseball bat as claimed in claim 1, wherein said handle portion of said covering member is made of foam plastic materials and said striking portion of said cover is made of wood materials.

5. The baseball bat as claimed in claim 1, wherein the end of said second section of said core has an inner shoulder to complementedly connect with an outer shoulder formed on said ring like device.

6. The baseball bat as claimed in claim 1, wherein said second section of said core is taperedly formed.

7. The baseball bat as claimed in claim 1, further comprising a protecting layer made of fiber-reinforced material and wrapping around the surface of said striking portion of said covering member.

8. The baseball bat as claimed in claim 1, further comprising at least one shock-absorbing device respectively and tightly inserted inside said core.

9. The baseball bat as claimed in claim 1, further comprising at least one weight device respectively and tightly inserted inside said core.

10. The baseball bat as claimed in claim 2, wherein the end of said second section of said core has an inner shoulder to complementedly connect with an outer shoulder formed on said ring like device.

11. The baseball bat as claimed in claim 3, wherein the end of said second section of said core has an inner shoulder to complementedly connect with an outer shoulder formed on said ring like device.

12. The baseball bat as claimed in claim 4, wherein the end of said second section of said core has an inner shoulder to complementedly connect with an outer shoulder formed on said ring like device.

recordation is not required to make an assignment valid. Issues relating to joint inventors, patent ownership, and transfer are further discussed in chapter 19.

If anyone other than the actual inventor is filing the application, a power of attorney will be needed to authorize the patent attorney or patent agent to act on the inventor's behalf. The power of attorney may be a separate form or may be included as part of the oath or declaration. The USPTO supplies a form for powers of attorney.

The requirements for preparing and filing design and plant patents are nearly identical to those discussed earlier for utility patents. Design patent applications, however, usually include a preamble stating the name of the applicant and the title of the design and a brief description of the nature and intended use of the article, and plant patent applications require the inventor's oath or declaration to confirm that the plant was reproduced asexually. Design and plant patent applications include only one claim.

Filing the Application.   After the application has been thoroughly reviewed to ensure it complies with USPTO regulations (such as requirements relating to the size of the paper used and that all pages be numbered and one and one-half or double-spaced), the application package should be assembled for filing with the USPTO. A transmittal letter should be prepared (the USPTO provides a form—see Exhibit 18–2), and it informs the USPTO as to what is being filed, identifies the applicant, and indicates if any other documents accompany the application. The applicant typically checks boxes indicating that a specification is included, an oath or declaration is included, and so forth. If the application is being simultaneously assigned at the same time it is filed, a recordation form should be included and the appropriate box should be checked on the application transmittal form.

Applicants may also submit an Application Data Sheet, a sheet supplied by the USPTO that contains bibliographic data such as information about the applicant, correspondence information, and information as to whether the applicant is represented by a patent attorney or agent. Use of the Application Data Sheet allows the USPTO to input records more accurately by scanning the information and thereby reducing errors in filing receipts. The USPTO supplies a form for the Application Data Sheet.

If the application is being simultaneously assigned at the same time it is filed, a recordation form should be included. (The recordation form used for patent assignments is nearly identical to that used for trademarks shown in chapter 5 as Exhibit 5–4.)

To obtain a filing date for an application, all that is needed is the specification (including claims) and drawings, if needed. The oath and fee can be submitted later, although an additional fee will be assessed as a surcharge.

Any document sent to the USPTO by regular or express mail should include a certificate consisting of a single sentence verifying the date the document was placed in the mail/express mail. In the event of a later dispute about filing dates of documents, the certificate of mailing will be accepted as proof of mailing on the date alleged. If there is no certificate of mailing, the filing date of the document will be deemed to be the date the USPTO received it.

In October 2000, the USPTO implemented its **Electronic Filing System (EFS)** for securely submitting utility patent applications and pre-grant publication submissions to the USPTO. EFS allows applicants to prepare patent applications and assemble the various parts of the patent application and transmit the application to the USPTO over the Internet. Applicants, however, have resisted filing their applications electronically; in fiscal year 2006, only about 14 percent of the more than 443,000 patent applications filed were submitted through EFS. (In contrast, nearly 94 percent of all trademark applications filed with the USPTO are filed electronically.) The USPTO continues to strive to encourage electronic filing, and in 2006 deployed a Web-based electronic filing system (referred to as EFS-Web) that accommodates PDF attachments and launched a marketing program to inform applicants of the benefits of using the system. EFS-Web (a more updated and easy-to-use system than EFS) has already significantly increased electronic filing of patent applications from 1.5 percent per month to 33 percent per month, and the USPTO hopes to achieve electronic filing of 40 percent of patent applications in fiscal year 2007. In May 2007, the USPTO announced it had reached a significant milestone: Each week more patent applications were being filed electronically than by the traditional paper method. Not all patent-related documents can be submitted using EFS-Web; for example, patent assignments must be filed using a slightly different electronic system. Paralegals working under the direction of others may file applications using EFS-Web if they provide their name and email address. One of the advantages of using EFS-Web is that senders receive immediate notification that their submissions have been received.

Since mid-2003, all patent applications are electronically scanned and loaded into a USPTO system called the **Image File Wrapper** system. This paperless system provides applicants and others the opportunity for unprecedented access to USPTO records.

The USPTO also offers its **Patent Application Information Retrieval (PAIR) System,** which allows patent applicants and their representatives to review the status of their pending patent applications online. There is both a "private" side to PAIR, allowing attorneys, patent agents, and inventors to securely access the USPTO's internal database and track the status of applications, and a "public" side to PAIR, allowing members of the public to access issued patents and published applications. Access to PAIR's private side requires registration by the inventor or her representative.

Fees and Small Entity Status. In order to provide encouragement to individual inventors, small entities or businesses, universities, and not-for-profit organizations, most fees for these applicants are reduced by 50 percent of the standard fees. For businesses, a **small entity** is one with fewer than 500 employees. While the small business cannot be the inventor, it is possible that, due to assignment, it is the owner of the patent rights, including the right to prosecute the application.

To claim the benefit of the reduced fees, the party must make a simple written assertion that it is entitled to small entity status. Specific forms are no longer required by the USPTO, and a simple statement that "the applicant is a small entity" is sufficient. The assertion can be prepared and filed at the same time as the application and

the reduced fee paid at that time. In fact, the Utility Patent Application Transmittal form (see Exhibit 18–2) allows the applicant to check a box to claim small entity status, and payment of the small entity fee is deemed to be an assertion that the applicant claims such status. The applicant must notify the USPTO if it loses entitlement to small entity status when fees for issuance or maintenance of the patent are due. To encourage electronic filing using EFS-Web, the USPTO reduces the basic filing fee for utility patents by $80 for small entities that file their applications electronically.

Effective September 30, 2007, the basic filing fee for a utility application is $310; the fee for a small entity is $155. Applications are subject to the payment of the basic filing fee and additional fees that include search fees ($510/$255) and examination fees ($210/$105) that are due at the time of filing, for a total fee of $1,030/$515. Additional fees are due if there are more than three independent claims ($210/$105), more than 20 total claims ($50/$25), multiple dependent claims ($370/$185), or if the total number of sheets in the specification and claims exceed 100 ($260/$130). The basic filing fees for a design or plant patent application are $210/$105. The USPTO offers forms to help applicants calculate and determine the appropriate fees due.

USPTO fees change each fall, so be sure to check the USPTO Web site to verify various fees. Fees may be paid by cash, cashier's check, money order, credit card, electronic fund transfer, or by **deposit account,** an account established with the USPTO for the convenience of attorneys and inventors, against which fees are charged. Generally, frequent USPTO filers deposit money into this account, and then charges for filing fees and other services are charged against this account. Replenishments are made as needed. For EFS-Web filers, payment may be made online.

As will be discussed later in this chapter, additional fees are also charged by the USPTO for issuance of a patent and to maintain a utility patent. (See Exhibit 18–3 for a listing of some patent fees.)

PTO/SB/05 (07-07)
Approved for use through 06/30/2010. OMB 0651-0032
U.S. Patent and Trademark Office. U.S. DEPARTMENT OF COMMERCE
Under the Paperwork Reduction Act of 1995, no persons are required to respond to a collection of information unless it displays a valid OMB control number.

UTILITY PATENT APPLICATION TRANSMITTAL

(Only for new nonprovisional applications under 37 CFR 1.53(b))

Attorney Docket No.	
First Inventor	
Title	
Express Mail Label No.	

APPLICATION ELEMENTS
See MPEP chapter 600 concerning utility patent application contents.

ADDRESS TO: Commissioner for Patents
P.O. Box 1450
Alexandria VA 22313-1450

ACCOMPANYING APPLICATION PARTS

1. ☐ **Fee Transmittal Form** (e.g., PTO/SB/17)
   (Submit an original and a duplicate for fee processing)
2. ☐ **Applicant claims small entity status.**
   See 37 CFR 1.27.
3. ☐ **Specification**   [Total Pages_____]
   Both the claims and abstract must start on a new page
   (For information on the preferred arrangement, see MPEP 608.01(a))
4. ☐ **Drawing(s)** (35 U.S.C. 113) [Total Sheets _____]
5. **Oath or Declaration**   [Total Sheets _____]
   a. ☐ Newly executed (original or copy)
   b. ☐ A copy from a prior application (37 CFR 1.63(d))
      (for continuation/divisional with Box 18 completed)
      i. ☐ DELETION OF INVENTOR(S)
         Signed statement attached deleting inventor(s)
         name in the prior application, see 37 CFR
         1.63(d)(2) and 1.33(b).
6. ☐ **Application Data Sheet.** See 37 CFR 1.76
7. ☐ **CD-ROM or CD-R** in duplicate, large table or
   Computer Program *(Appendix)*
   ☐ Landscape Table on CD
8. **Nucleotide and/or Amino Acid Sequence Submission**
   (if applicable, items a. – c. are required)
   a. ☐ Computer Readable Form (CRF)
   b. ☐ Specification Sequence Listing on:
      i. ☐ CD-ROM or CD-R (2 copies); or
      ii. ☐ Paper
   c. ☐ Statements verifying identity of above copies

9. ☐ **Assignment Papers** (cover sheet (PTO-1595) & document(s))
   Name of Assignee_____
   _____
10. ☐ **37 CFR 3.73(b) Statement**   ☐ **Power of Attorney**
    (when there is an assignee)
11. ☐ **English Translation Document** *(if applicable)*
12. ☐ **Information Disclosure Statement** (PTO/SB/08 or PTO-1449)
    ☐ Copies of foreign patent documents,
    publications, & other information
13. ☐ **Preliminary Amendment**
14. ☐ **Return Receipt Postcard** (MPEP 503)
    (Should be specifically itemized)
15. ☐ **Certified Copy of Priority Document(s)**
    (if foreign priority is claimed)
16. ☐ **Nonpublication Request** under 35 U.S.C. 122(b)(2)(B)(i).
    Applicant must attach form PTO/SB/35 or equivalent.
17. ☐ **Other:**_____
    _____

18. If a CONTINUING APPLICATION, *check appropriate box, and supply the requisite information below and in the first sentence of the specification following the title, or in an Application Data Sheet under 37 CFR 1.76:*

☐ Continuation   ☐ Divisional   ☐ Continuation-in-part (CIP)   of prior application No.: ....

Prior application information: Examiner _____   Art Unit: _____

19. CORRESPONDENCE ADDRESS

☐ The address associated with Customer Number: _____   OR   ☐ Correspondence address below

Name	
Address	

City		State		Zip Code	
Country		Telephone		Email	

Signature		Date	
Name (Print/Type)		Registration No. (Attorney/Agent)	

This collection of information is required by 37 CFR 1.53(b). The information is required to obtain or retain a benefit by the public which is to file (and by the USPTO to process) an application. Confidentiality is governed by 35 U.S.C. 122 and 37 CFR 1.11 and 1.14. This collection is estimated to take 12 minutes to complete, including gathering, preparing, and submitting the completed application form to the USPTO. Time will vary depending upon the individual case. Any comments on the amount of time you require to complete this form and/or suggestions for reducing this burden, should be sent to the Chief Information Officer, U.S. Patent and Trademark Office, U.S. Department of Commerce, P.O. Box 1450, Alexandria, VA 22313-1450. DO NOT SEND FEES OR COMPLETED FORMS TO THIS ADDRESS. **SEND TO: Commissioner for Patents, P.O. Box 1450, Alexandria, VA 22313-1450.**
If you need assistance in completing the form, call 1-800-PTO-9199 and select option 2.

EXHIBIT 18–2
Utility Patent Application Transmittal

EXHIBIT 18–3
Schedule
of Patent
Fees (as of
9/30/07)

Description	Fee	Small Entity Fee
Provisional application filing fee	$210	$105
Utility application filing fee	$310	$155
Utility application search fee	$510	$255
Utility application examination fee	$210	$105
Utility application total fees due:	$1,030	$515
Design application filing fee (including search and examination fees)	$440	$220
Plant application filing fee (including search and examination fees)	$680	$340
Submission of IDS	$180	$180
Issue fee for utility patent	$1,440	$720
Issue fee for design patent	$820	$410
Issue fee for plant patent	$1,130	$565
Publication fee	$300	$300
Statutory disclaimer	$130	$65
Request for continued examination	$810	$405
Notice of appeal	$510	$255
Filing brief in support of appeal	$510	$255
Request for oral hearing for appeal/interference	$1,030	$515

Duty of Candor. Patent applicants (and any individual associated therewith) are subject to a **duty of candor** and good faith in their dealings with the USPTO and must therefore disclose to the USPTO any information that is relevant to the patentability of a claimed invention. Violation of this duty may result in loss of patent rights. The applicant must therefore disclose, in writing, prior art references that bear on the novelty or nonobviousness of the invention, printed publications that describe the invention, any possible use or sale of the invention, related domestic or foreign applications or patents, litigation involving the invention, and any other matter that bears on patentability. The USPTO does not have the capabilities of fully researching all patent applications and thus relies on applicants

to disclose prior art and other matters material to patentability.

Under USPTO rules, information is material to patentability when it is not cumulative to information of record and (1) it establishes a *prima facie* (literally, "on its face") case of unpatentability of a claim or (2) it refutes or is inconsistent with a position taken by the applicant. To comply with this duty, applicants file an **Information Disclosure Statement (IDS)** with the USPTO listing and identifying material information. The USPTO provides a form (see Exhibit 18–4) for such disclosure. The IDS can be filed with the application or within three months of its filing. If the IDS is not filed during these time limits, it may be filed later, but generally additional fees will be charged and other documents may

PTO/SB/08A (12-07)
Approved for use through 12/31/2007. OMB 0651-0031
U.S. Patent and Trademark Office; U.S. DEPARTMENT OF COMMERCE
Under the Paperwork Reduction Act of 1995, no persons are required to respond to a collection of information unless it contains a valid OMB control number.

Substitute for form 1449/PTO

INFORMATION DISCLOSURE STATEMENT BY APPLICANT
(Use as many sheets as necessary)

Sheet _____ of _____

Complete if Known

Application Number	
Filing Date	
First Named Inventor	
Art Unit	
Examiner Name	
Attorney Docket Number	

U. S. PATENT DOCUMENTS

Examiner Initials*	Cite No.[1]	Document Number Number-Kind Code[2] *(if known)*	Publication Date MM-DD-YYYY	Name of Patentee or Applicant of Cited Document	Pages, Columns, Lines, Where Relevant Passages or Relevant Figures Appear
		US-			
		US-			
		US-			
		US-			
		US-			
		US-			
		US-			
		US-			
		US-			
		US-			
		US-			
		US-			
		US-			
		US-			
		US-			
		US-			
		US-			
		US-			

FOREIGN PATENT DOCUMENTS

Examiner Initials*	Cite No.[1]	Foreign Patent Document Country Code[3]¨Number[4]¨Kind Code[5] *(if known)*	Publication Date MM-DD-YYYY	Name of Patentee or Applicant of Cited Document	Pages, Columns, Lines, Where Relevant Passages Or Relevant Figures Appear	T[6]

Examiner Signature		Date Considered	

*EXAMINER: Initial if reference considered, whether or not citation is in conformance with MPEP 609. Draw line through citation if not in conformance and not considered. Include copy of this form with next communication to applicant. [1] Applicant's unique citation designation number (optional). [2] See Kinds Codes of USPTO Patent Documents at www.uspto.gov or MPEP 901.04. [3] Enter Office that issued the document, by the two-letter code (WIPO Standard ST.3). [4] For Japanese patent documents, the indication of the year of the reign of the Emperor must precede the serial number of the patent document. [5] Kind of document by the appropriate symbols as indicated on the document under WIPO Standard ST.16 if possible. [6] Applicant is to place a check mark here if English language Translation is attached.

This collection of information is required by 37 CFR 1.97 and 1.98. The information is required to obtain or retain a benefit by the public which is to file (and by the USPTO to process) an application. Confidentiality is governed by 35 U.S.C. 122 and 37 CFR 1.14. This collection is estimated to take 2 hours to complete, including gathering, preparing, and submitting the completed application form to the USPTO. Time will vary depending upon the individual case. Any comments on the amount of time you require to complete this form and/or suggestions for reducing this burden, should be sent to the Chief Information Officer, U.S. Patent and Trademark Office, P.O. Box 1450, Alexandria, VA 22313-1450. DO NOT SEND FEES OR COMPLETED FORMS TO THIS ADDRESS. **SEND TO: Commissioner for Patents, P.O. Box 1450, Alexandria, VA 22313-1450.**

If you need assistance in completing the form, call 1-800-PTO-9199 (1-800-786-9199) and select option 2.

(continues)

EXHIBIT 18-4
Information Disclosure Statement

PTO/SB/08B (12-07)
Approved for use through 12/31/2007. OMB 0651-0031
U.S. Patent and Trademark Office; U.S. DEPARTMENT OF COMMERCE
Under the Paperwork Reduction Act of 1995, no persons are required to respond to a collection of information unless it contains a valid OMB control number.

Substitute for form 1449/PTO

INFORMATION DISCLOSURE STATEMENT BY APPLICANT

(Use as many sheets as necessary)

Complete if Known

Application Number	
Filing Date	
First Named Inventor	
Art Unit	
Examiner Name	

Sheet | | of | | Attorney Docket Number |

NON PATENT LITERATURE DOCUMENTS

Examiner Initials*	Cite No.[1]	Include name of the author (in CAPITAL LETTERS), title of the article (when appropriate), title of the item (book, magazine, journal, serial, symposium, catalog, etc.), date, page(s), volume-issue number(s), publisher, city and/or country where published.	T[2]

Examiner Signature		Date Considered	

*EXAMINER: Initial if reference considered, whether or not citation is in conformance with MPEP 609. Draw line through citation if not in conformance and not considered. Include copy of this form with next communication to applicant.
1 Applicant's unique citation designation number (optional). 2 Applicant is to place a check mark here if English language Translation is attached.
This collection of information is required by 37 CFR 1.98. The information is required to obtain or retain a benefit by the public which is to file (and by the USPTO to process) an application. Confidentiality is governed by 35 U.S.C. 122 and 37 CFR 1.14. This collection is estimated to take 2 hours to complete, including gathering, preparing, and submitting the completed application form to the USPTO. Time will vary depending upon the individual case. Any comments on the amount of time you require to complete this form and/or suggestions for reducing this burden, should be sent to the Chief Information Officer, U.S. Patent and Trademark Office, P.O. Box 1450, Alexandria, VA 22313-1450. DO NOT SEND FEES OR COMPLETED FORMS TO THIS ADDRESS. **SEND TO: Commissioner for Patents, P.O. Box 1450, Alexandria, VA 22313-1450.**

If you need assistance in completing the form, call 1-800-PTO-9199 (1-800-786-9199) and select option 2.

EXHIBIT 18–4
Information Disclosure Statement (continued)

be required. If a party discovers additional material information during the course of the application process, the new information must be disclosed. In many instances, an application may be withdrawn so the newly disclosed information can be considered in a continuation-in-part application.

Breach of the duty to disclose may result in refusal to issue a patent, invalidity of the patent, and possible sanctions against the patent attorney.

PROSECUTING THE APPLICATION

Examination of the Application

Once the application is filed and a **filing receipt** is sent by the USPTO to the applicant (usually within 30 days after the application is filed), the application will be assigned to a patent examiner who is trained in the field to which the invention pertains. Examiners work in specialized groups or technology centers. The examiner will review the application, conduct a search in the patent files of the prior art, and determine if the invention is patentable. USPTO examiners rely heavily on the *Manual of Patent Examining Procedure* in examining applications; it includes excellent information, examples, commentary, and forms. It is available at the USPTO Web site at http://www.uspto.gov/web/offices/pac/mpep/mpep.htm.

If the examiner finds defects in the application or rejects some of the claims, he or she will issue an office action (similar to the office action issued by trademark examiners in rejecting trademark applications). If the examiner determines there are no bars to patentability, a notice of allowance will be issued for the application. Relatively few applications are allowed as filed. It generally takes about 22 months for the USPTO to issue a first office action.

It is far more likely that at least one office action will be issued, often indicating that based on the prior art, the subject matter claimed is either not novel or is obvious or that not enough information is disclosed in the application to enable another to practice what is claimed. The maximum time limit to respond to an office action is six months. Typically, however, the examiner demands that a response be filed within one, two, or three months, depending upon the type of reply required. The applicant may then obtain extensions upon filing a petition asking for an extension and payment of a fee. If a written response to an office action is not timely filed, the application will be deemed abandoned (unless the delay is shown to have been unavoidable or unintentional). If the final day for a response falls on a nonbusiness day or holiday, the applicant has until the next business day to file the response. The applicant may also request either a telephonic or in-person interview with the examiner to discuss the office action.

An applicant's response to an office action may include amendments to claims, drawings, or portions of the specification. Although amendments may be added to make explicit a disclosure that was implicit in the application as originally filed, amendments adding "new matter" are normally not allowed. Thus, claims may be amended and even added as long as they are supported by the original specification in the application. If the applicant believes the examiner's rejection of some claims to be sound, those may be canceled and the applicant may proceed on the remainder. Alternatively, the applicant may submit argument attempting to demonstrate patentability (often called a "traverse") and may submit evidence of secondary considerations, such as evidence of commercial success of the invention or its long-felt need.

After reply by the applicant, the application will be reconsidered, and the applicant will be notified as to the status of the claims, that is, whether the claims are rejected or allowed, in the same manner as after the first examination. If the application is now acceptable, a notice of allowance will be issued and the application will proceed to grant. If the application is not acceptable, the examiner will issue a second office action, which is usually made final and is referred to as a **final action.**

An applicant may appeal a final action (or may initiate an appeal when his or her claims have been rejected twice) to the Board of Patent Appeals and Interferences in the USPTO. An appeal fee ($510/$255) is required, and the applicant must file a brief to support his or her position, necessitating another fee of $510/$255. An oral hearing will be held, if requested, upon payment of a specified fee ($1,030/$515). If the board affirms the examiner's decision, the applicant may file a civil action in the U.S. District Court for the District of Columbia or may file an appeal with the Court of Appeals for the Federal Circuit (CAFC), located in Washington, DC. Many experts believe the Federal Circuit defers too readily to the board, noting that CAFC affirms approximately 95 percent of the board's determinations. The Federal Circuit can set aside USPTO findings only when the findings are arbitrary, capricious, an abuse of discretion, or unsupported by substantial evidence. *Dickinson v. Zurko,* 527 U.S. 150 (1999). Decisions by CAFC may be appealed to the U.S. Supreme Court; however, the Supreme Court has the discretionary power to deny certiorari and may refuse to hear the case.

While the USPTO ordinarily examines patent applications in the order in which they are received, an applicant can file a **Petition to Make Special** to accelerate the examination process. Common reasons for requesting expedited examination include the age or health of the applicant, applications involving HIV/AIDS and cancer-related patents, applications that contribute to the conservation of environment or energy resources, and applications that contribute to countering terrorism. Additionally, an expedited procedure is available for applications for design patents in view of their sometimes short economic life. Requests to obtain expedited treatment usually require payment of a fee.

Accelerated Examination of Applications

A new program implemented by the USPTO in 2006 allows applicants to file petitions for **accelerated examination.** Applicants must search and submit relevant prior art (rather than waiting for the examiner to do so), explain what the prior art teaches and how their invention is different, limit their claims to three independent claims and no more than 20 claims total, accept shortened time periods for responding to most USPTO communications, and file electronically. In return, these applicants will be given a final decision by the examiner within 12 months on whether their application for a patent will be granted or denied. In brief, the additional information given by the applicants helps examiners more quickly make decisions about patentability. The USPTO provides a form for the petition for accelerated examination. The first patent issued under the accelerated examination program was granted in just 6 months, a time savings of 18 months for the applicant.

Restriction Requirements and Divisional Applications

If an inventor claims two or more independent and distinct inventions in one application, the examiner will issue a **restriction requirement,** requiring the applicant to restrict or limit the application to one invention. The other invention may be pursued in a divisional application for which a separate application fee must be paid. Independent inventions are those that are unconnected in their design, operation, or function. For example, combining a shoe with a locomotive bearing, two articles that are not capable of being used together, would result in a restriction requirement. An applicant may argue against the examiner's requirement that an application be restricted to one invention.

If the applicant agrees with the examiner that the application includes two independent and distinct inventions and agrees to restrict the application to one invention, the second invention is usually protected or covered by the creation of a divisional application, a separate and distinct application for which a fee is required. The divisional application retains the filing date of its **parent application.** It is possible that creation of the divisional application may require changes in inventors inasmuch as the claims in the newly created divisional application may be the product of different inventors from those claims set forth in the original parent application.

Continuing Applications

If the examiner continues to refuse some claims in an application while accepting others, the applicant may wish to divide the application and allow the approved claims to proceed to issuance while continuing to do battle with the examiner on the rejected claims. Such a "continuation application" requires a separate filing fee.

Because patents cannot be enforced until they are issued, and the period of protection runs for 20 years from the date of application, an applicant should consider the strategy of moving forward with whatever he or she can to obtain patent protection as soon as possible. Filing a continuation application affords the applicant the opportunity to continue argument on the disputed claims while allowing the permitted claims to proceed to issuance. Moreover, because the continuation application retains the same date as the earlier "parent" application, the continuation application may be able to circumvent prior art that came into being after the original filing date and that would bar an entirely new application. A continuation application contains no new material.

If an applicant wishes to proceed on allowed claims and pursue rejected and additional matter that differs from that in the parent application, the applicant will file a "continuation-in-part" application. Because the continuation-in-part application includes additional information not in the original application (often, new improvements recently discovered), it requires a new fee, oath, and declaration. A continuation-in-part application may have one of two filing dates: If its claims are supported by the disclosure of the parent application, it will retain the parent application's filing date; if, however, its claims are not fully supported by the parent application, its filing date will be the date it was filed and not the earlier filing date of the parent application.

The distinction between a continuation application and a continuation-in-part application is that the former contains no new information while the latter includes new matter.

As an alternative to filing a continuation application, the **American Inventors Protection Act (AIPA)** of 1999 allows patent applicants to request continued examination of a utility or plant application for a fee without requiring the applicant to file a continuing application. This process, called **Request for Continued Examination** (RCE), may be used even if the application is subject to a final rejection, appeal, or notice of allowance. The fee is $810/$405.

Unlike the forms of continuation applications, an RCE is not a new application but rather a request that the USPTO make another full examination of the same application. In effect, the USPTO's final rejection is withdrawn and the patent claims are examined as if presented for the first time. Thus, new fees are required. RCEs are limited to applications for utility and plant applications although a somewhat similar process (the continued prosecution application) exists for applications for design patents.

Double Patenting

Another basis for refusal to issue a patent is double patenting. An applicant may not obtain two patents for the same invention. The doctrine prohibiting double patenting is an attempt to ensure that inventors do not apply piecemeal for patents in an effort to extend the term during which they may preclude others from making, selling, using, or importing the invention.

A rejection based on double patenting may arise because of an applicant's related application or already issued patent for the same subject matter or subject matter that is an obvious variation of that in the application.

If the subject matter is identical, the applicant must cancel one set of claims. If the examiner states that the subject matter is not identical but is rather an obvious variation of that in another application or issued patent, and the examiner cannot be persuaded otherwise, the applicant may enter a terminal disclaimer, agreeing that the term of the second patent will not extend beyond the term of the first. Both patents will simultaneously terminate. A terminal disclaimer will remedy a refusal based on double patenting only if the refusal alleges that the second invention is an obvious variation of another. A refusal alleging that two identical inventions have been applied for or patented cannot be remedied by a terminal disclaimer. The duplicate claims in the second application must be canceled, and if a patent has issued, it is invalid.

Protests

During prosecution, a member of the public may file a written protest against a pending application. Protests are filed to provide the USPTO with information that shows that the granting of a patent would be improper. The timing for protests is fairly restricted. They must be submitted prior to publication of the application or before the mailing of a notice of allowance, whichever occurs first. Once the protest is filed, the protestor has no further participation in the application procedure. Active involvement by the protestor ends with filing the protest. The patent examiner will consider any evidence submitted (e.g., prior art or evidence that the invention was in use more than one year before the application was filed) on the same basis as any other evidence bearing on patentability. If the examiner decides to allow the patent, the protestor cannot appeal, and there is no right to argue the protest before the USPTO.

Interference Practice

In the course of examination, an examiner may discover that another party's pending application or issued patent conflicts with the application in that the subject matter claimed in the application under examination is substantially the same as that claimed in a prior application or existing patent. In such cases, an **interference** will be declared or initiated by the USPTO, and a determination will be made regarding priority of invention by the Board of Patent Appeals and Interferences. About 1 percent of applications filed with the USPTO become involved in an interference proceeding. In many of those cases, interferences are declared because, due to the initial confidentiality of USPTO application proceedings, applicants may not know of other conflicting inventions at the time they file their applications. Because patents are typically issued to the "first to invent," a determination must be made by the USPTO in regard to which invention has priority.

Generally, the inventor who proves to be the first to conceive the invention (the one who had the idea for the invention) *and* the first to reduce it to practice either by filing the application (constructive reduction to practice) or by making and testing an embodiment of the invention (actual reduction to practice) will be held to be the first inventor. If an inventor is the first to conceive of the invention but the second to reduce it to practice, he or she may still prevail upon a showing that reasonably diligent efforts were made to reduce the invention to practice.

After holding a hearing and receiving testimony, the board will issue a decision. Appeal may be made to CAFC. A dissatisfied party also has the option of initiating a civil action in the U.S. District Court for the District of Columbia to determine the matter. Alternatively, during the course of any interference proceeding, the parties may reach a private settlement that will be binding on the USPTO if they file their agreement resolving the matter with the USPTO.

Notice of Allowance and Issuance of Patent

If the USPTO allows the claims and determines that the applicant is entitled to a patent, a notice of allowance will be sent to the applicant. The notice of allowance will specify a sum for an issue fee, which must be paid for the patent to be granted. The sum specified in the notice of allowance will also include the publication fee ($300), both of which must be paid within three months to avoid abandonment of the application (unless late payment is unavoidable or unintentional). You will recall that effective November 2000, all utility patent applications are published 18 months after filing (unless the applicant requests nonpublication and alleges there will be no equivalent foreign filing). At present, the issue fee for a utility patent is $1,440 ($720 for a small entity), $820/$410 for a design patent, and $1,130/$565 for a plant patent. When the issue fee is paid, the patent will be granted and a patent number and issue date will be given to the application. The applicant, now the **patentee**, may enforce its rights to exclude others from making, selling, using, or importing the invention. Furthermore, once a patent is issued, there is a statutory presumption of its validity. 35 U.S.C. § 282. On the date of the grant by the USPTO, the entire patent file becomes open to the public.

It now takes an average of 31 months for a patent to be issued, compared with three to four months for registration of a copyright and approximately 15 months to secure trademark registration.

(See Exhibit 18–5 for a flowchart illustrating the patent prosecution process.)

Portions of the issued patent will be published in the *Official Gazette*, the weekly publication of the USPTO, which was originally published in paper form and has been published exclusively electronically since 2002 (for patents). While the purpose of publishing trademarks in the *Official Gazette* is to provide notice so those who may be damaged by registration of a mark may oppose registration, publication of patents in the *Official Gazette* is done merely to provide information about patents, including patents that may be available for sale or license. The *Official Gazette* will include a claim and a selected figure of the drawings of each patent granted on that date, notices of patent lawsuits, a list of patents available for license or sale, and other general information such as changes in patent rules.

Utility patents are assigned numbers such as 4,999,904. Design patents are assigned a number as well as the letter "D," such as D339,456. Plant patents are assigned a number and the letters "PP," as in PP4,074.

(See Exhibit 18–6 for a sample of an issued patent.)

Notice of Patent

During the time that the application for the patent is pending, an inventor may mark the invention with the term *patent pending* or *patent applied for*. These notices have no legal effect, although they do provide notice that a patent application has been filed with the USPTO. Use of these terms or any other implying that an application for a patent has been made, when it has not, is a violation of statute and is punishable by fine. 35 U.S.C. § 292.

Once a patent has been issued, its owner may give notice that an article or invention is patented by using the word *patent* or its abbreviation *pat.*, together with the number of the patent. The notice may be placed on the article or on a label attached to the article. Use of the notice is not mandatory; however, in the event of failure to use the notice, no damages may be recovered by the patentee in any infringement action, unless it is proved that the infringer was notified of the infringement and continued to infringe thereafter. Marking of the patented invention constitutes such notice. Thus, although use of the notice is not required, it is always recommended. False marking is prohibited and is punishable by fine. The patent marking statute applies only to

EXHIBIT 18–5
Patent
Prosecution
Flowchart

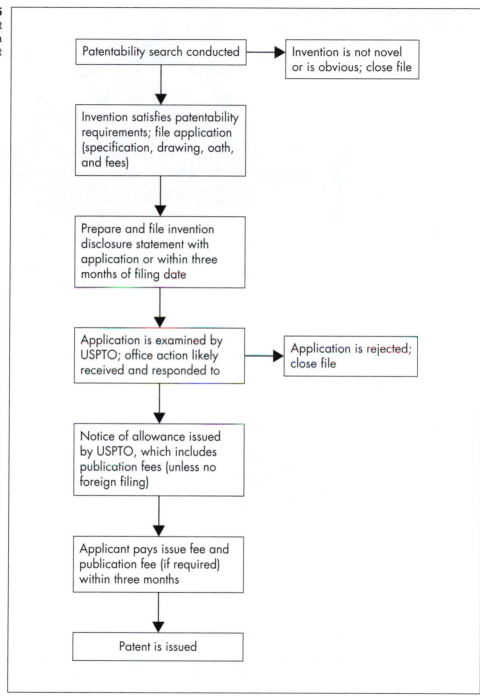

Patentability search conducted → Invention is not novel or is obvious; close file

Invention satisfies patentability requirements; file application (specification, drawing, oath, and fees)

Prepare and file invention disclosure statement with application or within three months of filing date

Application is examined by USPTO; office action likely received and responded to → Application is rejected; close file

Notice of allowance issued by USPTO, which includes publication fees (unless no foreign filing)

Applicant pays issue fee and publication fee (if required) within three months

Patent is issued

EXHIBIT 18–6
Issued Patent

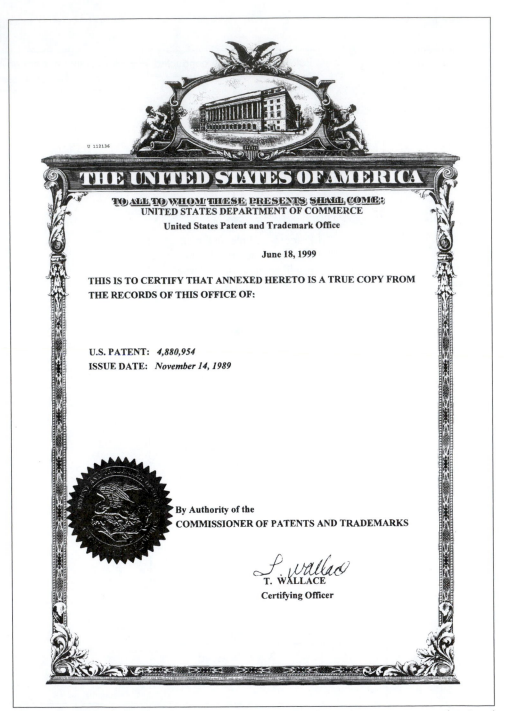

(continues)

EXHIBIT 18–6
Issued Patent
(continued)

United States Patent [19]

Bennett et al.

[11] **Patent Number:** **4,880,954**

[45] **Date of Patent:** **Nov. 14, 1989**

[54] **COMBINED REFRIGERATOR AND MICROWAVE OVEN WITH TIMED OVERLOAD PROTECTION**

[76] Inventors: **Robert P. Bennett,** 49 Francis Wyman Rd., Burlington, Mass. 01803; **Kunimitsu Ozaki,** 721 Mikan Dr., Richmond, Ind. 47374

[21] Appl. No.: **201,903**

[22] Filed: **Jun. 3, 1988**

[51] Int. Cl.⁴ H05B 6/68
[52] U.S. Cl. .... **219/10.55 M;** 219/10.55 B; 219/10.55 R; 221/150 HC; 307/41; 307/30; 361/22
[58] **Field of Search** .... 219/10.55 B, 10.55 R, 219/10.55 E, 10.55 C, 10.55 M, 10.55 D, 485, 486; 307/38, 41, 35, 30; 221/150 HC; 361/22, 31, 195

[56] **References Cited**

U.S. PATENT DOCUMENTS

T973,013	8/1978	Ferrara et al.	219/10.55 E X
3,482,509	12/1969	Gardner	219/10.55 R
4,004,712	1/1977	Pond	219/10.55 B
4,045,640	8/1977	McQueen, Jr. et al.	219/10.55 B
4,068,781	1/1978	Toth	219/485
4,129,769	12/1978	Takagi et al.	219/10.55 B
4,225,204	9/1980	Bellavoine	219/386
4,227,062	10/1980	Payne et al.	219/10.55 B
4,398,651	8/1983	Kumpfer	219/10.55 B
4,592,485	6/1986	Anderson et al.	221/150 HC

Primary Examiner—Philip H. Leung
Attorney, Agent, or Firm—Morris Fidelman; Franklin D. Wolffe

[57] **ABSTRACT**

A microwave oven and a refrigerator are combined in a single cabinet and share line power supplied to the cabinet. Door interlocks and a manually settable time are provided for disconnecting electrical supply to the compressor of the refrigerator during operation of the magnetron of the microwave oven. The circuitry provided ensures that electrical supply is reconnected to the compressor upon expiration of the timer setting, even if the door of the oven is incidentally left open after use.

3 Claims, 2 Drawing Sheets

(continues)

articles because processes and business methods cannot be marked.

Statutory Invention Registrations

A **statutory invention registration (SIR)** is not a patent. It is an invention "registration." It has the defensive attributes of a patent but not the enforceable attributes of a patent. An applicant may file a request for a SIR (under the provisions of 35 U.S.C. § 157) at the time of filing a standard nonprovisional patent application or later during the pendency of a nonprovisional application.

EXHIBIT 18–6
Issued Patent
(continued)

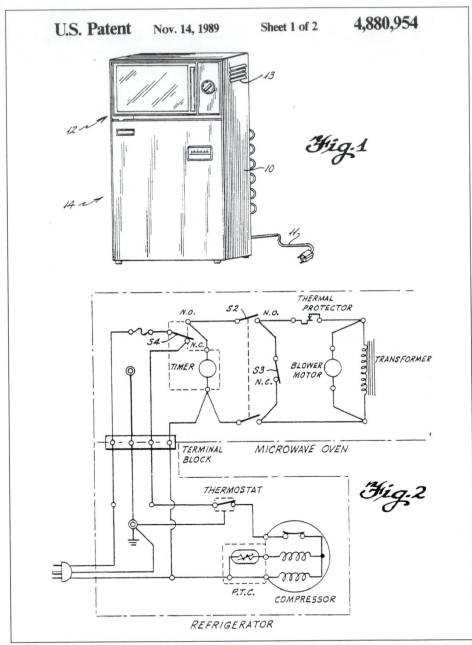

U.S. Patent   Nov. 14, 1989   Sheet 1 of 2   4,880,954

Fig.1

Fig.2

(continues)

Generally, an applicant will request an SIR to prevent someone else from obtaining a patent on his or her invention. An inventor may request a SIR

to place the invention in the public domain for others to use and to ensure another cannot obtain a patent on the invention. The SIR owner will

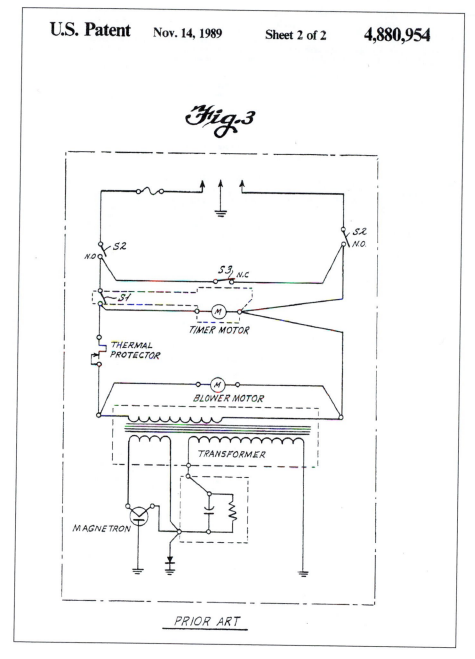

U.S. Patent   Nov. 14, 1989   Sheet 2 of 2   4,880,954

Fig.3

TIMER MOTOR

THERMAL PROTECTOR

BLOWER MOTOR

TRANSFORMER

MAGNETRON

PRIOR ART

EXHIBIT 18–6
Issued Patent
(continued)

(continues)

not be able to preclude anyone else from making, using, or selling the invention. Owners of SIRs are precluded from using the word "patent" in connection with their inventions. Upon publication of the SIR, the inventor waives all patent rights to the invention. Because inventors seldom

EXHIBIT 18–6
Issued Patent
(continued)

4,880,954

1

COMBINED REFRIGERATOR AND MICROWAVE OVEN WITH TIMED OVERLOAD PROTECTION

PRIOR ART CROSS REFERENCES

U.S. Pat. No. 3,482,509 Gardner, SANDWICH COOKING AND DISPENSING MACHINE, issued Dec. 9, 1969.

U.S. Pat. No. 4,225,204—Bellavoine, CUPBOARD FOR STORING PREPARED MEALS, WITH COLD-STORAGE AND REHEATING BY MICROWAVES, issued Sept. 30, 1980.

U.S. Pat. 4,398,651 Kumpfer, MICROWAVE FOOD DISPENSING MACHINE, issued Aug. 16, 1983.

U.S. Pat. No. 4,592,485—Anderson, et al, MEAL VENDING APPARATUS, issued June 3, 1986.

U.S. application Ser. No. 097,680—Bennett, REFRIGERATOR AND MICROWAVE OVEN AND OVERDEMAND INTERRUPT CIRCUIT, filed Sept. 17, 1987.

BACKGROUND OF THE INVENTION

This invention relates to a refrigerator and microwave oven enclosed in the same cabinet with unique electrical circuitry, so as to provide the convenience of storing and cooking food simultaneously in the same unit, while avoiding the peak power demands of simultaneous operation of the refrigerator compressor and the microwave magnetron. The invention finds particular application in buildings having older wiring and fewer circuits, by minimizing the possibilities of overloading such circuits while providing safe uninterrupted service. It also prevents overloading a more modern circuit which is "dedicated" to the apparatus by preventing start-up of the compressor during operation of the magnetron.

Microwave ovens are now commonly available in quick stop grocery stores and lunch rooms for heating and cooking foodstuffs purchased across the counter and from vending machines. Prior to the above-referenced Bennett application though, it had not been proposed to combine a microwave oven and refrigerator on a smaller scale in the same cabinet, particularly with provision for limiting the peak instantaneous power consumption so as to make the combination useful and attractive for use by students in dorm rooms, resort hotel rooms, tractor trailer cabs, recreational vehicles, so-called pullman efficiencies and the like.

The remaining prior art teaches refrigerated storage and a microwave oven combined in the same vending machine cabinet, and provision for transporting a selected item to the microwave oven for heating and subsequent removal from the machine. In particular, U.S. Pat. No. 4,398,651 discloses a switch, associated with a stack of food containers and actuated upon insertion of the uppermost container from the stack into a microwave oven, which causes a motor to drive a screw which, in turn, raises the stack until the next uppermost container changes the state of the switch. The amount of time that it takes for the switch to be changed by the raising stack determines the time of de-energization of a relay 56 which, in turn, determines how long the refrigerator is off and the microwave oven is on.

It is among the objects of the instant invention to combine prior art appliances into a single more convenient apparatus by utilizing a single molded, insulated shell containing both a microwave oven and a refrigera-

2

tor, while at the same time providing adequate ventilation of both and limiting instantaneous peak power consumption by the combination.

SUMMARY OF THE INVENTION

A microwave oven and a refrigerator are combined in a single cabinet and share line power supplied to the cabinet. Door interlocks and a manually settable time are provided for disconnecting electrical supply to the compressor of the refrigerator during operation of the magnetron of the microwave oven. The circuitry provided ensures that electrical supply is reconnected to the compressor upon expiration of the timer setting, even if the door of the oven is incidentally left open after use.

BRIEF DESCRIPTION OF THE DRAWINGS

FIG. 1 is an isometric view of a microwave oven and refrigerator sharing a common housing.

FIG. 2 is a schematic diagram illustrating an electrical circuit providing features of the instant invention.

FIG. 3 is a schematic circuit diagram of a conventional microwave oven.

DETAILED DESCRIPTION OF THE INVENTION

Referring to the drawings, cabinet 10 houses a microwave oven upper section 12 and a refrigerator lower section 14, with louvers 13 for venting the microwave section and cord 11 for supplying power to the combined refrigerator and microwave device from the standard receptacle.

The basic housing 10 comprises molded inner and outer shells with appropriate insulation therebetween, and these shells may be comprised of several panels defining sides, top, bottom, front and back of the device. The construction of the refrigerator section generally is well known and includes a freezer compartment. Below or at the rear of the refrigerated compartment and above the bottom panel is a refrigeration unit including condenser coils (not shown), while heat transfer mesh or screen is attached at the rear of the unit.

Above refrigerator section 14, and thermally insulated therefrom, is the microwave oven section 12 having the cooking compartment thereof surrounded by an absorptive layer. The absorptive layer is for preventing microwave energy from (1) reflecting from the outer wall and back to the magnetron of the microwave oven and thus damaging the magnetron, (2) warming foodstuffs in adjacent refrigerator compartments, and (3) escaping from the unit to the surrounding environment.

Of particular importance in the invention is the provision of a timing circuit 30 for controlling power to the magnetron and the compressor of the refrigerator.

Referring to FIG. 3. the magnetron of a conventional microwave is supplied with power via a transformer. In FIG. 3, the door of the oven is open and, upon closing thereof, the interlock switches S2 are closed and switch S3 is opened. Thus, the door must be closed in order for line power to be supplied to the timer switch S1 and to the transformer.

However, in order to combine a microwave oven and refrigerator in the same cabinet, while sharing line power supplied to the cabinet in the least costly and most efficient manner, it is necessary to ensure that the magnetron of the oven and the compressor of the refrigerator are not operated at the same time.

(continues)

desire to waive such rights, SIRs are seldom requested. In fact, in 2006, only 41 SIRs were published/granted (most of which were granted to the U.S. Air Force and the U.S. Navy). SIRs are searchable in the USPTO's database and are classified with the letter "H," as in "H2,100."

4,880,954

3

As seen in FIG. 2, the instant invention provides that the manually settable timer of a microwave oven interrupts line power to the refrigerator compressor by means of switch S4 whenever the timer is operating, while providing that same line power to the microwave oven and magnetron thereof in a manner that ensures the availability of line power to the refrigerator compressor upon completion of the timing function, even if the door of the microwave has been left open. In other words, with the timer manually set and actuated so that power is supplied to the timer motor via switch **54** according to a desired cooking time by the microwave oven, and with the door of the oven closed so that the interlock switches S2 and S3 allow supply of line power to the transformer of the microwave, opening the door of the prior to completion of the timing function will open switches S2 and interrupt power to the magnetron, but not to the timer. Thus, if the door is left open, line power can again be supplied to the compressor via switch S4 at the end of the previously selected timing period.

Having described the invention, it will be seen that the objects set forth above, among those made apparent from the preceding description, are efficiently obtained and, since certain changes may be made in carrying out the above method and in the construction set forth without departing from the scope of the invention, it is intended that all matter contained in the above description or shown in the accompanying drawings shall be interpreted as illustrative and not in a limiting sense.

It is also to be understood that the following claims are intended to cover all of the generic and specific features of the invention hereindescribed, and all statements of the scope of the invention which, as a matter of language, might be said to fall therebetween.

Now that the invention has been described, I claim:

1. In a method of operating a compressor of a refrigerator and a magnetron of a microwave oven, said re-

4

frigerator and microwave oven being combined in a single cabinet, the improvement comprising the steps of:

providing said microwave oven with manually settable means for timing supply of operating power to said magnetron for different, selectable periods of time;

setting said timing means according to each desired period of operation of said magnetron;

starting and operating said timing means according to said setting; and

preventing operation of said refrigerator compressor by and during said operating of said timing means.

2. In an electrical supply control circuit for a compressor of a refrigerator and a magnetron of a microwave oven, said refrigerator and microwave oven being combined in a single cabinet and sharing line power supplied to said cabinet, the improvement comprising:

manually settable means for timing supply of operating power to said magnetron for different, selectable periods of time; and

means for interrupting a power path to said refrigerator compressor during said operating of said timing means.

3. In an electrical supply control circuit for a compressor of a refrigerator and a magnetrom of a microwave oven, said refrigerator and microwave oven being combined in a single cabinet and sharing line power supplied to said cabinet, said microwave oven being provided with a door having interlock means for interrupting power to said magnetron when said door is open, the improvement comprising:

manually settable means for timing supply of operating power to said magnetron for different, selectable periods of time;

means for interrupting a power path to said refrigerator compressor during said operating of said timing means; and

circuitry means for reestablishing said power path upon cessation of said timing means even when said door is open.

* * * * *

EXHIBIT 18–6
Issued Patent
(continued)

POSTISSUANCE ACTIONS

Correction of Defective Patents

There are four separate ways to correct an issued patent: a certificate of correction, a reissue patent, a disclaimer, or a reexamination.

Errors occurring through the fault of the USPTO, minor errors (such as typographical errors), and errors in the naming of inventors can be corrected by asking the USPTO to issue a **Certificate of Correction.** Mistakes made by the USPTO will be corrected without charge.

Mistakes made by the applicant will be corrected upon the payment of a $100 fee.

Errors that are more significant, such as defects in the specification or drawings, that cause the patent to be partially or wholly inoperative or invalid are corrected by a **reissue patent.** A reissue patent may also be sought for the purpose of enlarging claims. The patentee's attorney may have failed to state the claims broadly enough or the patentee may discover that the claims stated in the issued patent are narrower than the prior art would require the patentee to make. In cases in which the patentee seeks to broaden claims, a reissue application must be filed within two years of the grant of the original patent. A reissue application can be made only if the error was committed without deceptive intent. While claims may be enlarged because the patentee originally claimed less than he or she had a right to claim, no new matter may be allowed.

An application for reissue must contain the same parts required for an application for an original patent (namely, a specification that includes claims, drawings, and oath of inventor). Moreover, the fee submitted must include a basic filing fee, search fee, and examination fee. Reissue proceedings involve a surrender of the original patent, filing of a reissue application, and reprosecution of the patent's claims (in the same manner as non-reissue applications).

If the application for reissuance is granted, the original patent is surrendered. The reissue patent is identified by the prefix "RE" in the USPTO records, for example, RE35,312, and its term is the same as that of the original patent inasmuch as it is granted to replace the original patent. In 2006, only 500 reissue patents were granted.

It is possible that during the two-year period before a reissue application is made, a third party has begun offering a device that did not infringe the original patent claims but that now infringes the reissue patent with its broader claims. In such a case, the third party may continue offering the device without liability for infringement. According to 35 U.S.C. § 252, no reissued patent shall affect the right of such an intervening party to continue to use or sell a device or invention unless the device or invention infringes a valid claim of the reissued patent that was in the original patent as well; otherwise, the significant investment an innocent third party might make in bringing a product to market would be lost. The intervening party, however, may continue to make or sell only the same specific thing; no additional devices can be offered.

Disclaimers

A patent owner who discovers that a claim in a patent is invalid may cancel the claim by filing a *disclaimer*. 35 U.S.C. § 253. The other claims remain valid and are unaffected by the disclaimer of the affected claim. A patent owner is not required to cancel an invalid claim, but cannot recover costs in an infringement suit alleging infringement of the valid claims unless the invalid claim is canceled prior to commencement of the lawsuit. 35 U.S.C. § 288. This type of disclaimer (often called a **statutory disclaimer**) is different from the terminal disclaimer discussed earlier (which is used to overcome a double patenting objection); it is a relinquishment of rights to one or more claims of a patent. It is not a vehicle for adding or amending claims.

Reexamination

When trademarks are published for opposition in the *Official Gazette,* third parties who believe they may be harmed by registration of the mark may oppose registration of the mark. Similarly, even after trademark registration, a registration may be canceled on certain grounds, including confusing similarity to a prior mark. Federal law affords no equivalent rights to a party to oppose the issuance of a patent or to cancel a patent on the basis he or she would be harmed by its issuance. In fact, because almost all pending patent applications are kept confidential until at least their time of publication 18 months after initial filing, parties seldom know whether an application has been filed for a patent.

Nevertheless, 35 U.S.C. §§ 301 and 302 provide that any person, including either the patent owner or an accused infringer of a patent, may file an ex parte (literally, a request "by one side" only) request for reexamination of any claim in an issued patent based upon the prior art, namely, patents or printed publications that may have a bearing on the patentability of a claim. An ex parte request for reexamination may be made at any time during the term of enforceability of the patent and must be accompanied by a filing fee of $2,520.

Within three months following the filing of a request for reexamination, the USPTO will determine whether a substantial new question of patentability affecting any claim of the patent has been raised. If the USPTO determines that a substantial question is raised, **reexamination of the patent** will be ordered so the question may be resolved. Reexamination procedure is identical to the procedure for initial examination of a patent application. The patent owner is permitted to amend his or her claims to distinguish them from the prior art, although no new matter enlarging or broadening the scope of a claim is permitted. If a reexamined claim is determined to be unpatentable, it will be canceled. If a reexamined claim is confirmed as patentable, a certificate of confirmation or reexamination certificate will be issued by the USPTO. The Patent Act requires that reexamination procedure be conducted with "special dispatch."

In 1999, Congress expanded the reexamination process by providing for inter partes (literally, "between parties") reexamination. Congress was concerned over the volume of expensive patent litigation and recognized that ex parte reexamination was infrequently used because a third party's involvement was so limited. After hearing testimony from witnesses that the volume of patent lawsuits would be reduced if third parties could argue their cases for patent invalidity before the USPTO, Congress enacted the American Inventors Protection Act, which amended the

Patent Act to provide for optional inter partes reexamination of patents. 35 U.S.C. §§ 311–318.

Like ex parte reexamination proceedings, inter partes reexamination proceedings are initiated by a request for reexamination; however, they may be initiated only by third-party requesters (and not by the patent owner). The filing fee is very high, $8,800 (probably due to the enhanced participation of third parties in the process). Just as with ex parte reexamination, the only basis for seeking inter partes reexamination is prior art, consisting of patents or printed publications that bear on patentability.

As is the case with ex parte reexamination, the USPTO will determine within three months whether a substantial new question of patentability is raised by the request. If such a determination is made, a reexamination will be ordered to resolve the question. Reexamination is conducted according to the procedures established for an initial examination of a patent application. If a claim is determined to be unpatentable, it will be canceled. If a claim is determined to be patentable, a certificate confirming such will be issued.

The primary difference between ex parte reexamination and inter partes reexamination is that in inter partes reexamination, the third party plays an active role. Every time that the patent owner files a response to an office action issued by the USPTO, the third party has the right to file written comments addressing issues raised by the office action or the patent owner's response. Moreover, the third party may appeal an adverse decision to the Board of Patent Appeals and Interferences ("BPAI") and thereafter to CAFC (just as may the patent owner).

The reexamination procedures can provide an alternative to litigation. Prior to commencing an infringement action, either the patent owner or the potential defendant may request ex parte reexamination, and a third party requester may request inter partes reexamination of an issued patent. Reexamination is less expensive and more expeditious than patent infringement litigation, confirms that claims are patentable, and may thus provide impetus for the parties to settle a dispute. The recently enacted inter partes reexamination procedures allow third parties to play an expanded role in the reexamination process and afford them appeal rights, thus placing these third parties on a more equal footing with patent owners in the reexamination process. Inter partes reexamination requests lag significantly behind requests for ex parte reexamination: In fiscal year 2006, 511 requests for ex parte reexamination were filed while only 70 requests for inter partes reexamination were filed.

TERM AND MAINTENANCE OF PATENTS

Term of Patents

For many years, the term of a utility patent was 17 years from the date of issuance. To align the U.S. patent system with that of most European countries and Japan, effective June 8, 1995, the term of utility and plant patents was changed from 17 years from issuance to 20 years from the date of filing of the application. The new provisions thus encourage inventors to prosecute applications in a timely manner. Under special statutory provisions, patents in existence or issued under applications filed before June 8, 1995, have a term of 17 years from issuance or 20 years from filing, whichever is longer. The term for design patents is 14 years from the date of issuance. After the term for any patent expires, anyone in the public has a right to make, use, sell, or import the invention or process (assuming no other government agency approval, such as that of the FDA, is required).

Under AIPA, there are some statutorily mandated extensions to patent terms, typically called *patent term adjustments,* usually granted to compensate for certain USPTO processing delays and for delays in the prosecution of applications pending more than three years. Subtitled, "The Patent Term Guarantee Act of 1999," this portion of the AIPA guarantees diligent applicants

a minimum 17-year patent term. The term of a patent is extended one day for each day lost as a result of various USPTO administrative delays or delays caused by interferences, secrecy orders, or successful appeals.

In addition to patent term adjustments, which are made to compensate for USPTO delays, a patent owner may apply for a **patent term extension,** which is granted to compensate patent owners of new drug products, medical devices, and the like, to recoup some of the time these owners lose when their products cannot be marketed because they are awaiting regulatory review (usually by the FDA). In such cases, the patent term may be extended by an amount equal to the time of the regulatory review; however, the period cannot exceed 14 years from the product's approval date.

Maintenance Fees

To maintain a utility patent in force, certain fees must be paid to the USPTO three times throughout the term of the patent. **Maintenance fees** are due at the 3½-, 7½-, and 11½-year anniversaries of the date of issuance. If the maintenance fees are not paid on or within six months before the due date or within a six-month grace period thereafter, the patent will expire at the end of the grace period. A surcharge is assessed if payment is made within the six-month grace period.

Patents that expire for nonpayment of maintenance fees may be reinstated within 24 months after the six-month grace period if the delay is shown to be unintentional, and expired patents may be reinstated at any time after the six-month grace period if the delay is shown to be unavoidable. Generally, an unavoidable delay is one that occurs because of reasonable reliance on mail delivery, employee conduct, or docketing systems; if through unforeseen events an error or delay occurs, it is viewed as unavoidable.

Imposing maintenance fees serves an important public policy: Patents that are not maintained are then released to the general public for all to use the invention without fear of infringement.

Maintenance fees may be paid by mail or over the Internet by electronic funds transfer, credit card, or through a deposit account established with the USPTO.

At present, the maintenance fees are as follows:

Due Date	Regular Fee/ Small Entity Fee
Due at 3½ years:	$930/$465
Due at 7½ years:	$2,360/$1,180
Due at 11½ years:	$3,910/$1,955

The surcharge for late payments made within six months of the due date is $130/$65. The USPTO estimates that most patentees will pay the USPTO a minimum of $4,000 over the life of a patent.

No maintenance fees are due for design or plant patents.

Trivia

- The youngest person granted a patent was a 4-year-old from Texas whose patent was for an aid for grasping around knobs.
- During fiscal year 2001, the USPTO became the first intellectual property office in the world to offer electronic filing for patents over the Internet.
- 2006 saw an increase of 8.7 percent over fiscal year 2005 in utility, plant, and reissue patent applications filed at the USPTO.
- The top three companies granted patents in 2006 were IBM (3,651 patents), Samsung Electronics (2,453 patents), and Canon (2,378 patents).
- At the end of fiscal year 2006, the USPTO had a backlog of more than one million patent applications pending.
- The USPTO reports that about 93 percent of patents issued are maintained at 3½ years, about 69 percent are maintained at 7½ years, and only 44 percent are maintained at 11½ years.
- In fiscal year 2006, the USPTO received 36 percent of its revenue from maintenance fees, the largest source of revenue for the USPTO.
- The design patent for the Congressional Medal of Honor was granted in 1904.

CHAPTER SUMMARY

Once a patent search has been conducted to determine an invention is novel and nonobvious, a patent application can be prepared. The patent application consists of a specification describing the invention and the inventor's oath or declaration. Applicants have a duty of candor in their dealings with the USPTO and must disclose anything that bears on the patentability of the invention. Applications filed at the USPTO are maintained in confidentiality until their publication. Once a patent issues, the entire file wrapper is available for review and copying. Once the application is filed, it will be examined by an examiner who will review the specification and determine patentability. One or more office actions may be issued that may necessitate amending or clarifying the claims. No new matter can be added to a pending application. Once the examiner allows the application, an issue fee must be paid for the patent to be granted. Utility and plant patents have a term of 20 years from the date of application while design patents have a term of 14 years from the date of grant. Patentees must pay fees at three different intervals to maintain a utility patent. The invention may be marked with a notice of patent, which will assist the inventor in recovering damages from infringers. After a patent has been issued, the patentee may request reissuance to correct a defective patent or to broaden claims if the application for reissuance is filed within two years after the original patent was granted. Either the patentee or a third party may request reexamination of a patent at any time during its term to determine if the patent or any of its claims are invalid.

CASE ILLUSTRATION—DUTY OF CANDOR

Case: *Buzzelli v. Minnesota Mining and Manufacturing Co.*, 521 F.2d 1162 (6th Cir. 1975)

Facts: A patentee, a professional hairstylist, brought an action for infringement of his patented method for retaining hair using adhesive tape. The lower court held that the defendant (owners of Scotch® brand tape) had infringed the patent, but the patent was unenforceable because of the patentee's conduct during examination of the patent.

Holding: The judgment of the lower court was affirmed. During the examination process, the patentee failed to clearly disclose material prior art and falsely asserted that no such art existed. This conduct was inequitable and rendered the patent unenforceable. Applicants have an "uncompromising duty" to disclose material prior art. Applicants owe the highest degree of candor and good faith to the USPTO. Only in this way can the USPTO act to safeguard the public interest against fraudulent patent monopolies. Because the applicant breached his duty of candor and truthful disclosure, his patent was unenforceable.

CASE STUDY AND ACTIVITIES

Case Study.   Vision's design engineers recently invented a new type of adjustable golf tee and filed one application for a patent for this invention and a new type of microwave oven to be used in the hotels' restaurants. The microwave oven is a variation of Vision's original microwave oven patented five years ago. After the application was filed, the USPTO refused some of the claims relating to the golf tee although most of the claims were approved. During the prosecution process, the USPTO temporarily lost the application file for the golf tee. Finally, once the patent was issued for the golf tee, Vision noticed a USPTO error in the spelling of the inventor's name and also noticed that one of the claims was invalid.

Activities.   Discuss any likely USPTO objections to Vision's application and any possible strategies Vision could adopt to obtain patent protection as expeditiously as possible and for the longest period of time. Discuss also how the errors in the issued patent should be handled.

ROLE OF PARALEGAL

Paralegals are involved in a variety of tasks in the patent search and prosecution process, including the following:

- conducting online searches to locate and retrieve patents that may bar a client's application for a patent
- gathering information from clients about their inventions so that searches can be targeted to the relevant prior art
- conducting research in nonpatent resources to locate relevant prior art
- obtaining copies of prior art, patents, and records from the USPTO
- assisting attorneys in reporting results of patent searches to clients
- drafting claims and preparing patent applications
- coordinating and assembling drawings for application
- verifying small entity status
- assisting in the patent application process by drafting and securing inventor's oath or declaration and drafting descriptions of drawings
- assembling the application packet and preparing the transmittal letter
- preparing assignment of patent application and invention and recordation document for same, if applicable
- preparing and filing Information Disclosure Statements
- coordinating the filing of the application (either in paper form or through EFS-Web) and the payment of fees
- docketing the date to ensure filing of a standard utility patent application 12 months after provisional application is filed, if pertinent
- maintaining and replenishing USPTO deposit accounts
- docketing dates for responding to office actions and preparing requests for extensions, if necessary
- assisting in preparing responses to office actions
- amending application to omit inventors if their claims have been dropped from the application
- notifying clients of status of patent prosecution
- preparing terminal disclaimers if a double patenting rejection is made
- assisting in preparing divisional, continuation, and continuation-in-part applications
- reporting notices of allowance and publication to client and docketing date for payment of issue and publication fees
- reviewing issued patent and making requests for correction, if necessary
- assisting in notifying client of issuance of patent, term of duration, marking of patent, and necessity to maintain patent
- docketing dates for maintenance fees for utility patents and maintaining patents in force

INTERNET RESOURCES

Federal laws relating to patents:

http://www.law.cornell.edu
http://www.findlaw.com

USPTO's information on how to search patents:

http://www.uspto.gov/main/profiles/acadres.htm

Patent search tutorial offered by Pennsylvania State University:

http://www.libraries.psu.edu/instruction/business/Patents/index.html

U.S. Patent and Trademark Office:

http://www.uspto.gov (general information about patents, filing fees, frequently asked questions, forms, and new rules and regulations)

Manual of Patent Examining Procedure:

http://www.uspto.gov/web/offices/pac/mpep/mpep.htm (USPTO's guide and manual to patent application, prosecution, and appeal process)

General information:

http://www.ipmall.fplc.edu (Pierce Law's IP Mall with excellent information and articles and links to other IP sources)
http://www.megalaw.com
http://www.findlaw.com

DISCUSSION QUESTIONS

1. Why should a law firm never inform a client, "We have reviewed all of the relevant prior art relating to your invention"?
2. Discuss why courts and statutes do not impose a duty on inventors to perform a patent search prior to filing a patent application.
3. Why is Boolean searching usually considered more precise than non-Boolean searching?
4. Sarah is the inventor of a new baby crib. She is concerned that a competitor is nearing completion on a similar invention and wishes to be the first to file a patent application. What should Sarah do?
5. Why must Sarah fully describe her invention in her application?
6. What are some advantages to Sarah in filing her patent application electronically with the USPTO?
7. Assume that the USPTO has issued a final rejection of Sarah's application. Sarah does not wish to appeal the rejection or institute an action in court. What should Sarah consider in order to have her application reviewed again?
8. Sarah's patent application was filed on December 1, 2005, and issued on June 1, 2007. What is the term of the patent and identify Sarah's obligations to maintain the patent in force.

9. One year after the patent was issued, Sarah realized that she could have stated her claims more broadly and would like to broaden the claims. What should Sarah do? During this period of time, Phil began offering a baby crib that did not infringe Sarah's original patent claims but will infringe the broader claims. Is Phil liable for infringement? Discuss why or why not.

USING INTERNET RESOURCES

1. Access the USPTO Web site and identify the Patent and Trademark Depository Library that is nearest to you.
2. Access the USPTO Web site and locate the *Official Gazette* notices for patents for December 19, 2006. Review the section called "Expiration of Patents." Give the number of the first patent listed that expired on October 25, 2006, and give the reason it expired.
3. Access the USPTO Web site, and locate the listing of class numbers and titles. What goods are in Class 036?
4. Access the USPTO Web site and locate information about patent attorney Linda Shapiro. Specifically, what city does Ms. Shapiro practice in, and what is her patent attorney identification number?
5. Access the USPTO Web site and review the fee schedule.
   a. What is the fee if a utility patent application is filed electronically by a small entity?
   b. What is the surcharge assessed if a maintenance fee is paid late (within six months)?
   c. Calculate the fee to be paid by Sarah for her application for her new baby crib, assuming the application has four claims (include the basic filing fee, search fee, and examination fee).
6. Access the USPTO Web site and review Chapter 1400 of the MPEP. When a patent is reissued, what is its term? What section of Chapter 1400 governs your answer?
7. Access the USPTO Web site and use the Glossary. What is the definition of "inter partes reexamination"?

For additional resources, go to www.paralegal.delmar.cengage.com.

Chapter 19

Patent Ownership and Transfer

CHAPTER OVERVIEW

Because patents have the attributes of personal property, they may be sold, licensed, or made subject to security agreements. Patent applications must be signed by the inventor of the discovery, namely, the person who conceived the invention. In many instances, inventions are the product of more than one inventor. Joint inventorship exists even when the contributions are not equal and the parties do not work in the same physical location. Disputes over priority of invention are typically determined by the principle that the first to invent is presumed to be the one who first reduced the invention to practice. Laboratory notebooks kept by inventors assist in determining the efforts inventors have made in reducing the invention to practice. Inventions made by an employee are owned by the employee, subject, however, to a "shop right," a nonexclusive royalty-free license to use the invention in favor of the employer. Nevertheless, if an employee is specifically hired to make an invention, the invention will belong to the employer. In most cases, employees and employers enter into written agreements by which employees agree that any inventions will be owned by and assigned to the employer. Patents may be assigned to others (an outright sale) or may be licensed to others, in which case permission to use the invention is granted to another.

OWNERSHIP RIGHTS

Patents are items of personal property and thus may be owned, sold, licensed, or devised by will. Applications for patents must be filed by the actual inventor of the article, process, design, or plant. If there is more than one inventor, the application must be signed by all inventors. Although the application must be signed by the actual inventor(s), it is possible that another party may already own the invention and any rights arising from it. For example, in many instances, employees are required to sign agreements with their employers whereby they agree that any invention or discovery invented by them while on the job will belong to the employer and that they will agree to assist and cooperate in any manner, including signing applications for patents, to ensure the employer's rights are protected. In such cases, although the oath in the patent application is signed by the individual inventor, when the application is filed, a simultaneous assignment is also filed, transferring the application and any rights under it to the employer. (See Appendix D, Form 13, for an agreement including provisions relating to ownership of inventions and work product by employers.)

SOLE AND JOINT INVENTORS

Sole Inventors

An invention may be the product of one person or more than one person. If one person conceives of the invention, he or she is the sole inventor. A directive given by an employer to an employee to solve a problem or invent an article does not make the employer an inventor. It is finding a solution to a problem rather than articulating it that determines whether one is an inventor. Similarly, giving suggestions, making minor contributions, or helping to build a model or embodiment of the invention do not make a person an inventor.

Joint Inventors

When more than one person contributes to an invention, they are **joint inventors.** Persons may be joint inventors even though they do not physically work together or at the same time, do not make the same type or amount of contribution to the invention, or do not make a contribution to the subject matter of every claim of a patent. 35 U.S.C. § 116. Each, however, must have made some contribution of inventive thought to the resulting product.

Joint inventors must apply for a patent jointly and each must make the required oath or declaration in the application. If one of the joint inventors cannot be found or refuses to join the application, the application may be made by the others on behalf of themselves and the omitted inventor. The U.S. Patent and Trademark Office (USPTO) will grant the patent to the inventor making the application, but the patent will remain subject to the rights of the omitted inventor. Errors in the naming of inventors can be readily corrected by amendment to the application or by correction to an issued patent as long as the errors occurred without any deceptive intent. Similarly, amendments occurring during prosecution that result in deletion of certain claims may require changing the named inventors if those inventors contributed only to the deleted claims.

DISPUTES OVER INVENTORSHIP

In the United States, patent rights are awarded to the first to invent. Almost all other countries follow a "first to file" system and award patent rights to the first person to file a patent application. Disputes over inventorship are usually determined in interference proceedings, as described in chapter 18. When a dispute occurs over inventorship, generally, the first to conceive the invention and to reduce it to practice (either actually or constructively) will be held to be the prior inventor. **Conception of an invention** refers to the formation in the mind of the inventor of a definite and permanent idea of the complete invention. For example, in one case it was held that an inventor's "hope" that a certain process would work did not establish conception because the inventor did not have a definite and permanent understanding as to whether and how the process would work. Generally, conception is complete only when the idea for the invention is so clearly outlined in the inventor's mind that mere ordinary skill would be required to reduce the invention to practice, without the need for elaborate experimentation or further developmental research.

An invention is not finished when it is conceived. It must be reduced to practice, meaning that it must be made and tested to ensure it works.

Reduction to practice may be actual or constructive. **Actual reduction to practice** involves construction of the invention in physical form or making or testing the invention or a prototype thereof. **Constructive reduction to practice** occurs when an application for a patent, completely disclosing the invention, is filed with the USPTO.

A person who reduces the invention to practice second may prevail and be found to be the first inventor only by showing that he or she conceived the invention first and made continual diligent efforts to reduce it to practice. Under TRIPs, and since January 1, 1996, inventive activity abroad may be considered in determining who is the first to invent.

To determine when an invention is reduced to actual practice and which inventors worked on which claims, inventors should keep **laboratory notebooks.** Inventors should make routine entries and sketches in notebooks as work on an invention progresses and as contributions are made by others. The safest course is to have the entries witnessed by the signature of a disinterested third party. Documents relating to the work, such as telephone bills, copying charges, emails, correspondence, and receipts for expenses for materials and supplies, should also be maintained with the notebook. Such notebooks are often critical pieces of evidence in determining conception, reduction to practice, diligence, and collaboration by joint inventors.

To provide evidence of the date an invention was conceived, an inventor previously could file a disclosure document with the USPTO. A disclosure document was not a patent application but was rather an informal document filed with the USPTO that described the invention and included sketches or photographs. Its sole purpose was to provide evidence of the date of an inventor's conception of an invention.

Note that the disclosure document was not the same as the Information Disclosure Statement patent applicants must file with the USPTO to identify information relating to their invention and to comply with their duty of candor. See

chapter 18 and Exhibit 18–4 for additional material on Information Disclosure Statements.

Effective February 1, 2007, the USPTO eliminated the Document Disclosure Program, which allowed inventors to file an informal document with the USPTO to provide evidence of the date of an inventor's conception of an invention. The USPTO concluded that few, if any, inventors obtained any actual benefit from a disclosure document, and some inventors who filed them mistakenly believed they were filing an application for a patent. Because a provisional patent application affords far more benefits and protection to inventors than did a disclosure document, the USPTO eliminated the program.

As discussed in chapter 21, proposals for patent reform would change the U.S. system from a "first to invent" to a "first to file" one. Such a change would harmonize U.S. law with that of most foreign nations and would eliminate or reduce interferences and reduce litigation over priority of inventorship and the complicated process of determining conception and reduction to practice.

INVENTIONS MADE BY EMPLOYEES AND INDEPENDENT CONTRACTORS

Employers and universities engaged in the business of developing inventions, drugs, processes, and other matter subject to patent protection typically require their employees to sign agreements by which the employees agree that anything discovered or invented by them during employment will be owned by the employer. The employee also usually agrees to assign the invention and any patent rights therein to the employer and to cooperate in filing documents and taking any other action to assist the employer in obtaining a patent. If the employee later refuses to sign an application for a patent as the inventor, the employer may do so upon a showing to the USPTO of his or her proprietary interest in the invention, and a patent will issue in the employer's name (see Appendix D, Form 13).

If an employer and employee do not agree in advance about which party will own inventions conceived by the employee during the course and scope of employment, the general rule is that the employee retains ownership rights, subject to a **shop right** in favor of the employer. A shop right is a nonexclusive, royalty-free, nontransferable license of the employer to make and use the invention in the employer's business whether or not the employee remains employed by the employer. The invention must result from efforts of the employee during his or her working hours and with material belonging to the employer. The employee may grant other licenses, may file a patent application and own any issued patent, and may sue for infringement by parties other than the employer. Typically, shop rights arise when an employee who is not hired to invent something nevertheless improves some machine or process at the place of employment. If an employee is specifically hired to solve a certain problem, however, and an invention results from the employee's work, the employee must assign the invention and any patent rights to the employer, regardless of the existence of any express agreement between the parties. In such a case, the parties have impliedly agreed that the employee's salary is intended to compensate him or her for making or developing the invention.

Employees who invent some article "on their own time" and which is not related to the employer's business generally own the resulting invention.

Companies that engage or commission independent contractors to work on projects or create inventions should always require that the contractor assign all inventions, discoveries, and any other intellectual property rights to the company.

Inventions made by federal employees while working for the U.S. government are generally owned by the employee. Nevertheless, the government will have a shop right to use the invention. Inventions made by companies or individuals working for the federal government pursuant to contract are usually governed by the terms of the contract. Typically, the government has the burden of demonstrating that it owns the invention. In many instances, particularly for educational, not-for-profit, or small business organizations, the government waives its patent rights. Government contracts relating to energy, nuclear propulsion, weapons programs, and other special topics generally provide that the government retains title to inventions arising from such contracts.

ASSIGNMENT OF PATENT RIGHTS

Because patents have the attributes of personal property, they may be transferred or assigned, just as may other items of personal property, and may be bequeathed by will. Patents or applications for patents may be assigned to another; a written instrument is required. 35 U.S.C. § 261. The written instrument should identify the patent by application or issue number, date, and title of the invention. An **assignment** is a transfer of a party's entire ownership interest or a percentage of that party's ownership interest (see Exhibit 19–1). A few states have prescribed certain formalities to be observed in connection with the sale of patent rights.

Although recording the assignment with the USPTO is not required for an assignment to be valid, recording is recommended because if the assignment is not recorded with the USPTO within three months from its date, it is void against a subsequent purchaser for a valuable consideration who acquired the patent without notice (unless the assignment is recorded prior to the subsequent purchase). The USPTO provides forms for recording assignments (see Exhibit 19–2), and the patent recordation form is highly similar to that used for recording assignments of trademarks. Additionally, for pending applications an assignee needs to make an assignment of record in the file wrapper to allow the assignee to take action with regard to the patent. The USPTO provides a form for this statement. The patent will then issue in the name of the assignee, and the assignee will be entitled to maintain the patent in force. Recorded assignments since 1980 may be viewed on the USPTO Web site by patent number or name of assignee or assignor.

Pursuant to 35 U.S.C. § 262, in the absence of agreement to the contrary, each of the joint owners of a patent may make, use, license, offer to sell, or sell the patented invention without the consent of and without accounting to the other owners. Thus, similar to copyright law, each owner has the right to assign or license the patent to a third

party without agreement of the other co-owners. Unlike copyright law, however, which requires accounting of profits, patent law does not require a joint owner to account to the others for monies received from such sale. Thus, it is critical that joint inventors be subject to a written agreement detailing their rights to use, make, sell, and license the invention to others.

LICENSING OF PATENT RIGHTS

A **license** differs from an assignment in that it is not an outright grant or transfer of ownership. The licensing of a patent transfers a bundle

EXHIBIT 19–1
Patent Assignment

Assignment of Patent

WHEREAS, _____, with an address at _____ (hereinafter referred to as "Assignor"), did obtain a United States Patent for _____, No._____, dated _____ (the "Patent"); and

WHEREAS, Assignor is now the sole owner of said Patent; and

WHEREAS, _____ (hereinafter referred to as "Assignee"), with an address at _____ is desirous of acquiring the entire, right, title, and interest in the Patent.

NOW, THEREFORE, for good and valuable consideration, the receipt and sufficiency of which are hereby acknowledged, Assignor does hereby sell, assign, and transfer to said Assignee the entire right, title, and interest in and to the said Patent, the same to be held and enjoyed by Assignee for his use and behalf, for his legal representatives and assigns, to the full end of the term for which said Patent was granted, as fully and entirely as the same would have been held by Assignor had this Assignment not been made.

Assignor further assigns to Assignee all right to sue for and receive all damages accruing from past infringements of the Patent herein assigned.

Assignor represents that he is the legal owner of all right, title, and interest in and to the Patent and has the right to assign the Patent and that there are no pending legal proceedings involving the Patent.

This Assignment shall be binding upon the parties, their successors and/or assigns, and all others acting by, through, with, or under their direction, and all those in privity therewith.

Assignor agrees to cooperate with Assignee and take any further action and execute any documents required to effect the purposes of this Assignment and the intent of the parties hereto.

Assignor   Assignee

_____   _____
Date: _____   Date: _____

Form **PTO-1595** (Rev. 07/05)
OMB No. 0651-0027 (exp. 6/30/2008)

U.S. DEPARTMENT OF COMMERCE
United States Patent and Trademark Office

EXHIBIT 19–2
Recordation
Form Cover
Sheet

RECORDATION FORM COVER SHEET
PATENTS ONLY

To the Director of the U.S. Patent and Trademark Office: Please record the attached documents or the new address(es) below.

1. Name of conveying party(ies)

Additional name(s) of conveying party(ies) attached? ☐ Yes ☐ No

2. Name and address of receiving party(ies)

Name: _____

Internal Address: _____

_____

Street Address: _____

_____

City: _____

State: _____

Country: _____ Zip: _____

Additional name(s) & address(es) attached? ☐ Yes ☐ No

3. Nature of conveyance/Execution Date(s):

Execution Date(s)_____

☐ Assignment   ☐ Merger

☐ Security Agreement   ☐ Change of Name

☐ Joint Research Agreement

☐ Government Interest Assignment

☐ Executive Order 9424, Confirmatory License

☐ Other_____

4. Application or patent number(s):   ☐ This document is being filed together with a new application.

A. Patent Application No.(s)   B. Patent No.(s)

Additional numbers attached? ☐ Yes ☐ No

5. Name and address to whom correspondence concerning document should be mailed:

Name:_____

Internal Address:_____

_____

Street Address:_____

_____

City: _____

State:_____ Zip:_____

Phone Number:_____

Fax Number:_____

Email Address:_____

6. Total number of applications and patents involved:_____

7. Total fee (37 CFR 1.21(h) & 3.41) $_____

☐ Authorized to be charged by credit card

☐ Authorized to be charged to deposit account

☐ Enclosed

☐ None required (government interest not affecting title)

8. Payment Information

a. Credit Card   Last 4 Numbers _____
              Expiration Date _____

b. Deposit Account Number _____

Authorized User Name _____

9. Signature:

_____   _____
Signature   Date

_____   Total number of pages including cover sheet, attachments, and documents: ☐
Name of Person Signing

Documents to be recorded (including cover sheet) should be faxed to (571) 273-0140, or mailed to:
Mail Stop Assignment Recordation Services, Director of the USPTO, P.O.Box 1450, Alexandria, V.A. 22313-1450

of rights, which is less than the entire ownership interest. A license is merely a permission to use. The permission or license may be limited in its scope, duration, terms, or territory. A patent license is, in effect, a contractual agreement that the patent owner will not sue the licensee for pat-

ent infringement if the licensee makes, uses, offers for sale, sells, or imports the claimed invention, as long as the licensee fulfills its obligations and operates according to the terms of the license agreement. Licenses may be exclusive (meaning that only one party has the ability to exploit the invention) or may be nonexclusive (meaning that more than one party may be given rights in the invention or patent). Similarly, licenses may be for the term of the patent (20 years from the date of filing) or may be for a limited time period. Licenses may be granted to one party to make the invention and to another party to sell the invention. They may be restricted to specific geographical areas, so that one party has rights west of the Mississippi while another (or the patent owner) has rights east of the Mississippi. Licenses are not usually recorded with the USPTO because they are viewed as private contractual relationships between parties that do not affect the ultimate ownership of the patent.

The patent owner may charge a one-time lump-sum payment for the license or may receive royalties or periodic payments during the term of the license. Typically, royalty payments are based upon sales of the invention. For example, an owner might receive 5 percent of the sales price of each patented item sold. Restrictions may be imposed on the licensee requiring the licensee to sell a certain number of units or forfeit the license or pay developers an increased amount therefor. As a sign of the value of patents, consider that from 1980 to 1999 royalties on patents in the United States increased from $3 billion to nearly $110 billion. IBM alone generates more than $1 billion annually in income generated by patent royalties.

Security interests may also be granted in patents to secure an obligation so that in the event of a default, the patent may be seized by the secured party. For example, the owner of a patent may wish to borrow money from a lender. The lender may be unwilling to lend money without some property being pledged as collateral for the loan. If a patent is pledged as collateral, and the patent owner defaults in any payments due to the lender, the lender may seize all rights in the patent. Although recordation with the USPTO of security interests in patents is not required, recordation is advised inasmuch as it provides notice to the public of the various interests claimed in a patent. The same recordation cover sheet used for assignments is also used for recording security interests. When the loan is repaid, another document is then filed with the USPTO confirming the security interest has been released.

INVENTION DEVELOPERS AND PROMOTERS

0In fact, due to the poor track record of invention promotion firms, the Inventors' Rights Act of 1999, part of the American Inventors Protection Act of 1999, helps protect inventors against deceptive practices of invention promotion companies. The act (see 35 U.S.C. § 297) requires invention promoters to disclose in writing the number

ETHICS EDGE: Drafting Assignments, Licenses, and Employment Agreements

Drafting a patent assignment or license or employment or joint inventors' agreement requires more than merely finding a similar form and filling in the blanks or changing the names of the parties. You must perform research (both factual and legal) and then modify preprinted forms or previously used agreements to comply with the law and to include any matters specific to the particular transaction involved. Because the law and USPTO rules and fees change frequently, using an outmoded form or document from a form file may be malpractice. In addition, proofread carefully to ensure that errors from one document are not imported into another.

of positive and negative evaluations of inventions they have given over a five-year period and their customers' success in receiving net financial profit and license agreements as a direct result of the invention promotion services.

Customers injured by a promoter's failure to disclose the required information or by any material false or fraudulent representation by the invention promoter can bring a civil action to recover statutory damages up to $5,000 or actual damages. Damages of up to three times the amount awarded are available for intentional or willful violations.

Additionally, while the USPTO does not investigate complaints against invention promoters or participate in legal proceedings, it does accept complaints against invention promoters (and provides a form for complaints) and then fowards the complaint to the invention promoter. Both the complaint and the response of the invention promoter are publicly available on the USPTO Web site.

Additionally, the Better Business Bureau can check the background of an invention promoter or developer. Similarly, the Small Business Administration may be of assistance. Finally, for $25, the USPTO will publish a notice in the *Official Gazette* that a patent is available for licensing or sale.

Trivia

- Abraham Lincoln is the only U.S. president to hold a patent (Patent No. 6,469 for A Device Buoying Vessels Over Shoals, granted in 1849).
- Someone receives a patent in the United States every three minutes.
- In 2000, Qualcomm reported royalty and licensing fees totaling $705 million for its technology used for cell phones.
- In 2005, Microsoft paid $54 million to extend a patent-sharing agreement with Sun Microsystems for one year.
- In 2000, IBM earned $1.7 billion from licensing and transferring patents.
- Many universities share patent license income with their scholar-inventors. For example, after Rice University recovers all of its costs involved with development of an invention, the inventor (a university employee) will receive 40 percent of income produced from the licensed patent. Other universities share on a sliding scale (for example, paying the university employee 40 percent of the first $50,000, 35 percent of the next $50,000, and so forth).

CHAPTER SUMMARY

Because patents have the attributes of personal property, they may be sold, licensed, or bequeathed by will. A person who conceives of an invention and reduces it to practice is a sole inventor. In many cases, however, more than one person will work on an invention. Those parties may be joint inventors even though they do not contribute equal efforts to the invention and do not physically work together. If a dispute over priority of inventorship arises, the general rule is that the first to invent is the one who conceived of the invention and first reduced it to practice, either actually (by building a model or embodiment of the invention) or constructively (by filing a patent application for the invention). Notebooks describing work done by inventors often assist in determining priority disputes.

Generally, inventions made by employees (who are not subject to agreements granting rights to employers) are owned by employees, subject, however, to a "shop right," namely a nonexclusive royalty-free license in favor of the employer to use the invention. In most instances, however, employers require employees to enter into agreements assigning any inventions and rights therein to the employer. Nevertheless, even without a written agreement, if an employee is hired specifically to create a certain work, the employer will own the resulting work.

As items of personal property, patents may be assigned or sold to others, as long as the instrument is in writing. Recordation with the USPTO is not required for an assignment to be valid but is recommended. Patents may also be licensed by agreements granting another the right to use, make, or sell the invention for a specified period in a specified territory in return for which the licensee will give consideration (usually in the form of periodic royalty payments) to the licensor. Patents may also be used to secure obligations so that in the event of a default by the patent owner, the secured party may seize the patent and exercise all rights of ownership. The USPTO provides numerous resources for independent inventors to protect them from unscrupulous invention promoters.

CASE ILLUSTRATION—JOINT INVENTORSHIP

Case: *On-Line Technologies, Inc. v. Perkin-Elmer Corp.*, 428 F. Supp. 2d 67 (D. Conn. 2006)

Facts: Plaintiff alleged that defendant infringed its patent for an improvement to a device. Defendant moved for summary judgment to dismiss the case on the grounds, among others, that plaintiff's patent failed to name a coinventor and was thus invalid.

Holding: Defendant's motion for summary judgment was denied. The alleged coinventor merely explained the state of the art to plaintiff's employee. An inventor may solicit the assistance of others when perfecting an invention without losing patent rights. To be a joint inventor, one must contribute in some significant manner to the conception of an invention. One cannot be a coinventor if one does no more than explain to the real inventor concepts that are well-known and current state of the art without ever having a firm and definite idea of the claimed combination as a whole. When the alleged coinventor explained the state of the art, the key aspect of the invention was already developed in the true inventor's mind, and thus the alleged coinventor was not a joint inventor.

CASE STUDY AND ACTIVITIES

Case Study. Two engineers employed by Vision in its New Research and Engineering Group invented a new card device that will allow hotel guests to more readily and securely access their hotel rooms. One of the engineers worked in Vision's Atlanta office and one worked in the Boston office. The Boston employee contributed far more to the invention than did the Atlanta employee. The two individuals never met each other, although they often talked on the telephone and sent e-mail communications to each other. Neither signed any agreement with Vision regarding ownership of any inventions. One of the individuals has left Vision's employment and cannot be located. Vision also owns a patent for a device that schedules golf tee times and alerts hotel guests accordingly. Vision would like to enter into an arrangement whereby it would allow other golf courses to use the invention. Finally, Vision would like to borrow a great deal of money to finance expansion of its hotels. The lender is insisting on obtaining security for any loan.

Activities. Discuss ownership of the card device and whether a patent application can be filed when one of the inventors cannot be located. Are the two individuals who worked on the card joint inventors? Discuss. What arrangements should Vision enter into with regard to the tee-time scheduling invention and obtaining new funding for planned expansion? What documents will be recorded with the USPTO and why?

ROLE OF PARALEGAL

Paralegals typically engage in the following activities related to ownership of patents:

- monitoring the progress of patent prosecution and the addition and deletion of claims to ensure inventorship is accurate for all claims
- reviewing issued patents to confirm all inventors are correctly identified
- assisting in drafting clauses for employment or other contracts confirming that inventions developed by employees will be owned by and assigned to employers or the commissioning party
- reviewing the *Official Gazette* to determine whether clients should be informed of patents offered for sale or license
- assisting in drafting assignments and security agreements relating to patents and recording same with the USPTO and assisting in drafting licenses of patent rights
- checking the chain of title of records at the USPTO to determine ownership of patents
- checking the reputation of invention promotion firms and preparing complaints against promotion firms

INTERNET RESOURCES

Federal laws relating to patents:	http://www.law.cornell.edu http://www.findlaw.com
U.S. Patent and Trademark Office:	http://www.uspto.gov (forms are provided for statements by assignees and for recording assignments)
Manual of Patent Examining Procedure:	http://www.uspto.gov (access MPEP chapter 300 for information about assignments and chapters 200 and 400 for information about joint inventors)

INTERNET RESOURCES (CONT'D)

USPTO's Inventor Resources Web page: http://www.uspto.gov/web/offices/com/iip/ index.htm (links to complaint forms and brochures on invention scam prevention)

General information: http://www.ipmall.fplc.edu (Pierce Law's IP Mall with excellent information and articles and links to other IP sources); http://www.findlaw.com http://www.megalaw.com

Forms: http://www.allaboutforms.com (forms for patent assignments, licenses, and joint inventor agreements)

DISCUSSION QUESTIONS

1. Tim and Steven have often discussed making better watchbands. Discussions have been informal and sporadic. Last year, Tim applied for a patent for a watchband of the type he and Steven often discussed. Steven is claiming he is a joint inventor of the watchband. Discuss.

2. Renee and Rick are working on a new, complex invention. Any patent that results from the invention will likely have numerous claims. Work is generally performed at Rick's house, and Rick does far more work on the invention than Renee. To ensure that each party knows what each has contributed to the invention, what should they do? Discuss.

3. Renee and Rick have received a patent for their invention. Without Renee's knowledge, Rick licensed the invention to another. Is this permissible? Will the license be recorded with the USPTO? What are Renee's rights? Discuss.

4. Harry was hired by his employer to invent a new remote control for televisions. During weekends, at home, and on his own time, Harry also invented a new type of resealable plastic bag. Discuss who owns the two inventions.

5. Nancy, an individual inventor, has decided to use the services of an invention promotion developer to help her market her invention. What resources does the USPTO provide to help ensure that the invention promoter is reliable and reputable?

USING INTERNET RESOURCES

1. Access the Patents home page on the USPTO Web site and select "Glossary." What is the definition given for "assignment"?

2. Access the USPTO Web site and locate Patent No. 7,114,223. Who is the inventor and who is the assignee? Now locate the USPTO Assignments Database and review the information for this assignment. When was the assignment recorded?

3. What is the fee required to record three assignments with the USPTO?
4. Access the Patents home page on the USPTO and select "Inventor Resources." Select "Complaints." Review the complaint filed by "Whitcomb" in September 2006. Who was the complaint filed against, and what was the nature of Ms. Whitcomb's complaint?
5. Access the USPTO Web site and select the *Official Gazette*. Review the *Official Gazette* notices for November 14, 2006. Review Section 14 (entitled "Patents available for License or Sale"). What is the first patent listed?

Chapter 20

Patent Infringement

CHAPTER OVERVIEW

Any person who, without authority, makes, uses, offers to sell, sells, or imports any patented invention infringes the patent. Innocence is not a defense to a claim of direct infringement, although it may serve to ensure punitive damages are not assessed. A person can also be liable for encouraging or inducing infringement or for contributory infringement by selling a component of a patented invention knowing it will be used to infringe a patent.

In determining whether infringement has occurred, the infringing device will be compared against the claims of a patent. If the accused invention falls within the language used in a patent claim, infringement is literal. Even if the accused invention differs from the claims in some way, it may still infringe under the doctrine of equivalents if it performs substantially the same function in substantially the same way to reach substantially the same result as the patented invention. A patentee is bound by the prosecution history of the patent process and cannot assert a position inconsistent with one taken during prosecution of the patent. In an infringement action, a defendant can raise a variety of defenses, including asserting there was no infringement,

that the patent is invalid or was procured by fraud, that the patentee has misused the patent to abuse his or her position, that the alleged infringer is using the invention solely for research purposes, laches, or estoppel. If infringement is found, a court may order injunctive relief, compensatory damages in an amount necessary to compensate the patentee for injury, costs, interest, and, if bad faith is shown, punitive damages up to three times the amount of compensatory damages and attorneys' fees. If parties cannot resolve infringement disputes amicably, litigation takes place in federal district court and is governed by the Federal Rules of Civil Procedure.

DIRECT INFRINGEMENT, INDUCEMENT TO INFRINGE, AND CONTRIBUTORY INFRINGEMENT

Direct Infringement

A patent issued by the USPTO does not grant a party any right to make, use, offer to sell, sell, or import an invention but rather *excludes* others from engaging in such acts. Under the Patent Act, any person who, without authority, makes, uses, offers to sell, or sells any patented invention within the United States or imports into the United States any patented invention during the term of its patent, infringes the patent (35 U.S.C. § 271(a)). A patent is effective and enforceable only after it is issued. Thus, making, using, selling, or importing devices prior to the time of a patent's issuance do not constitute acts of infringement. Nevertheless, recall from chapter 18 that under the American Inventors Protection Act (AIPA) of 1999, patentees may obtain reasonable royalties if others make, use, sell, or import their invention during the period between publication of their patent application (18 months after filing of most applications) and grant of the patent.

Liability for patent infringement may arise from one's acts in making, using, or selling the patented invention, referred to as **direct infringement,** or from encouraging or inducing another to infringe, often referred to as **indirect infringement.** One critical distinction between the two is that liability can be imposed for direct infringement without regard to the infringer's intent; however, liability for indirect infringement requires that the defendant know that infringement will occur because of his or her conduct.

Direct infringement occurs when a person violates 35 U.S.C. § 271(a) by making, using, selling, offering to sell, or importing the patented invention without the patent owner's permission. Note the use of the word *or* in the statutory language. Thus, a person may directly infringe another's patent if he or she makes the device without doing any further act, such as selling it. Similarly, merely using the patented invention without authority is an act of infringement even if the infringer did not make the device. Although the language of the statute is broad, there are several activities that do not constitute direct infringement.

THE FIRST SALE DOCTRINE

Under the **first sale doctrine** (also called the **exhaustion doctrine**), once the patent owner unconditionally sells a patented item, the buyer has the right to sell it or use it as desired. It is said that the first sale of the invention "exhausts" the patentee's rights to control the purchaser's use of the device thereafter. Thus, if you buy a patented espresso machine, you may use it as you see fit, resell it at a garage sale, or give it to a friend. The theory underlying the first sale doctrine is that when a patent owner sells an invention without any restrictions, he or she impliedly promises the buyer that the buyer may fully enjoy the invention. Of course, if the patentee imposes restrictions, conditions, or limitations on the sale (e.g., instructing a buyer that the patented invention may only be resold at a minimum price), then the buyer must comply with these agreed-upon terms.

Repair and Reconstruction

An adjunct of the rule that a buyer has a right to use the patented invention under the first sale doctrine is that the buyer has the right to repair the patented invention in order to prolong its use. Courts, however, draw a distinction between repair of a patented invention, which is permissible, and reconstruction of it, which is impermissible infringement. Courts often view purchasers of patented products as having been granted an implied license by the patentee to use the product, which use includes repair or replacement of its parts. While an owner of a patented invention thus has the right to repair and restore the article, activities that amount to rebuilding it such that the invention is being made anew are infringements. For example, if a party lawfully acquires a patented television, replacing components or reconditioning it is acceptable as a repair of the invention so long as the complete invention is not reconstructed.

IMPORTS AND SECTION 337 INVESTIGATIONS

Under 35 U.S.C. § 271(a), the patent owner has the exclusive right to exclude others from importing the patented invention into the United States.

In brief, one cannot import into the United States, or sell, offer to sell, or use in the United States a product made abroad by a process patented in the United States. Thus, a company cannot use a patented process abroad to make a product and then bring that product into the United States to compete with the patent owner. Although using the process abroad is not an infringement (because rights granted by a U.S. patent extend only throughout the territory of the United States and have no effect in a foreign country) subsequent importation of an article produced by a process patented in the United States is an infringement.

As an alternative to suing for patent infringement in the United States for another's act of importing the patented invention (and identical to the approach a trademark or copyright owner may take, see chapters 6 and 14, respectively) a patent owner may bring a proceeding before the International Trade Commission ("ITC") to block the infringing device from entry into the United States. Under section 337 of the Tariff Act of 1930 (19 U.S.C. § 1337), the ITC conducts investigations into allegations of unfair practices in import trade, including patent infringements. After a party files a complaint with the ITC alleging an act of patent infringement, the ITC examines the complaint and determines whether a Section 337 investigation should be conducted. Recall that a Section 337 investigation is somewhat similar to a trial in that motions will be made, discovery will occur, parties will testify, and an evidentiary hearing will be held. An administrative law judge will render an initial decision as to whether section 337 has been violated.

If section 337 has been violated, the ITC may issue an **exclusion order,** which bars the products from entry into the United States (which order is enforced by the U.S. Customs and Border Protection) or may issue a cease and desist order, which directs violators to cease certain actions. An award of money damages is not available as a remedy for violation of section 337.

In recent years, section 337 investigations have become increasingly popular with patent holders, primarily because of the strong remedies the ITC can order and because the proceedings are far less expensive and more expeditious than infringement trials in U.S. courts. The ITC has become an increasingly popular forum for blocking imported goods that infringe U.S. patents. Decisions may be appealed to the Court of Appeals for the Federal Circuit.

In addition to enforcing exclusion orders issued by the ITC, the U.S. Customs and Border Protection also allows owners of U.S. patents to order an **import survey** to provide the patent owner with the names and addresses of importers of merchandise that appears to have infringed the patent. The Customs survey does not stop infringement or importation, but it does provide information relating to the importer, who can then be sued for infringement or named in a complaint filed with the ITC to initiate a Section 337 investigation.

INDIRECT INFRINGEMENT

A person may be liable for patent infringement even if he or she never makes, uses, or sells the patented invention; liability may rest upon acts of encouraging others to infringe. Such acts are often referred to as indirect infringement. Indirect infringement is covered by two separate subdivisions of the Patent Act.

- Under 35 U.S.C. § 271(b), whoever actively induces infringement of a patent shall be liable as an infringer.
- Under 35 U.S.C. § 271(c), whoever offers to sell or sells within the United States a nonstaple component of a patented invention, knowing it to be especially made or adapted for use in infringement of a patent, shall be liable for contributory patent infringement.

In order for one to be liable as an indirect infringer, there must first exist liability for direct infringement. Without direct infringement by one party, there can be no indirect infringement by another. Moreover, to be liable, a defendant must know that infringement will occur because of his or her inducement or contribution.

Inducement of Infringement under Section 271(b)

If a person actively and intentionally encourages a third party to infringe a patent, and the patent is so infringed, the person who solicited the infringement will be liable for **inducement of infringement.** For example, selling a product with instructions on how to use the product in a manner that would infringe is inducement of infringement in violation of 35 U.S.C. 271(b). Similarly, if a corporation encourages and assists an employee in making another's patented invention, the corporation (together with any officer or director who induced the act) will be liable for infringement. Some experts refer to inducement as activity that aids and abets infringement, analogous to aiding and abetting a crime.

Although the Patent Act does not expressly require that the inducer know that he or she is encouraging infringing activity, courts have required that the plaintiff prove that the defendant had actual intent to cause the acts that constitute infringement.

Contributory Infringement under Section 271(c)

If a person offers to sell or sells within the United States (or imports into the United States) a component of a patented invention or process, or material for use in practicing a patented process and the component has no substantial use apart from use in the patented invention or process, knowing the same to be especially made or adapted for use in an infringement of such patent, he or she will be liable for **contributory infringement** under 35 U.S.C. § 271(c).

Selling some common or staple article that can be used for purposes other than in the inven-

tion does not constitute contributory infringement. For example, if a patented invention uses a common type of wire, a person who supplies the wire to the accused infringer cannot be liable for contributory infringement because the wire is a "staple" that has numerous uses other than in the invention.

In many instances, contributory infringement cases involve disputes regarding permissible repair and impermissible reconstruction. For instance, in *Aro Manufacturing Co. v. Convertible Top Replacement Co.*, 365 U.S. 336 (1961), the patent owner's patent was for a top for convertible cars, consisting of a metal frame and fabric. Consumers discovered that the fabric tops wore out much more quickly than the cars did and began ordering replacement fabric tops from the defendant. The patent owner sued the defendant supplier for contributory infringement. The Court held the car owners had a right to repair the cars and that replacement of the fabric top was not an impermissible reconstruction. Because the consumers were not direct infringers, the defendant (who supplied the replacement tops) could not be a contributory infringer.

INFRINGEMENT ABROAD

Acts committed abroad have posed special problems in infringement cases. For example, suppose that Pete owns a U.S. patent for a digital camera. Now suppose that Irv gathers together all of the component parts of Pete's camera and ships them to France to be assembled back into a workable camera. Has Irv infringed the patent? In *Deepsouth Packing Co v. Laitram Corp.*, 406 U.S. 518 (1972), the Supreme Court held that exporting unassembled components of a patented invention for assembly and use abroad was not infringement because the acts of finally assembling the invention had not occurred in the United States. To close this loophole in infringement law, Congress added section 271(f) to the Patent Act to clarify that one who exports all or a substantial portion of the unassembled components or a nonstaple component of a patented invention in such a manner as to actively induce the combination of the components outside the United States in a way that would infringe the patent if such acts were done within the United States is liable for infringement. Thus, section 271(f) parallels sections 271(b) and (c); acts that would constitute infringement in the United States under sections 271(b) and (c) also constitute infringement under section 271(f) if done abroad.

A recent U.S. Supreme Court ruling clarified *Deepsouth* by holding that abstract software code shipped by Microsoft to foreign manufacturers in the form of master disks was analogous to a blueprint and not a tangible "component" of the invention, and thus Microsoft would not be liable for patent infringement that occurs when copies of Windows software were made and installed on computers abroad. The master disk Microsoft sent from the United States was never installed on any of the foreign-made computers; foreign manufacturers rather used the disks to make copies, which were installed on the foreign-made computers. Because the master disk was never installed, the law prohibiting the exportation of patented "components" was thus not violated. *Microsoft Corp. v. AT&T Corp.*, 127 S. Ct. 1746 (2007). After *Microsoft* most experts believe that prototypes, templates, and intangible "blueprints" must thus be combined with something physical in order to infringe.

CLAIMS INTERPRETATION

The claims in a patent determine its exclusive rights. The skill required in claims drafting comes into play both before and after a patent is issued. Drafting a claim in a patent application is done to demonstrate patentability of an invention by distinguishing the invention from prior art. If the inventor later believes the invention is being infringed, the claims are again examined for determining whether such infringement has occurred. Thus, determining infringement requires interpreting the claims language in the patent and then comparing and contrasting the allegedly infringing article against those claims.

Literal Infringement and the Doctrine of Equivalents

If the accused invention, device, or process falls within the language used in a patent claim, there is **literal infringement** because the accused invention is the same as that protected by the grant of patent. A patent owner need not prove that every claim in a patent is infringed (remember that most patents include several claims). It is sufficient to prove that only one claim of the patent has been infringed.

Each element of the claim must be present in the accused device for literal infringement to exist. If the claim includes elements or steps that are not present in the accused device, there is no literal infringement. Thus, if Claim 1 in a patent is for a widget consisting of elements A, B, C, and D, and the accused device consists of elements A, B, and C, there is no literal infringement because the specified element D is not present in the accused device. For literal infringement to exist, the accused device must infringe all elements of the patent or claim.

In some cases, a party has made some change to a patented invention, for example, substituting one ingredient known to be an equivalent to that used in the patented invention. Because such a change would not constitute a literal infringement inasmuch as a claim has not been exactly copied, courts developed the **doctrine of equivalents** to protect the patented invention from misappropriation and ensure that a fraud is not committed on a patent. Courts will thus examine the accused invention to determine if it is "equivalent to" the patented invention in that it performs substantially the same function in substantially the same way to reach substantially the same result as the patented invention. If so, the two inventions are the same even though they may differ in name, form, or shape, and the second invention will be held to infringe the patent. *See Warner Jenkinson Co. v. Hilton Davis Chem. Co.*, 520 U.S. 17 (1997). Thus, a minor and obvious improvement on a patented invention can be an infringement. The doctrine of equivalents thus protects inventors by ensuring that latecomers do not profit by making an insubstantial alteration to a patented invention.

For a device to infringe under the doctrine of equivalents, it must have an equivalent of each element of the patented invention. Thus, if one element of a claim in the patented invention is not present in or has no equivalent in the accused invention, there is no infringement, even if the accused device as a whole performs substantially the same function in substantially the same manner as the patented invention.

The doctrine of equivalents reflects the tension between two competing policies. While claims should be drafted clearly and interpreted somewhat strictly so that the patentee is not given a broader scope of protection than that set forth in the patent itself, a patentee's efforts and invention should not be allowed to be circumvented by another person who makes some minor change in the invention or process.

Determining equivalency is a difficult task and generally depends upon the facts of each particular case rather than any set formula or rules. Moreover, the range of equivalents varies according to the significance of the patented invention: A **pioneer patent** (one that is an important advance or significant breakthrough in the art) is usually given a wide range of equivalents so that protection is broader; if the accused invention is generally equivalent to the patented invention, it infringes. Similarly, a patented invention that represents a marked improvement over prior art is given a wide range of equivalents. Conversely, a patented invention that is only a modest improvement is given a limited range of equivalents; the accused invention must be convincingly equivalent to the patented invention for infringement to be found. This theory is somewhat comparable

to the one used in trademark infringement cases that holds that distinct and unique trademarks such as XEROX® or EXXON® are given a broader scope of protection than weak or descriptive ones such as TASTEE BITES.

Reverse Doctrine of Equivalents

An accused device may fall within a claim's literal language and yet not infringe if it is so changed in principle from the patented article that it performs the same or similar function as the patented invention but in a completely different way. *Graver Tank & Mfg. Co. v. Linde Air Prods. Co.*, 339 U.S. 605 (1950). Known as the **reverse doctrine of equivalents,** this theory holds that despite literal infringement of claims, if the resulting device is different from the patented device, there is no infringement. The reverse doctrine of equivalents is not commonly encountered.

Prosecution History Estoppel

During the patent application process, the inventor or applicant may amend his or her claims and make various arguments to the examiner relating to the claims in the application. In the course of the patent prosecution, the applicant may omit certain claims or narrow them to avoid rejection on the basis they are precluded by prior art. The inventor/patentee is bound by this prosecution history in a later action alleging infringement under the doctrine of equivalents and is estopped from alleging that the claim was intended to be broader or asserting a position inconsistent with one taken earlier.

The principle is inapplicable to literal infringement cases inasmuch as literal infringement exists when the accused invention copies the actual claims in an issued patent; what occurred during the course of prosecution is thus not relevant. For example, during the application process, and in order to satisfy an examiner's objection, a patent applicant may narrow a claim. Once the claim is narrowed to be more specific, any invention that falls within the scope of the initial claims (but not the amended ones) does not infringe. The principle rests on the theory that a patent owner cannot narrow the scope of a claim and exclude certain subject matter in order to obtain a patent and then later recapture the excluded subject matter using the doctrine of equivalents. While the patentee has the right to appeal, a decision not to appeal and submit an amended or narrowed claim is viewed as a concession that the invention as patented does not reach as far as the original claim.

The doctrine, variously called **prosecution history estoppel** or **file wrapper estoppel,** applies not only to prosecution of the original patent but to reissue and reexamination proceedings. Underlying the doctrine is the principle that an applicant who disagrees with an examiner's position should appeal. The applicant is the one who drafts the claims, submits arguments, and makes amendments and should therefore be bound by his or her own actions, even if it is later determined that the examiner's position was incorrect.

The *Festo* Case

In late 2000, the U.S. Court of Appeals for the Federal Circuit sent shock waves through the patent community when it held that any narrowing amendment to claims made by a patent applicant during the patent prosecution process effected a complete bar to the doctrine of equivalents for the amended claim element. *Festo Corp. v. Shoketsu Kinzoku Kogyo Kabushiki Kaisha,* 234 F.3d 558 (Fed. Cir. 2000). Thus, applicants who narrowed claims in response to rejections by the USPTO subjected those claims to a complete bar and eliminated the doctrine of equivalents for the amended claim elements. Prior to *Festo,* only the particular subject matter surrendered would be lost through estoppel. After *Festo,* the patentee was limited to the strict scope of the amended claim element with no protection against equivalents.

Festo was appealed to the U.S. Supreme Court where it continued to attract attention with more

than 20 amicus curiae ("friend of the court") briefs filed. The U.S. Supreme Court vacated the Federal Circuit's decision in *Festo* and held that a narrowing amendment does not effect a complete bar but instead raises a rebuttable presumption that the complete bar applies. *Festo Corp. v. Shoketsu Kinzoku Kogyo Kabushiki Kaisha,* 535 U.S. 722 (2002). In fact, the Supreme Court chided the Federal Circuit and reminded the court that "courts must be cautious before adopting changes that disrupt the settled expectations of the inventing community." *Id.* at 739.

The Court held that estoppel need not bar suit against every equivalent to the amended claim element. Rather, prosecution history estoppel must be applied in a more flexible manner although the patentee should bear the burden of showing that the amendment does not surrender the particular equivalent in question. In brief, a patentee who amends a patent and narrows a claim gives up protection only for those things that were foreseeable by those skilled in the art covered by the patent. A patentee should not be expected to surrender that which he does not know or foresee. Consequently, a patent holder who could not have foreseen that changing the description in a patent application would limit coverage would still be able to sue those making equivalent products.

Patent practitioners have expressed relief at the Supreme Court's confirmation that the doctrine of equivalents is alive and well (although subject to a rebuttable presumption that estoppel applies and that equivalents have been surrendered), and at least one commentator has stated that *Festo* is likely the most significant U.S. Supreme Court patent case in a generation.

DEFENSES TO INFRINGEMENT

Defendants in infringement actions generally assert one or more of several affirmative defenses. The most commonly asserted defenses are noninfringement, patent invalidity, fraud, patent misuse, experimental or research use, the recently enacted "first inventor defense," laches, and estoppel.

A defendant may assert that its acts do not constitute infringement, either literally or under the doctrine of equivalents. An accused infringer may also assert that the patent is invalid and thus cannot be infringed. An invalidity defense alleges that the invention fails to meet statutory subject matter, is not novel or useful, or is obvious, such that the patent for the invention should not have been issued by the USPTO. Because issued patents are presumed to be valid under 35 U.S.C. § 282, a defendant asserting invalidity must prove invalidity by clear and convincing evidence. A party using an invention under a license from the patentee may assert patent invalidity and is not estopped from raising such a defense even though he or she has agreed in a license agreement not to contest the validity of the patent, primarily because the policy favoring the negation of invalid patents outweighs contract law policy.

Fraud or inequitable conduct by a patentee during prosecution will render a patent resulting therefrom unenforceable. Such conduct may consist of omissions or material misrepresentations during the patent application process. This fraud usually takes the form of a failure to disclose prior art during the patent prosecution. Recall that patent applicants owe a duty of candor to the USPTO in connection with their patent applications. A violation of this duty may render the patent entirely unenforceable.

An accused infringer may assert **patent misuse,** namely, that the patent owner has abused his or her position to exploit a patent improperly and thus should be precluded from suing for infringement. Common examples of patent misuse include price fixing, tying arrangements (generally, tying or conditioning the sale or license of a patented item to the sale of another item, unless it is a nonstaple item, meaning an item that has no significant commercial use except in connection with the patented invention or process), and other antitrust violations. Other examples of pat-

ent misuse that will preclude a patentee from suing for infringement are threatening or initiating patent infringement suits without probable cause or attempting to extend a patent beyond its term by requiring a licensee to pay license fees even after expiration of a patent.

A person accused of infringement may assert that unauthorized making or using of a patented invention was solely for research or experimental purposes. Making or using the patented invention for commercial purposes will defeat this defense.

As will be discussed further in chapter 21, under the AIPA, in actions involving business methods patents, an accused infringer may assert a defense called the **first inventor defense,** that he or she had, in good faith, actually reduced the subject matter of the patent to practice at least one year before the effective filing date of the patent and commercially used the subject matter before the effective filing date.

Although there is no statute of limitations in the Patent Act requiring that suits for infringement be instituted within any set time period, 35 U.S.C. § 286 provides that no monetary recovery may be had for any infringement committed more than six years prior to the filing of a claim of infringement. Although action may be initiated for infringement after six years (perhaps to enjoin further acts of infringement), monetary damages cannot be awarded for infringing acts committed more than six years before litigation is begun.

Even if the patentee initiates suit within six years after infringement, an action may still be barred by the doctrines of laches or estoppel. Laches is an unreasonable delay in bringing suit that causes prejudice to the defendant. A laches defense might be successfully asserted if a patentee knew of infringement and his delay in acting allowed the infringer to build up her business, market her accused device, and expend time and money expanding her business.

An estoppel defense might be successfully asserted if a patentee knew of infringement and yet led the infringer to believe he would not enforce the patent. Mere silence will not amount to estoppel. In the typical case, a patentee who informs an infringer that he or she objects to the infringer's activities and then fails to take action, leading the infringer to believe the patentee has decided not to enforce his or her patent rights, may be estopped or precluded from asserting infringement.

Some specific acts do not constitute infringement. For example, 35 U.S.C. § 271(e) allows persons to make, use, offer to sell, and sell certain patented inventions relating to genetic manipulation techniques for the purpose of submitting information to federal regulatory agencies such as the FDA. Thus, using certain patented inventions to perform experiments in order to obtain FDA approval of certain drugs is permissible. This exception allows individuals and companies to position themselves to enter the market as soon as a patent expires for a product. For example, the maker of a drug can engage in acts that would ordinarily be infringement in order to obtain regulatory approval of the drug so the maker can compete with the patented product as soon as the term of the patent expires. Similarly, use of another's patented biotechnical invention is not an infringement if the use is strictly for research purposes. Likewise, medical practitioners may perform certain medical activities (such as the performance of medical or surgical procedures), and these do not constitute infringement as long as the performance has no commercial application.

REMEDIES FOR INFRINGEMENT

A plaintiff who is successful in a suit for patent infringement may obtain injunctive relief, monetary damages, interest, costs of litigation, and, possibly, triple damages and attorneys' fees.

- **Injunctive relief.** In many instances, a patentee is as interested in ensuring that infringing activities cease as in recovering damages. A court may grant a preliminary injunction pending the final judgment in the case upon a showing that the patentee is reasonably likely to prevail in the action and that irreparable harm would result to the patentee unless an injunction were granted. For years, once courts determined that patent infringement had occurred, injunctions were ordered nearly automatically. In a groundbreaking recent case, *eBay Inc. v. MercExchange, L.L.C.*, 126 S. Ct. 1837 (2006), the U.S. Supreme Court noted that the Patent Act expressly provides that injunctions *may* issue in appropriate cases and that injunctions should not automatically follow a determination of infringement. To obtain a permanent injunction, patent holders must satisfy the traditional test discussed earlier. This ruling is being heralded as a significant blow to patent trolls who have been able to extort settlements from others by using the threat of injunctive relief.

- **Compensatory damages.** The Patent Act provides that upon finding infringement, a court shall award a claimant damages adequate to compensate for infringement, but in no event less than a reasonable royalty for the use made of the invention by the infringer, together with an award of interest and costs. 35 U.S.C. § 284. If a patentee can prove actual damages, such as lost profits, those damages will be awarded. If such damages are highly speculative or cannot be proven because the infringer has only made rather than sold the invention, courts will then use the reasonable royalty rate as the measure of damages. Amounts paid as royalties by authorized licensees using the invention or other comparable inventions will be used to determine the rate to be paid by the infringer. Under 35 U.S.C. § 287, if a patented product is not marked with a notice of patent, no damages may be recovered by the patentee in an infringement action, unless there is proof that the infringer was notified of the infringement and continued to infringe thereafter, in which case damages are recoverable only for infringement occurring after notice. Filing an action for infringement constitutes notice. The patentee should always mark the invention with a notice of patent so he or she may recover damages from the time the patent is first infringed. To compensate a patentee fully, prejudgment interest is usually awarded, meaning interest from the date of actual infringement rather than from the date judgment is entered by the court. Costs of litigation are awarded to a successful patentee. However, if the patent includes an invalid claim together with a valid claim, no costs may be recovered unless a disclaimer of the invalid claim is entered with the USPTO before suit for infringement is commenced. Two fairly new types of damages are often sought: damages for price erosion (damages incurred by a patentee forced to lower its prices to meet competition by the infringer) and collateral sales damages (damages on sales of items that are used with the patented item, for example, recovering damages for sales of patented remote controls when a patented television has been infringed). Because these damages are based on the entire market value of the product, they are sometimes awarded under a rule called the "entire market value rule." Proposals for patent reform would limit damages to the value of the infringed technology itself.

- **Punitive damages.** Under 35 U.S.C. § 284, courts are authorized to increase compensatory damages up to three times the amount assessed. An award of such **punitive damages** (those meant to punish

the defendant rather than compensate the plaintiff) is made only upon a showing of willful infringement or bad faith by the defendant. Persons have affirmative duties to use due care in avoiding infringement of another's rights. This duty can be satisfied by an alleged infringer by obtaining advice of counsel that a patent is invalid or that defenses exist to a claim of patent infringement. Thus, good faith reliance on counsel may be used to defend against a claim of willful infringement or bad faith. Bad faith infringement might occur when an infringer duplicates a patented invention or obtains a sham opinion of counsel only for the purpose of using it as a shield against a later charge of willful infringement. Such conduct might justify the imposition of punitive damages. Thus, obtaining an infringement opinion (see chapter 18) is critical because it may protect an infringer from punitive damages by showing an exercise of due care to avoid infringement.

- **Attorneys' fees.** A court may award reasonable attorneys' fees to the prevailing party "in exceptional cases." 35 U.S.C. § 285. If the patentee is the prevailing party, attorneys' fees might be awarded when the infringer's conduct is willful or in bad faith. If the accused infringer is the prevailing party, he or she may be able to recover attorneys' fees if the patentee instituted or continued the litigation in bad faith or was guilty of inequitable conduct, either in procuring the patent or in the course of litigation. Attorneys' fees awarded in some cases have reached $1 million.

- **Design patents.** In addition to the usual remedies available for infringement, one whose design patent has been infringed is entitled to recover all of the total profit of the infringer (but not less than $250). h35 U.S.C. § 289.

RESOLVING AN INFRINGEMENT DISPUTE

Lawsuits for patent infringement are among the most expensive and time-consuming of all litigation cases. Not only must the acts of the defendant be evaluated, but the entire file wrapper and prosecution history of the patent are open for examination. Moreover, because the subject matter of most patents is highly technical, experts and professionals must be retained for claim interpretation. If infringement is found, damages can run into the millions of dollars. For example, one case relating to a Hughes Aircraft Company patent for satellites produced 16 separate decisions, took more than 25 years to resolve, and resulted in an award of more than $100 million. Thus, many parties try to resolve patent disputes between themselves either before or during the pendency of litigation.

Typically, a party who believes its patent is being infringed will send a "cease and desist" letter to the accused infringer, notifying the infringer of its rights to the patent and demanding that any further infringing activities cease. (The sample cease and desist letter shown in chapter 6, Exhibit 6–4, may be easily modified for purposes of patent infringement.)

There is some risk to the patent holder in sending a cease and desist letter. In some instances, upon receiving the cease and desist letter, the recipient may immediately file a declaratory judgment action in the district court in the locality in which he or she is located. A declaratory judgment action is initiated when parties have a controversy over some matter and ask the court to declare their rights and obligations. If the declaratory judgment action is initiated, the patent owner will now be forced to assert his or her patent claims in a venue he or she would not have selected and which may be inconvenient for him or her.

A cease and desist letter should be carefully crafted to avoid triggering a declaratory judgment action. Such a carefully worded letter will not affirmatively allege that infringement is occurring but rather simply identify the patent and invite the recipient to discuss the matter or perhaps enter into licensing negotiations with the patent owner. Courts have held that if a cease and desist letter causes the recipient to have a "reasonable apprehension" that it will be sued for infringement, the recipient will have a legitimate right to file an action for a declaratory judgment. Additionally, there is a risk that the party receiving the letter may contest the validity of the patent and prevail.

Thus, in many instances, the tone of a cease and desist letter is highly civilized, and the letter may contain no overt or subtle threats of litigation, leading an unsophisticated recipient to believe that there is no urgency in responding to the letter. The worst thing a recipient of any cease and desist letter can do is ignore it because continuing infringement after actual notice of a patent owner's rights may give rise to a finding of willful infringement and resulting punitive damages.

Even if the cease and desist letter does not achieve the goal of convincing the infringer to cease his or her activities, it provides actual notice of the patent so that if the patented invention is not marked with a patent notice, the patent owner may recover damages for infringement after the date of letter notice. Moreover, the cease and desist letter generally triggers the accused infringer's duty of due care to avoid patent infringement so that failure to obtain advice of competent counsel in the face of an allegation of infringement might result in the imposition of punitive or increased damages against the infringer if infringement is found.

However, in a groundbreaking recent case, the Federal Circuit held that a party's refusal to disclose its attorney's advice (on the ground that such would violate the attorney-client privilege) or failure to obtain advice of counsel could no longer create a negative inference or presumption that the advice would have been unfavorable. *Knorr-Bremse Systeme Fuer Nutzfahrzeuge*

GmbH v. Dana Corp., 383 F.3d 1337 (Fed. Cir. 2004). (See Case Illustration later in this chapter.)

The accused infringer often responds to the cease and desist letter by denying its allegations, asserting various defenses, or suggesting a compromise. The parties might agree that the accused infringer should modify the invention in some way or gradually phase the invention out of use. They may enter into a licensing arrangement whereby the accused infringer pays royalties to the patent owner to be able to make, use, or sell the patented invention. One party might acquire the other's rights by outright purchase. The parties may agree to have an arbitrator resolve the dispute rather than go to federal court. One of the parties may initiate a reexamination proceeding before the USPTO to have the patent reexamined to determine the validity of any claim in a patent on the basis of prior art. A determination by the USPTO that a claim is valid (or, conversely, that it is unpatentable) may give the parties some impetus to settle their dispute inasmuch as the determination constitutes another full review of the patent and its validity. As discussed earlier, either party involved in an actual controversy may initiate an action in federal court for declaratory relief, asking a court to review the matter and declare the parties' respective rights and obligations with respect to the patent.

Alternatively, as discussed earlier in this chapter, patent rights may be enforced by the ITC, which will conduct a Section 337 investigation, and which may exclude products that infringe U.S. patents from entering the United States.

PATENT INFRINGEMENT LITIGATION

If the parties cannot resolve their dispute, the plaintiff will likely file an action for infringement in federal district court. Federal courts have exclusive jurisdiction over patent law cases, although if the matter only peripherally relates to a patent (e.g., a case involving whether a patent

licensee has paid its license fees under the terms of a written contract), the matter may be heard in state court. Questions relating to validity of the patent and infringement must be initiated in federal court. Moreover, state regulation of intellectual property must yield to the extent it conflicts with federal patent law. *Bonito Boats, Inc. v. Thunder Craft Boats, Inc.,* 489 U.S. 141 (1989).

The action will be governed by the Federal Rules of Civil Procedure relating to federal civil actions generally. These rules set the times for responding to the complaint, matters pertaining to motions and discovery, and any other litigation-related matters. The action should be filed in the federal district court where the defendant resides or where the defendant committed the acts of alleged infringement and has an established place of business.

After the complaint for infringement is filed, the defendant will respond by filing an answer, usually denying that infringement has occurred and asserting various defenses. If the defendant has a cause of action to assert against the plaintiff relating to the patent, it must be asserted by way of a counterclaim in the litigation so that all disputes between the parties relating to the patent can be resolved at the same time. Claims that another induced patent infringement or committed acts of contributory infringement may also be asserted.

Within one month after the filing of an action for patent infringement, the clerk of the court must provide notice of the suit to the USPTO, identifying the parties, name of the inventor, and the patent number of the patent at issue. Similarly, within one month after judgment is entered in the case, the clerk must provide notice thereof to the USPTO, so that records relating to the patent are complete.

After the complaint, answer, and counterclaim have been filed, various motions may be made. Discovery will commence. The plaintiff and defendant will take depositions to obtain testimony from those who may have information about the case. For example, the plaintiff may depose individuals in the defendant's company to determine whether they were instructed to copy the patented invention. Interrogatories may be served on either party to obtain information, such as to inquire about experts either side intends to call, how damages such as lost profits were calculated, or to determine the existence of pertinent documents, including e-mails and electronic documents.

Ultimately, if the matter cannot be resolved by private agreement, it will proceed to trial. The patent owner must prove infringement by a preponderance of the evidence. Either party may request a jury trial; otherwise, a judge will render the decision. Although juries determine whether infringement has occurred, the issue of claims construction is determined by the trial judge, not the jury. *Markman v. Westview Instruments, Inc.,* 517 U.S. 370 (1996). The need for uniformity in patent law requires that courts, not juries, interpret patent claims, including terms of art used within those claims. The testimony of witnesses may be received when needed, but per *Markman,* judges, not juries, are "better suited" to find the acquired meaning of patent terms. *Id.* at 388. The parties will file their briefs, often called Markman briefs, and the court will hold a Markman hearing outside the presence of the jury to determine the scope of the patent's claims.

The losing party in a patent infringement case may appeal the decision to the Court of Appeals for the Federal Circuit, established in 1982 in the District of Columbia to bring about consistency in patent cases, which hears all appeals from infringement cases brought in any of the federal district courts. Thereafter, the matter may be appealed to the U.S. Supreme Court if the Court, in its discretion, grants certiorari and decides to take the case.

If the U.S. government has allegedly infringed a patent, action is brought in the U.S. Court of Federal Claims in Washington, DC.

ETHICS EDGE: Unauthorized Practice of Law

Paralegals may engage in a broad array of legal tasks and are used more in connection with litigation-related tasks than probably any other task. Following are some permissible and prohibited activities.

Permissible Activities

- Paralegals may communicate with clients (both orally and in writing) so long as clients understand the paralegal's role and position.
- Paralegals may draft pleadings and other litigation-related documents.
- Paralegals may meet with clients.
- Paralegals may assist at trial.

Prohibited Activities

- Paralegals may not give legal advice, set fees, or agree to represent a client.
- Paralegals may not sign certain legal documents (e.g., pleadings such as complaints or answers).
- Paralegals may not negotiate settlements (although they may relay offers and responses to parties and may draft settlement agreements).

Although the patentee is entitled to obtain compensation for use by or for the government, an injunction cannot be ordered against the government to compel it to cease making, using, or selling the invention. If a patent is infringed by a state, a patentee may obtain the same remedies (including injunctive relief) as may be obtained against other infringers.

As technology progresses and the value of certain communication, health-related, and entertainment inventions increases, patent litigation is becoming an increasingly common and high-stakes occupation. Patent infringement cases increased by more than 110 percent between 1991 and 2000. Damage awards may run into the millions. For example, in 1997, a court awarded Procter & Gamble Company $178.4 million in lost profits and royalties arising out of the sale of diapers that infringed Procter & Gamble's patent. Legal fees for both companies exceeded $10 million.

In what is believed to be the largest patent verdict in U.S. history, in 2007, Microsoft was ordered to pay Alcatel-Lucent $1.52 billion for infringing digital music patents. Some of the damages assessed related to overseas sales of Microsoft's Windows product. At the time of the writing of this text, Microsoft planned to appeal the verdict. Microsoft's appeal will undoubtedly rely on the recent U.S. Supreme Court case involving it (although unrelated to the Alcatel-Lucent dispute), which held that Microsoft was not liable for patent infringement that occurred when copies of Windows were made and installed on computers abroad. See discussion of *Microsoft v. AT&T* earlier in this chapter.

In a rather distressing recent development, companies and individuals often purchase patents (frequently from bankrupt firms) and then sue or threaten to sue other companies claiming that one of the newly purchased patents has been infringed. Called **patent trolls,** these companies or individuals often do not practice or commercialize the patents themselves, and their sole business is pursuing potential infringers to obtain money through making claims of infringe-

ment. Many experts believe that patent trolls are one of the biggest IP challenges corporations currently face. By threatening to obtain an injunction (which would halt or shut down a legitimate business), the trolls have been able to effectively "shake down" many companies. For example, Intel recently faced a troll who requested $8 billion and a permanent injunction after purchasing a patent for $50,000. The trolling problem has become so significant that Intel's top patent attorney has urged Congress to pass legislation to crack down on the trolls. Patent trolls are discussed further in chapter 21.

Some experts have questioned whether juries should decide complex patent infringement cases. Because many patent cases involve questions of chemistry, physics, and biotechnology, courts and attorneys are trying a variety of novel approaches to make cases more understandable to jurors. Some courts have limited the number of hours that a plaintiff or defendant may use to present a case, and in one significant case, *Litton Sys. Inc. v. Honeywell, Inc.,* Nos. CV-90–93 MRP and CV-90–4823 MRP, 1995 WL 366468 (C.D. Cal. Jan. 6, 1995), *aff'd in part and rev'd in part,* 140 F.3d 1449 (Fed. Cir. 1998), attorneys used both a 45-second cartoon and a science fair type of experiment to argue that Honeywell had not infringed Litton's patent. Honeywell was ultimately found liable for infringement in the amount of $1.2 billion, at the time the largest patent infringement verdict in the United States. The verdict was later set aside, and Honeywell agreed in 2001 to settle the case for $420 million.

Although the role of juries is limited after *Markman,* few experts expect the United States to follow the European model in which juries are not used in patent trials, and infringement is decided by a special patent court consisting of judges and scientific experts.

To protect against patent suits, which can be costly to a litigant even when no infringement is found, many companies now procure insurance either to cover the costs of defending a patent infringement suit or for the costs of prosecuting a suit to enforce a patent. Such insurance is extremely expensive, especially for companies owning several patents or patents in high-tech areas.

Parties may agree in any contract involving a patent that any dispute relating to patent validity or infringement will be arbitrated. 35 U.S.C. § 294. Alternatively, the parties to any existing patent dispute may agree in writing to settle the dispute by arbitration rather than litigation. *Id.* Arbitration is often attractive because it is usually faster and more economical than litigation. Moreover, the parties may select a neutral arbitrator with experience in the relevant technology, rather than gambling the company's existence with an inexperienced lay jury. In an effort to promote arbitration, the American Arbitration Association (AAA) created a National Patent Board Center for Dispute Resolution to administer patent disputes. The AAA has adopted Patent Arbitration Rules and serves as a forum for out-of-court resolution of patent disputes. In 2000 alone, 160 patent disputes were filed with the AAA. More information is available at AAA's Web site at http://www.adr.org.

Trivia

- Because ITC proceedings are speedy, the remedies are harsh, and the ITC commissioners are well versed in intellectual property law, Section 337 investigations doubled in 2001 over 2000.
- Microsoft is a frequent patent defendant, spending close to $100 million each year to defend an average of 35–40 patent litigation suits at any time.
- Only about 7 percent of all patent infringement cases filed actually go to trial.
- The number of patent lawsuits filed in the United States is growing more than three times as fast as the number of nonpatent lawsuits.
- The costs of the average patent infringement trial are estimated at between $1.5 million and $3.5 million.

CHAPTER SUMMARY

A patent can be infringed even if the infringer does not intend to infringe and does not know a patented invention exists. Liability for inducing infringement or contributory infringement, however, requires intent.

If parties cannot resolve a patent dispute amicably, litigation will be instituted in federal court. The claims of the patent will be construed, and the accused invention will be compared against the claims to determine if infringement has occurred. If the accused invention falls within the language used in a patent claim, literal infringement exists. Under the doctrine of equivalents, infringement can also exist if the accused invention performs substantially the same function as the patented invention in substantially the same way to reach substantially the same result. The patentee is bound by arguments made and amendments entered during the history of prosecution of the patent and cannot later argue a position inconsistent with one reflected by the USPTO file wrapper.

An accused infringer may assert that there is no infringement, that the patent is invalid, that the patent was procured by fraud, that the patentee is guilty of patent misuse, that the accused device is being used solely for research purposes, or that the patentee is barred by laches or estoppel.

Remedies in infringement actions may include injunctive relief, compensatory damages, costs, interest, and, if bad faith is shown, attorneys' fees and increased damages of up to three times compensatory damages.

CASE ILLUSTRATION—NO NEGATIVE INFERENCE MAY BE DRAWN FROM FAILURE TO OBTAIN OR DISCLOSE ADVICE OF COUNSEL

Case: *Knorr-Bremse Systeme Fuer Nutzfahrzeuge GmbH v. Dana Corp.,* 383 F.3d 1337 (Fed. Cir. 2004)

Facts: The plaintiff owned a patent for air disk brakes. Two defendants were sued for patent infringement. One defendant said it had consulted counsel, but refused to produce its counsel's opinions, claiming attorney-client privilege. The second defendant did not consult counsel but relied on the first defendant's counsel's advice.

Holding: The Court of Appeals for the Federal Circuit overturned its prior precedent and held as follows:

- No negative inference could be drawn from a defendant's refusal to disclose its attorney's opinion because it asserted the attorney-client privilege. The court reviewed the historic importance of the attorney-client privilege and stated that to allow a jury or court to draw an adverse influence that the opinions were or could have been unfavorable because a party would not disclose them would chill the attorney-client relationship, which must be one of full and frank disclosure.
- Similarly, no adverse inference should be drawn from a party's failure to obtain any legal advice regarding willful patent infringement. Failure to obtain an exculpatory opinion from counsel does not create an inference or presumption that such an opinion would have been unfavorable. However, the court reaffirmed a party's duty of due care to avoid infringement of the known patent rights of others.

CASE STUDY AND ACTIVITIES

Case Study. Vision has discovered that a competitor is making and selling a heater for outdoor use that is substantially similar to that of Vision, which heater is patented although it is not marked with a patent notice. During the patent prosecution process, Vision narrowed some of the claims in the application. The heater, however, represents significant innovation in the industry. Coincidentally, Vision has just received a letter from

CASE STUDY AND ACTIVITIES (CONT'D)

Gregson Hotels alleging that one of Vision's swimming pool covers infringes Gregson's patented swimming pool cover. Vision made and used the swimming pool cover for a few years but has not made it or used it for eight years. Vision has discovered that during the patent prosecution process, Gregson did not disclose all of the prior art regarding the swimming pool cover to the USPTO.

Activities.   Discuss the issues facing Vision arising from these facts.

ROLE OF PARALEGAL

Paralegals are typically involved in a variety of interesting and challenging tasks related to patent infringement, including the following:

- ordering and reviewing file wrappers from the USPTO to review patent claims and prepare a summary of the prosecution history (because prosecution history will bind a patentee from later taking an inconsistent position)
- reviewing client materials to ensure patented items are properly marked with notice of patent
- assisting in preparing complaints to initiate Section 337 investigations before the International Trade Commission and participating in all phases of the investigation
- ordering Customs surveys to locate importers who may be infringing clients' patents
- assisting in preparing or responding to cease and desist letters
- preparing requests for reexamination of patents, complaints for infringement, or responses or answers thereto
- docketing all relevant dates in infringement proceedings, such as dates for close of discovery, submission of written briefs, and so forth
- assisting in discovery by drafting interrogatories, reviewing documents produced, summarizing depositions, and so forth
- conducting patent searches and investigations to determine the existence of other patents and whether a patent is a pioneer patent and thus entitled to a broader scope of protection than one that represents only a modest improvement in the art
- assisting in drafting settlement agreements
- providing general assistance in infringement trials such as locating witnesses, organizing exhibits and documents, conducting research, serving as a liaison with clients, helping to prepare for Markman hearings, and preparing jury instructions

INTERNET RESOURCES

Federal laws relating to patents: http://www.law.cornell.edu
                                           http://www.findlaw.com

U.S. Patent and Trademark Office: http://www.uspto.gov (access MPEP Chapters 2200 and 1200 for information about infringement actions and appeals, respectively)

International Trade Commission: http://www.usitc.gov (for information on Section 337 investigations)

U.S. Customs and Border Protection: http://www.customs.ustreas.gov

Other information: http://www.bustpatents.com (Web site relating to patent issues and providing table listing patent lawsuit awards and patent buyouts by companies)
http://www.findlaw.com and
http://www.megalaw.com (offering general information about patents and patent litigation)

DISCUSSION QUESTIONS

1. Dan, an employee of Jackson Inc., was instructed by his employer to develop a new type of ladder. The ladder infringes that of another. Dan developed the ladder, but it has not yet been sold. Are any parties liable for infringement? Discuss.

2. Sam purchased a patented snowboard. Because the bindings wore out, Sam replaced these on several occasions. Later, Sam sold the snowboard to his roommate. Are any parties liable for infringement? Discuss, and identify the name of the principle that governs your answer.

3. David's patent contains elements A, B, C, and D. Tyler's invention contains elements A, B, and C, and element X, which is substantially equivalent to element D in David's patent. Has infringement occurred? If so, is infringement literal? Discuss, and identify the name of the principle that governs your answer.

4. During prosecution of a patent application for a new lamp (which is significantly better than other lamps), Tom, the applicant, narrowed claims 4 and 6. The patent was granted, and Tom now believes that a similar and equivalent lamp infringes claims 4, 11, and 12 of his patent. What is the effect of Tom's actions during the patent prosecution process? May Tom sue for infringement? Discuss and identify the legal principles, cases, and doctrines that govern your answer.

5. Paul is the owner of several patents, one of which he intends to license to Lon. Paul has informed Lon that Paul will not grant the license to Lon unless Lon also purchases some other items from Paul, which items are easily obtainable from many other suppliers. If Lon is accused of patent infringement by Paul, what defense might Lon assert?

6. Anna's patented moisturizer was sold without any notice of patent. Anna has written the alleged infringer, Meg, and requested that Meg cease and desist from any further infringement of the patented moisturizer. Meg has ignored the letter and continued making and selling her moisturizer. Do Anna's and Meg's actions have any effect on the remedies they may seek or that may be imposed on them? Discuss. Discuss also what risks Anna may run in sending a strongly worded, threatening cease and desist letter.

USING INTERNET RESOURCES

1. Access the Web site for the USPTO and review the Glossary. What is the definition for "patent infringement"?
2. Access the Web site of the International Trade Commission.
   a. What types of patents may be the subject of an ITC investigation?
   b. Review the Frequently Asked Questions. How may a party intervene in a Section 337 investigation? Are Section 337 investigations open to the public?
3. Access the Web site of the U.S. Customs and Border Protection. Review the seizure statistics for Intellectual Property Rights violations.
   a. Review the yearly comparisons. What was the total domestic value of intellectual property rights seizures in 2004?
   b. Review the statistics by Top Trading Partner Commodity. In fiscal year 2004, what was the top source country for intellectual property rights seizures for infringing products? What was the top commodity seized?
4. Access the Web site of the American Arbitration Association. Review the Supplementary Rules for Resolution of Patent Disputes. Describe the expertise of the individuals who are on the National Panel of Patent Arbitrators.

For additional resources, go to www.paralegal.delmar.cengage.com.

Chapter 21

New Developments and International Patent Law

CHAPTER OVERVIEW

Many of the new developments in patent law relate to the increasing number of patent applications filed for computer software and business methods, reflecting the somewhat more limited scope of protection afforded to software under copyright law. Other new developments relate to medicine, science, pharmacology, and patents for new varieties of seeds and agricultural food products.

In regard to international patent law, because patents granted in the United States have no effect outside U.S. territorial borders, inventors desiring patent protection in foreign countries must comply with the laws of the countries in which they desire patent protection. Alternatively, however, they may rely on three treaties to which the United States adheres. Under the Paris Convention, a U.S. inventor who files a pat-

ent application in any of the more than 170 Paris member nations has 12 months to file applications in any of the other member nations and yet claim the priority date of the first filing. Under the Patent Cooperation Treaty (PCT), an inventor may file one "international" application, thereby receiving the benefit of one centralized filing, searching, and examination process and receiving protection in any PCT member nation, as long as the application is ultimately prosecuted in those nations. Prosecution in the other countries may be delayed for up to 30 months, affording the inventor significant time to gather funds, consider the commercial application of the invention, and evaluate market conditions. Under the Agreement on Trade-Related Aspects of Intellectual Property Rights (TRIPs), member nations must afford patent protection to citizens of member nations on the same basis they do for their own citizens. Foreign inventors may apply for patents in the United States as long as they comply with the provisions of the Patent Act.

NEW DEVELOPMENTS IN PATENT LAW

The Patent Act has proven remarkably flexible in accommodating changes and developments in technology. Thus, advancements in technology generally have not necessitated changes in the statutes governing patent protection. This situation is somewhat different from that encountered in trademark law with the conflict over domain names creating much turmoil and in copyright law with the ramifications of publication on the Internet creating similar turmoil.

Business Method and Software Patents

Many of the cutting-edge issues in patent law relate to patents for computer software. For several years, the conventional wisdom was that unless a computer program had significant commercial value and application, patent protection was often counterproductive or ineffective in that the USPTO often took more than two years to issue a patent, roughly the same time it took for the software program to become obsolete. Thus, protection of the program under copyright law was viewed as the most effective means of protection for software.

Some experts believe that in 1995, when the First Circuit held in *Lotus Development Corp. v. Borland International Inc.*, 49 F.3d 807 (1st Cir. 1995), *aff'd*, 516 U.S. 233 (1996), that Lotus's menu command system did not constitute copyrightable expression (being an unprotectable method of operation), courts clearly signaled that copyright law provides insufficient protection for computer software. Major companies apparently felt the same way: More than one-third of the patents issued to IBM in 1998 were software-related and nearly one-fourth related to network computing. Similarly, in the wake of losing a $120 million patent infringement suit (see chapter 20), Microsoft received nearly 200 patents for software in 1997 alone. The USPTO has reported that approximately 10 percent of all patents issued are for software.

The courts and the USPTO have historically struggled with the issue of patentability for software programs. Programs that are "processes" or "machines" are patentable; programs that are purely mathematical principles or algorithms are not. Nevertheless, in what many observers believe to be a groundbreaking decision, in *State Street Bank & Trust Co. v. Signature Financial Group Inc.*, 149 F.3d 1368 (Fed. Cir. 1998), *cert. denied*, 525 U.S. 1093 (1999), the Federal Circuit held that a data processing system designed to make financial calculations (calculating daily changes in the allocation of certain assets and tracking data relevant to determining year-end income, expenses, and capital gains and losses) was patentable because the calculations produced a useful, concrete, and tangible result. In 1996, guidelines for computer-related inventions (often called "software patents") were adopted by the USPTO to aid examiners in determining the patentability of software. Under the guidelines (available at the USPTO Web site at http://www.uspto.gov), the following are patentable: a machine that is directed by a computer program; a computer-readable memory; and a computer-implemented process. Algorithms that manipulate only abstract ideas remain unpatentable. In brief, patent applications for computer-related inventions must be carefully drafted by attorneys knowledgeable in the art, the developing case law, and the new USPTO guidelines.

In sum, *State Street* is seen as a deathblow to the older view that business methods were not patentable. Under *State Street*, software, mathematical algorithms, and business methods are patentable as long as they produce a useful, tangible, and concrete result. In the wake of *State Street*, the USPTO experienced an avalanche of patent applications related to business methods.

In 1996, two years before *State Street,* only 584 applications were filed claiming business methods; in 2001, three years after *State Street,* 8,700 applications were filed claiming business methods, approximately a 14-fold increase. While applications for business methods are down somewhat from their peak in 2001, application filings in business method–related arts continue to be substantial, and the USPTO continues to increase hiring and staffing levels for workgroup 2160 (the workgroup that handles business method–related applications, most of which are filed in Class 705). Moreover, the applications are sufficiently complex that to obtain a patent for software takes an average of 44 months (compared with the average length of time of 31 months for non-software patents).

The explosion of applications for business method patents and software patents led to the granting of some broad and unusual patents. Consider the following:

- U.S. Patent No. 6,004,596 is for a sealed crustless sandwich; the upper and lower fillings are preferably comprised of peanut butter and the center filling is comprised of at least jelly. In other words, the patent is for a crustless peanut butter and jelly sandwich, namely, Smucker's UNCRUSTABLES®; the patent was ultimately rejected by the Federal Circuit Court of Appeals.
- U.S. Patent No. 6,368,227 (for a method of swinging side-to-side on a swing, "invented" by a 5-year-old child whose patent documents stated "licenses are available from the inventor upon request"; upon reexamination, the patent was rejected, likely ending numerous infringing backyard activities).
- U.S. Patent No. 5,443,036 (for a method for inducing cats to exercise, consisting of directing a beam of invisible light produced by a handheld laser apparatus onto the floor or wall in the vicinity of the

cat, then moving the laser so as to cause the bright pattern of light to move in an irregular way fascinating to cats).

In 2002, the USPTO itself recognized that too many business method patents had been wrongfully awarded in the past and advocated a more careful approach. While previously the USPTO was granting approximately 65 percent of the applications for business method patents, the rejection rate was approximately 65 percent by late 2002.

In 2000, the USPTO issued a "Business Method Patent Initiative" designed to ensure high-quality patents in this fast-emerging technology field. The USPTO hired new examiners, provided additional training to the examiners, held roundtable meetings with patent practitioners, began subjecting business method applications to expanded prior art searches, and imposed a second review, usually called the "second pair of eyes review," for those applications. Coupled with the thorough and detailed USPTO Examination Guidelines for Computer-Related Inventions (with numerous training examples), the USPTO and many experts believe the USPTO has made significant progress in meeting the criticisms directed at the early business method and software patents. The USPTO maintains a separate Web page within its site for the exclusive purpose of providing information and updates on business method patents (see http://www.uspto.gov/web/menu/pbmethod).

When patents are issued without adequate review of prior art, too many patents are issued, causing technology owners to stumble over each other's intellectual property and producing an avalanche of litigation. Each year Microsoft spends between $75 million and $100 million simply to defend the patent lawsuits brought against it. In early 2006, Research in Motion Limited paid NTP, Inc. $612.5 million to settle the parties' long-term dispute over whether Research in Motion's popular BlackBerry wireless e-mail system infringed on NTP's patents.

In addition to the drain on resources and time caused by high-stakes patent litigation, a number of companies expend additional sums to patent inventions of questionable use solely for defensive purposes. **Defensive patenting,** the practice of obtaining patents not because of a desire to exploit the invention but solely to thwart efforts by others who might claim rights in similar methods and processes, has become increasingly common. Some experts refer to this as the patent practitioners' equivalent of mutually assured destruction. Cisco Systems, Inc. has gone from obtaining a few patents annually to approximately 1,000. Cisco's general counsel has stated that a significant part of this investment is to ensure that if Cisco is involved in litigation, it will have some "countervailing tools" and patents to assert in the litigation. An additional public policy issue raised by defensive patenting is that a company that obtains a patent merely because it is concerned a competitor will obtain the patent first (and then use it to extort a settlement or a license fee), rather than for the purpose of exploiting the patented invention, will likely "lock up" the patent by not using it, which prevents others from using the underlying technology, a practice that impedes the advancement of knowledge.

There is some indication that the business method patent application frenzy has abated. Perhaps as a result of the more rigorous examination of those applications at the USPTO, after reaching their peak in 2001, patent applications for business methods in Class 705 have shown a slight decline every year thereafter, with only 6,226 applications filed in fiscal year 2005 (and 1,001 granted).

In Europe, business method patents are not favored, and business methods and software are specifically excluded from the list of patentable inventions by the European Patent Convention, the governing law for the European Patent Organization (EPO). Nevertheless, despite the ban, the EPO has granted patents for computer programs with "technical effects." Likewise, experts predict that the EPO will allow business method patents if they are "dressed up" as another type of invention and specify a technical type of apparatus used to carry out the business method.

Patent Trolls

Patent owners have long used their patents to produce revenue streams by licensing the right to use patented inventions or technology to others. The licensee might pay a flat fee to use the patented technology or might pay a royalty based on the amount of sales of the patented invention or process.

In a twist on patent licensing, a number of companies now secure patents for inventions they have no intention of using or commercializing, solely for the purpose of initiating litigation against claimed infringers. Known as **patent trolls,** these companies acquire patents (often from bankrupt companies) and then begin looking or "trolling" for potential infringers. When the patent troll is unable to secure a quick settlement or licensing agreement, it initiates patent litigation, often threatening to obtain an injunction and shut down the other company's business. Injunctions may be sought and granted even though the trolls have no market share or customers to lose. One wonders whether the inventor of the patented "method of swinging on a swing" described previously intended to enjoin infringers or compel them to seek licenses to swing on their backyard swings.

Many observers viewed NTP, the owner of the BlackBerry-related patents, as a troll. Its only asset was the e-mail patents it accused Research in Motion of violating. In addition, the USPTO found that NTP's three disputed patents should not have been granted. Yet Research in Motion settled for more than $600 million to ensure that its three million users could continue to use their BlackBerry devices.

Experts are concerned over the rise of the patent trolls, believing that inventors will not seek to develop and market new ideas and inventions if those can be so easily thwarted by the trolls. Some of the reforms suggested for dealing with patent trolls include additional USPTO staffing and resources to ensure that "bad" patents are weeded out, giving competitors the right to submit arguments against and challenge patent applications, and encouraging patent owners to band together to share strategies and prior art to "bust" the trolls' patents.

Biotechnology Patents

Medicine, science, agriculture, and pharmacology present other cutting-edge issues in patent law. Research into genes may hold the key to curing disease throughout the world. Agricultural research may hold the key to providing sufficient food for the world's ever-increasing population. The USPTO continues to see increases in patents in these fields. In one interesting case, the USPTO issued a patent on Basmati rice lines and grains. The government of India requested reexamination of the patent and submitted 50,000 pages of information to the USPTO arguing that the patent should not have been issued because it was not novel. India was concerned that the patent would damage exports from its own farmers to the United States, a type of "biopiracy" that would carry off the genetic material and biological resources of India. Most of the claims in the patent were declared invalid.

The development of strains of plants and crops that are resistant to drought and disease has also led to an increasing number of patents issued, and attendant litigation, in the field of "agbiotech." Genetically modified varieties of crops have been quickly adopted by U.S. farmers. By 2004, approximately 45 percent of U.S. corn crops were genetically modified to be resistant to insects or herbicides, or both.

In *J.E.M. Ag Supply v. Pioneer Hi-Bred International, Inc.*, 534 U.S. 124 (2001), a case involving 17 sexually reproduced corn seed patents, the Supreme Court held that utility patents may be granted for plants even though plants are also pro-

tectable under the Plant Patent Act and the Plant Protection Variety Act. The Department of Justice supported the decision, stating that providing such protection would promote incentives for research and development in the agricultural fields.

Because scientific and technological advances now permit researchers to rapidly identify large numbers of gene sequences, and some of the sequences are more than 300 pages, the prosecution of applications for these gene sequences presents unparalleled search and examination challenges for the USPTO. Thus, in 2001 the USPTO issued its Final Guidelines for Determining Utility of Gene-Related Inventions. The guidelines are applicable to all areas of technology, but they are particularly relevant in areas of emerging technologies, such as gene-related technologies.

Genes and other genomic inventions are patentable so long as they meet the requisite statutory criteria of utility, novelty, and nonobviousness and fully disclose the use to which the gene can be put. Isolated and purified DNA is patentable because this form differs from the naturally occurring compound.

The intersection of the Patent Act's requirements that an invention be "useful" with patents in the biotech and chemical fields has led to much discussion. If drugs are experimental, how can their utility be proven to satisfy the Patent Act? Thus, drugs aimed at the most difficult diseases, such as AIDS and cancer, often face the most difficult challenges in meeting the requirements of utility. New USPTO guidelines now provide that sufficient utility is shown when a patent application explicitly describes a use for a drug that is credible to a person ordinarily skilled in the art.

Nearly insatiable consumer demand continues to fuel activity in the biotech arena. Just a few years ago, drugs were known by name only to the physicians who prescribed them. Today, patients routinely request or demand prescriptions for PAXIL®, NEXIUM®, or VIAGRA®, all patented products, whose effects are advertised with as much vigor as any other consumer product. Pharmaceutical companies invested approximately $50 billion in 2005 to discover and develop new medicines. Without patent protection for drugs, the pharmaceutical industry could not exist. The process of drug invention is lengthy, costly, and risky. Unless protection were provided by patent, manufacturers would not expend the time and effort in developing drugs that ultimately support public health. Thus, the public is benefited by the limited monopoly a patent gives to its inventor.

Other Cutting-Edge Patent Issues

Following are some of the other cutting-edge patent issues that have arisen in the past few years.

- **Human organism patents.** Effective January 23, 2004, federal law prohibits the USPTO from issuing patents on human organisms, such as genetically engineered embryos. The USPTO submitted a statement in favor of the law, noting that the law was fully consistent with the USPTO policy on the nonpatentability of human life forms.

- **Animal-related patents.** While a patent application for a part-human part-animal chimera was rejected in 2005 by the USPTO, a number of patents have been granted for animals and for animals with some "humanized" components, such as a patent granted for a mouse with a human immune system. As newer scientific techniques allow researchers to combine human and nonhuman life forms, a deputy commissioner for patents has remarked that it would be helpful to have guidance from Congress or the courts on which inventions are "human" and which are not. Most of these animal patents are for xenografts, namely, developing cells, tissues, and organs in animals for transplantation to humans.

- **Biopiracy.** Another critical issue is the patenting of the plant products of indigenous peoples, a form of biopiracy. For example, when the South African Council for Scientific Research discovered that the hoodia cactus plant, chewed by the San peoples of southwest Africa to reduce hunger, might have uses as an appetite suppressant, it patented the plant and then licensed the patent to British pharmaceutical company Phytopharm, which then licensed it to American drug company Pfizer for $32 million. When the San discovered the arrangement they negotiated a profit-sharing agreement.

- **Compulsory licensing.** Under certain conditions, countries may require that patent owners license the use of their patents to the government or to others. In a process similar to the government's eminent domain power, used to seize real property for the public good, the government thus intervenes in the market and requires that the patent owner grant a **compulsory license** to another. The patent owner usually receives royalties to compensate him or her for the loss of patent rights and control. Compulsory licensing is usually used to serve some public policy reason. For example, some African nations have issued compulsory licenses to allow certain manufacturers to produce additional supplies of patented AIDS-related drugs and vaccines. In the United States, the Attorney General has the authority to issue a compulsory license for air pollution prevention inventions. The topic of compulsory licenses is a hotly debated one as countries struggle with pandemics, widespread diseases, and other health-related threats. For example, the only known vaccine for the avian flu is made by Roche, the giant Swiss pharmaceutical company, which owns the patent for the Tamilflu vaccine. Thus, an outbreak of the avian flu would leave members of the public unprotected if Roche could not produce sufficient quantities of the drug. Additionally, Roche could charge whatever amount it wished for the drug. A compulsory license would allow government entities to require Roche to allow others to manufacture the drug as well.

- **Third-party submissions of prior art.** A new patent project, spearheaded by New York Law School law professor Beth Noveck and backed by IBM and others, proposed an online peer review system in which experts would submit prior art to be ranked by other experts and commented upon with relevance to published patents. Experts would advise the USPTO on prior art and assist with determining patentability to reduce the number of "junk" patents issued. Established in conjunction with the USPTO, the program, called the "Community Patent Project" or the "Peer-to-Patent Group," encourages experts to review pending patent applications and to provide feedback to the USPTO on existing prior art that may not have been discovered by the applicant or examiner. As of the writing of this text, the system has not been fully implemented, but it is anticipated that IBM and others will develop an online system that could then be used by patent examiners in searching prior art. The USPTO launched a one-year pilot program in 2007. Experts have called it the first significant change to the patent examination system since the 19th century. Under the project, some companies filing patent applications will agree to have them reviewed via the Internet. Anyone who believes he knows of information relating to the application will be able to post the information online and solicit comments from others. Because this might result in a flood of information, the program includes a ranking system so that others will evaluate the quality of the posters' information (much like eBay users evaluate the credibility of buyers and sellers). Patent examiners will award "gold stars" to those who submit the most useful information. In addition to improving prior art resources available to the USPTO, the group has agreed to develop a system to alert the public when USPTO publishes certain software-related applications so that interested parties can submit related prior art in accordance with relevant rules and law, and to explore developing additional criteria for measuring the quality of software patents. Patent reform legislation pending in the 110th Congress would also allow third parties to submit relevant information about prior art.

- **Patent donations.** In recent years, a number of patent owners who have no further use for their patents have donated them to universities and other nonprofit organizations and then taken a tax deduction for the value of the donation. For example, in 1999 DuPont donated a number of patents to universities and claimed a tax deduction of $64 million, likely depriving the U.S. treasury of tax revenue. To ensure that such donations do not constitute tax abuse, the IRS carefully scrutinizes patent donations to verify that the appraisal of their value is objective and reliable. One proposal for reform recommends civil and criminal proceedings in cases in which patents that are known to have no value are transferred for the sole purpose of obtaining tax deductions. In 2004, Congress changed the rules governing donations of intellectual property so that the tax deduction allowed is no longer the fair market value of the property but the lesser of the property's fair market value or its cost basis.

- **Collaborative patent efforts.** In another collaborative effort, in 2005, a number of companies, including IBM and Sun Microsystems, Inc., formed The Patent Commons Project, intended to serve as a central repository for patents that can be used without threat of infringement by individuals and groups working on open source software. IBM itself pledged open access to 500 of its software patents. Patent owners contribute their patents to The Commons and agree not to enforce these patents against those working on open source software. The Commons thus serves as a "preserve" where patents are used to encourage innovation and collaboration.

- **Patent pools.** In some instances, companies agree to contribute their patents to a **patent pool** and then share any revenue derived when others license use of the patents, which usually relate to complementary technologies. Generally, revenue is shared based on the relative importance of a patent. This approach to using patents to raise revenue is similar to the various licensing arrangements songwriters enter into with companies such as ASCAP, whereby the songwriters and composers obtain royalties based on licenses granted to restaurants, bars, and so forth to play their copyrighted music. Patent pools improve access to patents to those who license them and provide the patent owners with revenue. However, because of the possibility that patent pooling might have an anticompetitive effect, in 1995 the Federal Trade Commission and Department of Justice issued various guidelines relating to such patent licensing arrangements.

- **Counterfeiting of patented products.** Piracy of intellectual property is a global challenge because global trade in pirated and counterfeit products threatens the U.S. economy. For example, it has been estimated that 35 percent of the software in the world is pirated. In China, the rate of software piracy is 90 percent. According to the FBI and other sources, U.S. companies lose between $200 billion and $250 billion each year due to IP piracy. The Chamber of Commerce estimates that IP theft costs 750,000 jobs each year. Many countries lack strong intellectual property laws. Products from Callaway golf clubs to Rolex watches are counterfeited. One of the most dangerous counterfeit operations is the trade in pharmaceutical drugs such as Viagra. At best, the "fake" drugs are harmless. At worst, they present a serious health hazard to consumers. The World Trade Organization estimates that 10 percent of all pharmaceuticals available are counterfeit. The U.S. Trade Representative works diligently to protect U.S. trade and has implemented a program called Strategy Targeting Organized Piracy (STOP!) to stop pirated goods at the U.S. borders and strengthen intellectual property rights around the world.

- **Appointment of intellectual property "czar."** In mid-2005, President Bush created a new position in the Commerce Department, an international intellectual property enforcement coordinator, often referred to as the "IP czar," to help combat intellectual property violations on a global basis. The total global trade in illegitimate goods throughout the world was more than $600 billion in 2004.

American Inventors Protection Act of 1999

The AIPA was signed into law in 1999 and represents the most significant changes to patent law in 20 years. Although some of the provisions of AIPA have been discussed earlier, its key sub-titles are as follows.

- **Inventors' Rights Act of 1999.** AIPA helps protect inventors against deceptive practices of certain invention promotion companies. The act requires invention promoters to disclose information about their customers' success in receiving financial gain as a result of the invention promotion services and allows injured customers to bring a civil action to recover statutory damages up to $5,000 or actual damages.

- **The First Inventor Defense Act of 1999.** Because many individuals were using business methods prior to the stampede by companies to obtain patents for business methods, the act provides a defense against charges of patent infringement for a party who had, in good faith, actually reduced the subject matter of the invention to practice at least one year before the filing date of the patent and commercially used the subject matter before the filing date. This defense is available only in actions relating to business method patents.

- **The Patent Term Guarantee Act of 1999.** This portion of AIPA extends the terms of patents to compensate for certain USPTO processing delays and delays in the prosecution of applications pending for more than three years. Diligent applicants are guaranteed a minimum 17-year patent term.

- **The Domestic Publication of Foreign Filed Patent Applications Act of 1999.** This subtitle provides for publication of patent applications 18 months after their filing unless the applicant requests otherwise upon filing and certifies that the invention has not and will not be the subject of an application filed in a foreign country.

- **The Optional Inter Partes Reexamination Procedure Act of 1999.** This subtitle establishes a reexamination alternative that expands the participation of third parties by permitting those parties to submit a written response each time the patent owner files a response to the USPTO. Those third-party requesters who choose to use the optional procedure may also appeal adverse decisions beyond the Board of Patent Appeals and Interferences to CAFC.

Proposals for Patent Reform

The increasing number of patent applications and their complexity, the numerous patents granted for seemingly obvious inventions, the rise of the patent trolls, and the flood of patent litigation have all given rise to a number of proposals for reform of the patent system and to improve patent quality, including the following, currently pending as S. 1145 and H.R. 1908 in the 110th Congress at the time of the writing of this text: adopting a first to file system (rather than our current first to invent system); allowing assignees to file applications (rather than requiring that applications be filed by the actual inventor); requiring all applications to be published 18 months after filing; allowing third parties to submit prior art bearing on an application; providing for a post-grant review to consider challenges to a patent's validity; and limiting remedies for infringement, including making it harder for patent owners to obtain treble damages. A number of experts have suggested other patent reform measures, including the following: creating a special court whose sole function is hearing patent cases; limiting the use of injunctions in patent litigation; tightening the standard for nonobviousness (to eliminate "junk" patents); halting the practice of diverting USPTO fees to other government agencies (so the USPTO could use the fees to "beef up" its examiner corps, engage in additional

ETHICS EDGE: Staying Current

The duty of competence imposed on legal professionals requires that they stay current in legal developments they would reasonably be expected to know. To keep informed of changes that affect patent law and practice, consider the following:

- Track pending legislation through THOMAS (http://thomas.loc.gov).
- Subscribe to an IP-related newsgroup (such as GigaLaw.com at http://www.gigalaw.com) that will send you daily e-mail alerts on emerging issues in the IP field.
- Routinely visit the USPTO Web site and access "News" or "Emergency Notices" for changes in USPTO practice and procedures.
- Review any magazines or journals such as *Journal of Intellectual Property* to which your office may subscribe.

training, and ensure that all patent applications are provided a thorough review); limiting the role of juries in patent cases so that technical issues are resolved by special "Masters" with expertise in patent law; and allowing experts to assist the USPTO in evaluating patent applications.

INTRODUCTION TO INTERNATIONAL PATENT PROTECTION

The rights granted by a U.S. patent extend only throughout the United States and have no effect in a foreign country. Therefore, an inventor who desires patent protection in other countries must apply for a patent in each of the other countries or in regional patent offices. Nearly every country has its own patent law, and a person who wishes to obtain a patent in a particular country must make an application for patent in that country, in accordance with its requirements. A directory of more than 50 foreign patent offices can be found at http://www.uspto.gov/web/menu/other.html.

The laws of most other countries differ in various respects from the patent law of the United States. In most foreign countries, publication of the invention before the date of the application will be an absolute bar to the right to a patent, while in the United States, the one-year grace period applies, so that if the invention was described by the inventor in a printed publication, the inventor has one year thereafter to file the patent application for the invention. Most foreign countries require that the invention be manufactured in that country within a certain period of time, usually three years, after grant of the patent or the patent will be void, while in the United States there is no requirement that the invention ever be manufactured, used, or sold. Additionally, nearly all foreign countries grant patents to the "first to file" the application. In the United States, however, a patent is usually granted to the "first to invent."

There are several **international patent** treaties to which the United States adheres, primarily the Paris Convention, the PCT, and the Agreement on TRIPs.

THE PARIS CONVENTION

The Paris Convention for the Protection of Intellectual Property of 1883 is a treaty adhered to by more than 170 nations and is administered by WIPO, discussed in chapter 8.

The Paris Convention requires that each member country guarantee to the citizens of the other member adherents the same rights in patent and trademark matters that it provides to its own citizens (the principle of "national treatment"). The treaty also provides for the right of priority in the case of patents, trademarks, and industrial designs (design patents). The right of priority means that, on the basis of a patent application filed in one of the member countries, the applicant may, within one year, apply for patent protection in any of the other member countries. These later applications will then be regarded as if they had been filed on the same day as the first application in the first country, assuming the first application adequately disclosed the invention. (See Appendix A for a table of the countries adhering to the Paris Convention.)

Recall from chapter 8 that after a trademark application is filed in the United States (or any Paris Convention member country), the applicant has six months to file an application for the same mark in any Paris Convention member country. The later-filed application captures the filing date, called the "priority date," of the earlier-filed application. The same principle is true for patents, although the time period for filing a patent application is one year (six months for a design patent). Thus, a later application will have priority over an application for the same invention that may have been filed during the 12-month period of time. For example, if an inventor files a patent application in the United States on January 1, 2008, he or she will have until January 1, 2009, to file an application for the same invention in any Paris Convention member country, which application will then be treated as if it were filed in that country on January 1, 2008. Filing either a provisional application or a standard utility patent begins the Paris Convention priority year.

Additionally, the later-filed application, because it is based on the date of the first applica-

tion, will not be invalidated by some act accomplished in the interval, such as publication or use of the invention. Similarly, the earlier priority date is the date of invention for determining whether prior art precludes granting of a patent for the invention. Finally, for purposes of determining priority of inventorship, the earlier priority date will be deemed to be the date of constructive reduction to practice of the invention.

There are, however, a few conditions that must be satisfied if an applicant is to be allowed to claim the date he or she first filed an application in a foreign country as the priority date in a later-filed U.S. application.

- The foreign country in which the application was first filed must afford similar privileges to citizens of the United States or to applications first filed in the United States.
- No patent will be granted on any application for patent for an invention that has been patented or described in the inventor's printed publication in any country more than one year before the date of the actual filing of the application in the United States or that has been in public use or on sale in the United States more than one year prior to such filing. Thus, if *A* offers an invention for sale in the United States on January 1, 2007, files an application in Spain on April 1, 2007, and then files an application in the United States on February 1, 2008, claiming the foreign priority date of April 1, 2007, the application will be barred because the invention was offered for sale in the United States more than one year prior to the filing of the application in the United States, regardless of the fact that A is entitled to the benefit of the priority date of April 1, 2007.
- The applicant must submit a certified copy of the original foreign application, specification, and drawings to the USPTO.

• The priority application must be for an invention by the same inventor(s) and for the same invention as identified in the later U.S. application.

The priority right is based on the filing of the application in the foreign country and timely filing in the United States. The prosecution status or history of the application in the foreign country is irrelevant. If the foreign country refuses to grant a patent, or the applicant abandons the application, such is irrelevant to the later U.S. application.

The Paris Convention affords patent applicants the opportunity to file a patent application in a member country and then take 12 months to determine whether foreign protection will be sought. An applicant may determine that the invention is not marketable in certain countries and thus decide not to apply for patents in those countries. In this way, the Paris Convention saves an applicant the time and expense of having to file simultaneous patent applications in several nations before it has had an opportunity to evaluate the likelihood of obtaining patent protection and exploiting the invention commercially.

THE PATENT COOPERATION TREATY

Introduction to the Patent Cooperation Treaty

While the Paris Convention allows applicants to defer decisions about filing in member countries for 12 months, it still requires that applicants file separate applications in each country in which they desire protection. For an inventor who wishes to market his or her invention on a global basis, this process is time-consuming and expensive in the extreme. The PCT, which was negotiated in 1970 and came into force in 1978, responds to these concerns by providing a centralized way of filing, searching, and examining

patent applications in several countries simultaneously. Moreover, a standardized application format is used, saving applicants substantial time and money that is ordinarily incurred in ensuring that a patent application complies with the procedural and formatting requirements imposed by each country. The PCT is adhered to by more than 135 countries (called "contracting states"), including the United States, and is administered by WIPO. In sum, the PCT allows an inventor to file one "international" application and seek protection for the invention simultaneously in several countries. (See Appendix A for a table of the countries adhering to the PCT.)

The one application filed with the PCT does not automatically mature into a patent that affords patent rights in several countries. The applicant must eventually prosecute the application in the countries elected in the **national phase.** The PCT process, however, affords a significant window of time for the applicant to keep his or her options open while a determination is made whether protection should be sought in various foreign countries. The USPTO Web site (http://www.uspto.gov) provides a great deal of information about the PCT process, including a list of PCT member countries, fee schedules and PCT fees, and tutorials relating to the PCT application process.

Phases in the PCT Application Process

There are two main "phases" for PCT applications: the "international phase," which begins with filing the application and includes an international search report and written opinion and which may consist of two parts or "chapters," mandatory Chapter I and an optional Chapter II (collectively referred to as the "international phase"); and the "national phase," which involves prosecution of the application in each country in which the applicant desires patent protection.

The PCT Application Process

Filing the Application. The "international" application may be filed with the patent office of the member country of which the applicant is a national or resident or, if the applicant desires, with the International Bureau of WIPO in Geneva, Switzerland. When filed with a national patent office, such as the USPTO, the office is said to act as a PCT **receiving office.** Typically, applicants file their PCT applications with their own national patent offices. Thus, the USPTO acts as a receiving office for most international applications filed by nationals or residents of the United States, and the application may be filed electronically using EFS-Web (which provides an instant serial number and increases the visibility of the application on Private PAIR). Effective January 1, 2004, the filing of an international application automatically constitutes the designation of *all* contracting countries to the PCT on that filing date.

Ultimately, the applicant will designate or elect those countries in which the applicant desires patent protection. For example, a citizen of the United States could file a PCT application with the USPTO and later elect Spain, Brazil, and the United Kingdom as countries in which he or she also desires patent protection. Only one filing fee is paid for filing the PCT application, which is called an "international patent application." The amount of the filing fee generally depends upon the length of the application. The application is similar in form to utility patent applications in that it contains claims and drawings of the invention.

A PCT application may claim priority, under the Paris Convention, of an earlier patent application for the invention. Thus, if an application was filed in Hungary on January 4, 2007, and an international PCT application was filed with the USPTO on June 4, 2007, which later designates Spain, Brazil, and the United Kingdom, the effective filing date for the PCT application for all of those countries will be January 4, 2007. If priority is not claimed under the Paris Convention (usually because no prior application has been filed in any foreign country), the priority date will be the date the PCT application was filed.

Many applicants file a standard patent application with their home patent office and then, near the end of the 12-month period afforded by the Paris Convention, file a PCT application with their home office (now acting as a "receiving office").

Chapter I. The filing of the international patent application triggers the first phase of the PCT process, called **Chapter I.** During Chapter I, the international application is subjected to an international search by an "international searching authority," which are experienced patent offices designated by WIPO to conduct searches. The international searching authorities designated by WIPO are the national offices of Australia, Austria, Canada, China, Finland, Japan, the Republic of Korea, the Russian Federation, Spain, Sweden, the United States, and the European Patent Office. The applicant selects the international searching authority it desires, and it may be different from the office that is serving as the receiving office. The international searching authority will conduct an extensive search of the relevant prior art. The results of the search are set forth in an "international search report" that is provided to the applicant four or five months after the international application is filed (which is also 16 months after the Paris Convention priority date). The search report typically lists and identifies documents and references that may affect patentability. Additionally, the international searching authority will provide a written opinion, which is a preliminary (and nonbinding) opinion as to whether the invention is patentable. The applicant may amend claims in the international patent application, if necessary to avoid prior art. The applicant is generally given two months to amend his or her claims. If the report discloses prior art that would bar the application, the applicant may decide to abandon the PCT application.

The PCT application and the international search report are published 18 months after the filing date or priority date. Publication serves to notify the public that an international patent application has been filed for the invention and affords an opportunity for third parties to obtain copies of the application. After April 1, 2006, publication is solely in electronic form (and is available through WIPO's Web site at http://www .wipo.int). The written opinion is not published and is not publicly available until 30 months from the priority date. The publication date should be docketed so that the inventor can ensure applications are timely filed in countries that are not members of the Paris Convention inasmuch as this publication will foreclose patent applications in those countries that bar applications for inventions that have been published (unless they afford a one-year grace period such as the United States). Until publication, the application is maintained in confidence. In a later infringement case, in most PCT countries, a patent owner may recover damages arising from the date of publication (rather than from the date the patent issues).

The Chapter I phase of the PCT process lasts for 20 months from either the filing date of the international patent application with the receiving office or the claimed priority date if the application claims priority under the Paris Convention. This 20-month period affords the inventor the opportunity to evaluate the marketability of the invention and gather funds in order to enter foreign markets.

Participation in Chapter I of the PCT process does not require participation in Chapter II.

Chapter II.   After completion of Chapter I, the applicant may now elect to prosecute the application in individual countries in which patent protection is desired (the "national phase"). Alternatively, the applicant may take the optional step of entering Chapter II and requesting or demanding an international preliminary examination. This demand is filed 22 months after the priority date and identifies or elects the countries in which protection is desired. Filing fees are required. An international preliminary examining authority (which are the same as the international searching authorities identified earlier) will issue

a preliminary report on patentability (and which states whether the claims satisfy the criteria of novelty, nonobviousness, and industrial application) and communicate it to the various national offices in which the applicant desires patent protection. Although the report is not binding on any specific nation, it is highly authoritative. If the report is favorable, it provides a strong basis on which to continue with the application in various countries. If the report is unfavorable, the applicant may modify his or her claims or decide not to proceed further.

The PCT has experienced a consistent growth rate each year, which growth has generated tremendous increases in the workload for various PCT offices. In many cases, applicants entered Chapter II and demanded an international preliminary examination merely for the purpose of buying time, namely, an additional 10 months while the examination was conducted. As a result, the PCT was modified effective April 1, 2002, to provide that the time limit for entering the national phase (and prosecuting the individual patent applications in the desired countries) will be 30 months from the date of filing of the PCT application whether the applicant enters under Chapter I (and forgoes an international preliminary examination) or under Chapter II (and demands the international preliminary examination). Thus, applicants who wish to buy time no longer need to file a demand for the international preliminary examination. This new modification has resulted in fewer demands for international preliminary examinations, which in turn reduces the workload for the various patent offices.

In brief, until this modification, under Chapter I, applicants entered the national phase 20 months after filing, and the only way to gain additional time was to request an international preliminary examination (whether it was truly desired or not). Effective April 1, 2002, an applicant may enter the national phase 30 months after filing the PCT application whether entry is under Chapter I or Chapter II. Although the United States has adopted the modified rule, not all PCT contracting states have changed their national laws to adopt this new 30-month period.

The additional time afforded by the PCT process (20 months from filing of the application plus an additional 10 months whether or not a preliminary examining report is requested) is significantly more than the 12 months afforded under the Paris Convention. This additional time is useful for allowing inventors to determine whether the invention is commercially exploitable in various countries and whether protection is needed in certain countries.

The National Phase. If, after the duration of Chapter I (and the international preliminary examining report, if elected through Chapter II), the applicant decides to go forward with the application in the countries designated in the application, the applicant commences the "national phase" of the PCT application process.

As of April 1, 2002, an applicant must enter the national phase and begin prosecuting the application in individual countries 30 months from the date of filing of the PCT application or the priority date, whether the applicant enters the national phase after Chapter I (and forgoes an international preliminary examination) or after Chapter II (and demands the international preliminary examination). The additional time afforded by the PCT process (30 months from the date of filing of the PCT application or its priority date, whether or not a preliminary examining report is requested) is significantly more time (i.e., 18 months more) than the 12 months afforded under the Paris Convention. Note, however, that an applicant may always request early entry into the national phase.

National fees must be paid to each country in which protection is desired, and often translations must be obtained of the PCT application. In many instances, the applicant will decide to forgo protection in some countries and will not pursue the patent application in those countries. Thus, the application will lapse in those countries. Each national office in which the application is pur-

sued will now conduct its own search and examination procedure, although the process is both easier and faster due to the fact that the highly credible international search report and written opinion from Chapter I and possibly an international preliminary examination report from Chapter II have already provided interpretations regarding the patentability of the invention. Each of the countries will either grant or reject the application. The term of a patent designating the United States is 20 years from the filing date of the PCT application.

See Exhibit 21–1 for PCT timeline and Exhibit 21–2 for a summary of the PCT application process.

Advantages of the PCT Application Process

The most significant advantage provided by the PCT application process is time. If an application is filed in the United States and the applicant wishes to file an application for the same invention in Japan, under the Paris Convention, the applicant has only 12 months from the U.S. filing date to file in Japan. The filing in Japan will require filing fees, translations, and the costs of prosecution as the process proceeds in Japan. On the other hand, under the PCT, the applicant can later file one application in the United States (which is deemed to designate all PCT countries) and later elect to prosecute the application solely in Japan. The applicant then has 20 months during Chapter I while a search is done, and, whether or not an examination is requested under Chapter II, a total of 30 months before he or she must decide whether to pursue the application by entering the national phase in Japan and pay the filing fee, arrange for a translation, and prosecute the application in Japan. In addition to the benefits afforded by this time, the PCT process also affords the benefits of a single application format and a centralized filing, searching, and examination system. The PCT, however, is not applicable to design patents, and therefore, the

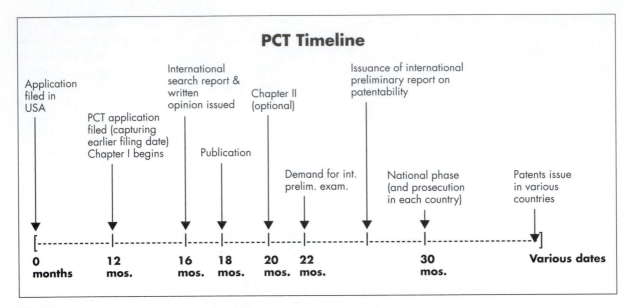

EXHIBIT 21–1
PCT Timeline

EXHIBIT 21–2
The PCT Process in a
Nutshell

1. **Filing.** An application is filed in a standardized form in a "Receiving Office." Since 2004, the application is deemed to constitute a designation of all PCT contracting states. Filing the application commences mandatory Chapter I of the PCT, which includes an international search and examination. Priority may be claimed under the Paris Convention.

2. **Examination.** The application is examined by an International Search Authority, which will issue an international search report and a written opinion.

3. **Publication.** The application and the international search report are published 18 months after the application filing date.

4. **Option A: Proceed to National Phase.** The applicant may now forgo Chapter II and proceed directly to the National Phase and begin prosecuting the application in the countries in which protection is desired. Entry into the National Phase must occur 30 months after filing of the application.

5. **Option B: Chapter II.** If the applicant desires to enter Chapter II, a "demand" is filed, an international preliminary examination will be conducted, and an international preliminary report on patentability will be provided. The applicant must enter the National Phase 30 months after filing of the application.

6. **National Phase.** The patent offices of the countries in which patent protection is desired will now examine the application and grant or deny the patent.

maximum delay afforded an applicant for a design patent to decide whether to make foreign patent applications is the six months provided for design patents under the Paris Convention.

The time afforded by the PCT allows an inventor additional opportunity to reflect on whether protection is actually desired in certain countries and to gather funds necessary to prosecute the applications during the national phase and to market and exploit the invention. Additionally, due to the highly authoritative nature of the international search report and written opinion (from Chapter I) and international preliminary examination report (from Chapter II), the PCT process provides an indication to the inventor about the likelihood whether a patent will be granted in various countries. Finally, the time and costs involved in the national phase are likely to be significantly reduced because much of the searching and examination work required has already been conducted in Chapters I and II.

The success of the PCT process is demonstrated by the fact that in 1979, only 2,625 PCT applications were filed, while in 2005, the number had grown to 135,602. The United States is the country of origin for approximately 34 percent of PCT applications, followed by Japan (18 percent), Germany (12 percent), the United Kingdom (4 percent), and France (4 percent).

THE EUROPEAN PATENT ORGANIZATION

The **European Patent Organization** (EPO) was founded in 1973 to provide a uniform patent system in Europe. A European patent can be obtained by filing a single application with the EPO headquartered in Munich (or its subbranches in The Hague or Berlin or with the national offices in the contracting nations). Once granted, the patent is valid in any of the EPO countries designated in the application and has the same force as a patent granted in any one of the contracting nations. The EPO contracting nations are Austria, Belgium, Bulgaria, Croatia, Cyprus, Czech Republic, Denmark, Estonia, Finland, France, Germany, Hellenic Republic (Greece), Hungary, Iceland, Ireland, Italy, Latvia, Liechtenstein, Lithuania, Luxembourg, Malta, Monaco, Netherlands, Norway, Poland, Portugal, Romania, Slovakia, Slovenia, Spain, Sweden, Switzerland, Turkey, and the United Kingdom. Although they are not contracting nations to the European Patent Convention, Albania, Bosnia and Herzegovina, the former Yugoslav Republic of Macedonia, and Serbia (legal successor the former state union of Serbia and Montenegro) have extension agreements with the Convention, allowing them to participate as EPO countries and to be designated in an EPO patent application.

After the application is filed, a search will be conducted, the application will be examined, and the application will be published. Within six months after publication, the applicant must decide whether to pursue the application by requesting an examination. It generally takes nearly four years to obtain a European patent. Within nine months following the date of grant of the patent, a party may oppose the grant on the basis the patent does not comply with the substantive provisions of the European Patent Convention. A binding decision will be issued by the opposition division of the EPO. The European patent is valid for 20 years from the date the application was filed. Since the filing of the first European patent application in 1978, more than four million European patents have been granted. In 2005, the EPO received more than 190,000 patent applications.

An applicant who is a national or resident of a nation that is a party to the European Patent Convention may file a PCT application with the EPO. A party from outside the European Patent Convention countries who designates a contracting state in a PCT application may opt for the effect of a European patent application. Thus, if a citizen from the United States files a PCT application and desires patent protection in Germany, the applicant may opt for the effect of a European patent application to cover all of the European contracting nations, rather than merely later electing Germany.

As discussed earlier, the EPO takes a far more conservative view in granting patents for software and for business methods than does the United States.

AGREEMENT ON TRADE-RELATED ASPECTS OF INTELLECTUAL PROPERTY RIGHTS

The World Trade Organization's Agreement on Trade-Related Aspects of Intellectual Property Rights (TRIPs) was accepted by the United States in 1994. In addition to providing enhanced protection for trademarks (by requiring all adhering nations to allow registration of service marks as well as trademarks and prescribing an international standard for determining likelihood of confusion of marks) and copyrights (by specifying that computer programs must be protected as literary works), TRIPs also strengthens international patent law.

To comply with its obligations under TRIPs, the United States was required to amend the Patent Act in several respects. The most significant change was the revision relating to the term of a patent. Until adherence to TRIPs, the U.S. utility patent term was 17 years from the date the patent was issued. Because the term of the patent did not start until issuance, applicants in some instances delayed prosecution of their patents (sometimes called "submarine patents" because they lurked below public view) while they tested the market, gathered funds, and made plans to bring the invention to the marketplace. To harmonize U.S. law with that of most foreign nations, the term of a utility patent was changed to 20 years from the date of filing of the application, thus encouraging applicants to pursue prosecution diligently. Additionally, the publication of most patents in the United States within 18 months of filing avoids the problem of submarine patents. Another sig-

nificant change in U.S. patent law related to determining the first to invent in priority disputes. Until TRIPs, the United States ignored evidence of inventive activity abroad, thus discriminating against foreign inventors. TRIPs requires the United States to make patent rights available without discrimination in regard to the place of invention. Thus, the United States now generally considers evidence of inventive activity abroad equivalent to evidence of inventive activity in the United States in determining which party is the first to invent for purposes of priority. TRIPs is administered by the World Trade Organization, headquartered in Geneva, Switzerland.

THE PATENT LAW TREATY

Negotiations in WIPO in the latter half of the 1990s produced the Patent Law Treaty (PLT), which was adopted in June of 2000 and entered into force in April 2005. The goal of the PLT is to harmonize the formal requirements established by the individual patent offices around the world and streamline the procedures for obtaining and maintaining patents. The PLT is primarily concerned with patent formalities. The PLT eliminates overly burdensome requirements and establishes limits on the requirements that can be imposed by the various national patent offices throughout the world. It simplifies and standardizes application procedures that at present vary from nation to nation. For example, the PLT signatories have agreed to a set of standardized forms and have agreed that a failure to comply with various formalities at the time of filing of a patent application will not result in a loss of the filing date. Additionally, the signatories have agreed to offer electronic filing of applications and other communications. These simplified procedures will make it easier and less expensive for individual inventors to apply for patents. Additionally, the PLT provides that in the event of a late filing (meaning one that is beyond a priority period), restoration is possible if it is found that the failure to file was unintentional or due care was exercised. Finally, the PLT does not require that a representative be employed during all stages of prosecution; however, a legal representative must still be engaged to provide translations, often the costliest part of the patent application process.

Nearly 60 countries have signed the PLT (including the United States), which continues the trend of harmonizing patent law throughout the world so that inventors have easier access to patent protection on an international basis. (See Appendix A for a Table of Treaties, identifying the member nations of various treaties and organizations.)

FOREIGN FILING LICENSES

To ensure that national security is not impaired, a person may not file a patent application in another country for an invention made in the United States unless the Commissioner for Patents grants a license allowing the foreign filing or until six months after the filing of the U.S. application for the invention. 35 U.S.C. § 184. The six-month waiting period allows the USPTO to review applications that might affect matters of national security.

Filing an application with the USPTO is deemed to be a request to the Commissioner for a license to file an application in a foreign country. The official USPTO filing receipt will indicate to the applicant whether the license is granted or denied. If the inventor does not wish to file an application in the United States but prefers to file immediately in a foreign country, he or she may file a petition to the Commissioner for Patents requesting that a **foreign filing license** be granted.

If the foreign filing license requirements are violated, any corresponding U.S. application is invalid. Additionally, criminal penalties and fines may be imposed. The violation may be cured, however, and a retroactive foreign filing license may be granted if failure to obtain the license was through error and without deceptive intent.

It is possible that the Commissioner may refuse the applicant permission to file an application in a foreign country and may order that the invention be kept secret. A secrecy order prohibits publication or filing in another country until the order is lifted. No patent can issue on an application subject to a **secrecy order.** The applicant may, however, obtain compensation from the government for damages caused due to his or her inability to secure a patent for the invention.

APPLICATIONS FOR U.S. PATENTS BY FOREIGN APPLICANTS

The patent laws of the United States make no discrimination with respect to citizenship of the inventor. Any inventor, regardless of his or her citizenship, may apply for a patent in the United States on the same basis as a U.S. citizen. In fact, approximately 47 percent of the patent applications received by the USPTO come from abroad. Compliance with U.S. patent law is required; thus, no U.S. patent can be obtained if the invention was patented abroad on an application filed by the inventor more than 12 months before filing of the application in the United States.

If the applicant is a citizen of a Paris Convention nation and has first filed the application in a foreign country, the applicant may claim the filing date of the earlier filed application (as long as the U.S. application is filed within 12 months after the filing of the foreign application). The U.S. application will then be treated as if it were filed on the earlier filing date.

An oath or declaration must be made with respect to the U.S. application. This requirement imposed on all applicants for U.S. patents is somewhat different from that of many foreign nations in that foreign nations often require neither the signature of the inventor nor an oath of inventorship.

Trivia

- U.S. resident inventors accounted for more than 60 percent of all biotechnology patents issued since 2001.
- Approximately 10 percent of all patents issued are related to software. In 1981, 1,100 software patents were issued. In 2003, more than 19,000 were issued.
- In 2006, four U.S. companies (IBM, Hewlett-Packard, Micron Technology, and Intel) were on the USPTO's top 10 list of private sector patentees. Samsung, a South Korean company, was the number two recipient. The remaining five recipients were Japanese companies.
- In 2005, U.S. citizens filed 218,472 patent applications with the USPTO. Citizens of foreign nations filed 191,060 applications with the USPTO, with citizens of Japan filing the most applications, followed by citizens of Germany, Taiwan, the Republic of Korea, the United Kingdom, and France.
- In fiscal year 2006, the USPTO received more than 52,000 international or PCT applications, representing nearly 12 percent of all applications filed with the USPTO and representing a 13 percent increase over 2005.

CHAPTER SUMMARY

The most significant new development in patent law is likely the Federal Circuit's decision in *State Street* to largely discard the business method exception to patentability. So long as they produce a useful, concrete, and tangible result, mathematical algorithms, software, and business methods are patentable. In the wake of *State Street*, patents for Internet business methods, software patents, and e-commerce technologies have been applied for in tremendous numbers. Other new developments in patent law relate to inventions in the areas of medicine, pharmacology, and ag-biotech.

Because patents granted by the USPTO have no effect in a foreign country, inventors desiring patent protection in other countries must apply for patents in each of the countries in which protection is desired. Because applying for and prosecuting patents on a country-by-country basis is expensive and cumbersome, inventors often rely on the protection afforded by the Paris Convention, a treaty adhered to by more than 170 nations. On the basis of an application filed in one of the member countries, the applicant may, within one year, apply for protection in any or all of the other member countries, and claim as its priority date the date the application was first filed. This 12-month period of time allows inventors to gather funding and engage in marketing analysis to determine in which countries patent protection should be sought.

Another treaty, the PCT, facilitates the filing of applications for patents in member countries by providing a centralized filing procedure and standardized application format. The filing of an "international" application under the PCT affords applicants an international filing date and provides a later time period (up to 30 months) within which individual national applications must be filed.

Other international conventions also exist, principally the EPO (a centralized patent system affording patent protection in as many of the member countries as the applicant designates in a single patent application), and TRIPs, by the terms of which the United States revised the duration of utility patent protection from 17 years from date of grant to 20 years from the date of filing of a patent application. The new PLT aims to simplify and streamline the process for international patent filings.

Under U.S. law, it is necessary to obtain a license from the Commissioner of Patents before applying for a patent in a foreign country. Filing an application in the United States is equivalent to requesting a license, and when the USPTO issues a filing receipt, it will indicate whether the request is granted or denied. The USPTO may order an invention to be kept secret if national security concerns are implicated.

CASE ILLUSTRATION—PATENTABILITY OF BUSINESS METHODS APPLIED IN USEFUL WAYS

Case: *State Street Bank & Trust Co. v. Signature Financial Group, Inc.,* 149 F.3d 1368 (Fed. Cir. 1998), *cert. denied,* 525 U.S. 1093 (1999)

Facts: The plaintiff bank brought an action against an assignee of a patent for a computerized accounting system (used to manage mutual funds) seeking a declaratory judgment that the patent was invalid because it was a pure mathematical algorithm. The district court granted summary judgment for the bank and the defendant assignee appealed, arguing that the patent was valid.

Holding: Reversed and remanded. Mathematical algorithms are unpatentable if they are mere abstract ideas constituting disembodied concepts or truths that are not useful; to be patentable an algorithm must be applied in a useful way. "[T]he transformation of data, representing discrete dollar amounts, by a machine through a series of mathematical calculations into a final share price, constitutes a practical application of a mathematical algorithm, formula, or calculation, because it produces 'a useful, concrete and tangible result'—a final share price . . . ." *Id.* at 1373. Business methods are subject to the same legal requirements for patentability as are applied to any other process or method; there is no per se rule that business methods are not patentable.

CASE STUDY AND ACTIVITIES

Case Study.   Vision is considering opening new resort hotels in various countries in Europe and Asia. The hotels would use Vision's newly developed hydrotherapy spa, for which Vision filed a patent application three months ago. Vision is in the process of conducting marketing surveys to determine in which countries the hotels would be most successful. The hotels will also use Vision's newly invented ornamental design for a fiberglass swimming pool that will be used at some hotels and for which Vision filed a design patent application four months ago. Finally, Vision has also recently invented a computer-based hotel reservation system, a method that makes it easier for guests to make hotel reservations.

CASE STUDY AND ACTIVITIES (CONT'D)

Activities.   What type of strategy should Vision consider to ensure that it has patent protection for its new inventions in the various countries in which it may operate its hotels?

ROLE OF PARALEGAL

Paralegals may be involved in a variety of activities relating to international protection of patents. Some of the more common tasks include the following:

- docketing filing dates and notifying clients that they have 12 months from the filing date of a patent application in the United States to file applications in Paris Convention nations and claim the earlier filing date as a priority date
- docketing filing dates and ensuring clients are notified that foreign applications cannot be filed without receipt of a foreign filing license
- preparing PCT applications and surveying clients for designations of countries to be elected in the national phase of PCT applications
- docketing critical dates involved in PCT applications to ensure rights to pursue patents in foreign countries are preserved
- reviewing PCT search reports and written opinions and assisting in reporting results to clients
- docketing critical dates to ensure the option to pursue a Chapter II international preliminary examination is preserved, if desired by clients
- reviewing PCT examination reports and assisting in reporting results of the reports to clients
- assisting in prosecution of national phase for PCT applications in desired countries

---

INTERNET RESOURCES

Federal statutes governing patents:	http://www.law.cornell.edu
USPTO's business method Web pages:	http://www.uspto.gov/web/menu/pbmethod
THOMAS:	http://thomas.loc.gov (Congress's Web site, allowing tracking of legislation by sponsor, key word, or bill number)
Electronic Frontier Foundation:	http://www.eff.org (information on cutting-edge patent and IP issues)
GigaLaw.com:	http://www.gigalaw.com (Web site providing legal information on Internet and technology-related issues and allowing users to subscribe to free, daily updates on breaking IP and patent news)

Information about, and text of, treaties:	http://www.wipo.int (information about and text of the Paris Convention, PCT, and PLT) http://www.wto.org (information about and text of TRIPs) http://www.european-patent-office.org (information about and text of the European Patent Convention and European Patent Organization)
USPTO information about PCT:	http://www.uspto.gov (See PCT home page and Chapter 1800 of MPEP)
Lists of patent attorneys and patent offices around the world:	http://www.piperpat.com http://www.uspto.gov/web/menu/other.html

DISCUSSION QUESTIONS

1. Phil has invented a computer software program that provides a method for "matchmaking." Is this patentable in the United States and in Europe? Discuss.

2. Samantha has discovered a new strain of wheat, which she has reproduced from seed. Samantha has also discovered a new type of asexually reproduced rose, with a distinctive color and fragrance. How may these two new inventions be protected under patent law?

3. Francine has invented a new barbeque grill. She applied for her patent in the United States on May 14. She would like to file an application in Spain for the same invention. What is the advantage to Francine in filing the application in Spain by May 14 of next year? What treaty or convention governs your answer?

4. Assume that Francine desires protection for her barbeque grill in several countries. What is the most efficient way for Francine to seek protection in multiple countries?

5. Why might a PCT applicant enter Chapter II and request an international preliminary examination even though an international search report and written opinion were provided in Chapter I?

6. Jack, a citizen of the United States, filed a patent application in Japan on July 10 and two months later filed a patent application for the same invention in the United States. What statute has Jack violated, and what penalties might be imposed against Jack?

7. Kate, an inventor, was ordered by the Commissioner for Patents to keep her invention secret. Does Kate have any remedies? Discuss.

8. Paul filed a patent application for a design patent in the United States on February 15. When must Paul file applications in foreign countries for this invention?

9. Dan has been using a business method for determining interest calculations. Charles filed a patent application for this same business method 13 months after Dan began using the business method. Charles obtained a patent and has sued Dan for infringement. What defense should Dan assert?

USING INTERNET RESOURCES

1. Access the USPTO Web site and locate information relating to the PCT.
   a. What is the telephone number for the PCT Help Desk?
   b. What is the basic national stage fee?
2. Access the Web site for WIPO.
   a. Review the list of PCT contracting states. When did the PCT enter into force for Belgium, Guatemala, and the United States?
   b. Access the PCT Glossary. What is the definition of "international search"?
   c. Access the PCT Time Limit Calculator. Enter the date November 8, 2007, and give the earliest date for international publication for an application filed on November 8, 2007.
   d. Review the PLT. What does Article 11 cover?
3. Access the European Patent Convention and review Article 52. What does this article provide with regard to the patentability of computer programs?

PART
V

The Law of Trade Secrets and Unfair Competition

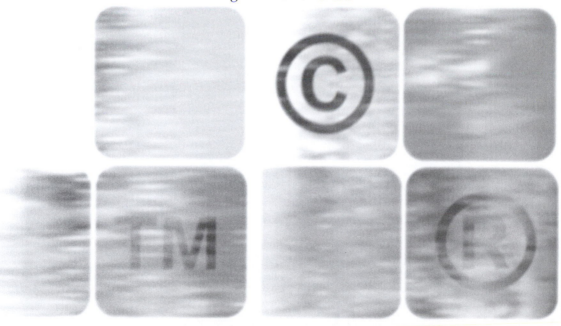

Chapter 22

Trade Secrets Law

CHAPTER OVERVIEW

Trade secrets consist of any valuable business information that, if known by a competitor, would afford the competitor some benefit or competitive advantage. To be protected, trade secrets must be protected by their owner from unauthorized discovery. If properly protected, trade secrets may last forever.

Although many companies and employers require employees to sign agreements promising to keep key information confidential, trade secrets can be protected even in the absence of written agreement if parties occupy a relationship of trust and confidence to each other, as is the case in the employer–employee relationship. Thus, employees who learn trade secrets while in the scope of their employment cannot misappropriate those secrets, even after termination of their employment.

Trade secrets are also protected from being appropriated by improper means, such as theft or espionage. Employers typically require certain employees, generally those with access to the employer's valuable information, to sign agreements promising not to disclose confidential information and not to compete with the employer after leaving the job. Covenants not to compete restrict an employee's ability to earn a living and are strictly scrutinized by courts to ensure they are reasonable in regard to time, scope, and subject matter.

A company whose trade secrets are misappropriated may seek injunctive relief to prohibit further use or disclosure of the information as well as monetary damages. Defendants typically assert that trade secret protection has been forfeited due to the owner's failure to employ reasonable efforts to protect the information.

INTRODUCTION

Definition of Trade Secret

Legend has it that the formula or recipe for COCA-COLA® is locked in a vault with no one person having access. Whether true or not, this legend illustrates a critical business reality: Information that is proprietary to a company and gives it certain advantages over competitors must be protected. Release or dissemination of the information to others may cause economic hardship to (or even total elimination of) the first owner who would then be faced by competitors trading off and using the information to compete with the owner. The type of information that must be kept confidential in order to retain its competitive advantage is generally called a "trade secret." In fact, the secret recipe listing 11 herbs and spices developed by Kentucky Fried Chicken founder Harlan Sanders "is safe and sound, locked in our vault," according to a spokeswoman for the company. The company has stated that only a few people know the recipe, and they have signed strict nondisclosure agreements.

A trade secret is any information that can be used in the operation of a business or other enterprise that is sufficiently valuable and secret to afford an actual or potential economic advantage over others. Restatement (Third) of Unfair Competition § 39 (1995). A recipe, a formula, a method of conducting business, a customer list, a price list, marketing plans, financial projections, and a list of targets for a potential acquisition can all constitute trade secrets. Even negative information can be protectable as a trade secret. For example, information that a certain operating process or technique is *not* effective or that a product is *not* profitable can qualify for protection. There is no requirement that a trade secret be unique or complex. Even something simple and nontechnical, such as a list of customers, can qualify as a trade secret as long as it affords its owner a competitive advantage and is not common knowledge. Generally, to qualify for trade secret protection, information must:

- be valuable
- not be publicly known
- be the subject of reasonable efforts to maintain its secrecy

The rapid pace of technology advances the ease with which information can now be rapidly disseminated, and the mobility of employees require businesses to devote significant effort to protecting their trade secrets. One survey showed that within 138 responding companies, the incidents of trade secret theft represented between $53 billion and $59 billion in combined losses.

If trade secrets were not legally protectable, companies would have no incentive for investing time, money, and effort in research and develop-ment that ultimately benefits the public at large. Trade secret law not only provides an incentive for companies to develop new methods and processes of doing business but also, by punishing wrongdoers, discourages improper conduct in the business environment.

The Law Governing Trade Secrets

While trademarks, copyrights, and patents are all subject to extensive federal statutory schemes for their protection, there is no federal law relating to trade secrets, and no registration is required to obtain trade secret protection. Most trade secret law arises from common law principles, namely, judge-made case law. The first reported trade secret case in the United States was decided in 1837 and involved manufacturing methods for making chocolate. *Vickery v. Welch,* 36 Mass. 523 (1837). In 1939, the Restatement of Torts adopted a definition of a trade secret, and many states relied on that in developing their body of case law, leading to greater consistency in the development of trade secrets law. Trade secrets are now discussed in the Restatement (Third) of Unfair Competition, which restates in a simple and clear fashion the law relating to trade secrets. Additionally, in 1979, the National Conference of Commissioners on Uniform State Laws drafted the Uniform Trade Secrets Act (UTSA) to promote uniformity among the states with regard to trade secrets law. The UTSA was amended in 1985. The UTSA has been adopted in more than 45 states. Although modifications to the UTSA have been made by various states, in general, most states now share similar trade secret legislation largely patterned after the UTSA. There are some differences between the Restatement and the UTSA. For the most part, however, the Restatement position and the UTSA are consistent in their treatment of trade secrets law. The following definition of *trade secret* has been adopted by the UTSA.

Trade secret means information, including a formula, pattern, compilation, program, device, method, technique, or process that:

(i) derives independent economic value, actual or potential, from not being generally known to, and not being readily ascertainable by proper means by, other persons who can obtain economic value from its disclosure or use, and

(ii) is the subject of efforts that are reasonable under the circumstances to maintain its secrecy.

In sum, the law related to trade secrets is derived from case law, state statutes modeled after the UTSA, and the various pronouncements made on trade secrets law by the Restatement.

In addition to the various state statutes and cases that provide a body of trade secrets law, additional protection is often gained through contractual arrangements. Companies routinely require employees with access to confidential information to sign agreements promising not to disclose that information to others and to refrain from using that information to compete with the employer, even after employment has terminated. Similarly, companies that enter into business relationships with each other generally require contractual confidentiality obligations to ensure neither party will use confidential information gained through their business relationship for improper purposes. Terms and breaches of those agreements (variously called "confidentiality agreements" or "nondisclosure agreements") are generally governed under standard contract law principles. (See Appendix D, Form 15, for a sample confidentiality agreement.)

Interplay of Trade Secrets Law with Copyright and Patent Law

Copyright rights often intersect with trade secrets. For example, a company may be in the process of developing a new software program. While the program is being developed, any documents or material relating to it are likely trade secrets. Employees of the company might be required to sign agreements promising not to disclose information about the software to others. If software is developed for internal use only or is intended for limited distribution, it may retain its character as a trade secret. Once the program is completed or "fixed," it is automatically protected under copyright law. If the owner wishes to apply for copyright registration, certain deposit materials must be supplied to the Copyright Office. The Copyright Office, however, expressly recognizes that the source code for a computer program might constitute a trade secret and allows the copyright owner to deposit less than all of the source code or to deposit blocked-out portions of the source code, thereby preserving the trade secret status of the program. Similarly, marketing materials for the program might constitute trade secrets while they are being developed. Once created, they are subject to copyright protection and the owner may apply for copyright registration for the written materials and advertisements. Once the marketing materials are distributed to consumers, they will lose their status as trade secrets but will remain protectable as copyrighted works.

In regard to patents, patent applications remain confidential until a patent is published 18 months after its filing date (unless the applicant certifies there will be no corresponding foreign filing for the invention). Thus, during the first part of the patent application process, an invention might well be protected by trade secrets law. Once a patent is published or issues, however, the invention is fully disclosed, and it cannot be a trade secret. Any protection for the invention arises under patent law. Information that is properly protected as a trade secret may maintain that status indefinitely. In contrast, patents are of a definite duration (20 years from the date of filing of a utility application). Thus, the formula for COCA-COLA is well protected under trade secret law, and protection can last indefinitely, while under patent law, the formula or process would be disclosed upon publication or issuance of the patent and would be protected for only 20 years from the date of filing of the patent application. In fact, Coca-Cola Co. has approximately 800 U.S. patents (primarily in technologies complementary to the beverage industry such as packaging and vending equipment); however, the product formulation for the COCA-COLA beverage is a trade secret.

Thus, trade secrets may be copyrightable or patentable. In fact, during the initial process of development of either copyright material or inventions, the material being developed or invented may well be a trade secret. Once a work is published, copyright protection continues, but trade secret protection is lost. Once a patent is published or is granted, patent protection is available, but trade secret protection is lost. An invention cannot be protected under both trade secret and patent law. Thus, companies should consider a variety of strategies to obtain the most protection for their proprietary materials. Because trade secrets (if properly protected) are eternal, a company may well wish to forego seeking copyright registration or patent protection and rely on trade secret law to protect the information indefinitely.

Like patents and copyrights, trade secrets can be transferred outright to others or may be licensed to others for use under specified conditions, generally in regard to territory and duration. Such license agreements, however, must contain adequate provisions to protect the confidential nature of the information or its trade secret status will be lost.

DETERMINATION OF TRADE SECRET STATUS

There are several factors to be considered in determining whether information qualifies as a trade secret. Courts routinely examine these factors to determine whether a company's information constitutes a trade secret. None of the factors alone are determinative; courts balance these factors and weigh them against each other in determining whether information qualifies as a protectable trade secret.

- **The extent to which the information is known outside the company.** Although information may be known to others outside the company and still qualify as a trade secret, the greater the number of people who know the information, the less likely it is to qualify as a trade secret. Secrecy need not be absolute. The owner of a trade secret may, without losing protection, disclose it to a licensee or a stranger if the disclosure is made in confidence. However, the more widely disseminated the information is, the less likely courts are to protect it. In sum, if information is publicly known or known within a specialized industry, it does not qualify for trade secret protection. Publication of information on the Internet will cause a loss of trade secret status.

- **The extent to which the information is known within the company.** Although an employer or company is permitted to disclose confidential information to those with a demonstrated "need to know" the information, if the information is widely known within the company, especially among those who have no business need to know the information, it may not qualify as a trade secret. Companies should implement policies to prevent the inadvertent disclosure of trade secret information and limit dissemination of the material to those who need it to do their work. Thus, while the information may no longer be technically a "secret," as long as those in possession of the information need to know it to be able to perform their duties, such limited disclosure will not preclude information from trade secret protection.

- **The extent of the measures taken by the company to maintain the secrecy of the information.** One claiming trade secret protection must take reasonable precautions to protect the information. Courts are unlikely to protect information a company has not bothered to protect.

A company is not obligated to undertake extreme efforts to protect information, but reasonable precautions are required. Thus, companies that require employees to sign nondisclosure agreements, keep confidential information in locked desks or rooms, restrict access to the information, and mark information with legends relating to its confidentiality are more likely to demonstrate successfully that information is a trade secret than those that fail to take such ordinary and reasonable precautions against inadvertent disclosure. Some experts predict that courts will likely require advanced security measures to protect trade secrets transmitted electronically, including encryption and protocols to ensure confidentiality of messages, authentication of the source of the message, and devices that ensure the recipient cannot deny receiving the message.

- **The extent of the value of the information to the company and its competitors.** If information has little value either to its owner or to the owner's competitors, it is less likely to qualify as a trade secret. Conversely, information that is valuable to a company, such as the recipe for its key menu product, and that would be of great value to the company's competitors is more likely to be a protectable trade secret. Nonprofit entities can also claim trade secret protection for their economically valuable information (e.g., their lists of donors).
- **The extent of the expenditure of time, effort, and money by the company in developing the information.** The greater the amount of time, effort, and money the company has expended in developing or acquiring the information, the more likely it is to be held to be a protectable trade secret.

- **The extent of the ease or difficulty with which the information could be acquired or duplicated by others.** If information is easy to acquire or duplicate, it is less likely to qualify as a trade secret. Similarly, if the information is readily ascertainable from observation or can be easily reproduced, it is less likely to be a trade secret. If it would be a straightforward matter to reverse engineer the product, it may not qualify for trade secret protection. On the other hand, if it can be reverse engineered only with significant expenditures of time, effort, and money, the product may retain its status as a trade secret.

Not all information qualifies for trade secret protection. In *Buffets, Inc. v. Klinke*, 73 F.3d 765 (9th Cir. 1996), the court held that a restaurant's recipes for barbequed chicken and macaroni and cheese were not trade secrets because they were so basic and obvious that they could be easily duplicated or discovered by others.

LIABILITY FOR MISAPPROPRIATION OF TRADE SECRETS

Misappropriation of a trade secret occurs when a person possesses, discloses, or uses a trade secret owned by another without express or implied consent and when the person:

- used improper means to gain knowledge of the trade secret
- knew or should have known that the trade secret was acquired by improper means
- knew or should have known that the trade secret was acquired under circumstances giving rise to a duty to maintain its secrecy

The term *improper means* includes bribery, theft, misrepresentation, breach or inducement of a breach of duty to maintain secrecy, or espionage through electronic or other means. Thus, misappropriation occurs either when a trade secret is lawfully acquired but then improperly used or when the trade secret is acquired by improper means.

Examples of trade secrets obtained through proper means include independent invention of the trade secret (such as would occur if a person independently created a recipe or method identical to one protected as a trade secret), discovery by reverse engineering (assuming the product being reverse engineered was lawfully obtained), public observation of the item or method, or obtaining the trade secret from published material.

Absence of Written Agreement

While a written agreement prohibiting misappropriation of trade secrets can be enforced through an action for breach of contract, a company's trade secrets can be protected against misappropriation even in the absence of any written agreement between the parties. A party owning trade secrets can bring an action in tort for misappropriation or for breach of the duty of confidentiality, which duty can arise even without an express agreement. Courts will impose a duty of confidentiality when parties stand in a special relationship with each other, such as an agent-principal relationship (which includes employer–employee relationships) or other fiduciary or good faith relationships (such as relationships among partners, or between corporations and their officers and directors, or between attorneys and clients). Courts have consistently held that employees owe a duty of loyalty, fidelity, and responsibility to their employers. Other persons found to be subject to a duty of confidentiality are customers, suppliers, trainees and students, licensees, and independent contractors. In fact, more trade secret cases are brought in tort for breach of confidentiality than in contract for breach of written agreements.

Similarly, courts can find that the parties had an implied contract arising out of their common understanding. For example, if ABC Company is attempting to make a sale to Jones and informs Jones that the ABC product is superior to that of competitors because it involves a new breakthrough in technology and explains the trade secret, courts would likely find that Jones is subject to a duty not to disclose the information. Similarly, if ABC Company explains its trade secrets to its bankers in an attempt to obtain financing, the bankers would likely be precluded from disclosing or using the information. Such implied contracts to protect the information generally arise when the parties' conduct indicates they intended the information to be kept confidential or impliedly agreed to keep it confidential.

Misappropriation by Third Parties

A number of other parties may also have liability for misappropriation of trade secrets if they knew or should have known they were the recipients of protected information. For example, assume Lee is employed by XYZ Company. In the course of his employment with XYZ Company, Lee learns valuable trade secret information. If Lee leaves his employment with XYZ Company and begins working for New Company, Lee and New Company may be prohibited from using the information. Lee may not misappropriate the information because he was in an employee–employer relationship with XYZ Company, and New Company may be prohibited from using the information if it knows or should know that the information was acquired by Lee under circumstances giving rise to a duty to maintain its secrecy or limit its use. In such cases, XYZ Company would generally prefer to sue New Company inasmuch as it is far likelier to have deep pockets, meaning it is more able to pay money damages than is an individual such as Lee.

If New Company has no reason to know the information was secret or that Lee may not reveal it, New Company would not have liability for such innocent use of the information. Similarly, if trade secret information were innocently obtained by New Company by mistake (e.g., by a misdirected package or letter), New Company would have no liability for subsequent use or disclosure of the information. A mistake or accident that is caused by a lack of reasonable precautions will always destroy trade secret status. Note, however, that if the accident occurred despite reasonable precautions, and New Company is given notice of the secrecy of the information (e.g., by a letter from XYZ Company informing New Company of the nature of the trade secret and demanding that New Company cease use) New Company may not thereafter use the information unless it has so changed its position based on the information that to preclude New Company from further use would be unjust. For example, assume that after acquiring information from Lee, New Company, mistakenly believing it may use the information, incurs great expense in building a new plant facility so it may use the information in a complex manufacturing process. In such cases, courts often attempt to fashion relief for both parties by requiring the party in New Company's position to pay a royalty or license fee to XYZ for continued use of the information. Companies in New Company's position should protect themselves by requiring employees to verify in writing that they will not use information gained in confidence from previous employers.

One who obtains trade secrets by improper means, such as espionage, theft, bribery, or placing one's own employees at a competitor's place of business, cannot use or disclose the information. For example, in one case, a court prohibited a party from using information gained by hiring a plane to make a low-altitude flight over a competitor's half-completed plant to determine its layout and features. While the plane was properly flying in public airspace, the court held that improper means, namely, means that fell below the generally accepted standards of commercial morality and reasonable conduct, subjected the actor to liability. To require the owner of the plant to erect a roof over the half-completed plant

would impose an unreasonable burden and expense on the owner, and thus the measures it took to protect its plant at ground level were reasonable and sufficient. *E.I. du Pont de Nemours & Co. v. Christopher*, 431 F.2d 1012 (5th Cir. 1970).

Finally, a recipient of trade secrets may be liable for misappropriation even if modifications or improvements are made to the original confidential information if the resulting product or information is substantially derived from the owner's original trade secret.

EMPLOYER–EMPLOYEE RELATIONSHIPS

Ownership of Trade Secrets in the Absence of Written Agreement

Use or disclosure of trade secrets by employees and former employees is a frequently litigated area. While employers should require employees who will have access to trade secrets to sign agreements promising not to disclose the information, even employees who may not be subject to written nondisclosure agreements have an implied duty not to use an employer's trade secrets learned by the employee within the scope of employment. Moreover, this duty survives termination of the employment relationship. Generally, the higher the level of expertise possessed by the employee, the more likely it is that a confidential relationship exists between the employer and employee. Thus, senior executives, engineers, and scientists are typically subject to a higher duty of trust and confidence than more junior employees, such as file room clerks. In no event, however, may an employee steal an employer's trade secret.

If confidential information is learned by or disclosed to an employee in the course and scope of employment, the employee is subject to an implied agreement to maintain the information in secret. Information or an invention discovered by the employee on his or her "own time" (e.g., on weekends or in the evenings) or before or after the employment relationship is owned by the employee. If an employee is specifically hired to develop certain information or to invent, the employer will own the resulting information or invention. In many cases, courts find that if an employee makes a discovery during employment that is related to his or her duties (even if the employee was not hired for that specific task), the employer is automatically granted a nonexclusive "shop right" in the discovery or trade secret, such that the employer can use the information, royalty-free, both during and after the employee's employment. Because the license to the employer is nonexclusive, the employee is free to market or license the information to others. Note that this shop right concept is a borrowing from patent law (see chapter 19).

Written Agreements

Employers are generally free to require employees, independent contractors, and consultants to sign express agreements relating to the confidentiality of information. These agreements are usually enforced by courts as long as they are reasonable. The agreements usually include four specific topics: (1) ownership of inventions; (2) nondisclosure provisions; (3) nonsolicitation provisions; and (4) noncompetition provisions.

These provisions may be set forth in separate "stand-alone" nondisclosure agreements or they may be included as part of a more comprehensive employment agreement. Provisions relating to the confidentiality of company information should also be placed in the company's employee handbook or manual and employees should be required to confirm in writing that they have received the manual. Departing employees should be reminded of their duties to protect the company's proprietary information.

Ownership of Inventions. Most agreements expressly state that any information, inventions, or material created by the employee in the course of employment are owned by the employer. Better agreements go one step further and state that if for some reason such a clause is not sufficient to vest ownership in the employer, by the terms of the agreement, the employee irrevocably assigns the information or invention to the employer. Some agreements go even further and include a **trailer clause,** whereby an employee assigns to the employer not only the inventions made during the period of employment but those invented for some period thereafter. Typically, reasonable trailer clauses are enforceable. Some states have statutes that restrict an employer's ability to require an assignment of inventions.

Nondisclosure Provisions. The agreement should prohibit the employee from using or disclosing the employer's trade secrets or confidential information whether during or after employment. The agreement should describe with specificity the information that is to be protected.

Nonsolicitation Provisions. Most agreements prohibit employees from soliciting or encouraging other employees from leaving the employer's business and from soliciting or attempting to "poach" clients or customers of the employer. Nonsolicitation clauses must be reasonable and should be limited in time.

Noncompetition Provisions. Most agreements include provisions prohibiting employees from competing against the employer both during and after the term of employment. Noncompetition clauses are also referred to as *restrictive covenants*, and they are enforceable in most states if they are reasonable. Because a covenant precluding an employee from exercising his or her only trade and earning a livelihood can be so detrimental to an employee, restrictive covenants are strictly construed by courts. In California, **noncompetition agreements** are automatically void as a restraint against trade because they preclude people from changing jobs and engaging in their lawful professions (unless they occur in connection with the sale of a business). In fact, in one California case, Aetna Inc. was ordered to pay a former employee $1.2 million after the employee was fired because she refused to sign Aetna's noncompete agreement that it used in all states. The jury found that Aetna knew such covenants were violations of California law but attempted to enforce the agreements anyway.

A variety of factors are taken into account in determining whether such covenants are enforceable.

- **Purpose.** Courts often consider whether the restriction is related to a legitimate business purpose of the employer. A restriction by McDonald's Corporation that its food handlers could not later work for any other restaurants would likely be unenforceable, while a restriction by United Airlines that its senior engineers could not later work for other competitor airlines would likely be enforced by a court. The restriction by McDonald's serves no legitimate public purpose and no legitimate business need of McDonald's. On the other hand, if United Airlines has carefully recruited its top personnel, trained them, and invested time and money in teaching them its techniques and processes, it would be inequitable for a competitor to reap the advantage of this investment of time and money. Thus, only employees with access to proprietary information should be required to sign noncompete agreements.
- **Reasonableness.** The restriction must be reasonable in regard to scope, duration, and geographic area. Thus, a prohibition by United Airlines that its senior engineers could not work for any other airlines in the United States in any capacity for 20 years would likely be struck down as unconscionable. A prohibition that senior engineers could not work for other competitor airlines for one year in a competitive capacity within a 100-mile radius of any United Airlines facility would be more likely to be enforced. In one case, a court held that a one-year

noncompete agreement was too long in the fast-paced and dynamic technology sector. The agreement should carefully define the type of business or competitor for whom the employee may not work.

- **Consideration.** Many states require that a covenant not to compete be supported by adequate consideration. Thus, noncompetition agreements are often entered into when the employee enters the employment relationship. In some instances, when employers award bonuses or salary increases, they use this fresh consideration as an opportunity to bargain for a noncompetition clause.

If a noncompete clause is struck down by a court (because it is too broad in regard to scope or territory or too long in duration), some courts will reform the covenant (a technique often called **blue penciling**) and enforce it in regard to a more reasonable territory or length, thus making it fit the parties' intentions rather than striking the entire covenant. Many noncompete clauses contain such built-in protection by providing that if the covenant is found to be unenforceable, a court may fashion an appropriate covenant or that if part of the covenant is struck down, the remainder will be valid. In the event of any doubt or ambiguity, the covenant not to compete will be construed against the employer and in favor of the employee.

Even those states that strictly scrutinize noncompete agreements will enforce them in certain situations, such as one bargained for in connection with the sale of a business. For example, if Long purchases Crosby's business at a substantial sum, it would be inequitable to allow Crosby to immediately reenter the market and compete against Long. Thus, a court would enforce a noncompete covenant made by Crosby.

Noncompete clauses must be carefully drafted to ensure they comply with state statutory and case law. Similarly, careful drafting is needed to ensure the employee does not find a loophole to circumvent the restriction. For example, if the covenant merely precludes employment with a competitor, the employee could establish his or her own business or could serve as a consultant to a competitor. Thus, the provisions in a noncompetition agreement or clause should be drafted to afford the employer the protection it needs.

Finally, courts generally will not enforce a restrictive covenant if the employee has left employment due to the employer's breach of the employment agreement. Otherwise, an employer could hire uniquely talented individuals, have them sign covenants not to compete, refuse to pay them, and still reap the benefits of precluding them from working for others. (See Appendix D, Form 13, for a sample nondisclosure and noncompetition agreement.)

PROTECTION FOR SUBMISSIONS

Submissions to Private Parties

In many instances individuals wish to submit an idea for an invention, process, game, or entertainment show to a company or business in the hope that the company will market and develop the idea and the individual will be compensated for the idea. For example, assume that Sanders has developed an idea for a new board game that he believes has great potential. Because Sand-

ers cannot mass-produce and mass-market the game, he decides to write a letter and submit the idea to Milton-Bradley, a well-known company in the game and entertainment field. Because ideas are not protected under copyright law, Sanders faces a dilemma: to pique Milton-Bradley's interest, he must describe the game in sufficient detail that it can fully evaluate the game; yet, by describing the game, he runs the risk that Milton-Bradley will appropriate the idea and develop it on its own, cutting him out of the picture.

Idea submission disputes frequently arise in the entertainment industry. In one case, an individual claimed that the producers of the *Cosby Show* misappropriated her idea for a television program portraying a wholesome and loving African American family. A court held there was no misappropriation inasmuch as Bill Cosby had earlier discussed the concept with a number of other people and the idea was so general as to lack the element of concreteness to be protectable. *Murray v. NBC*, 844 F.2d 988 (2d Cir. 1988). In another case, writer Art Buchwald claimed that the movie *Coming to America* with Eddie Murphy misappropriated his written submission for a similar movie, for which Paramount Pictures had agreed to pay him a royalty if a movie was made based upon his idea. Although the idea was changed slightly by the studio, the court held that the studio had misappropriated Buchwald's submission and entered judgment for Buchwald.

ETHICS EDGE: **Know the Law**

Because noncompete agreements are so strictly construed by courts, they must be drafted carefully and must be tailored to state law. Before preparing any noncompete agreement, thoroughly review any pertinent state statutes and case law. Rely on state-specific (rather than general) formbooks. Make a practice of reviewing others' noncompete agreements and considering whether language used may be appropriate for future use by clients.

The solution to such a dilemma is for the "inventor" to submit the idea pursuant to an evaluation agreement, or submission agreement, whereby the other party agrees to evaluate the idea only for the purpose of considering a future transaction between the parties and further agrees not to circumvent the submitter or to disclose the idea to others. The parties agree that if the recipient decides to develop and use the idea, the parties will negotiate further for compensation to the submitter. (See Appendix D, Form 14, for a sample evaluation agreement.)

Unsolicited manuscripts and ideas present unique problems. Many producers and companies do not accept unsolicited submissions for fear of lawsuits and often return packages unopened. In many cases involving unsolicited ideas that arrive with no contractual terms or language limiting their future use, courts allow the recipient to develop and market the idea, based on the concept that a person who discloses an idea without first seeking protection has only himself or herself to blame. Other courts find an implied contract exists, and hold that the recipient has impliedly agreed that he or she will compensate the submitter if the idea is used. Still other courts rely on a theory of unjust enrichment, holding that the recipient would be unjustly enriched if he or she could take the idea, develop it, market it, and make a profit from it, all without compensating the submitter. In those cases, courts award some reasonable compensation or royalty to the submitter. Finally, some courts consider industry practice and custom, and if submitters are routinely compensated in the industry, even for unsolicited submissions, courts may find an implied contract to compensate the submitter. In any event, the idea must be sufficiently developed or concrete that it can be protected, and it must be something novel rather than something so ordinary that anyone could have conceived of it. In sum, the only way for a submitter to be assured protection for an idea is by written agreement.

Submissions to Government Agencies

Private companies that present bids to government agencies in the hope of obtaining a government contract are often required to disclose confidential or trade secret information to the agency. Under freedom of information acts (both at the state and federal levels), the proposal might later be released to any member of the public requesting the document, thus resulting in loss of confidential information to possible competitors. To protect companies against such disclosure, many freedom of information acts contain exceptions so that parties can designate certain information as a trade secret and thus prevent its release. The protected information is usually blocked out. If a government agency discloses trade secret information, the owner may have a cause of action for an unconstitutional taking of private property and may be awarded compensation if the owner had a reasonable expectation of confidentiality.

DEFENSES TO TRADE SECRET MISAPPROPRIATION

A variety of defenses may be raised by a party accused of misappropriating another's trade secrets. The most commonly asserted defenses are as follows.

- **Lack of secrecy.** A defendant may assert that the owner of the trade secret failed to take appropriate and reasonable measures to protect the trade secret and the information has thus entered the public domain. Courts will then examine the measures taken by the trade secret owner and determine if they were reasonable under the circumstances. If the information could have been readily protected but was not, courts are likely to hold the owner has lost its rights to the information. Thus, discussions of information at conferences or in publications may result in loss of trade secret protection. Some recent cases have examined whether memorization of information is a defense, holding that reconstruction of a trade secret, such as a customer list, through memorization (as opposed to physically taking or copying the list) is not a defense and is another form of misappropriation.

- **Independent creation.** Just as independent creation is a defense to a claim of copyright infringement, independent creation of information that is a trade secret of another is permissible. As long as a party did not breach a duty of confidentiality or an agreement to hold information in confidence, and did not use improper means in acquiring the information, independent creation will be a defense to a claim of misappropriation. Reverse engineering, namely, the inspection or analysis of a product to determine the method by which it was developed, is generally a protected form of independent creation assuming the product was lawfully acquired. An assertion that the information lacks protection because it *could have been* reverse engineered is generally successful only when others have in fact reverse engineered the item or when reverse engineering could be easily accomplished.

- **Privilege.** A party may be compelled to disclose a trade secret in the course of some judicial or administrative action. Such disclosure is privileged and is nonactionable. Many written confidentiality agreements require that one called to testify about a trade secret provide notice to the owner of the trade secret so it may attempt to protect itself by seeking some judicial relief, such as exclusion of bystanders and the media from the courtroom during disclosure.

- **Unclean hands or laches.** A defendant may assert that the trade secret owner's conduct is so reprehensible that its "unclean hands" bars any recovery. Additionally, a defendant may assert that the trade secret owner has so delayed in bringing the action that the defendant has been prejudiced by such delay and thus the action should be barred. Laches (an unreasonable delay that prejudices the other party) is often asserted when a defendant has innocently acquired the trade secret and then expended a great deal of time and money in promoting or marketing the information. To require the defendant to cease use in such circumstances may be inequitable.

REMEDIES FOR MISAPPROPRIATION

A trade secret owner may request a variety of remedies from a court. Among them are the following.

- **Injunctive relief.** In many cases, a trade secret owner is more interested in ensuring the defendant cease use of the trade secret (or is precluded from commencing use) than in recovering damages. In cases in which money damages are not sufficient to protect a trade secret owner, a court may issue an injunction. Injunctions can be issued to prohibit a party from further using or disclosing the information or to ensure the party does not begin to use or disclose the information if disclosure is threatened, imminent, or inevitable. A court may issue a preliminary injunction during the pendency of the action; if the plaintiff prevails, the injunction may be made permanent. Because trade secrets can endure forever, the length of the injunction is often difficult to calculate.

A court may also issue an injunction to compel the defendant to surrender or destroy trade secret information. In fact, courts may issue injunctions to prevent **inevitable disclosure,** reasoning that even if a former employer cannot show a particular secret has been taken, it is inevitable that key employees will eventually disclose what they know to a new employer. In such cases, even in the absence of a covenant not to compete, courts have enjoined employees from working on particular projects, imposed time limits during which the new employee cannot work for another, or even prohibited employees from working for a new company in any capacity. *Pepsico, Inc. v. Redmond*, 54 F.3d 1262 (7th Cir. 1995). Not all courts acknowledge the inevitable disclosure doctrine.

- **Money damages.** A trade secret owner whose information has been misappropriated may recover money damages from the defendant. The plaintiff may recover its lost profits as well as the profits made by the defendant. Alternatively, the plaintiff may seek and recover a reasonable royalty arising from defendant's use of the trade secret. Punitive damages may also be awarded in cases in which the defendant's conduct is reckless, willful, and malicious. The UTSA provides that punitive damages not exceed more than twice the compensatory damages awarded. Damages can run into the millions. For example, in 2005, a California jury ordered Toshiba Corp. to pay $380 million in compensatory damages and $84 million in punitive damages for the theft of Lexar Media's trade secrets related to digital cameras and camera phones.
- **Attorneys' fees and costs.** In most cases, the parties bear their own attorneys' fees and costs. The UTSA, however, provides

that reasonable attorneys' fees and costs may be awarded to the prevailing party if bad faith or willfulness is shown.

TRADE SECRET LITIGATION

If a trade secret is disclosed in violation of a confidentiality agreement and the parties cannot resolve the dispute themselves, an action for breach of contract may be brought, similar to any other breach of contract action. The plaintiff may add other causes of action as well, for example, for misappropriation in violation of a state trade secret law. If no written agreement exists, the plaintiff must rely upon case law or state statutes protecting trade secrets, or both.

To protect itself against a lawsuit by another alleging trade secret violations, companies should require new employees who will have access to confidential information to acknowledge in writing that accepting employment with the new company does not violate any other agreement or violate any other obligation of confidentiality to which the employee may be subject. Additionally, employees should be required to represent that work they perform for the employer will be original work and will not infringe any other party's rights.

If grounds for federal jurisdiction exist (the parties have diverse citizenship and the claim exceeds $75,000), the action may be brought in federal court. If the action also involves copyright or patent, it must be brought in federal court. Otherwise, the action will be brought in a state court. If the action is instituted in federal court, a federal court will apply state law inasmuch as there is no federal trade secret law. The UTSA provides that an action for misappropriation must be brought within three years after misappropriation is discovered or reasonably should have been discovered.

In federal court, the action will be governed by the Federal Rules of Civil Procedure relating to federal civil actions generally. These rules set the times for responding to the complaint, matters pertaining to motions and discovery, and any other litigation-related matters. Most states have rules relating to civil procedure that are modeled substantially after the Federal Rules of Civil Procedure and likewise govern the litigation. After the complaint is filed, the defendant will respond by filing an answer, usually denying that any breach of agreement or misappropriation has occurred and asserting various defenses. If the defendant has a cause of action to assert against the plaintiff relating to the trade secret, it must be asserted by way of a counterclaim in the litigation so that all disputes between the parties relating to the information can be resolved at the same time.

After the complaint, answer, and counterclaim have been filed, various motions may be made. Discovery will commence. The plaintiff and defendant will take depositions to obtain testimony from those who may have information about the case. For example, the plaintiff may depose individuals in the defendant's company to determine whether they were instructed to use the plaintiff's information. Interrogatories may be served on either party to obtain information, such as to inquire about experts either side may intend to call, how damages such as lost profits were calculated, or to determine the existence of pertinent documents.

Ultimately, if the matter cannot be resolved by private agreement, it will proceed to trial. The trade secret owner must prove misappropriation by a preponderance of the evidence. Either party may request a jury trial; otherwise, a judge will render the decision. Appeals may follow.

One of the difficult issues in trade secret litigation arises from the fact that the trade secret sought to be protected often must be disclosed in the litigation so the judge or jury can evaluate whether the information is sufficiently valuable that it affords its owner a competitive advantage. Similarly, the owner's methods of protecting the information often must be disclosed so the fact finder can determine whether the owner has taken reasonable measures to protect the alleged trade secrets. Thus, the dilemma faced by trade secret owners in litigation is that they must disclose the very information they seek to protect. Courts can fashion a variety of means to protect the information, from issuing protective orders (prohibiting the parties and their counsel from any further disclosure), to holding private hearings in the judge's chambers, to closing the courtroom to the public, to sealing court records.

As technology progresses and the value of certain communication and entertainment inventions increases, trade secret litigation is becoming an increasingly common and high-stakes occupation. Damage awards may run into the millions. For example, the *National Law Journal* reported in September 1997 that the U.S. Court of Appeals upheld a $45.6 million judgment against Polaris Industries for the theft of a design for a fuel-injection engine for snowmobiles. The total litigation loss was $61.4 million. *Injection Research Specialists, Inc. v. Polaris Indus., L.P.*, No. 90-Z-1143 (D. Colo. 1997).

TRADE SECRET PROTECTION PROGRAMS

Because trade secrets are legally fragile and may be lost by inadvertent disclosure or failure to reasonably protect them, companies should implement trade secret protection programs to safeguard valuable information. While it is common for businesses to assume that only scientific and technical data constitute trade secrets, protection is available for a much broader range of subjects, such as customer lists, marketing plans, hiring tactics, and other information that would be valuable to a competitor, and that are common to many companies, not merely those engaged in scientific endeavors.

Because trade secret protection can last indefinitely, businesses should devote proper attention to the methods used to ensure confidentiality of information. Companies that value their trade secrets should implement trade secret protection programs. Developing programs and measures to protect trade secrets is an easy way to demonstrate to a court that an owner values its information and takes appropriate measures to maintain its secrecy. Such programs consist of several elements.

Physical Protection

There are a variety of tangible measures a company can implement to protect trade secrets, including the following:

- safeguarding information under lock and key
- protecting the information from unauthorized access
- conducting background checks of employees who will have access to key information
- forbidding removal of protected information from the company premises or certain rooms
- retaining adequate security during evenings and weekends either through alarm systems or security services
- ensuring tours of the company premises do not expose outsiders to valuable processes or information
- marking materials with legends or stamps such as "Confidential—Trade Secret Information"
- using checkout lists when valuable equipment or information is removed from its normal location
- monitoring activities of former employees who had access to confidential information and monitoring trade journals for articles that may show a competitor has gained access to company trade secrets
- ensuring no one person has access to critical information but rather that several people "share" parts of the information
- implementing inventory control systems (such as numbering each copy of valuable written materials and retaining a log showing which employee received which document)
- securing computers with password or encryption protection
- requiring use of paper shredders for disposal of sensitive documents
- designating a person to be responsible for trade secret information and release to others (including the media), and for reviewing bids, proposals, marketing materials, and plans by employees to publish articles or speak at conferences
- implementing photocopying policies and maintaining logbooks or electronic monitoring of copying
- monitoring employees' use of e-mail and the Internet to ensure confidential information is not being disseminated (as long as employees are notified beforehand that use of e-mail and the Internet must be for business purposes only and that the employer may monitor use)
- conducting exit interviews with employees to remind them of their obligations not to use or disclose proprietary company information
- including notices on facsimile coversheets and e-mail communications that the communication is intended only for the designated recipient, and if it is received in error, the party who mistakenly received it must return it to the sender
- using encryption technology and antivirus protection programs to protect information stored on computers
- making sure computers and handheld devices such as BlackBerrys are "wiped" before they are disposed of
- educating employees on trade secrets and protection of trade secrets
- requiring visitors to the premises to sign in and wear badges
- ensuring information retained on computers is available only on company networks so that access can be easily tracked

Most companies will not need to implement all of the measures described. Courts do not require absolute secrecy or that extreme measures be taken to protect information. Rather, reasonable measures will be sufficient to protect the status of information as trade secrets.

Some new high-tech devices are gaining popularity in the race to protect trade secrets, including electronic chips that track the location of sensitive documents and software that monitors content inside computer networks and also monitors employee activity. Home Depot Inc. operates a "secret" 88,000-square-foot Innovation Center, where it tests new products and marketing. The lab is in an unmarked building in a typical office park, and visitors must pass through a metal detector that scans for camera phones.

Contractual Protection

Another method of protecting trade secrets is by contract, namely, requiring those with access to the information to agree in writing not to disclose the information to others or use it to the owner's detriment. Similarly, in licensing arrangements, trade secret owners should ensure the license agreements contain sufficient protection for trade secret information. Employers should use noncompetition agreements to ensure former employees do not use material gained on the job to later compete against the employer. Even without formal contracts, a company should include protection policies in its employee handbooks, routinely publish reminders about confidentiality in company newsletters and through e-mail messages, and remind employees of their duties during their initial orientations and during exit interviews conducted when the individuals leave the company's employment.

With the advent of the Internet and the increased ease of electronic communications, employers have become concerned about the loss of trade secrets through dissemination over the Internet. It has been held that "once a trade secret is posted on the Internet, it is effectively part of the public domain, impossible to retrieve." *Religious Tech. Ctr. v. Lerma*, 908 F. Supp. 1362, 1368

(E.D. Va. 1995). Thus, employers have a legitimate interest in monitoring the electronic communications of their employees. Generally, employers have broad discretion to regulate the use of electronic communications in the workplace so long as the employees have been informed that the employer may do so. Many employers now adopt Internet use policies (see chapter 5) to inform employees that their electronic communications may be monitored and to set forth appropriate guidelines for use of the Internet and e-mail.

Intellectual Property Protection

Companies can also rely on other complementary methods of protection to safeguard trade secrets. Any material that qualifies for copyright protection should be protected by registration or, at a minimum, by ensuring a copyright notice is placed on the material or document to afford notice to others of the owner's right and interest in the material. Inventions may be subject to patent protection, and trademarks should be fully protected by applying for registration.

NEW AND INTERNATIONAL DEVELOPMENTS IN TRADE SECRETS LAW

New Developments

Perhaps the newest developments in trade secrets law have arisen out of the ease of electronic communication. Because information can be readily obtained by computer and then similarly disseminated to others with a stroke of the keyboard, companies are investing greater time and money in ensuring their communications systems are secure. While physical methods of protecting trade secrets (such as locked drawers, restricted access to information, marking information with legends, and so forth) have always been favored by courts, companies should now consider protecting their information by electronic security measures. Methods such as use of passwords, encryption and coding of documents, and restricting access to information placed on computers are now being examined by courts in attempting to determine whether an owner has taken sufficient measures to protect its proprietary information.

Another newer development in trade secrets law is the use of criminal statutes to punish wrongdoers. In 1996, Congress enacted the Economic Espionage Act of 1996 (18 U.S.C. § 1831), which provides criminal penalties for the theft or attempted theft of trade secret information that will benefit foreign governments and for the theft of trade secrets related to products produced or placed in interstate commerce. Theft of information by physical as well as electronic means is prohibited. The U.S. Attorney General can initiate a civil action to enjoin threatened theft, violators may be imprisoned, and fines can be imposed of up to $10 million for foreign espionage and $5 million for other trade secret theft. The criminalization of the theft of trade secrets was likely due to the increased incidence of economic espionage. The increasing importance of intellectual property has led to a shift from the theft of tangible physical property to theft of intellectual assets. A 2002 report for ASIS International, an organization for security professionals, concluded that of the companies that participated in its comprehensive IP survey, 40 percent reported incidents of known or suspected loss of proprietary information. The FBI estimates that as much as $200 billion is lost annually in the United States due to economic espionage.

Theft of tangible property containing trade secrets (such as documents or discs) and transporting it across state lines may be a violation of the National Stolen Property Act (18 U.S.C. § 2314). Federal mail and wire fraud statutes are also used to punish theft of trade secrets. Many states have similar statutes that are used to deter and punish misappropriation of trade secrets.

International Developments

Because trade secret information is generally lost once it is disclosed (assuming proper precautions have not been taken), companies intending to do business internationally must ensure that their trade secrets are protected in foreign countries so that inadvertent disclosure abroad does not cause worldwide loss of protection. Just as is the case in the United States, theft of trade secrets is a crime in most foreign countries. Moreover, the North American Free Trade Agreement (NAFTA), entered into by the United States, Canada, and Mexico in 1991, complements U.S. trade secrets law and requires member countries to protect trade secrets from unauthorized disclosure or use. In response to NAFTA, Mexico amended its laws to allow litigants to bring civil actions to enjoin threatened or existing trade secret violations.

In 1994, the General Agreement on Tariffs and Trade (GATT) was concluded by the major industrialized nations of the world, including the United States. GATT provides for adjudication of trade secret disputes, and under Trade-Related Aspects of Intellectual Property Rights (TRIPs), promulgated in accordance with GATT, member countries must provide effective remedies for misappropriation of trade secrets owned by residents of other member countries. Thus, all member nations of GATT have measures similar to those in the United States for protecting trade secrets, thereby ensuring that companies that wish to do business in other GATT member countries can do so with the knowledge that their valuable trade secret information will be protectable.

Note that the Economic Espionage Act of 1996 discussed earlier applies not only to conduct within the United States but also to conduct occurring outside the United States if the offender is a natural person who is a citizen or permanent resident alien of the United States or if an act in furtherance of the offense was committed in the United States.

Additionally, safeguards such as employment and nondisclosure agreements and limiting access to confidential information through both internal and physical measures may help to maintain the status of trade secrets in foreign countries.

Trivia

- Only four people know the recipe for Krispy Kreme donuts.
- Reportedly, no one is allowed to watch the process of making the creamy center in Oreo cookies.
- In May 2007 a former Coca-Cola secretary was sentenced to eight years in prison for conspiring to steal Coke's trade secrets and offering them to PepsiCo (which reported the matter to Coke).
- According to the Society for Human Resource Management, about one-half of all companies require employees to sign nondisclosure agreements.
- It is estimated that 80 to 90 percent of all inventions in the United States are made by employees.
- According to a 2005 survey by the American Management Association, about 75 percent of large U.S. companies actively monitor and review employee e-mail and Internet usage.

CHAPTER SUMMARY

A trade secret consists of any information that its owner has reasonably protected and that, if known by a competitor, would afford some commercial advantage or benefit. If properly protected, trade secrets may exist forever. Trade secrets are protectable even in the absence of written agreement if the parties enjoy a relationship of trust and confidence (as is the case in employer–employee relationships). Trade secrets are also protected from appropriation by improper means such as theft, bribery, or espionage.

Although trade secrets can be protected even without a written agreement, such an agreement is advisable. Agreements with key employees should also include noncompete clauses. While strictly scrutinized by courts as possible restraints against trade, such noncompete provisions are enforceable in most states as long as they are reasonable in time, territory, and scope.

A trade secret owner may obtain injunctive relief or monetary damages, or both, if a trade secret has been misappropriated. Criminal penalties may also be assessed against the violator. A trade secret, however, will not be protected by a court if its owner has not exercised reasonable efforts to maintain its secrecy.

Companies should implement aggressive trade secret protection programs to ensure the protectability of valuable information. Information can be protected by physical barriers (such as lock and key), contractual provisions prohibiting disclosure, and by taking advantage of protection available under copyright and patent laws.

CASE ILLUSTRATION—COVENANTS NOT TO COMPETE

Case: *Bed Mart, Inc. v. Kelley*, 45 P.3d 1219 (Ariz. Ct. App. 2002)

Facts: A salesperson signed a noncompete clause when he went to work for a mattress superstore by which he agreed that upon leaving his employment he would not work for any business for which the sale of mattresses accounted for more than 50 percent of its sales revenue. The restriction was for six months and prohibited the employee from working within 10 miles of any location in which the employer conducted business. The employee left the employer's business and went to work for a competitor. The former employer then filed a lawsuit alleging misappropriation of trade secrets and breach of contract. The trial court held that the noncompete clause was unenforceable and suggested that its length was overly long.

Holding: The noncompete provision was reasonable. A covenant not to compete is enforceable if it serves an employer's legitimate business needs and is not unreasonable as to time and space. In this case, the employee could have worked for various entities (such as department stores), and the noncompete provision was thus reasonable in its scope. Moreover, it was reasonable in its duration in light of evidence that the employer needed six months to train new employees and revised its various marketing materials and pricing schedules every six months.

CASE STUDY AND ACTIVITIES

Case Study.   Vision is developing its plans to open several hotels in Asia and Europe. It has commissioned several marketing studies and has been consulting with engineers, property developers, and contractors regarding the planned hotels. Vision's plans are known to only a few senior-level executives, all of who have signed confidentiality agreements that also include provisions prohibiting the employees from working for any direct competitor of Vision for 18 months after employment with Vision. Vision recently discovered that one of the engineers has leaked its plans to Westpark, a competitor hotel chain, which bribed the engineer to leak the plans. Additionally, Carolyn, one of Vision's senior executives is leaving Vision to go work for Westpark.

Activities.   Discuss whether and how Vision can protect the information relating to its planned expansion and whether Vision can prohibit Carolyn from going to work for Westpark.

ROLE OF PARALEGAL

Paralegals engage in numerous activities related to trade secret protection, including the following:

- conducting trade secret audits to ensure confidential information is protected
- drafting guidelines for clients to follow in implementing trade secret protection programs
- reviewing client documents to ensure materials are clearly marked with notices regarding their confidentiality
- drafting notices for clients to place in newsletters, near photocopy machines, and in prominent locations throughout offices reminding employees of the need to keep company information confidential

ROLE OF PARALEGAL (CONT'D)

- reviewing confidentiality clauses and employment agreements entered into with key employees to ensure client information will be maintained in confidence
- drafting nondisclosure and noncompete agreements
- conducting state-by-state research regarding enforceability of noncompete clauses

INTERNET RESOURCES

Uniform Trade Secrets Act:	http://www.nccusl.org (Web site of the National Conference of Commissioners on Uniform State Laws)
Trade Secrets Home Page:	http://my.execpc.com/~mhallign (Web site of attorney Mark Halligan offering excellent information about trade secrets, articles, and links to other resources)
Employment agreements:	http://www.allaboutforms.com (Web site offering sample forms for noncompete agreements, confidentiality agreements, and employee invention agreements, which can be used as models and drafting guides)

DISCUSSION QUESTIONS

1. TechCo is a high-tech company with 1,000 employees that specializes in the development of cutting-edge software. Its trade secret protection program consists of the following measures: a log by the photocopy machine, marking documents "confidential," and occasional e-mail reminders to employees to safeguard company information. Discuss whether these measures constitute "reasonable efforts" to maintain the secrecy of TechCo's information.

2. Patterson Inc. has invented a new process for transmitting digital images. Discuss the advantages and disadvantages of protecting this invention as a patent and as a trade secret.

3. Cellular Co. is negotiating with Breyer Co. to sell all of its assets to Breyer Co. Breyer Co. has inspected Cellular's plant and reviewed a significant amount of materials relating to Cellular's processes and methods. Is Breyer subject to any duties not to disclose Cellular's proprietary information? Discuss.

4. Harris Co. inadvertently sent an important document by facsimile to its adversary's law firm rather than to its own law firm. Within minutes, Harris Co. contacted the recipient and informed it of the mistake and instructed the recipient that it was not authorized to use the information. Is the information still protected? May the recipient use the information?

5. Jackson Inc. is an old, established company with a great deal of history. The company has kept many of its original, older documents, such as letters to and from its founders and

other materials that have purely "sentimental value" in a locked vault. An employee has stolen these documents. Is the employee liable for theft of trade secrets?

6. Peterson Inc., a large trucking company, requires its most senior employees to sign non-competition agreements, agreeing that if they leave employment with Peterson, they will not engage in any work related to the transportation industry for 12 months. Is such a provision enforceable? Discuss.

7. One month ago, Hal, an employee of ABC Co., inadvertently posted one of the company's critical documents on the company's Web site. Has trade secret protection for the documents been lost? Discuss.

8. Tina, a senior employee with XYZ Inc., has decided to leave the company and go to work for one of XYZ's competitors. Tina is not subject to any confidentiality agreements. Tina has been able to memorize XYZ's pricing strategies and plans to take this information to her new employer. Discuss whether Tina has misappropriated a trade secret.

9. ABC Co. has an aggressive trade secret protection program, including encrypting its documents when they are transmitted electronically. Through an unanticipated development, a company has been able to "crack" ABC's encryption technology and has intercepted many of its documents. Were ABC's efforts to protect its materials reasonable? Discuss.

USING INTERNET RESOURCES

1. Access the Web site of the Copyright Office. If an applicant for copyright registration for a computer program believes that depositing the computer program's source code would disclose its trade secrets, what deposit should it make?

2. Review the UTSA on the Web site of the National Conference of Commissioners on Uniform State Laws.
   a. Review the Legislative Fact Sheet. Which organization has endorsed the UTSA?
   b. Review the text of the Final Act relating to injunctive relief. Will an injunction be terminated when a trade secret ceases to exist?
   c. Review the text of the Final Act relating to attorneys' fees. When may attorneys' fees be awarded in trade secret litigation cases?

For additional resources, go to www.paralegal.delmar.cengage.com.

Chapter 23

Unfair Competition

CHAPTER OVERVIEW

The term *unfair competition* is a broad term covering a wide variety of deceptive practices in the marketplace. The law of unfair competition continues to evolve with changes in the marketplace so that deceptive infomercials and false advertising on the Internet can be prohibited, just as their earlier print counterparts are.

The most commonly alleged forms of unfair competition are:

- passing off (selling one's goods as those of another)
- misappropriation (the taking of another's intangible commercial property right)
- infringement of the right of publicity (appropriating another's identity or persona for commercial purposes)
- false advertising (making false or deceptive representations about the nature of one's own goods or services)
- product disparagement (making false or deceptive representations about another's goods or services)

- dilution (weakening or tarnishing the value of another's famous trademark or service mark if the use is likely to cause confusion)
- infringement of trade dress (causing confusion with the distinctive product image or overall appearance of another's product or service)

There is considerable overlap in the theories used by injured parties to protect their business property interests against deception and fraud, and the same act may give rise to several causes of action. Thus, a misleading advertisement may constitute passing off, false advertising, and product disparagement. For example, the Fifth Circuit Court of Appeals held in 1998 that a tavern's unauthorized use of the name "The Velvet Elvis" constituted trademark infringement, unfair competition, trademark dilution, and violation of the right of publicity. *Elvis Presley Ent. Inc. v. Capece*, 141 F.3d 188 (5th Cir. 1998). Moreover, section 43 of the Lanham Act (15 U.S.C. § 1125), often referred to as a "national unfair competition statute," also protects against a wide variety of false and misleading commercial practices. Finally, the Federal Trade Commission (FTC) may also take action to protect consumers from false and deceptive trade practices. Thus, injured parties often rely upon a wide variety of theories to protect their business goodwill or intellectual property from unfair tactics in the commercial arena.

INTRODUCTION

The law of unfair competition is based upon the notion that individuals should be protected from deceptive and improper conduct in the marketplace. The law of unfair competition is found in case law, in state statutes prohibiting unfair business practices, in specific federal statutes, and in regulations promulgated by the FTC, the federal regulatory agency charged with protecting consumers from unfair or deceptive acts and practices. The law of unfair competition continues to evolve as new methods of conducting business arise, such as electronic offers and sales through telemarketing, television infomercials, and the Internet.

There are a number of theories and actions that can be used by injured parties to protect against unfair competition. For the most part, the remedies are designed to protect intangible interests, such as one's interest in one's business reputation, goodwill, and so forth. For that reason, unfair competition law often protects intellectual property rather than real property or personal property and promotes a well-functioning marketplace.

In many instances, actions for unfair competition will be combined with other actions (such as those alleging trademark, copyright, or patent infringement) to provide a plaintiff a wide array of possible remedies. In other instances, a plaintiff may not have a protectable trademark, copyright, or patent, and thus must rely entirely on unfair competition theories to provide relief against unscrupulous business practices. For example, a designer of scarves imprinted with fanciful designs

may decide against applying for a design patent due to the expense involved and the short life cycle of fashion products. Protection against copying of the design may thus be available under the umbrella of unfair competition rather than under design patent law.

Section 43 of the Lanham Act (15 U.S.C. § 1125) provides a federal cause of action to protect consumers against unfair competitive business practices. It is effectively a national unfair competition statute prohibiting a broad range of wrongful business activities and providing a wide array of remedies to plaintiffs. Moreover, section 43(a) protects unregistered marks and names, such as those that do not qualify for federal trademark registration because they are descriptive or perhaps used only in intrastate commerce.

The most common types of unfair competition are discussed more fully in this chapter but can be briefly summarized as follows.

- **Passing off (or palming off).** "Passing off" occurs when one party attempts to pass off or sell his or her goods or services as those of another.
- **Misappropriation.** Misappropriation exists when one party takes or uses another's property that the original owner created or secured at effort and expense.
- **Right of publicity.** A person's name, identity, voice, likeness, or persona are protected against unauthorized commercial exploitation through the right of publicity.
- **False advertising.** Making false or deceptive representations about the nature of one's goods or services is actionable as false advertising.
- **Product disparagement.** Making false representations about the nature of another party's goods or services is actionable as product disparagement.
- **Dilution.** Using another's famous mark in a way that is likely to cause blurring of its distinctive quality or tarnishing it by

harming its reputation is actionable as dilution.

- **Infringement of trade dress.** Adopting the overall concept of another's distinctive packaging or product image, generally called its "trade dress," so as to deceive consumers is an infringement of trade dress.

Generally, injured parties notify the wrong-doer prior to initiating litigation. A cease and desist letter is usually sent, detailing the wrong-doer's acts and demanding that the wrongdoer cease and desist his or her activities. (See chapter 6, Exhibit 6–5, for a sample cease and desist letter used in trademark infringement matters.) If there is no resolution, the injured party may initiate legal action. In many instances, a plaintiff will allege several causes of action. For example, if a competitor of Nike uses a "swoosh" symbol similar to that registered to Nike, Nike may allege trademark infringement, passing off, dilution of its famous mark, and violation of section 43(a) of the Lanham Act, prohibiting a false designation of origin. If another shoe-maker sells an athletic shoe that copies the overall appearance or image of Nike's shoes, such conduct may be prohibited as infringement of trade dress.

PASSING OFF

Passing off (also referred to as *palming off*) occurs when one party attempts to pass off its (usually inferior) goods under the pretense that they are the goods of another. Passing off may exist when one party affixes another's trademarks to its goods, adopts a trademark or trade name that is so similar to that of another that consumers are deceived about the source of the product or service, or copies features of another's goods so that its goods are confusingly similar to those of the other. The essence of the action is some representation by a defendant, whether direct or indi-

rect, that causes consumers to be deceived about the source of their purchases. For example, if a tavern owner sells a lower quality cola as COKE® or a merchant sells its own inferior headphones as BOSE® headphones, passing off has occurred because the sellers have represented their own goods as those of someone else.

A variety of passing off is *reverse passing off*, which occurs when a defendant markets a plaintiff's product as his own, in essence, "taking credit" for the plaintiff's goods. Reverse passing off typically occurs when a defendant purchases a plaintiff's goods, removes the plaintiff's mark, and then resells the item with the defendant's own mark (or with no mark at all).

Actions alleging passing off are often brought when a case of trademark infringement does not lie. For example, a business owner may not be able to secure trademark protection for his or her business name because the name is primarily merely a surname or it is so descriptive it does not qualify for protection as a trademark. The use of a similar name by another party in connection with similar products and services that causes confusion and deception may thus be remedied by bringing an action alleging that the second party is passing off his or her goods as those of the plaintiff. Passing off may be enjoined and damages may be awarded to compensate the plaintiff for damages suffered, including lost profits.

Passing off is the earliest form of unfair competition, and the term is used to describe a wide variety of deceptive trade practices. Passing off can occur when a party suggests that its products or services are somehow associated with or sponsored by another, as when a retailer advertises that it is "an authorized dealer of Maytag® products," when it is not. Such conduct is harmful to Maytag, which has not only lost a sale but may suffer damage to its reputation inasmuch as improper conduct by the retailer could reflect badly on Maytag. Such a blatantly untrue statement also constitutes false advertising as well as a violation of section 43(a) of the Lanham Act, which prohibits false designations of origin. In fact, because much of the conduct formerly attacked as passing off is also prohibited by section 43 of the Lanham Act, the federal unfair competition statute, fewer actions alleging passing off are brought nowadays, inasmuch as those actions are dependent upon individual state court interpretations of cases. An action brought under the Lanham Act, however, is federal in nature and provides expanded remedies to plaintiffs such as enhanced damages and attorneys' fees, which are often unavailable under state law.

In brief, passing off one's goods or services as those of another is a form of unfair competition. Actions alleging palming off or passing off are brought less frequently now, because most plaintiffs prefer to bring actions under section 43 of the Lanham Act, which statutorily prohibits such conduct and provides a federal cause of action with expanded remedies.

The most blatant form of passing off is counterfeiting, namely, selling a product with a "fake" trademark that is an intentional copy of the true trademark. Counterfeiting is common with respect to high-end status products, such as Rolex watches, Louis Vuitton and Kate Spade handbags, and certain types of blue jeans. The Lanham Act (15 U.S.C. § 1127) defines "counterfeit" as a spurious mark that is identical with, or substantially indistinguishable from, a registered mark. Thus, the knockoff handbags sold by street vendors as Burberry bags, complete with a trademark or label identical to that used by Burberry, are counterfeits. In some cases, counterfeit goods can be dangerous. For example, in 1995, the FTC warned against the use of counterfeit infant formula labeled as "Similac" formula, but which did not have the nutritional content of the "real" Similac formula. Similarly, the FTC is now concerned about counterfeit drugs sold over the Internet that do not contain the medicinal compounds of their "real" counterparts. It has been estimated that counterfeit drugs make up 10 percent of the pharmaceutical market and that $3 billion in fake auto parts are sold in the United States each year.

Trademark counterfeiting is a federal crime under 18 U.S.C. § 2320, which imposes fines up to $2 million and jail terms up to 10 years for individuals who engage in counterfeiting activities. Enforcement of these laws is difficult, however, as street vendors often merely move their location to another corner when confronted. In many cases, trademark owners prefer to deposit their trademark registrations with the U.S. Customs and Border Protection (as discussed in chapter 6) so it can seize illegally imported goods.

Newer enforcement efforts focus on those in the supply chain that leads to counterfeit goods, such as landlords, shipping companies, and credit card companies. For example, in January 2006, to settle a lawsuit brought by Louis Vuitton, landlords for seven Canal Street properties in New York City promised to evict tenants found selling fake Louis Vuitton bags and agreed to regular inspections of the leased premises by the company's representatives.

In the United States, it is not illegal to buy counterfeit goods, although it is in some other countries, such as France and Italy.

MISAPPROPRIATION

The doctrine of misappropriation as a form of unfair competition first arose in *International News Service v. Associated Press*, 248 U.S. 215 (1918), in which the Supreme Court held that an unauthorized taking of another's property, in that case, news information, that it invested time and money in creating was actionable as misappropriation of property. In *INS*, news information originally gathered by the Associated Press relating to World War I was pirated by International News Service and sold to its customers. Because the news itself, as factual matter, could not be copyrighted, the plaintiff could not sue for copyright infringement. Instead it alleged that its valuable property right had been taken or misappropriated by the defendant. The Supreme Court agreed, noting that the defendant was "endeavoring to reap where it has not sown and . . . is appropriating to itself the harvest o those who have sown." *Id.* at 239–40. Because the defendant was not attempting to convince its subscribers that its news reports were from the plaintiff, an action for passing off would not lie. The defendant was misappropriating rather than misrepresenting.

In recent years, the doctrine of misappropriation has fallen into disfavor due to its somewhat amorphous nature, and many courts have followed *INS* only when nearly identical fact patterns are presented, namely, cases involving the taking of news, event results, mathematical formulae (such as golf handicapping systems), and indices (such as stock market index report and averages) that are not addressed by copyright or patent law and in which one party has wrongfully exploited another's effort and labor.

RIGHT OF PUBLICITY

Introduction

Some of the most interesting cases in the intellectual property field relate to the rights of individuals to protect their identities from unauthorized commercial use. The **right of publicity** gives individuals, not merely celebrities, the right to control commercial use of their identities or personas. Nevertheless, because the right of publicity protects a commercial interest, the vast majority of cases involve celebrities inasmuch as they can readily show economic harm when their names, photographs, or identities are used to sell products or suggest a sponsorship of merchandise.

Publicity rights are governed by state law. Nearly 20 states have specific statutes dealing with the right of publicity. Others recognize the right through case law. A few states do not recognize any right of publicity. On the other hand, California, with its large population of celebrities, has extensive statutes and significant case law recognizing the right of publicity.

The right of publicity has evolved from the right of privacy, which protected against unreasonable invasions upon another person's solitude and provided remedies for the disclosure of private information. While the right of privacy, however, protects one's *personal* interests against indignity, hurt feelings, and invasion, the right of publicity protects one's *commercial* interests against wrongful exploitation. The right of publicity allows individuals to protect the marketability of their identities (a property right) and punishes those who would unjustly enrich themselves by appropriating another's fame for profit-making purposes. Unpermitted commercial exploitation of an individual's persona would dilute the value of the persona, making it more difficult for the individual to commercialize his or her identity. Thus, remedies for infringement include injunctions to prevent further exploitation and monetary relief to compensate the individual whose right of publicity has been appropriated (including damages for injury to reputation, recovery of the defendant's profits, and punitive damages in extreme cases).

Courts have articulated a number of reasons for upholding an individual's right to publicity, including the need to protect against confusion that would arise if consumers were led to believe individuals sponsor or approve products when they do not, the need to incentivize performers who provide entertainment and benefit to society and should thus be provided with a protectable property right in their identities, and the need to prevent unjust enrichment of those who seek to profit from another's talent and often hard-earned fame.

The right of publicity does not apply to noncommercial uses; thus, using another's name, likeness, or identity for news reporting, scholarship, or research is permissible, as long as there is no invasion of privacy or defamation. Most cases involve the unauthorized use of another's identity to promote some product or service, thus suggesting that the individual sponsors or approves the item being advertised. It is not necessary to prove falsity, deception, or likelihood of confusion in order to prevail in an action for infringement of the right of publicity.

Appropriation of Identity

Most states protect more than just a person's name. Thus, unauthorized use of a nickname, voice, likeness, portrait, signature, appearance, identity, or personal attribute (such as customary gestures, clothing, or hairstyle) is prohibited if that use is understood to identify a particular person. Neither intent to deceive nor consumer confusion must be proved. The essence of an action for misappropriation of one's right to publicity is that one's identity was used without permission. Nevertheless, wrongfully using a celebrity's name or likeness to advertise a product may also be actionable as false advertising and unfair competition.

Although it is clear that unauthorized use of a person's name or picture is actionable, there are a variety of other ways in which the right of publicity or related rights can be infringed.

- **Phrases and nicknames.** In *Carson v. Here's Johnny Portable Toilets,* 698 F.2d 831 (6th Cir. 1983), a court prohibited a portable toilet company from using the phrase "Here's Johnny" in connection with advertising its services, holding that the phrase had become sufficiently identified with the entertainer Johnny Carson to be protected, even though neither his full name nor his picture was used. Disguising a name, such as varying a few letters, will not protect a defendant. Even nicknames are protectable if they are understood to identify the plaintiff. For example, in *Hirsch v. S.C. Johnson & Sons, Inc.,* 280 N.W.2d 129 (Wis. 1979), the use of the word *Crazylegs* to advertise moisturizer was held to infringe the right of publicity of football star Elroy "Crazylegs" Hirsch.
- **Likeness.** A person's "likeness," including a variety of physical features, is protectable against unauthorized use,

whether by drawing, cartoons, or look-alikes. Thus, in *Ali v. Playgirl, Inc.,* 447 F. Supp. 723 (S.D.N.Y. 1978), a cartoon drawing of a black man in a boxing ring that included the phrase "The Greatest" was held to have identified the boxer Muhammad Ali and violated his right of publicity. Similarly, in *Allen v. National Video, Inc.,* 610 F. Supp. 612 (S.D.N.Y. 1985), Woody Allen was able to prohibit the use of a look-alike's photograph in advertisements for video rental stores inasmuch as the advertisements falsely suggested that Woody Allen endorsed the advertised services. The case was later settled out of court. In yet another case involving a look-alike photo of Woody Allen, a court stated that certain photos could be used only if accompanied by bold-faced disclaimers identifying the person displayed as a look-alike and stating there was no connection with Woody Allen.

- **Voice.** In *Midler v. Ford Motor Co.,* 849 F.2d 460 (9th Cir. 1988), the Ford Motor Company's use of an impersonator to imitate the singer Bette Midler's vocal style in advertisements for Ford's cars was held to be unlawful. The Ninth Circuit held that while it would "not go so far as to hold that every imitation of a voice to advertise merchandise is actionable . . . when a distinctive voice of a professional singer is widely known and is deliberately imitated in order to sell a product, the sellers have appropriated what is not theirs . . . ." *Id.* at 463.
- **Roles and associated objects.** Imitating a distinctive performing style or persona is actionable. Thus, the roles associated with Groucho Marx and Charlie Chaplin (the "Little Tramp" persona) have been protected from unauthorized commercial exploitation. In *White v. Samsung Electronics America, Inc.,* 971 F.2d 1395

(9th Cir. 1992), the use of a mechanical robot wearing a wig, jewelry, and evening wear posed near a game board similar to that used on the television game show *Wheel of Fortune* was held to create a triable issue of fact regarding whether such use violated game show hostess Vanna White's right of publicity because the display evoked her identity. Similarly, Fred Rogers ("Mister Rogers") sued a store for selling T-shirts showing him wearing his well-recognized sweater and bearing a pistol, arguing that the image was wholly inconsistent with his child-friendly persona and violated his right of publicity.

One of the most famous recent right of publicity cases involved robots that appeared to resemble Norm and Cliff from the *Cheers* television sitcom. The robots, named Hank and Bob, were placed at airport bars. The actors who portrayed Norm and Cliff in the television show sued *Cheers*'s trademark and copyright owner for violations of their right of publicity. After seven years of litigation and an appeal to the U.S. Supreme Court, the parties ultimately settled out of court. The Ninth Circuit Court of Appeals, however, had ruled that the actors' case could proceed and that it was ultimately up to a jury to determine whether the rights of publicity were violated. An earlier court had dismissed the actors' lawsuit but the Ninth Circuit reversed that decision. *Wendt v. Host Int'l Inc.*, 125 F.3d 806 (9th Cir. 1997).

Duration and Descendibility of Right to Publicity

The duration of the right of publicity is subject to much variation. Some states do not provide any protection for deceased individuals. For example, in New York, the right can be asserted only by a living individual. Many experts believe that this view stems from the association of the right of privacy with the right of publicity. Because the right of privacy is personal to the individual and does not survive death, some states similarly hold that there is no postmortem right of publicity.

The majority of states, however, recognizing that the right of publicity is an economic property right, hold that just as one can pass one's other property to one's heirs so that they receive the fruit of one's labors, so too the right of publicity should survive death. To hold otherwise allows others, generally advertisers, to reap a windfall upon the death of a celebrity. Moreover, because an individual can license the right to another to use his or her name or likeness (e.g., the use of athletes' names or photos on sporting goods equipment), clearly indicating the nature of the right of publicity as a property right, the better-reasoned view appears to be that of the majority: The right of publicity is a property right, and like other property rights, it can pass to one's heirs upon death.

On the other hand, there is no real need for the right to exist in perpetuity. It serves little purpose today for the heirs of Benjamin Franklin to be able to control the use of his likeness or name. Thus, in most states, the right of publicity survives death for a stated period of time. For example, in California, the right survives for 70 years after a person's death. Other states recognize varying terms for protection, ranging from 10 years to 100 years. Still other states that recognize postmortem rights allow heirs to allege infringement only when the individual commercially exploited his or her identity during life. In those states, unless a person has exploited his or her likeness or identity during lifetime, heirs cannot sue for infringement after the person's death. This is a minority approach.

State laws that do not recognize postmortem rights of publicity can often be circumvented. For example, New York will apply the law of a deceased individual's domicile at death. Thus, celebrities often make sure to claim California or some other state as their domicile. Indiana, another state that is highly protective of the right of publicity, authorizes application of its law as soon as an advertisement enters the state. Not surprisingly, one company that represents the estates of more than 100 deceased celebrities is headquartered in Indiana. Similarly, in today's climate of national communication and advertising, heirs of celebrities may be able to avoid states that do not recognize postmortem rights by asserting that the infringing act was committed in some other state and therefore its laws should apply.

Defenses in Right of Publicity Cases

A variety of defenses may be asserted in actions alleging infringement of one's right of publicity. One defense raised is that the plaintiff is not specifically and readily identified by the usage. For example, in *T.J. Hooker v. Columbia Pictures Industries, Inc.*, 551 F. Supp. 1060 (N.D. Ill. 1982), the plaintiff, a woodcarver named T. J. Hooker, was unable to prove he was the specific person identified in the defendant's television program concerning a fictional police officer.

Another defense asserted is that the usage is protected speech under the First Amendment. News reports using a person's name or identity are protected by the First Amendment's freedom of speech clause as long as the use does not extend beyond what is necessary to inform the public of a newsworthy event. Similarly, use in connection with research and scholarship, because it is not commercial use, is permissible. Courts have clearly held that false or misleading commercial speech is not protected under the First Amendment. Thus, once falsity or deception is shown, a First Amendment defense is generally eliminated.

Use of a person's name, identity, or likeness for purposes of satire, commentary, or parody is protected "fair use." Thus, the biting portrayals of President Clinton and Frank Sinatra by the late comic Phil Hartman on *Saturday Night Live* would likely not support actions for infringement of the right of publicity.

In a 2001 case, the California Supreme Court held that T-shirts decorated with an artist's drawing of the Three Stooges violated the rights of publicity of the heirs of the Stooges because the product containing their likeness did not so transform their image that it became the artist's own expression. The work did not contain significant creative elements but was rather a realistic reproduction of their image. The court noted that by contrast, Andy Warhol's famous silkscreens of celebrities are permissible because they go beyond mere commercial exploitation of celebrity images and provide ironic social commentary. *Comedy III Prods. Inc. v. Gary Saderup, Inc.*, 21 P.3d 797 (Cal. 2001).

Because individuals can license the right to use their names, likenesses, and signatures to others, defendants often assert that use was authorized. Actors typically grant studios the right to use their names and identities to promote movies in which they appear. The right generally extends to future re-releases of the movie, even on television, and may extend so far as to allow the studio to use the individual's name or likeness in connection with collateral products, such as toys and other related merchandise. Similarly, athletes often grant or license sporting goods and card companies the right to reproduce their names, signatures, and photos on goods in return for license or royalty fees.

New Developments in the Right of Publicity

As is common with intellectual property rights in today's society, some of the new issues relating to the right of publicity stem from increasing technological advances. Through digital technology, President Clinton appeared in the movie *Contact*, John Wayne has sold beer, and Fred Astaire has danced with a vacuum cleaner. Some actors, such as Tom Cruise, already insist that their contracts prohibit the modification of their digital images without prior permission. Vanna White's success in presenting a triable issue of fact in seeking to enjoin the use of a robot that evoked her likeness indicates that the right of publicity can extend beyond conventional infringement to misappropriation through digital and electronic means.

Another issue is whether the Copyright Act preempts (to takes precedence over) individual state statutes relating to the law of publicity. In some instances, the two fields coexist. For example, if a scene from a movie with Harrison Ford (protected by copyright) is later used without permission in another movie, Harrison Ford's copyright rights as well as his right to publicity have been violated. At least one court has held that in such a case, federal copyright preempts state laws relating to rights of publicity. *Fleet v. CBS*, 58 Cal. Rptr. 645 (Ct. App. 1996). In the Bette Midler case, because voices cannot be copyrighted, Midler sued solely for misappropriation of her identity and violation of her common law right to publicity. Similarly, names, gestures, and likenesses are unprotectable under copyright law because they are titles or ideas rather than expressions. Thus, in some instances federal copyright law may control a plaintiff's rights, while in other instances only the right to publicity will provide protection. In another new development, California recently passed the Astaire Celebrity Image Protection Act (Cal. Civ. Code § 3344.1) to allow heirs of celebrities to block commercial uses of deceased celebrities' likenesses while allowing a "safe harbor exemption" to artistic uses, such as the digital insertion of President Kennedy's image into the movie *Forrest Gump,* or uses for news, public affairs, and so forth.

FALSE ADVERTISING

Introduction

In 1943, the federal trademark law, the Lanham Act, was passed. Section 43(a) of the act (15 U.S.C. § 1125) prohibited false designations of origin, namely descriptions or representations tending falsely to describe or represent goods or services. Until the passage of the Lanham Act, actions involving unfair competition tended to allege passing off or trade disparagement. Passing off, however, was limited to instances in which a party misrepresented the *source of* goods or services. Thus, it was not an effective vehicle to use when a party made misrepresentations relating to the *nature* or *quality* of goods or services. Moreover, until the passage of the Lanham Act, plaintiffs were generally required to prove that the defendant's acts were the direct cause of loss of sales and profits, an element that was often difficult to demonstrate. Finally, courts were reluctant to let business competitors bring actions against each other to assert what was often a harm done to consumers and not to them. In *Ely-Norris Safe Co. v. Mosler Safe Co.,* 7 F.2d 603 (2d Cir. 1925), *rev'd on other grounds,* 273 U.S. 132 (1927), Judge Learned Hand stated that the law did not allow a plaintiff-competitor to sue as a "vicarious avenger" of the defendant's customers.

Although the individual states enacted statutes prohibiting **false advertising,** these statutes varied from state to state and were often ineffective to prohibit false advertising that was national in scope. The expansive language of section 43 of the Lanham Act, however, soon began to be used to protect not only against unregistered trademarks but also against nearly all forms of false advertising. In 1989, Congress amended the Lanham Act and broadened the scope of section 43. As presently written, one portion of the statute allows parties to bring actions in federal courts for infringement of trademarks (both registered and unregistered marks) and trade dress, while the other portion of the statute allows the assertion of claims for false advertising and trade libel.

Under section 43(a), whoever uses a false or misleading description or representation of fact or false designation of origin in commercial advertising or promotion or misrepresents the nature, qualities, or geographic origin of his or her or another person's goods, services, or commercial activities is liable to any person likely to be injured by such act (if the act is committed in interstate commerce). Thus, the statute protects competitors as well as perhaps consumers and allows recovery if the plaintiff can show he or she is *likely* to be damaged, thereby eliminating the prior requirement that a plaintiff show *actual damage*. Most plaintiffs are business competitors, injured celebrities, and others who can show direct injury. Most cases that have considered the issue have held that defrauded consumers have no standing to sue for false advertising under section 43(a).

The broad and sweeping scope of section 43 has been used to protect the distinctive uniform of the Dallas Cowboys cheerleaders, the color and shape of a drug capsule, the overall look of a line of greeting cards, and the sound of singer Tom Waite's voice from use by a sound-alike to falsely suggest Waite endorsed DORITOS® chips.

Remedies for false advertising include injunctive relief to prohibit further false statements or to correct falsities, as well as monetary relief.

Examples of False Advertising

An advertisement that is literally false is clearly actionable. Even advertisements that are implicitly false or unclear, however, are actionable if they are nevertheless likely to mislead or deceive consumers. False advertising is actionable under section 43 of the Lanham Act, which prohibits advertisements that falsely represent the nature, characteristics, or qualities of one's own or another's goods or services. In many cases, surveys of consumers are used to prove that the message conveyed, even if literally true, is deceptive to the public at large. Courts generally require, in cases involving implicit rather than literal falsity, that an "appreciable" or "substantial" number of consumers must be misled by a claim. If scientific, medical, or technical claims are made in an advertisement, experts are usually called to demonstrate truth or falsity. Following are some examples of advertising held to be false.

- a failure to disclose that advertised prices did not include additional charges
- a statement that a pregnancy test kit would disclose results in "as fast as 10 minutes" when a positive result would appear in 10 minutes but a negative result might take 30 minutes
- a claim that a certain motor oil provided longer life and better engine protection than a competitor's product when that claim could not be substantiated
- a claim that orange juice was pure, pasteurized juice as it came from the orange and showing a celebrity squeezing an orange and pouring the juice directly into the carton when the juice was heated and sometimes frozen prior to packaging
- a false claim that automobile antifreeze met an automobile manufacturer's standards

ETHICS EDGE: Seeing the Whole Picture

Try to serve the client's interests in everything you do. When reviewing its advertising materials to determine copyrightability, consider also whether the materials could subject the client to liability for false advertising or some other form of unfair competition. If you observe conduct or documents that might constitute acts of unfair competition, review the matter with your supervisor. Many clients desire to "push the edge of the envelope" when it comes to their promotional activities. Serve the client's whole interest, and review materials and issues from a variety of perspectives—not only to protect the client's intellectual property but also to ensure the client stays within the bounds of ethical conduct in the marketplace.

- falsely claiming a whiskey to be "scotch" whiskey when it was not
- covering up a label stating "Made in Taiwan" that appeared on goods
- ads for GLAD-LOCK® resealable storage bags that did not accurately portray the leakage rate of a competitor's bags and did not indicate that only a certain percentage of the competitor's bags leaked

Many cases involve **comparative advertising** claims in which one party claims its products are superior or equivalent to those of a competitor. The competitor need not be specifically identified for an action to lie. In comparative advertising cases, a plaintiff must in fact show that the claimed product is inferior or not equivalent. Claiming that a product is "compatible with" or "works with" another product is permissible as long as the claim is true.

Defenses to False Advertising

Clearly, the truth is a defense to a claim that an advertisement is false or misleading. Note, however, that an advertisement that is literally true can still constitute false advertising if it is likely to mislead consumers. Truth can be shown by survey evidence (showing consumers are not misled), statistical evidence, or expert opinion. Another common defense asserted in false advertising cases is **puffing.** Puffing is an exaggerated and highly subjective statement upon which no reasonable person would rely. Courts generally hold that such puffing is vague and is opinion only rather than misrepresentation and is thus not actionable. Thus, stating that elves make KEEBLER® cookies is not false advertising because no reasonable person would believe such a statement to be true. Vague statements such as that a product is a "major breakthrough" or represents "new technology" are likewise permissible puffing inasmuch as they are more in the nature of boasting than representation. Similarly, general statements that a product is "superior" are usually held to be nonactionable puffing;

however, if a statement purports to rely on test results that demonstrate superiority, such a claim may be false advertising if superiority cannot be proven.

Another defense often raised is that the speech involved in an allegedly false advertisement is protected speech under the First Amendment. Courts have typically held, however, that commercial speech is not constitutionally protected from regulation and that the government has the right to ban deceptive and false speech.

Regulation by the Federal Trade Commission

The **Federal Trade Commission (FTC)** is charged with enforcing a comprehensive law, section 5 of the FTC Act (15 U.S.C. § 45), which prohibits unfair or deceptive acts or practices in or affecting commerce. Similar to section 43 of the Lanham Act and most state statutes relating to false advertising, section 5 requires that objective claims made in advertising and marketing be truthful and substantiated. The FTC will not pursue subjective claims or puffing, such as a claim that a suntan lotion is the "best in the world," but will pursue claims that include an objective component, such as "our suntan lotion lasts longer than other popular brands." Almost all states have statutes similar to section 5 of the FTC Act that prohibit deceptive and unfair trade practices. The state statutes are usually referred to as little **FTC acts.**

Most of the advertising cases challenged by the FTC involve health and safety claims inasmuch as these pose the most risk to consumers. Alcohol and tobacco advertising is subject to particular scrutiny. Many recent cases involve health and nutrient claims for foods and dietary supplements and weight loss and disease prevention claims. Health and safety claims typically require competent and credible scientific evidence. Claims such as "clinical studies show that our brand is better than . . ." are permissible only if they are true. If other studies exist that contradict claims or if the methodology of the studies is defective, there is likely a violation of the FTC Act.

The FTC also vigorously enforces its "Do Not Call" rule and has been paying increased attention to consumer protection on the Internet, including privacy rights and identity theft. Section 5 of the FTC Act applies to electronic commerce, and thus the FTC is charged with prohibiting unfair and deceptive practices on the Internet. FTC staff routinely monitor the Net and online services. In 1995, the FTC brought its first case involving an online scam, and with the cooperation of the Internet service provider (AOL), the FTC shut the scam down and achieved complete redress for injured consumers. In 2006, identity theft was the leading consumer fraud complaint received by the FTC. The FTC is currently targeting abusive and deceptive lending schemes and other credit practices.

The FTC has a wide array of remedies it uses to protect consumers. While cease and desist orders, injunctions, and monetary penalties are common, the FTC is increasingly using more innovative remedies designed to protect consumers. For example, the FTC often requires that restitution be made to injured consumers, rescinds contracts that are deceptive, and has required corrective advertising and affirmative disclosures about product safety claims. In one case involving false claims relating to sunscreen, the FTC required that the respondent design, produce, and print brochures about the importance of sunscreen usage by children. Similarly, in 2000, the FTC required Bayer Corp. to embark on a $1 million consumer education program to settle charges that Bayer advertisements made unsubstantiated claims that regular aspirin could help prevent heart attacks and strokes in the general population. The FTC itself uses the Internet to protect consumers. By accessing the FTC's home page (http://www.ftc.gov), consumers can obtain consumer protection information electronically and participate in online seminars regarding selected topics.

PRODUCT DISPARAGEMENT

At common law, an action can be brought for making intentional and untrue statements about another company or its products or services that cause monetary harm to the company. The action is variously called **product disparagement,** *commercial disparagement,* or *trade libel.*

The statements, which can be written or oral, must be false and must clearly communicate a disparaging message about the plaintiff. Mere puffing does not give rise to an action for product disparagement. Similarly, merely expressing a negative opinion about a company in an Internet chat room does not constitute disparagement. Most jurisdictions require that the defendant act with intent to injure the plaintiff or, at the least, with a reckless disregard for the truth or falsity of its statements. Finally, specific economic harm must be pleaded and proven. It is not sufficient for a plaintiff to show that it is likely to be harmed by a defendant's false representations. The plaintiff must generally demonstrate specific economic harm, such as the loss of a contract or loss of customers.

Actions for product disparagement are seen less frequently today inasmuch as plaintiffs would generally prefer to rely upon section 43(a) of the Lanham Act. Relying on section 43 rather than individual state judicial decisions affords a plaintiff several advantages, chiefly that the plaintiff need not prove specific economic harm inasmuch as relief is provided to anyone who is *likely* to be damaged. Moreover, under section 43, a plaintiff need not prove that a defendant had the specific intent to injure the plaintiff or that the defendant acted in reckless disregard of the truth or falsity of misrepresentations.

In defending an action for product disparagement (whether brought under common law or section 43(a)), a defendant may allege that its statements are permissible comparative advertising (as long as the statements are true), that its statements are mere opinion or puffing, or that its statements are protected as speech under the

First Amendment. As discussed earlier, however, commercial speech is provided a lower level of protection than other forms of speech.

DILUTION

Dilution is another form of unfair competition. Dilution occurs when a famous trademark loses or is likely to lose its distinctive quality due to tarnishment or blurring. As previously discussed in chapter 6, the Federal Trademark Dilution Act (FTDA) and its 2006 revisions (15 U.S.C. § 1125(c)) provide remedies for the dilution of famous marks. Under the act, the owner of a famous mark that is distinctive (either inherently or through acquired distinctiveness) is entitled to an injunction against one who uses a mark or trade name in commerce that is likely to cause dilution (by blurring or by tarnishment) of the famous mark, regardless of the presence or absence or actual or likely confusion, of competition, or of actual economic injury. The 2006 revisions to the act clarified that *actual* dilution is not required; a *likelihood* of dilution is sufficient. The revisions also clarified that marks must be famous to the general consuming public, not merely in a niche market.

The FTDA is intended to provide a remedy for the owners of famous marks when the owners of those marks would not otherwise be able to establish likelihood of confusion and thus avail themselves of the many avenues available to protect marks from confusingly similar uses. In one famous case, the use of TIFFANY for a restaurant was prohibited inasmuch as it diluted the famous TIFFANY® mark used in connection with jewelry. The court noted that confusion was not likely inasmuch as no reasonable person would believe that the restaurant services were somehow affiliated with or sponsored by the jewelers. Nevertheless, the use of the famous mark TIFFANY, even in connection with unrelated services and goods, whittled away or diluted the strong association consumers make between the TIFFANY mark and fine jewelry. The

goodwill inherent in the famous TIFFANY mark would evaporate if junior users were allowed to use the mark even on unrelated goods. *Tiffany & Co. v. Boston Club Inc.*, 231 F. Supp. 836 (D. Mass. 1964).

Dilution can occur in two ways: blurring or tarnishment. Blurring occurs when a mark's distinctive quality is eroded through use on dissimilar products. Both inherently distinctive marks and those that have acquired distinctiveness are protected. Examples of blurring would be TIFFANY RESTAURANT, KODAK BICYCLES, or CHRYSLER SOUP. Tarnishment occurs when a mark is linked to products of inferior quality or when the mark is portrayed in an unsavory manner, such as a poster reading "Enjoy Cocaine" in the distinctive colors and script used in the famous "Enjoy Coca-Cola" advertisements. Dilution by tarnishment "harms the reputation of the famous mark." 15 U.S.C. § 1125(c).

Many of the recent cases involving dilution focus on uses of Internet addresses. For example, the address "http://www.candyland.com" for sexually explicit services and goods was held to dilute the famous CANDYLAND mark owned by Hasbro Toys. *Hasbro Inc. v. Internet Entertainment Group, Ltd.*, 40 U.S.P.Q.2d 1439 (W.D. Wash. 1996). Similarly, the address "http://www.adultsrus.com" used for sexual paraphernalia was held to dilute the famous TOYS "R" US mark owned by Toys "R" Us, Inc. *Toys "R" Us, Inc. v. Akkaoui*, No. C-96-3381, 1996 WL 772709 (N.D. Cal. Oct. 29, 1996).

One of the difficult tasks presented to courts is determining what constitutes a "famous" mark. The FTDA provides some factors for courts to consider in determining whether a mark is famous, including the following: the amount and extent of sales of goods or services under the mark; the duration and extent of advertising and publicity of the mark; the degree of recognition of the mark; and whether the mark is federally registered. To be famous a mark must be widely recognized by the general public. After the 2006 revisions to the FTDA, fame in a "niche" market no longer suffices.

If a plaintiff can show willful intent by the defendant to trade on the plaintiff's famous mark or to cause dilution of a famous mark, a plaintiff can obtain monetary relief, the defendant's profits, costs, and attorneys' fees, in addition to injunctive relief.

Under the FTDA, some uses of famous marks are not actionable, such as fair use of a famous mark in comparative advertising, noncommercial use of a famous mark, parody, and use of a famous mark in news reporting and commentary.

INFRINGEMENT OF TRADE DRESS

The total image and overall appearance of a product or service is protectable as its "trade dress." Trade dress, like trademarks, can be registered with the USPTO. Trade dress refers to the distinctive appearance of a business or product and may include a product's distinctive packaging, the interior design of a restaurant, the layout of a business, and other nonfunctional features of a product or service. Trade dress may include features such as size, shape, color or color combinations, texture, graphics, and even particular sales techniques. Trade dress protection does not extend to utilitarian or functional aspects of a product or service inasmuch as such would tend to reduce or stifle competition. Functional products may be protected under patent law (assuming they meet the tests of patentability, such as novelty and nonobviousness), which provides a limited period of duration for utility patents. To allow a functional product or service to be protected as trade dress would allow a monopoly on a useful feature or product in perpetuity.

In *Two Pesos Inc. v. Taco Cabana, Inc*, 505 U.S. 763 (1992), the Supreme Court held that the inherently distinctive trade dress of a Mexican restaurant could be protected under section 43(a) of the Lanham Act against infringement by another restaurant that used confusingly similar décor and design elements. The trade dress in-

cluded the shape and general appearance of the exterior of the restaurant, the signage, the interior kitchen plan, the décor, the menu, the equipment, servers' uniforms, and other features that reflected the total image of the restaurant. The Court held that as long as a party's trade dress is distinctive (either inherently or upon a showing of secondary meaning), it will be protected against a junior user's use that is likely to cause confusion among consumers. The Court expressly noted that protection of trade dress, like protection of trademarks, serves the Lanham Act's purpose of securing to owners the goodwill of their businesses and protecting the ability of consumers to distinguish among competing goods and services.

In a relatively recent case, *Samara Bros. Inc. v. Wal-Mart Stores, Inc.*, 165 F.3d 120 (2d Cir. 1998), *rev'd on other grounds*, 529 U.S. 205 (2000), the plaintiff was awarded $1.2 million against Wal-Mart for selling (under Wal-Mart labels) knock-offs of the plaintiff's children's clothing line. The court held that the clothing, which displayed large collars and bold appliques of hearts and flowers on seersucker, was sufficiently distinctive to be entitled to trade dress protection. Thus, although clothing per se is not protectable under copyright law because it is a useful article, distinctive elements of clothing can be protected under trade dress theory. The U.S. Supreme Court held that product design is not inherently distinctive, and thus trade dress cases based upon product design must show that the design has acquired distinctiveness through secondary meaning. 529 U.S. at 211–13. Moreover, clothing design embellishments, such as the hearts and flowers, can be protected under copyright law, although the scope of protection for such familiar elements will be narrow and only nearly identical copying will be prohibited.

To prevail in a trade dress case a plaintiff must show that its trade dress is valid and protectable, that it is nonfunctional, and that the overall impression of the defendant's trade dress is likely to cause confusion with that of the plaintiff.

Most cases for trade dress infringement are brought in federal court under section 43(a) of the Lanham Act. Trade dress that is inherently distinctive is protectable under the Lanham Act without showing that it has acquired distinctiveness or secondary meaning. If a plaintiff alleges infringement of an unregistered *product design*, it must be shown that the product design has acquired secondary meaning. Finally, under the 2006 revisions to the FTDA, owners of unregistered trade dress may bring actions for *dilution* of their trade dress, but the burden of proof is on them to show that their trade dress is famous and is not functional. Thus, trade dress may be infringed (nearly identically to infringement of trademarks) or trade dress may be diluted under section 43(a).

INTERNATIONAL PROTECTION AGAINST UNFAIR COMPETITION

The United States has assumed certain obligations under international agreements in the arena of unfair competition, chiefly under the Paris Convention. The Paris Convention seeks to afford citizens of each of the more than 170 member nations protection against unfair competition and trademark infringement and requires that member nations provide the same level of protection against unfair competition to citizens of other member nations as they do for their own citizens. (See Appendix A for a table of countries adhering to the Paris Convention.)

The Paris Convention expressly prohibits acts that create confusion by any means with a competitor, false allegations that discredit a competitor, and indications that mislead the public in regard to the nature or characteristics of goods.

Section 44 of the Lanham Act (15 U.S.C. § 1126) implements the Paris Convention and expressly provides that any person whose country of origin is a party to any convention or treaty relating to the repression of unfair competition, to which the United States is also a party, is entitled to effective protection against unfair competition, thus affording citizens of Paris Convention member nations the wide variety of protection afforded under section 43 of the Lanham Act.

Trivia

- In 2007, the U.S. Chamber of Commerce stated that counterfeiting costs U.S. businesses as much as $250 billion annually.
- To deter counterfeiting of its golf clubs, Nike places ultraviolet markings on the shafts so Customs inspectors can identify them as legitimate.
- Research has found that more than 90 percent of the "Tiffany" jewelry offered on the Internet as genuine is fake.
- In 2004, computer company Gateway was able to prevent a company from marketing stuffed animals that wrapped around the edges of computers and televisions because they created a likelihood of confusion with Gateway's trade dress in its distinctive black and white cow spots.
- The FTC currently receives more complaints about identity theft than any other type of fraud.

CHAPTER SUMMARY

The term *unfair competition* refers to a wide variety of acts and practices that constitute improper commercial conduct. Because the property interests being protected are often intangible, such as reputation, image, and goodwill, the interests are classified as "intellectual property."

Injured parties can rely on a host of theories to protect their commercial interests: passing off (selling one's goods as those of another); misappropriation (the taking of another's valuable commercial interests); false advertising (making false representations about the nature or quality of one's own goods or services); the right of publicity (protecting one's image or persona from commercial appropriation); product disparagement (making false representations about another's goods or services); dilution (weakening or likely weakening another's trademark or service mark); or infringement of trade dress (causing a likelihood of confusion with the overall appearance or image of another's product or service). Additionally, section 43 of the Lanham Act provides a federal cause of action for a broad range of anticompetitive activities (including passing off, false advertising, product disparagement, trademark dilution, and infringement of trade dress). Finally, the FTC regulates commercial acts and practices. Under the Paris Convention, the United States is required to protect citizens of member nations against unfair competition, and U.S. citizens are treated in other countries equivalently to nationals of those member nations with regard to unfair competition.

CASE ILLUSTRATION—FALSE ADVERTISING AND PUFFING

Case: *American Italian Pasta Co. v. New World Pasta Co.*, 371 F.3d 387 (8th Cir. 2004)

Facts: American Italian Pasta Co. used the phrase "America's Favorite Pasta" on its packaging and instituted a declaratory relief action to declare it had the right to use such phrase. Defendant, its competitor, counterclaimed that the use of such a phrase was false advertising. The lower court ruled in favor of American.

Holding: The Eighth Circuit Court of Appeals affirmed. To be false, a claim must be a specific and measurable claim capable of being proved false. On the other hand, puffing is exaggerated statements or boasting upon which no reasonable person would rely or vague and highly subjective claims of product superiority. Puffing and statements of fact are mutually exclusive. In this case, the court held that the phrase "America's Favorite Pasta" was not a statement of fact but rather subjective and vague puffing.

CASE STUDY AND ACTIVITIES

Case Study.   Vision has observed that Vacation Vista, a competitor hotel chain, has begun decorating its lounges, common areas, and restaurants in the same color schemes as Vision. The overall appearance and impression created by Vacation Vista in its hotels is highly similar to that of Vision's. Vacation Vista has also begun advertising that its hotel spas are "more luxurious" and "five times more relaxing" than those of Vision. Vacation Vista has also advertised that its room prices are "lower than" those of Vision. Vision is currently

CASE STUDY AND ACTIVITIES (CONT'D)

planning an advertising campaign, featuring a Donald Trump look-alike who will promote the luxuriousness of Vision's hotels. Finally, Vision has noticed that many children visiting its hotels are carrying backpacks with Vision's logo, registered with the USPTO. These backpacks are "knockoffs" and are likely sold by street vendors.

Activities. Discuss whether any of the foregoing acts constitute unfair competition.

ROLE OF PARALEGAL

There are a number of tasks in which IP paralegals are engaged in the unfair competition arena. Some of those activities are as follows:

- reviewing advertisements and publications to alert clients to possible instances of passing off, misappropriation, false advertising, product disparagement, or dilution
- reviewing the products and services of competitors of clients to ensure that the trade dress of clients is not being infringed
- preparing and responding to cease and desist letters that demand the cessation of unfair competitive practices
- conducting legal research relating to unfair competitive practices
- preparing and responding to complaints alleging acts of unfair competition
- engaging in the discovery process in unfair competition actions, including preparing and responding to interrogatories and requests for production of documents, preparing notices of depositions, and coordinating survey results
- assisting in trial preparation by preparing exhibits and jury instructions and assisting in the preparation of briefs for court
- assisting in the drafting of settlement agreements

INTERNET RESOURCES

Federal and state laws relating to unfair competition:

http://www.law.cornell.edu
http://www.findlaw.com

Federal Trade Commission:

http://www.ftc.gov

General information:

http://www.findlaw.com
http://www.megalaw.com
http://www.ipmall.fplc.edu

DISCUSSION QUESTIONS

1. A customer in a bar orders a martini made with GREY GOOSE® vodka and instead is served a martini with an inferior brand of vodka. What type of action may the owner of the GREY GOOSE® trademark bring?

2. An unauthorized picture of actor George Clooney has appeared in the following:
   a. an article in *Newsweek* about Hollywood power brokers
   b. an advertisement for men's cologne
   c. a review by *The Today Show* of Mr. Clooney's latest movie
   Discuss whether Mr. Clooney has any remedies for these uses of his photograph.

3. Pop singer Britney Spears would like to stop publication of an unauthorized biography of her. Ms. Spears intends to assert that the book will infringe her right to publicity. Is such a claim likely to succeed? Discuss.

4. The maker of DURACELL® batteries is advertising that its batteries are "longer lasting" than those of ENERGIZER®. Is such a statement actionable? Discuss.

5. Disney World's advertisements state that its parks are "more fun" and contain more "thrills and adventures" than other amusement parks. Are such statements actionable? Discuss.

6. The maker of GRACO® child safety seats has begun advertising that its seats are the "safest on the market" and are being sold at "great prices." Are such statements actionable? Discuss.

7. ABC Inc. has begun marketing a series of stuffed animals that are highly similar to BEANIE BABIES® in their size, color, and overall impression. What sort of action should the maker of BEANIE BABIES® bring? Would it make a difference if there were no federal trademark registration for "Beanie Babies"?

8. Discuss what type of trademark dilution is involved for each of the following:
   a. Kraft sunscreen
   b. Barbie's Pleasure Palace (for adult-oriented materials)
   c. Nike mascara

9. A company advertises that its products "work with" SWIFFER® tools and products." The claim is true, and the company that makes SWIFFER® products suffers a loss in its sale. Is the advertisement actionable? Discuss.

USING INTERNET RESOURCES

1. Access the Web site of the FTC. How would you go about filing a complaint with the FTC about false advertising?

2. Access WIPO's Web site and review the Paris Convention, specifically Article 10. If one makes a false allegation discrediting a competitor, what section of the Paris Convention has been violated?

3. Access the Web site of the World Trade Organization. Review its Glossary. What does the term "counterfeit" mean?

4. Access the USPTO's Web site, specifically its section called "StopFakes.gov." Review the materials that can be downloaded, and access the FAQs. What is the difference between "counterfeit" and "piracy"?

Chapter 24

Intellectual Property Audits and Due Diligence Reviews

CHAPTER OVERVIEW

Clients are often unaware of the importance of their intellectual property. To help clients realize the value of such assets and exploit them, law firms often conduct intellectual property audits for clients. The audit reveals the intellectual capital owned by a client and assists in developing a strategy so the client can maintain its valuable intellectual capital. Once clients fully understand *what* they own, they can then protect it, license it, or sell it. The audit should be repeated on a periodic basis to reflect the changing nature of intellectual property. Audits are also conducted when a company is sold, when it borrows money, or when it acquires another company. This type of audit is usually referred to as a "due diligence" review.

INTRODUCTION

Although clients are always aware of the value of their tangible assets (such as their stock and inventory), they are often unaware that they own other valuable assets: their intellectual property. They may use distinctive names for certain products or services, may possess creative marketing materials, or may have developed a novel method of conducting business. All of these developments are assets that can and should be protected as intellectual property. Distinctive names should be registered as trademarks, written materials should be protected by copyright notices and registration, inventions should be protected by patents, and trade secrets should be protected so they can endure perpetually. At least one expert has estimated that tangible assets represented 80 percent of the value of most U.S. companies in 1975. By 2007, 80 percent of these companies' market value consisted of intangible assets (including brand name, reputation, and intellectual property).

If intellectual property is not protected, it may be lost. Failure to monitor and police infringing activities may also lead to a loss of rights. Competitors may acquire rights to valuable property that formerly provided a competitive edge to a company, resulting in a loss of market share and profits.

Companies not only should protect their intellectual property in order to ensure business survival but also should use their intellectual property to create revenue. Trademarks, copyrights, patents, and trade secrets can all be licensed to others. The owner of intellectual property can achieve a continual revenue stream through licensing of rights to others for either a fixed sum or recurrent royalty payments. Alternatively, intellectual property may be sold outright to another. Intellectual property can also be used as collateral so its owner can secure a loan from a bank or other institution. Just as real property or personal property such as inventory is pledged as collateral when money is borrowed, so too can intellectual property (trademarks, copyrights, and patents) serve as collateral. Intellectual property can also be used as donations. For example, a number of companies have donated patents to universities and other nonprofit institutions. The donors then take an income tax deduction for the donation, although the Internal Revenue Service has begun subjecting such claims to increased scrutiny, and Congress has limited deductions for such donations. Recall that some companies now contribute patents (and pledge not to assert their patent rights) to the Patent Commons Project, a collaborative environment that serves as a "preserve" for patents. (See chapter 21 for additional information about patent donations and the Patent Commons Project.)

The failure to capitalize on the value of intellectual property is generally caused by a lack of awareness of just what can be protected. Many companies believe that copyright extends only to important literary works and therefore fail to secure protection for their marketing brochures or other written materials. Similarly, companies often fail to implement measures to ensure valuable trade secrets maintain their protectability. Because clients are often unaware of the great potential and value of this property, law firms often offer their clients an **intellectual property audit** to uncover a company's protectable intellectual property. The IP audit is analogous to the accounting audit most companies conduct on an annual basis to review their financial status.

Another type of IP investigation is usually conducted when a company acquires another entity. At that time, a thorough investigation should be conducted of the intellectual property of the target company to ensure the acquiring company will obtain the benefits of what it is paying for and will not inherit infringement suits and other problems stemming from the target's failure to protect its intellectual property. This type of intellectual property investigation is generally called a **due diligence** review inasmuch as the acquiring company and its counsel have an obligation to duly and diligently investigate the target's assets. Due diligence reviews are also conducted when a company offers its securities for public sale inasmuch as potential investors must be informed of the offeror's assets (including its intellectual property) and any claims that may arise against the offeror. Similarly, when a company is being sold, it is generally required to identify its intellectual property and make certain representations and warranties that it owns the property being sold and there are no defects in title or pending claims involving the property. Thus, due diligence must be conducted to ensure these representations and warranties can be made with respect to a seller's intellectual property.

Audits may also be triggered by changes in the law. For example, once the Federal Circuit clarified in 1998 that business methods could qualify for patent protection if they produced a useful, concrete, and tangible result, a number of companies discovered they owned such patentable business methods that required protection.

Finally, audits may identify defects in a client's intellectual property (such as a lack of an effective trade secret protection program or failure to register a trademark used by the client) so that measures may be taken to protect these valuable assets.

PRACTICAL ASPECTS OF INTELLECTUAL PROPERTY AUDITS

IP audits come in all shapes and sizes. Most importantly, the audit must fit the client and respond to its needs. If a client owns a small retail shop or provides auto repair services from only one location, the sole intellectual property may consist of the business name (which may be protectable as a trademark), any logos or designs used by the client, customer lists, and marketing materials, if any. On the other hand, if a client is engaged in software development, information technology, or telecommunications services, it may possess a wealth of IP assets. For example, in 2006 alone, IBM Corp. was granted 3,651 patents, helping to generate about $10 billion in royalties for IBM over the past 10 years.

In many cases, the first IP audit is the most extensive and expensive. Some clients conduct periodic audits, and law firms typically docket the dates for annual reviews and send reminder notices to clients. The annual reviews can focus on changes since the previous audit. While there is some expense involved in conducting any audit, the benefit of the audit outweighs the expense involved. Moreover, there are often intangible benefits to the audit. If the client later wishes to obtain a loan or sell some of its assets, the pre-

ceding audit need only be updated, eliminating costly delays in a transaction. Moreover, if new members join a company's IP legal team, an existing audit will help familiarize them with the company's IP assets. If the client is adequately prepared for the audit and actively assists in the audit, costs can be reduced.

Before the audit is conducted, the law firm and the client should agree on its scope and nature. Consideration should be given in regard to whether the firm will conduct the audit on an hourly fee basis or for a fixed fee. In most instances, the law firm will need to send IP professionals to the client site, resulting in disruption to the client's operations. Again, with careful preparation, such disruption can be kept to a minimum.

The following issues should be clearly addressed before the audit begins.

- Who will conduct the audit? Usually, counsel (inside or outside), together with IP paralegals, will conduct the audit, relying on company representatives for assistance. The law firm and the client should each designate a person who will serve as the team leader and to whom questions and concerns can be addressed. If a client is unusually large, it may designate various leaders, for example, one from its research and development department, one from its marketing department, and so forth.
- What scope will the audit have? Should only U.S. rights be explored? Should consideration be given to protecting intellectual property on an international basis?

CONDUCTING THE AUDIT

The first step in the audit should be a face-to-face meeting of the legal team and company managers. The legal team should make a brief presentation on what intellectual property is, why it is important to the company, and why and how the audit will be conducted. Managers will be more likely to cooperate if they fully understand the importance of the audit. Obtaining this kind of "buy in" from the client's managers and employees will speed the audit and reduce costs. Moreover, education about the importance of intellectual property helps ensure that managers consider ways to further protect a company's valuable assets and remain alert to possible infringements of the company's intellectual capital or infringements by the company of others' rights. Finally, having outside counsel involved in the process will ensure that confidential communications related to the audit are protected by the attorney-client privilege.

Once the company's managers have been advised of the need for the audit, the legal team should provide a worksheet or questionnaire (see Exhibit 24–1) to the company specifying the type of information that the firm is looking for so that company files can be reviewed and materials assembled for inspection by the firm and its representatives. Although it is not strictly necessary that the client do this kind of preparatory work, the more work the client does, the faster, cheaper, and less disruptive the audit will be.

Once the materials that are responsive to the questionnaire are gathered, the legal team can review them. The review is generally done at the client site. Files are pulled, brochures gathered, and contracts assembled. The legal team will review these materials and often make copies of pertinent documents, marking them as confidential.

After review of the materials is completed, another face-to-face meeting should be held to ensure that all of the materials were gathered and that there are no other contracts, license agreements, or other documents or software that should be reviewed. Questions may have arisen during the course of the audit for which the legal team needs responses. For example, the legal team may ask whether a certain brochure or trademark is still in use or whether the company logo was designed in-house or by another company. The legal team will generally check the records of the USPTO and the Copyright Office to determine whether there are any records on file showing the company's ownership of trademarks, copyrights, and patents. A follow-up questionnaire may be sent to the client to obtain the answers to questions that arose in the course of the audit.

ETHICS EDGE: Confidentiality and Competence

Throughout this text, many of the ethics tips have focused on two critical duties of paralegals: the duty to maintain confidential information and the duty to provide competent service to clients. Those two core duties play a significant part in IP audits. Consider the following.

- IP audits routinely disclose the most important assets that many companies own. Be scrupulous in maintaining the confidentiality of the information to which you will gain access. Don't discuss the results of the audit with others, keep the information securely protected, and mark all documents with notices of confidentiality.
- As you work on clients' IP matters, maintain and update your own IP audit list. For example, when a client secures a trademark registration, note the particulars on your own client audit sheet. When it comes time to conduct a full-fledged IP audit or to update a prior audit, you will already have much of the information at your fingertips, saving the client time and money.

EXHIBIT 24–1
Intellectual
Property Audit
Questionnaire

Identified below is a list of subjects to be covered in connection with our review of the intellectual property rights of your company (the "Company"). Please gather any materials and documents relevant to the subjects listed below so they can be reviewed. If no materials or documents exist with respect to a particular subject, please confirm that in writing next to the relevant question.

For all relevant questions, give the name of the person who assisted in the design, development, or implementation of any intellectual property rights; describe the nature of the relationship between the person and the Company (for example, employee, independent contractor, and so forth); and indicate whether the person signed any confidentiality or nondisclosure agreements with the Company.

A. General

1. Has the Company ever acquired another entity or the business or assets of another entity or person? (This party may have owned intellectual property that is now owned by the Company.)
2. Has the Company ever sold any assets or business to another entity or person?
3. Is the Company engaged in the development or design of any useful products or parts for useful products?
4. Is the Company engaged in the development, design, or modification of computer software?
5. Are there any individuals who may have developed or designed products or software for the Company who have left employment with the Company? If so, indicate whether each such person signed a confidentiality, nondisclosure, or employment agreement with the Company.
6. Does the Company have a Web site or are there links from other parties' sites to the Company's site? If so, provide Web site addresses.
7. Does the Company use a docketing system or calendar to provide reminders of due dates relating to any of its intellectual property?
8. Has the Company ever conducted an intellectual property audit, or does it maintain a list of its IP assets? If so, please attach a copy.

B. Trademarks and Service Marks

1. Does the Company use any trademarks, service marks, logos, slogans, trade dress, or designs (collectively "Marks") in connection with the offer and sale of its products or services? These Marks may have been displayed on products, labels, packaging, letterhead, business cards, in advertisements, brochures, or other marketing materials, including a Web site.
2. Has the Company ever applied for registration of any Marks with the United States Patent and Trademark Office (USPTO) or any state trademark agencies?
3. Has the Company ever allowed another party (such as an employee, client, vendor, or competitor) to use any of the Company's Marks?
4. Does the Company use any Marks that are owned by any third party? Review Company marketing materials, Web site, and other written documents to determine whether the Company displays or uses Marks belonging to another.

C. Copyrights

1. What written materials does the Company use to advertise its products and services? These may be written materials, scripts or copy for radio or television advertisements, or Web site materials. Were these developed by Company

EXHIBIT 24–1
Intellectual
Property Audit
Questionnaire
(continued)

employees or by independent contractors working for the Company? What agreements exist relating to the development of such materials?

2. What written materials does the Company use internally, such as employee handbooks, training materials, company policies, manuals, training or other videos, audios, or modules, relating to the way the Company conducts its business?

3. Do Company employees prepare written materials or electronic materials (such as PowerPoint slides) when presentations are made within the Company and outside the Company? If so, describe.

4. Do Company employees submit articles for publication to any journals, periodicals, or other publications? If so, describe.

5. Has the Company ever applied for registration of any copyrights with the U.S. Copyright Office?

6. Are articles from periodicals, magazines, trade journals, and other related written materials photocopied for distribution within the Company?

7. What policies exist regarding reproduction of books, articles, journals, and other materials that may be subject to copyright?

8. Is any music piped in through the Company's offices (whether through the use of CDs or music being simultaneously transmitted by a radio station)?

9. Is music played when callers to the Company are placed on hold?

D. Patents

1. Has the Company or its employees ever invented any useful article, product, method, process, or software? If so, do any inventor or laboratory notebooks exist that document the development of the invention? Does the Company have any present plans for any such inventions?

2. Has the Company ever made any improvements to another party's useful article, product, or invention?

3. Has the Company ever engaged in the reverse engineering or decompilation of another company's product or software?

4. Has the Company ever applied with the USPTO for issuance of any patent?

5. Does the Company mark all patented inventions with a patent notice?

E. Trade Secrets

1. What information does the Company possess that would be harmful to the Company if it were discovered by a competitor? Consider proprietary information relating to research and development plans; calculations and financial data; employee manuals and handbooks and personnel information; information relating to the Company's clients and customers; the Company's methods of recruiting; methods and processes of production; test results for Company products and services; data concerning the pricing for Company products and services; sales forecasts; research information; manufacturing information; marketing materials; surveys and data relating to customer needs and preferences; and business plans and forecasts.

2. Do employment, confidentiality, nondisclosure, or other agreements exist that protect such proprietary materials?

3. Does the Company conduct employee orientation for new employees and exit interviews for departing employees to ensure employees understand the need to maintain confidentiality of Company trade secrets?

(continues)

EXHIBIT 24–1
Intellectual
Property Audit
Questionnaire
(continued)

4. What measures does the Company take to protect confidential and proprietary information? Are documents marked "Confidential"? Are proprietary materials kept in locked cabinets? Are restrictions placed on the access to and copying of such materials?

5. What measures does the Company take to ensure electronic communications are protected and secure? Are any encryption methods in place for electronic communications? Describe restrictions on access to the Company's computer systems, including password protection methods.

6. Are any legal notices or disclaimers provided at sign-on when Company employees access the Company server or network?

F. Software

1. Has the Company designed, developed, or modified any software?

2. Does the Company have the right to use any software designed or developed by another party? If so, have licenses been obtained for each user?

3. Does the Company allow its employees to copy any software for their home use?

G. Claims

1. Are there any presently pending claims relating to any of the Company's intellectual property? Has any person alleged or claimed that the Company has violated or infringed its intellectual property rights?

2. What claims have been made (whether or not resolved or compromised) within the past five years against the Company relating to alleged infringement or violation by the Company of the intellectual property rights of others?

3. Has the Company observed or made any claims relating to any possible infringements by others of the Company's intellectual property rights?

4. Does the Company use any methods to detect possible infringing uses of its intellectual property?

H. General Documents

1. Please assemble all applications and registrations, and all license, royalty, security agreements or other agreements relating to trade names, Marks, copyrights, patents, trade secrets, software, licenses, or other similar rights relating to the Company's intellectual property rights.

2. Please assemble all agreements entered into by employees (including officers and directors) and any Company handbooks, manuals, or policies relating to Company employees.

3. Please assemble all agreements entered into between the Company and any consultants or independent contractors.

4. To the extent not already covered, please assemble all agreements or licenses entered into between the Company and any other parties that relate to the Company's intellectual property, which are essential for the operation of the Company's business, or by which the Company is allowed to offer or use another party's Marks, copyrights, patents, processes, software, or other related property, including contracts entered into with the government.

5. Does the Company offer its products or services in any foreign countries? If not, does the Company have any plans to offer its products or services in foreign countries within the next three years?

POSTAUDIT ACTIVITY

After the inspection is completed, the legal team will usually prepare a written report identifying the specific items of IP owned by the company, reviewing their status, and making recommendations for protection. The IP audit team may then proceed to take the following actions: filing applications for registration of trademarks, service marks, copyrights, and patents; drafting contracts to be used when the company retains independent contractors (to ensure that all work created by the independent contractors is "work made for hire" or is owned by or assigned to the company); preparing license agreements so the company can license its intellectual property to others; preparing nondisclosure and noncompetition agreements; and preparing policies for the protection of trade secrets.

The IP audit team may also assist the client's human resources department and provide instructions on conducting exit interviews and may redraft the employee manual to include a trade secret policy, Internet use policy, and instructions regarding use of the company's trademarks.

The legal team may also advise the company to engage appraisers and analysts to valuate the IP assets so they can be licensed at appropriate royalties or sold at their fair market value to produce revenue for the company.

The company is usually advised to initiate an aggressive campaign to locate others who may be infringing the company's intellectual property by reviewing competitors' materials and trade publications and by monitoring applications filed at the USPTO for marks that may be confusingly similar to those owned by the company and published patent applications for inventions that might infringe the company's patents. The legal team may help the company initiate a docketing system for reminder dates for renewals of licenses, trademark registrations, and patent maintenance, or may be retained to perform the docketing functions itself.

Once companies know what IP assets they own, they will be able to protect these valuable assets and mine them to produce a revenue stream by licensing or using the assets as collateral to obtain financing.

Trivia

- Dow Chemical reportedly used the results of an IP audit to increase its patent licensing by $125 million.
- Many experts estimate that about 80 percent of the value of American companies is attributable to their intangible assets, such as intellectual property.
- In 2005, *Forbes Magazine* estimated that the overall revenue achieved by the licensing of Star Wars memorabilia, action figures, spin-offs, and so forth was approximately $20 billion.
- Starbucks derives revenue from licensing its name to Jim Beam for a coffee-flavored liqueur.
- The COCA-COLA® trademark is the most recognized trademark in the world, and the company values its brands at more than $70 billion.

CHAPTER SUMMARY

Because clients may be unaware of the value of the intellectual property they own, law firms often conduct intellectual property audits for clients. The audit reveals valuable intellectual property assets that can then be exploited for the client's benefit. Audits should be conducted on a periodic basis to reflect the changing nature of intellectual property. Audits or reviews are also conducted when companies are sold, when they borrow money, or when they acquire other companies. In such instances, the review is often called "due diligence." Because almost all types of intellectual property can be lost through lack of protection (including nonuse, failure to monitor licensees properly, failure to renew or maintain registrations, and failure to protect against infringing activities), the intellectual property audit is a crucial tool that allows a company to understand and exploit the value of its intellectual property portfolio.

CASE ILLUSTRATION—VALUE OF TRADEMARK

Case: *United Drug Co. v. Parodney*, 24 F.2d 577 (E.D.N.Y. 1928)

Facts: Plaintiff conducted business for 25 years under the name "United Drug Company" and was one of the largest sellers of drug store merchandise in the world. Defendant intentionally changed its name to "United Drug Exchange," and plaintiff sought to prevent defendant from using such name.

Holding: The plaintiff may prevent the defendant from using "United Drug Exchange." The plaintiff has created recognition in its mark by expenditure of large amounts of money and honest and skillful management. "This hard-earned right is as important as money in the bank." *Id.* at 580. Defendant's use of a similar name causes confusion in the marketplace and should be prohibited.

CASE STUDY AND ACTIVITIES

Case Study. Vision owns a variety of names, inventions, and marketing materials that it seldom uses. It would like to explore the opportunity of either abandoning these IP assets or using them to produce revenue for the company. Additionally, Vision would like to borrow a significant amount of money from a bank to fund its planned European expansion. Finally, Vision recently purchased a small hotel chain.

Activities. Given Vision's plans and desires, discuss the advantages of an intellectual property audit for Vision.

ROLE OF PARALEGAL

Paralegals generally play an active and vital role in planning and conducting IP audits. Using nonattorney IP practitioners also helps reduce the costs associated with audits. In many instances, a paralegal serves as the liaison between the law firm and the client and coordinates all activities related to the audit. IP paralegals are generally involved in the following tasks:

- preparing the audit questionnaire and ensuring a company representative completes the questionnaire
- coordinating the time and manner of the audit by scheduling a convenient date for all team members and ensuring that a conference room or office near a photocopy machine is set aside for the audit team
- reviewing client files and documents
- preparing a follow-up questionnaire, if needed
- reviewing the records of the USPTO and Copyright Office to determine if trademarks and copyrights have been applied for or registered and whether patents have been published or have issued
- reporting the results of an IP audit
- preparing applications for registration of marks, copyrights, and patents; drafting policies for trade secret protection; drafting contracts, licenses, and assignments
- assisting in setting up a docket or calendar for maintenance of intellectual property
- providing reminders to clients of the need for annual or periodic updates to the IP audit

INTERNET RESOURCES

Statutes relating to intellectual property:	http://www.law.cornell.edu http://www.findlaw.com
General information:	http://www.findlaw.com http://www.ipmall.fplc.edu http://www.megalaw.com
Patent Commons Project:	http://www.patentcommons.org
Sites that value and assist in buying, selling, and licensing IP assets:	http://www.ipauctions.com http://www.Oceantomo.com

DISCUSSION QUESTIONS

1. Assume that an IP audit reveals that a client has acquired several registered copyrights and trademarks from another company. Although it is not required that one record a transfer of ownership of such assets, why should the appropriate documents be recorded with the USPTO and Copyright Office?

DISCUSSION QUESTIONS (CONT'D)

2. During the course of an IP audit, the legal team determines that a client is using only 10 of its 30 issued patents. What might the client consider doing with respect to the unused patents?
3. Your law firm conducts annual audits for its IP clients. One of the clients is being purchased by a large company. The acquisition must be effected within 10 days. What advantage does last year's IP audit afford the client?

USING INTERNET RESOURCES

1. Access the Web site for the law firm Fish & Richardson P.C. Locate a 1998 article written by firm lawyers and posted on the Web site relating to IP audits. What is the conclusion of the article?
2. Access the Web site for the Patent Commons Project. Review the information relating to contributors to the Project.
   a. What did Nokia pledge to the Commons (specifically, identify the document name)?
   b. What did Computer Associates International pledge to the Commons? Specify the document name and then retrieve the document. How many patents did Computer Associates International pledge?

Glossary

A

abandonment: Loss of trademark rights through nonuse coupled with an intent not to resume use; loss of patent rights through express intention to relinquish rights

abstract: A concise statement of an invention

access: Availability of a copyrighted work to a defendant so that the defendant had a reasonable opportunity to copy it

acquiescence: Conduct by a person that leads another to believe the owner will not assert certain claims against the other

acquired distinctiveness: See *secondary meaning*

actual reduction to practice: Construction of an invention in physical form, making or testing an invention or its prototype

actual use application: A trademark application based on an applicant's use in interstate commerce of a trademark

Affidavit of Continued Use: Document filed by a trademark registrant between fifth and sixth years and every 10 years after registration verifying the mark is still in use; also called *Declaration of Use* or *Section 8 Affidavit*

Affidavit of Incontestability: Document filed by the owner of a mark registered on the Principal Register after five years of continuous use that reduces the challenges that may be made to a mark; also called *Section 15 Affidavit*

Amendment to Allege Use: Document filed during prosecution of an intent-to-use trademark application, alleging that use of the mark has begun

American Inventor's Protection Act: A 1999 federal law providing significant changes to patent law

anonymous work: A copyrighted work in which the author is not identified

anticipation, doctrine of: See *doctrine of anticipation*

Anticybersquatting Consumer Protection Act (ACPA): Federal law intended to deter the practice of cybersquatting

arbitrary mark: A mark using a common dictionary word for an unrelated product, such as APPLE for computers

architectural work: The design of a building as embodied in any tangible medium of expression

article of manufacture: See *manufacture*

asexual reproduction: Growing something other than from a seed, often by grafting or placing cuttings in soil

assignment: Transfer of rights in a trademark, copyright, patent, or other property to another

assignment in gross: A purported transfer of a trademark without the business goodwill that the mark symbolizes; it is insufficient to transfer trademark rights

associates: Attorneys in foreign law firms who work with attorneys in U.S. firms regarding intellectual property matters

attribution: The right of an author to be known as the author of a work; also called *the right of paternity*

audiovisual work: A work consisting of a series of related images intended to be shown by the use of a machine such as a projector together with its accompanying sounds

author: For copyright purposes, a person who creates a work or, if the work is one made for hire, the employer or commissioning party

automated database: A body of facts, data, or other information assembled into an organized format suitable for use in a computer and comprising one or more files

B

background: The portion of a specification in a patent application that discusses how the invention differs from the prior art

Berne Convention: An international convention adhered to by more than 160 nations that requires its members to treat nationals of other countries as their own nationals for purposes of copyright

best edition: The deposit edition of a copyrighted work most suitable for purposes of the Library of Congress; generally, clean, legible, and superior deposit materials

blackout period: The period after approval of an application for publication in the *Official Gazette* within which an amendment to allege use of a mark cannot be filed

blue penciling: The revision of a noncompetition clause by a court to make it enforceable, generally because it is unreasonable in regard to scope, territory, or duration

blurring: A form of trademark dilution that whittles away the value of a famous trademarkthrough its unauthorized use on a dissimilar product or with a dissimilar service

Board of Patent Appeals and Interferences: Division of the USPTO that reviews adverse decisions by patent examiners and determines priority and patentability of inventions in interferences

business method patent: A patent allowed since 1998 that covers a business method that produces a useful, tangible, and concrete result

C

cancellation: A proceeding initiated after registration of a trademark seeking to cancel registration of a mark registered on the Principal or Supplemental Register

cease and desist letter: Correspondence sent to a party demanding that it cease and desist from certain action (in the intellectual property context, from further use of a trademark, copyright, patent, or trade secret)

Certificate of Registration: Document issued by the USPTO confirming registration of a trademark

certification mark: A word, name, symbol, or device used by one person (or a union) to certify that the goods or services of others have certain features in regard to quality, material, or some other characteristics

chain of title: Documentation of continuity of ownership or title to a trademark, copyright, patent, or other property right

Chapter I: The first phase of a patent application filed under the Patent Cooperation Treaty, consisting of a search of the application and which can now last for 30 months

Chapter II: The second phase of a patent application filed under the Patent Cooperation Treaty during which an International Preliminary Examination is conducted of the application, generally lasting 10 months

choreographic work: The composition and arrangement of dance movements and patterns

claim: The portion of a specification in a patent application that defines the scope of the invention

click-wrap license: A license of software that comes into existence by the clicking of a computer keystroke, by which act the licensee agrees to terms governing use of the software

coined mark: See *fanciful mark*

collateral use: Acceptable use of another's trademark, such as in comparative advertising

collective mark: A mark used by a collective membership organization to identify that the person displaying the mark is a member of the organization

collective work: A work such as a periodical issue or anthology in which a number of contributions, constituting separate and independent works, are assembled into a collective whole

combination patents: New inventions consisting of a combination of older, known elements

commerce: See *interstate* and *intrastate commerce*

commercial disparagement: See *product disparagement*

common law trademark: A mark used by a party without any governmental registration

Community Trademark (CTM) System: A trademark system allowing trademark owners to file one single trademark application that covers all members of the European Union

companion application: Related trademark applications by the same applicant

comparative advertising: Advertising that compares one product or service with another or that states that one product works with or is compatible with another

compensatory damages: Damages awarded to a plaintiff to compensate it for injury suffered

compilation: A work formed by the collection of preexisting material arranged in such a way that the resulting work is original; includes *collective works*

composite mark: A mark consisting of words and a design element

composition of matter: In patent law, a combination of two or more chemical or other materials into a product

comprehensive search: A search of trademarks registered or applied for at the USPTO, state trademark registrations, and common law sources such as periodicals, directories, and the Internet

compulsory license: The imposition of a statutorily set fee for use of a copyrighted work

computer program: A set of instructions used directly or indirectly in a computer to produce a certain result

conception of an invention: The completion of the devising of the means for accomplishing an invention's result

concurrent use proceeding: A proceeding initiated at the Trademark Trial and Appeal Board to determine specific geographic areas in which parties with confusingly similar marks can each use the mark

confidentiality agreement: See *nondisclosure agreement*

conflicting application: Trademark applications filed by different parties for conflicting or confusingly similar marks

consent agreement: Private agreement entered into between two trademark owners whereby each consents to the use of the other's mark, generally with some limitations or restrictions; also called *consent to use agreement*

constructive reduction to practice: The filing of a patent application that fully discloses an invention

constructive use: Use of trademark other than actual use; for intent-to-use trademark applications, the application filing date constitutes constructive use of the mark (assuming the mark achieves registration)

continuation application: A patent application that claims priority from a previously filed application and contains no new information

continuation-in-part application: A patent application that adds new matter to a previous patent application

contributory infringement: In the intellectual property context, causing, inducing, or assisting in infringement of another's trademark, copyright, or patent

copy: In copyright law, a material object (other than a phonorecord) from which a work can be perceived, reproduced, or communicated, either by human perception or with the help of a machine

copyhoarding: Retaining all rights in a work and refusing to allow others to use it

copylefting: Licensing users of software to use it for any purpose

copyright: Right protecting original works of authorship, including literary, musical, dramatic, artistic, and other works, from unauthorized reproduction, sale, performance, distribution, or display

copyright rights management: See *digital rights management*

counterfeiting: A form of trademark infringement in which a trademark is affixed to goods or services that do not originate with the trademark owner

creation: In copyright law, the fixation of a work in a copy or phonorecord for the first time

cybersquatting: A practice in which a person, without permission, registers another's name or mark as a domain name and then attempts to sell the domain name to its true owner

D.

deadwood: Unused marks that the USPTO desires to clear from its records

declaration: A statement by an applicant for a trademark registration acknowledging that statements in the application are true

Declaration of Use: See *Affidavit of Continued Use*

deep linking: The process by which an Internet user can proceed directly to certain information at another's Web site, bypassing the home page at the second site

defensive patenting: The practice of obtaining patents not for the purpose of using or exploiting and invention but for the purpose of avoiding claims of patent infringement by others

de minimis defense: A defense that excuses infringement when what is taken or infringed is trivial or slight

deposit: The best edition of a work provided to the Copyright Office in support of an application to register a copyright for the work

deposit account: Prepaid accounts established with the USPTO, against which application and other fees are drawn by applicants

derivative work: A work based on one or more preexisting works, such as a translation, fictionalization, revision, or abridgment; also called a *new version*

descriptive mark: A mark that merely describes some characteristic of the goods or services offered under it and is unregistrable unless secondary meaning is shown

design application: An application for a design patent

design patent: A patent covering new, original, and ornamental designs for useful articles

Digital Millennium Copyright Act (DMCA): A 1988 law updating copyright law for the digital age

digital rights management: Technologies used to control usage, distribution, or access of digital works (also called *copyright rights management*)

dilution: Unauthorized acts that tend to blur the distinctiveness of a famous mark or to tarnish it

direct infringement: In patent law, making, using, importing, or selling another's patented invention

disclaimer: In trademark law, an acknowledgment by an applicant that exclusive rights in certain wording in a mark, usually descriptive or generic wording, are not claimed; a notice placed on trademarked goods or advertising that the owner of the goods is not affiliated with another; in patent law, the cancellation of invalid claims in an issued patent

distinctiveness: See *secondary meaning*

divisional application: A patent application separated from another application when the original or parent application covers more than one invention

doctrine of anticipation: Theory that an invention was known or used by others such that its invention was anticipated

doctrine of equivalents: Principle that if an accused invention is equivalent to a patented invention in its purpose and achieves the same result, it infringes the patent even if a claim in the patent is not literally copied

domain name: Internet address used by a company or individual

domestic representative: A person or law firm in the United States designated by a foreign applicant to receive documents and notices affecting a trademark application

double patenting: In patent law, a principle prohibiting the issuance of more than one patent for the same invention

downstream infringement: Infringement by users who obtain copyrighted items from legitimate users

dramatic work: A theatrical performance or play performed for stage, movies, television, or radio

drawing: The display of the mark applied for in a trademark application; may be a *standard character drawing* (typewritten display) or *special form* (a design mark or a design mark with words); the display of an invention in a patent application

droit de suite: A doctrine in foreign countries that allows the authors of fine works to share in the appreciation of those works, even after they have parted with ownership of those works

due diligence: A type of audit of intellectual property, usually conducted when a company is sold, when it borrows money, when it offers securities, or when it acquires another company

duty of candor: Requirement that patent applicants disclose to the USPTO any information that is material to the patentability of a claimed invention

E

Electronic File Wrapper: Electronic record of documents filed with the USPTO

Electronic Filing System (EFS): USPTO electronic system allowing secure electronic filing of some documents with the USPTO

Electronic Trademark Assignment System (ETAS): The USPTO's system for electronically filing requests for recordation of assignments of trademarks and other similar documents

equivalents, doctrine of: See *doctrine of equivalents*

e-signature: An electronic rather than a conventional paper signature

estoppel: A defense often raised in infringement actions, alleging the plaintiff is precluded from making certain assertions due to the plaintiff's conduct or acquiescence in the infringement

European Patent Organization: An organization with 34 member nations founded in 1973 to provide a uniform patent system in Europe

European Union (EU): An association of 25 European nations

Examiner's Amendment: A written communication from the USPTO setting forth an agreed-upon clarification or correction to a trademark application

exclusion order: Order issued by the International Trade Commission to exclude items that infringe U.S. trademarks, copyrights, or patents from entry into the United States

exclusive license: A grant of rights to one party with no other party having any right

exhaustion theory: In trademark and patent law, the extinguishment or exhaustion of a trademark or patent owner's rights once a lawful first sale has been made of trademarked goods or a patented invention; in copyright law, the extinguishment of a copyright owner's right to distribute a copyrighted work once

a lawful first sale has been made; also see *first sale doctrine*

experimental use: Use of an invention to perfect it and which is not "public use" such as to trigger one-year grace period

F

fair use: A defense asserted in trademark or copyright infringement actions; a noninfringing use of copyrighted work such as a parody or for criticism, scholarly research, or educational purposes

false advertising: False or deceptive representations about one's own goods or services

Family Entertainment and Copyright Act: Legislation enacted in 2005 prohibiting camcording of movies in theatres, allowing copyright preregistration of movies before their release, and permitting individuals to "sanitize" movies to omit objectionable material

fanciful mark: A wholly invented mark; also called *coined mark*

fan fiction: Unauthorized fiction created about preexisting book and movie characters by those other than the original authors, likely infringing the owners' copyright rights and possibly trademark rights

Federal Trade Commission (FTC): The federal regulatory agency charged with protecting consumers from unfair or deceptive acts and practices

Federal Trademark Dilution Act: A 1995 federal statute (and its later amendments) that protects famous marks from uses that weaken or tarnish their distinctiveness, even in the absence of actual confusion; actual harm need not be shown to prevail against such uses

file wrapper: The official USPTO file containing all papers relating to a trademark or patent application

file wrapper estoppel: See *prosecution history estoppel*

filing receipt: Document mailed (or sent by electronic means) by the USPTO to an applicant to confirm filing and details of an application

final action: Action by the USPTO refusing a trademark or patent application; also called *final refusal*

first sale doctrine: In copyright and patent law, the principle that once the owner of copyrighted material or a patented item sells it, the buyer can treat the object as his or her own and freely sell, lease, or lend the work to another; in copyright law, the first sale doctrine only affects the right of distribution; also see *exhaustion theory*

fixation: The embodiment of a work in a sufficiently permanent or stable form to permit it to be perceived, reproduced, or communicated for more than a transitory period

foreign filing license: The grant by the USPTO of permission to an inventor to file a patent application in another country for an invention made in the United States, required before a foreign application may be filed

framing: Capture of content from another's Web site, often obscuring owner's content

freeware: Software that is allowed to be used for free but in which certain rights are maintained to ensure the work is not reverse engineered

functional feature: A feature that is essential to the use or purpose of the product or that affects the cost or quality of the product

G

General Agreement on Tariffs and Trade (GATT): Agreement adhered to by most industrialized nations aimed at increasing international trade and that resulted in some changes to U.S. trademark and patent law, notably relating to the duration of patent protection

genericide: Loss of rights in a trademark occurring when consumers begin calling a product or service offered under a mark by the mark itself

generic mark: An unprotectable common name for a product or service

generic top-level domain: The portion of a domain name to the right of a period, such as ".com" or ".gov"

goodwill: The value inherent in achieving consumer loyalty to a particular product or service through maintenance of consistent quality of the products or services offered under a mark

grace period: A period within which late documents are accepted by the USPTO; in patent law, the one-year period within which a patent application must be filed after the invention is in public use, on sale, or described in a printed publication anywhere

gray market goods: Unauthorized importation of goods into the United States for resale after the goods are distributed in foreign markets

H

homestyle exemption: Exemption allowing the mere reception of a copyrighted work in public from being considered an infringement

house mark: A mark used for a wide range of products or services

hyperlink: A symbol designating another's Web page

I

idea-expression dichotomy: Doctrine that ideas are not protectable by copyright although the expression of those ideas is copyrightable

idea submission: The submission of an idea for an invention, process, game, or entertainment show in the hope it will be developed and marketed by the recipient

import survey: Survey ordered by IP owners from U.S. Customs and Border Protection to help locate foreign IP infringers

impoundment: Seizure, generally of infringing goods

incontestable: A trademark registered on the Principal Register that is protected from certain challenges after its registrant files a Section 15 affidavit alleging continuous use for five years

independent contractor: One who renders services in the course of independent occupation; one who is not an employee of another

inducement of infringement: In patent law, actively and intentionally encouraging another to infringe a patent

industrial property: The term used in some foreign countries to refer to intellectual property

inevitable disclosure doctrine: Principle that if new employment will inevitably lead to disclosure of former employer's trade secrets, employee can be enjoined from working for new employer

Information Disclosure Statement (IDS): A document filed by an inventor with the USPTO identifying information material to patentability of an invention

infringement: A violation of some right; in the intellectual property context, a violation of a party's rights in a trademark, copyright, or patent

injunction: A court order prohibiting or compelling some act

innocent infringement: Infringement of another's intellectual property rights without any intent to infringe; not a valid defense in copyright or patent infringement actions

integrity: See *right of integrity*

intellectual property: The result or product of human creativity, including trademarks, copyrights, and inventions; generally, *intellectual property* consists of the fields of trademarks, copyrights, patents, and trade secrets

intellectual property audit: A review of the trademarks, copyrights, patents, and trade secrets owned by a person or company

Intent-to-use application: A trademark application for which no actual use of a mark has been made but rather alleging the applicant's bona fide intent to use the mark in the future

interference: A proceeding before the Trademark Trial and Appeal Board when marks in two pending trademark applications are confusingly similar or when a mark in a pending application may be confusingly similar to a registered mark that is not yet incontestable; a proceeding initiated by the USPTO and handled by the Board of Patent Appeals and Interferences to determine which of two or more patents has priority

International Classes: The categorization of goods and services into 45 separate topics for trademark purposes; class(es) of goods or services must be identified in a trademark application

international patent: A patent filed under the Patent Cooperation Treaty

International Trademark Association (INTA): A not-for-profit international association devoted to promoting trademarks

Internet Corporation for Assigned Names and Numbers (ICANN): Nonprofit corporation that oversees the domain naming system

Internet Treaties: Two international copyright treaties adopted by WIPO in 2002 to protect copyright works in the digital environment

inter partes proceedings: Literally, "between parties"; proceedings handled by the Trademark Trial and Appeal Board; may be oppositions, cancellations, interferences, or concurrent use proceedings

interstate commerce: Commerce between or among states

intrastate commerce: Commerce conducted within the borders of one state

invention developer: One who assists an inventor in bringing a discovery to market or negotiates with others for assignment or licensing of an inventor's rights; also called an *invention promoter*

invention promoter: See *invention developer*

issue fee: A fee required by the USPTO for a patent to be granted

J

Jepson claim: A type of claim in a patent specification used for improvements to existing inventions that identifies what is new to the invention

joint application: An application for a trademark, copyright, or patent registration made by more than one person

joint inventors: Two or more people who contribute to an invention

joint work: A copyrightable work created by two or more authors with the intent that their contributions be merged into a unitary whole

junior user: A party who adopts and uses a mark similar to that previously used by a senior user

K

keying: Practice of forcing an Internet user to view certain preselected ads when certain "key" terms are entered into a search engine

knockout search: A preliminary search of USPTO records designed to disclose identical or nearly identical marks; often followed by a *comprehensive search*

L

laboratory notebooks: Books and notes kept by inventors as work progresses on an invention, often used in determining conception of invention and reduction to practice of an invention

laches: An unreasonable delay in asserting one's rights that causes prejudice or harm to another; a common defense asserted in intellectual property infringement actions

Lanham Act: The federal statute found at 15 U.S.C. §§ 1051 *et seq.* governing the law of trademarks; also called the *United States Trademark Act*

Library of Congress: The agency charged with examining copyright applications, issuing registrations, and maintaining copyright deposits

license: A limited transfer of rights, such as permission to another to use a trademark, copyright, patent, or trade secret subject to some conditions, rather than an outright transfer of all rights

literal copying: Identical duplication or copying of another's copyrighted work

literal infringement: An accused invention that falls within the language used in a claim in an issued patent

literary work: A work expressed in words, numbers, or other verbal or numerical symbols, such as a book or computer program

little FTC acts: State statutes that prohibit deceptive and unfair trade practices

logo: A design used as a trademark

M

machine: In patent law, a device that accomplishes a result

Madrid Protocol: An agreement adhered to by more than 70 countries including the E.U. and U.S. that provides an "international trademark registration" that would be valid in all member nations

maintenance fees: Fees due at 3½, 7½, and 11½ years after issuance of a utility patent required to keep it in force

Manual of Patent Examining Procedure **(MPEP):** A USPTO publication containing rules and regulations relating to examination and issuance of patents

manufacture: In patent law, anything made by humans

mark: A trademark or service mark

Markman **hearing:** Hearing held in front of a judge in a patent infringement case to determine claims construction of a patent; the briefs submitted for the hearing are often called *Markman* briefs

mask works: Stencils used to etch or encode an electronic circuit on a semiconductor chip

merger doctrine: The principle that if there are few alternative ways of expressing something, only literal copying will infringe because the expression merges with the idea and ideas are uncopyrightable

mime: See *pantomime*

misappropriation: The taking or using of property created or secured at great effort by another

misuse: A defense often asserted in patent infringement actions alleging that the patentee has so misused its rights that its patent is unenforceable

moral rights: Personal rights retained by authors in their works (often works of fine arts) to protect their honor and reputation even after they no longer own the copyright in the work

motion picture: Audiovisual work consisting of a series of related images that, when shown in succession, impart an impression of motion, together with accompanying sounds

mousetrapping: Practice of trapping an Internet user into viewing a series of advertisements

musical work: Original musical compositions or arrangements, including lyrics

N

naked license: Granting permission to another to use a trademark and retaining no control over the nature or quality of the goods or services offered under the mark; a naked license results in a loss of the licensor's rights in a mark

national phase: The final phase of a patent application filed under the Patent Cooperation Treaty consisting of prosecution of the patent in countries in which patent protection is desired

national treatment: Principle that member countries adhering to a treaty guarantee to the citizens of other member adherents the same rights in intellectual property matters that they provide to their own citizens

new version: See *derivative work*

noncompetition agreement: An agreement prohibiting an employee from competing against the employer during and after the term of employment; also called *restrictive covenant*

nondisclosure agreement: An agreement requiring a party to maintain information in confidence; also called *confidentiality agreement*

nonenabling specification: A specification in a patent application rejected by the USPTO on the basis that it is not sufficient to teach or enable another to make or use the invention

nonexclusive license: A grant of rights to more than one party

nonobviousness: In patent law, the requirement that subject matter sought to be patented be sufficiently different from what has been used or described before such that it may be said to be nonobvious to a person having ordinary skill in the area of technology related to the invention

North American Free Trade Agreement (NAFTA): A trade agreement entered into in 1991 by the United States, Canada, and Mexico

Notice of Allowance: Document issued by the USPTO informing a trademark applicant that an intent-to-use application has been allowed and granting the applicant a specified time period within which to begin use of the mark in order to secure registration for it; document issued by the USPTO informing a patent applicant that a patent application has been allowed and granting the applicant a specified time period within which to pay an issue fee so a patent will be issued

notice of copyright: A mark informing the public that a work is protected by copyright and identifying its owner and year of publication

Notice of Opposition: The document that initiates a trademark opposition proceeding and that sets forth a short and plain statement of the reasons why the opposer believes he or she will be damaged by registration of a mark

novelty: In patent law, a new invention; one not known or used by another

novelty search: A search of prior art to determine if an invention is new and nonobvious

nunc pro tunc assignment: Assignment prepared on a later date to reflect an earlier transfer

O

object code: A computer language consisting of zeroes and ones that is machine-readable

office action: Written communication from the USPTO refusing registration of a trademark or issuance of a patent and specifying reasons for the issuance of a refusal

Official Filing Receipt: A document issued by the USPTO confirming the filing of a trademark application

Official Gazette: The weekly publication of the USPTO that publishes trademarks for purposes of opposition and publishes information about issued patents and patents available for sale or license

on sale bar: The doctrine precluding granting of a patent unless a patent application is filed less than one year from the time the invention is in public use, on sale in the United States, or described in printed publication anywhere

opposition: A proceeding initiated at the Trademark Trial and Appeal Board by one who believes he or she may be damaged by registration of a trademark

originality: In copyright law, a work that is independently created (not copied) and that exhibits a minimal amount of creativity

orphan drug: A drug needed to treat a disease affecting fewer than 200,000 people

orphan works: Works that may be subject to copyright protection but whose owners cannot be found and thus for which permission to use is nearly impossible to obtain

P

palming off: See *passing off*

pantomime: A performance using gestures as expression to communicate with no accompanying sound

parallel imports: See *gray market goods*

parent application: An original trademark or patent application that is the source or parent of a later separate application

Paris Convention: An agreement adhered to by more than 170 member nations providing that foreign trademark and patent owners may obtain in a member country the same protection for their trademarks and patents as can citizens of the member country

passing off: Attempting to sell one's goods or services as those of another; also called *palming off*

patent: A grant from the U.S. government permitting its owner to exclude others from making, selling, using, or importing an invention for a limited period of time

patent agent: A nonattorney engineer or scientist who passes a USPTO exam testing patent knowledge and may engage in patent prosecution but may not give legal advice or appear in court

Patent and Trademark Depository Libraries: Public libraries throughout the United States that maintain selected trademark and patent records

Patent Application Information Retrieval (PAIR) System: USPTO electronic system allowing applicants to review the status of pending patent applications; may be private or public

patent attorney: A licensed attorney who passes a USPTO exam testing patent knowledge and who may engage in patent prosecution, give legal advice, and appear in court

Patent Cooperation Treaty (PCT): A 1978 treaty adhered to by more than 130 countries that provides a centralized way of filing, searching, and examining patent applications in several countries simultaneously

patentee: The owner of a patent issued by the USPTO

Patent Law Treaty: WIPO treaty entered into force in 2005 to harmonize formal requirements for obtaining patents around the world

patent misuse: See *misuse*

patent pool: Collection of patents owned by various patent owners and which are used to raise revenue by licensing their use to others

patent term adjustment: Additional time granted to term of patent to compensate for certain USPTO delays, interferences, and other matters

patent term extension: Extension of time granted to term of patent to compensate for regulatory review of new drugs, medical devices, and so forth

patent troll: Individual or company that purchases a patent that it does not commercialize and then uses it offensively by threatening litigation to obtain money or licenses from other businesses

PCT application: A patent application that has applicability and effect in member nations adhering to the Patent Cooperation Treaty; often called *international application*

peer-to-peer file sharing: Trading of computer files, often songs, from one user's computer to another's

performing rights society: An organization of copyright owners (such as ASCAP or BMI) that licenses the rights to use copyrighted music to third parties, collects fees therefor, and remits those fees to its members, the authors of the works

Petition to Cancel: The document initiating a trademark cancellation proceeding that sets forth a short and plain statement of the reasons a petitioner would be damaged by continued registration of a mark

Petition to Make Special: Request for accelerated examination of patent application due to importance of patent or age or health of inventor

phishing: Practice of inducing computer users to reveal sensitive financial and personal information through the use of legitimate-appearing e-mails or Web sites

phonorecord: A material object in which sounds (other than those accompanying a motion picture or other audiovisual work) are fixed and from which the sounds can be perceived, reproduced, or communicated by human perception or with the help of a machine

pioneer patent: A patent representing an important advance or significant breakthrough

plant application: An application for a patent for a plant

plant patent: A patent covering asexually reproduced and distinct plant varieties

Plant Variety Protection Act: Federal law allowing quasipatent protection for certain sexually reproduced plants

posting of ports: Monitoring of ports of entry into the United States by U.S. Customs and Border Protection for the purpose of seizing unauthorized goods bearing a party's registered trademark

preregistration: New copyright procedure allowing owners to preregister certain works that have a history of infringement prior to their release, allowing owners to sue for infringement prior to a work's release

Principal Register: The most preferred roll or register for registration of trademarks conferring wide protection for a mark and indicating that the mark distinguishes the registrant's goods and services from those of others

prior art: In patent law, the generally available public knowledge relating to an invention at the time of its creation

process: A patentable method of doing something to produce a given result

product disparagement: Making false representations about another's goods or services; also called *trade libel*

progressive encroachment: Use of a trademark that becomes infringement although earlier it may have been permissible; often used by plaintiff to defeat a claim of laches, asserted by a defendant

prosecution: The process of moving a trademark or patent application through the USPTO

prosecution history estoppel: The principle that an inventor or patentee is bound by acts taken and statements made during the prosecution of a patent and cannot later take an inconsistent position; also called *file wrapper estoppel*

provisional patent application: A patent application that is less formal than a utility patent application; within 12 months of its filing, it must be followed by a standard utility patent application at the USPTO

pseudonymous work: A copyrighted work in which the author is identified under a fictitious name, such as the name "Mark Twain" used by Samuel Clemens

publication: The distribution of copies of a work to the public for sale or other transfer of ownership by rental, lease, or lending

public domain: A work or invention that is free for all members of the public to use

puffing: An exaggerated and highly subjective statement upon which no reasonable person would rely; generally, nonactionable opinion

punitive damages: Damages intended to punish a defendant rather than to compensate a plaintiff

R

receiving office: A patent office in which a patent application prepared in accordance with the Patent Cooperation Treaty is filed

recordation: Filing of certain documents with the USPTO, Library of Congress, or other official body to provide public notice of the contents of a document or a transaction, such as an assignment or transfer of intellectual property, a grant of a security interest in intellectual property, or a change in the chain of title of intellectual property

reduction to practice: Construction of an invention in physical form (called *actual reduction to practice*) or filing a patent application for an invention (called *constructive reduction to practice*)

reexamination of patent: Proceeding initiated at the USPTO to review or reexamine a claim in an issued patent to determine its validity

registered user agreement: Agreement by which an owner of a registered mark allows or licenses another to use its mark and is required to be filed by many foreign trademark offices for the grant to be effective

registrant: The owner of a trademark registration issued by the USPTO

registrar: Company that assigns domain names

reissue patent: A proceeding to correct defects in an issued patent or to enlarge the claims of an issued patent

renewal: Document filed with the USPTO or Library of Congress to maintain a trademark or copyright registration for an additional term

Request for Continued Examination: Request by applicant for continued examination of a utility or plant application

Request to Divide: Request by applicant to create a new trademark application, usually in intent-to-use applications, when applicant can proceed to registration for some goods or services and wishes to retain a separate application for goods or services not yet in use

restrictive covenant: See *noncompetition agreement*

restriction requirement: Requirement by the USPTO that a patent applicant limit a patent application to one invention when two or more distinct inventions are claimed in one application

reverse doctrine of equivalents: In patent law, the principle that even if there is literal infringement of claims, if the accused resulting device differs from the patented device, there is no infringement

reverse engineering: Disassembling an object, usually a computer program, to understand its functional elements

reverse passing off: A form of unfair competition in which a defendant misrepresents someone else's goods or services as his own

right of integrity: A personal right of a copyright author to ensure that his or her work not be distorted, mutilated, or used in a way that would injure the author's reputation

right of publicity: Protection of a person's identity, voice, likeness, or persona against unauthorized commercial exploitation

royalties: Periodic payments paid by one who uses or licenses property owned or created by another, usually based on sales or licenses of the property

rule of doubt: Policy followed by Copyright Office or USPTO to resolve doubts about copyrightability or trademark applications in favor of copyright applicant or existing trademark registrant, respectively

S

scenes a faire: Literally, "scenes which must be done"; stock characters and devices in a work that are uncopyrightable

secondary considerations: In patent law, nontechnical and objective factors considered in determining whether an invention is nonobvious, namely, its commercial success, the long-felt need for the invention, commercial acquiescence to it by others, and copying of it by others

secondary level domain: The part of a domain name to the left of a period, such as "ibm" in "ibm.com"

secondary meaning: An association by a consumer who has learned to link a mark with its source; also called *acquired distinctiveness*

secrecy order: An order issued by the USPTO requiring that an invention be kept secret and prohibiting publication of it or patent applications for it in another country, generally for national security reasons

Section 8 Affidavit: See *Affidavit of Continued Use*

Section 15 Affidavit: See *Affidavit of Incontestability*

Section 44(d) Application: Trademark application filed with the USPTO by a non-U.S. citizen based upon an application filed in a foreign country

Section 44(e) Application: Trademark application filed with the USPTO by a non-U.S. citizen based upon a registration secured in a foreign country

Section 337 investigation: Proceeding instituted at International Trade Commission aimed at blocking importation of articles that infringe U.S. trademarks, copyrights, or patents

security agreement: In intellectual property law, an agreement by which one party grants an interest to another in its intellectual property, usually in order to obtain or secure a loan; if the owner defaults on the loan, the lender usually obtains ownership of the intellectual property

semiconductor chip: A product having two or more layers of metallic, insulating, or semiconductor material placed on or removed from semiconductor material and intended to perform electronic circuitry functions

senior user: The first party to use a mark

service mark: A word, name, symbol, or device used to indicate the source, quality, and ownership of a service

shareware: Copyrighted software that has been released under the condition that if the user likes it, the user will pay a license fee therefor

shop right: An employer's nonexclusive royalty-free license to use an invention or trade secret when the employer and employee do not agree in advance about who will own the invention or trade secret conceived by the employee while on company time

shrink-wrap license: A license of software that comes into existence by the opening of the plastic wrapping on the software and by which act the licensee agrees to terms governing use of the software

small entity: A business with fewer than 500 employees, an individual inventor, a university, or a not-for-profit organization entitled to a 50 percent reduction in many standard patent fees

softlifting: The act of software piracy by which one makes unauthorized copies of computer software

sound recording: A work that results from the fixation of a series of musical, spoken, or other sounds

source code: An alphanumeric computer language that is human-readable

special handling: Expedited processing of copyright applications and other documents for specified reasons upon payment of a fee

specification: The part of a patent application that describes an invention and the manner and process of making and using it

specimens: Samples of tags, labels, packaging, or advertising materials showing how a trademark or service mark is used in commerce

standard character drawing: A trademark or service mark displayed in typed form, with no claim to any particular font style, size, or color; a mark that has no design element

Statement of Use: Document filed by an intent-to-use trademark applicant verifying that the mark is in actual use in interstate commerce; required to receive a trademark registration

statutory damages: Damages awarded by a court in an infringement action as specified by statute, generally elected when a plaintiff will have difficulty proving actual damages

streaming: See *Webcast*

suggestive mark: A mark that suggests something about the goods or services offered under it; a suggestive mark is registrable without proof of secondary meaning

Supplemental Register: The roll or register for marks not qualifying for registration on the USPTO Principal Register; registration on the Supplemental Register is an indication that the mark does not yet distinguish the registrant's goods or services from those of others

supplementary copyright registration: An application to correct an error or amplify information in a copyright registration

T

takedown notice: Notice served by a copyright owner on an Internet service provider asking it to remove or block access to allegedly infringing material posted on the Internet

tarnishment: A form of dilution in which a famous trademark is portrayed in an unsavory or embarrassing manner

TEAS Plus: Method of filing trademark applications electronically with stricter requirements than TEAS and allowing reduced filing fee

terminal disclaimer: An agreement by an inventor that the term of protection for a second patented invention will terminate upon expiration of the term for the first patented invention

trade dress: The overall image of a product or service

trade libel: See *product disparagement*

trademark: A word, logo, phrase, or device used to indicate the source, quality, and ownership of a product or service; technically, *trademark* refers to a mark that identifies a product, while *service mark* refers to a mark that identifies services

Trademark Applications and Registrations Retrieval (TARR): The USPTO's online search tool allows searching by application or registration number

trademark compliance policy: A guide to use of a trademark to ensure a mark is not misused or does not become generic or abandoned

Trademark Document Retrieval (TDR): The USPTO's electronic system allowing review and online retrieval of documents and specimens submitted to the USPTO

Trademark Electronic Application System (TEAS): The USPTO's system allowing electronic filing of many trademark documents

Trademark Electronic Search System (TESS): The USPTO's online search tool allowing searching of trademarks in the USPTO data-base

Trademark Manual of Examining Procedure: A USPTO publication containing rules and regulations related to the prosecution and registration of trademarks

Trademark Status Line: System maintained by the USPTO allowing telephonic checking of the status of trademark registrations or applications (800–786–9199 or 571–272–9250)

Trademark Trial and Appeal Board (TTAB): Department of the USPTO that resolves inter partes proceedings and other matters affecting trademarks

trade name: A name used to identify a business or company

Trade-Related Aspects of Intellectual Property Rights (TRIPs): Agreement promulgated in accordance with the 1994 General Agreement on Tariffs and Trade providing intellectual property protection for WTO members

trade secret: Any valuable commercial information that, if known by a competitor, would provide some benefit or advantage to the competitor

trailer clause: A clause in an employment agreement requiring employee to assign inventions to employer both during and after employment

traverse: Arguments made in response to objections by the USPTO to a trademark or patent application

TTAB Vue: The Trademark Trial and Appeal Board's system that allows access and viewing of opposition, cancellation, and other inter partes documents filed with the TTAB

typosquatting: Variation of cybersquatting in which one registers misspelled versions of others' domain names to attract visitors for profit

U

unclean hands: A defense often raised in infringement actions; an assertion that the plaintiff's own wrongful conduct precludes he or she from obtaining relief

unfair competition: A branch of law protecting against deceptive and improper conduct in the marketplace

Uniform Domain Name Dispute Resolution Policy (UDRP): Policy adopted by all ICANN registrars, allowing a streamlined and inexpensive dispute resolution procedure for domain name disputes

United States Patent and Trademark Office (USPTO): The agency within the Department of Commerce charged with registering trademarks and granting patents

United States Trademark Act: See *Lanham Act*

Universal Copyright Convention (UCC): An international convention relating to copyrights requiring that works originating in a member nation must be given the same protection in all member nations as is granted by the country of origin of the work

Uruguay Round Agreements Act: A 1994 act that implemented GATT and amended U.S. copyright law to provide remedies for pirated sound recordings of live performances and to provide automatic restoration of copyright in certain foreign works; amended U.S. trademark law relating to abandonment of marks and geographic designations for wines and spirits; and amended patent law to harmonize terms of patent protection with that of most foreign countries

useful article: An article having an intrinsic utilitarian value

usefulness: In patent law, a process or invention that is of some present value to humanity

utility application: A patent application for a new, useful, and nonobvious process, machine, article of manufacture, composition of matter, or some improvement thereof

utility patent: A patent for a useful article, invention, or discovery

V

Vessel Hull Design Protection Act: A portion of the Digital Millennium Copyright Act, providing copyright protection for original designs of boat vessel hulls

vicarious infringement: Liability imposed for infringement on a party due to its special relationship (such as employer-employee) with another infringer

W

warez: More than one piece of pirated software; a site that allows downloading of pirated software; slang term for all content traded on the Internet

watch service: Service provided by a private company, usually a trademark search firm, to review the *Official Gazette* and USPTO records for potentially conflicting marks

Webcast: The broadcast of a radio program over the Internet; also called *streaming*

work made for hire: A work that is presumed to be authored by an employer because it was created by an employee on company time or a work authored by a commissioning party when the parties have agreed in writing that the commissioning party will own the copyright and the work falls into one of nine statutorily enumerated categories

World Intellectual Property Organization (WIPO): A specialized agency of the United Nations with more than 180 member nations that promotes intellectual property throughout the world and administers various multilateral treaties dealing with intellectual property, including the Berne Convention

World Trade Organization (WTO): An international organization established in 1995 with more than 150 member countries, created by the Uruguay Round negotiations to handle trade disputes and monitor national trade policies

Index